COMPARATIVE EUROPEAN POLITICS

General Editors: Max Kaase and Kenneth Newton

Editorial Board: Brian Barry, Franx Lehner,
Arend Lijphart, Seymour Martin Lipset, Mogens Pedersen,
Giovanni Sartori, Rei Shiratori,
Vincent Wright

Parliamentary Representatives
in Europe 1848–2000

COMPARATIVE EUROPEAN POLITICS

Comparative European Politics is a series for students and teachers of political science and related disciplines, published in association with the European Consortium for Political Research. Each volume will provide an up-to-date survey of the current state of knowledge and research on an issue of major significance in European government and politics

Parliamentary Representatives in Europe 1848–2000

Legislative Recruitment and Careers in Eleven European Countries

Edited by

HEINRICH BEST and MAURIZIO COTTA

OXFORD

UNIVERSITY PRESS

OXFORD
UNIVERSITY PRESS

Great Clarendon Street, Oxford OX2 6DP

Oxford University Press is a department of the University of Oxford.
It furthers the University's objective of excellence in research, scholarship,
and education by publishing worldwide in

Oxford New York

Athens Auckland Bangkok Bogotá Buenos Aires Calcutta
Cape Town Chennai Dar es Salaam Delhi Florence Hong Kong Istanbul
Karachi Kuala Lumpur Madrid Melbourne Mexico City Mumbai
Nairobi Paris São Paulo Singapore Taipei Tokyo Toronto Warsaw

and associated companies in Berlin Ibadan

Oxford is a registered trade mark of Oxford University Press

in the UK and certain other countries
Published in the United States
by Oxford University Press Inc., New York

British Library Cataloguing in Publication Data

Data available

Library of Congress Cataloging in Publication Data

Parliamentary representatives in Europe, 1848–2000 : legislative recruitment and careers
in eleven European countries / edited by Heinrich Best and Maurizio Cotta.
p. cm. — (Comparative European politics)
Includes bibliographical references and index.
1. Legislative bodies—Europe—History. 2. Legislators—Europe—History. I. Best,
Heinrich. II. Cotta, Maurizio, 1947– III. Series.
JN8 .P37 2000   328'.094'09034—dc21   00-031354
ISBN 0-19-829793-9

1 3 5 7 9 10 8 6 4 2

Typeset by Best-set Typesetter Ltd., Hong Kong
Printed in Great Britain
on acid-free paper by
Biddles Ltd
Guildford and King's Lynn

PREFACE

Between the 1950s and the 1970s the 'behavioural revolution' in the social sciences had stimulated parallel efforts directed towards the collection of data on legislative recruitment in most European countries. However, in spite of the rich amount of basically similar data produced by these studies, Stein Rokkan's suggestion of using them as one of the instruments for a systematic comparative analysis of the processes of democratization in Europe remained unheeded. Moreover, since fashions change in academia, as in the outer world, in the 1980s empirical elite studies lost some of the attraction they had previously enjoyed and other themes became more fashionable in European political science. The full potential of these empirical studies was thus, to a great extent, left unexploited.

Yet those who had been involved in this type of research at the national level knew very well that, whatever the interest of single country studies, the real 'treasure' still waiting to be unearthed lay in their comparative potential. Bringing this treasure to light required (as treasure-hunting novels teach) a mix of boldness and daring. In order to embark on this adventure, data archives that had been dormant for decades had to be brought back to life; technical problems of data cleaning and standardization had to be tackled; and more fundamental questions of equivalence of indicators had to be answered. However, in spite of the scepticism of (probably) wiser colleagues, we felt the challenge to be one worthy of facing. The European Consortium for Political Research (ECPR) Joint Sessions in Rimini, 1988, offered an opportunity for the first discussion about the possibility of pursuing this enterprise; but it was in 1991 in the monastic seclusion of the Certosa di Pontignano near Siena that the project was finally launched. As we have discovered since then, through an extended series of meetings, workshops, get-togethers in different universities, conference centres, and mountain resorts, the task was much more daunting than first expected. Comparing across eleven countries is in itself a demanding challenge, but if one adds to this a time span of 150 years the problems inevitably grow exponentially. Yet if the problems have made the advance of our work slower, they have not persuaded us to abandon the search for the treasure and we are now able to present the first results of our work.

The first step of our research programme implied the creation of a comprehensive European data set out of the many national files. For the sake of the manageability of the data, a joint data set, or the CUBE, as we have come to call it, had to be constructed. This entailed the transformation of the national data sets, which had the individual parliamentarian as the unit of analysis, into a new data set where the unit is an aggregate one, that is, the parliamentary group during a parliamentary term. Currently, the integration of the national data into the CUBE format has been completed for Finland, France, Germany, Italy, the Netherlands, Norway, and the United Kingdom. In addition, data for Denmark, Hungary, Portugal, and Spain, while not yet fully transformed into the new format, are already usable for comparative analyses.

Our initial programme foresaw that, after having created the CUBE, we would be able to move immediately to the testing of hypotheses for explaining the long-term transformations of parliamentary elite profiles and recruitment patterns in Europe on a variable by variable basis. However, the realization that these developments were to a large extent path-dependent, and that they reflected specific historical circumstances and institutional settings, has convinced us to proceed first to an equally ambitious and innovative task, that of presenting and analysing the trends of change over the last 150 years on a country by country basis. The broad theoretical guidelines underpinning our work of creating a comparative database and revealing the long-term trends of European parliamentary recruitment are outlined in the introductory chapter. Although the comparison of eleven country patterns of development offered by this volume is not the end of our work, this book stands by itself and provides a comprehensive basis for a new interpretation of the strained relation between the development of democracy and parliamentary representation during the past 150 years.

The preparation and the making of this book could not have been possible without the help of many persons and institutions. We would like first of all to acknowledge our intellectual debt to the scholars whose theoretical and empirical contributions in the 1950s and 1960s opened this field of research: Mattei Dogan, Erwin K. Scheuch, Lewis J. Edinger, W. L. Guttsman, Dwaine Marvick, Stein Rokkan, Giovanni Sartori, Wolfgang Zapf, and later Moshe Czudnowski, Paolo Farneti, and Robert D. Putnam. Their works were a source of inspiration and a guide in our efforts. Hans-Dieter Klingemann always encouraged our work with his great friendship, and Jean Blondel, Hans Daalder, John Higley, and Wlodzimierz Wesolowski participated in the discussions of the drafts of the chapters and contributed to their improvement through suggestions and constructive criticisms.

The granting of an Exploratory Research Grant by the Standing Committee for the Social Sciences of the European Foundation in 1996 provided crucial financial support to organize two conferences, one in Jena and one in Siena, and to develop the data set. The Vigoni Fund of the German and Italian Conferences of University Rectors made it possible for the editors of this book, and for the two persons in charge of the CUBE data set, Christopher Hausmann and Luca Verzichelli, to exchange visits and to work on the standardization of the data sets. The Italian Centro Nazionale delle Ricerche (CNR), the Italian Ministry of University, the German Deutscher Akademischer Austauschdienst (DAAD), the British Council, the Nuffield Foundation, the Universities of Jena, Leiden, and Siena, the Norwegian School of Management of Sandvika have all supported the costs of the collection and refinement of data, and of the organization of preparatory meetings and workshops through allocation of grants. We are also grateful to the European Consortium for Political Research (ECPR) for enabling us to organize a workshop on 'Long Term Studies of Political Recruitment Patterns and Elite Transformation' during the 1995 Joint Sessions of Bordeaux and to meet at the 1994 Research Sessions of Gelsenkirchen.

Christopher Hausmann, Harald Klein, Joachim Loose, and Luca Verzichelli have helped to achieve the Herculean task of cleaning, standardizing, matching, and documenting the entries into the DATA CUBE, while Verona Christmas-Best had a similarly demanding task in preparing the contributions to this book for publication. The staff of the Institut für Soziologie of the University of Jena and of the Dipartimento di Scienze Storiche, Giuridiche, Politiche e Sociali of the University of Siena provided efficient support throughout the years. We would like to express special thanks to Sylvia Juhász and Susan Böhmer for their unstinting efforts to transform all the various and diverse contributions into the coherent whole that is our book.

Jena and Siena
May 1999

Heinrich Best
Maurizio Cotta

CONTENTS

NOTES ON CONTRIBUTORS

Heinrich Best is Professor of Sociology and Dean of the Faculty for Social and Behavioural Sciences at the University of Jena (Germany). His main research areas are the comparative study of political elites, information and knowledge processing in the social sciences, and the methodology of historical and comparative sociology. He is editor and author of 23 books and author of 74 articles and book chapters including *Social Sciences in Transition* (1996), *Elites in Transition* (1997), and *Parliamentary Representation in the Revolutions of 1848* (2000).

Maurizio Cotta is Professor of Political Science and Director of the Centre for the Study of Political Change at the University of Siena. He has written extensively on parliaments, executives, and on Italian politics. He has co-edited with P. Isernia, *Il gigante dai piedi di argilla. La crisi del regime partitocratico in Italia* (1996) and with J. Blondel, *Party and Government* (1996), and *The Nature of Party Government* (2000).

Valerie Cromwell is Director of the History of Parliament, Senior Research Fellow of the Institute of Historical Research, University of London, and Vice-President of the International Commission for the History of Representative and Parliamentary Institutions. She has published extensively on 19th and 20th century British administrative and parliamentary history, most recently 'The Fourteenth Earl of Derby' in Robert Eccleshall and Graham Walker (eds.), *British Prime Ministers* (London, 1998).

Kjell A. Eliassen is Director of the Centre for European and Asian Studies at the Norwegian School of Management. He has published 10 books and many articles on EU and European affairs, public management and political elites, including, *The European Union: how democratic is it? (1995)* and *Foreign and Security Policy in the European Union* (1998).

Pilar Gangas is currently Professor of Political Science at Salamanca University. She has been Visiting Scholar in the Center for European Studies, at Harvard University, and is currently working on the organizational development of political parties, and on political elites. Amongst others, she has published *El Desarrollo Organizativo de los Partidos Políticos Españoles de Implantación Nacional* (1995).

Daniel Gaxie is Professor of Political Sociology at the University of Paris and Director of the Centre for Political Research of the Sorbonne. Among others, he has published *Le cens caché* (1993) and *La démocratie représentative* (1999).

Christopher Hausmann is a researcher at the Institute for Sociology at the University of Jena. His research interests focus on electoral research, survey methods, sociology of crime and political elites. He has published on German electoral history, crime prevention, and East German political elites in a comparative perspective, including *Biographisches Handbuch der 10. Volkskammer der DDR* (1999) and *Wahlen nach dem politischen Wechsel 1998* (forthcoming).

Gabriella Ilonszki is Professor at the Department of Political Science at the Budapest University of Economic Sciences and her research interests include the development of parliamentary institutions in Central Europe. She was co-editor (with A. Ágh) of *Parliaments and Organized Interests in Central Europe: The Second Steps* (1996), and has recently published a comparative politics textbook in Hungarian (*Westminsteri változatok*, 1998).

Miguel Jerez Mir is Professor of Political Science at the University of Granada. He has been visiting scholar at Yale University, and Visiting Professor at the Universities of North Carolina (Chapel Hill) and Stetson (DeLand, Florida). He is the author of *Elites políticas y centros de extracción en España, 1938–1957* (1982), *Corporaciones e intereses en España* (1995) and *Ciencia política, un balance de fin de siglo* (1999).

Juan J. Linz is Sterling Professor of Political Science at Yale University. He has published extensively on the processes of regime change, democratization, presidential systems, federalism, and national identity. His books include *The Breakdown of Democratic Regimes* (co-editor with A. Stepan, 1978), *Problems of Democracy in Developing Countries* (co-editor with L. Diamond and A. Stepan, 1988–89), *The Failure of Presidential Demacracy* (with A. Valenzuela, 1994), *Democratic Transition and Consolidation in Southern Europe, Latin America, and Post-Communist Europe* (with A. Stepan, 1995).

José M. Magone, is Lecturer in European Politics at the Department of Politics and Asian Studies, University of Hull and was Karl W. Deutsch Guest Professor at the Wissenschaftszentrum für Sozialforschung Berlin (WZB), 1999. He has published on the impact of the European integration process on Southern Europe and among his recent publications are the books *The Changing Architecture in Iberian Politics* (1996) and *European Portugal: The Difficult Road to Sustainable Democracy* (1997). He is currently working on the theme of 'Democratic institutional transfer within and outside of the European Union'.

Alfio Mastropaolo is Professor of Political Science at the University of Turin and is currently a member of the Executive committee of the European Consortium for Political Research. He has published extensively on parliamentary elites and theory of political class including *Il ceto Politico* (1993) and *La repubblica dai destini incrociati* (1996).

Mogens N. Pedersen is Professor of Political Science and holds the chair of Political Science at the University of Southern Denmark at Odense. He has published widely in the fields of legislative behavior, political elite recruitment, parties and party systems, and methodology. Among his recent publications are *Kampen om Kommunen* (co-editor J. Elklit, 1995) and *Leksikon i statskundskab* (editors K. Goldman & Ø. Østerud, 1997).

Ilkka Ruostetsaari is an acting Professor of Political Science at the University of Tampere, Finland. His special fields of interests are elites, power structures, professionalisation of politics, and energy policy. He has published, amongst others, *Vallen ytimessä* (1992) and *Energia politiika käännekohdassa*.

Michael Rush is Politics Professor at the University of Exeter where he was Director of the Graduate School of Political and Administrative Studies. He is author, co-author and editor of a number of books and articles on British politics and of articles on Canadian politics. He is currently completing *From Gentlemen to Players: the role of the MP since 1868*, to be published by OUP.

Karl Schmitt is Professor of Political Science at the University of Jena. His research focuses on parties, elections, and political elites. Major publications include *Konfession und Wahlverhalten in Deutschland* (1989), *Parteien und regionale politische Traditionen* (co-edited, 1991), *Die Verfassung des Freistaats Thüringen* (edited, 1995), and *Handbuch der Parteien in Thüringen* (forthcoming).

Ineke Secker is Lecturer in Constitutional and Parliamentary History at Leiden University, the Netherlands. Her research interests focus mainly on governing and legislative elites. Her publications include a study on the background of the Dutch cabinet ministers from 1848 to 1990 and several biographical contributions. She is co-editor of the Dutch Parliamentary Yearbook.

Marit Sjøvaag Marino holds an MSc from the Norwegian School of Management, where she did her Master's thesis on European political cooperation. She is currently undertaking her PhD at the London School of Economics and Political Science. She has published *European Telecommunications Liberalisation* (1999) with Kjell A. Eliassen.

Luca Verzichelli is Assistant Professor of Political Science at the University of Bologna and secretary of the Centre for the Study of Political Change of the University of Siena. His main research interests are on parliamentary elites and budgetary processes in comparative perspective. Recent publications include *La politica di Bilancio* (1999) and several articles, in Italian and English, on the Italian transition, the transformation of the political class, and the budgetary policy in Italy.

1

Elite Transformation and Modes of Representation since the Mid-Nineteenth Century: Some Theoretical Considerations

HEINRICH BEST AND MAURIZIO COTTA

1. ROKKAN'S CHALLENGE

It is now approximately thirty years since Stein Rokkan developed his theoretical framework and empirical grid for a comparative study of nation building and state formation in Western Europe. His systematizations became the intellectual guideline for several generations of sociologists and political scientists and the point of departure for numerous research projects in comparative political sociology. In Rokkan's conceptual framework, political elites formed a central object of interest because their structure sets the stage for the formation of sociopolitical coalitions, which are in turn the decisive, explanatory factor for the variations among European party systems. In his initial proposal for a grid of indicators for the comparative study of political development, there was already a section on the recruitment of elite groups. Recruitment patterns were of particular interest for Rokkan because he maintained that the changing composition of elites reflects the processes of social and political mobilization, of societal integration, and the establishment of rules for access to positions and resources in a society (Rokkan 1967).

Although in 1967 Rokkan was already able to present an impressive list of databases and ongoing research projects concerning elite groups in various countries, no successful attempt was made to co-ordinate these efforts and establish an integrated database for comparative elite research until recently. Despite a continuing tradition of empirical research, whereby truly comparative studies into the development of the welfare state, the extension of suffrage, and the formation of party systems flourished well, elites remained a 'white spot' in the Rokkanian archipelago. Thus we have a field of study where the richness of empirical research covering most of the democratic countries and often long-term periods has not been matched by an equally developed exploitation of their potential for the use of comparative analysis. Descriptive and one-country studies have dominated the field.

It is interesting to consider why, until very recently, this well developed area of research could not be integrated into a comprehensive infrastructure and conceptual framework. The paradoxical answer may be that it was precisely because of its early take-off that research about political elites remained episodic and confined to national settings (Tardieu 1937; Marvick 1961; Thompson and Silbey 1985). Apparently, it is far more difficult to overcome the diversities and idiosyncrasies of existing coding standards, classification schemes, and data management techniques by an *ex post* effort than to start from scratch.

However, despite obstacles built up by a tradition of nationally fragmented and temporally episodic research into political elites, the demand for the integration of databases and a standardization of research concepts has persisted in the field of political elite studies. For example, twenty years ago, Robert D. Putnam in his seminal and still unmatched synthesis of political elite research, referred to the 'copious, but disparate findings' in this field of scholarship, and complained about the unusually large gap 'between abstract, general theories and masses of unorganised evidence'. He concluded that in important areas of elite research, generalizations remained 'merely plausible hunches' (Putnam 1976: p. ix). In his *ex post* synthesis of the then available knowledge of political elites, Putnam was aware of the inevitable disadvantages of his 'patchwork' approach, which used fragmented evidence from disparate sources rather to illustrate theoretical generalizations than to test them systematically. His joining in James Thurber's maxim that 'it is less important to know all the answers than to know some of the questions' had an undertone of resignation.

About ten years ago, Moshe Czudnowski and Gwen Moore were more interested in answers and more hopeful to get them. The collections of articles they published in 1982, 1983, and 1985 marked a considerable step forward to an *ex ante* co-ordination of comparative research about political elites. Contributors to their books were guided by sets of well-defined research questions and by stringent instructions as to how they might be answered. Nevertheless these publication projects were still far from a truly comparative approach to the analysis of trends and variations based on direct variable to variable comparisons. Nation states still formed the main objects of investigation in their own right and were not just contexts for the observation of the structure and change of political elites as proposed in Stein Rokkan's original research concept.

Even Pippa Norris's recently published work on legislative recruitment in contemporary democracies (1997) follows a country by country approach based on varying databases and dispersed empirical evidence, although an important attempt was made to integrate these studies in a common theoretical framework and to complement them by a cross-country study on candidates of the European Parliament. However, the aim to overcome the

' "patchwork approach" that has marked so much of European recruitment research both geographically and conceptually' (Patzelt 1999), has still to be achieved and with it Rokkan's call to integrate cross-cultural and cross-temporal comparisons in one comprehensive approach.

Behind Rokkan's agenda lurked an ambitious but simple idea. The description and analysis of diversity is only possible on the basis of a homogeneous database, that is, a set of identical or at least equivalent indicators covering a plurality of nations. Ideally such a set of indicators would be organized in a three-dimensional data-matrix of countries, time, and variables. In the 1980s, such a 'data cube' was still non-existent for the comparative research of political elites, although researchers in several European countries (such as Daalder, Dogan, Eliassen, Farneti, Pedersen, Sartori, and so on) had been working on databases at a national level with similar, in some cases almost identical, research agendas. Their convergence was owed partly to the restricted scope of primary data sources, partly to a socialization of the researchers involved by the eminent figures of classical political elite theory like Weber, Mosca, Pareto, Michels, or Schumpeter, and last but not least, by a common devotion to the great theoretical syntheses of Stein Rokkan.

It was on the basis of this convergence, which helped to overcome the fragmentation and the disparities of research about political elites, and which provided the common ground for co-ordinated efforts, that a group of scholars who had contributed in the past decades to national empirical researches in this field, thought that it was time to move forward along the lines suggested by Rokkan. They were convinced that it was both desirable and possible to launch a truly comparative study of the political elites of European countries and analyse their long-term transformations. This research collaboration is aimed particularly at the analysis of long-term trends in European parliamentary recruitment from the mid-nineteenth century to the present day. Its main focus is the interdependence between social change, political change, and the transformations of parliamentary representation, whereby representation is conceptualized as the 'hinge' between society and polity, through which social conflict and authority structures are translated into political action, but at the same time political actors guide, reshape, and reinterpret the demands of society.

A crucial task for this research is to set up an integrated database that incorporates a series of common variables for the countries included in this study. Such a database, covering 150 years of parliamentary history and involving different paths of development towards modern parliamentarism provides, for the first time, the empirical prerequisites for a comprehensive comparative research agenda. Following John Stuart Mill's 'Method of Differences' (Skocpol 1979), we intend to provide new insights into the effects on parliamentary representation resulting from the extension of suffrage, the emergence of organized mass parties, the social transformation of the electorate, the growing influence of mass media, and the declining role of the nation state. Divergent constitutional traditions and differences in the past performance of parliamentary assemblies provide the contrasting institutional background for the interpretation of long-term trends in the countries involved.

2. PARLIAMENTARY ELITES AND THE PROCESS OF DEMOCRATIZATION

The starting-point of our investigation was 1848, one of the 'critical junctures' (Lipset and Rokkan 1967) in European history and one which marks symbolically the birth of representative democracy in many areas of Western and Central Europe. The political mobilization of significant parts of the population, the granting of freedom of association and political expression, the establishment of elected parliaments, the extension of suffrage, which led to a convergence between the *pays légal* and the *pays réel*, the formation of parliamentary parties along ideological lines, their connection with support groups and even party organizations in the country, all formed a configuration which, for the first time, connected important elements of a new political order (de Tocqueville 1942; orig. 1893; Marx 1965; orig. 1852). It is true that this political configuration was in some cases ephemeral and remained confined for some time to restricted areas in Europe, but it set the agenda and marked the goal for a process of political development which eventually enveloped all European countries. The long historical cycle from the homogeneity of the monarchical order, which was re-established in Europe after the Napoleonic wars, through the divergent multilinearity of developments towards democratization and parliamentarization—including extended periods of authoritarian and even totalitarian rule in some countries—to the new homogeneity of present Europe, which has with few exceptions adopted the principles and practices of representative democracy, defines the temporal limits and provides the substantive content of our investigation. This view on the *moyenne durée* (Braudel 1958) of change in parliamentary representation, combined with a comparative approach based on identical or at least equivalent indicators, was the new and distinctive feature of our approach.

The comparative and long-term approach adopted by our study enables us to relate the study of elites more closely to one of the central themes of contemporary political science: the theme of democratization and of its internal variations. It is this theme which offers some of the crucial elements of the theoretical background of our investigation. It is obviously neither possible nor desirable to review in detail all the literature concerning democratization, but it is necessary to highlight some of the more salient points which have been raised. The first is that democratization processes have been a common experience for European political systems. Looking back at European political history from the vantage point of the end of the twentieth century, we can see significant elements supporting an image of convergence, whereby the fundamental ingredients of contemporary mass democracy have progressively become part of some kind of political *koinè*. The final result at least seems to support the existence of some sort of 'deterministic' trend towards democracy, whereby the process of democratization and parliamentarization in Europe seems to be guided by an 'iron' teleological mechanism working in favour of one type of political order and sweeping aside all others. Yet such a deterministic and linear view of the democratization process appears far too simple as soon as we analyse the paths through which the end result was approached in greater detail. Such an approach also ignores the variations in the timing of the process, the crises, the discontinuities and setbacks as well as failing to take account of the fact that the end result itself, the democratic regime, can encompass significant variations (Lijphart 1984).

Already some of the pioneering studies of democratization, from Dahl, to Rokkan and to Linz, have drawn attention to important variations existing in Europe (and to even more outside Europe) within the common experience of democratization. Such differences have concerned both the formal institutional steps required for the attainment of democracy and the extension of citizenship by processes of political mobilization and participation. Some years ago, in an attempt to produce a scheme for the analysis of such variations, Dahl proposed focusing on differences in the relative timing and speed of the evolution of two main dimensions of the democratization process—liberalization and inclusion—which enabled him to distinguish between different paths of democratization (Dahl 1971). In addition, Rokkan for his part, having conceptualized the process of democratization as the passing of a number of thresholds (legitimation, incorporation, representation, executive power), has discussed the reasons and implications of variations in the sequences of the thresholds and in the timing of their overcoming (Rokkan 1970). These authors, and others following in their foot steps, have documented how the process through which voting rights have been extended to the whole adult population has varied significantly among European countries. But it has also been shown that the political mobilization of the newly enfranchised voters has not automatically followed at the same speed: in some countries it has taken place more promptly while in others it may have lagged behind. The same can also be said for the development of the main agents of political mobilization and participation, the parties. A good deal of the literature devoted to parties has challenged the view of a uniform and deterministic trend in the evolution of parties leading everywhere towards the 'supreme form' of the mass organized party (or later of the catch-all party) and has proposed a more indeterminate view according to which distinctive developmental paths may appear in different countries, or even within the same country, thus producing significant variations in the organizational models of a central actor of democratic life. Even more radical variations in democratization paths appear as soon as we take into consideration the existence both of continuous and of discontinuous patterns of development at the regime level. While in some European countries democratization has developed without major breaks and as a gradual process, in an even greater number of countries the process has faced one or more interruptions. In these cases, a democratic breakdown (Linz 1978) has opened the way for a non-democratic regime (of variable nature and length) and only at a later stage could the democratization process be resumed. Thus, the processes of democratization are best viewed as a complex interweaving of common and divergent threads.

The significant variations existing among European countries in the developmental paths towards democracy have been fairly thoroughly documented by many analyses of the steps in suffrage extension, of the trends of political mobilization, of the processes of party formation and transformation, of the transformation of institutions and of inter-institutional relations (in particular the relations between government and parliament). Crises and breakdowns of democracy have also been studied systematically and their connections to the previous dimensions have been investigated. Our view is that the empirical study of parliamentary elites can add a new dimension to these analyses by documenting how and to what extent the representatives, that is, those actors which are at the same time the main products and producers of the democratization processes and of the democratic institutions, have changed in parallel with the other dimensions of that great transformation. As a result, the study of the European processes of democratization will ideally have at its disposal the empirical data for the parallel sequences of developments concerning: (*a*) the rules of admission to the political arena (suffrage rights and other political rights); (*b*) the extent and patterns of political mobilization of the citizenship (turnout); (*c*) the main agents of political mobilization (parties); (*d*) institutional arrangements (parliamentarization of governments, and so on); (*e*) characteristics of political elites. Quite obviously such different aspects into which the democratization process can be broken down are linked together by important connections. In particular, it is clear that the recruitment of political elites will be affected in significant ways by all the other phenomena mentioned above. At the same time, we have enough evidence to suggest that there is some degree of 'flexibility' in such linkages. The synchronism of these developments is not always the same. Leads and lags among the different aspects are a real possibility and contribute to the variability of democratization processes. Extensions of suffrage may not be followed immediately by the political mobilization of the new enfranchised strata; new voters may not necessarily be channelled by new parties; old elites may survive and manage to adapt to the new conditions. Such variable interrelations (synchronisms, leads, lags) between the different aspects are at the same time a scientific puzzle (particularly *vis-à-vis* oversimplistic interpretations of democracy and democratization) and the starting-point for a more satisfactory understanding of the mechanics of the great political phenomenon of the last two centuries, the process of democratization.

3. REPRESENTATION AS THE CENTRAL FOCUS OF OUR RESEARCH

The subject of our comparative study is parliamentary representation at national level. This is a conventional choice, which can be superficially justified with well-established research traditions in many countries and by a comparatively rich availability of data. Of greater importance, however, are theoretical considerations. Representation is a central element of modern democracy (Sartori 1987); therefore, the study of the members of parliament, that is, of that section of the elite which embodies the representational element of the regime, offers a strategic point of view for the understanding of democracy and of the processes through which it has been established, developed, and consolidated. The importance of studying the representatives is better understood when we reflect upon their two-sided position, that is, being both on the borders between the political institutions of governance and society, and at the same time 'inside' the architecture of democratic government.

Parliamentarians by the fact of being 'the' elected are a crucial link in the exchange process between society and polity typical of contemporary democracy. On one side, they obviously are the 'projection' of society into politics. The elected members of parliament are the primary channel through which society, with its variety of conflicting values, needs, interests, identities, resources, demands, makes itself felt in the institutional arena of democracy. Therefore their individual and collective features are at least to some extent the reflection of society and of its changing structure. Yet, as the best studies of political representation have demonstrated, they cannot be viewed *sic et simpliciter* as a linear extension of societal structures of power and of social lines of conflict into the political arena. Representation is never a purely passive process of translation of society into politics. In fact, it is also a much more active process through which societal elements

are 'politicized' and thus in fact changed. The political actors of representation (be they individual leaders or organized groups such as parties) are
to be considered as a relatively independent variable which shapes the
political expressions of society (and to some extent society itself). In particular, it is quite clear that the enormous societal changes which have taken
place during the age of democratization have been not only reflected, but
also filtered, selected and reinterpreted, absorbed or dramatized, and generally transformed, by the processes of representation. As a consequence,
the group of people that has entered into the political game of democracy
through the process of representation has been significantly different from
the raw materials offered by social life in itself (to the extent that it can be
conceived as a new entity). Parliamentarians have played a very significant
role in this process. Being on the frontline of the representation process
they have been in some way also the 'projection' of politics into society, the
'terminals' through which politics (and its processes) have politicized and
shaped social demands. If this point of view is taken into account, they are
not simply to be seen as the product of society but also as a product of
(democratic) politics and of its specific dynamics. As we will discuss in more
detail later, the 'production' of parliamentary representatives, that is, the
recruitment process, is best interpreted as an interactive combination of
social and of political processes.

However, members of parliament are also placed in a crucial position
well inside the institutional architecture of democracy. Precisely because of
their role as representatives, they are endowed with a prominent position
in the law-making process, as well as (in all European forms of democracy)
in the democratic legitimization (and consequently also often in the recruitment) of the executive branch of government. The potential relevance of
the parliamentary elite, and of its properties for the working of democracy,
seems therefore to be a plausible assumption. Yet when it comes to speci-
fying a causal model of their influence, a number of questions arise. Which
features of the members of parliament should be considered as relevant:
personal characteristics, past experiences, linkages to organizations, or what
else? Which consequences or outputs should be explained: individual attitudes or behavioural patterns (such as votes)? Aggregate routine results
(such as the legislation passed by parliament) or systemic outcomes (such
as regime crises or regime consolidation)? And how direct and simple can
the relationship between elite features and political outputs be? Within this
perspective, the range of studies has gone from short-term microanalyses
of correlations between personal features (such as gender, race, class, education) of individual members of parliament and their political attitudes
or their legislative behaviour (Schleth 1971; Matthews 1985; Norris and
Lovenduski 1995), to the attempts to infuse them with a longer-term
perspective (von Beyme 1982), to the macroanalyses of the relationship

between systemic features of elites and regime dynamics (Field and Higley 1980, Higley and Gunther 1992). Different *explananda* have obviously guided such studies: it makes a difference to study 'normal' current outputs of the political systems (such as legislation) or much broader fundamental features of them (such as the characteristics and persistence of regimes). But differences do not pertain only to the explanandum. They often also have to do with the theoretical models of political action upon which elite studies are based. In some cases, it is a simplified individualistic model which assumes that outputs can be related immediately to the character- istics of the individual members of the elites. Against this point of view, other models contend that only under very special conditions is reality accu- rately represented by this description and that more commonly, between the individual properties of elite members and political outputs, we must take into account the intervening effect of parties, organizations, hierar- chies, institutional solutions, and so on (von Beyme 1982).

Summing up, we can view parliamentary representation as the intersec- tion of two sets of relations: on one side, relations with society (the input side), on the other side, with the decision-making processes of democracy and their outcomes (the output side). Thus, the study of the (individual and collective) characteristics of parliamentarians may be seen as an instrument for investigation in both directions and also for attempting to understand the connections of the two sets of relations. In the most simplified scheme of interpretation, a linear causal direction links the three elements: societal factors will explain the features of the representative elite and these will determine the outputs of the political process (Fig. 1.1*a*). If this scheme may in some marginal or extreme cases reproduce reality, in most cases more complex schemes are needed. On both sides of the scheme the impact of intervening variables must be taken into account (Fig. 1.1*b*). Therefore elite features cannot normally be interpreted as a simple indicator of societal factors nor as simple predictors of political outputs. Yet they allow infer- ences about both if we can relate them meaningfully to the other inter- vening variables.

4. THE RECRUITMENT FUNCTION

On the 'input side', the study of parliamentary elites must be related to a clearer understanding of the processes through which they are 'produced', that is, the recruitment mechanisms. Recruitment can be conceptualized as the intersecting point between the 'supply' of candidates, the 'demand' of selectorates—that is, those organizations and support groups which send the contenders for public offices into the arena of electoral competition— and the choice of the voters. Supply and demand models of legislative

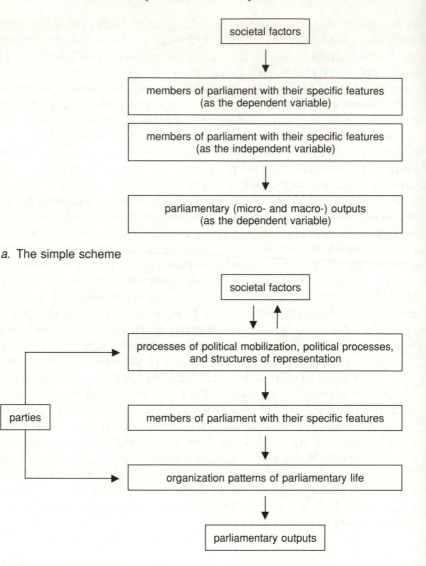

a. The simple scheme

b. The refined scheme

Fig. 1.1. Two schemes for the analysis of parliamentary elites

recruitment have reached a certain degree of popularity among researchers in the past few years (Patzelt 1999: 243), whereby a 'new institutionalist design' prevails focusing on the rules on the game defined by the legal system, the electoral system and the party system (Norris 1997: 2, 8–14). Our work, which is guided by a long-term perspective reaching back into

the pre-party era, extends the study of contextual factors influencing legislative recruitment to changes in the structure and prevailing normative
orientations of whole societies over extended periods, and asks how these
changes translate into changes of legislative recruitment patterns.

It has to be taken into consideration here that actual recruitment is a
highly improbable event when seen against the numbers of those who wish
to stand for public office at some stage of their life, or against those who
actually run for a placement on a party list, or even against those whose
names eventually stand on the ballot-paper. Attributes and affiliations of
contenders give a favourable or unfavourable momentum to their passage
through the recruitment process. The given makeup of a parliament can
therefore be regarded as the final balance of advantageous and disadvantageous factors working in the (self-) selective process preceding the act of
recruitment. Divergent modes of parliamentary representation are therefore indicative of variations between opportunities, norms, and institutional
settings interacting in the process of recruitment. Since this model of parliamentary recruitment had a direct impact on the selection and use of indicators for intertemporal and intercultural comparisons used in our study,
its elements and their combinations should be further specified.

We can distinguish four basic elements in the recruitment-process.

1. The *contenders*, who are stimulated to enter the competition for offices
by individual incentives like prestige, power, material rewards, spiritual or
ideological commitments, and who dispose of certain resources qualifying
them for entry into the electoral competition, such as availability for office,
relevant qualifications formally acquired in the educational system, certain
skills informally acquired through personal experience, access to material
resources to pay for electoral campaigns and to provide for clienteles or
their own maintenance during or after a political career, credibility as an
advocate for material and non-material interests, and finally, a 'social
capital' invested in reputation, in 'strong ties' such as relationships of
patronage and allegiance, and 'weak ties' like acquaintances of a more
casual but wider being. These contenders represent the 'offer' on the
recruitment market. The strength of the incentives and the value of their
resources for those who are on the demand side determines their starting
position in the race for office (Black 1970; 1972).

2. An important intermediary actor in the process of recruitment are the
selectorates, that is, the party organizations, the personal cliques, the groups
of dignitaries or state officials involved in the selection of candidates and
in their presentation to constituencies. Selectorates select candidates
according to the result of complex choices considering the probable value
of the contender's resources for electoral success, their ideological fit with
and their practical function for the selectorates themselves and their likely

loyalty, that is, their expected obedience to the implicit and explicit expectations of the selectors after becoming a parliamentary actor. Since selectorates have not only a demand position on the recruitment market but must also make convincing offers to the electorate, the relative weight of factors working in the selective process is variable: for example, in a situation when a selectorate is in secure control of a significant part of the electoral support market, campaign qualities of contenders will be of less importance than their expected loyalty or their ideological fit. When analysing the role of selectorates we must keep in mind that the meaning of the concept of selection itself is susceptible of significant variations. Selection may vary from a substantially reactive mode (the contenders are there and compete for selection) to a more active mode (the contenders have to be searched for, convinced, stimulated to stand for office). In some contexts, selection comes very near to the meaning of 'production'. For instance, in the case of some highly organized mass parties, the contenders that are selected for parliament had been in fact 'produced' through a long process of socialization within the ranks of the selectorate itself. In other cases, selection means simply choosing and 'labelling' someone from within a pool of contenders which have been formed completely outside the field of influence of the selectorate.

3. The *end consumer* of offers on the electoral support market and the final judge of legislative recruitment is the electorate. Factors such as the candidates' credibility, competence, impact, charisma, and conformity with essential values and interest concerns are part of the electors' demand function when they evaluate the competing offers on the support market. The effect of some of these factors can be directly inferred from the social and political background of representatives, for example, a noble title of a representative is indicative of a connection to the traditional sources of political and social authority, whereas an occupational career as a trade union official hints at an affiliation to the aggregations of organizational power in an industrial society. Such attributes have not only functional relevance for the representatives themselves, they have also symbolic significance for the electorate. Changes of such background attributes can therefore be interpreted as shifts in the relative weight of factors in the demand function of the electorate. However, it must again be kept in mind, that the prominence of candidates' personal attributes in the recruitment process is dependent on the position of selectorates in the electoral support market: if a party has a strong and loyal electoral support in a given constituency, 'symbolic' qualities of candidates attracting a wider audience are of less importance than their intra-organizational qualities such as loyalty or managing skills.

4. All the three elements previously mentioned are strongly influenced by the *formal structure of opportunity* for parliamentary representation. This is the fourth factor in our model of parliamentary recruitment. Here are to be considered the laws and administrative practices regulating access to legislative offices and the competition for these offices in different ways as, for example, the extension of franchise and eligibility, the opportunities for organizations to intervene in the recruitment process through list systems, laws and practices favouring or impeding governmental intervention in the process of recruitment, and so on. It is obvious that such rules of the game have a direct impact on the supply of and demand for contenders for legislative recruitment. To give just one example, the denial of allowances to representatives favours those candidates who either dispose of a regular independent income of their own or who are dependent on transfers from supporting organizations such as parties or trade unions. The resulting representation will be at once more 'plutocratic' and 'oligarchic' (in Michels' sense) than in a parliament which offers allowances to its members.

It is clear that time is a central element of our research design and that we are particularly interested in the dynamics of change. This causes something of a dilemma since our model of parliamentary recruitment is static, as are all simple demand and supply models. According to such a model, after the establishment of representative institutions, an equilibrium will emerge between the demands of selectorates and electorates on the one hand and offers from interested contenders on the other. Historical analyses of European parliaments show that such a balance can indeed be very stable; in some cases the makeup of parliaments hardly changed for decades and even withstood deep changes in other areas of society. Nevertheless, changes can occur and have occurred in all cases under observation. These changes must be the result of internal or external factors, which affect the choices of the actors in the recruitment market. In order to understand those factors of change, we must go back to the four elements of the recruitment function previously outlined: they can be seen as potential sources of variations in the output of recruitment within countries, across countries, and over time.

The pool of the available (realistic) contenders is likely to vary very significantly and it is obviously the element that will be more directly influenced by societal differences (within and across countries) and transformations (over time). In particular, which resources are likely to be relevant for success as a potential candidate, and how they are distributed depends in a significant way on the general makeup of society (a traditional agricultural society versus a dynamic industrial and then a post-industrial one, and so on). For example, being noble or not, owning a large piece of land or not, controlling the networks of clients typical of practising lawyers or having the prestige that derives from writing for newspapers, having or not a university education, being a man or a woman, may acquire rather different meanings in different societies.

The fact that the nature of the selectorates has changed over the last 150 years and that cross-country variations are very significant needs hardly be mentioned. An extensive comparative literature on parties from Ostrogorski to Katz and Mair, through Duverger and Kirchheimer provides sufficient evidence for that purpose. The substitution of parliamentary cliques with organized parties (Sartori 1976); the variable models of organization of the parties—from Duverger's mass party to the catch-all party of Kirchheimer, to the cartel party of Katz and Mair—and the different patterns of competition among them—are all elements which result in selectorates operating differently, with different priorities and constraints. And when talking about selectorates, we should not simply consider parties but also a variety of interest and pressure groups which interact with them in performing the selective function. Different selectorates will probably choose contenders with significantly different properties.

As for the end 'buyers' in the representation market, that is, the voters, we need only recall the fundamental transformations that this element has undergone in the period we are considering. As a consequence of suffrage extensions which have brought the propertyless lower middle classes, peasants, workers, illiterates, and women into the electoral market in successive waves, the original narrow pool of middle and upper class, educated (and propertied) males has been severally diluted. We must also keep in mind the important variations in the predisposition of electors to make use of their voting rights. High or low (and possibly differentiated along some lines of social demarcation) levels of turnout may result in different electorates, but these quantitative elements are only the beginning of possible variations. Qualitative aspects such as the existence of segmented identities (based on region, ethnicity, language, religion, gender, and so on) or, vice versa, the predominance of a common sense of belonging, may guide the attitudes of the voters *vis-à-vis* the parliamentary candidate in a very powerful way. Where one such identity plays a major role, the voters will choose primarily on such grounds; otherwise, they may be guided by quite different criteria (such as opinions, interests, competence, and so on).

Finally, the rules and the institutional system of opportunities must be considered. Variations in electoral systems (single member versus larger constituencies; first-past-the-post versus proportional representation (PR) systems, the existence of preference vote, and so on) are the most obvious factors that, by affecting all the other elements of the game (contenders, selectorates, and voters) and their strategies, may influence the recruitment of parliamentarians. But one should not forget also the potential import-ance of other institutional aspects, such as the role of the parliament *vis-à-vis* the executive. During the period examined, parliaments have generally moved from a position of limited influence upon the legitimization and recruitment of the governments to a position of dominance. It is plausible to expect that the attractiveness of the position of parliamentarian for the contenders, the consequences (and thus the criteria) of the selection for the selectorates, the meaning of their vote for the voters will also change substantially.

The transformations of some of these elements may have originated from processes of change internal to the social and political system of one country, but in some cases also under the impact of external events and actors. The most extreme examples of the second possibility are those coun-tries, such as Germany and Italy, where democracy was re-established after World War II under the close scrutiny of the winners, which, as such, had a significant influence upon the new institutional structure of opportunity, the parties, and even some societal aspects. In other countries too, perhaps in a less visible way, external variables have probably contributed to stimu-lating the dynamics of change in some of the elements of the recruitment function.

The social makeup of a parliament can in the end be viewed as a 'sedi-ment' of norms, values, interests, and opportunities of those involved in the recruitment process and of their respective strategies to achieve their goals. Certain contenders dispose of qualities and resources which equip them better than others to establish themselves on the recruitment market. Pre-ceding processes of selection and self-selection should result in a structure depicting such advantages, whereby selectorates and electorates decide what will be considered as an 'advantage' and which weight should be attached to it. It is obvious that the value of advantages varies over time, between countries and between parties. To be of noble origin will be advan-tageous in a society which maintains 'deference' as a criterion shaping class and power relationships, whereby such political parties will promote noble candidates who defend the idea of a 'natural' order of social inequality based on ascriptive criteria and may accordingly try to capitalize on the prestige, and the privileged access to resources of power, attributed to noble status. On the other hand, in a society where egalitarian principles predominate and achievement has been established as a criterion for access to positions of power, noble status will be of no advantage or even disadvantageous in the recruitment process. For a party favouring nobles as political leaders, it will be difficult to impose them as legislators against the resistance or even the mere indifference of a constituency which has become more egalitarian. These considerations may illustrate how legislative recruitment can be used to reveal the mechanisms which generate a certain structure of social and political power and to identify the driving forces behind its change.

Following Raymond Aron's invitation to elite research (1950), the study of leadership groups provides us with a characteristic insight into the social structure of a society. Or, as Robert D. Putnam (1976: 166) put it: 'Because elite composition is more easily observable than are the underlying patterns of social power, it can serve as a kind of seismometer for detecting shifts in the foundations of polities and politics'. The picture we obtain is not representative in the statistical sense of an equal opportunity for each unit of observation to enter a sample, but it is authentically depicting the inequalities, advantages, and disadvantages inherent in the process of recruitment. The main problem of this approach is not to define a field of observation, but rather to relate outcomes—the given composition of a parliament—to causes—the mechanisms generating a certain structure. If we find a rising proportion of female legislators in a parliament, various explanations are on offer as, for instance, an improved availability of qualified and motivated women competing for seats, a higher concern in a given selectorate or electorate for gender equality or even—paradoxically—a lower attractiveness of legislative positions, making them more easily accessible to hitherto disadvantaged social categories. Within the logic of an inductive research design, there is no easy solution to the dilemma of competing explanations. One way would be to change the level of observation and seek for additional evidence in the micro-worlds of selective bodies. The other way is to make use of the comparative method and to use variations across countries, between party families, and diachronically within countries in order to control the influence of different explanatory variables. Research assembled in the present volume prepares the ground for this work of attributing 'causes' to certain phenomena by interpreting their variations over time, between nations or party families.

5. ON THE OUTPUT SIDE

So far we have treated legislative recruitment as a dependent variable to be explained, as an indicator of the general structure of social power. As an independent variable, legislative recruitment is present in research designs which relate social background of parliamentary leadership groups to their integration, stability, and performances. A *locus classicus* for such an approach is Otto Hintze's famous article on *Das monarchische Prinzip und die konstitutionelle Verfassung*, where he outlined why parliament in Imperial Germany had not succeeded in gaining the 'ruling influence in the state' as it did in contemporary Britain or France, and as it was hoped by leading German liberals after the foundation of the German Empire. The main reason he gave was that German parliamentary elites were 'completely lacking in the necessary inner unity and solidarity which would, under all conditions, be the prerequisite for a role in political power'. He attributed these divisions to their lack of social homogeneity and their acting as 'agents of special interests of singular social classes, occupational groups, branches of the economy, regions and religious denominations'. He concluded that

with us parties are, properly speaking, not political but rather socio-economic or religious-confessional formations. This is connected with the fact that it is actually the life of the bourgeois society—as opposed to the actual political operation—which finds expression in our representative bodies. That is, however, a formation of the party system which leads more to a monarchical leadership of the state than to parliamentary influence. (Hintze 1970; orig. 1911: 337–8 our translation)

Although Hintze restricted his argument to Imperial Germany at the turn of the century, we have here concisely a more general theoretical model which links social structure at large, the party system, the social makeup of parliamentary elites, and their ability to establish parliamentary democracy. Elements of this model can be found in modern political theories and explanatory schemes such as the Lipset–Rokkanian cleavage concept (Lipset and Rokkan 1967) or Lijphart's Consociational Democracy model (Lijphart 1968). More recently, Field and Higley (1980, 1985) proposed a taxonomy linking states of elite structure with the stability or instability of representative institutions. Both, elite structure and regime stability, were connected in a deterministic relationship: 'As a causal variable an elite state always predates the stability or instability of political institutions' (1985: 30). The ability of elites to develop and to maintain a culture of peaceful competitiveness is the prerequisite for a stable representative democracy, whereby high structural integration and value consensus of elites are the bases of their consensual unity. Incidentally, it is interesting to note that characteristics of political elites which were considered by authors like C. W. Mills (1956) to be incompatible with pluralist democracy were treated by Field and Higley as its cornerstones. Field and Higley's taxonomy became a widely accepted point of departure and a framework for interpretation in elite studies. Research on the processes of democratic consolidation in Southern European and Latin American countries (Higley and Gunther 1992) and, recently, also in the post-communist polities of Central and Eastern Europe (Best and Becker 1997) has drawn from their proposition.

As we mentioned before, other studies have also proposed relating attributes of parliamentary elites to more specific outputs of parliamentary institutions such as legislation. Robert D. Putnam's sceptical question 'Does social background matter?' should thus be answered with 'yes!' provided we don't establish a direct link between origin and outlook of legislators and our explananda. If we use social and political background variables as independent variables, we should treat them as 'structural parameters' establishing or weakening links between factions of political elites or between elites and constituencies, pressure groups, or mass organizations. It should make a difference whether representatives are closely related through origin and communal offices to their local constituency or whether they entered parliament gaining a safe seat provided by a national party list when local affairs are on the agenda of a legislature. It should make a difference if members of different parliamentary parties are recruited from mutually exclusive social settings and devoted to divergent political norms if it comes to parliamentary compromising and the formation of coalitions.

The design of the DATA CUBE allows us to confront such statements with empirical evidence and particularly to research into the connections between elite structure, regime stability, and performances of representative institutions. If Otto Hintze was right to propose that it was the strong correlation between social background of legislators in the broadest sense and their parliamentary party affiliations which incapacitated the Imperial Reichstag, we should be able to verify this proposition by a series of 'second order comparisons' (Rokkan 1967), combining cross-national and cross-temporal designs.

6. THE CUBE AND ITS PRESENTATION

At the beginning of our research effort was the building of the CUBE. This is an integrated European data set, with countries, time, and variables as its three dimensions (Fig. 1.2). The creation of the data set was the result of a process that can be described as the finding of the minimum common denominator between already existing empirical research. When this process was started, we faced three questions:

1. For how many European countries would systematic empirical data be available?
2. Which time periods would be covered by the data?
3. Which variables concerning the personal features, the social and political background, the career of members of parliament would be present in the national data sets?

Thanks to the influence of the founding fathers of European political science, and to the predisposition of researchers to follow established paths of research, we soon found that, in spite of a number of problems, the

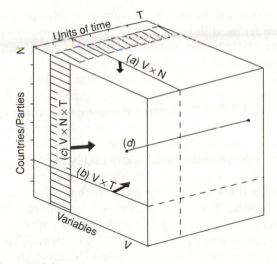

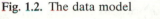

Fig. 1.2. The data model

Note: (d) = The axis for time-series analyses.

Source: Andress (1985); Best and Ponemereo (1991).

answers to the three questions were such that they allowed us to move forward. In most European countries, systematic empirical research about parliamentary elites had been done at some stage; typically, such analyses had covered a long-term perspective or at least a medium-term one; at worst, in some countries, there was the problem of 'stitching' together separate time series. As for the indicators, we found that together with a number of rather idiosyncratic variables due to special peculiarities of one or more countries, there was a good number of common variables and also their operationalization had not been too different. Thus, the conditions for the building of the CUBE existed.

Having selected the variables (see appendix to this chapter), the next step was that of transforming individual-level data into aggregate data. The unit in the CUBE is the parliamentary party of a given parliamentary term. More precisely, that means that the values of individual members in each category were transformed into an aggregate value of the parliamentary party to which they belonged (for instance, if the variable is 'education' and one of its features is 'university level', the value assigned to the 'x' parliamentary group in the 'y' parliamentary period is the percentage of MPs of that group who have reached that educational level). The countries covered completely at this point are Finland, Germany, France, Great Britain, Italy, the Netherlands, and Norway. For Denmark, Hungary, Portugal, and Spain, either the data collection or the data conversion into the CUBE format are under way but still not fully complete.

When data is available in the CUBE format, results are graphically represented as standardized time series, exhibiting the long-term variation in percentage shares of selected traits of MPs such as, for example, gender or local politics background. A small subset of indicators, for example, age and tenure, is based on the mean. Alterations in the composition of legislatures occurring after an election are depicted as step changes in the trend lines. Data are presented for all MPs and for members of main party families, provided they had obtained at least ten seats in five consecutive elections. To avoid the interruption of otherwise continuous time series, the threshold of ten seats was ignored when a party family failed to meet the entry criterion for just one or two elections. The graphs are meant to delineate main trends and periodizations in the data which is why the time axis of the graphs is not broken down into periods of legislatures. In the case of extended interruptions of competitive parliamentary elections by authoritarian or dictatorial regimes (like those of the *Deuxième Empire* in France, of Fascist Italy after the mid-1920s, and of Nazi Germany after March 1933), the trend lines connect the legislatures elected prior to and after these regime discontinuities in order to give a clearer picture of erratic changes in the composition of parliaments following such interim periods. In some time series, singular legislatures are missing due to a lack or an incompatibility of data. In such cases, and when only one or two legislatures were affected, the nearest valid observation points were connected. When data was missing for more extended periods, the time series were interrupted for the legislatures in question.

Most time series start in 1848 for reasons given in preceding parts of this chapter. However, in countries where neither the basis for parliamentary representation was dramatically expanded nor a national parliament became established in this year of European revolutions (as in Italy, Finland, and Great Britain) other, more appropriate starting-points were chosen by the authors of the country chapters. In most countries, the time series end with the parliaments actually convened at the time of writing and with the likelihood of continuing their terms into the next millennium. Exceptions are Finland and Norway where elections were held after the respective country chapters were finished. In cases where data is not yet available in the CUBE format, authors have made efforts to provide evidence which approaches the scope and standards of the CUBE as closely as possible, thus extending our basis for comparison to an even broader variety of European polities.

7. THIS BOOK

Our research effort aims at producing two complementary books. This first book has the purpose of preparing the ground for the more ambitious goals of the second. In the second book, we want to test, within a truly comparative research design, a number of propositions explaining (on the input side) transformations over time, and variations across countries and across parties in the social and political makeup of parliamentary elites and to explore (on the output side) relations between some of the characteristics of parliamentary elites and the performances of democratic regimes. In order to move in that direction, the first book, based on national chapters, provides a rich mapping of long-term transformations and of inter-party variations of parliamentary elites, complementing them with basic information about the different national contexts and processes of democratization. Starting from the analysis of a number of common variables concerning the personal properties (age, gender, education), the social origin (nobility, occupation, economic sector), the political background (local and party offices), and the institutional entrenchment (turnover rates) of members of parliament, special attention will be devoted to the following points:

1. *The starting point of the process.* What is the profile of members of parliament in the first years of liberal parliamentarism? To what extent do their social features conform to a standard model? More concretely, there is the problem of assessing the characteristics of the representatives of the original political establishment on one side and of the first challengers on the other. With regard to the first, it is important to evaluate whether a more 'societal' type of establishment (based on land-owning and aristocracy) or else a more 'etatist' one (based on high bureaucratic positions) prevails.

2. *The decline of the original establishment and its substitution with professional politicians during the process of democratization* (and particularly in connection with the extension of suffrage). In discussing this theme we may go back to the schemes of Figure 1.1. We know that democratization processes have affected the relationship between society and members of parliament through a transformation of the intervening variables. To put it simply, one could say that their overall effect has been that of 'widening the gap' between societal variables and the features of parliamentary elites, and of enhancing the weight of political intermediation. From a situation where 'society' could represent itself in a fairly direct way (and parliamentarians were predominantly persons with high social prestige), we have increasingly moved to a different situation where society came to be represented only through highly developed political organizations such as parties. This transformation of representation mechanisms is also reflected in a transformation of the social makeup of representatives. The key concepts for interpreting this process are the concepts of 'political professionalization' and of 'partyness of recruitment'. Democratization has entailed a substitution in the role of representatives of the members of the societal

establishment with an autonomous breed of professional politicians rooted much more in political organizations than in societal positions. The process can be gauged with a combined use of social background and political career variables, which indicate the relative importance of social and political resources available for the representatives. Professional and social background qualifications, suggesting a strong weight of social resources in the selection and career of parliamentarians, should decline. Weaker professional qualifications or professional qualifications with a 'democratic potential' should take their place, but will increase still further the weight of political qualifications linked with the processes and structures of political mobilization. Within this general tendency, we must assess more accurately the correlation between the two processes. How promptly does the first follows the second? How significant are the lags in elite transformations?

3. *The degree to which political professionalization takes the form of party professionalization.* The point here is to evaluate to what extent the career inside party organizations becomes the dominant component of political professionalism, and to what extent other forms of political professionalization (for instance, one based more on local politics resources) can survive.

4. *Differences in the upper levels of political professionalization reached.* Of relevance here are several questions; is there a convergence towards similar levels of political professionalization or, on the contrary, do systematic differences among countries persist and, within countries, what are inter-party differences and to what extent do they persist over time or give way to a process of homogenization?

5. *Is there an 'end' in the history of professionalization?* In our perspective, the one question becomes central: what happens once a high level of political professionalization is reached; up to what point will the trend go; when will it start to level off; and, is a reversal of the trend foreseeable? Finally, given the strong linkage between political professionalization of parliamentarians and the development of strong party organizations, can we interpret some recent signs of a weakening of parties as organizations as factors also of a decline in political professionalism? Party-centred political professionalization, which has entailed the substitution of ascription and social prestige with the active involvement in party organizational networks as the fundamental resource for political careers, has sometimes been considered as the end stage of parliamentary elites development in the past. This idea requires more open discussion and empirical control. There are good reasons to question this view: it may be that the growing interconnection of established parties (Katz and Mair's 'cartel parties') with the

state (and its bureaucracy) have contributed to a weakening of party organizations as the focal centre for the production of political personnel. The state apparatus (in an extended sense) could be a competitive source. But the challenge to party organizations may also come from other directions: for instance, society and its specific agencies of interest representation. The proliferation and growth of associations, interest groups, and movements capable of acting with greater autonomy *vis-à-vis* the parties both in the electoral arena and in the decision-making processes, should also have an impact in the recruitment of parliamentary elites. The growing importance of the media in the processes of interest articulation and political mobilization may be a further intervening variable (celebrities versus more obscure *apparatchiks*).

Appendix: DATA CUBE Coding Instructions

Aim: to create for analytical purposes a database containing legislative recruitment and elite transformation data from as many European countries as possible and for as long a period as feasible. For each country, the partial objective is to derive from existing/reorganized data files a DATA CUBE, i.e. a three-dimensional data matrix (variables by time by party).

Thus each case in the data set should be identified by a composite number, i.e. the string of VAR01, VAR02, and VAR03.

A. Technical Variables

VAR01   country code: each country will be identified by numbers 01–nn

1	Denmark
2	Germany
3	Italy
4	Netherlands
5	Norway
6	United Kingdom
7	France
8	Austria
9	Spain
10	Portugal
11	Finland

VAR02   year of election: six digits with one decimal, first election with 0, second election with 1, e.g. 1868.0 or 1932.1

VAR03   party at time of election: the following modified, Gallagher *et al.* categorization should be used in order to maximize comparability. Consult the relevant tables in Gallagher *et al.*, *Representative Government in*

Western Europe (1992) in case of doubt about the proper position. The following table shows combined party codes.

301   Communists
302   New Left
303   Socialists/Social Democrats
304   Greens
305   Agrarians
306   Left Liberals
307   Right Liberals
308   Christian Democrats, Protestant
309   Christian Democrats, Catholic
310   Conservatives
311   Extreme Right
312   Nationalists and Regionalists
313   Other
314   No party
315   All Parties (=N)
350   *Destra storica* (right liberals)
351   *Sinistra storica* (right liberals)
398   Liberals
399   Christian Democrats

B. Legislator-Related Variables

Values of each of the following variables will be percentages, unless otherwise indicated. All percentages should be given with one decimal point.

Calculation method:

1. On the basis of information on individual legislators, calculate for each election period/legislature the relevant value for each variable (all parties).
2. For each party/family of parties and for each period/legislature, calculate the relevant value for each variable.

1. Educational Background: Non-academic

VAR04   basic education: includes all cases where no information is available about further education or further education is not plausible
VAR05   intermediate education: any level of education above basic education and below full academic degree
VAR06   university or comparable degree: military education included unless otherwise specified

2. Educational Background: Academic

VAR07   law degree
VAR08   humanities, social sciences, theology
VAR09   technical, engineering, natural sciences, medicine

3. Political Background of Legislators

VAR10   local/regional political background: local/regional politics local elective position before and/or at first election; including also appointed mayors

VAR11   other leading party position: legislators with leading position in party organization, national or local, including youth and women's organizations before and/or at first election

VAR12   cabinet positions: cabinet positions of various types before and/or at first election

VAR13   other parliamentary experience: all other types of noteworthy political experience at national level—to be specified by national expert—before and/or at first election

4. Political Background Index

The following index variables are counts on the variables VAR10 to VAR13.

VAR14   none of above types, unknown inclusive
VAR15   one of above types
VAR16   two of above types
VAR17   three or more of the above types

5. Regional Background

The following variables state the combination of the regions of birth, living, and election at the time of election. All values are percentages, # means not.

VAR18   region of birth = region of living at entrance = region of election
VAR19   region of birth = region of living # region of election
VAR20   region of birth # region of living = region of election
VAR21   region of birth = region of election # region of living
VAR22   region of birth # region of living # region of election
VAR23   region of birth = region of election
VAR24   insufficient information

6. Gender Information

VAR25   female legislators

7. Social Background Indicators

These variables are not mutually exclusive and are valid for the time of first election. All values are percentages.

VAR26   noblemen legislators, if applicable, and as defined by national expert
VAR27   teachers and professors, all sorts of
VAR28   journalists and other writers, including publishers and editors
VAR29   full-time, paid political party employees as well as other political organization employees, all types—including trade unions—as defined by national expert

VAR30   higher administrative-level civil servants, excluded are military, judges, professors, and clergymen
VAR31   public sector employees, all levels paid by public institutions, state-owned companies included according to national experts
VAR32   military persons, all levels
VAR33   priests, all clergymen
VAR34   lawyers, practising
VAR35   judges, prosecutors included if independent judicial organ
VAR36   primary sector, agriculture, fishermen
VAR37   blue-collar workers, industrial sector
VAR38   managers, 'businessmen'

8. Age and Seniority

VAR39   mean age: in years, one decimal, rounded, exact calculation if possible, otherwise difference between year of election and year of birth
VAR40   mean age of newcomers: in years, one decimal, rounded, newcomer means elected for the first time on the election day
VAR41   elections: mean number of 'normal' elections in which member stood successfully, periods with one decimal
VAR42   percentage of newcomers: members entering as newcomers, only newly elected without previous legislative careers

9. Other Variables

VAR43   number of members of party groups/total number for each category in VAR03
VAR44   professions other than the law
VAR45   small independent craftsmen and merchants
VAR50   religion: Protestant
VAR51   religion: Catholic
VAR52   non-aligned
VAR53   Jewish

References

Andress, H.-J. (1985). *Multivariate Analyse von Verlaufsdaten*. Mannheim: Zuma.
Aron, R. (1950). 'Social Structure and the Ruling Class'. *The British Journal of Sociology*, 1: 1–16, 126–43.
Best, H., and Becker, U. (eds.) (1997). *Elites in Transition: Elite Research in Central and Eastern Europe*. Berlin: Leske & Budrich.
——and Ponemereo, R. (1991). 'The German Parliamentary Data Base: Catching the Complexities of Political Life-Histories', in H. Best, E. Mochmann, and M. Thaller (eds.), *Computers in the Humanities and the Social Sciences: Achievements of the 1980s—Prospects for the 1990s*. Munich, London, New York, and Paris: K. G. Saur, 163–71.

Beyme, K. von (1982). 'Elite Input and Policy Output: The Case of Germany', in Czudnowski (1982).

Black, G. (1970). 'A Theory of Professionalisation in Politics'. *American Political Science Review*, 64: 865–78.

——(1972). 'A Theory of Political Ambition: Career Choice and the Role of Structural Incentives'. *American Political Science Review*, 66: 144–59.

Braudel, F. (1958). 'Histoires et sciences sociales: la longue durée'. *Annales*, 13: 725–53.

Czudnowski, M. M. (ed.) (1982). *Does Who Governs Matter?* De Kalb, Il.: Northern Illinois University Press.

Daalder, H., and van den Berg, J. T. (1982). 'Members of the Dutch Lower House: Pluralism and Democratisation 1848–1967', in Czudnowski (1982), 214–42.

Dahl, R. (1971). *Polyarchy: Participation and Opposition.* New Haven: Yale University Press.

Dogan, M. (1961). 'Political Ascent in a Class Society: French Deputies 1870–1958', in Marvick (1961).

Field, G. L., and Higley, J. (1980). *Elitism.* London: Routledge and Kegan Paul.

————(1985). 'National Elites and Political Stability', in Moore (1985), 1–44.

Gallagher, M., Laver, M., and Mair, P. (1992). *Representative Government in Western Europe.* New York: McGraw-Hill.

Higley, J., and Gunther, R. (eds.) (1992). *Elites and Democratic Consolidation in Latin America and Southern Europe.* Cambridge: Cambridge University Press.

Hintze, O. (1970; orig. 1911). 'Das monarchische Prinzip und die konstitutionelle Verfassung', in *Staat und Verfassung. Gesammelte Abhandlungen*, i. Göttingen: Vandenhoeck & Ruprecht.

Lijphart, A. (1968). *The Politics of Accommodation: Pluralism and Democracy in the Netherlands.* Berkeley: University of California Press.

——(1984). *Democracies.* New Haven: Yale University Press.

Linz, J. (1978). *The Breakdown of Democratic Regimes.* Baltimore: The Johns Hopkins University Press.

Lipset, S. M., and Rokkan, S. (1967). *Party Systems and Voter Alignments.* New York: Free Press.

Marx, K. (1965; orig. 1852). *Der Achtzehnte Brumaire des Louis Bonaparte.* Berlin: Dietz.

Marvick, D. (ed.) (1961). *Political Decision Makers.* Glencoe, Il.: Free Press.

Matthews, D. R. (1985). 'Legislative Recruitment and Legislative Careers', in G. Loewenberg, S. C. Patterson, and M. E. Jewell (eds.), *Handbook of Legislative Research.* Cambridge, Mass.: Harvard University Press, 17–55.

Michels, R. (1925). *Zur Soziologie des Parteiwesens in der modernen Demokratie.* Stuttgart: Kröner.

Mills, C. W. (1956). *The Power Elite.* New York: Oxford University Press.

Moore, G. (ed.) (1985). *Studies of the Structure of National Elite Groups.* Greenwich and London: JAI Press.

Norris, P. (ed.) (1997). *Passages to Power: Legislative Recruitment in Advanced Democracies.* Cambridge: Cambridge University Press.

——and Lovenduski, J. (1995). *Political Recruitment.* Cambridge: Cambridge University Press.

Patzelt, W. J. (1999). 'Recruitment and Retention in Western Europe an Parliaments', *Legislative Studies Quarterly*, 24: 239–79.

Putnam R. (1976). *The Comparative Study of Political Elites*. Englewood Cliffs, NJ: Prentice Hall.

Rokkan, S. (1967). 'Models and Methods in the Comparative Study of Nation-Building'. Paper prepared for a Preparatory Meeting on Problems of Nation-Building. Brussels: UNESCO.

——(1970). *Citizens, Elections, Parties*. Oslo: Universitesforlaget.

Sartori, G. (1976). *Parties and Party Systems*. Cambridge: Cambridge University Press.

——(1987). *The Theory of Democracy Revisited*. Chatham: Chatham House Publishers.

Schleth, U. (1971). 'Once Again: Does it pay to study Social Background in Elite Analysis?' in *Sozialwissenschaftliches Jahrbuch für Politik*. Munich: Günter Olzog, 99–118.

Skocpol, T. (1979). 'Emerging Agendas and Recurrent Strategies in Historical Sociology', in T. Skocpol (ed.), *Vision and Method in Historical Sociology*. Cambridge: Cambridge University Press.

Tardieu, A. (1937). *La Profession parlementaire*. Paris: Flammarion.

Thompson, M. S., and Silbey, J. H. (1985). 'Historical Research on 19th Century Legislatures', in G. Loewenberg, S. C. Patterson, and M. E. Jewell (eds.), *Handbook of Legislative Research*. Cambridge, Mass. and London: Harvard University Press, 701–37.

Tocqueville, A. de (1942; orig. 1893). *Souvenirs*. Paris: Gallimard.

2

The Incremental Transformation of the Danish Legislative Elite: The Party System as Prime Mover

MOGENS N. PEDERSEN

A parliament was introduced into Danish politics in 1849. Before that time, royal absolutism had allowed only a limited—and controlled—'popular' participation, and no traditions for representative bodies existed. But since that year, the *Folketing* has met continually, its activity only briefly interrupted during World War II. Long lines of newcomer-politicians have entered Parliament for their respective parties and have served for a short time or for an extended period. Some moved in and out of the parliamentary 'career', others were—or succeeded in being—more faithful servants. A few spent a lifetime in the legislature—the all-time record being fifty years of service. Many put their mark on Danish politics. Their names are still remembered, and their marble bust, a painting, or another memorial may still remind today's citizens of their existence. Many more have, however, left very few traces apart from their name and scattered pieces of biographical information. But data exist for each and everyone, at least enough to make it possible to trace the development and slow transformation of the collective profile of the *Folketing* over almost 150 years.[1]

The story that can be told on the basis of the data available is basically a simple one. It is not very different from the story which is being told in other chapters in this book. The findings can be summarized in the following five propositions:

[1] Biographical information for the first 100 years can be found in Elberling (1949–50), which also contains information about members of the upper house, the *Landsting*. For the following period the Danish *Folketing* has published volumes with information after each election (e.g. *Folketinget efter valget den 12. December 1990*). A list of members 1949–89 is also available (*Folketingets medlemmer i 40 år 1949–1989*. 1992). A comprehensive (42 variable) data set, covering the period 1849–1968, is available from Danish Data Archive (reference number DDA-0018). Data were originally collected by the author of this chapter. Due to the fact that the data were ordered sequentially after the date of the politician's first entry into the *Folketing*, this data set is not directly comparable with other data sets used in this volume. For this chapter, the author has therefore used other, less comprehensive, data sets, several of which have not been reported before. The reader is referred to legends in connection with the tables.

1. In terms of its educational, social, and political background character-
    istics, the collective profile of the Danish legislative elite has developed
    over time in an *incremental* but not in all respects *uni-directional*
    way.
2. *Ascriptive values* were dominant as the basis for recruitment in the early
    days of the Parliament. Later on some kind of *achievement-based values*
    became important as political activity in a party or another organiza-
    tion turned out to be a *conditio sine qua non* for entry into legislative
    politics. In other terms, this transformation also lends itself to descrip-
    tion as a move from a collective profile dominated by *amateur politi-
    cians* to the modern profile with its predominantly *professional* outlook
    and with its gradual tendency to be dominated numerically by members
    recruited from *public sector occupations.*[2]
3. If a more systemic perspective is taken, one may also say that this
    transformation comprises an *institutionalization* of the process of leg-
    islative recruitment. This process has gradually produced a specific
    pattern, a *cursus honorum* which most new political recruits will tend
    to follow. *Gatekeepers* in the party organizations demand special qual-
    ities from the ambitious recruits and these tend to supply what is in
    demand.[3]
4. *The development of the party system* is by far the most effective explana-
    tory variable with regard to this transformation process, and this
    statement holds true irrespective of stability or instability in the
    explanandum, the collective profile of the parliamentary elite.[4]
5. Thus an *adaptive party system* and *an adaptive collective profile* go
    together and the interplay between these two variables account for
    the long-time incremental trend in the social, educational, and political
    background characteristics of the members of the *Folketing*.

The following sections of this chapter will provide basic documentation
for these descriptive generalizations. For more comprehensive analyses
the reader is, however, referred to other sources, identified in notes and
references.

In Section 1, I shall give some introductory contextual political background information about the Danish political system and its development.
This is followed in Section 2 by a discussion of the pattern of emergent
institutionalization in Danish legislative recruitment, and some of the

---

[2] The theoretical terminology in this paragraph is the same as has been used in Eliassen
and Pedersen (1978). The reader is referred to this article for further elaborations.

[3] The concept of institutionalization is in this context used as proposed by Nelson Polsby
in his influential article on the institutionalization of the US House of Representatives (1968).

[4] For lack of space, this chapter will not contain a comprehensive discussion of the effects
of *realignments* and *critical elections* on elite transformation. Long trends are highlighted
at the expense of the *critical junctures*. The latter aspect is discussed at length in Pedersen
(1994).

critical historical junctures will also be identified. In Sections 3–5, assorted indicators of social and educational background characteristics will be presented, and finally, in Section 6, the development of the party system, especially its long-term transformation, will be brought to bear on the discussion.

1. A HEURISTIC PERIODIZATION OF DANISH POLITICAL HISTORY

When the first *Folketing* met in 1849 its members had been recruited in a process which still has to be charted by historians. Due to the restricted suffrage, the electorate was rather small, comprising of approximately 75% of all males above 30 years of age, that is, at most 15% of the total population (Elklit 1988: 49–50). Curiously enough the age of eligibility was lower—25 years—than the minimum age required for the suffrage. The ruling elite—those who had engineered the events of 1848 that led to the abolition of royal absolutism—apparently did not wish to set up obstacles for election of bright young men like themselves.

Elections took place in public in 100 single-member constituencies. In most cases, townspeople and farmers from the countryside met at the town hall square, prospective candidates were presented and presented themselves to the audience, and the election took place by a show of hands. Behind the scenes, various local notables were active. Various social and political networks were active as well, but there were no parties yet, only—in some parts of the country—political 'clubs' of like-minded citizens or some loosely organized associations, embryonic interest organizations. As far as is known, there was not a shortage of candidates. On the other hand, the pattern of supply and demand is not known. What is known is, for example, that between 1849 and 1866 more than half of all elections in the individual constituencies were decided by means of a show of hands, and in those elections where votes were counted, the average turnout was as low as 31% (Holm 1949: 10). What is also known is that well-educated and mostly well-to-do national notables ('personalities') played an important role in the local processes, but in particular in the first parliaments, where they dominated the proceedings: 56% of the first 'class' of 1849 have been characterized as coming from an upper-class family background; 50% had an academic education; and no less than 68% were civil servants, other officials of the state, or belonged to the liberal professions. Wealthy farmers comprised about a fifth of the total number of 101 members of the *Folketing* (Elberling 1950).

This situation at the outset of parliamentary history has been depicted in some detail, because it is important to note the absence of party organizations and most other institutional structures for recruitment. It is also important to note the absence of experience and political knowledge of a stable and institutionalized kind. Those who already belonged to the social elite also had easy access to the new political elite. The new democracy still had to experiment with the processes of nominations and elections. Behavioural patterns had to develop. First and foremost, mobilization of the new voters had to take place.

The following decades witnessed the slow widening of the electorate, the gradual mobilization of the lower—and especially middle—classes in the countryside, and later on the same mobilization process among the working class in the cities. From approximately 1870, a gradual political organization and mobilization process took off which in due time led to the formation and crystallization of a party system with several parties. This process, which lasted several decades, was characterized by a bitter constitutional conflict between 'left' and 'right' in Danish politics, but also by internal conflicts within parties. The 'classical' Danish party system with its four— 'old', as they are still called—parties, was a long time in the making. It only became a reality and a stable feature as late as 1910–20. During the same decade' constitutional reforms opened up universal suffrage. From 1915, most Danish citizens above the age of 25 years had the right to vote and stand for election, meaning that parties could attract voters—and had to cater for voters—from all social classes and categories.

Without doing serious harm to work of Danish historians, it is possible to condense this development in a summary table which may serve as a background for the presentation which follows of parliamentary elite data from the various periods (see Table 2.1). It is of course hardly possible to make a theoretically relevant periodization and condensation of major events without theory. In the case of Table 2.1, I have without much hesitation suggested that the party system and changes in that system should be seen as the major causal agent for the transformation of the parliamentary elite. During 150 years, the scene has shifted from that of a non-partisan, upper-class-dominated, 'caucus' situation (Duverger 1951), through an emergent party system, to a full-fledged mass-party system, towards a situation in which parties are characterized as 'media parties' (Pedersen 1994: 105), sometimes even—following Katz and Mair (1995)— as 'cartel parties' (Bille 1997). This development has had profound effects upon recruitment conditions. First and foremost, it has created a movement towards institutionalization of career patterns in all the parties. In this connection it is, however, more important to stress the changes that have taken place in the format and the numerical distribution within the party system. We shall see in Section 6 below that the gradual shift from bourgeois dominance in Danish politics, through dominance by the agriculturally based parties around the turn of the century, to the era of the Social Democratic

Table 2.1. Periods in Danish history since democratization 1849–1990: major political events and party system characteristics relevant for understanding parliamentary elite transformation

Period	Characteristics of party system and life in the parliament	Major political events
1849–70	Restricted suffrage and eligibility. Parliamentary factions crystallize slowly in to 'left' and 'right'. No significant organizational activity in country.	First democratic constitution 1849. National homogeneity after 1864 military defeat. Constitutional reaction and 'left–right' conflict after 1866.
1870–1901	Constitutional conflict polarizes parliament and country. Party organizations develop during 1880s.	Social Democrats gain representation 1884. Parliamentarism accepted as principle 1901.
1901–20	'Classical' party system comes into existence. National interest organizations emerge.	Constitutional amendments 1915–20 lower suffrage thresholds, including female suffrage and eligibility.
1920–45	Parties develop auxiliary organizations. Institutionalization of parties and parliament. Party system survives but partly suspended 1940–5.	PR introduced in 1920. First Social Democratic cabinet 1924. 'Stauning era' 1929–41. 'Non-partisan' election 1943. Major gain for Communists 1945.
1945–68	The era of the mature party system (four to five parties). Towards the end of period beginning reshuffle of the party system and weakening of party organizations.	New constitution 1953 removes Upper House. Gradual lowering of suffrage age. Small-scale public support for parties introduced 1965.
1968–90	Continued decay of party organizations. Party system becomes an eight to ten party system. Building up of new cleavages (EU issue).	Major realignment 1973. Ten elections 1971–90. Introduction of full-scale public support for parties 1986.

near-dominance, is the most important explanatory factor for the gradual transformation of the collective profile.[5]

By stressing party system change as the prime factor of elite transformation I have deliberately played down other causal models, especially those which are based upon assumptions about a direct linkage between social/class structure and political elite. Institutional reforms, such as constitutional amendments, electoral system reforms, and so on have been identified in Table 2.1, partly because they may have an autonomous impact upon the recruitment process, partly because of their relationship with developments within the party system.

---

[5] For a much more developed argument about the relationship between party system change, institutional factors, and elite transformation, the reader is referred to Pedersen (1976).

During the period under inspection, Danish society has changed profoundly from being a society ridden with class conflicts—from 1849 until 1864 even with a national conflict—to a society which is dominated by consensus—and equality values. Danes see themselves—together maybe with the Swedes—as the inventors of the modern welfare state. Some scholars would expect such a dominant value shift to produce visible changes in the parliamentary profile. Some scholars would also expect to see some of the major—deliberate—changes in the political status of various social categories strike through. The introduction of female suffrage and eligibility (1908–18) should in particular be traceable in the collective profile of the *Folketing*.

I do, however, consider the internal politics of the parties and of the party system a much more powerful dynamic factor than the changing social/class structure and the legal institutional structure. The impact of the first is 'translated'—with delays—through the transformation of the party system more than through any other medium. The impact of the latter, for example, in the form of female suffrage and eligibility, has, as we shall see later, only become visible after almost fifty years, and only when the parties and the party system allowed the impact to take place. These are some of the themes that will be pursued in the following sections.

2. CIRCULATION AND INSTITUTIONALIZATION OF THE PARLIAMENTARY ELITE

One of the basic truths about parliamentary elite transformations is that such transformations will only happen, if and when incumbent legislators leave parliament. Such departure may for the individual be due to a genuinely voluntary decision to retire or to—more or less forced—eviction as a candidate. It will also in some cases be due to defeat in an election.[6] In some countries, the large proportion of ever-victorious incumbents, because they bar the entry of new politicians, is even seen as a *potential threat to democracy*, to quote a recent book on this topic (Somit *et al.* 1994) Whatever the cause, a member with certain identifiable characteristics and legislative experiences will leave the parliament, thereby opening up space for a new recruit to enter, or for an 'old-timer' to return. The incoming member may be like the departing member in many respects—or he may be totally different. On the micro-level, this is how elites may or may not be transformed. On the macro-level, the tendency to return members with the same characteristics as the departing members is what results in a stable or an

---

[6] At each election the following equation holds true: number of voluntary retirements *plus* number of electoral defeats *equals* number of newcomers *equals* (number of seats in parliament *minus* number of re-elected incumbents).

only incrementally changing collective profile. By saying so, we also say, that even rapid personal 'circulation'— high turnover rates—may coincide with great stability in the collective profile over time. Conversely, it is possible to see considerable change in the collective profile, even when electoral volatility is low and/or when the career of Members of Parliament is characterized by institutionalized stability.

A first step in describing the changing collective profile of the Danish *Folketing* since 1849 consists in mapping the personal circulation characteristics of the parliament. The numbers in Table 2.2 tell at the same time a story about incremental development and rapid change. When the circulation indicators are followed over the first 120 years of parliamentary history, the tale undoubtedly is one of institutionalization of the pre-parliamentary career as well as the career in parliament (Pedersen 1977; cf. also Polsby 1968). In the course of more than a century of non-interrupted development of procedures and unwritten norms, a pattern of institutionalized recruitment and de-recruitment gradually emerged.

It became more and more difficult to enter the parliamentary elite, not to say 'parachuting in' as one could still do during the first decades. The 'quick' careers gradually gave way to a more regulated party-organized career. Candidates had to spend more and more time qualifying for the seat. They had not only to run for office more times before they succeeded, but they also had—on average—to move among constituencies in order to qualify for a seat, and especially so, if they were looking for a 'safe' seat. In most cases, the successful candidate would also have had a previous career in municipal politics. He might have served in some capacity in his party's

Table 2.2. Selected indicators of personal circulation of the Danish parliamentary elite: period averages 1849–1968 and selected sessions 1971–1990

Period	Average no. of times nominated before first elected	Turnover rate (%)	Mean Seniority (years of service in *Folketing*)	Mean age at final departure from *Folketing*	Percentage leaving for 'non-political' reasons
1849–70	1.3	30	4	49	11
1870–1901	1.5	20	11	54	25
1901–20	2.1	22	12	57	28
1920–45	2.5	22	11	58	36
1945–68	2.5	21	12	60	41
1971	n.d.	34	7	n.d.	20
1973	n.d.	45	5	n.d.	11
1981	n.d.	26	6	n.d.	9
1990	n.d.	24	8	n.d.	6

Sources: For 1849–1968, figures are based on secondary analysis of a data set, used in an unpublished conference paper; values for the period 1968–90 are estimates; 'n.d.' means that no data are available at present.

organization or in an affiliated interest organization. No wonder that the newcomer was also a mature person. The average age at first entry slowly increased, until in the 1950s it reached the high forties.

When candidates then arrived at the *Folketing*, they could expect a fairly long and safe career. Their parliamentary mandate was not as often brought to a temporary halt as had been the case during the nineteenth century. They did not quite as often have to move from one constituency to another in order to continue and to safeguard their political career. For many, it was almost as if they had been appointed to a tenured position. They would also tend to retire from legislative service at a ripe age. Considering the fact that several parties required their members to retire from politics before they turned 70 years old, an average age of departure such as was reached during the postwar decades (see Table 2.2), is very high indeed.

Although data for the period after 1968 are not as complete, it is nevertheless beyond doubt that this picture was shattered within a few years, at least momentarily, when Danish politics went through electoral realignment and turbulent years during the 1970s. A combination of generational change in several party groups, which started around 1970, and instability created by sharply increasing electoral volatility and consequent disruption of the hitherto stable party system, produced considerably increased circulation rates, whatever measure is used. After some elections, the turmoil came to a halt, but the party system never returned to its former shape and format, and the stable recruitment patterns had apparently also become a phenomenon of the past, at least in terms of the variables highlighted in Table 2.2.[7]

I have argued that it is logical to start a mapping of the developmental patterns of the parliamentary elite by studying circulation rates. This is so, because the turnover rate will set an upper limit to social transformation in its widest sense. First, as has already been said, one legislator has to go for another to enter. Secondly, the new recruit may, or may not, be different from the one who was de-recruited. Since one would further expect that a period with a stable party system would also tend to produce an institutionalized, hence stable, recruitment pattern, while party system instability will be expected to go hand in hand with higher social transformation rates (Putnam 1976: 166–8), we may end the inspection of Danish circulation patterns by suggesting that transformation rates would be higher at the beginning and at the end of the period under inspection than in the middle period, which is also incidentally the era of the maturing and the mature mass party. We shall return to this question later in this chapter.

---

[7] For more thorough analyses of the personal circulation of the Danish *Folketing* the reader is referred to Pedersen (1977, 1994). An analysis of the 1973 election can be found in Pedersen (1988).

3. WHERE DID THEY COME FROM?

Denmark is a small country. Today it is possible for a member of the *Folketing* to live in the provincial parts of the country and travel 'up to Copenhagen', the seat of the parliament, every day. This was not so 150 years ago. Nor was it possible fifty years ago. Before the era of fast ferries, bridges, and domestic air flights, the working and living conditions for members were very unequal and very unfavourable for the politicians who lived in the Danish provinces. The Member of Parliament, who lived and worked in Copenhagen, could relatively easily pursue a political as well as a professional/occupational career. For the MP, who came from peripheral Jutland, election to the *Folketing* meant having to take up hotel-room residence in the capital for most of the time, only returning to home and constituency with irregular intervals, at weekends, or even more seldom. It was often difficult to pursue an occupational career—or just to 'stay in business'. The personal costs for the politicians from the provinces were considerable.

Given these conditions and assuming a certain individual rationality of candidates, one would expect a particular geographical pattern of recruitment to manifest itself in the data, at least in earlier times. A study of all newcomers to the *Folketing* between 1920 and 1968 provided a very clear picture, when all Danish constituencies were roughly rank-ordered with regard to travel distance to Copenhagen (Pedersen 1975). It was found, first, that the typical representative in every type of constituency was a local resident. Secondly, by far the largest proportion of candidates with local residence was found in the constituencies of the Copenhagen area. Thirdly, the further one moved away from the political centre, the smaller the probability that the representative would have a metropolitan background, and the higher the probability that he would be a local resident in the constituency. Thus, to some extent, a polar pattern existed in which 'metropolitan' members were pitched against 'peripheral' members. The pattern was visible also in the individual party, at least in the major parties.

This pattern constitutes a theoretically important piece of information. Even in a small country, where residency in the constituency is not mandatory, most members still had—at least during most of the period under inspection—a close relationship to their constituency. On the other hand, the Copenhagen residents were favoured considerably in the recruitment process, since they would not only compete on their 'home turf' for the metropolitan seats, but also in the provincial constituencies, including those in the very periphery of Denmark. Even if the 'local son' was often given favourable treatment in the latter constituencies, there were also quite a few constituencies in which the 'king-makers' preferred to be represented in parliament by a 'high-flyer' or a senior politician, even if that meant a

Table 2.3. The degree of over/underrepresentation of the capital, the provincial towns, and the rural districts in the Danish *Folketing*: the residential background of newcomers compared to the residential background of the population 1850–1968 (percentage Differences)

Decade	Copenhagen area	Provincial towns	Rural districts
1850s	+17	+9	−26
1860s	+11	+9	−19
1870s	+17	−4	−13
1880s	+26	−3	−23
1890s	+8	−4	−4
1900s	+2	+4	−5
1910s	+6	+2	−8
1920s	+7	+4	−12
1930s	+6	+3	−9
1940s	+11	+1	−12
1950s	−2	+15	−13
1960s	0	−1	+1

Source: Pedersen (1976: 47).

person, who lived in Copenhagen. And between 1920 and 1968, no candidate living in Jutland was ever elected in a Copenhagen constituency—and only 9% of those elected in Copenhagen had their residency outside that city—mostly in the neighbouring county, which today is an integral part of the metropolitan area.

The main effect of these recruitment mechanisms was to create an imbalance: the population of the Copenhagen area was overrepresented in Parliament, and so to some extent was the population of provincial towns. The losers were the rural parts of Denmark (see Table 2.3). The imbalance was significant during the first decades of democratic representation. During the heyday of the Agrarian Liberal Party it tended to diminish, but it reappeared later in the twentieth century.[8] This pattern of urban overrepresentation and rural underrepresentation characterized not only the lower house, the *Folketing*, but also, though to a lesser extent, the upper house. Not surprisingly, it also reflected itself in the educational as well as the occupational profile of the Parliament, and thus it is quite vital for an understanding of the political elite transformation to keep the geographical pattern in mind. On the other hand, one should not just jump to the conclusion that Danish politicians were—and are—divided up into an elite with a Copenhagen background and a 'counter-elite' from rural Denmark.

[8] Unfortunately, no comparable data from most recent periods are available. Municipal reforms *inter alia* have made direct comparisons dubious. An estimation does, however, suggest that the overrepresentation of the metropolitan area was still a reality in 1990: the proportion of the population living in the area was 33%, while the percentage of MPs with residency in the metropolitan area was—at the very least—39%.

Table 2.4. Selected indicators of parliamentary elite transformation: percentage of MPs with various geographical backgrounds 1849–1968 (period averages)

Period	Members living in constituency	Members born in constituency	Members born and living in constituency	Members living in Copenhagen area
1849–70	69	40	36	26
1870–1901	68	48	43	30
1901–20	68	38	36	25
1920–45	57	34	29	29
1945–68	63	35	29	24

Source: Unpublished data, DDA-0018.

The picture is much more complicated. Most important of all, the recruitment system tended to maintain a close relationship between the constituency and the member. Even if members were not legally forced to live there, many of them still did so, or they had other close connections to 'their' constituency of election.

The close relationship between constituency and member has existed throughout the entire period. One may suggest that to some extent this reflects the rural cultural heritage with its low degree of geographical mobility. It is not only a pattern of congruence between constituency and area of residence.[9] There has also always been a connection between constituency and place of birth and upbringing (see Table 2.4). Approximately two-thirds of the members were elected in their home constituency throughout the period 1849–1968, and a third of all members were not only living there, but had even been born, in the constituency from which they were elected, thus in a sense being the 'true locals'. But it is also noteworthy that a considerable proportion of the representatives were already living in the metropolitan area, when they were elected for the first time.[10] The relative population size of this area has increased over the period from approximately 7% to 20–25%, and from this perspective the overrepresentation of Copenhagen-based politicians during the nineteenth century becomes even more conspicuous. It was also to a considerable extent a pattern which reflected the conflict in the old party system between the forces of 'right' and 'left', between the educated/academic/upper class and the farmers, who challenged the former group.

[9] The location of residence and constituency has been found to be highly correlated (coefficient of determination = 0.61 for the period 1920–68) (Pedersen 1975: 11).

[10] Upon election and after the career has taken off, it quite often happens that the MP takes up residence in Copenhagen. As a result, for example, of rules about individual remuneration of members, it also happens that members keep—more or less—pro forma residence in their provincial constituency. Documentation for these patterns is, however, difficult to obtain.

4. HOW WERE THEY TRAINED?

After this brief discussion of the pattern of geographical background of members of the *Folketing*, the time has come to shift the focus to the educational background in the widest sense, that is, the training which precedes first entry into parliament. Although information about this aspect is often of a dubious nature, since it relies heavily on information given by the members themselves, it is still possible to focus on a few relevant facts.

In a collective portrait of Danish politicians fifty years ago it was said that

A majority among them have, before they were ever elected, been on their way for considerable time, carried forward by the trust of their fellow-citizens from parish council to county council, from the board of the co-operative bakery to the town council, from the local farmers' wholesale association to the regional leadership, from the local workers' club to the pinnacle of the trade union. (Thorsen 1949: 129)

In this quotation, the author, a shrewd observer of Danish political history, gives special emphasis to that kind of education which is acquired 'on the job', not to formal education and school attendance. Phrased another way, it is the process of moving ahead, stepwise, through selection or self-selection, which is important in the career, more than the formal education, and more than the family background. The early career moves are probably the most important steps in many a political career, also because 'The very fact of having been elected or selected—having been "elevated" through some mechanism of choice from one position to another—makes the "chosen" fundamentally different from their choosers' (Eulau 1969: 101). Flowing from this statement, many lines can be pursued. Thus we can see that a considerable proportion of the Members of Parliament had a career behind them in local politics, when they entered the *Folketing*. At the very least, they had political experience from an elective position in their home municipality (see Table 2.5).

During the last decades of the nineteenth century, it may have been an exaggeration to speak about a local political 'career', for politics in parish councils and town councils was still in its infancy. One could certainly not make a living out of serving there. But local participation meant that one belonged to a network, and that network as well as the fact that the holder of a position acquired some valuable political experiences, was what mattered, especially for those who came from the proverbial 'log cabin'—in Danish often described as 'the village school with the thatched roof', or from an industrial proletarian upbringing. Even today local politics is an important factor in recruitment, not least for politicians from the provincial parts of the country.

Table 2.5. Education and socialization: selected parliamentary sessions: percentage of MPs with particular backgrounds

Parliamentary session	Primary school only	Academic degree (all)	Law degree	*Folk High School*	Local politics experience
1855	33	33	21	1	48
1887	43	26	17	10	41
1901	67	16	8	39	50
1920	57	23	7	26	55
1935	54	18	4	26	55
1950	48	21	7	33	50
1966	39	25	10	29	49
1990	15	31	7	12	48

Sources: 1855–1966: unpublished data (Pedersen 1968). 1990: *Folketinget 1990*.

Another important training ground was that very special Danish institution, the *Folk High School*. These private, general-purpose schools, which in particular recruited their adolescent or adult pupils from among the sons and daughters of farmers, mushroomed during the final decades of the nineteenth century—from two schools with eight pupils in 1850 to seventy-four schools with more than 5,000 pupils half a century later (Pedersen 1976: 43). Schools providing more specific agricultural/professional skills were also important for the young men from the villages, and very often attendance at both types of schools became the most important educational background for these youngsters, who, given the backward school system in the Danish countryside, did not always obtain an adequate, systematic educational training in the primary school system. Around the turn of the century, the Danish working-class movement established its own variation of the *Folk High School*, and many Social Democratic shop stewards and 'political apprentices' acquired an equivalent training and experience in these schools as well. In more recent times, this channel of mobilization has lost some of its earlier importance, as the general educational level has improved.

The general national system of education changed its profile several times during the period that we are observing. Most of the time, the system comprised three levels as in most other countries. Primary school (approximately seven years' duration) could be followed by training at a middle level, eventually leading to the artium exam, which gave the student access to an academic education at one of the—few—universities and professional schools. During the nineteenth century, pupils from the countryside would still have found it difficult to advance beyond the first level, and recruitment to the highest levels of the school system was very narrow throughout most of the period. It only started to expand in about 1960 beyond a definite minority (4–5% of a cohort entering the *Gymnasium* and 2% continuing to the universities). Until the 1970s, but especially before the World War II, many of the members of the *Folketing* had only a primary school background with seven to eight years of formal schooling, and in Parliament they were then confronted with the other large group of politicians, those with an academic background and training. During the first decades of Danish democracy this juxtaposition, not to say confrontation, of those with the lowest and the highest educational levels was a primary source of conflict in Danish politics, compounded by the fact that this juxtaposition correlated highly with variations in residential background, social background, as well as the politicians' occupational background.

It is also in this perspective that the Danish *Folk High Schools* must be seen as politically important. In the short run, they may have added to the confrontation, since their ideological programme was often almost anti-academic. In the longer run, they may have served as an intellectual bridge and as forerunners for the present-day educational system with its less pronounced barriers.

In a comparative perspective, probably the most interesting fact to note about the formal educational background of the Danish members of the *Folketing* is the relatively low overrepresentation of members with a law degree. Academics have always been heavily overrepresented in Danish politics, in particular at the very beginning, but also towards the end of the period under inspection. But whereas in most countries the lawyers in the widest sense of the word comprise only a infinitesimal proportion of the population, but are still often very conspicuous participants in legislatures, this is not at all so in Denmark. In the *Folketing*, they were prominent during the early decades, but later on their numbers were decimated. There are many explanations that can be given for this 'comparative abnormality'.[11] It is noteworthy that lawyers have never recaptured the position they had during the first decade of representative government. Lawyers in private practice are still rare creatures in Danish politics.

5. OCCUPATIONAL PROFILE

A thorough analysis of the occupational profile of the *Folketing* is beyond the scope of this brief chapter. It has to be found elsewhere (Pedersen 1976). It suffices here to map the profile for selected sessions by means of

---

[11] This special feature and its general theoretical implications are discussed at length in Pedersen (1972). The reader should also notice that Table 2.5 contains information about holders of a law degree from the universities, not about practising lawyers, whose numbers are and always have been considerably smaller.

Table 2.6. Occupational background of MPs: selected parliamentary sessions (percentage of members)

Parliament-ary session	Agriculture	Educational positions	Public administrations	Politics and organiza-tions	Liberal professions	Mass media	Urban sector/residual
1855	40	12	9	2	16	4	17
1887	47	16	7	3	10	8	9
1901	54	14	3	6	5	12	6
1920	29	13	8	3	9	25	12
1935	32	13	6	15	5	15	14
1950	22	12	7	16	7	8	28
1966	14	14	16	20	6	4	26
1990	7	30	14	11	3	6	28

Sources: Unpublished data (Pedersen 1968, 1972; *Folketinget 1990*).

a crude categorization which will highlight the most prominent categorical groups (see Table 2.6). The following six general statements can be derived from an inspection of these as well as other available data:

- The representation of farmers and 'agricultural Denmark' in the widest sense of the word culminated around the turn of the century and has decreased since then. During the period 1849–1990, the proportion of the population living off agriculture has dwindled from more than 50% to somewhat less than 10%. The linear trend in the population thus has to be compared to a decidedly curvilinear trend in the elite population.
- There has been a steady growth in the proportion of members with a background in positions in politics and the world of organizations. The figures are probably somewhat underestimated, since this kind of information is hard to find and difficult to interpret.
- Teachers and educators of all kinds have been well represented, not to say significantly 'overrepresented' in Parliament throughout the period, and in recent times their numbers have even increased considerably. While primary school teachers, especially from rural Denmark, played an important role during the nineteenth century as agents for the mobilizing rural population, the more recent advances in several parties of educators reflect a differentiation of the educational system—but also the still important fact that teachers as dispensable public employees will find it relatively easy to pursue a more or less risky political career.
- Starting in the late nineteenth century and lasting until the middle of the twentieth century, a background in mass media—the newspaper world—was quite frequent. This group, who like teachers belong to a population category characterized by a central location in local

networks, have played a role in all major parties. In more recent times, the differentiation of the media structure has opened up recruitment opportunities for 'television personalities' who are in demand in several parties.

- As primary sector representation has decreased, a wide array of urban sector occupations have proliferated among the representatives. In Table 2.6, the last column gives the aggregate size of this sector but it is almost impossible to categorize further, hence the term 'residual'. Upon closer inspection it turns out, however, that the most conspicuous increase is not related to the private urban sector. It is related to the considerable growth of a Welfare State with a relatively strong component of employment-heavy institutions.

- The most important development over the last decades thus has been the mushrooming of public sector employees of various kinds. This group includes not only a rich variety of educators, but also administrators at various levels, many categories of service personnel, military personnel, political professionals, and so on. In 1990, public sector white-collar employees comprised 42% of all Members of Parliament—as against only 18% of the entire population (*Folketinget* 1990: 268). This group representation now has the same relative weight as the agricultural/rural representation had during the nineteenth century. But it is much more differentiated in its composition.

The most conspicuous change in the collective profile has, however, not been identified yet. It concerns the representation of gender. Women were entitled to vote and to stand for election as early as 1915. But as in most other countries, where women's formal political rights were introduced, it took quite some time before the women mobilized as political activists, candidates, and representatives. Until after World War II, the proportion of female legislators was very low: less than 5%. Over the next decades, there was a gradual increase in the proportion of women who became politically active, locally as well as nationally. It was, however, only towards the end of the 1960s that women mobilized considerably at all levels in Danish politics, but then the process was rapid, and with no significant setbacks. Since 1990 the proportion of female members in the *Folketing* has been more than 30%, and in two of the parties a clear majority of legislators are women. When women enter legislative politics, they mostly tend to come with an occupational background in the public sector, primarily the educational or the social service sectors. Gender representation is thus closely linked to the increasing representation of public sector employees. Although doubts are being raised about the prospects for further increases in the representation of women, their number still grows. In the 1998 election, the propor-

Table 2.7. Some indicators of political mobilization and party system development

Period	Number of seats in *Folketing* (period average)	Electorate as % of total population (period average)	Turnout (period average) (%)	Average Conservative strength[1] (%)	Average Agrarian Liberal strength[1] (%)	Average Social Democratic strength[1] (%)	Strength of other parties/ groups[1] (%)
1849–70	100	15	28	53	47	—	—
1870–1901	103	16	56	27	70	3	—
1901–20	119	17	72	13	46	24	17
1920–45	148	55	80	19	25	40	16
1945–68	148–175	62	84	17	23	39	21
1968–90	175	71	87	15	14	33	38

Note: [1] Figures are approxmiate.

Sources: Høgh (1972: 43); Elklit (1988: 34); Holm (1949); Rokkan and Meyriat (1969: 73 ff.); *Folketinget 1990*.

tion was 37%. Similar increases are found in most elite positions, including local politics.[12]

6. THE PARTY SYSTEM AS PRIME MOVER

Some decades ago, a Danish historian summed up the period under inspection, using simple metaphors:

If we wish to illustrate the long trends in the domestic politics of Denmark, the curve would have to be drawn as three big waves, indicating the long movements created by the political maturing of three social classes. Separately, the appearance of the bourgeoisie, the farmers, and the working class on the political arena were the result of profound social and economic upheavals in society, and each wave washed over the previous one, thus dominating for a time . . . Democratic thinking so to speak filtered down through the layers of population and triggered the political process (Hvidt 1960: 9).

The main story is one about social classes and their democratic representation. Representation means party representation, and therefore we should now return to the discussion which was opened up in the introductory parts of this chapter. In Table 2.7 which, following Table 2.1, provides some rough indicators of party system change, we are able to follow the political mobilization that took place in Denmark after 1849.

The electorate increased gradually, and so did the turnout of voters in

[12] This statement is very well documented in the context of Norwegian and Swedish politics, see e.g. SOU (1990: 44), but it is probably as true with regard to Denmark. The study of the representation rates of women in Danish politics and society will be given special priority in coming years.

Folketing elections. The three 'waves' are easily spotted, when we follow the changing strength of the old *Højre* and its successor, the Conservative People's Party, the changing strength of the Agrarian Liberal party (parties), and the development of the major socialist party, the Social Democrats. We even find a trace of the dramatic upheavals in the Danish party system around 1973 (cf. Pedersen 1988), which meant that the three oldest parties lost out for a long period to some new parties.[13]

In the preceding section, the collective profile of the legislative elite was mapped onto some simple indicators. It was evident that the class/occupational composition fitted the description quite well: from a period in which bourgeois occupational and educational backgrounds dominated the profile, one moved through a long period in which occupations—and educational levels and forms—characteristic of the farming community became dominant. In the twentieth century, the profile gradually 'urbanized' and 'democratized', both in terms of educational and occupational backgrounds of the members. The relative growth of the public sector was also reflected in the collective profile.

In an earlier analysis of this transformation, the process was mapped in much greater detail (Pedersen 1976). It was demonstrated, first, that one could observe the three waves not only in the composition of the lower house, the *Folketing*, but also in the upper house, the *Landsting*, until its abolition in 1953. Even the changing composition of the Cabinets was reflecting the macro-sociological trends in Danish society, albeit with a considerable time lag. Secondly, it was documented that long-term changes in the collective profiles of these three bodies was caused predominantly by changes in the party system. Each of the major parties in Danish politics had fairly stable or at most only incrementally changing profiles over time, and the overall change in the collective profile of the Parliament thus was primarily a result of changes in the distribution of parliamentary—and Cabinet—seats among parties.

Fluctuations in party strength from one election to another have been found to correlate highly with fluctuations in the occupational profile of the parliament, and the long-term trends in party strength to correlate as well with the secular trends in collective profile. The main conclusion from the 1976 study accordingly was that

As long as one party dominates the legislature in numbers, it will also dominate its profile . . . But when the party system changes and new parties with differing opportunity structures begin to attack the position of the dominant party, this is bound to have an effect at the level of the elite as such . . . Just as the addition of new magnets to an existing magnetic field will force an iron object to move, so the consecutive

---

[13] Since the author has elsewhere analysed the effects upon the parliamentary elite of the 1973 events, this aspect will not be dealt with here, but see e.g. Pedersen (1994).

appearances of two new major forces in Danish politics after 1849, the agricultural class and the urban industrial class, caused the changes in the socio-economic composition of the political elites. (Pedersen 1976: 35–6)

The 1976 study did, however, also suggest that the relationship between socio-economic change and elite transformation was closer during the nineteenth century and the early decades of the twentieth century than later on. During the nineteenth century and well after 1950, farmers were comprising a majority in the parliamentary group of the Agrarian Liberals. At the peak, they counted more than two-thirds of all members. In 1990, this proportion was down to one-quarter. In its infancy the Social Democratic Party recruited almost all its legislators among the employees of the party press and among trade union employees, later on also from other political organizations within the working class movement. These groups may still be seen, but they do not play the same dominant role as they did (cf. also what was said in the previous section about the increasing differentiation within the public sector) (see Table 2.8).

Gradually, and especially during the last five decades, the differentiation of the occupational structure, the emergence of new positions with special affinity to politics and the political career, the differentiation of the educational structure, and the institutionalization of the major parties, have also created a more differentiated structure of demand as well as supply in the recruitment process. Most of the parties will today try to appeal to a wide

Table 2.8. Highlights of the occupational differentiation in two major parties

a. Agrarian Liberals

Occupational Category	1887	1901	1920	1935	1950	1966	1990
Farmers, all categories	56	63	59	68	53	57	30
Teachers, Primary School	10	11	12	11	9	—	7
Newspaper men	11	6	8	3	6	6	7
Others, all categories	23	20	21	18	31	37	56
All	100	100	100	100	100	100	100
N	72	91	51	28	32	35	30

b. Social Democrats

Occupational category	1887	1901	1920	1935	1950	1966	1990
(Party) Newspaper men	—	50	57	25	10	—	1
Employee, labour movement	—	43	8	22	29	19	20
Politics, elective position	—	—	4	6	5	17	7
Others, all categories	100	7	31	47	56	64	72
All	100	100	100	100	100	100	100
N	1	14	48	68	59	69	71

array of voters, and since Danish voters have become increasingly influential with regard to the actual selection of candidates as well as the actual election of members, it has also become more and more important for the party organizations, centrally as well as locally, to take into consideration that the collective profile of the parliamentary party has to reflect to some extent the influential groups within the wider electorate, not just those groups that dominate the party organizations. With a large and still growing public sector, and with the highest employment rate for women in the Western world, it is in particular not surprising to find that most of the parties lay special emphasis on these categories when they consider the composition of their parliamentary groups.[14]

References

Bille, L. (1997). *Partier i forandring*. Odense: Odense University Press.
Danish Statistical Yearbook, various volumes.
DDA-0018 (1984). *Danske politiker-arkiver, MF-arkivet 1849–1968*. Odense: Danish Data Archives.
Duverger, M. (1951). *Les Partis politiques*. Paris: Armand Colin.
Elberling, V. (1949–50). *Rigsdagens medlemmer gennem 100 år*, i–iii. Copenhagen: J. H. Schultz Forlag.
——(1950). 'Rigsdagsmændenes Livsstilling', in H. Frisch, K. Fabricius, H. Hjelholt, M. Mackeprang, and A. Møller (eds.), *Den Danske Rigsdag*, iv. Copenhagen: J. H. Schultz Forlag, 349–92.
Eliassen, K. A., and Pedersen, M. N. (1978). 'Professionalisation of Legislatures: Long-Term Change in Political Recruitment in Denmark and Norway'. *Comparative Studies in Society and History*, 20: 286–318.
Elklit, J. (1988). *Fra åben til hemmelig afstemning*. Aarhus: Politica.
Eulau, H. (1969). *Micro-Macro Political Analysis: Accent of Inquiry*. Chicago: Aldine Publishing Company.
Folketinget efter valget den 12. december 1990. Copenhagen: Schultz Information.
Folketingets medlemmer i 40 år 1949–1989 (1992). Copenhagen: Folketingets Informations- og Dokumentationsafdeling.
Holm, A. (1949). *Rigsdagsvalgene i hundrede år 1849–1947*. Copenhagen: Fremad.
Hvidt, K. (1960). *Venstre og forsvarssagen 1871–1901*. Aarhus: Universitetsforlaget.
Høgh, E. (1972). *Vælgeradfærd i Danmark 1849–1901*. Copenhagen: Jørgen Paludans Forlag.
Katz, R., and Mair, P. (1995). 'Changing Models of Party Organisation and Party Democracy: The Emergence of the Cartel Party'. *Party Politics*, 1: 5–28.
Narud, H., and Johansson, J. (eds.) (forthcoming). *Nominations in the Nordic Countries*.

---

[14] The last paragraph opens up a discussion which cannot be pursued here. The author will deal with the issue of nominations and preferential voting in a chapter for a forthcoming book (Narud and Johansson forthcoming).

Pedersen, M. N. (1972). 'Lawyers in Politics: The Danish Folketing and United States Legislatures', in Samuel C. Patterson and John C. Wahlke (eds.), *Comparative Legislative Behavior: Frontiers of Research*. New York: John Wiley & Sons, 25–63.

——(1975), 'The Geographical Matrix of Parliamentary Representation: A Spatial Model of Political Recruitment'. *European Journal of Political Research*, 1–19.

——(1976). *Political Development and Elite Transformation in Denmark*. London and Beverly Hills, Calif: Sage.

——(1977). 'The Personal Circulation of a Legislature: The Danish Folketing 1849–1968', in William O. Aydelotte (ed.), *The History of Parliamentary Behavior*. Princeton.: Princeton University Press, 63–101.

——(1987). 'The Danish "Working Multiparty System": Breakdown or Adaptation', in H. Daalder (ed.), *Party Systems in Denmark, Austria, Switzerland, The Netherlands, and Belgium*. London: Frances Pinter.

——(1988). 'The Defeat of All Parties: The Danish Folketing Election 1973', in K. Lawson and P. H. Merkl (eds.), *When Parties Fail*. Princeton: Princeton University Press, 62–81.

——(1989). 'En kortfattet oversigt over det danske partisystems udvikling'. *Politica*, 21: 265–78.

——(1994). 'Incumbency Success and Defeat in Times of Electoral Turbulences: Patterns of Legislative Recruitment in Denmark 1945–1990', in Somit *et al.* (1994), 218–50.

Polsby, N. (1968). 'The Institutionalisation of the U.S. House of Representatives'. *American Political Science Review*, 62: 144–68.

Putnam, R. D. (1976). *The Comparative Study of Political Elites.* Englewood Cliffs, NJ: Prentice-Hall.

Rokkan, S. and Meyriat, J. (eds.) (1969). *International Guide to Electoral Statistics.* Paris: Mouton.

Somit, A., Wildenmann, R., Boll, B., and Römmele, A. (eds.) (1994). *The Victorious Incumbent—A Threat to Democracy?* Aldershot: Dartmouth.

SOU (1990). *Demokrati och Makt i Sverige—Maktudredningens huvudrapport*, 44. Stockholm: Allmänna Förlaget.

Thorsen, S. (1949). *Danmarks Rigsdag.* Copenhagen: Fremad.

3

From Political Amateur to Professional Politician and Expert Representative: Parliamentary Recruitment in Finland since 1863

ILKKA RUOSTETSAARI

Several studies concerning political leaders have indicated that changes in social and economic circumstances caused by industrialization have simultaneously effected the social background and characteristics of political decision-makers. Moreover, different kinds of electoral systems and gradual democratization of the franchise have been seen to cause changes in political leadership (Matthews 1954: 18, 42–3). Thus, the aim of the present study is to find out whether different kinds of changes concerning political, social, and economic development are also reflected in the composition of the Finnish parliamentary elite. We can presume that the effects of variations concerning franchise and electoral system are most strikingly seen when the whole system of representation of the people changes suddenly (Noponen 1964: 18–19). In Finland, preconditions for comparison are excellent because of a dramatic change: by a parliamentary reform in 1906, Finland moved directly from a four-chamber assembly (the Diet) representing the estates—which was the last of its kind in Europe—to the most modern unicameral Parliament in Europe elected by a universal and equal suffrage.

The following analysis is divided into five periods according to major crises and turning-points in Finnish political life: (1) the Diet under Russian rule, 1863–1906, (2) unicameral Parliament during the autonomy, 1907–17, (3) the first period of independence, 1919–39, (4) the era of reconstruction after World War II, 1945–62 and (5) the period of the welfare state, 1966–95. The purpose of the study is to analyse in what way these periods of political life and the breaks between them have an influence on representatives' social structure and characteristics. We also expect to show an influence of the political elite itself on such developments.[1]

---

[1] The material of the present study covers the whole period of the unicameral Parliament, 1907–95. As material for comparison, we can use the doctoral dissertation of Martti Noponen (1964), which deals with the social background of representatives of the last Diet, 1905–6 and Members of Parliament, 1907–39. The composition of Parliaments elected since World War II

1. THE DIET UNDER RUSSIAN RULE 1863–1906

The birth of the history of the Finnish Parliament can be seen in the convening of the estates in March 1809. However, the roots of the representative assembly and experiences of the principle of representation are older, stretching back to the fourteenth century under Swedish rule (see Renvall 1962). The convening of the estates in 1809 was a result of Finland's annexation to Russia, which severed the centuries-old connection between Finland and Sweden. Finland got not only autonomy, the position of an internally independent state, but also her own estates. The Diet, which convened for the second time as late as 1863, was divided into four chambers, although at this time in Sweden the estates were replaced by a bicameral representative assembly.

According to the Parliament Act of 1869 'The Estates of the Grand Duchy of Finland which are convened in session and represent the people of Finland, are constituted from the estates of the nobility, the clergy, the burgesses and the peasantry' (art. 1; my translation). Although the estates had been mentioned as early as the Parliament Act of 1617, the Constitutional Committee, which prepared the new Constitution, now added a statement according to which all Finnish people would be represented by the estates. The amendment was seen as necessary in order to prevent 'misunderstandings' which might have arisen due to former beliefs whereby members of the Diet were seen to be representatives only of local interests and their own estates.[2]

Representatives of the estate of the nobility were not elected by general elections but taken from the heads of families or persons delegated by them. The estate of the clergy was represented *ex officio* by bishops as well as the lower clergy. Civil servants, university teachers, and secondary school teachers could also elect their representatives to the estate. The representatives of the estate of burgesses were elected by merchants, practitioners

has not been studied systematically, except for some elections (e.g. Noponen 1989; Ruostetsaari 1995). The major source of the material is *Members of the Finnish Parliament 1907–1982* along with the *Parliament Calendar*, the *State Calendar*, and *Who's Who in Finland*, all for 1907–95.

[2] According to the committee, 'the conception was not compatible with the opinion of the people of Finland and those principles which are nowadays universally applied to representative bodies. The estates had to represent "the interests of the whole country and the whole people", despite that as a result of historical development the representative body of the people of Finland was still divided into four estates, each of which consisted of representatives of different classes of the population' (Krusius-Ahrenberg 1981: 263). In fact, there was a contradiction in the Parliament Act; according to the Act, members of the Diet were representatives of the people, but as far as their mandates were concerned they were still only representatives and delegates of their own estates. Moreover, 'representatives in office are directed by nothing but the regulations of the constitution' (Sect. 7), i.e. the imperative mandate was explicitly denied. This statement, which is still valid, was included in the Constitution as early as 1634.

of certain occupations and crafts, mayors, and magistrates. The corporatist principle of representation was abandoned in the estate of the burgesses in 1879 by admitting to the constituency and candidates all town residents whose taxation exceeded a certain limit. The franchise was not equal but the number of votes depended on the amount of tax paid whereas, in the peasant estate, the number of votes was based on land-ownership. The estate of the peasants was elected indirectly, that is, representatives were elected by electoral colleges of jurisdictional districts (i.e. *tuomiokunta*) which were elected in municipalities by independent landowners and some tenant farmers. All in all, political power was centralized on a very small part of the population: in 1890, more than 70% of the whole population were outside the constituency of estates represented in the Diet. In particular, women and manual workers living in towns had no influence over the composition of the estates (Noponen 1964: 26–9).

When regular sessions of the Diet began, there were no national parties in the modern sense. However, grouping into parties did take shape, the first being the Finnish Party, which originated in the 1860s. This was primarily a language party eager to make Finnish an official language and the language of education. In the 1870s, in an intensified language conflict and in order to counterbalance this Finnish movement, the Swedish Party was formed. The second period of party activity began in the 1890s when the assembly parties started to form national electoral organizations, which in turn led to the formation of national parties (Rommi 1971: 373). At the turn of the century, a stand against the Russian government's policy of oppression acted as a watershed in political life. The Swedish Party adopted the policy of passive resistance to Russian oppression and the Finnish Party split into two factions, the (old) Finnish Party and the Young Finnish Party. The former represented a more conservative and more submissive orientation, while the latter was more radical and pursued the policy of passive resistance in relation to Russia (Rantala 1981: 9). The Social Democratic Party of Finland (SDP), which was established in 1899, was, with its comprehensive organization, the first modern political party in Finland. However, under estate rule, the party was practically unable to recruit any representatives to the Diet.

If we analyse the representatives of all chambers of the last Diet, 1905–6, by occupation, the 45% share of all representatives who were also public officials is strikingly high. As the share of the whole population holding public office was only 2%, this means that the overrepresentation of the public sector in the Diet was about twenty-fold (Jutikkala 1974: 24–7). Among the nobility, state officials were the largest group: in the 1870s and 1880s more than two-fifths of the nobility were civil servants. Besides the nobility, almost half of the estate of burgesses worked in public office and all members of the clergy also belonged to the public sector. The dominant

Table 3.1. Population of Finland by sector 1880–1990 (%)

Sector	1880	1900	1920	1940	1950	1960	1970	1980	1990
Agriculture and forestry	77	68	64	51	42	31	18	9	9
Manufacturing and construction	6	11	15	21	29	30	30	27	29
Commerce	1	2	3	5	7	9	13	14	26
Transport and communication	2	3	3	5	6	7	7	7	7
Services	3	3	3	6	9	11	14	18	27
Other	11	13	12	12	7	12	18	25	2
Total	100	100	100	100	100	100	100	100	100
Population (millions)	2.0	2.6	3.1	3.7	4.0	4.4	4.6	4.8	5.0

Note: 1880–1980 total population including retired and unemployed; in 1990 only employed people.
Source: Waris (1974: 21); SVT (1983, 1995).

position of public office as a profession of members of the Diet was influenced, naturally, by the fact that the three above-mentioned estates covered between them four-fifths of all representatives. However, in 1890, the constituency of these estates covered only 3.5% of the whole population (Jutikkala 1974: 20–6). The second largest professional group (a quarter of all representatives) in the last Diet was formed by landowners and small farmers, including fishermen and foresters. But, as agriculture was the chief occupation for 71% of the population in 1900 (Noponen 1964: 35) in contrast to the situation of public officials, the underrepresentation of agriculture is obvious (see Table 3.1). From 1863 to 1906, the number of representatives from free professions, that is, lawyers, medical doctors, journalists, and authors, increased noticeably, so that by the end of the Diet period, they formed 8% of all representatives. However, this again did not reflect the share (0.2%) of the population working in these professions. Also, every eighth representative of the Diet had a background in trade, whereas the equivalent share of the population was less than 2%. In industry and the crafts, the equivalent share was 7% and 13% respectively. Thus, the disproportion of occupations between members of the Diet and the population is very clear—especially when the exclusive social composition of the estates is considered (Jutikkala 1974: 35–6). This disproportion is even better demonstrated by an analysis of the social stratum of members of the Diet. Eight out of ten members of the estates can be located in the uppermost social stratum whereas the equivalent share of the population was less than 2%. In addition, less than one-tenth of all representatives comprised the middle class and the peasant estate, and representation of the working class was almost totally absent (Jutikkala 1974: 25; Noponen 1964: 38–9).

Finnish class structure at this time was peculiar in two respects. First, although ultimate control was exercised in St Petersburg, domination in Finland—political, economic, and cultural—was in the hands, not of the Russians, but of the Swedish-speaking upper class. Thus, although linguistic, social, and educational barriers overlapped within Finland, the Finnish elite was not an extension of the metropolitan elite. This situation was not common in Eastern Europe, where the aristocratic upper classes often identified themselves both politically and culturally with the metropolitan power. Secondly, during the Swedish period, a non-feudal class structure with a large and strongly independent peasantry had consolidated itself in Finland. Consequently, the upper classes in Finland had no solid basis in land-ownership; rather, their position was based almost exclusively on the central role they played in the administration of the emerging state (Alapuro 1988: 90–1). This is perhaps the most important divergence in the Finnish situation. Elsewhere, the power of the upper classes rested on a seemingly solid basis, thanks not only to the guarantees of the metropolitan power but also to the prolongation of feudal class domination. As a result of this, the Finnish state-centred elite was coherent, because the administrative elite had no competitors in other sectors of society. This coherence and state-centredness of the Finnish elite structure remained until the 1990s as far as attitudes of the political culture are concerned (see Ruostetsaari 1993; 1994). We can thus conclude that Finland's power structure was closest to the pattern of Eastern Europe but, as far as class structure is concerned, better resembled other Scandinavian societies (Alapuro and Stenius 1987: 12).

Accordingly, the dominating position of the state officials in the estate of the nobility can be explained by the transformation of the class structure which resulted from Finland's annexation to Russia in 1809. The nobility, whose status was based on the profession of military officer rather than on land-ownership, lost its ability to reproduce the estate status when the Finnish army was suppressed. This crisis was settled, however, by the establishment of a central administration in Finland at about the same time, and by the nobility subsequently turning to university degrees, particularly those in law. Thus a law degree quickly achieved dominant status as the qualification for a state office and the nobility was transformed from an estate of military officers to an estate of public officials (Konttinen 1991).

As might be expected with the majority of representatives coming from the upper social strata and free professions, and with opportunities for education being primarily an upper-class privilege, the representatives' level of education was very high: at least 88% of representatives were educated to a level higher than basic (primary school). This can be compared to only

Table 3.2. Social stratification and descent of representatives (%)

Stratum	The Diet	The Parliament			
	1905–6	1907–17	1919–39	1945–58	1966–70
Own stratum					
Top stratum	82	37	43	46	
Middle class	8	30	26	28	
Peasantry	10	20	24	20	
Working class	—	13	7	6	
Total	100	100	100	100	
Father's stratum					
Top stratum	77	24	22	17	14
Middle class	4	10	9	14	17
Peasantry	16	33	39	39	37
Working class	3	33	30	30	28
Total	100	100	100	100	96

Source: Noponen (1964: 15, 304); Alestalo and Uusitalo (1972: 201).

5%, at most, of the population over 15 years having the same level of education (Noponen 1964: 41–2). In the last Diet, 68% of members had a university degree (including three-quarters of the nobility representatives) or the education of a regular military officer, and only 12% had had a basic education. Even one-fifth of the representatives from the peasantry estate had a university degree. It is also interesting to note that the degree held by every fourth representative was in law. The mean age of representatives at this time was 45 years, the same as for the total population over 25 years of age (Noponen 1964: 44–5).

When oppression by the Russian government began at the end of the nineteenth century, the turnover of representatives increased. Of all representatives in 1899, newcomers comprised 10% of the clergy estate, 9% of the burgess estate, and no less than 30% of the peasant estate. However, the last elections in 1905 showed a move towards more stability: only every fifth representative of the last Diet was a newcomer and every third, although not having participated in the preceding session of the Diet, had been involved in some previous session (Noponen 1964).

Membership of the Diet was not a profession although, according to the Parliament Act of 1869, representatives of the Diet were entitled to a sufficient living for the time the Diet convened as well as to a remuneration for travel expenses.[3] This regulation, however, did not apply to representatives of the nobility (who had to pay their own expenses), but to the

---

[3] According to the Parliament Act of 1869, the duration of the yearly session of the Diet was no more than four months. After parliamentary reform, the duration of the session was first regularly 90 days, which was sufficient in 1907–14. After 1918, this was no longer felt to be enough and the session was lengthened to 120 days (although in practice it was often longer).

expenses of representatives from the other estates, which had to be met by the estates themselves. These payments were small, and economic profit was certainly not the motive for a representative's career. On the contrary, in most cases the income of the representative decreased due to membership of the Diet. For instance, civil servants elected as members of the estate of the clergy had to pay from their daily allowance not only their own living expenses in the capital city, Helsinki, but also the salary of their substitutes, which was about one-third of the representative's own civil salary. The constituency of the estate of burgesses paid for the representative's travel expenses and daily allowance, the extent of which varied between towns and elections. Inevitably, this led to speculation over a candidate's costs and often to the candidate who would be the least expensive being selected (Jutikkala 1974: 108–10). In fact, this kind of 'social selection' could have been even more decisive at the stage of nomination for candidates than the behaviour of the constituency as far as recruitment to the Diet is concerned (Lilius 1974: 163–4; Noponen 1989: 56, 176). According to Noponen (1964: 321–3), it may have been one of the reasons that the Diet neither mirrored the establishment nor the constituency.

2. UNICAMERAL PARLIAMENT DURING THE PERIOD OF AUTONOMY 1907–1917

The introduction of universal and equal suffrage in Finland in 1906 was far more the result of the outcome of the Russo-Japanese war, which momentarily paralysed the Russian Empire, than the struggle of the Finnish labour movement (Alapuro and Stenius 1987: 11). The general strike, which had spread from Russia to Finland, also persuaded the Russian government to moderate its policy of repression. The ensuing reform, which meant moving directly from an assembly of four estates to a unicameral parliament, elected through universal and equal suffrage, was the most radical in the whole of Europe. The reform, however, did not change the relationship between the Russian Tsar and the Finnish Diet in that, while all people now elected the representatives, the government was still appointed by the Tsar. Thus, although Finland enjoyed universal suffrage, in reality, the Finnish Diet cannot be said to have been truly characterized by the principle of parliamentary government (Jussila *et al.* 1995: 77–8).[4]

The electoral system, introduced in 1906, was based on the proportional

---

[4] From 1907, the age of franchise and eligibility was set at 24 years. This was, however, with the exception of officers in regular military service, who were neither eligible for candidacy nor enfranchised, even though there were no requirements for candidates to have a permanent residence in the electoral district (Nousiainen 1989: 163–4).

Table 3.3. Representation women of in general elections 1954–1987 (%)

	1954	1962	1970	1975	1987
Share of women of					
enfranchised	54.1	53.6	52.9	52.6	52.7
candidates	15.2	14.5	17.3	24.2	35.2
elected MPs	15.0	13.5	21.5	31.0	31.5
Successful male candidates	21.7	14.8	19.4	14.1	9.3
Successful female candidates	22.0	16.2	14.8	15.1	11.4
MPs of all candidates	22.0	16.0	15.6	14.8	10.4

Source: Noponen (1989: 142).

representation of party lists of candidates in which seats are distributed among the individuals parties in accordance with the d'Hondt rule of highest average. For the distribution of seats within each list, candidates were ranked according to the number of personal votes they had polled.[5] As a result of parliamentary and franchise reform, the electorate increased tenfold to 1.3 million compared to the previous Diet period. This resulted in an immediate change in the social structure of the constituency. Besides the lower social strata, that is, blue-collar workers in towns, tenant farmers, and the rural population with no landed property, women were given both franchise and eligibility. This made Finnish women the first in Europe to get the vote and, apart from women in New Zealand (1893), Australia (1902), and some states of the United States (1890s), the first in the world (Kuusipalo 1994: 57).

This early inclusion of Finnish women in politics has several underlying factors. At the turn of the century, Finland was an agricultural country with three-quarters of the population living from primary production and, in Finnish farming culture, women have always had an equal position along-side men. On the other hand, the proportion of women among the few industrial workers was remarkably high at the beginning of industrialization: for example, in 1910, almost one-third of industrial workers were women (Saarinen 1992). This strong input into the country's production, which was crucial to the financial well-being of a relatively poor country, and their early established paid employment, gave them a legitimate position as agents of political change (Julkunen 1990). At the turn of the century, women also participated alongside men in nationalist movements, such as youth associations, and the temperance and labour movements

---

[5] In 1906–35 party lists of three candidates were used, i.e. an elector could vote for not more than three persons with the same ballot. Party lists of two candidates were used in 1935–54, after which only lists of one candidate have been allowed (Tarkiainen 1971: 19–20). Finland has been divided into at least 12 but no more than 18 electoral districts, in practice 15 to 16 according to the size of the whole population. The same electoral system is still used today, which indicates the strong continuity of Finnish political institutions.

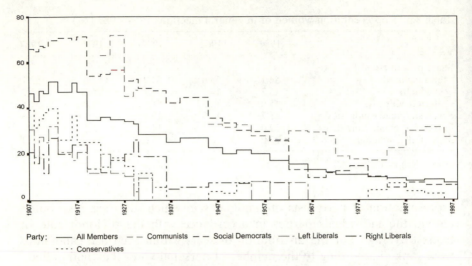

Fig. 3.1. Finland 1907–1998: basic education

Note: In Fig. 3.1 to 3.2, Left Liberals refers to the Liberal Party and its predecessors, while Right Liberals refers to the Swedish People's Party.

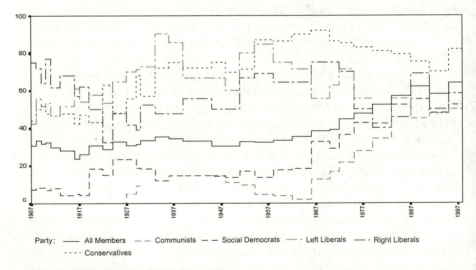

Fig. 3.2. Finland 1907–1998: university degree

(Sulkunen 1990). In fact, a characteristic feature of the social organization of Finnish women which differed from countries such as Great Britain and the United States, was their active participation in the same associations as men (Sulkunen 1987: 169). The international women's movement had also

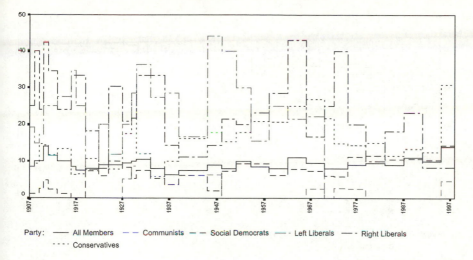

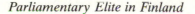

Fig. 3.3. Finland 1907–1998: law degree

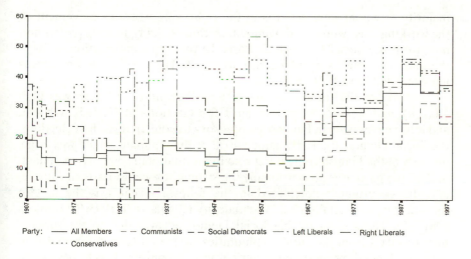

Fig. 3.4. Finland 1907–1998: humanities, social sciences, theology

provided an incentive for the founding of several women's associations in Finland, such as the Finnish Women's Association, which had been established as early as 1884. The suffrage campaign of the women's movement, which was supported by both right-wing and working-class women's movements (Kuusipalo 1993: 14) also had an important effect on the results of universal suffrage. Women's organizations saw it as their duty to mobilize women to the polls, and with good results; after the first democratic elections in 1907, 9.5% of the MPs were women. Of these 19 female MPs, the

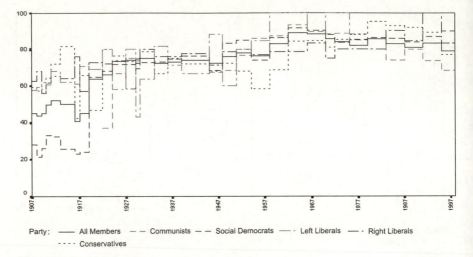

Fig. 3.5. Finland 1907–1998: local politics background

majority of whom were activists in the right-wing women's movement or the working-class women's movement, 10 came from right wing parties and nine from the Social Democratic Party. In the following election of 1908, the share of women's mandates rose to 12.5%. This early achievement was not exceeded until 1951 (Fig. 3.9).

The level of the turnout of the first parliamentary elections was high (70.7%), and was not surpassed until the elections in 1945. It was not, and it has never been in Finland, compulsory to vote. In these first elections, the Social Democratic Party gained 40% of the mandate, which was large, not only in the Finnish context but also in international comparison. In fact, in 1907 the party was proportionally the strongest socialist party in Europe, and the government nominated in the following year was the first in the world where socialists held the majority (Jussila *et al.* 1995: 89; Rantala 1981: 12). The success of the Social Democrats was due to the support they received from the rural communities, above all from the population with no landed property and agricultural labourers, which became a characteristic feature of the SDP. However, the average turnout for the entire period, 1907 to 1919, was no more than 69.2% (Rantala 1971: 467). This was mainly due to the people becoming tired of the continual elections which resulted from the almost annual dissolution of Parliament by the Russian Tsar through his frequent dissatisfaction with it.

The expansion of the constituency's social structure also had an impact on the occupational composition of the new unicameral Parliament (Figs. 3.10–3.18). The largest occupational group of representatives elected in 1907–17 still consisted of persons working in the public sector, but at 29%

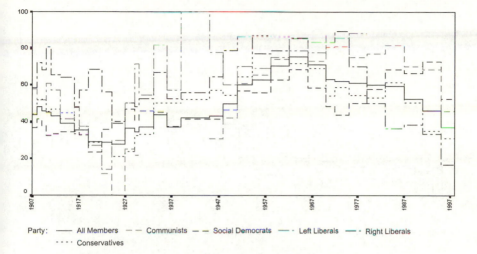

Party: ——— All Members —·· —·· Communists — — Social Democrats —— · Left Liberals —— · Right Liberals
- - - - Conservatives

Fig. 3.6. Finland 1907–1998: other parliamentary experience

this was approximately one-third less than in the last Diet of 1905–6 (cf. Noponen 1964: 55). However, it must also be noted that at this time the size of the public sector was very small in Finnish society; state expenditure as a proportion of GNP was less than 10% from the 1860s to World War I. Even the combined outlays of the state and municipalities were only 12–13% (Hjerppe 1988: 111–13). A dominating group in the public sector, and accounting for more than half of Members of Parliament coming from this sector (15.6%), consisted of teachers,[6] from primary school to university level.

Representatives with backgrounds in agriculture and forestry, including independent farmers, tenant farmers, and agricultural workers, increased to 29%, bringing them in line with the share from the public sector. Independent farmers formed the largest single occupational group, and in this case, the share was about the same as in the whole population.[7] An even more extensive change was in the proportion of lawyers, medical doctors, journalists, and officials of associations. These groups now accounted for almost one-quarter of all MPs, while previously the share had been less than one-tenth. The greatest part of this group consisted of labour union officials or the permanent officials and journalists of the SDP, whose previous occupation most often had been tenant farmer, agricultural worker, or

---

[6] The clergy is also part of the public sector, because the Evangelical Lutheran Church and the Orthodox Church have the position of state churches in Finland.

[7] In 1906, the Agrarian League was established to articulate the interests of the agrarian people. The share of agriculture, especially small-scale farms, among all occupations was one of the highest in Europe (Noponen 1964: 51–2; Jussila *et al.* 1995: 78).

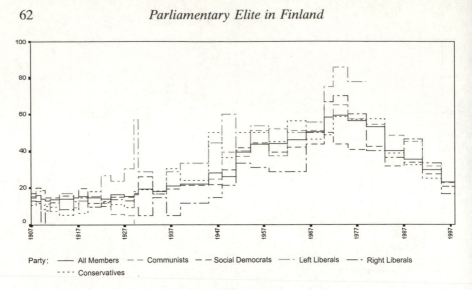

Party: —— All Members — — Communists — — Social Democrats ⋯⋯ Left Liberals —⋅ Right Liberals
- - - - Conservatives

Fig. 3.7. Finland 1907–1998: leading party position

blue-collar worker. In fact, at this time, as a result of the consolidation of party organization connected to parliamentary reform (Noponen 1964: 55–6), these professional politicians often accounted for almost half of Social Democrat MPs (Figs. 3.16, 3.17).[8] In the Social Democratic Party itself, one-quarter of all members were industrial workers. However, as the parliamentary party was dominated by party officials, labour union officials, and representatives coming from the public sector, they accounted for only 11.4% of Social Democratic MPs (Fig. 3.18).

The most important point of the parliamentary reform was that it ended the domination of Finnish politics by educated people at the top of the social stratum. This transformation, indicating democratization of society, occurred suddenly in the political sphere, whereas in other respects, the disintegration of the estate society had already happened gradually. Although the share of representatives from the upper stratum was still the largest, it had diminished from four-fifths to one-third of all MPs (ibid. 59–63). Nobles, that is, individuals who had represented the nobility in the Diet at any time, accounted for 3.7% of Members of Parliament elected in this period

---

[8] The large proportion of professional politicians and journalists of the Social Democratic parliamentary faction found at this time can be explained by a general pattern presented by Maurice Duverger (1954). While the party organizations of the right-wing parties were established after the introduction of parliamentary groups, the reverse was true for left-wing parties. In Finland, the right-wing parliamentary parties were established after the parliamentary reform of 1866 and they only started to establish national electoral organizations after the 1890s. The Social Democratic Party was established later, eight years before the first general elections of the unicameral Parliament, so that their party organization was already in place. Some social democratic newspapers were established even before this.

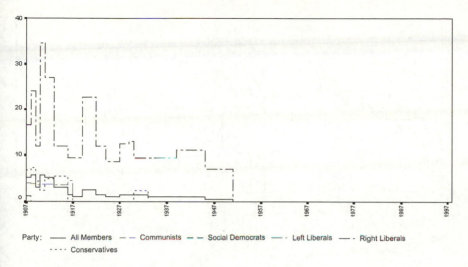

Fig. 3.8. Finland 1907–1998: nobility

Note: Nobility refers here to MPs who have represented the nobility at anytime in the Diet.

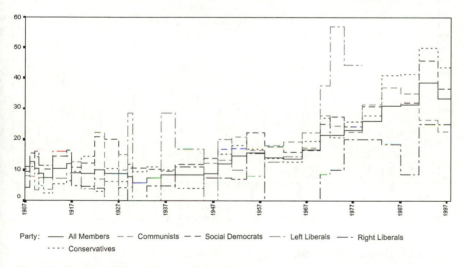

Fig. 3.9. Finland 1907–1998: female legislators

(Fig. 3.8). Blue-collar workers and agricultural labourers still accounted for no more than 12% of all MPs, although in 1910 they comprised 73% of employed people.

In sum, the most important transformation in the Parliament's social composition during the autonomy period was that the two middle strata (the middle class and the farmers) grew, while the top stratum and the

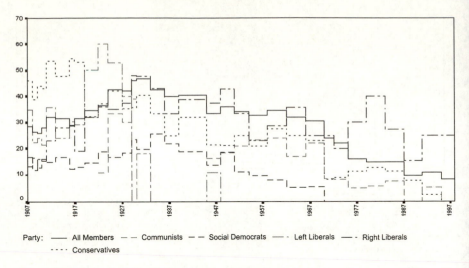

Party: —— All Members --- Communists — — Social Democrats — · Left Liberals —— · Right Liberals
···· Conservatives

Fig. 3.10. Finland 1907–1998: primary sector

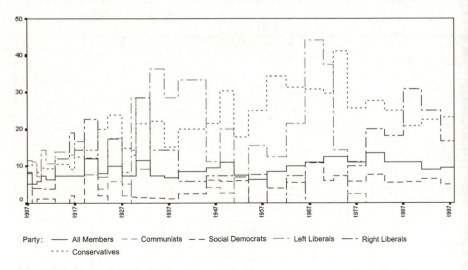

Party: —— All Members --- Communists — — Social Democrats — · Left Liberals —— · Right Liberals
···· Conservatives

Fig. 3.11. Finland 1907–1998: managers, businessmen

working class diminished—a phenomenon which can be explained by the continued growth of support for the new political parties, the Social Democrats and the Agrarians. This development of a more egalitarian character in the unicameral Parliament becomes even more marked when upward mobility is considered. At least one-third of representatives elected in 1907–17 had risen from lower social strata to the topmost stratum, or from the working class to the middle class, including the independent peasantry (Noponen 1964: 65–6).

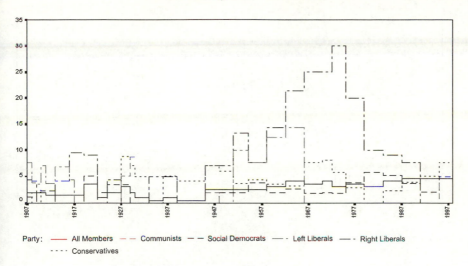

Fig. 3.12. Finland 1907–1998: practising lawyers

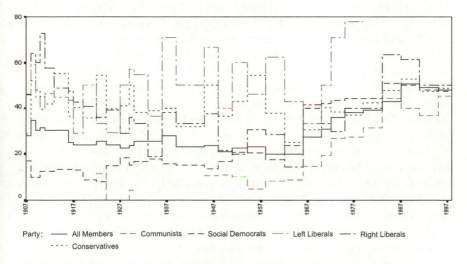

Fig. 3.13. Finland 1907–1998: public sector employees

In estate society, education was the main distinguishing feature, some-thing which was also reflected in the membership of the Diet (Figs. 3.1–3.4). In 1907, due to the parliamentary reform and introduction of universal and equal suffrage, representatives' level of education lowered remarkably. While 88% of representatives of the last Diet of 1905–6 were educated beyond the basic level, the equivalent share in the Parliaments elected

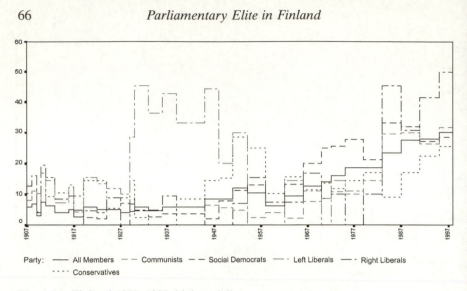

Fig. 3.14. Finland 1907–1998: higher civil servants

between 1907 and 17 was, on average, only just over 50%. Representatives with university or military officer backgrounds decreased from 68.3% to 29.3%, while those with only basic-level education, or less, increased from 11.9% to as much as 47.5%. However, regardless of the decreased level of education, Members of Parliament were generally still much better educated than the average population. For example, in 1910, only 5% of people older than 15 years had education higher than primary school level. Compared to the Diet of 1905–6, the highest decrease was in representatives with law degrees, falling from 24% to 10%, which is particularly small by international comparison. For instance, in France about 35% of MPs in 1898–1940, and more than half in the United States, were lawyers (Blomstedt 1967: 915). Rather, representatives had a university degree from the humanities, the social sciences, or in theology. In contrast, only 5% of representatives had technical, natural science, or medical degrees.[9]

The reasons for the relatively weak role of the legal professions (Fig. 3.12) and those with law degrees in the wielding of political power in Finland after 1906 deserve special attention. First, humanists had an important position in the establishment of the Finnish nation at the end of the nineteenth and the beginning of the twentieth century, as well as in the resistance movement against Russian oppression. Indeed, many of these activists, who were specialists of cultural life and national identity, such as historians, philosophers, and philologists, had remained politically active in the period

---

[9] As far as the education of cabinet ministers is concerned, the proportion with law degrees was higher, being 34% in 1898–1917.

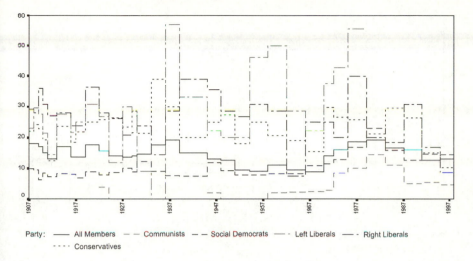

Party: —— All Members —— Communists —— Social Democrats ——- Left Liberals ——- Right Liberals
· · · · Conservatives

Fig. 3.15. Finland 1907–1998: teachers and professors

of independence and subsequently risen to top political positions. Also, joining the rather low-status position of the intelligentsia did not attract lawyers, who had generally higher-estate status (Ylikangas 1996: 500). The second reason for the weak position of the legal professions and holders of law degrees in political life lies within the party system itself. As the profession of a lawyer has traditionally been connected mainly to upper social groups, which rarely support left-wing parties, the share of legal academic degrees, as well as the share of lawyers, has traditionally been smaller on the Left than on the Right. Hence, if political support for the Left is high in the country, the share of lawyers in politics is generally small. This general pattern can be seen clearly in the reduction of the dominating position of lawyers which occurred after the first elections (1907) when the Left gained important political positions.[10]

A representative's competence is not only affected by formal education and experience in Parliament, but also by their degree of prior experiences as an elected or appointed representative in other bodies before

---

[10] Actually, the role of lawyers in politics has been explained by several theoretical models (e.g. Eulau and Sprague's professional convergence model (1961), Pedersen's a career-linkage model (1972), and Czudnowski's critical linkage position model (1975), which have been analysed by Eliassen and Pedersen (1978). Of these, Eliassen's model, which is based on the idea that political systems differ with regard to the occupational options they provide for their politically ambitious citizens, can best be applied to the Finnish case. An ambitious individual will pursue a political career if such a career is either worthwhile in itself or if, by pursuing it, no harm is done to alternative career possibilities. As, in some Finnish parties, there exists a certain, historically founded, hostility towards practitioners of law, so that consequently they are less likely to reach high political positions, it may be that lawyers etc. are not enticed to join. In short, the two career ladders are not linked together (Pedersen 1972).

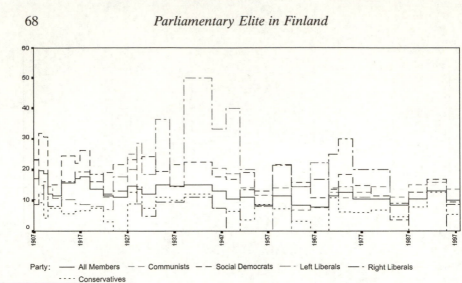

Party: —— All Members ······ Communists — — Social Democrats —— · Left Liberals —— · Right Liberals
        ···· Conservatives

Fig. 3.16. Finland 1907–1998: journalists and writers

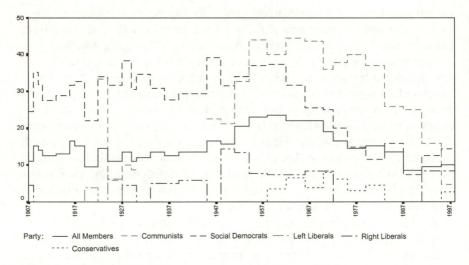

Party: —— All Members — — Communists — — Social Democrats —— · Left Liberals —— · Right Liberals
        ···· Conservatives

Fig. 3.17. Finland 1907–1998: party and pressure group officials

recruitment (Figs. 3.5–3.7). Active participation in party activities furthers
political upward mobility in two ways; by virtue of the education and training offered, and by virtue of the relationships which it creates (Dogan 1961:
82). For example, of the MPs elected between 1907 and 1917, 14.1% had
held leading party positions (referring here to chairmen of national,
regional, or local party organizations) prior to recruitment. Indeed, a
leading party position was the most common channel for recruitment to

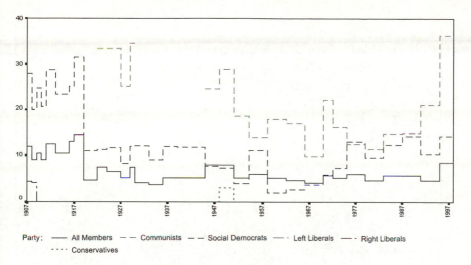

Party: —— All Members — — Communists — — Social Democrats —— · Left Liberals —— · Right Liberals
- - - - Conservatives

Fig. 3.18. Finland 1907–1998: blue-collar workers

Parliament for the Agrarians (one-fifth), and for the Social Democrats (one-sixth). However, it must be noted that while most MPs in well-organized parties, especially labour parties, had had leading party positions before nomination as a candidate (Dogan 1961: 82), for those in cadre parties, which all early Finnish right-wing parties could be called, having held a leading party position was not always a decisive factor in nomination as a candidate (see Duverger 1954: 63–4; Hamon 1961).

A more common channel of training for recruitment to Parliament has been other political experience referring to membership in party executive committee, party council, or the electoral college of the President of the Republic. In Finland, success in elections of the electoral college has generally preceded recruitment to Parliament. By contrast, the career of a minister does not precede recruitment to Parliament in Finland. Previous experience as an elected representative at the municipal level, that is, membership of the parish council, municipal board, or municipal council, had also preceded the recruitment of almost half of the Members of Parliament (46.3%). In this respect, there were small divergences between parties. However, more than three-fifths of right-wing Members of Parliament had had a local political background prior to parliamentary recruitment, but this was true for only a quarter of Social Democrats.[11] This pattern remained stable during the whole period of the unicameral Parliament. To conclude, taking into account all the above-mentioned types of political background,

---

[11] In Finland there are no representative bodies at regional level elected directly by the constituency.

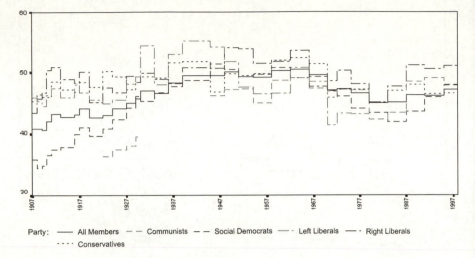

Fig. 3.19. Finland 1907–1998: mean age

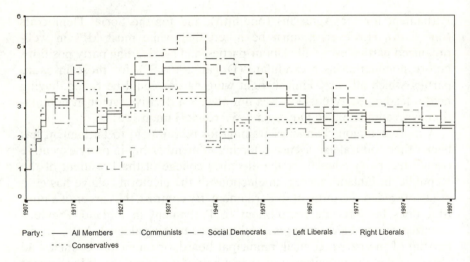

Fig. 3.20. Finland 1907–1998: mean number of elections

under Russian rule, Members of Parliament with the most political experience are found in cadre parties representing the traditions of estate society, that is, the Swedish People's Party, the Liberals, and the Conservatives. On average, of MPs elected between 1907 and 1917, 30.5% were without any form of political background before recruitment.

The representatives' rather slow turnover quickly added experience and continuity to parliamentary work (Figs. 3.20–3.21). In 1907, the fear that was

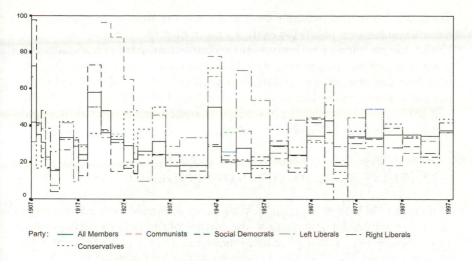

Fig. 3.21. Finland 1907–1998: newcomers

felt because of the new unicameral Parliament's inexperience was relieved somewhat by the fact that 27.5% of its members had previously been members of the Diet. In 1907–17, this share was, on average, 20.8%. Taking into account the almost annual dissolution of Parliament, turnover of the unicameral Parliament was rather slow in 1907–17, compared to the turnover of the unprivileged estates (i.e. burgesses and peasants) in the years 1863–1906. During the last-mentioned period, a representative was elected to the Diet on average 2.3 times (Noponen 1964: 73–4). In 1907–17, the number was on average 2.6 times, and the share of newcomers was 32.4%. Nevertheless, the tenfold growth of the electorate and the establishment of new parties not only lowered the mean level of representatives' education but also noticeably reduced the mean of their age. Of MPs elected to the first unicameral Parliament in 1907, the mean age was 40.8, that is, about four years lower than in the last Diet one year earlier. Paradoxically, the mean age rose quickly despite the almost yearly dissolution of Parliament. Constituencies felt that this behaviour by the Tsar was not legitimate, and thus deliberately voted back the same MPs. Consequently, the mean age of MPs elected for the whole period of 1907–17 was 42.2, which was several years higher than in the Diet in 1863–1906.

As a result of the parliamentary and suffrage reform, more than half of all women (52%) were regularly enfranchised. Moreover, based on proportional representation, the Finnish electoral system was favourable to women's success, and the personal electoral system, which is applied in Finland, enabled the concentration of votes for women candidates over and above the preferences of party leaders (e.g. Rule 1981: 73–6). However, in the general elections between 1908 and 1916, the turnout of women was 8.6–10.5 percentage points lower than that of men (Noponen 1964: 79–80). Even taking women's low turnout into account, their share of mandates was low, one-tenth on average (Fig. 3.9). This may have been linked to the fact that the share of women candidates was smaller than that of men, and para-doxically, even smaller than among elected Members of Parliament. At the end of the period, the number of women increased, mainly due to the rapid growth of the Social Democratic faction.

3. FIRST PERIOD OF INDEPENDENCE 1917–1939

The period 1917–18 was a clear turning-point in Finnish political develop-ment and heralded a new phase in the history of the Finnish party system. In December 1917, Finland became independent and true parliamentarism was introduced. The Civil War broke out at the beginning of 1918 and, in July 1919, the Constitution of the Republic was confirmed. The Finnish Party and the Young Finnish Party were dissolved, as a result of a consti-tutional dispute; the National Progressive Party was established by sup-porters of the Republic and the National Coalition Party by supporters of a monarchy. The Coalition Party formed itself into the Conservatives, defending inherited values and strong governmental power, while the Pro-gressive Party formed itself into the Liberals. The right-wing radical Patri-otic Popular Movement, which was influenced by European totalitarian ideologies, broke away from the Coalition Party, taking almost half of its support. The beginning of independence was also characterized by increased political activity of the left-wing parties, especially the Commun-ists, who, as a result of the Civil War, had split away from the Social Demo-cratic Party. Because of charges of high treason, the Communist Party and its newspapers were suppressed and the whole parliamentary faction was arrested. However, the representation of the Communist movement con-tinued in Parliament, although under other names, until 1930 when the party activities were finally forbidden by law.

Changes of the party system and the varying successes of parties were reflected in the recruitment patterns of the Finnish Parliament and of the post-independence era. The proportion of party and union officials decreased slightly between the wars, compared to the previous period. This was a dominant occupational group in the Social Democratic faction, while in the Communist faction it was exceeded by industrial workers and those from the primary sector. The break caused by the Civil War and inde-pendence is clearly seen in the data presented here (Figs. 3.17, 3.18). The proportion of union and party officers diminished even more than that of blue-collar workers, which fell by half to 5.4% in this period. However, there was less than one-third of blue-collar workers in the Communist faction, and one-ninth in the Social Democrats. Compared to the previous period, when the SDP alone represented the political Left, the party had lost half of its blue-collar MPs. This development is surprising, even if we take into account the fact that the number of labourers had decreased since the nineteenth century and following 'the crofter liberation' in 1918 when tenant farmers were able to buy farms themselves, so that a large portion of the population moved from the group with no landed property to the group of more or less independent small farmers.

Despite democratization and an increase in the support for parties representing blue-collar workers and the peasantry, a rather large number of MPs were still recruited from the upper social strata. Indeed, an analysis of representatives' social origin at this time indicates that parliamentary reform had introduced a type of representative who had experienced social advancement through new channels of mobility. Thus, in Finland, realization of universal suffrage did not lead immediately to an increase of representation directly from the lower social strata, but rather to the emergence of new types of politicians who had been socially upward mobile from these groups (Noponen 1964: 122, 128–9).

During this time, Finland not only remained primarily an agrarian society but actually recorded an increase for this sector (41.2%). This was mainly due to an increase in land-ownership by small farmers, when, following the law of 1918, crofters bought some 123,000 farms (Jussila *et al.* 1995: 112). In previous years, the number of people employed by this sector had fallen steadily for some time. The massive increase in land-ownership clearly influenced the results of the general elections in 1919. The share of the primary sector increased in both the Social Democratic and Communist factions, and, more surprisingly given its upper-class nature, within the Swedish People's Party, where its share doubled from one-fifth to two-fifths (Fig. 3.10). This rise in representatives from the primary sector meant that the Finnish parliament more closely resembled other Nordic parliaments than most Western ones (Jussila *et al.* 1995: 148, 151).

By contrast, the number of representatives coming from the public sector continued to decrease; so that for the period 1919–39, it was no more than 24.6% (Fig. 3.13). This proportion fits quite well with the size of the public sector at this time; total outlays by the state and municipalities was slightly more than one-fifth of GNP between the world wars (Hjerppe 1988: 114). A feature somewhat peculiar to Finland between the world wars was the large number of representatives from the clergy, especially when compared to other Scandinavian countries. They were mainly located in parties on the right, being evenly divided between the Conservatives and the Extreme Right, so that 15.8% of Conservative MPs, and one-fifth of the Extreme

Right, were priests. There were none in the factions of the labour parties .

With regard to level of education, given the decrease in representatives from the old parties, who traditionally had had higher levels of education, it would seem logical to assume that overall levels of education in Parliament would have declined. But, on the contrary, the level of MPs' education actually increased (Fig. 3.2). This can at least partly be explained by the general increase in levels of education in the country as a whole. During this period, the level of education was highest in the Extreme Right, where almost nine out of ten had a university degree, and reached its peak at the end of the 1930s, mainly due to the absence of the Communists.

In terms of turnover during this period, it is not surprising that the first Parliament elected after independence and the Civil War changed radically (Figs. 3.20–3.21). Many party activists and MPs, overwhelmingly Social Democrats, had either been killed, escaped to Russia, committed to prison, or were ineligible for Parliament because of loss of civil rights. Consequently, these events resulted in a break in continuity. While newcomers accounted for 21% of representatives in the general elections of 1917, in the elections of 1919, the share stood at 58%. This effect was even more dramatic in the social democratic faction; in 1917, newcomers made up 12% of the party but in 1919, accounted for as much as 73.2%. The Conservatives fared slightly better with newcomers only accounting for one-third of representatives. However, at the beginning of the 1930s, changes in party groupings, for example, the suppression of the Communists, electoral success of the Extreme Right and small farmers' parties, increased the rotation of MPs across all parties. Establishment of new parties in the restless 1930s also created cross pressures at constituency level and lowered turnout. In fact, the mean turnout for this period was only 61.3% (Rantala 1971: 469).

As time proceeded, newcomers tended to have been better trained politically, especially when compared to those of the Diet under Russian rule, and the career of representative became more structured. Prior experience in a leading party position was becoming somewhat more common, whereas the share of other parliamentary experience at national level decreased. However, MPs with a wealth of political experience prior to recruitment were still a minority, accounting for no more than 8.1%. MPs who had no political background before recruitment decreased from 30.5% under Russian rule to 18.6% at this time.

Although the share of women of the enfranchised population was regularly about 53% between the world wars, that is, slightly more than the last period, the number of women representatives in Parliament became smaller (Fig. 3.9). This was not because support for women had been noticeably lower than that for men, or that women were more passive voters. Women's low representation was affected decisively by the fact that women's share of candidates was only 7%–8%. During this period, the maximum number of women representatives was in 1922 when they accounted for 10%, due mainly to the recruitment of the Communists to Parliament as a new party. Conversely, it was lowest in 1930, at 5.5%, when the Communist Party was suppressed. Generally, across all parties, the largest number of women representatives was to be found in the left-wing parties (see also Duverger 1954; Ross 1955).

4. PERIOD OF RECONSTRUCTION 1945–1962

After World War II, Finland's political life and international position again reached a turning-point which affected the political system as a whole, and the relative power of political parties in particular. The political atmosphere was characterized by the term 'years of danger', referring to the aspirations of the Communists for usurpation of power. This era of reorientation has been called 'The Second Republic', differing from 'The First Republic' in its friendly relations with the Soviet Union, as well as the state's more extensive role in society and economy (e.g. Alasuutari 1996: 11). However, in spite of significant transformations concerning the political constellation, there occurred surprisingly few changes in the political system: on the grounds of the truce agreement, the Patriotic Popular Movement was suppressed as a fascist organization and, reciprocally, activity of the Communists was legalized.

Generally, Finland saw an increased interest of the general population in politics, and turnout rose to European levels with a mean of 77.9% between 1945 and 1962, that is, 17 percentage points higher than during the previous period. In 1945, turnout at the parliamentary elections was particularly high (74.9%) and provided the extreme left with a quarter of all mandates. However, the highest turnout was in the elections of 1962 (85.1%) which has not yet been exceeded in Finnish political history, following the crisis caused by the Soviet Union's delivery of a letter concerning Finnish foreign policy. On the other hand, increased turnout after World War II was also, to a certain extent, due to measures which had originated in order to ease participation; the audience of the mass media had grown, parties' election organizations were strengthened, and the number of voting districts increased. By contrast, the lowering of the age of enfranchisement to 21 in 1944 resulted in a lowering of the overall percentage turnout rather than an increase.

As far as MPs' social recruitment is concerned, during the period after World War II, a striking feature is that the overrepresentation of the top stratum increased further. Almost half of all Members of Parliament were drawn from the upper classes while, in 1950, they comprised only 3% of the occupied population. It is important to note that the overrepresentation of the top stratum originated already in the selection process of candidates inside parties. For instance, in 1958, 37% of candidates could be allocated to the top stratum, 32% to the middle class, 18% to the peasant estate, and only 12% to blue-collar workers. The relationship between Members of Parliament coming from the working class and the equivalent share of the population (52%) was just the reverse. The numbers of MPs belonging to the working class diminished slightly compared to the previous period, as did those from the primary sector where their share decreased in all parties, except in the Agrarian League (Figs. 3.10, 3.18). In fact, the overrepresentation of MPs with an agrarian background disappeared during this period, so that their share corresponded in some degree to the equivalent share of the population (see Table 3.1). The public sector was also further diminished after World War II, again coinciding with changes in public sector volume. Whereas total consumption expenditure as a proportion of GNP at the end of World War II was 14%, it fell to 13% in 1960 (Tiihonen 1990: 129, 215). However, total outlay by the state and municipalities from the 1950s to the 1970s was slightly more than one-third of GNP (Hjerppe 1988: 117).

As far as occupation is concerned, the most important change lies in the professionalization of politics and of the office of representative. The share of party officials and union officials increased from one-eighth to one-fifth during this period and, at more than one-third, was largest in both left-wing parties (Fig. 3.17). However, professionalization did not only apply to labour parties, but also to some right-wing parties. Besides the above-mentioned professionalization, after World War II, a further increase in the level of education can be observed. However, the rise is associated more with intermediate-level education than to academic degrees (Fig. 3.1). This is due to the return of Communists to Parliament, as only 7.5% of their representatives had a university degree. By contrast, in other parties, the number of academic degrees increased, with the Conservatives having the highest share at eight out of ten members of Parliament (Fig. 3.2). Further, accumulation of MPs' training was also seen with an increased experience of elective or appointed representatives prior to recruitment to Parliament (Figs. 3.5–3.7).

Generally, turnover of representatives has been particularly large when a longer than usual time has passed since the previous elections, or the number or the relative power of parties has varied exceptionally, such as may happen during a major political crisis (Noponen 1964: 314). All these requirements were fulfilled in the first general elections in 1945, especially the time element: six years had passed since the previous elections, that is, twice as long as usual. Moreover, a speech by Prime Minister Paasikivi, just before the elections, in which he stressed the importance of having 'new faces' in Parliament as an indicator of change of direction concerning foreign policy, was particularly effective (Tarkiainen 1971: 344). Thus, half of the Members of Parliament elected in 1945 were newcomers and the divergence between parties was remarkable (Fig. 3.21). Whereas seven out of ten Conservatives, and as many as three-quarters of the Communists were newcomers, in the Social Democratic faction, the equivalent share was only three out of ten. While MPs elected in 1939 had been elected on average 4.3 times, in the elections of 1945 that number was less than 3.1. However, after these elections, the turnover of representatives decreased (Fig. 3.20).[12] This was not only due to the state of peace after the war, but also to a law passed in 1948 which entitled a person to a half pension if she or he had been a Member of Parliament for at least ten years, continuously or not, and to a whole pension after twenty years when she or he reached 60 years of age, or the mandate expired. This provided an incentive for former MPs to stand as candidates and generally increased interest in the continuity of a representative's career. Because of this law, the third or fourth elections of an MP was an important test as far as the entitlement to a pension was concerned (ibid. 345).

Whereas women represented 53.9% of the total enfranchised population in 1954–62, women only accounted for 14.7% of candidates, and for 14.3% of members elected to Parliament (Fig. 3.9).[13] However, although female candidates did not succeed as well as men in elections, nevertheless the mean share of women of all Members of Parliament rose to 13% in 1945–62 (Noponen 1964: 319; see also Tarkiainen 1971: 356–7). This smaller than might have been expected number of women MPs, given the length of time women had been eligible and enfranchised, was not a result of male domination of nominations. According to Tarkiainen (1971: 356–7), there became established some kind of standard in parties, according to which there should be at least one woman candidate in each electoral district. On the other hand, political parties set limits to the number of female candidates in order to make sure that not less than one women would be elected in each electoral district. This policy was adopted by, for example, the Liberals and the Agrarians as well as the Social Democratic women's organization at the end of the 1940s.

With regard to the social background of MPs at this time, overrepresentation of the top stratum and an almost total absence of blue-collar workers in Parliament were not directly caused by economic factors associated with availability for office. Previously, the length of the parliamentary session being short, MPs had been able to hold another full-time occupation.

---

[12] During the whole period 1945–62 the proportion of newcomers fell to 29.1% and the mean age of representatives rose to 49.8 years.
[13] At this time, 19.2% of male candidates and 18.1% of female candidates were elected.

Consequently, for a long time, MPs' salary was paid as a daily allowance. However, in 1928, the time during which the Parliament convened was extended from 90 to 120 days, and after the mid-1930s the number of issues which had to be handled in the Parliament multiplied so that Parliament actually had to convene for seven to eight months a year. Although the daily allowance of representatives who were living far away from the capital city was raised in 1941, after World War II, total reform was needed, especially as MPs living far away from Helsinki found it increasingly difficult to have a second occupation. At least in this way, we can consider that the office of MP was transformed into a profession. In 1947, the remuneration was changed to an annual salary, and the daily allowance began to be paid for the time the Parliament convened and for travelling days (Tarkiainen 1971). However, standing as a candidate requires good capital backing because, since the 1950s, candidates have had to pay more and more of the costs of election campaigns themselves. A significant consolidation of the position of Members of Parliament and raising of their salary was intended when, in 1956, MPs were ranked in the same salary category as top civil servants. Since 1977, representatives' salary has been tied to that of cabinet ministers, being seven grades lower.

5. PERIOD OF THE WELFARE STATE SINCE 1966

After 1966, Finnish politics was characterized by the return of the Social Democrats and Communists, together with the Agrarians, to government. At the same time, there were major structural changes in the population, increased industrialization, rising politicization, and the extension of many welfare services. These welfare provisions were made possible by a victory of the Left in the elections of 1966 whereby the combined left-wing parties had an overwhelming majority, something which had only occurred twice before, in 1916 and 1958, and has never happened since. The exceptional nature of these elections was also reflected in the turnout, which rose to 83.9%.[14]

At the beginning of the 1970s, the party system went through a period of fragmentation which resulted in the formation of many small parties. One major factor in this process was the so-called *protest elections* of 1970, the results of which were strongly affected by both changes in society at this time, and by social reaction to change. An example of the latter was the formation of the Christian League. This was formed as a protest against what was seen as the growing secularization and the decline of basic Christian

---

[14] The mean turnout 1945–95 was 78.7%, i.e. two percentage points higher than during the previous period.

values.[15] Although many political groupings had appealed to electors' religiousness at the beginning of the century (Tarkiainen 1971: 211), by 1970, religion had assumed a marginal role in Finnish politics due to the religious homogeneity of the country. Indeed, except for the Conservatives, religion had had no important effect on the success of a candidate in general elections in the first period after World War II. Also at this time, the Agrarian party was split with the formation of the Finnish Rural Party (the Regionalists).

Overall, during the period 1966–95, the number of newcomers to Parliament increased slightly to 33.8% and on average, representatives were elected 2.6 times, reminiscent of the period of Russian rule (Fig. 3.20). However, there were extreme variations between elections. In the 1966 elections, turnover was exceptionally high, being some 10 percentage points higher than in previous elections. Likewise, in the protest elections of 1970 when there was a generational change in parliament, 42.5% of Members of Parliament were newcomers (Fig. 3.21). In contrast, in the next premature elections of 1972, turnover declined to 18%. Changes concerning social structure of the society, value systems, and party system are also reflected in the reduction of the mean age to 46.7 years, which, however, was not as low as during the period of Russian rule, or the period between the two world wars (Fig. 3.19).

During the period of the welfare state, Finland moved in rapid succession from an agrarian, to an industrial, and then to a post-industrial society. Actually, the phase of industrial society was almost non-existent as far as the occupational structure of the population is concerned (see Table 3.1). This transition is reflected in the decrease of farmers and agricultural workers and the immediate rise of the public sector, whereas there was little change in the numbers of blue-collar workers. The effect on the composition of Members of Parliament was that the share of those coming from the primary sector declined very quickly: by the elections of 1995 it had dropped from 30.5% of MPs elected in 1966 to just 8% (Fig. 3.10). In other words, in the middle of this period, the primary sector still had a slight overrepresentation, but by the end it reflected that of the population more evenly. In terms of party representation, the primary sector was channelled almost exclusively through the Agrarians. During this period, neither the Liberals and the Greens, nor the Labour parties, had MPs representing the primary sector.

A particular feature of the period of the welfare state is the dramatic growth of public sector representation, which almost doubled compared to the previous period (40.2%) and was particularly marked in the left-wing

---

[15] The party was not related to the Christian Workers' Party at the beginning of the century nor to European Christian Democratic parties but to Scandinavian counterparts.

parties (Figs. 3.13–3.15). This growth quite accurately mirrored developments in public sector volume, whereby consumption expenditure as a proportion of GNP was 15% in 1965 and rose to 25% in 1992. Likewise, the
total outlay of the state and municipalities was 39% of GNP in 1980 and as
much as 62% in 1992 (Tiihonen 1990: 215; SVT 1995). In terms of MPs
recruited from public sector professions, the number of higher civil servants
doubled to 21% and the share of teachers increased by a third (14.9%)
before declining somewhat in the 1980s. Representatives from the clergy,
however, only accounted for 1% in the Parliament of this period, indicating the increased secularization in Parliament. The growth of public sector
representation was accompanied by a decrease in the share of party officials and functionaries of labour organizations by a quarter to 14.3%. The
number of industrial workers also declined so that, on average, they
accounted for only 5.4% of Members of Parliament. However, the elections
of 1995, which were the first since the breakdown of the Finnish economy,
were an exception and the share of industrial workers in Parliament rose
to 8.5% (Figs. 3.17, 3.18).[16] Regarding level of education, by this time
(1966–95) every second member of Parliament had a university degree
compared to every third in the last period (Figs. 3.2–3.4). In particular, the
number of humanities, social science, and theological degrees doubled
(29.7%). Thus, Members of Parliament in this period, especially since the
beginning of the 1970s, received less training for their work as officials of
parties or labour unions than their predecessors, but this was compensated
for by increased formal education. This development indicates a new type
of politician, that is, an expert representative who is highly educated, has
seldom served political parties or labour unions as a functionary, but who
has served either as a locally elected representative, or has held a leading
party position, or has had other parliamentary experience prior to entry
into Parliament. In fact, there has been polarization among MPs as far as
political background is concerned. From 1983, representatives with
no political background have increased, as has the share of MPs with multiple political experience (Figs. 3.5–3.7).[17]

[16] In 1991, Finland's role as a Nordic Japan was cut short with a drop in industrial production of 10%, and GNP of 6.5%. Bankruptcies, mass unemployment (20%), and a bank crisis
followed, and the state rapidly incurred debt so that maintenance of the welfare state itself
was in danger. As a result of losing hundreds of millions of Finnish marks through speculation on the exchange markets and purchasing real estate, the Communist Party was forced
into bankruptcy (Nevakivi 1995: 305–7).

[17] The proportion of representatives who had had a leading position at any level of party
organization peaked at 59.5% in 1972, declining to 23% in 1995. Other parliamentary experience became more and more rare during the period of the Welfare State: 56.9%, compared to
the previous period. The share was at its largest as early as 1966. Of MPs elected 1966–95, a
slightly bigger share had functioned as a local elective representative compared to the previous period (83.6%). The maximum was reached in 1979; after that the share declined. The
share of MPs with no political experience prior to recruitment to Parliament is larger (7.7%)
during 1966–95 than the previous period. On the other hand, accumulation of such a background became more general in the sense that the number of MPs who have had three or

Compared to the previous period, the proportion of women MPs doubled to 27%, reaching a maximum of 38.5% in 1991 (Fig. 3.9). That share was the highest in the world. It is evident that this increase has been affected by the selection stage in the electoral process, and that there are links, especially evident in the earlier part of this period, between the share of women candidates and the number of women representatives elected to Parliament. Although the number of candidates multiplied in the period, a smaller share of candidates continued to be elected. This development was unfavourable especially for women because the proportion of elected woman candidates fell more than that of men. For instance, of male candidates in 1987, 2% more were elected than of woman candidates (see Noponen 1989: 142). In fact, women's access to top-level politics hinged on the development of social policy and the welfare state. Since the first phase of the unicameral Parliament, there have been two peaks in women's participation in Finnish politics. The first occurred immediately after World War II when the first steps in welfare policy were being taken. During the postwar period, women's representation in the Finnish government became almost regular, but there were still only one or two women in the government at the same time. Women's ministerial posts centred regularly on the Ministry of Social Welfare and Health and the Ministry of Education (Kuusipalo 1994: 13). A real take-off occurred in the early 1970s. This was a period when the Finnish welfare state was developing rapidly with an expanding public service sector. This enabled women to enter the resulting, numerous new jobs, such as those in the health and social service sector and in education. Their emerging contradictory position between home and paid labour resulted in the Nordic debate about sex roles in the 1950s and 1960s but it was not until the late 1960s that equality between sexes was taken into account seriously in national politics. Growing demands for equality and institutionalization of equality policy also had its effect on the increasing representation of women in politics (ibid).[18] The increase of women in the labour force resulted in women being recruited into politics through political parties as well as labour unions and being increasingly involved in the highly politicized sectors such as employment, education, and health.

6. CONCLUSIONS

The present study analysed, on the one hand, transformations concerning the social and political background of the Finnish parliamentary elite from

more types of political background rose to 29.7%. However, in this respect, too, a sharp change occurred in the 1970s: whereas in 1972 two-fifths of representatives had had many types of political background, in 1995 the share was no more than one-eighth.

[18] Also relevant is the reduction of the age of enfranchisement to 18 in 1972.

the end of the nineteenth century to the present day. On the other hand, it has examined to what degree the parliamentary elite was itself affected by changes in the political and economic structure of Finnish society. The Parliament Act of 1869 established the ideal, which is still valid today, that representatives should represent all people and not simply the interests of the electoral districts and groups which have elected them. However, this ideal is still yet to be fully realized. The social stratum and the level of education of representatives have always been higher than that of their electors, even if the gap has narrowed in the late twentieth century. However, as far as social origin is concerned, Members of Parliament have been much closer to both supporters and the general population since they have also been socially upwardly mobile to a considerable degree. In fact, the democratization of Finnish society seems to have had little effect on the number of representatives coming directly from the lower social strata but rather on the degree to which they have their origins there. One of the reasons behind the seeming lag between transformations of society at large, extension of suffrage, and the actual composition of Parliament, concerns to a considerable degree the selection of candidates by the party organizations. Indeed, the selection of candidates can be seen to function as a filter mechanism between Parliament and the people, resulting in the overrepresentation of the upper social strata and those with academic education, as well as in the underrepresentation of women.

In Finland, the most important transformations concerning the structure of parliamentary recruitment have centred on turning-points in both governmental and political systems; the parliamentary and suffrage reforms of 1906; Independence in 1917 and the ensuing Civil War of 1918; the restless 1930s; the end of World War II in 1945; and the radicalization and politicization of society at the end of the 1960s. Most of these transformations are also strongly connected to the growth or decline of mandates of the Communist faction; an increase in the Communists' mandates strengthened the representation of blue-collar workers and women, but lowered the mean levels of education and age. On the other hand, it seems evident that these turning-points were evoked rather by external factors and circumstances than by the parliamentary elite. According to Moring (1989: 162), the basis for Finnish policies has been to adjust to contextually determined conditions inherent in the geopolitical situation and in international developments as a whole. Political leaders have lacked the means of power to change the contextual frame by force. On the other hand, as the contextual frame was formed through continuous adjustments, the parliamentary elite had some scope for influence by their reactions to the external actors who set the frame. However, despite these periods of change, since the parliamentary reform of 1906 and Independence in 1917, the Finnish

Constitution and political institutions have been characterized by astonishing continuity.

As regards the direction of influence between the parliamentary elite and
the electorate, a top-down authoritarian relationship has been the dominating feature in Finland. The line of action taken in times of crisis cannot
be seen to have been in response to either the voters' or parties' wishes.
This gives quite a clear indication of a relative autonomy enjoyed by the
political elite in Finnish politics. This autonomy was possible because the
elite was able to remain in power despite changes in their political support,
that is, general elections were only partly effective in terms of influencing
government coalitions. In fact, it is clear that these elite configurations
inhibited change in the Finnish political structures which prevailed throughout the postwar period (Moring 1989: 162–4; see also Ruostetsaari
1993). This started to change at both the elite and electoral level in the early
1980s. In the elections which followed the resignation of President Urho
Kekkonen in 1982, changes at the electoral level enabled changes at the
elite level. This change to a bottom-up direction of influence was reinforced
when Martti Ahtisaari, who was an outsider to the established parties, was
elected in the presidential elections of 1994.

Taking the period as a whole, from the last Diet of 1905–6, to the
Parliament of 1995, it is interesting to note that some of the more notable
characteristics of the Finnish Parliament in the period of the welfare state
(1966–95) mirror those of the last Diet. The public sector has risen to be
the largest single occupational group, so that it accounts for half of all MPs,
and has thus reached a similar proportion to that of the last Diet. Also,
almost as many representatives as in the Diet have a university degree.
Again, looking at the whole period, a loose but not fully consistent connection can be seen between the development of public sector representation, and the development of the public sector at large. After the parliamentary reform of 1906, the share of MPs recruited from professions in
the public sector decreased—excluding the temporary increase caused by
the depression in the 1930s—until the parliamentary elections of 1966, after
which the share rose sharply. On the other hand, state expenditures as a
proportion of GNP increased slowly—excluding the temporary acceleration at the beginning of the 1930s—from the parliamentary reform to the
mid-1960s when it also started to rise sharply (Hjerppe 1988). The specific relationship between the number of MPs recruited from professions in
the public sector and state expenditures' share of GNP, as well as the
general share of public sector employees in the labour force, cannot be
determined here. However, as a general trend, there was a simultaneous
increase in the share of MPs recruited from the public sector, and the degree
of state expenditure during the 1930s Depression and then following the
elections of 1966. Moreover, the proportion of MPs recruited from the

public sector coincides roughly with the growth of the number of government employees, which peaked at the beginning of the era of Independence (1917), in World War II, and in the mid-1960s (Talkkari 1979: 57). In terms of party effect, it is evident that the return of the Left to government, following the victory of the Social Democratic Party in 1966, influenced the growth of the public sector, especially in welfare services. However, this was supported by the more general increase in MPs recruited from public sector professions into both factions of the Left and the Right. By contrast, the development of the primary sector has been the reverse. While the share of MPs coming from the public sector decreased until the late 1960s, the share of representatives coming from the primary sector increased, at least until the beginning of the 1930s. In other words, the overrepresentation of the public sector in Parliament disappeared between the world wars (1919–39) and the underrepresentation of the primary sector was removed during the era of reconstruction after World War II (1945–62).

With regard to political background, there has been a polarization among Members of Parliament. On the one hand, since the beginning of the 1970s the number of representatives with no political experience at all prior to recruitment has increased. However, the number of MPs with an accumulation of several types of political experience has also increased. This indicates the growth in Finland of, not only political professionals, but also a new type of politician—the expert representative. This is a highly educated professional, more frequently female, who works in the public sector as a civil servant. But such expert representatives have seldom served in either political parties or labour unions as a functionary or held a leading party position, or had any other parliamentary experience. Although more than four-fifths of MPs since the late 1950s have had experience in local politics before recruitment to Parliament, the share began to decline as early as the beginning of the 1980s.

This trend fits very well with the discussion regarding image politics and the growing role of the media in politics; success in elections requires more publicity and prominence in the public arena than active and prolonged activity in party organization. In that sense, this route of development is positive: the expert representative does not 'live off' politics like the professional politician and is able to be more independent of political parties, thus being a more independent representative of the electorate. Alternatively, because the politician must pay continuous attention to the vagaries of popular opinion, as measured by opinion polls, in order to harmonize his or her own statements with changes in popular opinion, the development might lead both to the short-term policy-making and to a lessened inclination to take responsibility.

References

Alapuro, Risto (1988). *State and Revolution in Finland.* Berkeley and Los Angeles: University of California Press.

——and Stenius, Henrik (1987). 'Kansanliikkeet loivat kansakunnan', in Risto Alapuro, Ikka Liikanen, Kerstin Smeds, and Henrik Stenius, *Kansa liikkeessä.* Helsinki: Kirjayhtymä.

Alasuutari, Pertti (1996). *Toinen tasavalta. Suomi 1946–1994.* Tampere: Vastapaino.

Alestalo, Matti, and Uusitalo, Hannu (1972). 'Eliittien sosiaalinen tausta ja yhteiskunnan muutokset Suomessa'. *Sosiologia*, 5/9: 193–207.

Blomstedt, Yrjö (1967). '*Lakimiehet ja poliittinen valta itsenäisessä Suomessa. Lakimies*', 914–18.

Czudnowski, Moshe (1975). 'Political Recruitment', in F. I. Greenstein and N. Polsby (eds.), *Handbook of Political Science*, ii. Reading: Addison-Wesley Publishing Company.

Dogan, Mattei (1961). 'Political Ascent in a Class Society: French Members of Parliament 1870–1958', in Dwaine Marvick (ed.), *Political Decision-Makers*. Glencoe, Ill.: The Free Press, 57–89.

——(1979). 'How to Become a Cabinet Minister in France? Career Pathways 1870–1978'. *Comparative Politics*, 12/1: 1–25.

Duverger, Maurice (1954*). Political Parties*. New York: John Wiley & Sons.

Eduskunnan kalenteri (1907–95). Helsinki: Valtion Painatuskeskus.

Eliassen, Kjell, and Pedersen, Mogens (1978). 'Professionalisation of Legislatures: Long-Term Change in Political Recruitment in Denmark and Norway'. *Comparative Studies in Society and History*, 20: 286–318.

Eulau, H., and Sprague, J. D. (1961). *Lawyers in Politics: A Study in Professional Convergence*. Indianapolis: Bobbs-Merrill Company.

Gosnell, Harold F. (1948). *Democracy: The Threshold of Freedom*. New York: John Wiley.

Hamon, Leo (1961). 'Members of the French Parliament'. *International Social Science Journal*, 13/4: 545–66.

Hjerppe, Riitta (1988). *Suomen talous 1860–1985: Kasvu ja rakennemuutos*. Suomen pankin julkaisuja. Helsinki: Valtion painatuskeskus.

Julkunen, Raija (1990). 'Women in the Welfare State', in M. Manninen and P. Setälä (eds.), *Lady with the Bow: The Story of Finnish Women*. Keuruu: Otava.

Jussila, Osmo, Hentilä, Seppo, and Nevakivi, Jukka (1995). *Suomen poliittinen historia 1809–1995*. Helsinki: WSOY.

Jutikkala, Eino (1974). 'Säätyvaltiopäivien valitsijakunta, vaalit ja koostumus', in *Suomen kansanedustuslaitoksen historia*, 4. Helsinki: Eduskunnan historiakomitea.

Konttinen, Esa (1991). *Perinteisesti moderniin*. Tampere: Vastapaino.

Krusius-Ahrenberg, Lolo (1981). 'Uutta luovaa valtiopäivätoimintaa vanhoissa puitteissa (1863–1867)', in *Suomen kansanedustuslaitoksen historia*, 2. Helsinki: Eduskunnan historiakomitea.

Kuusipalo, Jaana (1993). 'Women's Positions and Strategies in Political Arenas', in Hannele Varsa (ed.), *Shaping Structural Change in Finland*. Helsinki: Ministry of Social Affairs and Health. Equality Publications. Series B: Reports 2.

——(1994). 'Finnish Women in Top-Level Politics', in Marja Keränen (ed.), *Gender and Politics in Finland*. Aldershot: Avebury.

Lilius, Patrik (1974). 'Säätyvaltiopäivien työmuodot', in *Suomen kansanedustuslaitoksen historia*, 4. Helsinki: Eduskunnan historiakomitea.

Matthews, Donald R. (1954). *The Social Background of Political Decision-Makers*. Garden City, NY: Random House.

Moring, Tom (1989). 'Political Elite Action: Strategy and Outcomes'. *Commentationes Scientarum Socialium*, 41: Helsinki.

Nevakivi, Jukka (1995). 'Jatkosodasta nykypäivään', in Osmo Sussila, Seppo Hentilä, and Jukka Nevakivi, *Suomen Polittinen Historia 1809–1995*. Helsinki: WSOY.

Noponen, Martti (1964). *Kansanedustajien sosiaalinen tausta Suomessa*. Helsinki: WSOY.

——(ed.) (1989). *Suomen kansanedustusjärjestelmä*. Helsinki: WSOY.

Nousiainen, Jaakko (1989). *Suomen poliittinen järjestelmä*. 7th edn. Helsinki: WSOY.

Pedersen, Mogens (1972). 'Lawyers in Politics: The Danish Folketing and United States Legislatures', in S. C. Patterson and J. C. Wahlke (eds.), *Comparative Legislative Behaviour: Frontiers of Research*. New York: Wiley-Interscience.

Rantala, Onni (1971). 'Äänestysosanotto', in *Suomen kansanedustuslaitoksen historia*, 9. Helsinki: Eduskunnan historiakomitea.

——(1981). 'Suomen puolueiden muuttuminen 1945–1980'. *Turun yliopisto, valtio-opillisia tutkimuksia*, 40: Helsinki.

Renvall, Pentti (1962). 'Ruotsin vallan aika', in *Suomen kansanedustuslaitoksen historia*, 1. Helsinki: Eduskunnan historiakomitea.

Rommi, Pirkko (1971). 'Puolueet ja valtiopäivätoiminta', in *Suomen kansanedustuslaitoksen historia*, 4. Helsinki: Eduskunnan historiakomitea.

Ross, J. F. S. (1955). *Elections and Electors*. London: Eyre and Spottiswoode.

Rueschemeyr, Dietrich (1973). *Lawyers and Their Society: A Comparative Study of the Legal Profession in Germany and in the United States*. Cambridge, Mass.: Harvard University Press.

Rule, W. (1981). 'Why Women don't Run? The Critical Contextual Factors in Women's Legislative Recruitment'. *Western Political Quarterly*, 34/1: 60–77.

Ruostetsaari, Ilkka (1993). 'The Anatomy of the Finnish Power Elite'. *Scandinavian Political Studies*, 16/4: 305–37.

——(1994). 'Recruitment to Elites in Finland'. Paper presented at the twelfth annual joint sessions of the ECPR, 17–22 April, Madrid.

——(1995). 'Transformation of the Finnish Parliamentary Elites in the 20th Century'. Paper presented at the thirteenth annual joint sessions of the ECPR, 27 April–2 May, Bordeaux.

Saarinen, Aino (1992). *Feminist Research—An Intellectual Adventure*. Centre for Women's Studies and Gender Relations. Research Institute for Social Sciences. University of Tampere, Publication Series no. 4.

Sulkunen, Irma (1987). 'Naisten rjestäytyminen ja kaksijakoinen kansalaisuus', in Risto Alapuro, Ilkka Liikanen, Kerstin Smeds, and Henrik Stenius, *Kansa liikkeessä*. Helsinki: Kirjayhtymä.

——(1990). 'The Mobilisation of Women and the Birth of Civil Society', in M.

Manninen and P. Setälä (eds.), *Lady with the Bow: The Story of Finnish Women*. Keuruu: Otava.

Suomen kansanedustajat 1907–1982 (1982). Helsinki: Valtion painatuskeskus.

Suomen virallinen tilasto (SVT) (1907–95). Helsinki.

Talkkari, Antti (1979). *Valtionhallinnon henkilöstön määrällinen ja rakenteellinen muutos itsenäisyyden aikana Suomessa*. Tampereen yliopisto. Julkishallinnon julkaisusarja, No. 3. Tampere.

Tarkiainen, Tuttu (1971). 'Eduskunnan valitseminen 1907–1963', in *Suomen kansanedustuslaitoksen historia*, 4. Helsinki: Eduskunnan historiakomitea.

Tiihonen, Seppo (1990). *Hallitusvalta*. Helsinki: Vapk-kustannus, hallintohistoria-komitea.

Uusitalo, Hannu (1980). *Valtion korkeimpien hallintovirkamiesten ja talouselämän johtajiston sosiaalinen tausta 1970-luvulla*. Turun kauppakorkeakoulun julkaisuja A8. Turku.

Valtiokalenteri (1907–95). Helsinki.

Who's Who in Finland (1954–96). Helsinki.

Waris, Heikki (1974). *Suomalaisen yhteiskunnen rakenne*. Porvoo: WSOY.

Ylikangas, Heikki (1996). 'Autonomisen Suomen virkamieseliitti', in *Suomen keskushallinnon historia 1809–1996*. Helsinki: Edita.

4

Detours to Modernity: Long-Term Trends of Parliamentary Recruitment in Republican France 1848–1999

HEINRICH BEST AND DANIEL GAXIE

1. INTRODUCTION

Looking at the political history of modern France since 1789, the most obvious, and to some extent stereotypical, characteristics are discontinuity and division: popular upheavals and frequent changes of constitutional settings, extended periods of governmental instability and fierce conflict between opposing political currents dominate the historical record. However, underneath this choppy surface, we find more steady undercurrents which manifest themselves in astonishingly stable substructures of political processes. One of these continuous elements is the practice of representative government, which for a long time held its own against challengers from the top and bottom of the political order, or at least offered a fall-back position when the holders of supreme power were troubled and the institutions of government dissolved. For long periods after 1830, 1871, and again after 1945, this regime was formally institutionalized as a Parliamentary Monarchy or a Parliamentary Republic.

Related to these parliamentarian traditions are specific channels of transfer between social and political power, which were also part of the more stable substructure of the polity. It has been assumed that such links between society and polity will manifest themselves in the results of parliamentary recruitment processes and associated patterns of political

The data relating to the Second Republic were collected by Heinrich Best. Data for the Third Republic have been adapted by Heinrich Best from a data set originally collected by James Q. Graham (ICPSR data set: *French Legislators 1871–1940*). Thanks are due to the International Consortium for Political and Social Research (Ann Arbor, USA) and the Central Archive for Empirical Social Research (Cologne, Germany) for providing the data. Data relating to the Fourth and Fifth Republics were collected by Daniel Gaxie. We thank Dominique Anglès d'Auriac from the Archives Departement of the French National Assembly for allowing us access to his personal data file from which some information about the post-World War II period was taken. We also want to thank Arnaud Richez and Ivana Obradovic for their efficient and friendly help in the collection and entry of data.

careers. They should be shaped, on the one hand, by the formal structure of opportunity for access to parliament—such as, for example, electoral laws, eligibility rules, or financial provisions for MPs—and, on the other hand, by the transformation of society in general, influencing the offer of, and the demand for, representatives with certain qualities and qualifications (cf. the introductory chapter). Of particular significance in the process of recruitment and the development of career patterns are the selectorates and caucuses involved at different regional levels. Here, local groups and more extensive networks of dignitaries—the notorious *notables*—and emerging party organizations come into focus, being both part of the opportunity structure and translators of social into political change.

In the following chapter, although a comprehensive account will be given of parliamentary recruitment and career patterns in Republican France after 1848, the period of the Second Empire will be omitted, since it was a time of strict governmental control of parliamentary recruitment and manipulative or even repressive interventions into electoral processes. Also omitted will be the *Assemblée nationale législative* of 1849 and the Constituent Assemblies of 1945 and 1946 due to a lack of data at the level and of the quality required for this study. With these exceptions, continuous time series can be produced for the whole period of modern French parliamentary history where universal suffrage was applied. Thus, a central element of the formal opportunity structure—the right to vote and eligibility—was almost constant throughout the period of investigation. There is, however, one significant point to note: the gender barrier to full citizenship was maintained in France until 1944, so that references to universal suffrage prior to this time refer only to males (Huard 1991). The following chapter divides the period under investigation into two parts, separated by World War II and the Vichy regime (also not included for obvious reasons). This division, as will be shown, is plausible not only because of constitutional changes, particularly those associated with the establishment of the Fifth Republic, but also due to major changes in the substructure of the French political system.

2. STRUCTURES AND TRANSFORMATIONS OF LEGISLATIVE RECRUITMENT 1848–1940

2.1. *Structures of Opportunity for Legislative Recruitment 1848–1940*

The Revolution of 1848 marks the ascent of mass politics in France. One of the immediate consequences of the fall of the 'July Monarchy' (1830–48) was the abolition of an electoral law based on a strict census: after some extensions following the Revolution of 1830, the right to vote had still been restricted to men who paid a direct tax of least 200 f., and eligibility was bound to an even stricter threshold of 500 f. Although some exceptions were made in favour of retired officers and members of the Institute de France, the French electoral laws before 1848, which were among the most restrictive in Europe, effectively excluded about 99.3% of the population from the fully enfranchised *pays légal* (Bastid 1954). This was to change after February 1848 when the newly established Provisional Government introduced suffrage for all males aged 21 and over to elect the National Constituent Assembly. Eligibility was granted on the same terms, only fixing the age limit at 25. To break away from the politics of parochialism and cliquishness, the new electoral law also abolished voting on the basis of single nominees at the level of *arrondissements*. Voting was now to take place within a departmental framework and for a list of names (Agulhon 1993).[1]

Majority franchise in multimember constituencies (*scrutin de liste*), as had been decreed by the Provisional Government, was confirmed with only minor changes by the Constituent Assembly in March 1849 for the election of the Legislature to be held in May 1849. After an interruption of nearly twenty years during Napoleonic rule, the same electoral law was reintroduced in January 1871 to elect the National Assembly of the Third Republic. This was, however, the last application of the *scrutin de liste* in French national elections for some time, since in 1875 the *Assemblée nationale* voted a new electoral law, based on a majority franchise in single-member constituencies (*scrutin uninominal*), with a second run if no candidate had won an absolute majority in the first. During the Third Republic, its application was only interrupted in the elections of 1885, 1919, and 1924 which saw a brief return to list balloting, with some elements of proportional voting in 1919 and 1924 (Huard 1991). These episodic changes were intended, as was the original introduction of list balloting in 1848, to break up the influence of local power groups and, motivated by more recent experiences, to stop the somewhat underhand dealings between local political groupings (*marchandages*) before second runs. On the other hand, list balloting and particularly proportional voting systems were expected to strengthen national party organizations and to react more sensitively than single-member majority voting to structural changes in the electorate. Not surprisingly, the emerging Socialist and Communist Parties were advocates of electoral reform. However, modifications of electoral laws always contain elements of a somewhat experimental nature, often with unintended

---

[1] Although universal male suffrage had been initially introduced in France during the First Republic and formally applied in the 1793 elections, it was not adopted by the population before April 1848. In the elections of 1793, less than 10% of the entitled population cast a vote, whereas in those of 1848, 83.3% of the registered voters took part (Garrigou 1992).

consequences, taking into account the resistance and adaptability of established behavioural patterns of voters and selectorates to institutional change. Empirical evidence shows to what extent and in which ways parliamentary recruitment in France was actually influenced by these changes of the voting system.

Although the electoral laws of the Third Republic established and maintained the principle of universal suffrage as the basis for parliamentary representation, there were some restrictions which effectively excluded major parts of the population from the *pays légal*. The most obvious was the denial of women's suffrage and eligibility. Although several attempts were made to overcome this gender discrimination, something which gained momentum after the turn of the century, resistance remained strong, even within the radical republican camp, which suspected that the female vote would favour conservative and pro-clerical political currents.[2] Eligibility was granted to those over 25 who had the right to vote, except that some incompatibilities between public service positions and the exercise of the parliamentary mandate were established; some public functionaries were even excluded from standing for election. However, the number of exceptions to these incompatibility rules were also large, including ministers, ambassadors, members of the high clergy, and even the *préfet de la Seine* (Mayeur 1984).

In general terms, the institutional setting for parliamentary recruitment was relatively stable until the end of the Third Republic, with 14 of the 18 elections under investigation being held under a majority voting system in single-member districts (the *arrondissements*) with two runs, and the remaining elections being held according to a list ballot system at *département* level. The return to *arrondissement* and *uninominal* in 1928 shows to what extent this electoral system conformed to the 'habits and tastes' of the established political class, that is, to the interests and the modes of parliamentary recruitment that, from a phrase coined by Robert de Jouvenel, has became enduringly known as 'La République des camarades' (1913).

Another element of continuity related to the process of parliamentary recruitment was the granting of allowances for MPs. In 1848, a daily sum of 25 f. was introduced amounting to an overall payment of 9,000 f. per year. This mode and level of pay was reintroduced in 1871, confirmed in 1875, and maintained until 1906. Although it secured an income directly linked

---

[2] Another, less obvious discrimination was established by a clause in the electoral law of 1875 which made the right to vote dependent on at least six months of residence in the electoral district and consequently disenfranchised a considerable population of migrant workers. The exclusion of active soldiers also disenfranchised a good part of the young adult male population. Finally, the demarcation of constituencies favoured rural areas and disfavoured the big cities, particularly Paris.

to public office, it was rather moderate: less than the pay of an Inspector of Public Education (12,000 f.) and far less than what a State Councillor received (25,000 f.). No adjustments for inflation were made for nearly sixty years. Money was a continual problem for many deputies, due to the considerable expenses incurred when carrying out their office, particularly for campaigning. In 1906, a new level of payment was introduced, raising allowances to 15,000 f. per year.[3] Although this was a major step towards a full professionalization of the parliamentary mandate, and was criticized by the socialists as being indecently high, it was still considerably less than was needed to maintain a refined bourgeois lifestyle in the capital. Consequently, the temptation to top up this basic income by accumulating offices, exploiting 'outside interests', and even corruption, remained strong. It also advantaged those deputies who could reconcile their public office with their private occupation, which particularly held true for those from the free professions (Mayeur 1984: 216).

Another important element of the opportunity structure for parliamentary recruitment and parliamentary careers was bicameralism. While the political practice and the constitution of the Second Republic was based on the opposition between just two strong and independently legitimized political forces—the *Assemblée nationale* and the President—in 1875 the Third Republic introduced a second chamber, the Senate, which was based mainly on electoral bodies emerging from regional and local councils. Constitutionally, the Senate formed a counterweight to the Chamber of Deputies and socially it was an element of personnel continuity in the political process, since it was less exposed to changing electoral fortunes. The term of office for Senators was nine years, while deputies were elected for a four-year period.[4] In terms of career opportunities, the Senate offered an attractive alternative or—as was more often the case—a sequel to the risk-laden existence of a deputy.

Whereas the constitutional order and electoral laws are key elements of the formal structure of opportunity for parliamentary recruitment and political careers, the party system is part of a semi-formal setting of selectorates and supporting agencies involved in the formation of parliamentary leadership groups. The French party system was throughout the period under investigation, and for most parties, characterized by weak and unstable central organizations, fuzzy borders between parties, low cohesion, frequent splits and mergers. This general picture holds true for parliamentary as well as national parties. However, notwithstanding their low degree of institutional consolidation, political parties and their forerunner organizations were part of the political game since 1848, and were

[3] Further increases were voted by the Chamber after World War I.
[4] Between 1875 and 1884 one-third of the Senators were elected for life.

important actors when it came to the selection and allocation of political personnel. They were even present in the wheeling and dealing among the networks of local dignitaries—'la France des notables'. Beyond the borders of singular parties, the great ideological controversies and related opposi-tions of interest were channelled and expressed by more comprehensive political currents—*les tendances*—which form the basis for the definition of party families in our study: Conservatives, Left Liberals, Right Liberals, Christian Democrats, Socialists, Communists, and populist right-wing parties.

The Second Republic, the 'apprenticeship of the republic' (Agulhon 1993), saw the emergence and first organizational consolidation of some of these groupings, although in many cases they were the continuation of older and sometimes clandestine forerunners from the pre-1848 era.[5] In order to prepare electoral campaigns, extra-parliamentary political organizations were established, which co-ordinated extended networks of local associ-ations and informal caucuses: the conservative *Parti de l'ordre* directed its campaigns by a *Comité de l'union électorale*, while the republican left formed the *Solidarité républicaine* as a highly efficient propaganda agency. However, the post-1848 heyday of intra- and extra-parliamentary party formation soon ended, with the first restrictions on democracy being voted by the *Assemblée nationale constituante* after the Paris insurrection of June 1848, and being further tightened by its successor parliament. These measures succeeded in their intention to remove radical democrats, particularly Socialists, from the arena of legal political competition. None the less, the Second Republic anticipated (in terms of intra- and extra-parliamentary political aggregation) the *summa divisio* which is still famil-iar to French political life under the descriptions of left and right: 'Indeed it was the true ancestor of the ideology of the left while . . . it provided a precedent and model for all the centre-rightists of the future' (Agulhon 1993: 192).

After an interruption of nearly twenty years, which had been imposed by the dictatorial regime and the *Restauration Impériale* of Louis Napoléon Bonaparte, in 1871 a political landscape re-emerged which very much resembled the situation of the Second Republic, that is, a republican left opposing a predominantly monarchist right, with a split centre taking a middle position and shifting its political weight incidentally to either side (Mayeur 1984: 39–42). Particularly in the centre, there were no parliament-

---

[5] In the ranks of the *Assemblée nationale*, 'reunions' formed to co-ordinate and control the parliamentary process. As early as May 1848, a 'conservative coalition' (Bastid 1945: i. 115–217) gathered in the rue de Poitiers, consisting of monarchists adhering to one of the branches of the Bourbon dynasty, together with other conservatives having no explicit commitment to a restoration of the monarchy. Moderate republicans assembled in the 'Réunion du Palais National', while the radical republican left, among them some Social Democrats, formed the 'Societé des réprésentants républicains'.

ary parties proper, rather ephemeral *réunions* formed which were in a continuous process of reshaping and drifting to the more coherent groupings on the wing positions of the political spectrum. As a result of the harsh suppression of the Paris commune, Socialists were effectively excluded from the parliamentary arena until the mid-1880s. The reappearance of socialism as a serious competitor after the 1885 elections was accompanied by extensions and modifications of right-wing political groupings, which were partly due to the failure of a restoration of the Bourbons and the fading prospects for Bonapartism: populist anti-parliamentarian and authoritarian political concepts were expressed by the Boulangist movement, while Christian Democratic groupings combined an acceptance, in principle, of democratic procedures with close links to the Catholic Church. However, these new actors on the political stage could not challenge the strong Republican majority which was first gained in the 1876 elections and which provided the lasting, solid political basis of the *République parlementaire*, particularly in its fight for the secular state (Rudelle 1982). After a rapid strengthening of the Socialists (1885: 8 MPs; 1914: 133 MPs), the Republicans formed the new centre in the parliamentary arena, being split into a radical left wing and a more moderate (or 'opportunist' as adversaries preferred to label it) right wing. However, after World War I, which can be seen as a successful trial of democratic institutions, values, and the leading personnel, a new challenger appeared that put the wartime consensus into question and further extended the width of the political spectrum. Formed in 1920, the French Communist Party became a noteworthy parliamentary force after the 1924 elections and, after an electoral breakthrough in 1936, even a party upholding the government. On the right of the political spectrum, the appearance of Communism after the World War I was complemented, but not, however, counterweighted in terms of electoral successes, by the emergence of authoritarian and anti-parliamentarian groupings and movements, some of which adopted Fascist ideologies and strategies of mass mobilization (Mayeur 1984: 251–94).

Although, in terms of underlying ideologies and the emergence of fundamental political alternatives, the development of the French party system was very much in line with the experience of other European countries, with the exception of Communist and Socialist Parties, the cohesion of French political parties and their organizational strength remained lower than elsewhere. Indeed, throughout the whole period under investigation, most parties, particularly those in the centre and on the right, remained rather ephemeral umbrella organizations for caucuses and committees operative at constituency level. In addition, the electoral laws fostered a personalized and rather fragmented regime of candidate selection and campaigning, which was further enhanced by a modification of the law in 1889, formally prohibiting multiple candidatures. In the context of the Chamber of Deputies, the concept of party was even more ephemeral, with parliamentary parties not being included in the standing orders until 1910, and multiple memberships being possible until 1911. Connections between national party organizations and parliamentary parties were loose or non-existent, again with the exception of the Communist and Socialist Parties: 'Les groupes expriment une réalité proprement parlementaire, distincte de la vie partisane' (Mayeur 1984: 218). Still, in the last chamber of the Third Republic, which was elected in 1936 in a highly polarized political climate, approximately 4% of the deputies did not join a parliamentary party. Indeed, the notorious instability of French governments until the end of the Third Republic was largely due to a lack of party discipline and coherence. Contrary to this, however, the unpredictability of parliamentary majorities provided the Chamber of Deputies with a central role in the political process, which was another element of continuity in an otherwise discontinuous setting.

The outline of structures of opportunity for parliamentary recruitment and political careers reveals a somewhat contradictory picture of continuity and change. On the one hand, since the 1880s there had been a transformation and extension of the party system, which resulted in a 'partial modernization' with coherent and centralized party organizations particularly emerging on the left of the political spectrum. In addition, political development resulted in a thorough secularization of the political order, a lasting involvement of the 'popular classes' in political processes, and a gradual drift of the centre of gravity in elections towards the left. Also, between 1848 and 1940, French society underwent a thorough change with the share of the agricultural sector dropping from 53% to 37%, the proportion of people living in 'cities' (i.e. municipalities with more than 5,000 inhabitants) rising from 18% to 47%, and a decrease in the illiterate adult population from about 50% to virtually 0% (Dupeux 1972; Charle 1991), all of which worked in favour of a change in parliamentary recruitment and political career patterns. On the other hand, continuity in the basic principles of electoral laws and eligibility rules can also be seen, namely: universal male suffrage and territorial majority voting systems with some proportional elements in only two elections; a party system which was, for most of the political spectrum, weakly organized and only loosely linked to the parliamentary arena; and finally, a strong constitutional and actual position of the assemblies and chambers in the processes of political decision-making. With regard to societal change, until 1940, France transformed more slowly and to a lesser extent than other advanced European societies, particularly the UK and Germany, which was partly due to the stagnation and temporary decrease of the French population at this time. These latter factors, then, worked in favour of a continuity of parliamentary recruitment and career patterns.

2.2. Continuity and Change in French Parliamentary Recruitment and Career Patterns 1848–1940

2.2.1. Elements of Continuity

The most dramatic change in the formal structure of opportunity for parliamentary recruitment took place at the beginning of the period of observation. The February Revolution of 1848 and the electoral law subsequently decreed by the Provisional Government increased the constituency from 240,000 to 8.2 million registered voters and extended eligibility correspondingly. Thus, in terms of size and composition, a completely different *pays légal* emerged within weeks of the fall of the July Monarchy, and it is plausible to expect that this would also have produced a completely different representation to the pre-revolutionary chamber. This was, however, not the case, since the popular vote resulted in an assembly which was manned by representatives who were largely recruited from the same social couches as the preceding chamber, had predominantly (56%) held office in representative bodies on the national, regional, and local levels of the July Monarchy, and consequently met the corresponding census criteria (Figs. 4.4 and 4.21). According to another estimate, approximately 75% of the Members of the Constituent Assembly had paid 500 f. of direct taxes and thus belonged to the 0.13% of the population which had been eligible for the pre-Revolutionary chamber (Best 1984). The socio-professional makeup of the Constituent Assembly points in the same direction: proprietors of large estates, persons of independent means, entrepreneurs, and members from the free professions contributed 72% to its total of 900

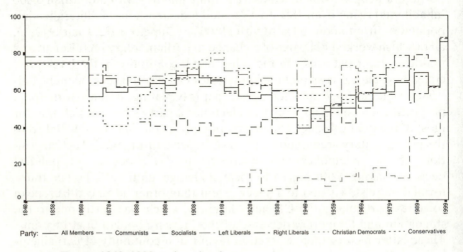

Party: —— All Members — — Communists — — Socialists ······ Left Liberals —— Right Liberals ···· Christian Democrats ···· Conservatives

Fig. 4.1. France 1848–1999: university degree

members. The share of representatives from the petty bourgeoisie, the working class, and the unpropertied 'intelligentsia' was only 12% (Figs. 4.8–4.18).

What we see here is a remarkable resistance by the existing organization of social power against a fundamental change of its formal mode of reproduction, and a democratic confirmation of the former *pays légal* as a source for the recruitment of the political class—even without the safeguard of the census and after the exit of its monarchical patron. The share of members

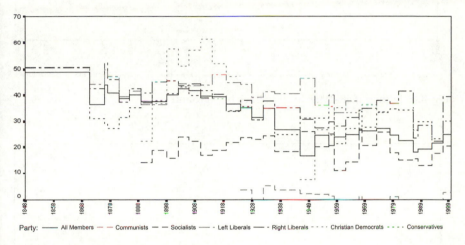

Fig. 4.2. France 1848–1999: law degree

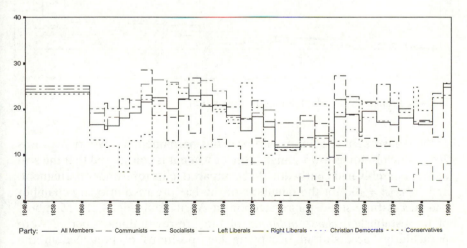

Fig. 4.3. France 1848–1999: engineering, sciences, medicine degree

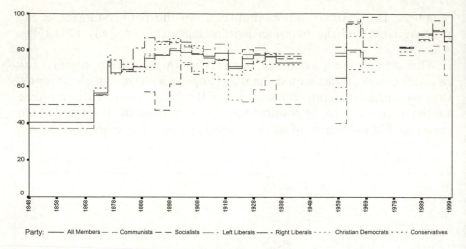

Party: —— All Members — — Communists — — Socialists —— · Left Liberals —— · Right Liberals · · · · Christian Democrats · · · · Conservatives

Fig. 4.4. France 1848–1999: local politics background

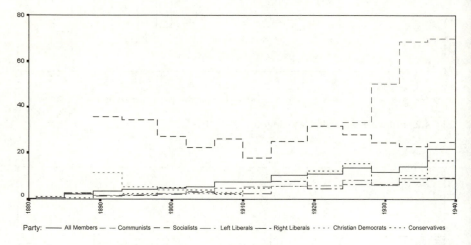

Party: —— All Members — — Communists — — Socialists —— · Left Liberals —— · Right Liberals · · · · Christian Democrats · · · · Conservatives

Fig. 4.5. France 1880–1940: leading party position

of the Constituent Assembly with previous parliamentary experiences was 20%, which is not as low as might appear when it is considered that the size of the Assembly had nearly doubled compared to its forerunner parliament, and 28% (n = 130) of the members of the last pre-revolutionary chamber had successfully stood for re-election in April 1848 (Fig. 4.21). Members of the established *classe politique* of the pre-revolutionary period were particularly successful in occupying key positions of influence in the Constituent Assembly and the various governments formed after February

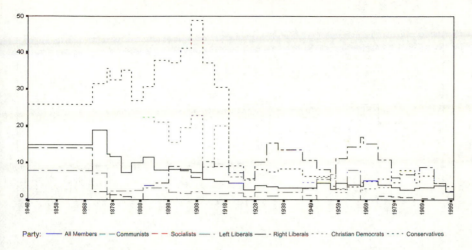

Fig. 4.6. France 1848–1999: nobility

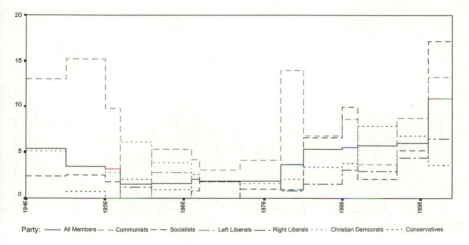

Fig. 4.7. France 1946–1999: female legislators

1848. In fact, no fewer than 60% of the members of the Provisional Government established in February 1848, 55% of the ministers in the first cabinet formed by President Louis Napoléon Bonaparte, and 47% of the members of the various committees entrusted with drafting the new constitution had been members of previous chambers. Compared to this, members of the counter-elites of the forerunner regime were less successful. Overall, only 17% of the members of the Constituent Assembly had a record of illegal or at least nonconformist oppositional behaviour, even if

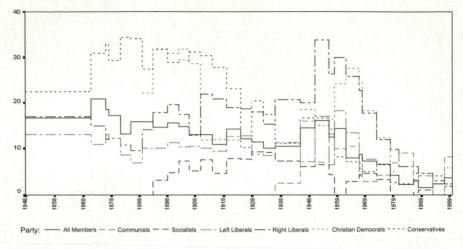

Party: ——— All Members — — Communists — — Socialists ······· · Left Liberals ——— · Right Liberals · · · · Christian Democrats · · · · Conservatives

Fig. 4.8. France 1848–1999: primary sector

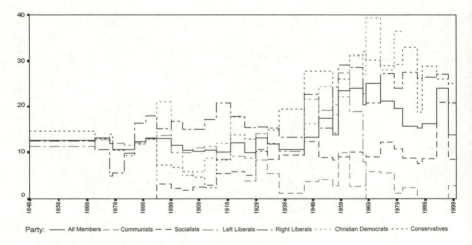

Party: ——— All Members — —Communists — — Socialists ——— · Left Liberals ——— · Right Liberals · · · · Christian Democrats · · · · Conservatives

Fig. 4.9. France 1848–1999: managers, businessmen

we include such moderate activities as participation in the banquet move-ment (Best 1990: 192).

If we look at occupational background, we see even more continuity with the previous regime, particularly with regard to the high proportion of free professions (above all lawyers), which formed the modal group in the Con-stituent Assembly as well as in the Chamber of 1846 (38%). Compared to this, the share of members from the civil service and the judiciary was rather low (15% respectively), contrary to contemporary parliaments in other

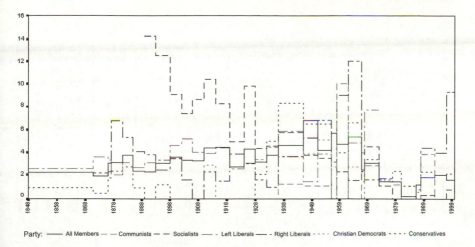

Party: —— All Members — — Communists — — Socialists —— · Left Liberals —— · Right Liberals - - - - Christian Democrats · - - · Conservatives

Fig. 4.10. France 1848–1999: small businesses

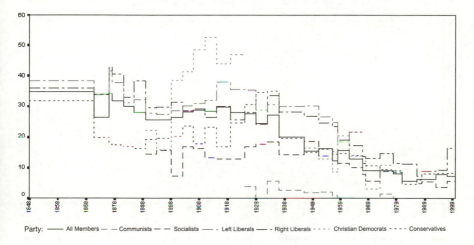

Party: —— All Members — — Communists — — Socialists —— · Left Liberals —— · Right Liberals - - - - Christian Democrats · - - · Conservatives

Fig. 4.11. France 1848–1999: practising lawyers

countries (Figs. 4.13–4.15).[6] Even with regard to age structure we do not see a particularly 'revolutionary' profile in the Constituent Assembly of 1848 compared with its predecessor: the elections of April 1848 even increased slightly the share of members who were over 50 years of age from 53% to 56%, instead of bringing in a new generation of young contenders

[6] With regard to the Chamber of 1846, this is also contrary to the inflated figures of other studies, which include holders of honorary and electoral offices in the share of state officials (Best 1984: 678).

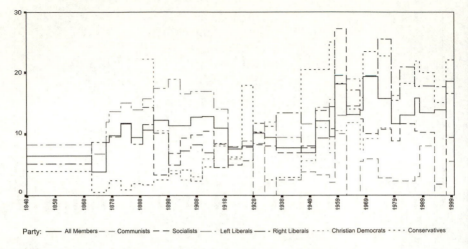

Fig. 4.12. France 1848–1999: professions other than the law

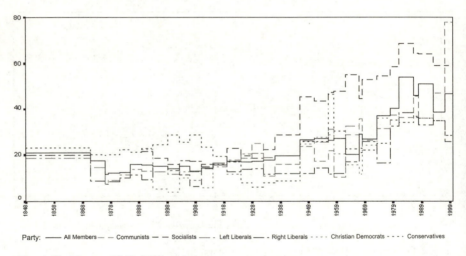

Fig. 4.13. France 1848–1999: public sector employees

(Fig. 4.19). The greatest change between the last chamber of the *régime cen-sitaire* of the July Monarchy and the democratically elected Constituent Assembly concerned the nobility, whose share decreased from 33% in 1846 to 15% in 1848 (Fig. 4.6). However, this decline becomes less spectacular when absolute numbers are examined, which just dropped from 156 to 135. In terms of Harold D. Lasswell's (1952) distinction between 'personal cir-culation'—that is, the rate of individual turnover—and 'social circulation'—

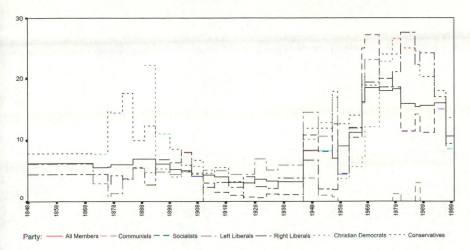

Fig. 4.14. France 1848–1999: higher civil servants

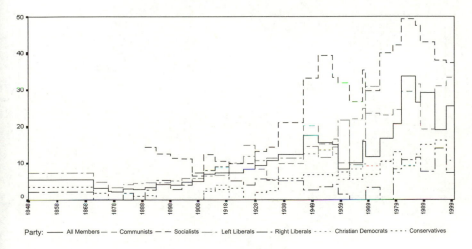

Fig. 4.15. France 1848–1999: teachers and professors

that is, the amount of change of crucial background characteristics of elite groups—we see in neither respect a revolutionary break-up of recruitment or career patterns. If we include the intermediary levels of the political order of the July Monarchy and consider the increase of available mandates in the Constituent Assembly of 1848, overall circulation was rather moderate and gradual. Instead of producing a revolutionary exchange of the elite, the elections of 1848 formed just one step (although a significant one) in shaping the gestalt of French parliamentary leadership groups which

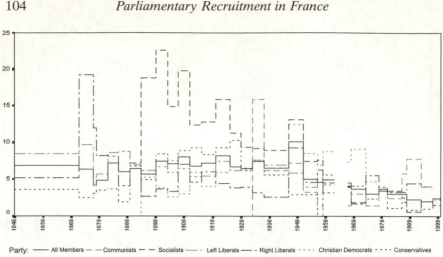

Fig. 4.16. France 1848–1999: journalists and writers

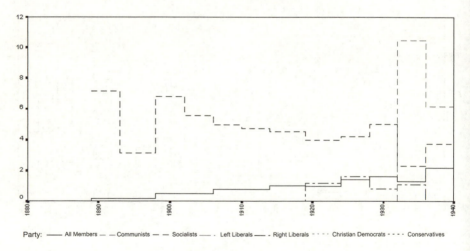

Fig. 4.17. France 1880–1940: party and pressure group officials

remained quite stable for nearly ninety years until the final years of the Third Republic.

Continuity of recruitment patterns reveals itself in most indicators available for French parliamentary leadership groups and even connects the Constituent Assemblies of 1848 and 1871, which were separated by profound regime discontinuities and a time gap of more than twenty years. A striking example is the representation of lawyers, who attained 26% in the Assembly of 1871. After an increase to more than 30% in the late 1870s

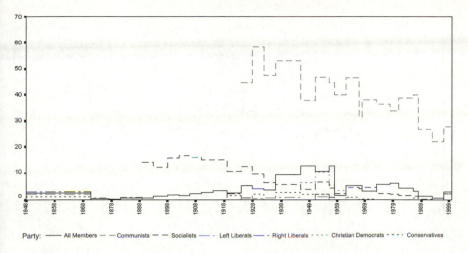

Fig. 4.18. France 1848–1999: blue-collar workers

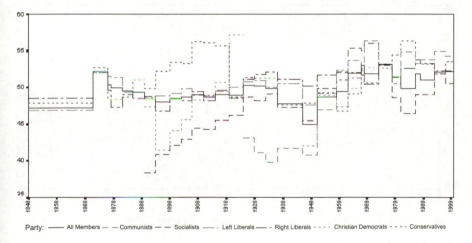

Fig. 4.19. France 1848–1999: mean age

and early 1880s, this share returned to its original level and remained there from the second half of the 1880s until 1936 (27%). Lawyers were the modal occupational group among French MPs throughout the whole period under investigation (Fig. 4.11). Together with other free professions, they formed the wider category of what in contemporary France was called *les capacités*, that is, a class of people who earned their potential political status through academic training, through their embeddedness

Fig. 4.20. France 1848–1999: mean number of elections

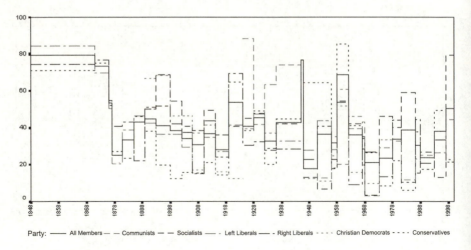

Fig. 4.21. France 1848–1999: newcomers

in heterogeneous social networks, and through their authority to advise others or to represent them in private matters.[7] Their independent position of trust, and their location at *critical linkage positions* in their constituencies, designated them to become political representatives too (Weber 1947, orig. 1919). The compatibility between their professional roles and the

---

[7] The pre-1848 use of the term *capacité* referred to those who were excluded from the *pays légal* according to the criterion of wealth but contested this disadvantage by referring to their cultural capital, i.e. education (Charle 1991: 47).

demands of public office enhanced their availability and readiness to stand for elections. With a share of more than 40% for extended periods, and one which approached 50% at the turn of the century, members of the free professions formed the core of French parliamentary leadership groups. The fact that this type of free political entrepreneur is known to flourish particularly well in institutional settings where parties are weak, and where representative–constituency relations are strong and direct, suggests that these favourable conditions existed throughout the whole period under investigation.

The enduring dominance of the *capacités* in French parliaments until the end of the Third Republic defines the limits for members of other occupational categories to gain access to the parliamentary arena. Within these limits, we see again a predominant pattern of continuity. This holds true for primary sector representation, which was astonishingly low in a country where agriculture remained the leading economic sector until after World War II, while landed property formed a significant source of income and an important attribute of elevated social status (Fig. 4.8). Even so, only in the 1871 Assembly did the share of agriculturists slightly exceed the 20% threshold, while it fluctuated around 15% in most chambers before the turn of the century and approached the 10% level in the following decades. Although these proportions and developments should be interpreted while considering that our data reflect involvement in agriculture as the main occupation, and not landed interests in the broader sense of property rights, it indicates that direct or symbolic interest representation of the primary sector was a secondary feature in the overall composition of the assemblies and chambers under study. In the setting of French representative institutions, the Senate included a stronger agricultural element than the Chamber and thus provided an additional platform for primary sector interests.

With regard to business representation, a similar pattern to agriculture can be seen, whereby stability over time was even more pronounced: from 1848 to 1940 the share of business representatives fluctuated between 10% and 15% without any trend in the data (Fig. 4.9). If we include small independent business (Fig. 4.10), the range is between 14% and 16%. In a graphical display, these time series look as if they were frozen or as if an invisible hand had intervened in parliamentary recruitment processes to fulfil a fixed quota of business representation. Since there was obviously no central authority to enforce a master plan of direct business representation, we can only infer that the supply and demand function, and the structures of opportunity for the recruitment of owners from large and small business, remained constant over such an extended period of time. The result was a dissociation between the spheres of business and politics in terms of direct personal interlockingness, which went beyond the levels of the July Monarchy and the Second Empire (Best 1984: 675; Charle 1991: 75). This is even more astonishing when we consider that in France economic pressure group associations were less consolidated than in other countries with stronger corporatist traditions. It seems that the system of what can be called care-taker representation, exerted by the notorious *capacités*, allowed for an indirect and informal influence on parliamentary decision-making which satisfied the needs of business interests into the interwar period, and which enabled them to maintain a comparatively moderate presence in the parliamentary arena.

Another sphere where overall continuity of recruitment patterns can be seen is the public sector (Fig. 4.13). Its share fluctuated between 12% and 20%, whereby the highest values were reached in 1848 and 1936. In 12 out of 18 elections the spread was between 14% and 18%, including extended periods without any significant change (1885–1906, 1919–36). Again, the time series look as if they were frozen at a certain level, with a distinct barrier separating the public sector from the parliamentary arena.[8] Contrary to other European countries, where the higher civil service was a major source of parliamentary recruitment throughout extended periods during the second half of the nineteenth century, in the Second and Third Republics it never exceeded 7% (1885: 6.9%) and dropped to about 3% after World War I (Fig. 4.14). However, these low figures can only be partly attributed to formal incompatibilities because they also applied to the Assemblies of 1848 and 1871, where no such rules were effective. They rather hint at an established division of power and associated careers between the administrative and legislative sectors of the state apparatus.

If we break the public sector into different subcategories, the general diagnosis of continuity has to be somewhat modified: after their share had peaked with 8% respectively in the first parliaments under investigation (judges 1848; officers 1871), judges and officers gradually died out as noteworthy categories of parliamentary recruitment. In the Chamber of 1936 they had virtually disappeared, with the exception of a few MPs with a military background. Again, the mechanisms of selection and self-selection worked in favour of a factual dissociation between different spheres of power and authority in French society, whereby the legislature became increasingly separated from the judiciary and the executive without major legal changes being introduced to enforce this process. The inverse development can be seen with regard to the parliamentary recruitment of teachers, including the whole range of the teaching profession from elementary school teachers to university professors (Fig. 4.15). Since the turn of the

---

[8] This was literally true for some higher civil servants to whom formal incompatability rules were applied from 1876 onwards.

century, their share has always exceeded the 4% threshold and from 1906 onwards has risen continuously, increasingly replacing other categories of the public sector, until it attained 12% in 1936. By then, they had become one of the largest professional categories in the Chamber of Deputies, and started to transform 'la république des avocats' (Le Béguec 1996) into a 'république des professeurs' (Thibaudet 1927).

Notwithstanding such shifts within the group of deputies with a public sector background, which indeed hint at a tendency to reduce recruitment from the executive and judiciary branches of the state apparatus, the overall picture of the occupational background of French parliamentary elites remains remarkably stable until the second half of the 1930s. Whereas in other European polities, the advent of mass politics from the late nineteenth century was accompanied by an influx of representatives from a working-class background or a position as trade-union and party official, this process was quite restrained in France. Until 1936, the share of blue-collar workers had peaked at a moderate 5% in 1924, while after the 1898 elections that of the *permanents* of parties and pressure group organizations fluctuated between 1% and 2% (Figs. 4.17 and 4.18). Even if we assume that a considerable number of self-styled workers in the Chamber were employed by party or trade-union organizations, the penetration of parliamentary politics by representatives from the 'apparatus' of mass organizations, which fundamentally transformed the political scene of countries like Germany and Great Britain after World War I, did not take place in France. Only after the 1936 elections, when the share of deputies from a working-class background rose to a significant 9% and that of party or pressure group functionaries exceeded the 2% threshold for the first time, did this process also gain some momentum in France. Together with teachers (12%) (approximately one-third of them from the lower levels of the educational system) and owners of small businesses (5%), deputies with a petty bourgeois background or some sort of an affiliation to the 'popular classes' attained a share of between a fifth and a quarter of all members of the Chamber. Additionally, for the first time in French parliamentary history, the share of MPs with a university education fell below 50% (45%) and those with a law degree below 30% (27%), while the proportion of deputies with only basic education rose above 40% (Figs. 4.1–4.3). Not before the crisis-ridden final period of the Third Republic did changes in recruitment patterns start to show that the old days of uncontested dominance of the propertied and educated classes in the political arena had also come to an end in France, and that beside established channels for parliamentary recruitment, alternative pathways to power had opened for a new brand of politician.

However, in the French case, it is not change which requires explanation and attention, but rather continuity: while the transformations of the

Chamber of Deputies in the 1930s can be directly attributed to the successes of working-class parties, namely the Communists, earlier shifts in the party system and changes of electoral laws had left no significant traces in the makeup of the assemblies and chambers under study. This hints at a firmly established stability of the substructure of French political life: those deeper layers of a political order where polity and society are intimately intertwined and the ascent to national offices starts. It has been shown on the preceding pages to what an astonishing extent the informal and semiformal networks and caucuses on that level were even able to cope with and adapt to the introduction of universal suffrage in 1848, an experience which repeated itself in a situation of national crisis and revolutionary turmoil in 1871.

One stabilising element of the recruitment process which points directly to the substructure of the political system was the involvement of French MPs in electoral offices on the local and regional level. Even in the National Assembly of 1848 this had been a major channel for recruitment, although access to these offices was limited by rigid census criteria before the February Revolution (Fig. 4.4). Parliamentary representation during the Third Republic was dominated from the beginning by politicians with a background in local or regional offices. This pattern of recruitment was further reinforced during the formative period of the Third Republic when it became a trademark of the French political system. Since the early 1880s, between 70% and 80% of MPs had their roots in local or regional politics. The resources needed for the ascent to a national office were predominantly accumulated in these contexts and not in leading party positions, which gained some limited significance only after the turn of the century, and only for parties which were placed on the extremes of the political spectrum (Fig. 4.5).

If one attempts to assess the long-term development of parliamentary recruitment in Republican France between 1848 and 1940, one might come to the somewhat paradoxical conclusion that stability resulted in change, that is, in a gradual shift from progressiveness to backwardness. In the beginning, French parliamentary leadership groups had quite advanced features compared to neighbouring European countries, which was most notably indicated by a low representation of traditional elites, in other words, representatives from large landowning stock or the nobility. Even in the 1871 Assembly, which was derogatorily nicknamed by contemporaries as the 'Chamber of Dukes' (Dogan 1961: 73), the share of representatives with an aristocratic background was much lower than in the contemporary German *Reichstag*, which was also elected on the basis of universal suffrage (cf. Chapter 5 and Fig. 4.6). In France, the proportion of MPs from the nobility fell below 10% in 1877 when in most other European countries parliaments were still strongholds of aristocratic influence. On the other hand, the high proportion of the *capacités* (namely lawyers) in French parliaments resulted in the dominance of politicians who displayed some features of political professionalism and could claim that they had earned their office through achievement rather than ascription or deference. These traits can be clearly associated with 'modernity'. However, this pattern of representation became anachronistic when political parties in other European countries became the main link between society and parliament, in that their organizations developed into the most important support agencies and channels for parliamentary recruitment. France only followed this path reluctantly, whereby a wide segment of its party system retained the structures and procedures of an era when informal or semi-formal networks of local dignitaries directed electoral campaigns and the processes of candidate selection.

2.2.2. *Patterns of Change*

Although, until 1936, continuity was a dominant feature of French parliamentary leadership groups, both for the chamber as a whole and for broadly defined social and political background characteristics, considerable discontinuity can be seen concerning individual parliamentary careers, and in comparing recruitment patterns within and between parliamentary parties or political currents. To some extent, aggregation rather tends to inflate the notion of continuity and to obscure the dynamic equilibrium which materialized in countervailing processes of change and adaptation. The leeway for these shifts was opened up by a considerable turnover which continued after the turbulences related to regime discontinuities in 1848 and 1870 had calmed down, and which was in no way limited to the formation years of the 'long' Third Republic (Graham 1982). In eight out of the 16 elections since 1876 the percentage of newcomers was above 40%, peaking in 1876 and 1919 with 54% (Fig. 4.21). Although in some of these elections, irregular circumstances such as overlengthy sessions of preceding legislatures (1876, 1919), the turmoils of war (1919), or the impact of major changes of the electoral system (1876, 1885, 1919, 1928) took effect or even interacted, in other elections none of these factors was present (1893, 1924, 1936). In some periods, sequences of elections with turnover rates exceeding 40% (1885–93, 1919–28) can be seen, which must have resulted in a far-reaching renewal of the political personnel on the parliamentary stage. The interwar period in particular was a time of intense circulation, with only one election dropping below the 40% newcomers' threshold (1932: 33%).

However, high turnover affected primarily those MPs who were not firmly anchored in the political class and who had to compete for unsafe seats with little support from political parties. The necessity to distinguish between constant elements and 'drift sand' within French parliamentary leadership groups is confirmed by the observation that even during extended periods of high turnover, the overall level of legislative experience, indicated by the mean number of elections in which MPs stood successfully for parliament, increased or at least remained constant (Fig. 4.20). Between 1877 and 1914, the indicator for incumbency grew quite steadily from 2.2 to 2.9 and, after a steep drop to 2.2 in 1919, again reached 2.5 in 1932. It was particularly declining political currents like the Conservatives (after their last great electoral success in 1885) and the Christian Democrats (after 1902) which contributed to these developments. Obviously, a hard core of established politicians managed to navigate into the havens of safe seats and exposed newcomers to the risks of declining electoral fortunes. Again, we see a somewhat contradictory pattern combining continuity in the modes and procedures of parliamentary recruitment with discontinuity in the parliamentary careers of a large part of the personnel involved.

It conforms to the notion of a 'hidden' dynamism in French parliamentary recruitment that there was much more change at the level of political currents and parties than in the Chamber as a whole, whereby established parties tended to sharpen their particular sociopolitical profiles in periods of decline, while newcomer parties tended to adjust to prevailing recruitment patterns in the process of their expansion. The Conservatives are a case in point: on their way into the political diaspora, they transformed into a stronghold for the aristocracy (1906: 49%) and ex-officers (1906: 20%), something they had not been to the same extent during their heyday and which now separated them from the main trends of legislative recruitment prior to World War I. The Socialists are another case in point. During their rise, they adjusted their involvement in local and regional politics (1924: 80%), their degree of academic training (1902, 1932: 44%), their mean age (1932: 49), their level of incumbency (1914, 1919, 1932: 2.4), the representation of *capacités* (1932: 26%) and public service employees (1936: 29%) to the overall recruitment pattern of the chamber. The representation of small business (of a 'blue-collar' type) and journalists, which had been noticeable at the beginning of the Socialists' rise as a parliamentary party (1889: 14%; 1898: 23%), decreased to the same level as within the Left Liberals (1936: 6%; 9%).

The adjustment of the Socialists' sociopolitical profile to the 'grand mean' of the Chamber was the result of a two-way process whereby the Socialists themselves developed some traits of an established party, while at the same time, due to the influx of a new brand of MPs through the recruitment channels of parties on the outer wing positions of the political spectre, the Chamber as a whole gradually changed its outlook. This was particularly reflected in the share of MPs who held leading party positions, which

fluctuated in the Socialist camp between a fifth and a third of its representation, and which attained a stunning 70% in the Communist parliamentary
party after its great expansion in 1936 (Fig. 4.5). A similar pattern, although
on a considerably lower level, can be observed within right-wing parties,
starting with the Boulangist movement in the 1880s. These results seem to
illustrate M. Duverger's thesis that political entities become more coherent, more organized, and more centralized the further they are located
from the centre of the normative structure of a polity (1976: 293). The
French case conforms to this view in that the subjection of parliamentary
recruitment to organized parties was a process which started and took hold
at the outer fringes of the political spectre, particularly on the left. The
centre right and the centre left of the Chamber were hardly affected by
this process, and maintained their roots in the local networks of dignitaries
and caucuses to the end of the Third Republic. Even after the 1936 elections, just 9% of Right and Left Liberal MPs had a record of leading party
positions.

Undoubtedly, the ingrained traditionalism of the political groupings in
the centre contributed much to the overall continuity of French legislative
recruitment patterns until World War II, although even here disaggregation
exposes a more differentiated picture and hints at different strategies of
adaptation to social and political change. One distinguishing feature
between the centre right and the centre left became the representation of
agriculture and business, which had increased in the centre right after the
1880s, peaking at 42% in the 1914 elections (Figs. 4.8 and 4.9). At the same
time, only 18% of deputies in the centre left were recruited from these categories, while in 1914 the share of *capacités* in their ranks reached its all-
time high of 52% (centre right: 37%) (Figs. 4.11 and 4.12). The gap between
the direct representation of economic interests and a more universalistic
concept of political representation, as incarnated by the *capacités*, which
had opened in the centre, narrowed somewhat after World War I, but did
not disappear before the end of the Third Republic. In 1936, the centre right
had the strongest agricultural element of all parliamentary groupings in its
ranks (21%), even surpassing the right wing of the chamber, which had previously been the stronghold of agricultural interests (Fig. 4.8). At the same
time, the share of public sector employees in the centre left grew to about
20% and reached a similar level to that in the Socialist parliamentary party
(Fig. 4.13). Although in 1936 the two currents in the centre of the chamber
still shared important features, such as an insignificant penetration by party
organizations, a relatively high level of university training (60%), and a firm
entrenchment in the middle classes, their recruitment patterns had developed in different directions, bringing them increasingly closer to their
respective neighbours at the outer positions of the political spectrum.
Although one should be careful in inferring directly from the social and

political background of deputies to their behaviour in the parliamentary arena, it is tempting to associate the differentiation of recruitment patterns in the centre of the chamber to its declining ability to provide a firm base for the formation of governments. On the other hand, it possibly paved the way for the polarization of political conflicts in the final years of the Third Republic.

3. STRUCTURES AND TRANSFORMATIONS OF PARLIAMENTARY RECRUITMENT SINCE 1946

3.1. *Structures of Opportunity for Legislative Recruitment Since 1946*

Since the end of World War II, the social and institutional factors which influence the legislative recruitment processes have changed much faster than during the seven decades of the Third Republic. In particular, France lost its rural outlook, with the share of the agricultural sector dropping from 20.7% in 1954 to 5% in 1990, and urbanization gaining a share of around 42% of the population living in town centres, 32% in suburbs, 22% in peri-urban rural areas, and only 4% in truly rural areas. More recent developments entail a decline of the proportion of blue-collar workers (34% at the end of the Fourth Republic, 38% in 1968, 31% in 1981, and 29% in 1990) and the rapid increase in the number of both categories of white-collar employees, those at the medium level (increase of 17% between 1982 and 1990) and those at the upper level (increase of 40% between the same dates).

Institutional changes are also numerous. Women were given the vote in 1944, the age limit of eligibility of the members of National Assembly was lowered to 23 in 1946, and the age limit for entitlement to vote dropped from 21 to 18 in 1974. Since 1946, deputies are elected for a five-year period. As a result of the professionalization of parliamentary activities, problems relating to the setting of allowances were solved with their adjustment to the level of salaries of the highest civil servants. Additional advantages have been granted to MPs to help them in their work: they are provided with a secretary and two assistants, they are entitled to free travel, their mail is free of charge, and they have pension rights when they leave parliament. The Constitution of the Fourth Republic drastically reduced the powers of the Senate, but it was agreed to restore these gradually. Under the Fifth Republic, the legislative powers of the Senate are almost the same as those of the National Assembly, but the cabinet can reduce them by giving 'the last word' to the 'lower' house at the end of the legislative process. In order to fight localism and the persistence of local dignitaries in parliament, and to strengthen the political weight of mass parties in power after World War II, the electoral law of 1946 introduced proportional voting at an intermediate level (*département*) and banned incomplete lists and split tickets. Some majority elements were reintroduced in 1951 with the aim of weakening anti-regime parties (mainly the Gaullist and Communist Parties) and strengthening the governmental parties. The purported effects of proportional voting upon the cabinet's instability led the leaders of the newly established Fifth Republic to return in 1958 to a majority franchise in single-member constituencies, with a second run if no candidate had won an absolute majority and the votes of more than a quarter of registered voters (*scrutin majoritaire uninominal à deux tours*), which was very similar to the dominant electoral system of the Third Republic.

The party system did not change very much during the Fourth Republic. With the exceptions of the Communist and Socialist (SFIO) Parties, most political groupings located in the centre right or the centre left were still characterized by weak and ephemeral organization and fuzzy borders. As they often belonged to governmental coalitions, their low cohesion was a major factor in cabinets' instability. After 1958, dramatic changes occurred in the party system. First, the reduction of the number of political movements has favoured its simplification. On the left side, various groupings (SFIO, left socialists, left radicals) merged into a new party between 1969 and 1974. The amalgamated Socialist Party was able to establish a growing supremacy over the Communist Party and to lead left-wing governmental coalitions in 1981, 1988, and 1997. In 1958—in order to sustain the new regime and its head—General de Gaulle's supporters created a new party on the right of the political spectrum—the 'Union for the New Republic' (UNR), renamed 'Union for the Defence of the Republic' (UDR) in the turmoil of 1968, and 'Rally for the Republic (RPR)' in 1976. It gathered various conservative, nationalist, right liberal, and technocratic members and politicians and won a relative majority of seats in the National Assembly from 1958 to 1981 (and even an absolute majority in 1968) and again from 1986 to 1988 and from 1993 to 1997. In the early 1960s, the right liberals, right radicals, various more or less independent '*modérés*' merged with the declining Christian-Democrat MRP in the 'Democratic Centre'. In 1977, this movement allied with the right liberal 'Independent Republicans' who, under the leadership of Valéry Giscard d'Estaing, had stayed in the Gaullist governmental coalition since 1958. A new amalgamated grouping—'Union for French Democracy (UDF)'—was later created to counterweight the RPR. The party system was thus stabilized with four main parties in Parliament—PCF, PS, RPR, and UDF—until the rise of the National Front after 1983 and the recent split (1998) between the UDF and its right liberal component 'Liberal Democrats' introduced some disruptive factors.

Even if French political parties—especially the conservative and liberal ones—are still weaker than their British or German equivalents, they are presently much stronger than they were in the past. In the Fifth Republic, candidates who stand for Parliament have few chances of success if they are not supported by a major political group and almost all deputies are members of one of the main parties. Leaders of the parties in Parliament are more often able to impose discipline on their deputies, especially in voting, and cabinet coalitions are stronger than they were in the past.

3.2. The Common Features of Members of Parliament

3.2.1. An Assembly of Professional Politicians

All these changes must be taken into account to understand parliamentary recruitment since 1946. It brought a rather homogeneous political elite into the National Assembly, partly because of the various transformations it has undergone and in spite of differences in parties' selection processes. Beyond the ideological differences which distinguish the various political factions, Members of Parliament share common political and social characteristics. Some may be observed throughout Parliament's history; others are more specific to the most recent period. From a political point of view, most deputies are professional politicians. From a social point of view, they occupy dominant positions in the various divisions of labour which organize society.

Data related to age, local political background, or percentage of newcomers all reveal the consequences of the growing professionalization of deputies in political activity, which may be regarded as one of the major transformations of Parliaments since 1848 (Weber 1947, orig. 1919). Most deputies have long been involved in a career which has progressively led them to full-time political work. This does not mean that politicians enter politics to take up a career and to profit from the various privileges associated with high political positions. It rather means that entrance to Parliament is a step in a *cursus honorum* which is often marked by abandoning previous occupations and by making vast social investments in politics. In the French case, few deputies have been full-time salaried pressure group or party officials before their first election as a MP, mainly because political parties are too weak to afford large bureaucracies.[9] Rather it is the

---

[9] The only exception is the Communist Party whose leaders are often party officials. But Communist leaders rarely admit that they are salaried party officials. They prefer to define themselves by their previous occupation or by one of their previous occupations. Thus, they try to attest that they are true members of popular classes. Some of them declare the most 'proletarian' of their previous occupations. For example, they say they were a baker rather than a book-keeper when they successively carry on these jobs. They also use vague and equivocal denomination when their previous occupation is not 'proletarian' enough. They prefer

cumulation of local electoral mandates or the conquest of a parliamentary seat and the associated allowances which has led to professionalization in politics (Fig. 4.4). If this cumulation is familiar in French political history, its effects related to professionalization are rather new.

It has become progressively difficult to reconcile parliamentary activities and a non-political occupation. Unlike during the Third Republic, there are presently only few exceptions among MPs from the professions and other independent occupations, but it is difficult to assess how frequent they are. Members of Parliament need to reduce their previous occupational activities, because these are incompatible with their new parliamentary tasks. In the case of electoral defeat, they are not certain to recover their previous position and may therefore be unemployed. As an insurance against such an occurrence, some of them—a few physicians, for example—try to maintain their professional activities at a reduced level in addition to their parliamentary work. But professions which enable such arrangements are scarce so that many who are involved in occasional political activities are reluctant to extend these and to run for Parliament, especially when they work in the private sector.

Government officials and, more generally, members of the public sector, have a more secure job. Once elected, they get a special status (*position de détachement*) which ensures that in the case of electoral defeat, they can return to a position equivalent to the one they left when they entered Parliament. It is understandable, therefore, that between 40% and 50% of the present deputies come from the public sector, where their positions are secure by law (Fig. 4.13). Self-employed persons or independent business leaders are more exposed when they take on a political career, but they control financial and social resources which reduce the risks (Figs. 4.9–4.12). In contrast, managers of private firms are constantly less numerous in the Assembly than other leading categories. This is, at least partly, a consequence of their reluctance to face the risks of a precarious full-time political activity. The occupational composition of a Parliament and some aspects of its transformation (particularly the increase of the proportion of former state employees among deputies) are therefore partly a consequence of the professionalization of political actors.

As we have already said, in the French case, it is the cumulation of elective offices and their allowances, and not salaried positions in parties or pressure group organizations, which enable political actors to live for and from politics. Therefore, about 90% of the deputies are members of local or regional assemblies when they enter parliament (Fig. 4.4). Presently, holding a local or another elective office, has become an informal precon-

to say that they were a 'railway worker' (*cheminot*) or a 'clerk' rather than a station master or a journalist (Pudal 1989).

dition to running for parliament with some chance of success. Access to Parliament and the preceding nomination by a political party as a candidate are *de facto* reserved for those who have already demonstrated their ability to mobilize voters and who are well advanced in their political career. The burden of parliamentary work, in addition to growing local responsibilities, leads those who are not yet entirely professionalized in politics to give up their previous occupation and to become a full-time politician more often than did their predecessors. This is facilitated by the cumulation of elected offices and their associated allowances. The *cumul* is also a protection against the risks of a defeat in a parliamentary election since it enables former deputies to rerun for parliament from the relatively save haven of local and regional offices.

These days, professionalization is a factor in the stability of parliamentary personnel. Once elected, politicians tend to involve themselves fully in politics. Having given up their previous occupations, it is difficult and hardly rewarding to restart a private career and consequently they usually want to rerun for Parliament. Their position is often strong enough to renew their nomination as a party candidate, since party leaders are themselves professional politicians and understand their deputies' worries about their re-election (Gaxie 1996). Parties also prefer to support incumbents who have put down roots in their constituencies and have a better chance of winning. For all these reasons, the National Assembly's turnover is normally low and slightly lower than it was in the past. On average, about two-thirds of the deputies elected after a general election had been members of the previous assembly while about a third are newcomers (Figs. 4.20–4.21).

This state of things changes only in exceptional circumstances. In the past, elections held after both world wars and a long interruption of parliamentary elections have been characterized by a significant turnover of members of Parliament.[10] In the last fifty years, high turnover rates have been related to significant modifications in the balance of power between political forces. In the 1958 general election, which took place during the Algerian war and after an important political crisis comprising the collapse of the Fourth Republic, the discrediting of the governing parties in this regime, the foundation of the Fifth Republic, and the success of the supporters of General de Gaulle, an unusual proportion of 62% newcomers were elected. A lot of these new deputies were 'Gaullists', whose parliamentary grouping increased from 16 to 198 members. Among them, 78% entered the National Assembly for the first time. The large electoral successes of the Socialist Party in 1981 and 1997 as well as the landslide victory of the RPR–UDF

[10] The high point was reached in the first Constituent Assembly of 1945 where 76.8% of its members had no previous parliamentary experience.

coalition in 1993, also had important effects. In 1981, 38% of the deputies were newcomers, as were 61% of Socialist deputies. In 1993, 42% of deputies were newcomers, as were 50% of RPR deputies.

Professionalized politics, associated with growing competition between parties, became the main factor in the National Assembly's turnover. After general elections with a high renewal rate, most newcomers tend to become professional politicians and to put down roots locally. As with their colleagues, they generally want to keep their seat and are usually successful. Thus, the renewal rate of the dominant party deputies tends to decrease, while that of other parties remains low until another shift of the political equilibrium provokes the defeat of a main party and the victory of one of its opponents. In the case of a large defeat for their party, some deputies have to abandon their political career or take refuge at the local level or elsewhere while waiting for a new opportunity to enter Parliament. A new electoral success for their party will allow some of these former deputies to recover 'their' seat in the Parliament, as well as promoting the ascent of younger political actors who will, in turn, try to maintain themselves in Parliament and in the political field. One can, therefore, understand that the renewal of parliamentary personnel is more apparent than effective. In 1958, for example, only 28% of deputies were incumbents, but 10% were former MPs, 21% former candidates, 12% leaders of political parties, 18% holders of elective offices at local and departmental level, 4% members of ministerial staffs, and only 7% were truly newcomers in the political milieu.[11]

For the most part, it is this logic of professionalization which explains the age variations of members of Parliament (Fig. 4.19). Parties generally assign their safe constituencies to their leaders, so that, when parties are defeated, it is these deputies who survive. They are more often party hierarchs and rather old deputies with the result that the mean age of the defeated parties in parliament increases, as in 1968, 1986, or 1993 for the PS, or in 1981 and 1997 for right-wing parties. On the contrary, when a party has a clear electoral win, it gains seats in contested constituencies where its candidates are less advanced in their political career and thus usually younger. In this way, the mean age of MPs of the winning party declines, as did those of the PS in 1981 or 1997, or those of the right-wing parties in 1968, 1986, or 1993. Some of the new deputies will be able to continue their careers but the re-election of those in weaker positions, especially those MPs whose entrance to Parliament is a consequence of an unusually favourable conjuncture for their party, is less likely. When the circumstances become even more difficult, they may be defeated and forced to quit the political arena. The variation in the mean age of parliamentary parties is thus an indirect indicator

[11] Figures taken from Mattei Dogan (1960: 262).

of their electoral fortunes. Deputies of declining parties like the Communist Party are older than the other members of Parliament, while new parties, such as the National Front in 1986 or the Greens in 1997, mobilize a younger personnel.

Candidacy in an election is formally open to all citizens who fit the legal conditions, but only those few who are involved in a political career are really able to take part. When a party chooses its candidates, competitors cast covetous eyes on its most promising constituencies. When the competition for nominations increases, contenders will mobilize the full volume of resources available to them in order to win. The best constituencies are thus reserved for the leaders and older MPs. These leaders enter the government when their party wins general elections and are likely to keep their seats when their party returns to opposition. In such cases, backbenchers are more threatened and quit Parliament more frequently. The former government's members are proportionally more numerous in a parliamentary group when a party loses general elections such as the PS in 1986 and 1993, and the right-wing parties in 1981, 1988, and 1997.

3.2.2. An Assembly of Occupiers of Dominant Social Positions

Whatever the differences which separate them may be, the Members of Parliament share common features, not only as professional politicians but also in their social characteristics (Gaxie 1983). First, most deputies are male: whereas in the last 50 years, 53% of voters have been women, generally fewer than 10% of deputies in the National Assembly and in the various political groups are female (Fig. 4.7). Although women have been able to vote for more than fifty years, the National Assemblies of the Fourth and Fifth Republics have been (until now) almost as male dominated as were the Chambers of the Third Republic under the regime of male suffrage. While women are underrepresented in Parliaments in most European countries, they are possibly more disadvantaged in France. Most deputies also belong to intermediate generations. When the conjunctural variations analysed above are controlled for, the deputies' mean age is remarkably stable throughout the whole period, being a little over 50 (Fig. 4.19). This average is a consequence of an underrepresentation of older and, particularly, younger age groups. If we compare the weight of the various age categories in the National Assembly and in French society, we see that those under 30 are grossly underrepresented, whereas the 'index of representativeness' increases and crosses the threshold of proportional representation between 35 and 40, and reaches its maximum between 40 and 60. Those over 60 are also underrepresented.

Deputies are also better educated and from a higher social background than the population at large. After 1945, a high proportion—more than 60%

according to incomplete data—hold a university degree (Fig. 4.1). This share has been growing in all parties during the past decades (even if it remains lower in the Communist Party) and is now significantly higher than it was at the beginning of the Third Republic, before the ascent of parties linked with popular classes which lowered it between the two world wars. A university degree is thus a 'normal' characteristic for a member of the Assemblies of the Fourth and, even more so, of the Fifth Republic. Those who did not reach this educational level are more likely to be outsiders in a parliamentary milieu which may occasionally stigmatize them for that reason. With such an educational background, Members of Parliament distinguish themselves from the population they represent. The proportion of the population with university education was about 5.2% in 1974 and 7.8% in 1981, while the percentages of those with only basic education (*certificat d'études primaires, certificat d'aptitude professionnelle*) were 79.2% in 1974 and 72.5% in 1981.[12] In spite of the increase in the number of years of school attendance and of the proportion of the population which has been trained at university level, deputies still have a significantly higher level of education than the present generation of graduates. Among the age cohorts who left the school system in 1973, 17% were graduates of universities or similar institutions, with equivalent figures of 20% in 1980, and 24% in 1986 (INSEE 1990: 328).

With regard to types of university training, there was a decline in the proportion of deputies with law degrees, which was the dominant intellectual background during the Third Republic. Although it is difficult to depict this trend exactly with the data available, it seems that deputies with a university background increasingly have a degree in the humanities, economics, or public administration (Cayrol *et al.* 1973). However, with regard to these developments, deputies differ again from general trends in the educational system where mathematics and the natural sciences are particularly prestigious and expanding (Fig. 4.3). On the other hand, the proportion of holders of diplomas of *Grandes Écoles* is higher among MPs than it is among the most educated segment of the population. Since these educational establishments are independent from and more selective than the universities, they attract the best students. Those who have passed their difficult entrance exams can expect to reach the highest positions in the private and public sectors. Deputies with such prestigious qualifications have, however, more often graduated from the National School for Administration (*École Nationale d'Administration*—ENA) than from an institute of technology, such as the *École Polytechique*, which are generally regarded as the most difficult of the French educational system.

---

[12] The 1974 figures are taken from INSEE (1978: 35). Those for 1981 were published in 'L'Enquête sur l'emploi de mars 1981' (INSEE 1987: 117).

However, the high educational level of French MPs is just one component of their high social status. Most deputies are or are becoming professional politicians and the professionalization homogenizes their status, even
if important differences with regard to way of life, cultural levels and practices, incomes, fortunes, or social memberships, remain among them. A
Communist deputy who was an industrial worker thirty years ago is
presently a full-time politician paid by his party. The distance between such
a deputy and the dominant social circles has been reduced even if it has not
completely disappeared. A physician or a manager who enters the Parliament has frequently given up his or her former occupation and is more a
politician than a physician or a manager (Gaxie 1996).

On the other hand, differences in social background still have various
empirically observable consequences upon the way deputies perceive and
practise their parliamentary work and must therefore be taken into
account. Most deputies come from small occupational categories. They are
former industrialists or managers (about 20% of MPs since 1946; Fig. 4.9),
self-employed professionals (about 15%; Fig. 4.12), lawyers (about 10%;
Fig. 4.11), teachers, mainly secondary school or university teachers
(between 15% and 30%; Fig. 4.15), or higher civil servants (about 15%; Fig.
4.14). Less numerous, partly because of their smaller share in the general
population, are members of the clergy, judges (fewer than 1% of deputies)
and journalists (often fewer than 4%; Fig. 4.16). In sum, with some variations, which will be analysed further, about 80% of National Assembly
members come from social categories presently representing about 13% of
the whole population. These figures are approximately the same in all parliamentary parties, except the Communist Party.

The National Assemblies elected since 1946 are then not very different
from the Chambers of the Third Republic in which about three out of four
members came from upper social strata (Dogan 1961; Gaxie 1980). Differences exist, however, with regard to the weight of the various groups: the
proportion of MPs from the free professions (especially of lawyers), owners,
judges, military officers, and priests has declined, while the share of industrialists, business executives, higher civil servants, and teachers, has risen.
Members of all these categories are at the highest levels in terms of
incomes, fortunes, or education, and therefore occupy the highest social
positions in French society. Presently, deputies who come from upper social
strata are six to seven times more numerous in the National Assembly than
these groups are in the whole population and almost all categories belonging to these upper strata are overrepresented in the various political groups,
except the Communist Party.[13] Similar figures may be found in almost all

[13] For example, in 1993, after right-wing parties had gained a large majority, former industrialists and business leaders were 17 times more numerous in the Assembly than in the
population (former high-ranking civil servants 13 times, intellectual professions 10 times,

parties in Parliament, with the Communist Party being the only exception. This is because many upper categories are not or are only marginally represented in its group (business leaders, higher civil servants, managers, members of free professions). Furthermore, those who are 'present' (mainly members of intellectual and academic professions) are less overrepresented than in other parties. But, even in a party officially organized to favour more popular recruitment of its leaders, deputies coming from upper strata are nevertheless overrepresented.

The underrepresentation of other social categories is the obvious counterpart of the weight of upper social groups in Parliament. In recent years, only 3% of deputies are of popular origin, while the categories which may be classified in this category include 60% of the whole population. The development of the share of former blue-collar workers in the National Assembly is typical in this respect (Fig. 4.18). Deputies of working-class origin have always been very few in liberal and conservative groups. Some were present in Christian-Democratic parties like the MRP at the beginning of the Fourth Republic, but their number rapidly decreased and they disappeared completely after 1958. Likewise, former workers were not very numerous in the Socialist group during the Fourth Republic. Their proportion lowered progressively to nil in 1993 although they rose again very slightly to 2.3% in 1997. The Communist Party is the only organization which fosters the election of deputies with a working-class background, but their number and their proportion in its parliamentary group has also declined during the last fifty years (27.8% in 1997). Although the Communist Party has formerly heralded itself as the party of the working class, and although it still emphasizes its popular roots, even in its group, former blue-collar workers are underrepresented in comparison to their weight in the population (Pudal 1989).

Middle strata are also underrepresented in Parliament, although less strongly that of the lower classes. Deputies coming from the middle classes attained a share of 20% in 1988, 16% in 1993, and 14% in 1997, while 27% of the whole population belong to those categories. Again, this underrepresentation can be observed in all parties, except the Communist Party. With some conjunctural exceptions, all middle categories are underrepresented, except schoolteachers who are proportionally more numerous in the Communist, Socialist, and, sometimes, in centre or right-wing parties, than they are in the population (Fig. 4.15). The case of leaders of small businesses is typical: former small shop owners and independent craftsmen held a

secondary school and university teachers six times, and corporate managers three times). In 1988, when the Socialist Party led the relative majority and the government, higher civil servants were 16 times more numerous in the National Assembly, and business leaders 13 times, free professions 11 times, intellectual professions nine times, teachers eight times, and managers twice.

share of less than 5% in the various assemblies of the Fourth Republic and more than 10% in the population at the same period, but they presently make up less than 2% in Parliament yet represent almost 7% of the population (Fig. 4.10). This underrepresentation crosses all parties, although it is less in right-wing than in left-wing parties.

In sum, during the Fourth and Fifth Republics, the French Parliament has been mainly composed of men of intermediate generations, coming from upper social and more highly educated categories. Most deputies share an origin in dominant positions in the divisions of labour between genders, generations, and social groups. This 'iron law' of the selection of political personnel is at work in all parties, even in those which claim to fight against it. This is also true for the Communist Party, even though it was created, among other reasons, to end the bourgeois recruitment of the leaders of the Second International. This trend has become even stronger since the crisis of the Communist Party has brought its leaders to an adjournment in various fields. Although the concern of the French Communist Party with political inequalities is mainly focused on class origins, it has previously also criticized the underrepresentation of women. However, notwithstanding some attempts to raise the share of women in the ranks of its parliamentary party, it is not very different from other parties in this respect.

3.3. Changes in Legislative Recruitment Patterns

3.3.1. Parliamentary Consequences of General Social Transformations

If deputies' selection adheres to recurrent structures, it has also undergone changes. Some changes are the consequence of general social transformations, while others are more specifically political. Since the composition of a Parliament is partly an effect of the global societal organization, it is thus affected by some of the great social transformations, especially those which modify the morphology of social groups or the structure of the divisions of labour.

The number of deputies coming from the primary sector of the economy, mainly farmers, continued to decline during the Fourth and Fifth Republics from 12% in 1946 to 4% in the 1990s (Fig. 4.8). However, farmers are not presently less represented in Parliament than they were formerly. During the past fifty years, their relative (under-) representation (on average, farmers are half as numerous in the National Assembly as in the population) remains fairly stable. The decline of the number of former farmers is thus partly a consequence of the decrease of the workforce in agriculture from 21% of the whole working population in 1946 to little more than 5% in the 1990s.[14]

---

[14] It must be noted, however, that farmers are proportionally much more numerous, and

The decrease in the number of former blue-collars workers in Parliament can also be partly attributed to the decline of the industrial sector (Fig. 4.18). This development is an aspect of a more general process of the dissolution of the working class, due to the closing of big industrial estates, the disintegration of working-class neighbourhoods, the vanishing of working-class culture, and the decline of the trade unions. This deconstruction has played a part in the decline of the Communist Party and has also affected the selection of candidates by the PCF, since its former priority to chose candidates with a working-class background has been reduced in recent years. Symbolically, a former male nurse succeeded a former metalworker as head of the party a few years ago.

Changes in the social structure have also had some covert effects on the 'representativeness' of MPs, which can be demonstrated with regard to education. French society, like other comparable societies, has seen a strong increase of the number of years in school and of the educational level of its population. However, this transformation has not had dramatic effects on Parliament's composition, because since the Second and Third Republics, a university degree was an informal precondition for a seat in parliament and for the prestige necessary to occupy it. During the past fifty years, the proportion of deputies with university education has increased considerably. However, although the average level of qualification of MPs has not changed greatly, the social value of their degrees has been affected by the general qualification inflation. Even if they still have higher degrees than most of their constituents, modern deputies are less different from their fellow citizens, in this respect, than they were in the past.

The same argument can be pursued with regard to the occupational background of MPs. As we have seen above, most deputies come from a small number of high-ranking positions. About 55% of the Fourth Republic's deputies had their origins in upper social groups. This percentage increased after 1958 in parallel with the number of deputies belonging to centre or right-wing parties. At the beginning of the Fifth Republic, the percentage of deputies with upper social origins generally varied between 70% and 75%. This has increased even further during the last decade to levels between 75% and 80%, due to a transformation of recruitment patterns within left-wing parties. However, the overall share of most of these groups in the population has increased during the last decades as well. For example, within the same period, the proportion of higher civil servants (and equivalent positions in the public sector) has increased from 0.9% after World War II to 1.2% of the working population in 1990; that of members of free

even overrepresented, in the Senate. Their election into this assembly is favoured by indirect suffrage and by the important weight given to rural constituencies. There were 25% former farmers among Senators in 1959, 22% in 1968, 20% in 1977, 13% in 1989 and in 1996.

professions from 0.6% to 1.3%; of managers from 1% to 5.5%; of secondary school and university teachers from 0.2% to 2.3%; and of primary school teachers from 1.3% to 3.3%. Industrialists and business leaders are the only upper social group to have had a fairly stable membership during the last fifty years.

Altogether, the share of these categories rose from 5% of the whole working population after World War II to 13% in the 1990s. Therefore, although the overrepresentation of the various upper social groups in Parliament is still important, it is less important now than it was at the beginning of the Fourth Republic and, *a fortiori*, during the Second and Third Republics. In the 1990s, self-employed persons were 11 or 12 times more numerous in National Assembly than in the whole population, but they were 30 times more numerous in the assemblies of the Fourth Republic and more than 80 times at the beginning of the Third Republic. Secondary school and university teachers were eight times more numerous in the National Assembly elected in 1988, but this factor was 44 in the Parliaments of the Fourth Republic and more than 70 at the end of the Third Republic. If, on average, the social background of MPs is more elevated now than it was previously, it has also become more common. Deputies still distinguish themselves from most of their constituents, but the proportion of those constituents who are not very socially distant from their representatives is presently higher than it was. The social (and political) status of MPs remains high but it was relatively more elevated in the past than it is now.

The selection and recruitment of MPs is also affected by changes in the societal division of labour. A case in point is the restructuring of gender inequalities. Without disappearing, male domination, particularly the male monopoly in the political and social power structure, became less firmly established than it was before. After the struggle by feminist movements for a change in the status, especially the political status of women, parliamentary positions are now less defined as masculine. There is a slow and gradual progression of female presence in all parties in Parliament, although their proportion is still much smaller than in comparable countries. This proportion is slightly higher in left-wing than right-wing parties. This development is likely to continue through political cycles. When a party is in the opposition, its leaders may more readily select new candidates, including women, in constituencies where the respective party has no incumbent. These leaders will support the election of a women because they expect political benefits in return. This was the case in the Communist Party and, even more so, in the Socialist Party in 1997. Thus, after the 1997 general election, the share of women in the Socialist parliamentary party rose to 17%—the highest percentage in French political history so far (Fig. 4.7). These mechanisms show that the access of women to Parliament is not yet 'natural' and that it still depends on the will of party leaders to promote a 'gendered' representation. However, the adoption of a law currently under debate concerning the equal representation of genders in the various elected assemblies could change this.

3.3.2. *The Impact of Political Change on Legislative Recruitment*

Transformations of the political field have also changed the processes of legislative recruitment. The most significant development is the profession-alization of politics. This established trend has been reinforced during the last fifty years. We have seen an increase in all parties of the percentage of deputies who held local elected offices when they entered the Parliament, which is probably a symptom of this trend. Even parties traditionally hostile to the cumulation of electoral mandates, like the Communist Party, or parties with weak local roots when they first appeared on the national level, like the Gaullists, have copied their competitors (Fig. 4.4).

The nomination of candidates with elective mandates on the local level aims at improving party results. The entrance to Parliament is thus *de facto* reserved for politicians who have reached relatively high positions in local or national political hierarchies (Dogan 1967). Recent trends, especially a process of devolution of competencies to local institutions (*décentralisation*), also favoured political professionalization via local politics. Since powers of local elected assemblies have been increased, leaders of these institutions must spend a greater amount of their time on managing them and they receive bigger allowances in return. A growing proportion of candidates with good prospects in the competition for leg-islative recruitment are professionalized in local politics or on the way to professionalization.

This professionalization goes together with a unification of the 'political market', the centralization of powers in political organizations, and a strengthening of the role of political parties. During the Third and Fourth Republics, most candidates had local roots and had to gain the support of local caucuses to get into a favourable competitive position for legislative recruitment. National party leaders didn't have much to say about the nomination of candidates, except in the Communist Party and, to a lesser degree, in the Socialist Party. Since the beginning of the Fifth Republic, can-didates are nominated by an 'ad hoc' national committee. Its role is vari-able, according to the degree of centralization of party organizations and the strength of the position of political actors, but presently few candidates get elected without the nomination of one of the main parties or, at least, without the tacit support of a national party. Only a few dissident incum-bents or some public personalities may succeed without this support.

Since in order to gain a nomination for a parliamentary election, poten-tial candidates must control resources which give them some value from a party leader's point of view, central party markets have become often more important than local political or partisan markets. Among these valuable resources are friendship, clientelist, or exchange relationships with party leaders, rare social titles, degrees from universities or *Grandes Écoles* with a high reputation, expertise, and an ability to deal with current political issues. Other resources, such as roots in a constituency, local reputation, personal acquaintance with constituents, gratitude of voters for various favours they have received in the past have become less important. Although the high percentage of deputies with a background in local politics shows that ties between a candidate and his or her constituency are still crucial, local roots are not self-sufficient anymore and must be added to the support of party leaders. The local political work in a constituency, which was the starting-point of a political career in the past, is presently more often a strengthening element of a political position held within the ruling circles of a party. Many deputies have had no personal connection with their constituency before their first election. This form of 'parachute landing' is possible if party leaders give their support and are able to overcome local opposition to their candidates.

The expansion of the welfare state, public spending, and the personnel of the state sector might have also affected the process of political professionalization. In all parties, the number of deputies coming from the public sector, especially from higher civil servants' ranks, has increased (Fig. 4.13). This increase took place between 1958 and the beginning of the 1980s. Its stabilization during the last fifteen years, especially among right-wing parties, shows that the weight of former public sector employees in Parliament does not only depend on the various advantages given to those who belong to the public sector and are eager to enter a political career. One may wonder if this high-level stagnation might not be connected to a certain delegitimation of the state, its higher bureaucracy, and the National School for Administration (ENA) as a consequence of economic crisis, deregulation, globalization, and neo-liberalism. None the less, the public sector has maintained its position as the single most important source of legislative recruitment in France in recent elections. In the Communist Party, teachers are presently almost as numerous as former workers (Fig. 4.15). In the Socialist camp, the restructuring of the old SFIO and the amalgamation of a 'new' Socialist party in the early 1970s were accompanied by the emergence of a new personnel, partly coming from academic, especially university, circles. Although, traditionally, teachers have not been very numerous in right-wing parties, their number has recently increased. In the same way, from 1958 to the early 1980s, the proportion of former higher civil servants has notably increased in all parties, with the exception of the Communist Party (Ysmal 1985; Fig. 4.14). This growth may be partly a consequence of the professionalization of politicians but other changes in political career requirements such as new forms of rhetoric and skills, especially in economic and administrative fields, may also have had an influence. This trend is particularly strong in governing parties, while there are few former higher civil servants in outsider parties like the Communist Party, the Greens, or the National Front which have been (until now) less involved in governmental tasks.

A new political personnel with instrumental skills has become predominant. These political actors have acquired power and administrative techniques and knowledge about issues faced by the state and the government through university, administrative colleges (especially the ENA) and a career in public administration. On these grounds, they have captured the attention of state and party leaders, who have appointed them onto ministerial staffs, and partisan expert committees, or designated them as advisers. Afterwards, they acquire their nomination as a candidate for one of the main parties in promising constituencies: some of them enter the government and become party leaders. They have played an important role during the establishment of the Fifth Republic or in the formation of the governing parties (PS, RPR, UDF). As the ascent of this new personnel has relied more on the support of the state or party leaders than on local roots and ties, it has thus played a part in the relative decline of agents with local political capital.

All these contemporary transformations of political activity have contributed to the substitution of local notables by professional politicians (Garrigou 1992). Notables are sufficiently well to do to finance an electoral campaign and a political career by their own means. Their level of education and their degrees entitle them to run local politics whereby their social relationships in various local circles provide the necessary resources to solve the problems they are facing in this field. They are known by the local population for their skills, respectability, concern for the public good, and the various favours they have granted to their fellow citizens. Since they are often well to do, self-employed, big farmers, or industrialists, their social position helps them to accumulate a capital of confidence and reputation through their relationships with the local population. Notwithstanding all these advantages, deputies coming from occupations with a focus in local communities are in decline. This applies to farmers and is also the case for lawyers whose proportion in Parliament has been halved in the last twenty years after a more gradual decline in previous years, while there is no decline of members of other independent professions (Figs. 4.8, 4.11, and 4.12). The replacement of local dignitaries by professional politicians is a consequence of the strengthening of parties. Notables rely primarily on personal and patrimonial resources for their electoral mandates, while professional politicians exploit the collective resources offered by their party or other organizations, in addition to those they get from their local or national mandates once they have been elected.

Although there is a long-term trend which increases politicians' dependence *vis-à-vis* their party, this dependence on partisan resources and the subordination to the party is not equally distributed across the political spectrum. It is stronger in left-wing parties, which recruit leaders with lower social origins and are more articulated, than in right-wing parties. The Communist Party has been a strong organization for most of its existence, although its weakening in recent elections has reinforced the autonomy of some of its elected officials. In contrast, the Socialist Party has been strengthened and is stronger *vis-à-vis* its elected officials than was the former SFIO. The UDF is a confederation of small parties which gathered relatively autonomous officials at various levels. Even if UDF leaders are more powerful than they used to be, they remain weaker than other party leaders. The Gaullist movement, despite being more centralized than other right-wing parties, was often weak locally so that it was able to impose its collective discipline on its elected officials. According to these observations, the weight of deputies with former occupations in a local setting is greater in right-wing than in left-wing parties, greater in the UDF than in the RPR, and greater in the Socialist than in the Communist Party.

3.4. Differences in Legislative Recruitment Patterns between Parliamentary Parties

Beyond common features shared by most deputies in most parties, and general trends which affect almost all parties in a similar way, each political grouping has its own selection mechanisms which specify the characteristics of its legislative representation (Gaxie 1980). From this point of view, differences may be attributed to the relative strength of the various parties and to their position in social and ideological cleavages. Sharing characteristics with the vast majority of a legislative body has a legitimizing and integrating effect, while being different, for example, female, younger, less educated, lower or middle class often has a marginalizing effect on an MP's position in the parliamentary milieu. Thus there is a cleavage between 'legitimate' deputies who possess the attributes commonly associated with the status of a MP and less recognized deputies with atypical features. These individual differences typically relate to party cleavages.

Established parties—like the current PS, the RPR, and the UDF—have leaders who are or who have been members of government, and oppose outsider organizations which have never been in a government coalition—such as the *Union de Défense des Commerçants et Artisans* (UDCA) in 1956, or the National Front in 1986—or which have only been episodically in government—such as the Greens from 1997, or the Communist Party from 1945 to 1947, from 1981 to 1984, and since 1997. All things being equal, atypical deputies are proportionally more numerous in outsider parties, while dominant parties recruit proportionally more deputies with 'legitimate' features. Becoming an MP of an established party is in high demand and consequentially internal competition is harder, so that challengers must have a greater amount of social or political resources in order to win. Among other factors, those who occupy dominant positions in society, because of their gender, age, educational degree, or occupation, are more likely to reach the higher ranks of these dominant parties, which are also more attractive than others from their point of view. On the contrary, power positions in marginal parties are less in demand. Social elites would be discredited if they joined such organizations. The degree of internal competition is lower and thus good opportunities are on offer to agents with fewer social resources. Lower position holders are thus more or less supplanted in the course of political competition. In most cases, they may only hope for second-rank positions in dominant parties or for power positions in outsider parties. We may thus understand that members of marginal parties in Parliament share common features, even if they have opposite ideological points of view. Some properties of Communist deputies—like a level of education and a social origin lower than the parliamentary average—must be connected with the social basis and ideological orientations of their party but also with its (relatively) marginal position in the political field. The deputies of far right parties in Parliament show some resemblance to them—a lower social origin for example—even if they are different in other respects.

If deputies of opposing parties may thus share common features, they are also distinct in a systematic way, and these differences are related to social and ideological cleavages which structure political struggles. Seen from this angle, the differences between right-wing and left-wing parties translate into an opposition between 'low' and 'high'. A case in point is university education, where the proportion of socialist deputies with a university degree is slightly lower, and much lower in the Communist parliamentary party, compared to right-wing parties (Cayrol *et al.* 1973; Fig. 4.1). Similar differences appear if we look at occupational background. In a Parliament dominated by deputies coming from upper social strata, there is a non-negligible proportion of Communist deputies coming from popular classes (especially former industrial workers and low-ranking clerks) or middle strata (especially schoolteachers). Even if socialist deputies are socially less distant from right-wing MPs, they are nevertheless somewhat different in that deputies with middle-class origins are significantly more numerous than in right-wing parties. The opposition between lower and higher origins also translates into an opposition between subordinate and elevated positions, public and private sectors, employees and employers. Communist and, to a lesser degree, Socialist deputies are more often former wage-earners, while right-wing deputies have more often occupied positions of command as employers or elsewhere (Figs. 4.9, 4.14). Likewise, even if they are presently not numerous, former military officers or judges are more often members of liberal or conservative groups.

These oppositions between low and high, subordinate and elevated positions may be also found if one only considers deputies from upper strata. An important proportion of left-wing deputies are former teachers. The highest proportion can be found in the Socialist parliamentary party, but almost all Communist deputies coming from upper strata are former university or secondary school teachers (Fig. 4.15). Although less numerous, the former teachers in right-wing parliamentary groupings are different from their opponents and former colleagues in so far as they have occupied, on average, higher positions in academic hierarchies. When right-wing parties' deputies have been schoolteachers, they have more often been employed in private, particularly denominational, schools, or as head teachers. When left-wing parties' deputies were university professors, it was more often as associate professor, while symmetrically, right-wing party deputies coming from academic circles were more often full professors. Former university teachers in right-wing parliamentary groupings were also more often specialized in practical disciplines such as law, medicine, or technology, which open opportunities to supplement incomes as lawyers, physicians at hospitals, through expert advice or reports. They are typically familiar with the spheres of business or free professions. On the contrary, left-wing deputies with an academic background were more often specialized in intellectual disciplines, with fewer practical applications, like the humanities, basic natural sciences, or social sciences (Gaxie 1980).

The general conclusion is that Communist and, to a lesser degree, Socialist deputies are from a somewhat lower origin than Liberal or Conservative deputies. When left-wing deputies come from upper social strata, it is often from less prestigious and privileged groups like teachers. If they have an academic background, they have usually occupied lower and more esoteric positions, while right-wing deputies were in positions of command or of prestige, and/or were specialized in less intellectually prized but more socially valued fields, and were thus closer to the associated rewards in terms of power and money and to governing of economic circles.

Similar oppositions appear when one analyses the variations of public sector positions between parliamentary parties. Left-wing parties, especially the Socialist Party, recruit a high proportion of their deputies in the public sector (Fig. 4.13). Therefore, the proportion of deputies coming from the public sector increases when left-wing parties are gaining seats (1978) or are running the governmental coalition (1981, 1988, 1997), and decreases when right-wing parties are stronger (1968, 1986, 1993). These differences in deputies' origins are correlated with the predispositions of left-wing parties to advocate welfare state benefits and state regulation, while right-wing parties generally are more eager to assert the superiority of the market, the private sector, and business organization. However, the higher proportion of former public servants among the MPs of left-wing parties is also a result of the high number of former schoolteachers or lower or middle-ranking state officers in their ranks. Higher civil servants are proportionally more numerous in right-wing parties than in the Socialist Party and, *a fortiori*, in the Communist Party where they have always been very few (Fig. 4.14).

These differences are complemented by those related to the position occupied in the state apparatus. When Socialist deputies hold senior positions in the civil service—that means in the French case that they were in the *A* category or in an equivalent position—they were (proportionally) more often located at the bottom of these upper bureaucratic categories—for example, in the so-called *A'* categories—while symmetrically, Liberal or Conservative deputies were more often members of the highest and most powerful bureaucratic groups, in particular of the *Grands Corps* of the civil service. Notwithstanding their rank, socialist deputies also more often belong to the less reputable, wealthy, or powerful state agencies, like social, cultural, intellectual, or educational departments, while right-wing MPs with a civil service background have been involved in the inland revenue administration and therefore have been close to business and financial circles or in the 'regalian' offices in charge of core functions of state authority, such as internal security or foreign affairs (Gaxie 1980).

The main distinction between right-wing and left-wing MPs is the proximity of the former to business and independent professions. Among right and far right-wing parliamentary parties, former industrialists, managers, lawyers, members of free professions, and, to a lesser degree, shop owners and independent craftsmen are more numerous, while these categories are poorly represented in the Socialist Party, and missing altogether in the Communist Party (Figs. 4.9–4.12). If differences between left-wing and right-wing parties echo the opposition between low and high social status and between employees and employers, this should not be over-evaluated since it is mainly an opposition between lower and higher positions holders in the upper echelons of society, between intellectuals and business leaders, and between public and private sectors.

The same logic applies to differences between the prestige of degrees and educational establishments. In this regard, the main difference between MPs on the left and on the right is not that the former have only had a basic or an intermediate education, while the latter have reached degree level, although this difference exists, especially if we take Communist deputies into account. Rather, the main difference lies in the nature of university education. Left-wing party deputies—especially Socialist deputies—have followed less prestigious academic programmes, and had specialized in more intellectual fields, with fewer chances of financial rewards. Rightist deputies had a more practical curriculum, frequently in administrative, business, or technical *Grandes Écoles*, which usually leads to the highest social positions in state and economy. For example, in 1997, the proportion of deputies with degrees from one of the *Grandes Écoles* was 13.9% in the Communist Party, 30.1% in the Socialist Party, 41.8% among the Right Liberals (*Démocratie libérale*), 40.3% in the UDF group (mainly with Christian-Democrat background), and 34.3% in the RPR parliamentary parties.

Right-wing MPs are more often from upper-class families with links to the traditional and economic bourgeoisie. They tend to have religious education, often in private denominational schools. Some incomplete data show that many of them are still practising Catholics and attend church regularly. Socialist and Communist MPs have more often been educated in atheist families and in secular primary and secondary public schools. These differences in the socialization process help to understand why the state–church cleavage manifests itself as a left–right opposition and why struggles between religious defence movements and their lay opponents persist.

Although Socialist and Communist deputies have different origins, they have a relatively lower origin in common. For some Socialist and more Communist deputies, this means that they had held lower positions in French society, so that most of them could be referred to as the deprived of the privileged. Beyond those similarities, which favoured ideological proximities and political alliances, social differences and distances have opposite effects. The various oppositions between Socialist and Communist Parties have ideological, political, but also social foundations. Their opposite views have something to do with, among other factors, the differences between their leaders' backgrounds.

On the other hand, deputies of right and far right parties have more often held dominant positions in French society or in a given milieu and more frequently came from the private sector, independent professions, top-ranking civil service positions, or other positions of command. Differences between right-wing party deputies are much smaller than on the left. It is difficult, for example, to discover differences in recruitment patterns between Gaullist or Liberal Parties, whereas differences between right and far-right-wing deputies are easier to delineate, although in both cases many came from the private sector. On average, deputies of far right parties have a lower position in these circles, while moderate right-wing parties have a wider recruitment, extending to higher civil servants or teachers (who are almost entirely absent from the ranks of far right parties).

Sometimes inter-party differences in the recruitment of MPs are subtle and hard to discover, but a closer look reveals a hidden substructure of persistent cleavages in French political life. Indeed, it seems that political struggles obey many factors: the political and social backgrounds of deputies, who are often also party leaders, are two of them.

4. CONCLUSIONS

Analysis of the main features of French MPs since 1848 shows a mix of continuity and change. Across this long history, deputies have been recruited from the dominant categories in the divisions of labour between genders, generations, and social groups. As a result, the mean age of MPs has remained very stable during the last 150 years and if women were obviously excluded from Parliament before 1945 they are still not very numerous, in spite of universal suffrage. Another element of continuity is related to the weight of local elected officials in the French Parliament. MPs are thus inclined to approach cabinet members and administrators in order to defend their constituents' interests, and Parliament might be analysed as a mechanism of compensation for the centralization of the French political and administrative systems.

Various transformations have also appeared throughout French parliamentary history. One of major importance has been the progressive professionalization of MPs, the effects of which have been tangible since the end of the last century. This has contributed to the strengthening of political parties which, in turn, is one of the main factors in the decline of Parliament's powers. Combined with several general social changes, the substitution of *notables* for politicians explains the regular decrease in the number of nobles, landowners, farmers, military officers, and judges who were predominant in the Assemblies of the nineteenth century (Garrigou 1992; Dogan 1961). These have been replaced by new personnel linked to political parties. On the left of the political spectrum, the number of former blue-collar workers or party officials with working-class origins increased steadily from the end of the last century to the end of the Fourth Republic in 1958. The level of working-class representation in the National Assembly has, however, significantly decreased during the Fifth Republic and, as far as the background of their deputies is a pertinent indicator, Socialist and even Communist Parties are now more likely to be described as intellectual and public sector parties rather than working-class or even popular class parties.

An initial feature of the Fifth Republic is the rise of higher civil servants in all governing parties (PS, UDF, and RPR), although their share in the National Assembly has stagnated somewhat during the last two decades. A less well-known feature of current French politics is the direct representation of business interests and independent professions in right-wing parliamentary parties, which leads to the conclusion that cleavages between intellectuals and business leaders and between public and private sectors, might have become predominant in today's Parliament and political system.

References

Agulhon, Maurice (1993). *The Republican Experiment 1848–1852* (*The Cambridge History of Modern France*, ii). Cambridge: Cambridge University Press.

Aubert, Véronique, and Parodi, Jean-Luc (1980). 'Le personnel politique français'. *Projet*, 147.

Bastid, Paul (1945). *Doctrines et institutions politiques de la Seconde République*, 2 vols. Paris: Hachette.

——(1954). *Les Institutions politiques de la monarchie parlementaire française, 1814–1848*. Paris: Hachette.

Best, Heinrich (1984). 'Kontinuität und Wandel parlamentarischer Repräsentation im revolutionären Frankreich 1848/49'. *Francia*, 11: 667–80.

——(1990). *Die Männer von Bildung und Besitz: Struktur und Handeln parlamentarischer Führungsgruppen in Deutschland und Frankreich 1848/49*. Düsseldorf: Droste.

Cayrol, Roland, Parodi, Jean-Luc, and Ysmal, Colette (1973). *Le député français*. Paris: Pr. de la Foundation Nationale des Sciences Politiques.

Charle, Christophe (1987). *Les Élites de la République: 1880–1900*. Paris: Fayard.

——(1991). *Histoire sociale de la France au XIX siècle*. Paris: Éditions du Seuil.

Dogan, Mattei (1960). 'Changement de régime et changement de personnel', in Association Français de Science Politique (ed.), *Le Référendum de septembre et les élections de novembre 1958*. Paris: 241–79.

——(1961). 'Political Ascent in a Class Society', in Dwaine Marvick (ed.), *Political Decision Makers*. Glencoe, Ill.: Free Press, 57–90.

——(1967). 'Les filières de la carrière politique en France'. *Revue Française de Sociologie*, 8: 468–92.

Dupeux, Georges (1972). *La Société française 1789–1970*. Paris: Armand Colin.

Duverger, Maurice (1976). *Les partis politiques*. Paris: Armand Colin.

Garrigou, Alain (1992). *Le Vote et la vertu. Comment les Français sont devenus électeurs*. Paris: Presses de la Fondation Nationale des Sciences Politiques.

Gaxie, Daniel (1980). 'Les logiques du recrutement politique'. *Revue Française de Science Politique*, 30/1: 5–45.

——(1983). 'Les facteurs sociaux de la carrière gouvernementale sous la Cinquième République de 1959 à 1981'. *Revue Française de Sociologie*, 24: 441–65.

——(1996). *La Démocratie représentative*, 2nd edn. Paris: Montchrestien.

Graham, James Q. (1982). 'Legislative Careers in the French Chambers and U.S. House, 1871–1940'. *Legislative Studies Quarterly*, 7: 37–56.

Huard, Raymond (1991). *Le suffrage universel en France 1848–1946*. Paris: Aubier.

——(1996). *La Naissance du parti politique en France*. Paris: Presses de la Fondation Nationale des Sciences Politiques.

INSEE (1978; 1987; 1990). 'Données sociales'. Paris: INSEE.

——(1987). 'Enquête sur l'emploi de mars 1981 (D 87)'. Paris: INSEE.

Jouvenel, Robert de (1913). *La République des Camarades*. Paris: Grasset.

Lasswell, Harold D. (1952). 'The Elite Concept', in H. D. Lasswell, D. Lerner, and C. E. Rothwell, *The Comparative Study of Elites*, Stanford, Calif.: University Press, 6–21.

Le Béguec, Gilles (1996). 'De la république des avocats à la république des énarques', in Louis Dupeux, Rainer Hudemann, and Franz Knipping, *Elites en France et en Allemagne aux XIXième et XXième siècles: Structures et relations*, ii. Munich: Oldenbourg, 79–92.

Lewis, Edward (1970). 'Social Backgrounds of French Ministers, 1944–1967'. *The Western Political Quarterly*, 23: 564–78.

Mayeur, Jean-Marie (1984). *La Vie politique sous la Troisième République 1878–1940*. Paris: Éditions du Seuil.

Pudal, Bernard (1989). *Prendre Parti: pour une sociologie historique du PCF.* Paris: Presses de la Fondation Nationale des Sciences Politiques.

Rudelle, Odile (1982). *La République absolue. Aux origines de l'instabilité constitutionnelle de la France républicaine 1870–1889*. Paris: Publications de la Sorbonne.

Tardieu, André (1937). *La profession parlementaire*. Paris: Flammarion.

Thibaudet, A. (1927). *La République des professeurs*. Paris: Grasset/Albert.

Weber, Max (1947; orig. 1919). 'Politics as a Vocation', in H. H. Gerth and C. Wright Mills (eds.), *From Max Weber: Essays in Sociology*. London: Routledge & Kegan Paul Ltd.

Ysmal, Colette (1985). 'Élites et leaders', in Madeleine Grawitz and Jean Leca, *Traité de Science Politique*, iii. Paris: Presses Universitaires de France, 603–43.

5

Challenges, Failures, and Final Success: The Winding Path of German Parliamentary Leadership Groups towards a Structurally Integrated Elite 1848–1999

HEINRICH BEST, CHRISTOPHER HAUSMANN, AND KARL SCHMITT

1. INTRODUCTION

Changes in patterns of parliamentary recruitment are the result of an interplay between two agents of change: on the one hand, alterations of the formal structure of opportunity for access to office—determined by electoral laws, eligibility rules, or financial provisions for members of parliament—and, on the other hand, the transformation of society in general, influencing the offer of and the demand for representatives with particular qualities and qualifications (cf. introductory chapter). Although in theory both agents of change are independent of each other, in reality they interact, either providing the conditions for a smooth adaptation of recruitment markets to new societal needs, or causing tensions and inconsistencies in the relationship between polity and society. German political history between 1848 and the foundation of the Federal Republic has been widely considered to follow the second mode of change, being strained by a delayed, erratic, and disruptive adaptation of the political system to the modernization of society (Kocka 1988; Steinmetz 1997). The notion of an 'unusually extended delay of democratisation as against industrialisation' is also at the core of the theory of a German *Sonderweg*,[1] which claims a 'particular position of Germany in the history of democratisation and industrialisation' (Lepsius 1973: 56).

In this theory, political elites have a special significance, whereby the disturbances and delays in Germany's development towards parliamentary democracy are attributed to the failures of its leadership groups. It is their inability or reluctance to push forward a thorough modernization of society and polity that is seen as one of the main reasons for Germany's

---

[1] i.e. German exceptionalism.

inclination towards authoritarian government and even totalitarian rule for extended periods of its history. In terms of modernization theory, such an interpretation of German political history can be considered as a special case of partial modernization (Wehler 1995). Whereas Germany transformed into a highly industrialized and urbanized country, its power structure remained under the control of the old and particularly pre-industrial elites, so that the legitimizing bases of political authority continued to be tied to pre- or even anti-democratic ideologies. Put in an historical context, this line of argument suggests oppressive continuity: the betrayal of the democratic goals of the 1848 Revolution by the liberal bourgeoisie was followed by its failure in the Prussian constitutional conflicts of the 1860s and by the formation of a reactionary 'cartel of power' during the Wilhelminian Empire. In the 1930s, an alliance between this cartel and the plebeian contenders from the Nazi Party (NSDAP) brought about the overthrow of the Weimar Republic and its democratic institutions (Best 1990*a*: 16). Even in the early days of the Federal Republic, a heterogeneous 'cartel of angst' was supposed to have prevented a 'radical enforcement of civic equality as well as a rigorous implementation of economic liberty' (Dahrendorf 1979: 256). Not before the 1960s were German political elites attributed with a general ability and readiness to adapt peacefully and consensually to social change, and to accept democratic rules (Hoffmann-Lange 1985). On this line of argument, German parliamentary elites were a kind of toothless tiger: they were supposed to occupy the central position in the political decision-making process and to establish parliamentary democracy, but they failed to succeed during the nineteenth century and were unable to preserve what they gained after World War I.

It should be emphasized that this theory, or rather, this thesis, has been harshly criticized from various angles (Steinmetz 1997: 252). In particular, the early accomplishment of general male suffrage at national level, the development of a highly competitive party system, and the thorough politicization of German society soon after the foundation of the Empire, can all be considered as emerging traits of political modernity. Indeed, before the turn of the century, the proportions of adults being entitled to vote and actually voting were among the highest in Europe (1890: 21.7% and 71.6%), both approaching the corresponding values for the French Third Republic (1889: 27.1% and 76.5%; Kohl 1982: 493, 495). The proportion of votes cast for working-class parties by far outnumbered all other countries in Europe (1890: 19.7%; Ritter and Niehuss 1980: 40). What we see is a somewhat contradictory picture of early democratization in terms of formal suffrage requirements and actual political participation versus a late parliamentarization with regard to the formation of governments and the role of the *Reichstag* in determining the political course of the country. However, such inconsistencies were not uncommon in European political history. Although parliamentarization usually preceded the introduction of general suffrage, cases such as France (until 1871) and Denmark (until 1901) display a picture similar to the German case without, however, their deserving the epithet of a *Sonderweg* (Kohl 1982: 488). Obviously an analysis of constitutional set-tlements and eligibility rules is not enough to uncover the relationship between societal and political change. What is needed is a long-term study, which reconstructs the structural patterns of this relationship over time and which, through a comparative perspective, can reveal what was special or even unique in the German case. Here, the long period of democratic stab-ility and parliamentary performance after 1949 can serve as a contrasting frame of reference for a within-country comparison.

The study of political recruitment leads us directly to the connection between society and polity, since parliamentary representation is one of the most crucial linking points between both spheres. This subject will be approached in four steps. In Section 2, we will outline the structures of opportunities for parliamentary recruitment as they were determined by the territorial range, the social scope, and the formal application of suffrage and eligibility rules. In Section 3, we will reveal patterns of interlockingness between society and polity by studying affiliations of representatives to socio-economic interest groups, intermediary organizations, and the public sector. In Section 4, ascriptive and acquired prerequisites for parliamentary recruitment such as gender, aristocratic background, and religion will be discussed. Section 5 addresses patterns of interlockingness between levels and areas of the political system, and introduces data on seniority and turnover. In this final section, we will also deal particularly with the effects of discontinuities of formal recruitment requirements set by the legal context and the patterns of party competition on personal elite circulation and reproduction.

2. STRUCTURES OF OPPORTUNITIES FOR PARLIAMENTARY RECRUITMENT

2.1. The Changing Territory of the German Constituency

Structures of opportunity for parliamentary recruitment in Germany have been influenced by major constitutional and territorial changes since 1848. At the beginning of national parliamentary history in 1848, Germany consisted of 41 independent states with large non-German populations in Prussia and the Habsburg Empire. Following revolutionary outbreaks, the German Confederation (1815–66) called elections to a Constituent National Assembly in April 1848. For the first time, a national poll, based on a free and equal male suffrage (although using for the most part indirect balloting and applying the admission criterion of 'independence'), was held in what was supposed to become the German Empire (Botzenhart 1977: 141–62). The constituency extended beyond the limits of the future German *Reich* of 1871, since it comprised the western half of the Habsburg Monarchy, even including those parts with a predominantly non-German population like Trieste, most of what is today Slovenia, Bohemia, and Moravia.[2] All in all, 585 constituencies were represented in the National Assembly of 1848, but, by 1849, due to considerable turnover and replacement, some 809 deputies had taken seats as members (Best and Weege 1996).

Since the National Assembly finally failed to establish a nation state in 1849, national parliamentary representation was interrupted for nearly twenty years. Nevertheless, elements from the constitution and above all the electoral law drafted by the Frankfurt National Assembly influenced further developments. In 1867, the North German Union (1867–71) was founded after Austria had been defeated in the 'German War' of 1866 and the German Confederation was dissolved. In the following year, the Constituent North German *Reichstag* was elected according to the electoral law passed in 1849 by the Frankfurt Assembly. This Union, which comprised only the German states north of the River Main, was just an interlude on the way to a nation state. In 1868, Southern Germany was invited to elect 85 delegates for a German 'Customs Parliament' (*Zollparlament*, 1868–71) on the basis of the same free, direct, and equal franchise already in practice in Northern Germany. These delegates joined the members of the North German *Reichstag* already assembled in Berlin (n = 297; Pollmann 1985). Though the main task of the *Zollparlament* was to take decisions on economic matters, it was the first national representation for the whole of Germany since 1849. In 1871, the German Empire was formed by 25 German states, now fully integrating Southern Germany and the newly annexed Alsace-Lorraine, but excluding the western territories of the Habsburg monarchy. The constitution was mainly adopted from the North German Union. Elections for the first all-German *Reichstag* were held in 1871, only excluding Alsace-Lorraine which was not represented in the *Reichstag* before 1874 (Huber 1970: iii. 862–3). Although Germany now had a national representation based on universal male suffrage, it was by no means a parliamentary democracy. The governments of the singular states retained a pivotal position in the constitution through a Federal chamber, which was dominated by Prussia. The Chancellor of the *Reich* could not be elected or dismissed by the *Reichstag*, but only by the Emperor who,

---

[2] However, in those areas of Bohemia with a predominantly Czech population, the elections were boycotted. Elections were also organized in the eastern provinces of Prussia, which had not belonged to the German Confederation before 1848, and in Schleswig, which was then ruled by the Danish crown but had a predominantly German population.

together with the Federal Chamber, had the right to dissolve the *Reichstag* at any time. Even the budgetary rights of the *Reichstag* were limited, since military expenses were fixed for seven years in advance and remained a domain of the Emperor. Although the *Reichstag* played an important role in legislation and the design of economic policy, no serious attempt was made to shift the balance of constitutional powers and to implement parliamentary government fully before the outbreak of World War I (Wehler 1995: iii. 309 and *passim*).

The Weimar Republic started in troubled circumstances and with inner conflicts after the defeat of World War I. Vast areas of German territory were ceded by the Versailles peace treaty of 1919: Alsace-Lorraine, parts of Eastern and Western Prussia, Upper Silesia, and Northern Schleswig, while the Saar territory was administered by the Peoples League in Geneva until 1935. The new constitution increased the powers of the *Reichstag*. It could vote out the Chancellor and the cabinet, but was still restricted by a *Reichspräsident* furnished with the right to dissolve parliament and to govern by emergency decrees. From 1930 onwards, this became a continuous practice, so that parliamentary government was effectively abolished. Eventually, extreme right and left-wing parties prevailed, and in 1933 the Nazis brought the first German democracy to an end (Kolb 1993). For the twelve years which followed, a show parliament existed, 'elected' in non-competitive quasi-elections, and rubberstamping the decisions imposed by Adolf Hitler (Hubert 1992).

At the end of World War II, Germany was divided into four zones of occupation and lost its territories east of the Oder and the Neisse. Once again, the territory of the Saar was separated from Germany and stayed under French administration until it was reintegrated in 1957. In those parts of Germany which were under the control of the Western Allies, democratic institutions were gradually re-established, starting at the local and state level. The first *Bundestag* was elected in 1949 and became the hub of the German constitution, whereby all former elements of a presidential system were removed (von Beyme 1996: 247). Parliamentary government was implemented without restrictions, providing the chancellor with comprehensive powers. Today, the *Bundestag* can only be dissolved after a chancellor loses his parliamentary majority.[3] No substantial constitutional changes preceded or followed German Unification in 1990. The existing political institutions of the Federal Republic were expected to guarantee

---

[3] The dominance of the German *Bundestag* is limited, however, by the participation of the *Bundesrat*, a Federal chamber consisting of representatives of 16 state governments, in the legislative process, whereby some political decisions need a majority both in the *Bundestag* and the *Bundesrat*. The constitution of the Federal Republic thus revitalized an old tradition of German political life that had been interrupted only during the Weimar period (von Beyme 1996: 320–1).

further stability. In October 1990, after forty years of coexistence of two Germanys, the *Bundestag* became the representation of the whole German nation by including delegates from the first (and last) freely elected *Volks-kammer* of the GDR (von Beyme 1996: 47–57).

2.2. Development of Suffrage and Eligibility

Contrary to the widespread belief that Germany was politically backward in the nineteenth century, in 1867 suffrage was already advanced in comparison to most other European states since all German males over 25 years of age were granted an equal right to a direct and secret vote that was not limited by any property or census rule. This was the take-off point for mass participation and a fundamental politicization which gained momentum in the 1880s (Vogel, Nohlen, and Schultze 1969).

The second step to universal suffrage was taken in 1919, when full voting rights for women were established. Simultaneously, the age limit for eligibility and the right to vote was reduced to 20 years. This age limit for suffrage remained in force until 1970, when it was finally fixed at 18 years. However, the age of eligibility, which had been as low as 20 in the Weimar Republic was raised in the early Federal Republic to 25. This remained until 1969 when it was lowered to 21, remaining thus until it was synchronized with the right to vote in 1972. Women's suffrage and the reduction of age limits led to increased enfranchisement so that it rose from 22% at the end of the Wilhelminian Empire to 60% in the Weimar Republic and to 75% in the Federal Republic (cf. Graph 5.1).[4] With regard to turnout, full mobilization had already been reached by the end of the Wilhelminian Empire: starting with 51% in 1871, participation had risen to 85% by 1912. These elevated rates indicate contested elections and a high degree of mobilization among the voters in general and not just at crucial points in political development (1933/1972).[5] However, the general trend from the beginning of the 1980s has been, as in most other European countries, towards a decline in turnout.

With regard to eligibility for the *Reichstag*, there were no substantial exclusions based on economic criteria; only those who were on poor relief or bankrupt were not admitted as candidates. Even soldiers were eligible, though they did not have the right to vote during the time of their military service. However, as elsewhere in Europe, there were some restrictions on

[4] The decrease of the share of those enfranchised at the end of the 1980s was due to an increase in the non-German population combined with a decrease in the indigenous German population. Currently, about 9 per cent of adult German residents are not enfranchised, since suffrage is tied to German citizenship.
[5] For example, in East Germany, 93% of the voters participated in the *Volkskammer* election in March 1990, the highest rate in German electoral history to date (not included in Graph 5.1).

Graph 5.1. Turnout rates and share of voters in Germany 1848–1998

Note: For 1848, no official data are reported for the whole territory; for 1867, only the Prussian results for turnout are displayed (cf. Ritter and Niehuss 1980: 38–43; Falter *et al.* 1986; von Beyme 1996).

civil servants entering a political career: for example, to protect them from the temptations of patronage they had to resign from Parliament after being promoted but they could rerun immediately in a new election. Of much greater importance was the incompatibility which existed between membership of the *Reichstag* and the government of the *Reich* or a state government (Ritter and Niehuss 1980: 27). This only became redundant in 1918 with the establishment of parliamentary government as a failed last-minute attempt at constitutional reform. It was, however, the constitution of the Weimar Republic which ended completely any separation between the spheres of government and parliament born out of the idea of monarchical prerogative.

Until 1906, being elected into the *Reichstag* involved no financial rewards.[6] The constitution of the Empire explicitly forbade any kind of allowances or compensations in an attempt to prevent the emergence of professional politicians and to hamper the involvement of unpropertied

---

[6] The granting of allowances to the members of the Frankfurt National Assembly remained an episode (Jansen 1999).

contenders in politics (Butzer 1999). The Social Democratic Party, however, developed effective ways to circumnavigate this obstacle by employing its candidates as journalists or party officials, or by recruiting them from the cadres of trade union officials. When allowances were finally introduced in 1906, this had no real impact on professionalization, since other parties had adapted similar means of rewarding their full-time politicians. After their introduction, allowances increasingly resembled a real income. The amount of 3,000 marks per year granted in 1906 was quite generous: in 1912 only 5% of all taxable inhabitants of Prussia had an equal or a higher income (Hohorst *et al.* 1975: 106). Today, members of the German *Bundestag* receive yearly allowances amounting to approximately 160,000 marks (before tax), which places them in the same income bracket as their predecessors in the *Reichstag* of 1906 (Borchert and Golsch 1999: 133; Geißler 1996: 57). However, we have to consider that today's politicians also receive a generous pension scheme and a tax-free lump sum of approximately 80,000 marks per year—provided for expenses but difficult to distinguish from personal income. Although German parliamentarians belong to the privileged sector of the population, the rewards for their office are not spectacular and do not exceed international standards in Western Democracies like Italy, Switzerland, the United States, or Great Britain (Harenberg 1997: 105 ff.).

2.3. Electoral Systems

In German parliamentary history there have been two major electoral systems: first, until 1918, an absolute majority franchise in single-member constituencies with a run-off majority ballot was in practice. Secondly, after complaints from the Social Democrats, who had felt discriminated against in a majority system, a strict proportional voting system was applied during the Weimar Republic. This electoral system, although complemented by some elements from the majoritarian system, still exists in the Federal Republic today.

During the Wilhelminian Empire, when there were 397 single-member constituencies (382 until 1874), voters had a single vote (Huber 1970: iii. 861–78). If a candidate was elected in more than one constituency, a decision had to be made as to which constituency was to be represented and new elections held in those constituencies which were not chosen (*Neuwahlen*). In addition, substitutionary elections (*Ersatzwahlen*) had to be called every time an MP died, resigned, or became (or was promoted as) a civil servant. Run-offs, which were held in nearly half of the constituencies by the end of the Wilhelminian Empire, were necessary when no candidate gained an absolute majority in the first run. As a rule in these situations, the 'bourgeois' parties formed strategic coalitions against the socialist candidates. The Left Liberals profited most from this procedure, since they could win voters from both the left and the right, depending on the coalition chosen. By this means, they were able to win 80% of their run-offs, whereas the socialists won just 27% (Ritter and Niehuss 1980: 125–9). The retaining of constituency borders was another instrument by which certain parties were disadvantaged. Based on a census from 1864, con-stituencies each held originally around 100,000 inhabitants. However, although the territorial distribution of the German population had pro-foundly changed by 1914, the old constituency borders were not adapted before the end of the Wilhelminian Empire. Rural areas with slow demo-graphic growth and/or low immigration were advantaged by this policy, while it worked to the detriment of urban and industrialized areas. In terms of political representation, parties with a rural base were overrepresented whereas the Social Democrats were disadvantaged. Conservative parties were particularly successful in taking advantage of this situation by patron-izing their mostly rural clientele and controlling the voting act. The latter was furthered by the fact that voting in a booth was not introduced in many areas before 1903, so that pressure could be exerted to vote for the 'right man' (Ritter and Niehuss 1980: 27–9).

During the Weimar Republic, we find a pure proportional voting system, where voters could only vote for fixed party lists without any option to chose between candidates (Falter *et al.* 1986: 23–31). There were no substi-tutional elections and successors were taken from the party lists. The Weimar voting system worked on the basis of 35 large multimember con-stituencies (38 in 1919), which consisted of one or two minor *Länder* (states) or, as in the case of Prussia and Bavaria, of provinces. Votes were counted on three different levels: in the constituency, a party needed 60,000 votes to obtain a seat. Any surplus votes were transferred to the next higher level of 16 combined constituencies, where again the requirement for a seat was 60,000 votes. In case of further surplus, the same number of votes had to be reached at national level. Thus, the Weimar *Reichstag* did not have a fixed number of seats, but became smaller or bigger depending on the turnout (minimum 459, maximum 647). This electoral system worked to the advan-tage of small parties with a regionally dispersed electorate and, since there was no significant threshold, parties with a small share in the vote could win a seat much more easily than during the Wilhelminian Empire (Huber 1981: 350–2).[7]

In the Federal Republic, after 1953, every voter has two votes, the first to elect a candidate in a single-member constituency according to a simple plurality system, the second to vote for a fixed party list at *Länder* level

---

[7] Since 1919, Parliaments are elected for a four-year term. Prior to this, they were elected for periods of three (1867–87) and five years (1888–1912) respectively, though, up to 1933, pre-mature elections occurred more often than regular terms.

(Ritter and Niehuss 1987). Half of the seats in parliament (currently 328; 248 up to 1990), are distributed according to the results in the single member constituencies. The final number of seats for parties is distributed according to the proportions of the votes for party lists, with mandates obtained by the first vote being subtracted from the initial overall amount. However, under this combined system, a full proportional translation of votes into seats is not given, since a party which wins more direct seats than it should according to the proportions of the second vote, can keep these additional seats (*Überhangmandate*): there is no mechanism to redress this disproportion by giving additional seats to the other parties. These man-dates normally occur in regions where there is a stronghold of one party that can win most of the constituencies (von Beyme 1996: 82–92). Further-more, since 1953, a party has to exceed 5% of the second votes at national level to be admitted to parliament (in 1949, this 5% threshold was only at the *Land* level). Alternatively, since 1957, winning a minimum of three seats in single-member constituencies is also sufficient for a party to enter the *Bundestag* (until 1953, one was adequate).

The mixed system established in Germany after World War II has an impact on the recruitment of MPs whereby parties with a strong regional background recruit their candidates according to the perceived preferences in local constituencies, while small parties with a regionally dispersed elec-torate tend to compose their party lists with regard to more universal cri-teria, like gender or profession of the candidates (Anderson 1993: 85–91). Consequently, in single-member constituencies, male candidates are dis-proportionally favoured (especially in Catholic rural areas where a certain type of local politician is preferred by the selectorate), while women are much more likely to run on party lists.

2.4. Party Systems since 1848

In comparison to most other European polities, the party system in Germany developed relatively early with its origins dating back to the pre-revolutionary era of the late 1840s (Ritter 1990*b*: 30). From the 1870s until 1930, four main party families can be distinguished which, according to M. R. Lepsius (1973), represented basic social milieux (Rohe 1990: 9). For most of the period investigated here, the Liberal party family, although the social profiles of neither wing were clearly distinguished, was divided into a left, more democratic wing and a national right wing, which represented large parts of the Protestant upper and petty bourgeoisie. During this period, there was a Conservative party family, which consisted of two major parties, and was mainly rooted in the rural areas of Prussia, east of the river Elbe. A Catholic party was firmly established in 1870 and became the political representation of most of the Catholic population throughout the period, while a socialist party represented predominantly the non-Catholic working class in industrialized and urban areas. The Catholic and socialist parties succeeded in developing strong subcultural ties during most of this period while other parties remained only temporarily linked to specific electorates (Ritter 1990*b*). In addition to these main political groups, three other party families were only intermittently represented (communists and extreme right) or rather negligible (non-aligned MPs). Only during the Wilhelminian Empire were ethnic and regional parties of some importance, such as those representing the Polish and Danish minorities, or those expressing popular protest against the annexation of Alsace-Lorraine and the former Kingdom of Hanover to the German Empire or Prussia in 1866 and 1871. These regional parties together held barely more than 10% of the seats in the Wilhelminian *Reichstag*.

According to Maurice Duverger (1976: 338–51), there are certain mechanisms with which an electoral system may shape a party system. One is that a majoritarian system should lead to a two-party system, whereas a proportional system tends to evoke a multi-party system. Contrary to this assumption, different electoral systems in German history did not produce the expected outcomes. During the Wilhelminian empire, the majoritarian system led not to a two-party but to a rather stable multi-party system based on regional strongholds, while national party organizations—except for the Social Democratic Party—developed only slowly (Rohe 1990: 9). In effect, the electoral system rather reinforced the regional structures of the party system.

Although party organizations were reshaped after 1918 in general, during the early stages of the Weimar Republic, this multi-party system continued with only minor changes. An early and important extension was the emergence of the Communist Party in 1919 while regional parties disappeared due to the loss of peripheral territories. Although it appears that the proportional electoral system introduced in the Weimar Republic favoured an increase in parties and party families, most of the change in its final period was due to a dramatic disintegration of the protestant bourgeois parties. On the extreme right, the Nazi Party (NSDAP), a kind of 'catch-all party', finally caused the break-up of the traditional German party system by absorbing much of the electorates of liberal and conservative parties in the 1930s. Only Catholic and socialist milieu parties managed to keep large parts of their electorate until 1933 (Falter 1990; Lösche 1993: 65–82).

After 1945, the pre-1933 party system was dramatically 'simplified'. War, territorial dismemberment, and migration had intermingled German society, thus leading to a coalescence in the electorate. The newly formed Christian Democratic Union (CDU) and its Bavarian counterpart (CSU) overcame former denominational barriers and opened their ranks to both

Protestant and Catholic members. Some single-issue parties, which had flourished in the first years after the war, were absorbed by the CDU/CSU and just one Liberal party (FDP) was established, integrating both left and right-wing liberals. Only the Social Democratic Party (SPD) resumed its pre-1933 organizational tradition and kept its old party name. The extremes of the pre-1933 party system were cut off by an Allied decree dissolving the NSDAP and precluding the foundation of a successor party, while the Communist Party was formally banned by a rule of the Constitutional Court in 1956.

The process of reduction of party families in West Germany after 1949 was also fostered by the introduction of a 5% threshold in the electoral law at national level. Thus, a three-party system, in which the Liberals were able to enter into coalitions with both the Christian Democrats and the Socialists (Lösche 1993) existed for almost three decades, and it was not until 1983, after the Greens appeared as a new contender, that this equilibrium came to an end. After German unification in 1990, the German party system was further extended by the post-communist PDS, which has developed as a kind of a regional party so far restricted to East Germany. The elections of 1998 confirmed the establishment of a five-party system in post-unification Germany.

3. LINKS BETWEEN SOCIETY AND PARLIAMENT THROUGH THE OCCUPATIONAL BACKGROUND OF REPRESENTATIVES

3.1. Changing Patterns of Primary Sector Interest Representation

According to theories of political modernization, a shift of power from landed interests and rural leadership groups to urban elites and secondary or tertiary sector interests is a necessary step in the development towards a stable democracy. Following Marx and Engels, Barrington Moore (1967) maintained that it was the weakness of the German commercial and industrial bourgeoisie which prevented it from taking over power in the Revolution of 1848, and which forced it to act as a junior partner in a reactionary coalition with the landed aristocracy. In such a coalition, the landed interests try to defend their challenged social power position by political means, relying on authoritarian methods of government, social protectionism, and anti-democratic ideologies. Barrington Moore establishes a direct link between the formation of 'reactionary coalitions' and the success of fascism in various countries, including Germany. However, the early introduction of universal suffrage in Germany, and the significant role of the *Reichstag* in decisions on tariffs, taxes, social welfare legislation, and civil law, forced economic interest groups to attract mass support and to build up parliamentary bargaining power to promote their claims. Our data show to what degree, and through which political channels, they were able to translate social power positions into direct interest representation in the *Reichstag*.

The figure showing the share of representatives with an occupational background in the primary sector (Fig. 5.10) demonstrates that, indeed, for an extended period in the late nineteenth and early twentieth centuries, general social change and parliamentary interest representation developed independently of each other. In the Frankfurt National Assembly, landed interests were poorly represented, even if we consider that landed property ownership was often combined with other occupational positions, particularly in the public sector (Fig. 5.13 and Best 1990*a*: 49–117). Nevertheless, the Constituent Assembly in the *Paulskirche* primarily comprised propertyless but highly educated intellectuals, giving 'education' a strong predominance over 'wealth' as a criterion for parliamentary recruitment (Fig. 5.2). This picture changed dramatically in the founding period of the Second Empire. Already in the Constituent Northern German *Reichstag* of 1867, 26% of its members had their main occupation in agriculture, predominantly as large estate owners in the northern and eastern provinces of Prussia. This proportion rose steadily to 33% in 1881 and remained on this level until 1893. In a period when the share of the workforce employed in the primary sector fell from about 55% to about 38%, its share in parliamentary representation almost tripled.

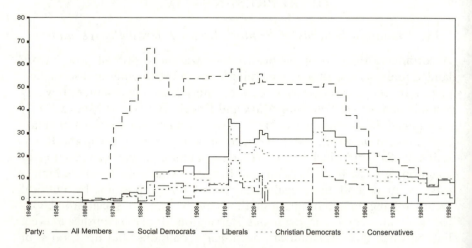

Fig. 5.1. Germany 1848–1999: basic education

Note: For the period between 1933 and 1949, see the comment on p. 20 of the Introductory Chapter.

Although this increase was due largely to the particular conditions for parliamentary recruitment during the Revolution of 1848, and to the specific function of the Frankfurt parliament as a constituent assembly, the subsequent additional rise of agricultural interest representation during the first decades of the *Kaiserreich* cannot be attributed to the same irregularities. This later rise rather suggests the resistance of the 'endangered classes' to a loss of power in a period of rapid social change and their ability to mobilize mass support under conditions of universal male suffrage. It is

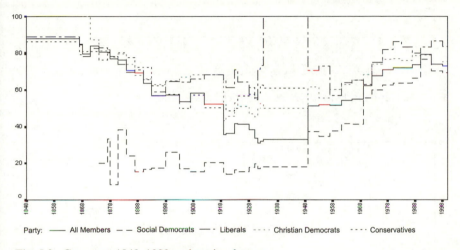

Party: —— All Members — — Social Democrats — · Liberals · · · · Christian Democrats · · · · Conservatives

Fig. 5.2. Germany 1848–1999: university degree

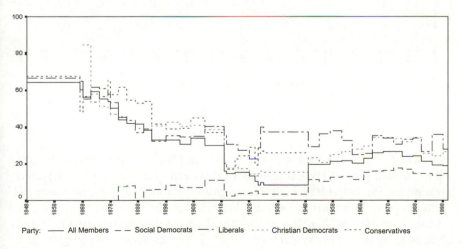

Party: —— All Members — — Social Democrats — · Liberals · · · · Christian Democrats · · · · Conservatives

Fig. 5.3. Germany 1848–1999: law degree

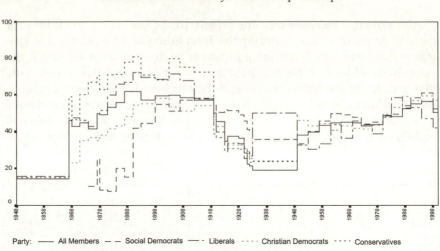

Party: —— All Members — — Social Democrats —— Liberals ···· Christian Democrats ···· Conservatives

Fig. 5.4. Germany 1848–1999: local politics background

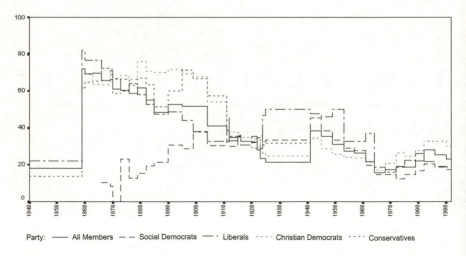

Party: —— All Members — — Social Democrats —— Liberals ···· Christian Democrats ···· Conservatives

Fig. 5.5. Germany 1848–1999: other parliamentary experience

noteworthy, however, that it was not only the Conservative Party—the traditional guardian of landed interests in eastern Germany—who provided a channel for agricultural interest representation but that the share of primary sector representatives also increased in the Catholic Centre Party (peaking in 1881 with 42%) and within the liberal parties, particularly the National Liberals (peaking in 1893 with 27%). However, during the late 1880s a different structure started to emerge: while the share of peasants

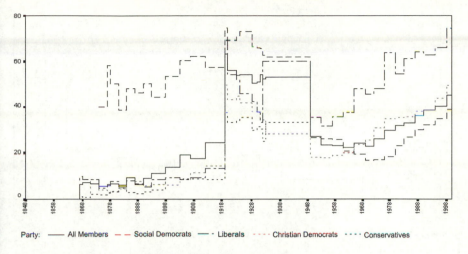

Party: —— All Members — — Social Democrats — · Liberals ···· Christian Democrats ···· Conservatives

Fig. 5.6. Germany 1848–1999: leading party position

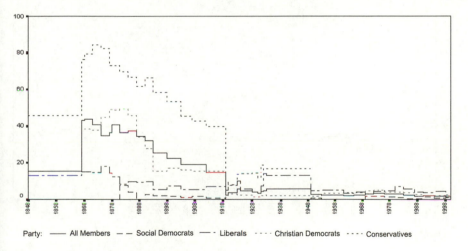

Party: —— All Members — — Social Democrats — · Liberals ···· Christian Democrats ···· Conservatives

Fig. 5.7. Germany 1848–1999: nobility

and landowners started to decline in other parties, and while the rapidly increasing Social Democratic Parliamentary Party provided no channel for agricultural interest representation at all, the Conservatives transformed overwhelmingly into an agrarian party. In the last Imperial *Reichstag* of 1912, 59% of their representatives had an agrarian background compared to 22% of the Catholic Centre Party, 16% of the National Liberals, and 12% of the Left Liberals. An increasing division of labour with regard to agrarian interest representation coincided with its overall

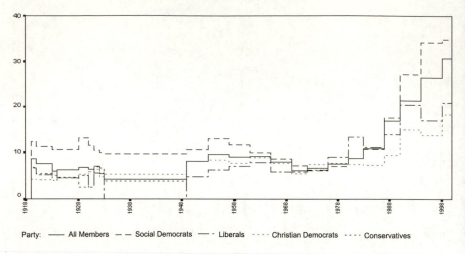

Fig. 5.8. Germany 1848–1999: female legislators

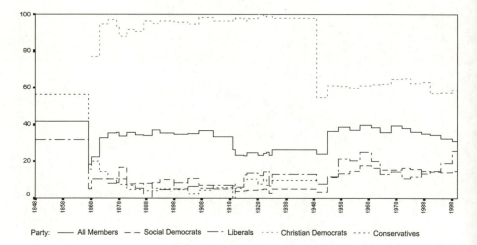

Fig. 5.9. Germany 1848–1999: religion: Catholic

decrease in terms of parliamentary representation to a level of about 20%. Although we have to be aware that this development was partly compensated for by the emergence of powerful agricultural interest organizations and their highly efficient lobbying practices, these trends show clearly that it became increasingly difficult to mobilize the support of selectorates and electorates for candidates with an agricultural background (Blackbourn 1984).

The Revolution of 1918 and the subsequent election of the Weimar

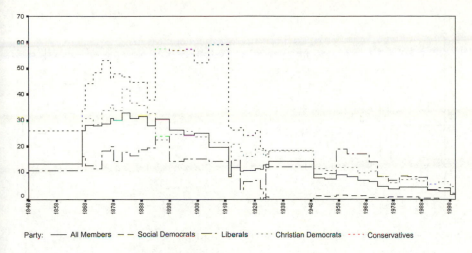

Fig. 5.10. Germany 1848–1999: primary sector

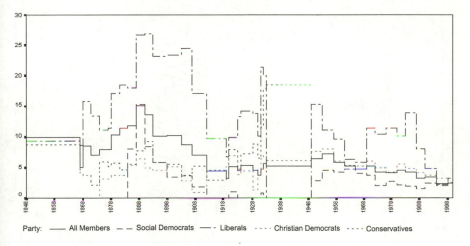

Fig. 5.11. Germany 1848–1999: managers, businessmen

Constituent Assembly resulted in a further sharp decline of agrarian interest representation. In 1919, the share of deputies with an agricultural background plummeted to 8%, while about 30% of the workforce was still
employed in agriculture and forestry. This breakdown of agricultural representation was brought about by the electoral success of socialist parties
with their traditional distance from the rural world, the ousting of the traditional elites (which had been drawn largely from the landed aristocracy),
the loss of predominantly agricultural territories in the east, and last but

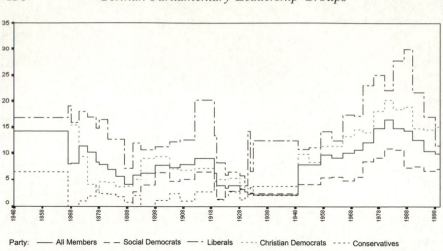

Party: —— All Members — — Social Democrats — · Liberals ···· Christian Democrats - - - Conservatives

Fig. 5.12. Germany 1848–1999: practising lawyers

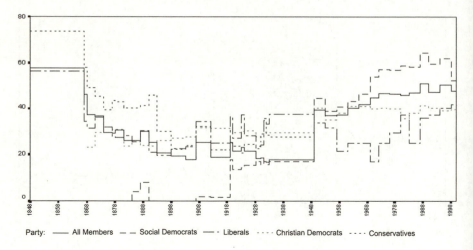

Party: —— All Members — — Social Democrats — · Liberals ···· Christian Democrats - - - Conservatives

Fig. 5.13. Germany 1848–1999: public sector employees

not least, the introduction of a new electoral law based on proportional representation, thus finishing with the former preference for rural constituencies. During the Weimar Republic, and partly as a reaction to this development, agrarian parties were formed, gaining up to 25 seats in the *Reichstag* (4% in 1930), while the Catholic Centre Party (CP) and the right-wing DNVP (re-)opened their ranks to a considerable number of deputies from agricultural backgrounds (CP 1920: 21%, DNVP 1924: 27%). However, by the 1930s, this share had again declined (CP, DNVP

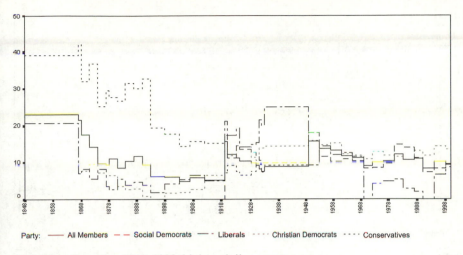

Party: —— All Members — — Social Democrats —‑ Liberals ···· Christian Democrats ‑‑‑‑ Conservatives

Fig. 5.14. Germany 1848–1999: higher civil servants

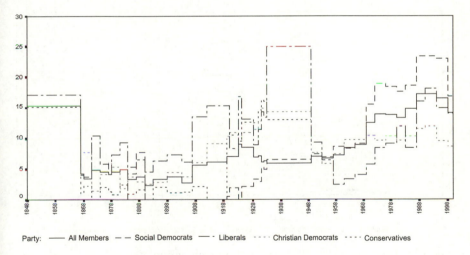

Party: —— All Members — — Social Democrats —‑ Liberals ···· Christian Democrats ‑‑‑‑ Conservatives

Fig. 5.15. Germany 1848–1999: teachers and professors

November 1932: 16%, 19%). At this time a new defender of agricultural interests and a successful contender for the rural vote had appeared: in the time of its escalatory electoral success, the NSDAP presented itself as a protector of the endangered middle classes with a special focus on the peasantry. The backward ideology of 'blood and soil', a protectionist agricultural policy programme, and a skilful infiltration of agricultural interest organizations went together with a strong symbolic representation of farmers in

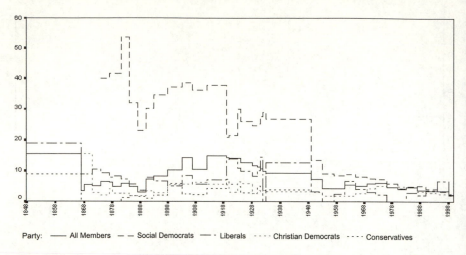

Fig. 5.16. Germany 1848–1999: journalists and writers

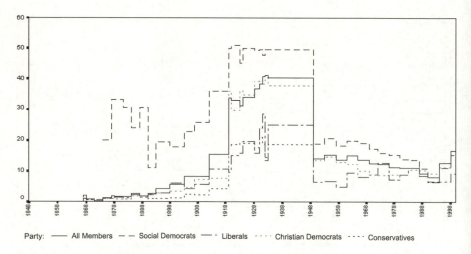

Fig. 5.17. Germany 1848–1999: party and pressure group officials

its parliamentary party (Best 1997). In November 1932, while purely agrarian parties had virtually disappeared, more than a fifth of NSDAP representatives in the *Reichstag* were from an agricultural background, outnumbering the same in all other parties. The mobilization of mass support against the hated system of the Weimar Republic heavily targeted a category of the population which could consider itself as a loser of the 1918 Revolution, at least in terms of interest representation. Although this loss had a strong symbolic dimension compared with the limited drawbacks

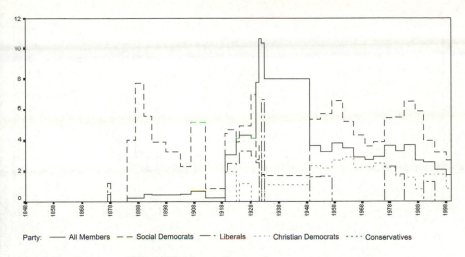

Party: —— All Members – – Social Democrats — · Liberals · · · · Christian Democrats - · · · Conservatives

Fig. 5.18. Germany 1848–1999: blue-collar workers

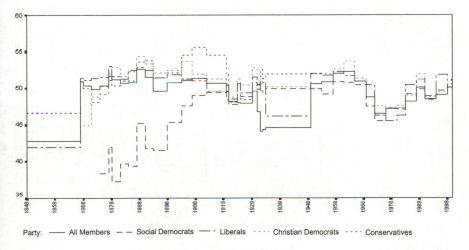

Party: —— All Members – – Social Democrats — · Liberals · · · · Christian Democrats - · · · Conservatives

Fig. 5.19. Germany 1848–1999: mean age

in terms of protection and support by the state, it paved the way for a party which promised to reinstate agriculture as the centrepiece of German economic and social policy. Since, in 1933, 29% of the workforce was still employed in agriculture, this was a potential support group worth wooing (Petzina *et al.* 1978: 56).

For the comparatively long history of the Federal Republic, the account of direct agricultural interest representation can be kept brief. Starting with a share of 8% in 1949 (as the Weimar Republic in 1919), the proportion of

Party: ——— All Members — — Social Democrats ——· Liberals ····· Christian Democrats ···· Conservatives

Fig. 5.20. Germany 1848–1999: mean number of elections

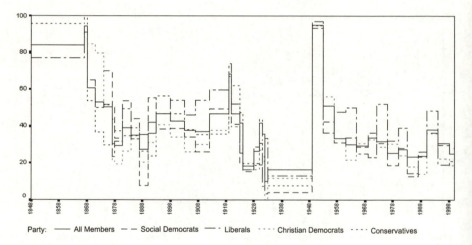

Party: ——— All Members — — Social Democrats ——· Liberals ····· Christian Democrats ···· Conservatives

Fig. 5.21. Germany 1848–1999: newcomers

members of the *Bundestag* with an agricultural background fell during the forty-five years which followed to about 3%. Only during the 1950s did the Liberals open their ranks to a considerable number of farmers and landowners, thus underlining their claim to be the political harbour of the old middle classes (*Alter Mittelstand*; Hein 1985). The proportion of 19% primary sector representation in 1957 was the highest in the Liberal camp since the early 1890s. However, this pattern disappeared completely in the 1970s, leaving only residual traces of agricultural experience and interest in the Liberal parliamentary party and approximating it to the same low level as in the Christian Democratic Party (Langewiesche 1988: 287–300), while by 1994, no member with a direct occupational link to the primary sector can be found in the SPD parliamentary party, nor among the representation of the post-communist PDS, nor in the ranks of the Greens, and their share in the Liberal Parliamentary Party had dropped to 2%. Among the Christian Democrats, their share was 5% in 1998. Thus, somewhat ironically, after approximately 100 years, the overall share of agricultural representation in the present *Bundestag* once again corresponds almost exactly to the share of the primary sector in the general working population, thereby finally meeting an old claim of advocates of agricultural interests. In parliament and federal administration, direct interest representation, through MPs with an immediate biographical and occupational link to certain sectors of the economy, has been almost completely replaced by corporate interest representation through professional lobbyists (Ullmann 1988: 247–55). Only the habit of having an agricultural minister who owns a farm or an estate remains as a somewhat nostalgic reminder of the past, which is still in practice in the present SPD-led government. Today, the main and ultimate addressees of agricultural interest mediation are to be found at the level of European institutions.

In the long history of agricultural representation in German parliaments, we see a pattern of retarded and erratic adaptation to social change and traces of party strategies trying to attract the rural vote, whereby neither the socialist nor the communist camp developed any distinctive or persistent interest in this direction. The conservatives of the German Empire, followed by their successors in the Weimar Republic, that is, the DNVP, the NSDAP in the 1930s, and the Liberals in the 1950s, presented themselves as champions of agricultural interests. During most of the time, the Centre Party, and to a lesser degree the Christian Democrats, had also a distinctive agrarian facet in their strategy to attract voters. A persistent and exclusive alliance between a party and a section of the electorate, as required by cleavage theory, did not emerge. Nor do we find strong evidence to support Barrington Moore's concept of a cartel of power between strong agrarian elites and a weak bourgeoisie paving the way for a fascist take-over. The gradual decline of agricultural parliamentary representation in the Imperial *Reichstag* since the 1890s, and its steep fall after the establishment of the Weimar Republic, rather suggests a growing difficulty to translate its fading social basis into political power.

3.2. *Entrepreneurs and Blue-Collar Workers: A History of Non-representation*

Structures and dynamics of economic interest representation beyond the primary sector can be interpreted against the background of what has been established with regard to agriculture. According to the somewhat naive concept of parliament mirroring society, a sequence of parliamentary sector representation, following J. Fourastié's (1959) stages of economic development (from primary through secondary to tertiary sector dominance) should be expected. That this expectation is misleading can be easily proved by the simple fact that the public service, that is, a set of occupational categories belonging to the tertiary sector, was by far the most important field of recruitment for the Frankfurt National Assembly (Fig. 5.13). What was supposed to be the end-point of development was actually its starting configuration. Another pattern deviating from the expectation of sector sequence emerges if we look at managers and business leaders (Fig. 5.11). The development of their parliamentary representation rather coincides with that of the primary sector than follows it. The historical peak of entrepreneurial representation in German parliaments was in 1887 with 15%, when primary sector representation attained 32%, the second highest score in German national parliaments. The late 1880s and early 1890s were a period in German parliamentary history when wealth, notwithstanding in which economic sector it was invested, played an exceptional role as a criterion for legislative recruitment. It was also a period when new legal and tariff conditions for the national economy, such as the introduction of protective tariffs and basic social insurance provisions, and the establishment of a national commercial law, dominated the agenda of the *Reichstag*. Simultaneously, corporate interests formed into powerful agencies exerting a growing influence on polity and society (Wehler 1995: iii. 610–99). These developments were clearly reflected in the social makeup of the *Reichstag*. If we include representatives from a small business background in our calculation, during the 1880s and 1890s, between 50% and 60% of its members were directly involved in some sort of economic activity, which is again the highest share in German parliamentary history.

This development was complemented by a growing division of labour between parties with regard to economic interest representation. While the Conservatives transformed into an agrarian party *pur et dur*, the Liberals opened their ranks to big business which proceeded to take up to 27% of Liberal seats in the *Reichstag* of 1890, gaining a particularly strong influence within the National Liberal parliamentary party (1890: 37%). The *Reichstag* of 1890 was also the first legislature in which the Social Democrats had a significant share of the seats (8%). Many of them were taken by representatives from small business which gave the socialist parliamentary representation of that time a distinctive petty bourgeois flavour.

If we look at the whole period from the mid-1880s to the beginning of the twentieth century, it emerges as a unique configuration in German parliamentary history when direct interest representation by deputies with an occupational background in business and agriculture was dominant. It is somewhat ironic that considerations of Bismarck to complement or even replace the *Reichstag* by an assembly of the estates, thus undermining the liberal principle of universal representation, were to some extent taken up in the actual patterns of parliamentary recruitment (Nipperdey 1993: 409 ff.). This was, however, a development which shifted the main focus of competence and interest in the *Reichstag* from an extension of parliamentary prerogatives and civil rights to economic matters and the associated conflicts about the (re-)distribution of wealth and income. If we interpret this reorientation in terms of Pierre Birnbaum's (1978) concept of changing patterns of fusions and dissociations of sectors of the elite system, we have here an example of a particularly intimate fusion between the economic and the political–parliamentary sphere. This was a strong push in the direction of class-based politics which particularly affected the Liberals. What they gained with regard to business connections and support, they lost with regard to inner coherence and popular support. In particular, the split of the National Liberals over the introduction of protective tariffs in the 1880s was directly linked to the impact of an increase of direct interest representation in their ranks (Sheehan 1978).

With the turn of the century, this pattern again started to change. By 1912, the share of business leaders in the *Reichstag* had dropped to 4%, agricultural representation to 20%, and representation from small businesses to 8%. This change was only partly the result of a shift of party strengths, namely the rise of the Social Democrats; changes within parties also had a major effect. For example, within the Liberals the accumulated share of business and agriculture had dropped from an overall peak of 47% in 1893 to 24% in 1912. The golden age of direct interest representation was over and, for the first time in the history of the *Reichstag*, members being fully paid as association officials, party journalists, and party functionaries outnumbered those with a direct involvement in economic activity (Figs. 5.16 and 5.17).

This process, which can be described in general terms as an increasing 'professionalization of politics', was driven by the growing opportunity costs for the acquisition and retention of parliamentary seats. Contemporaries such as Max Weber, who discussed the phenomenon under the heading of availability, maintained that it particularly affected contenders with a business background (1947; orig. 1919). Large estate owners, on the other hand, who were in a better position to accommodate the administration of their property with political involvement were affected less. Joseph Schumpeter, who diagnosed a social uprooting and political marginalization of entrepreneurial capitalism since the beginning of the twentieth century, deplored the fact that 'economic leadership does not extend to the leadership of whole nations. On the contrary, the accounting book and expense budgeting set limits' to a political career (Schumpeter 1943). The growing com-petitiveness of the German party system, indicated by an erosion of party strongholds and a rise of voting turnouts between 1871 and 1912, trans-formed canvassing into an absorbing activity (Ritter and Niehuss 1980:125). At the same time, the burden of parliamentary work increased and the freedom of action for single parliamentarians, set by the obligation to vote in accordance with party policy, shrank. Therefore it became more and more difficult to reconcile specific economic interests and activities with the requirements of the political role. At the beginning of the twentieth century, the share of business representatives in the *Reichstag* dropped to about 5% from which, despite various parties providing a temporary platform for business representation, it has never recovered. In the 1920s, it was the Lib-erals, particularly the Right Liberals from the DVP, who had a considerable business element in their parliamentary groups, but by the 1930s this was matched by the right-wing DNVP. After World War II, the Liberals regained their former stronghold position but, since the beginning of the 1980s, this again disappeared. By 1994, the overall share of business representatives in the *Bundestag* had dropped to its historical low of 2%, sharing this mar-ginal position with its counterpart on the other extreme of the class order, the blue-collar workers (Fig. 5.18).

If political modernization is associated with a lowering of social barriers for entry into political careers, in reality, it has never opened access either to the plenary chambers of the *Reichstag* or to those of the *Bundestag* for any meaningful number of recruits from working-class positions. Even in socialist parties, the claim to promote politics for the working classes was not complemented by actual political representation from the working classes, and the introduction of allowances in 1906 did nothing to remedy the situation. Indeed, the number of authentic workers actually fell from three members of the *Reichstag* in 1907 to one in 1912, even though the Social Democratic parliamentary group had more than doubled in size from 58 to 122 members during this time. Neither did the Revolution of 1918 make any real changes. By 1928, the share of working-class representatives had only risen to 4% in the *Reichstag* overall and to 7% within the Social Democratic Party, marking the historical peak in its parliamentary history. From the late 1890s until the end of the Weimar Republic, journalists of party newspapers and full-time trade union or party functionaries were by far the most important occupational categories from which the SPD drew recruits for its parliamentary party. Although most of these had a working-class background, they had passed through the filters of a career within party or trade union organizations, thereby adapting to the oligarchic world of the German working-class movement, which was analysed and criticized by Robert Michels at the beginning of the twentieth century (1987; orig. 1908). On the other hand, working-class representation in other parties was also rather more symbolic than authentic, even where it included 'real' workers.

The eventual rise of the overall share of workers in the *Reichstag* in the 1930s was very much the result of strategies of symbolic interest representation by the Communist Party (KPD) and the NSDAP, both of which included a considerable number of blue-collar workers in the ranks of their parliamentary parties (KPD July 1932: 34%, NSDAP July 1932: 13%). In the case of the NSDAP, this was part of a comprehensive attempt to tailor the social makeup of its parliamentary party to complement the party's economic and social programmes, particularly targeting farmers, small entrepreneurs, and blue-collar workers (Best 1997). After the July election of 1932, recruits from these three target groups had 54% of the NSDAP's parliamentary seats, seemingly re-establishing a representation of the German estates, reminiscent of the 1890s. However, it would be misleading to assume a return to the past, since the NSDAP addressed a wider range of interest groups than each of the political parties in the Wilhelminian era. It also used the appeal to economic interest to anchor itself in German society rather than to serve as a channel and clearing house for pluralist interest mediation, as did the democratic catch-all parties of the post-World War II era.

In the Federal Republic, the concept of socio-economic representativeness has disappeared as a criterion for parliamentary recruitment while, at the same time, strategies of symbolic interest representation have become obsolete. Even within the ranks of the post-communist PDS, which claims to be the legitimate heir of the socialist traditions of the German working-class movement, only one authentic blue-collar worker could be found in 1994 and 1998. If we aggregate the occupational categories of farmers, workers, small entrepreneurs, and business representatives, their overall share in the present (1998) *Bundestag* amounts to 9% compared to 41% in the March 1933 *Reichstag*. In the long course of German parliamentary history this is the final result of a gradual dissociation between economy and polity in terms of personal interlockingness, which started at the beginning of the twentieth century, was interrupted during the final years of the Weimar Republic, and was resumed after the foundation of the Federal Republic. To some extent, this development is a paradox, since during the same period economic and social policies occupied the agendas of German national parliaments. Even the process of German reunification, which was and still is dominated by problems of reallocating economic resources and social welfare benefits, did not reverse this development but rather accelerated it. Instead of direct interest representation inside parliament, we have external lobbying and the translation of pressure group claims into legislation by a personnel which is removed from the constraints and rewards of practical economic activity. We have shown that this development, driven by the requirements of political professionalization, the constraints of availability, and the need for compatibility between political and occupational activity, followed its own logic.

3.3. Political Professionalization: The Victory of the Functionary over the Free Political Entrepreneur

In his famous lecture on 'Politics as a Vocation', Max Weber (1947; orig. 1919) developed a typology of the political personnel of his time, based on the extent to which their life orientation, that is, time budget, intellectual capacities, and income, was dependent on or absorbed by their involvement in politics. Weber diagnosed a development towards the professional politician, who not only lives for politics but who also makes a living from it, thus replacing the political dignitary who is only temporarily involved in political offices and who makes a living through extra-political occupation or private means. According to Weber, it was the profession of lawyer which was particularly compatible with the role of the parliamentary representative. This independent position of trust, coupled with experience of everyday living conditions, qualified the lawyer to be an intermediary between society and polity. Being professionally involved in extended social networks and working from an office moulded a lawyer to become a kind of a free 'political entrepreneur'. In his analyses of the political system of the late Wilhelminian Empire, Weber deplored the low representation of lawyers in German politics, not only as a reason for a deficiency in rhetorical brilliance in the *Reichstag* but also with regard to a lack of mediating and integrating competencies (1971; orig. 1918). Our data show that the low representation of lawyers (low that is compared with France, the United States, and most Mediterranean countries of the time) was a persistent feature of German politics (Fig. 5.12). It was the salaried functionary who profited from the trend towards the professionalization of politics, while the free political entrepreneur remained rather marginal (Figs. 5.16 and 5.17).

In 1919, when Weber gave his lecture, this development had just been pushed forward by the Revolution of 1918 and the massive circulation of political elites which had brought it about. Exactly 50% of the members of the Weimar National Assembly were salaried party journalists or full-time functionaries of parties and pressure group organizations, thus fulfilling Weber's strictest criterion for political professionalism. The percentage of employees of intermediary organizations like political parties and trade unions had more than doubled since 1912, growing from 15% to 35%. Indeed, until the end of the Weimar Republic, the *Reichstag* was dominated by party journalists and functionaries, whose overall share fluctuated between 45% and 51%, peaking in November 1932.

The rise of the functionary to become the dominant political figure had started from a very low level in the formative years of the Empire. In the *Reichstag* of 1871 there were about 20 journalists and writers, and just one pressure group employee, nearly all of them in the ranks of the Left Liberals. This pattern started to change dramatically after the early 1890s when the Social Democratic Party greatly increased the number of its seats in the *Reichstag*. From the mid-1870s, its parliamentary group was interspersed with political professionals and particularly party journalists, who became the single most important occupational category in its ranks for much of the period until the end of the Wilhelminian Empire. This development was partly an unintended result of attempts to contain political professionalism by the government, but it also partly reflected the SPD's strategy to avert suppression of its party organization and media of propaganda by using the protection of parliamentary privilege.

Bismarck's constitution of the *Reich* extended the ban on all direct payments to members of the *Reichstag* not only to allowances paid out of public funds, but also to include all salaries or compensations paid by private bodies or individuals to support holding a parliamentary mandate (Huber 1970: iii. 893–5). The explicit intention of this regulation was to protect political amateurs from the 'professionalization' and 'bureaucratization' of parliamentary business; implicitly it was meant to prevent undesirable social categories from entering the *Reichstag*. However, these intentions failed completely; in fact, the professionalization of parliamentary representation in Germany was accelerated by the ban on allowances. Parties, particularly those in opposition to the established political order, built up powerful party organizations to compensate for legal outlawing and social ostracism. These organizations provided salaried positions and channels for upward mobility for the counter-elites of the Wilhelminian Empire, particularly for those of the working-class movement. Positions in the party apparatus proper were complemented by those in friendly organizations like trade unions and the party press (Schröder 1995: 59–85). Working-class officials (*Arbeiterbeamte*), who were in many respects modelled after public servants, became the backbone of the German working-class movement and formed the main reservoir for the recruitment of its parliamentary representation. By the end of the Wilhelminian Empire, this development led to the formation of a corps of functionaries which had become a world of its own and—to some extent—an end in itself. Robert Michels derived his law of the trend towards oligarchic rule in party organizations from these experiences (1949, orig. 1911). However, the involvement of the staff of working-class organizations in parliamentary representation cannot only be understood by the self-interest of those profiting from an accumulation of offices and a stabilization of their careers. To a large extent it was an inheritance of the legal suppression of social democracy between 1878 and 1890, when campaigning and the participation in parliamentary debates remained as the only lawful arena for party propaganda. Until after the turn of the century, parliamentary privilege served as a means to protect exponents of party and trade union organizations or the party press from persecution (Nipperdey 1993: 398–400). Although in the beginning, the development towards political professionalism can be seen as a means for ostracized political movements to compensate for their marginalization, it continued after these restrictions had ended, following an inherent dynamism and involving all parties to some degree. In 1912, 74% of the Social Democrats, 18% of the Left Liberals, 16% of the National Liberals, 23% of the Conservatives, and 13% of the members of Centre Party in the *Reichstag* were functionaries or party journalists.

This was only the starting-point for a virtual take-over of parliamentary representation by functionaries during the Weimar Republic, whereby most parties modelled their patterns of recruitment on the Social Democratic mould. After the November election of 1932, 44% of the Centre Party, 46% of the NSDAP, and 62% of the Communist parliamentary party's seats were taken by party journalists and functionaries, whereby the latter dominated by a ratio of four to one. This was the final triumph of the functionary over the dignitary, and it is significant that it was particularly the parties with a strong ideological commitment (*Weltanschauungsparteien*) which were in the front line of this development. The dominance of party organizations over parliament was exerted through the control over a parliamentary personnel which was ideologically committed to and economically dependent on extra-parliamentary political authorities. If this was political professionalization, it was definitely no help for parliamentary democracy which requires wide margins of action for parliamentary compromising and log-rolling (Best 1989: 215–22).

In the Federal Republic, from the very beginning, a completely different picture emerged; the share of party and pressure-group functionaries dropped to about 15% in the early 1950s. If we include journalists and writers, the overall share of 'political professionals' (according to this limited definition) has never surpassed the 1949 threshold of 21%. In the current *Bundestag*, 19% of its members can be found in these occupational categories, with the percentage in the 'old' parties, CDU/CSU, FDP, and SPD, being below this value, while those in the Greens (26%), and particularly of the post-communist PDS (39%) are much higher. This indicates that there might still be a compensatory mechanism working in the recruitment of party-connected functionaries and intellectuals. Since 1990, the share of full-time party and pressure-group employees has more than doubled from 8% to 17% (1998), indicating a return of the functionary as a noteworthy category of parliamentary representation, surpassing teachers for the first time since 1972.

3.4. State Builders and Redistribution Specialists:
The Repeated Dominance of Public Service Employees in
German Parliamentary Recruitment

Public sector employees, comprising, among others, judges, local administrators, university professors, and military personnel, occupied more than half the seats of the Frankfurt National Assembly (Fig. 5.13). It was somewhat paradoxical that an assembly which originated in a revolution and which was summoned to replace the supremacy of bureaucracy in a monarchical state by a regime based on parliamentary representation, was dominated by a personnel so closely tied to the established political order. On the one hand, in many areas of Germany, particularly in the heartlands of Prussia, Austria, and Bavaria, the elections to the Frankfurt National Assembly rather confirmed the old hierarchies and former authorities than replaced them. Local officials of the state, who exerted control over many areas of rural society and who had already acted before the Revolution as intermediaries between local communities and central government, were elected to fulfil a similar role under new conditions (Best 1990*a*: 59–73). On the other hand, universities and the personnel attached to them had played a major role in the oppositional movements before the 1848 Revolution. The migration of professors and students, the flow of ideas, and the circulation of publications had created a German *Kulturnation* (the nation based on culture) as an idea and a set of social networks, which was now supposed to be transformed into a *Staatsnation* (the nation state). 'Symbol specialists' (Lasswell 1952) in academic positions and local administrators provided the bulk of public sector employees in the Frankfurt National Assembly (Figs. 5.14 and 5.15). Specific academic skills and social network positions, either as intermediaries between the local level and the state level or as communicators in the emerging discourse about a German nation state, qualified them for a mandate. However, the failure of the Frankfurt National Assembly to implement its constitution, and the subsequent abduction of the German national movement by the Prussian government, persistently deprived the German 'political professor' of an important role, allotting him a rather marginal and subsidiary position in the following 150 years of German parliamentary history. After 1867, the whole educational sector did not exceed the 5% threshold until after the 1907 election, when it started to rise again, continuing until the mid-1920s (Fig. 5.15). However, by then, it had changed composition profoundly, with schoolteachers instead of university professors now dominating its ranks.

As recruitment from the educational sector plummeted during the formative period of the German Empire, that of the higher civil service and the judiciary, although also decreasing, retained some significance (Fig. 5.14). Again we see a clear differentiation between parties: while until the late 1880s the Conservatives had a great number of civil servants in their ranks, namely district administrators (*Landräte*) from the eastern provinces of Prussia, the Catholic Centre Party and the Liberals kept a stronghold among the judges. These differences reflected the attachment of parties to the established power structure of the state and the legal positions of civil servants and judges. Whereas the latter enjoyed the privilege of formal independence in the performance of their office, civil servants were curbed in their margins of action by formal requirements of loyalty and obedience to their superiors (Hattenhauer 1980). Up until the early 1890s, this special relationship marked the Conservatives for the part of the parliamentary representation of the authoritarian state. However, this relationship became fragile when the Conservatives started to oppose the governments of Prussia and the Empire from the right. This Conservative rebellion was answered by a 'muzzle decree' which restricted the political activities of Prussian civil servants to such an extent that it came close to formal incompatibility (Wehler 1995: iii. 863, 1031). On top of this, dissenting civil servants were no longer supported as governmental candidates in elections. Therefore the share of civil servants among the Conservative parliamentary parties halved in the 1890s, most of them now being elected outside Prussia and being recruited by the more nationally oriented *Deutsche Reichspartei*. Since the ostracized SPD had virtually no public servants in its parliamentary party until the Revolution of 1918 ended its disqualification, after the turn of the century the overall share of public sector employees in the *Reichstag* dropped to less than 20%. However, contrary to this general trend, in the Centre Party and among the Liberals the share of public servants rose, although only modestly, thus indicating the gradual integration of both political movements into the established power structure of the Empire.

The Revolution of 1918 also ended the exclusion of Social Democrats from positions in the public sector. Forming the 'Weimar coalition' with the Catholic Centre Party and the Left Liberals, they upheld the new German Republic during its formative years. From 1919, this was reflected in the parliamentary group of the SPD, where public sector employees from all ranks of the civil service and a growing number of teachers occupied between 14% and 18% of the seats. Although political parties who had been accused of being 'enemies of the *Reich*' by the power-holders of the Wilhelminian Empire now gained access to all echelons of the state apparatus, the overall share of public sector employees in the *Reichstag* further declined during the Weimar Republic. This was partly due to the fact that parties hostile to the democratic state gained a growing share of the seats in the *Reichstag*. In the Communist parliamentary group, public sector employees formed a tiny minority, only exceeding the 5% threshold in 1924 (Table 5.1). With regard to the extreme right, the situation was somewhat different, since during the formative years of the Nazi movement the share of public servants had been a little higher, and during the period of its electoral take-off in the 1930s only moderately lower than the overall average in the *Reichstag*. Actually, the Nazi movement used parliamentary privilege and the immunity it entailed to shield some of its members in the public service from the intervention of the Weimar Republic's legal authorities. Particularly after formal bans on civil servants joining the NSDAP had been established in the late 1920s and early 1930s, entry to parliament prevented disciplinary legal action and gave public sector employees in the NSDAP a protected scope for political action (Brustein 1996: 167–76). However, these were only marginal exceptions to a general trend towards a growing dissociation between parliament and the public sector in terms of personal interlockingness, which had started in the 1860s and culminated in the final years of the Weimar Republic. The requirements of loyalty and impartiality expected from civil servants were difficult to reconcile with the strong ideological commitments and the undivided devotion to the 'cause' which were demanded from party representatives in an increasingly polarized party system. The case of the Conservative Party in the 1890s shows that severe problems with conflicting loyalties could emerge, even within a parliamentary group which was closely connected to the established political order.

The fact that in the Federal Republic public sector employees are by far the most important occupational group from which members of the *Bundestag* are recruited, hints at a profound change in the relationship between parties, parliament, and the state (Hess 1976; 1995). From 39% in 1949, in the mid-1990s the share of public servants has risen to 50%, once again approaching its initial level of the mid nineteenth century. The SPD in particular, which has recruited up to 64% (1987) of its parliamentary group in the *Bundestag* from public service is the driving force behind this renewed fusion between parliament and the state sector. However, the CDU/CSU and the FDP, with a public service share of about 40% in their 1998 *Bundestag* representations, have also participated in this development, although on a somewhat lower level. It is a stunning fact that recent protest parties such as the Greens and the post-communists are conforming to this pattern: with a public service share of 50% (PDS) and 66% (Greens) in the 1998 *Bundestag*, these parties demonstrate that even questioning of the existing political and social order is perfectly compatible with employment in the public sector (Table 5.2).

This seeming take-over of parliament by recruits from the public sector has been harshly criticized as an undermining of the separation of powers and as an impoverishment of parliament with regard to the experiences and competencies embodied in its members. A direct connection was established between the extension and guarantee of material privileges for public

Table 5.1. Newcomers to the German party system 1919–1933: some selected traits of their parliamentary representation in the Reichstag

	University education		Local politics background		Female legislators		Public sector employees		Mean age		Religion: non-aligned or no information	
	Communist Party	Nazi Party	Communist Party	Nazi Party	Communist Party	Nazi Party	Communist Party	Nazi Party	Communist Party	Nazi Party	Communist Party	Nazi Party
1920	60.0*		60.0*		20.0*		0*		41.0*		100.0	
1924 I	19.0		25.4		7.9		6.3		37.2		100.0	
1924 II	21.3		36.2		8.5		2.1		37.3		100.0	
1928	16.4	61.5	36.4	0	5.5	0	0	7.7	38.9	42.1	96.4	0
1930	7.5	37.3	26.3	5.5	12.5	0	5.0	19.1	38.2	38.4	97.5	4.5
1932 I	6.8	32.8	22.7	6.9	10.2	0	3.4	12.5	37.6	38.7	97.7	1.7
1932 II	4.9	33.3	23.5	6.5	10.8	0	2.9	14.4	37.6	39.5	98.0	2.5
1933	6.2	32.6	26.2	6.9	10.8	0	3.1	14.9	39.2	40.1	96.9	1.4

Note: *Number of mandates below ten.

Table 5.2. Newcomers to the German party system since 1983: some selected traits of their parliamentary representation in the Bundestag

	University education		Local politics background		Female legislators		Public sector employees		Mean age		Religion: non-aligned or no information	
	Greens	PDS	Greens	PDS	Greens	PDS	Greens	PDS	Greens	PDS	Greens	PDS
1983	77.8		9.3		29.6		61.1		39.1		83.3	
1987	73.5		18.4		55.1		57.1		41.2		81.6	
1990	100.0*	100.0	14.3*	10.0	28.6*	55.0	28.6*	55.0	44.0*	44.4	42.9*	95.0
1994	85.4	63.3	41.7	26.7	60.4	43.3	70.8	46.7	41.9	48.6	77.1	93.3
1998	80.9	63.9	31.9	16.7	57.4	55.6	66.0	50.0	43.5	47.1	66.0	91.7

Note: *Number of mandates below ten.

sector employees and their representation in legislative bodies (von Arnim 1991; Scheuch and Scheuch 1992). Indeed, it can hardly be denied that the enormous advantages which candidates from the public sector enjoy with regard to availability and compatibility between occupational position and political office translate into a parliamentary representation which is distant from the productive sectors of the economy, the risks of the labour market, and the pressure of competition in achievement-oriented work environments. What we find in the *Bundestag* today are specialists in redistribution rather than in the creation of wealth. On the other hand, material interests and personal loyalty attached to the state, the latter usually reinforced by an oath of allegiance to the existing constitutional order, may prevent political extremism among deputies with a public service background. Their special bond to the 'real state' may thus be a stabilizing factor which was lacking in the *Reichstag* of the Weimar Republic. As in the nineteenth century, public service representation adds a conservative element to parliamentary life, although it is a very different state to which its servants are attached. Whereas in the mid-nineteenth century, civil service representation translated the power structure of the authoritarian state into parliamentary seats, we now find a close correspondence between legislative recruitment and the development of the welfare state.

4. QUALITIES AND QUALIFICATIONS: ASCRIPTIVE AND ACQUIRED CRITERIA FOR PARLIAMENTARY RECRUITMENT

4.1. Level of Education

At the beginning of parliamentarization in 1848, parliamentary representation was almost the exclusive *chasse gardée* of university-trained personnel (Fig. 5.2). This situation, whereby 80 to 90% of representatives were university trained, continued into the first national parliaments of Imperial Germany. After this time, the percentage began to decline, so that in the last Weimar Republic *Reichstage* of 1932 and 1933, only approximately 30% of MPs had a university degree.

This significant decline was due to two factors. First, it reflected the increasing weight of the Social Democrats (2 seats 1871, 122 seats 1912), who had few MPs with higher education in their ranks until the end of the Weimar era (mostly fewer than 20% with a university degree) (Figs. 5.1 and 5.2). Secondly, in the 1890s, there was a change in the recruitment patterns of the Conservatives who started to replace higher civil servants with non-academically trained personnel, most of whom were landowners. In the Catholic Centre Party, a similar pattern reflected the increasing weight of its petty bourgeois, agrarian, and working-class wings (most markedly in the Weimar Republic). In addition, the NSDAP, whose initially small parliamentary party (13 seats in 1924) had included a majority of university-trained MPs, changed its social makeup with its breakthrough in 1930 (110 seats). From now on, as a consequence of its electoral strategy to target farmers, small entrepreneurs, and blue-collar workers, the proportion of MPs with a university degree dropped to one-third of the NSDAP's parliamentary seats (Table 5.1). Contrary to the general trend, until 1933 Liberal MPs remained predominantly academically trained. The post-World War II period saw an opposite trend: within the forty years from 1949 to 1989, the proportion of university-trained MPs increased by 30% to 80%, thus reaching the level of the 1870s. Moreover, this change took place in all parties, but most dramatically within the Social Democrats, so that today only slight differences remain between the parties.

The overall decline of the importance of university training from the beginning of parliamentary representation in 1848 until 1933 is paralleled by a similar trend regarding academic legal training (Fig. 5.3). During this time, the German law faculties lost their dominant position for the recruitment of parliamentary personnel, so that by 1933 only 8% of MPs held a law degree compared to 64% of the Frankfurt National Assembly in 1848. In the Federal Republic, the law faculties, in contrast to university training in general, could not restore the dominant position they had held a century earlier. Although somewhat higher than in the Weimar *Reichstag*, the proportion of *Bundestag* members with a law degree remained moderate, decreasing further after the 1970s, from 29% in 1976 to 19% in 1998.

In sum, after 150 years, the findings regarding the educational background of representatives are similar to those concerning occupation, in that we can note a return to the point of departure. As in the Frankfurt National Assembly, the overwhelming majority of the current *Bundestag* members hold a university degree. If, given the close links between occupation and education, this observation is not surprising, it nevertheless confirms the main conclusions presented above regarding the interlockingness between society and polity. Indeed, the changes in educational background fit well into the sequence of leadership groups, which emerged from the analysis of occupation. It is evident that university (in particular, legal) training was a mandatory prerequisite for access to higher public service, that is, the main agent of state and nation-building in the first era of German parliamentarization. It is equally plausible that academic prerequisites lost ground in the subsequent periods of industrialization (Wilhelminian Empire) and mass democratization (Weimar Republic), when interest representatives and party functionaries became the modal occupational categories in parliamentary positions, access to which obeyed to other logics of recruitment. Again, there can be little surprise that the massive return of public service representatives as agents of interest mediation and redistribution of welfare state benefits in the Federal Republic reintroduced academic training as a major criterion of access.

Beyond this confirmation of the previously described general pattern, the findings regarding educational background highlight specific features of the present public service parliamentary representatives when compared to the same category one and a half centuries earlier. As our data show, legal training has not only lost its dominant position but is now largely represented by practising lawyers, that is, the private sector. To a considerable extent, legal training has been replaced by training in other academic disciplines: economics, business administration, humanities, social sciences, or engineering. This reflects a transformation of the public service which has since long transcended the realm of classical administration.

In addition to this, the role of education in German society as a whole has undergone a dramatic change over the last century. The rapid expansion of educational opportunities has created a large reservoir of academically trained personnel. The egalitarian structure of the German university system, which lacks the specific internal differentiation typical for the French and British systems (*Grandes Écoles* or Oxbridge based on public schools) was particularly functional in this respect. By creating new channels of upward mobility via higher education for lower strata of society formerly excluded from access to leadership positions, the chances for inheritance of elite positions from one generation to the next decreased considerably. Education lost its character of being merely an additional prerequisite acquired in order to obtain leadership positions for the offspring of the upper strata of society (Zapf 1965: 176 and *passim*; Hoffmann-Lange 1992: 125 and *passim*). Meritocratic elements gained weight for career opportunities. At the same time, the rapid expansion of higher education introduced the university degree as an almost universal prerequisite for leadership positions in society at large. Thus, non-academic personnel were also gradually excluded from political careers leading to or via parliamentary mandates. As our data demonstrate, academic training became mandatory even for those political parties such as the Social Democrats, who traditionally recruited their MPs largely from party or trade union functionaries with a working-class background.

4.2. Noble Title

In Imperial Germany, the traditional proximity of the nobility to state affairs and its general leadership position in society as a whole were the most important reasons for their comparatively easy access to parliament (Wehler 1995: ii. 805–25). This holds true for the Conservative parties, and to some extent for the Catholic Centre Party, which chose Catholic nobility as parliamentary leaders (Fig. 5.7). By contrast, nobles played a lesser role in the Liberal parties and were practically non-existent in the Social Democratic Party. Again, the decline of the proportion of legislators from the nobility, from the beginning of the *Kaiserreich* to its end (from 41% to 14%) is due to the rise of the Social Democrats and the declining tendency of both Conservatives and Catholics to select from the nobility for parliamentary positions.

When in 1918 the nobility lost its prominent position in society and politics with the fall of the monarchy at the *Reich* and *Länder* level, parliamentary representatives from the nobility disappeared almost entirely: in the Weimar Republic they held an average proportion of just 4%. Only the DNVP (a successor of the former Conservatives in representing agrarian interests, mainly in the eastern provinces of Prussia) and the contracting Liberal parties continued to include a significant number of noble representatives in their ranks (between 8% and 19%, and 4% and 13% respectively). German nobility lost what was left of its economic resources as a result of World War II. With Eastern Prussia, Pomerania, and Silesia being transferred to Polish administration, and with the communist agrarian policies in the Soviet Zone, the landed nobility was deprived of what had been its traditionally most important stronghold east of the Elbe and most of its members moved to West Germany where they had to engage in bourgeois occupations. While concentrating on the higher echelons of bureaucracy (particularly in the foreign service) and in the officer corps of the re-established military, political careers remained rather exceptional. Thus, the current proportion of nobles in the *Bundestag* (1–3%), mainly Liberal and Christian Democratic MPs, is the lowest in German parliamentary history.

The gradually vanishing position of the nobility in German parliaments can be interpreted as a result of a general shift from ascriptive to achievement-based criteria for elite recruitment. Today, those members of the nobility who engage in political careers can no longer rely on their 'social capital' as landed dignitaries or industrial magnates, but have to follow the requirements of political professionalization which have to be fulfilled by all of their competitors. Thus, the remaining tokens of this venerable political species tend to hide rather than to demonstrate their highborn origin: for example, the former leader of the Liberal parliamentary group in the *Bundestag*, a member of one of the oldest families of German aristocracy, has renounced his noble title.

4.3. Gender

As in most other European democracies, female MPs appeared in German national parliaments after World War I and the subsequent introduction of women's suffrage and eligibility (Fig. 5.8). In 1919, women made up 9% of all MPs, declining to 4% in 1933 with the loss of importance of the parties of the left, where women MPs had always been most numerous (SPD 1919: 12%). In accordance with its ideology of banning women from public leadership positions, the NSDAP refrained totally from nominating women candidates (Table 5.1). After World War II, the situation remained more or less unchanged, so that between 1949 and 1980 there was little variance in the average percentage of women in the *Bundestag* (6–9%). However, in the 1980s this situation began to change and the proportion of women grew from 11% in 1983 to nearly a third (31%) in the current *Bundestag* (Rebenstorf 1990; Hoffmann-Lange 1992: 132 ff.; *Deutscher Bundestag* 1993; Hoecker 1998). The initiative for this new trend can be attributed to the Greens, whose quota system (50% of all candidates have to be women) provides the highest proportions of women ever registered in a parliamentary group of the *Bundestag* (Table 5.2). The SPD took up quota nominations in 1987, which resulted in a substantial increase in the percentage of women in its parliamentary group: 35% in the present *Bundestag*. The Liberals and the Christian Democrats, who have so far refrained from taking this step on a mandatory basis, are lagging behind with 21% and 18% respectively.

Considering that women's suffrage and eligibility was introduced as early as 1919, a time lag of more than sixty years is evident before female representation in German national parliaments moved beyond the marginal threshold of 10% in 1983. This belated breakthrough is mainly due to the abolition of legal discrimination against women, substantial changes in the gender distribution in the occupational structure, and an increase in women's participation in politics (e.g. party membership) which only took place after World War II. On this basis, gender politics, which had been one of the traditional programmatic features of the political left, could for the first time find wide resonance in the electorate at large, resulting in a substantial impact on the market for political recruitment in all parties. Thus, at a time when the class conflict had gradually disappeared from the political agenda, gender politics could open a new scene for symbolic representation. This process has gained momentum with German unification, when some of the effects of the state-organized female emancipation, inherited from the former GDR, became part of the all-German scenario.

4.4. Religion

Undoubtedly, one of the specific features of the cleavage system of German society is the importance of the religious factor. Unlike confessionally homogeneous nations of Europe such as France, Italy, or the Nordic countries, where united religious and secular forces oppose each other, Germany experienced a religious conflict in the form of the confrontation between the Protestant and Catholic confessional groups themselves. This conflict was politicized in the second half of the nineteenth century and was institutionalized in the German party system. The Catholic Centre Party, which opposed the liberal, conservative, and social democratic party families who drew their support mainly from the Protestant part of the population, became one of the most stable German parties (Fig. 5.9). In the immediate post-World War II years, the traditional German party system, which had collapsed in the early 1930s, re-emerged in West Germany. However, the new Christian Democratic Party, which inherited the loyalties of the Catholic population from the defunct Centre Party, while integrating some sections of the former conservative Protestant circles, did not end the confessional split of the party system but only mitigated it. Moreover, all parties remained deeply rooted in their respective densely integrated subcultures (Schmitt 1990).

However, beginning in the 1960s, the landscape changed and the subcultures, among them that of the Catholics, began to disintegrate. At the same time, the parties loosened their ties to their associated subcultures and tried to become independent of them, steadily transforming their character from parties representing a *Weltanschauung* to catch-all-parties. In 1945, another important change, the partition of Germany, resulted in a shift of the ratio of the two-major confessional groups. Whereas the Protestants had previously held a two-thirds majority over one-third of Catholics in the *Reich*, there was now a roughly even distribution of both groups in West Germany. German unification in 1990 did not fully restore the pre-war situation: in East Germany forty years of communist rule had reduced church affiliation to about one-third of the formerly mainly Protestant population, with the effect that Protestant dominance in the population of unified Germany is now much less marked than in pre-war times.

One should expect that both major changes, the weakening of the ideological profile of the parties, and the shifts of the confessional ratio in the electorate, would result in tangible effects on the level of parliamentary representation; the first should result in a de-confessionalization of the parliamentary parties, the second should affect the confessional composition of parliaments at large. The overall distribution of the confessional groups in the first Imperial *Reichstag* reflects accurately the ratio in the electorate: roughly two-thirds of its members were Protestant, one-third was Catholic. Whereas the Catholics were able to hold their share until the fall of the Empire, Protestants lost ground steadily (1912: 45%) to the benefit of the religiously non-aligned, whose share had increased in 1912 to 18%. This was mainly due to the rise of the Social Democrats, whose parliamentary party was predominantly composed of non-aligned MPs (67% in 1912). At the beginning of the Weimar Republic, the electoral system was changed to proportional instead of majority rule. This change, combined with the increased strength of the left-wing parties, resulted in a new confessional composition of the *Reichstag*, which remained constant until 1933, when the Catholics' share dropped to 25%, the Protestants held a share of 40 to 45%, and the non-aligned held 30 to 35% (Table 5.1).

In the Federal Republic, the confessional ratio in the *Bundestag* reflected the balanced composition of the population at large; Catholics had finally reached 'parity', so that both Protestants and Catholics now held a share of about 40%. The non-aligned share amounted to 20 to 25%, which exceeded the proportion of religiously non-affiliated persons in the population (5–10%). As was to be expected, German unification did not bring about major changes in the confessional composition of the *Bundestag*, there being neither an increase in the Protestant nor a significant drop in the Catholic share. The only tangible effect has been an increase of the non-aligned to 36% up to 1998 (Table 5.2).

The de-confessionalization thesis is only partly confirmed by our data: both in the Imperial and in the Weimar Republic *Reichstage*, a clear confessional cleavage in the party system can be seen. The Centre Party recruited only a tiny minority of Protestant MPs, whereas the conservative and the liberal parties, as well as the Social Democrats, had only a few Catholics in their ranks. While this pattern of confessional cleavage had remained rather stable over more than sixty years, limited change occurred in the postwar period. Now, the new Christian Democratic Party recruits both Catholic and Protestant MPs. If this means de-confessionalization, it is worth noting that the original ratio of the 1950s (two-thirds Catholic, one-third Protestant) remained constant over more than four decades. The weakening of the ideological profile of the Christian Democratic Party in the 1960s and 1970s did not affect the confessional composition of its MPs, just as it also did not entail an analogous shift in its electoral basis (Schmitt 1989). Under the Federal Republic, the confessional profile of the other parliamentary parties is less sharp than it had been before 1933. Now the Liberal Party is more open to Catholics (10–25%) and, at the same time, it has loosened its Protestant profile. The Social Democrats, giving up their former secular or even anti-clerical positions, now recruit a considerable proportion of Catholic and even more of Protestant MPs. However, there is no steady and consistent trend of de-confessionalization throughout the entire postwar period. As with voting behaviour, the most significant elements of the new pattern of parliamentary recruitment date from the 1950s and remain stable even after German unification.

5. INTEGRATION AND CIRCULATION OF GERMAN PARLIAMENTARY LEADERSHIP GROUPS

5.1. Intertwining and Disentanglement: Changing Patterns of Interlockingness between Levels and Areas of the Political System

If the stability of democratic regimes is addressed, the extent and the modes of elite integration come into focus, whereby a distinction is made between normative integration—that is, the degree to which political elites share a set of fundamental norms, ensuring a culture of peaceful competitiveness—and structural integration—that is, the degree to which political elites are embedded in the framework of positions provided by a polity (Putnam 1976: 108–32). Since our data do not provide information about the attitudinal and normative orientations of elites, we are restricted to the structural aspects of elite integration. Although this is a recognized deficiency, the changing patterns of interlockingness between areas and levels of the German political system depicted in our data suggest that structural integration had an independent and significant impact on the course of democratic development. This is particularly striking with regard to the Weimar Republic where a career pattern emerged which tied members of the *Reichstag* closely to their party organizations but disentangled them from the local and intermediary levels of the political system.

In the Frankfurt National Assembly, the overall degree of interlockingness between levels of the political system was low. The percentages of representatives with previous experience in elective communal offices or of those who had been members of state parliaments was below 20% in each case (Figs. 5.4 and 5.5). This was primarily due to the fact that before 1848 communal self-administration had not been fully introduced in the rural areas of Eastern Germany, and that neither Prussia nor Austria had established parliamentary representation at state level (Best 1990a: 169–78). A distinctly different picture emerged in the small and medium-sized states of Southern and Central Germany, where constitutional traditions had started after the Napoelonic wars or the Revolution of 1830, and where up to 50% of the delegates to the Frankfurt parliament had been members of state parliaments before 1848. From this stratum of experienced delegates were drawn the political entrepreneurs who formed the core group of state and nation-builders in 1848. However, they remained a minority, whereas in the vast eastern hinterland of the German Confederation the traditional power structure had remained unshattered or had quickly recovered. To put it in Stein Rokkan's terminology (1975): the city belt was unable to integrate the secession states on the eastern periphery of the German Confederation under the umbrella of a democratic national state. The front lines of repressive military intervention and civil war, which broke up with the abortive attempt to implement the constitution of the Frankfurt parliament, followed roughly the political topography of pre-1848 traditions of constitutionalism and parliamentarism.

Although the national and democratic movement of 1848 was militarily defeated in 1849, it had irretrievably transformed the political topography of Germany. Prussia, which finally adopted a constitution in 1848, remained a constitutional state and retained its state parliament, although suffrage and parliamentary prerogatives were severely restricted after 1849 (Grünthal 1982). That Prussia shared essential constitutional features with its German neighbouring states was an important prerequisite for its future role in the process of German unification. The impact of the extension of the basis for institutionalized political participation after the Revolution of 1848 was revealed in the composition of the second generation of state and nation-builders who were elected into the *Reichstag* and the *Zollparlament* after 1867. With regard to previous parliamentary mandates and cabinet membership at state level, they were a highly experienced political elite, outstanding in the past and future course of German parliamentary history (Fig. 5.5). At the same time, the proportion of representatives with a background in local offices rose to a level above the 40% threshold.

Since most of the members of the *Reichstag* retained their elective offices at local and state level, they effectively intertwined different strata of the political order of the new national state. With regard to political background experience and the cumulation of offices, they were as much an integrated as an integrating elite. For the members of the second chambers of the Prussian State Parliament, there was a particular material incentive added to the topographical convenience in combining their mandate with a seat in the *Reichstag*: while the *Reichstag* and the Prussian State Parliament were within walking distance of each other, deputies of the Prussian second chamber (*Abgeordnetenhaus*) were entitled to receive allowances, thus drawing a direct income for their parliamentary activities (Huber 1970: iii. 97). Although parliamentary government was not formally implemented before 1918, neither at the state level nor on the level of the *Reich*, the cumulation of mandates factually helped to counterbalance the predominance of the executive powers and to integrate the federal structure of the Reich.

However, the halcyon days of the founding period of the Empire soon ended. Between 1867 and 1912, the share of members of the *Reichstag* with previous cabinet experience fell from 18% to 8%, while the proportion of members who had held mandates in state parliaments fell from 72% to 41% during the same period. These data disclose a growing disconnection between the state level and the national level of the German political system, which was partly the result of different electoral laws: while on the national level universal male suffrage was introduced in 1867, class-based electoral systems were retained at the state level until 1918, establishing a barrier which was particularly difficult for Social Democratic candidates to transcend. If we extend our observation into the Weimar Republic, we see, however, that the disconnection between levels of the German parliamentary system was driven forward by dynamics which were to some extent independent of formal structures of opportunity. Although census qualifications were abolished all over Germany after 1918, the disconnection between the state level and the national level increased rapidly, reaching the low point of intersection in 1933. This process was complemented by a steep decline of involvement in local politics, which had become the seedbed for parliamentary recruitment during the Wilhelminian Empire (Fig. 5.4 and Table 5.1). Between 1903 and 1933, the share of members of the *Reichstag* with previous experience in communal or regional self-administration dropped from 60% to 18%.

By the 1930s, when parliamentary democracy in Germany went into an anomic state, various indicators hinting at the structural integration of its personnel converged in an all-time low for the period after 1849. At the same time, affiliations to party organizations peaked (Fig. 5.6). Between 50% and 63% of the members of the Weimar National Assembly and the Weimar *Reichstag* held leading party positions, compared with 25% in the last *Reichstag* of the Wilhelminian Empire. Although working-class parties headed this development, it extended to other party families as well and took shape in the NSDAP, where in 1933 64% of its parliamentary party's members held leading positions in the NSDAP or its affiliated organizations, such as the SA and SS (Best 1997). By the end of the Weimar Republic, party organizations had become the main channel of access to the *Reichstag*, replacing the former *cursus honorum* through elective offices at local and state level.

It does not need much speculation to assume that this transformation of parliamentary recruitment contributed to an estrangement of voters from their representatives and to a renunciation of the principles of independent representation by the actors on the parliamentary stage. The fact that throughout the Weimar Republic the share of representatives without any biographical links to their electoral region reached its highest level in German parliamentary history points in the same direction. Contemporary criticism of parliamentary democracy, which was particularly fierce in the works of Carl Schmitt, found some obvious grounds in the structure of German parliamentary leadership groups of the time (Röhrich 1995). It would appear that the electoral law of the Weimar Republic, which was based on proportional representation and transferred the decisive say about the makeup of the final slates to national party organizations, contributed to this development and, in particular, cut through the local roots of the German party system. Our data suggest that it was not only the fragmentation of the party system of the Weimar Republic which contributed to its instability and final downfall, but also the detachment of its parliamentary leadership groups from the institutional substructure of the political system and the estrangement of their local bases.

With regard to the indicators discussed here, the parliamentary history of the Federal Republic started where the Wilhelminian Empire had ended. The shares of members of the first *Bundestag* with previous experiences in either *Länder* parliaments or local offices both reached 38%, thus reflecting the fact that the reconstruction of German democracy and the formation of a new political elite after 1945 had originated from the local and *Länder* level: 'Survivors' from the Weimar *Reichstag* were only a small minority. Further developments in the patterns of interlockingness between areas and levels of the German political system were incremental and rather resumed the trends of the late Wilhelminian Empire than the erratic shifts of the Weimar Republic. While the proportion of recruits to the *Bundestag* with roots in local and regional self-administration grew steadily to 56% in 1994,[8] thus approaching the level of the turn of the century, the share of former members of state parliaments had dropped to 16% by 1973. The increase of previous parliamentary experience in the 1990s is mainly a result of German reunification and the influx of former members of the last GDR *Volkskammer*. As a general trend, we see a differentiation of parliamentary careers at the *Länder* level and the federal level, while the nineteenth-century practice of simultaneously holding mandates on both levels has become extinct. After the 1970s, we see an increasingly intimate fusion between party hierarchies and parliamentary representation. By 1998, 48% of the members of the *Bundestag* held leading party positions with a particular peak among the Liberals. This indicates that party has again become a main career channel for parliamentary recruitment, although members of the *Bundestag* are still less tied up in party organizations than those of the Weimar *Reichstag*. Since the number of office holders on the local and regional level has also risen, an 'uprooting' of parliamentary leadership groups, as in the Weimar Republic, is not yet in store. Nevertheless, our indicators show that recent diagnoses of a growing estrangement between the political class and the population at large may have a pointer in the structural patterns of interlockingness between levels and areas of the political system.

5.2. Cycles and Transitions: Changing Patterns of Elite Circulation and Incumbency

In classical elite theories, the stability of a political order is closely related to the amount of its elite turnover (Bottomore 1993: 35–51). Whereas a very

---

[8] In the 1998 elections, this share has dropped again to 50%.

low turnover rate is expected to increase tension and conflict between established elites and contenders in non-elite positions, thus creating the preconditions for radical systemic change, a very high level of elite circulation is considered to be a symptom of an existing crisis, after an established regime of elite reproduction became desynchronized and the rules of the game were changed. Between sclerosis and an anomic state of elite reproduction, there is a middle way of elite adaption, ensuring a constant but limited influx of fresh elite members and creating some flexibility with regard to adapting the whole polity to new needs and changing circumstances. Elite turnover in representative democracies is expected to follow the middle way. In fact, the combination between competitiveness and pacification through procedural rules is considered to be a major advantage of parliamentary democracies in comparison with other regimes. Successful democracies should therefore develop a stable equilibrium between elements of elite incumbency and change, allowing for a moderate turnover while maintaining the advantages of career stability for their personnel (Squire 1988). After an interruption of the normal course of elite reproduction and renewal, this equilibrium should re-emerge within a limited time. Major deviations from this equilibrium hint at a crisis in an existing regime of elite recruitment and—more generally—at a failure in the system of transfers between polity and society.

Four indicators are available to depict patterns of elite turnover and career stability: the percentage of newcomers and the mean number of successive mandates held by members of a given parliament indicate the changing amount of elite circulation (Figs. 5.21 and 5.20), whereas the mean ages of members and newcomers in a parliament are indicators for career stability, that is, the average life-span passed before entry into and exit from parliament (Fig. 5.19).[9] An overview of the development of these indicators shows that, indeed, there seems to be a normal level of elite circulation and career stability, which is fairly constant over extended periods of time, with some cyclical change around this long-term constant, and erratic change preceding and following regime discontinuities.

With regard to the impact of systemic change, four levels of elite circulation can be distinguished in our data. Regime discontinuities, that is, complete changes of a political order, result in a near to complete exchange of the elite (e.g. the election of the first *Bundestag* with 95% percent turnover). However, after three normal elections, that is, approximately a period of eight years, turnover rates return to a normal level of exchange (20–40%). Restricted systemic changes as, for example, changes of the electoral system, have a more moderate impact, resulting in a turnover rate of about 60% (Weimar Constituent Assembly, 1919). On the other hand,

---

[9] The mean age of newcomers is not represented in a figure.

turnover rates exceeding 40%, which are not caused by a regime transition, indicate volatile elite structures linked to a transformation of the party system at large, as in the Wilhelminian Empire after 1890. At the other end of our scale, turnover rates of less than 20% mark a limit below which oligarchical structures can develop. In the Federal Republic, the two main parties showed very little renewal in the late 1970s and early 1980s, which is why changes of government were executed mainly by the old personnel.

Marked between-party differences are also recognizable in the indicators for incumbency. With regard to established parties, a mean age of between 46 and 52 is obviously a 'normal value', varying within the limits of a seemingly cyclical turnover as a result of generational replacement. Contenders from established parties enter parliament after a *cursus honorum* has been run in politics or elsewhere. Therefore, MPs of established parties come predominantly from the 'middle-aged' cohorts while a higher average age hints at an emerging imbalance, since there might be not enough supply from the lower ranks of contenders, or newcomers may be prevented from pursuing a political career due to an impermeable hierarchy within a party. Deputies of recently established parties tend to be considerably younger than the average representative, whereby the delegates of radical protest parties are even younger than those in a more moderate oppositional position within the system. Examples of the moderate variant are the Liberals in 1848, or the Social Democrats of the 1890s, both of which had a mean age below 42 years. As soon as new parties are integrated into a polity, differences from established parties start to disappear. The Greens of the Federal Republic are a case in point, with an initial age gap of about nine years compared to the established parties, gradually narrowing during the past decade (Table 5.2). During the late Weimar Republic, members of the KPD and NSDAP parliamentary parties were more than ten years younger than those from established parties (Table 5.1). A low degree of *carrièrisation* of preceding legislative recruitment and, particularly, a low frequency of previous offices held on the local and state level, hint at a poor integration of extremist parties in the political system of the Weimar Republic.

If we look at our data from a longitudinal perspective, we can identify four major periods of elite reproduction: from 1867 to 1890, we can observe an equilibrium of career stability and renewal after the process of initial institutionalization of the new political system was completed in 1878. During the late Wilhelminian Empire, partly caused by the increasing inflow of the Social Democrats, a process of decreasing career stability can be observed. Due to transformation processes of the whole party system, the average share of newcomers rose and the mean number of elections decreased. With regard to the latter, one also has to keep in mind that the period of the *Reichstag* was extended to a five-year term in 1888, one possible effect of which could have been that newcomers had a better chance of replacing incumbents. In line with this assumption are observations for the Federal Republic, when in 1969 and 1983, after two premature elections, incumbency increased.

Looking at differences between parties during the late Wilhelminian Empire, one can identify a tendency towards increased stability in the Catholic Centre Party, which was firmly rooted in its sociocultural milieu. Compared with this, the Liberals were affected by a higher turnover in combination with a growing instability of careers. The most stunning development, however, was a sharp increase of all indicators related to seniority and career stability within the Social Democratic Party, thus providing a model case for Robert Michels's 'iron law of oligarchy' (1987; orig. 1908). Renewal within the ranks of the Social Democratic parliamentary party was mainly due to its overall growth since the 1890s, whereby the mean age of its newcomers approached the overall mean by 1912.

During the Weimar period, no stable pattern of elite circulation emerged. The distinguishing feature of this period was the dramatic oscillations of indicators and growing differences between parties. In fourteen years, there were nine elections and only one normal election, that is, after a full term of the *Reichstag* in 1924. Legislative recruitment and campaigning became a continuous challenge for parties and their candidates and it is remarkable that this instability was complemented by an extreme increase of career stability and seniority, especially within the Social Democratic and the Catholic Centre Party. Eventually, turnover in these parties was very low, indicating an ultra-stability which failed to face rising extremism by offering new chances to a new personnel and by offering a new personnel to the electorate. On the other hand, extremist parties were poorly integrated in the established system, partly due to high rates of newcomers, and partly due to low levels of interlockingness with other areas of the political system (Best 1997).

In the Federal Republic, elite recruitment and elite circulation returned to a stable pattern, following a middle way between stability and change. It took three elections to reduce turnover to a level slightly below that of the Wilhelminian Empire, while the mean number of elections grew steadily until the late 1980s. It is remarkable how fast political parties in the Federal Republic reached a moderate level of renewal of their personnel, thus providing a continuous influx of newcomers, while increasing seniority. The proportion of newcomers remained relatively stable at between 20% and 30%, being raised only temporarily by German reunification, and the mean age fluctuated within the limits of an interval between 46 and 50 years. Here we can identify a cycle of generational change starting with the cohort entering the *Bundestag* in the formative years of the Federal Republic and being replaced after the early 1960s, while a second political generation, having entered parliament in the late 1960s and early 1970s, was mostly replaced by the late 1980s. Seniority increased period by period without differing greatly between parties and the declining rates in 1990 and 1994 can be explained by the 130 newcomers from East Germany for whom parliamentary experience in the *Bundestag* before 1990 was impossible; as expected, this trend was reversed in the 1998 elections.

Three reasons may have contributed to this success story. First, inter-party differences with regard to education, occupational background, and career styles decreased considerably. Modern politics requires a type of politician with certain skills and abilities, thus favouring certain qualities and qualifications of contenders, regardless of party affiliation. Secondly, politics becomes increasingly complex and demanding. Political elites accumulate specific knowledge and know-how and cannot be replaced as easily as in former times. Increasing seniority is therefore indicating a constant growth of professional potential in parliaments, which in turn supports stability and continuity of careers. Thirdly, interlockingness between polity and society increased again in the Federal Republic. Political elites could accumulate important functions on different levels of the political system, thus building up careers from the grass roots. All in all, the pattern of career stability and seniority in the Federal Republic hints at a stable framework of elite recruitment, where elements of competitiveness and continuity are combined rather efficiently.

6. CONCLUSION: TOO FAST, BUT NOT TOO LATE— THE GERMAN *SONDERWEG* RECONSIDERED

This chapter started with a reference to the *Sonderweg* as a general descriptive and explanatory scheme for the course of German political history, but particularly for its delayed and crisis-ridden development towards parliamentary democracy from the mid-nineteenth century onwards. The reason for Germany's deviation from what was considered by many to be the successful Western model of democratic development was seen to be the distorted relationship between social and political change, which could be expected to manifest itself and to be particularly effective at the level of elites. The question addressed in the concluding passages of this chapter is to what extent the notion of German exceptionalism is supported by our data, so that special emphasis will be given to its alignment with basic assumptions of political modernization theories. The notion that change is possible and even inherent in processes of parliamentary recruitment and modes of representation does not necessarily mean that change is focused in any particular direction. However, concepts such as professionalization and democratization imply an underlying pattern of progress guiding the development of parliamentary elites from a lesser to a more advanced state. In most general terms, this pattern has been conceptualized as modernization, or more specifically as political modernization, whereby the professionalization of political roles and the democratization of political participation can be seen as part of a more complex and comprehensive pattern of directed change (cf. introductory chapter and Badie 1988).

After a cycle of 150 years, the course of German parliamentary history has returned to a point from which it had departed in 1848, namely a legislature dominated by representatives from an occupational background in the public sector. However, in this cycle, two further stages can be distinguished: a period which extended from the 1880s until the beginning of the twentieth century, when direct interest representation through landowners, entrepreneurs, and small business prevailed, and an era which lasted twenty years from 1912 until 1933, when party functionaries and pressure-group officials were the modal occupational categories in the *Reichstag*. The sequence of these periods does not follow a linear trend which would fit easily into the concept of 'political modernization'. Not even the notion of 'political professionalization' can grasp fully what we find in our data. Because of their legal occupational status as members of the public service, the majority of representatives in the present *Bundestag* can easily return to their original occupational positions should they lose their seats, although in most cases this would mean a considerable loss of income. Nevertheless, they enjoy more independence and control over their careers than the functionaries of the Weimar Republic who, for good or ill, were at the mercy of their trade union or party organizations. Consequently, the modern public service representative, who is well protected from pressure by his former superiors, resembles more closely the traditional dignitary with independent means than most of the other occupational categories represented in parliament.

Rather than a linear development, following the transformation of social structure in general, we see a pattern of change in parliamentary leadership groups which reflects the sequence of main challenges for polity and society since Germany entered the era of democratization and industrialization. The first period of public service dominance in German national parliaments coincides with the era of state and nation-building. During this period, 'symbol specialists' and specialists in the application of executive power, both of which were to be found in the public sector, had a dominant role. The second challenge was the period of accelerated industrialization and urbanization, when Germany transformed fundamentally into an advanced industrial society. In this period, specialists in the creation and appropriation of wealth, such as entrepreneurs and landowners, prevailed in parliament. The third challenge was the development of mass democracy and the accumulation of organizational power outside the state apparatus. In this period, specialists in mass mobilization and the running of intermediary organizations dominated the *Reichstag* until 1933.

The history of the Federal Republic was marked by the consensus challenge which was connected to the mediation of conflicts and the integration of societies in the bipolar world after World War II. The establishment of a consensually unified polity and society was seen as a primary condition for the containment of communism. Corporate interest mediation and particularly the extension of welfare state benefits were the most important consensus-creating instruments. Redistribution specialists, who were predominantly found in the public sector, prevailed at this time. The end of communism, the crisis of the welfare state, globalization, and neo-liberalism seemed to usher in the end of consensus politics. It is not yet clear which new challenge will determine the structure of parliamentary representations in the future or what effect this will have on recruitment patterns. The rise of public service employees seems to have come to an end, while no other occupational category—with the remarkable exception of party and pressure-group functionaries—shows a clear upturn. Perhaps it is the pattern of political careers rather than a change in the patterns of recruitment which will be the most significant development in the future; whereby a growing volatility on the part of the voters might be answered by a more episodic involvement in politics on the part of contenders for political offices.

If we subject our data to the assumptions of theories of political modernization, a somewhat contradictory picture emerges. On the one hand, time series referring to the representation of the primary sector, of the nobility, of women, and of non-church members moved roughly in the expected direction. However, even in these areas, we see some significant deviations from the model of linear and progressive or degressive change: first, the nobility and the primary sector was able to defend or improve their position in parliamentary recruitment markets during the first decades of the German Empire. Secondly, female representation, after the introduction of women's suffrage and eligibility, remained rather marginal for more than sixty years, and, finally, the rise of non-church members ended with the Weimar Republic, turning into a temporary decrease after 1949. On the other hand, and contrary to the notion of a German *Sonderweg*, during the last decades of the Wilhelminian Empire and with the ascent of the Weimar Republic, some of these indicators changed most dramatically in a direction expected by modernization theory. Between the 1890s and the 1920s, we see a clear trend towards elite modernization, fundamentally transforming the patterns of recruitment and the social makeup of German parliamentary elites. This transformation extended to all party families, whereby newcomers to the party system, such as Social Democracy, acted as pioneers, followed sooner or later by all other major parties. At the end of the Wilhelminian Empire, a new type of parliamentary representation had already emerged in Gemany, dominated by 'political professionals' and closely tied to party organizations. The transition to the Weimar Republic continued these trends, but transferred them to a new level following an erratic increase (or decrease) after 1918. It was definitely not a lack of modernity, but an accelerated and erratic transition to modernity which marked the development of German parliamentary elites between the 1890s and the 1920s. Other indicators which, in the long run, follow a cyclical pattern of change also fit into this picture. At the end of the Weimar Republic, the decrease of university education, of public service representation, of mean age of newcomers, and of interlockingness between areas and levels of the political system converge, while representation by full-time party and pressure-group organization officials, and by high-ranking members of party hierarchies, peaked. The dignitary and the intermediary had virtually disappeared from the arena of German parliamentary politics, having been replaced by the functionary and the descendants of party careers.

The establishment of the Federal Republic in 1949 reversed some of these trends and a pattern of parliamentary representation resumed which resembles that seen in the late Wilhelminian Empire rather than that which had emerged at the end of the Weimar Republic. In 1949, the proportion of members of the *Bundestag* with university education reached a much higher level than in 1933 and increased further during the following period. The same is true of public service representation, the cumulation of electoral offices on the communal and regional levels, and personal ties to the region of election, while incumbency and the proportion of representatives directly employed by parties or party organizations decreased significantly up to the early 1990s. Although there has been no revival of the dignitary, parliamentary representation in the Federal Republic is more directly and more intimately linked to other areas of society and polity than during the Weimar Republic. This increase in integration is complemented by a decrease of volatility: changes in the indicators presented here became more incremental after 1949 and the average rate of renewal of parliamentary elites decreased to a level lower than that of the late Wilhelminian Empire, increasing only temporarily due to the influx of new members of the *Bundestag* following reunification. Apparently, the stability of the Federal Republic, and the performance of its parliamentary institutions, have a two-directional link to the stability of its political personnel, whereby elite stability enhances institutional stability and vice versa. The question as to whether the mutual reinforcement of stabilizing elements in the German political system leaves enough room for the adaptions necessary for change cannot be addressed here, although extensions of the German party system in the 1980s and 1990s indicate that there is sufficient flexibility in the modes of parliamentary recruitment to confront future challenges.

References

Anderson, Christopher (1993). 'Political Elites and Electoral Rules: The Composition of the *Bundestag* 1949–1990', in Christopher Anderson, Karl Kaltenthaler, and Wolfgang Luthardt (eds.), *The Domestic Politics of German Unification*. Boulder, Colo. and London: Lynne Rienner, 73–95.

Arnim, Hans Herbert von (1991). *Die Partei, der Abgeordnete und das Geld*. Mainz: Koehler.

Badie, Bertrand (1988). *Le Développement politique*, 4th edn. Paris: Économica.

Best, Heinrich (1989). 'Mandat ohne Macht. Strukturprobleme des deutschen Parlamentarismus 1867–1933', in Heinrich Best (ed.), *Politik und Milieu. Wahl- und Elitenforschung im historischen und interkulturellen Vergleich*. St Katharinen: Scripta Mercaturae, 175–222.

——(1990*a*). *Die Männer von Bildung und Besitz: Struktur und Handeln parlamentarischer Führungsgruppen in Deutschland und Frankreich 1848/49*. Düsseldorf: Droste.

——(1990*b*). 'Elite Structure and Regime (Dis)continuity in Germany 1867–1933: The Case of Parliamentary Leadership Groups'. *German History*, 8: 1–27.

——(1997). 'Strategien und Strukturen parlamentarischer Repräsentation einer antiparlamentarischen Partei: Die Reichstagsfraktion der NSDAP 1928–1933', in Arnd Bauerkämper, Jürgen Danyel, Peter Hübner, and Sabine Roß (eds.), *Gesellschaft ohne Eliten? Führungsgruppen in der DDR*. Berlin: Metropol, 231–48.

——and Weege, Wilhelm (1996). *Biographisches Handbuch der Abgeordneten der Frankfurter Nationalversammlung 1848/49*. Düsseldorf: Droste.

Beyme, Klaus von (1996). *Das politische System der Bundesrepublik Deutschland: Eine Einführung*, 8th edn. Munich: Piper.

Birnbaum, Pierre (1978). 'Institutionalisation of Power and Integration of Ruling Elites'. *European Journal of Political Research*, 6: 105–15.

Blackbourn, David (1984). 'Peasants and Politics in Germany 1871–1914'. *European History Quarterly*, 14: 47–75.

Borchert, Jens, and Golsch, Lutz (1999). 'Deutschland: von der Honoratiorenzunft zur politischen Klasse', in Jens Borchert (ed.), *Politik als Beruf: Die politische Klasse in westlichen Demokratien*. Opladen: Leske & Budrich, 114–40.

Bottomore, Tom (1993). *Elites and Society*, 2nd edn. London and New York: Routledge.

Botzenhart, Manfred (1977). *Deutscher Parlamentarismus in der Revolutionszeit 1848–1850*. Düsseldorf: Droste.

Brustein, William (1996). *The Logic of Evil: The Social Origins of the Nazi Party 1925–1933*. New Haven and London: Yale University Press.

Bürklin, Wilhelm, and Rebensdorf, Hilke (1997). *Eliten in Deutschland. Rekrutierung und Integration.* Opladen: Leske & Budrich.

Butzer, Hermann (1999). *Diäten und Freifahrt im Deutschen Reichstag: Der Weg zum Entschädigungsgesetz von 1906 und die Nachwirkung dieser Regelung bis in die Zeit des Grundgesetzes.* Düsseldorf: Droste.

Dahrendorf, Ralf (1979). *Society and Democracy in Germany.* Garden City, NY: Norton & Company.

Deutscher Bundestag (1993). 'Parlamentarierinnen im Deutschen Bundestag 1949–1993'. *Materialien,* No. 122. Bonn: Wissenschaftliche Dienste des Deutschen Bundestages.

Duverger, Maurice (1976; orig. 1951). *Les Partis politiques.* Paris: Armand Colin.

Falter, Jürgen W. (1990). 'The First German Volkspartei: The Social Foundation of the NSDAP', in Karl Rohe (ed.), *Elections, Parties and Political Traditions: Social Foundations of German Parties and Party Systems.* New York: Berg, 53–81.

——Lindenberger, Thomas, and Schumann, Siegfried (1986). *Wahlen und Abstimmungen in der Weimarer Republik. Materialien zum Wahlverhalten 1919–1933.* Munich: C. H. Beck.

Fourastié, Jean (1959). 'De la vie traditionelle à la vie tertiaire: recherches sur le calendrier de l'homme moyen'. *Population,* 417–32.

Geißler, Rainer (1996). *Die Sozialstruktur Deutschlands: Zur gesellschaftlichen Entwicklung mit einer Zwischenbilanz zur Vereinigung,* 2nd edn. Opladen: Westdeutscher Verlag.

Grünthal, Günther (1982). *Parlamentarismus in Preußen 1848/49–1857/58: Preußischer Konstitutionalismus—Parlament und Regierung in der Reformära.* Düsseldorf: Droste.

Harenberg, Bodo (1997). *Harenberg Lexikon der Gegenwart 1996.* Dortmund: Harenberg Lexikon Verlag.

Hattenhauer, Hans (1980). *Geschichte des Beamtentums.* Köln: Heymann.

Hausmann, Christopher (1999). *Biographisches Handbuch der 10. Volkskammer der DDR.* Köln, Wien, and Weimar: Böhlau.

Hein, Dieter (1985). *Zwischen liberaler Milieupartei und nationaler Sammlungsbewegung. Gründung, Entwicklung und Struktur der Freien Demokratischen Partei 1945–1949.* Düsseldorf: Droste.

Hess, Adalbert (1976). 'Statistische Daten und Trends zur Verbeamtung der Parlamente in Bund und Ländern'. *Zeitschrift für Parlamentsfragen,* 1: 34–42.

——(1995). 'Sozialstruktur des 13. Deutschen Bundestages: Berufliche und fachliche Entwicklungslinien'. *Zeitschrift für Parlamentsfragen,* 4: 567–85.

Hoecker, Beate (1998). 'Deutschland zwischen Macht und Ohnmacht: Politische Partizipation von Frauen in Deutschland', in Beate Hoecker (ed.), *Handbuch Politische Partizipation von Frauen in Europa.* Opladen: Leske & Budrich, 65–90.

Hoffmann-Lange, Ursula (1985). 'Structural Prerequisites of Elite Integration in the Federal Republic of Germany', in Gwen More (ed.), *Research in Politics and Society,* i. *Studies of the Structure of Elite Groups.* Greenwich and London: JAI Press, 243–83.

——(1992). *Eliten, Macht und Konflikt in der Bundesrepublik.* Opladen: Leske & Budrich.

Hohorst, Gerd, Kocka, Jürgen, and Ritter, Gerhard A. (1975). *Sozialgeschichtliches*

Arbeitsbuch. Materialien zur Statistik des Kaiserreichs 1870–1914. Munich: C. H. Beck.

Huber, Ernst Rudolf (1968–81). *Deutsche Verfassungsgeschichte seit 1789*, 7 vols., 2nd edn, ii: *Der Kampf um Einheit und Freiheit* (1968); iii: *Bismarck und das Reich* (1970); v: *Weltkrieg, Revolution und Reichserneuerung* (1978); vi: *Die Weimarer Reichsverfassung* (1981). Stuttgart: Kohlhammer.

Hubert, Peter (1992). *Uniformierter Reichstag: Die Geschichte der Pseudo-Volksvertretung 1933 bis 1945*. Düsseldorf: Droste.

Huntington, Samuel P. (1968). *Political Order in Changing Societies*. New Haven and London: Yale University Press.

——and Dominguez, Jorge (1975). 'Political Development', in Fred Greenstein and Nelson Polsby (eds.), *Handbook of Political Science*, iii. Reading, Mass.: Addison-Wesley, 1–114.

Jansen, Christian (1999). 'Selbstbewußtes oder gefügiges Parlament? Abgeordne-tendiäten und Berufspolitiker in den deutschen Staaten des 19. Jahrhunderts'. *Geschichte und Gesellschaft*, 25/1: 33–65.

Kocka, Jürgen (1988). 'German History before Hitler: The German Debate about the German *Sonderweg*'. *Journal of Contemporary History*, 23: 3–16.

Kohl, Jürgen (1982). 'Zur langfristigen Entwicklung der politischen Partizipation in Westeuropa', in Peter Steinbach (ed.), *Probleme politischer Partizipation im Modernisierungsprozeß*. Stuttgart: Klett-Cotta, 473–502.

Kolb, Eberhard (1993). *Die Weimarer Republik*, 3rd edn. Munich: Oldenbourg.

Langewiesche, Dieter (1988). *Liberalismus in Deutschland*. Frankfurt: Suhrkamp.

Lasswell, Harold D. (1952). 'The Elite Concept', in Harold D. Lasswell, Daniel Lerner, and Charles E. Rothwell (eds.), *The Comparative Study of Elites*. Stanford, Calif.: University Press, 6–21.

Lepsius, M. Rainer (1973; orig. 1966). 'Parteiensystem und Sozialstruktur: Zum Problem der Demokratisierung in Deutschland', in Gerhard A. Ritter (ed.), *Deutsche Parteien vor 1918*. Cologne: Kiepenheuer & Witsch, 56–80.

Lösche, Peter (1993). *Kleine Geschichte der deutschen Parteien*. Stuttgart.: Kohlhammer.

Michels, Robert (1949; orig. 1911). *Political Parties*. Glencoe, Ill.: Free Press.

——(1987; orig. 1908). 'Die oligarchischen Tendenzen der Gesellschaft: Ein Beitrag zum Problem der Demokratie', in Robert Michels, *Masse, Führer, Intellektuelle: Politisch-soziologische Aufsätze 1906–1933*. Frankfurt am Main and New York: Campus-Verlag, 133–81.

Moore, Barrington (1967). *Social Origins of Dictatorship and Democracy*. Boston: Beacon.

Nipperdey, Thomas (1993). *Deutsche Geschichte 1866–1918*, ii: *Machtstaat vor der Demokratie*. Munich: C. H. Beck.

Nohlen, Dieter (1997). *Wahlrecht und Parteiensystem*. Paderborn: UTB.

Norris, Pippa (ed.) (1997). *Passages to Power. Legislative Recruitment in Advanced Democracies*. Cambridge: Cambridge University Press.

Pappi, Franz Urban (1990). 'New Social Movements and the Traditional Party System of the Federal Republic of Germany', in Karl Rohe (ed.), *Elections, Parties and Political Traditions: Social Foundations of German Parties and Party Systems*. New York: Berg, 203–22.

Petzina, Dietmar, Kocka, Jürgen, Ritter, Gerhard A., Abelshauser, Werner, and

Faust, Anselm (1978). *Sozialgeschichtliches Arbeitsbuch*, iii: Materialien zur Statistik des Deutschen Reiches 1914–1945, Munich: C. H. Beck.

Pollmann, Karl Erich (1985). *Parlamentarismus im Norddeutschen Bund 1867–1870*. Düsseldorf: Droste.

Putnam, Robert D. (1976). *The Comparative Study of Political Elites*. Englewood Cliffs, NJ: Prentice-Hall.

Rebenstorf, Hilke (1990). 'Frauen im Bundestag—anders als die Männer?', in Hans-Georg Wehling (ed.), *Eliten in der Bundesrepublik Deutschland*. Stuttgart: Kohlhammer, 52–75.

Ritter, Gerhard A. (1985). *Die deutschen Parteien 1830–1914*. Göttingen: Vandenhoeck & Ruprecht.

——(1990*a*). 'The Electoral Systems of Imperial Germany and their Consequences for Politics', in Serge Noiret (ed.), *Political Strategies and Electoral Reforms: Origins of Voting Systems in Europe in the 19th and 20th Century*. Baden-Baden: Nomos, 53–75.

——(1990*b*). 'The Social Bases of the German Political Parties 1867–1920', in Karl Rohe (ed.), *Elections, Parties and Political Traditions: Social Foundations of German Parties and Party Systems*. New York: Berg, 27–52.

——and Niehuss, Merith (1980). *Wahlgeschichtliches Arbeitsbuch. Materialien zur Statistik des Kaiserreichs 1871–1918*. Munich: Beck.

————(1987). *Wahlen in der Bundesrepublik Deutschland: Bundestags- und Landtagswahlen 1946–1987*. Munich: C. H. Beck.

————(1995). *Wahlen in Deutschland 1990–1994*. Munich: C. H. Beck.

Rohe, Karl (1990). 'German Elections and Party Systems in Historical and Regional Perspective: an introduction', in Karl Rohe (ed.), *Elections, Parties and Political Traditions: Social Foundations of German Parties and Party Systems*. New York: Berg, 1–25.

Röhrich, Wilfried (1995). 'Staatsmacht und Demokratiezerfall. Eine Skizze zu Carl Schmitt', in Wolf R. Dombrowsky and Ursula Pasero (eds.), *Wissenschaft, Literatur, Katastrophe: Festschrift zum 60. Geburtstag von Lars Clausen*. Opladen: Westdeutscher Verlag, 307–16.

Rokkan, Stein (1975). 'Dimensions of State Formation and Nation Building: A Possible Paradigm for Research within Europe', in Charles Tilly (ed.), *The Formation of National States in Western Europe*. Princeton: University Press, 562–600.

Saalfeld, Thomas (1990). 'The West German Bundestag after 40 years: The Role of a Parliament in a Party Democracy', in Philip Norton (ed.). *Parliaments in Western Europe*. London: Frank Cass, 68–89.

Scheuch, Erwin K., and Scheuch, Ute (1992). *Cliquen, Klüngel und Karrieren*. Reinbek: Rowohlt.

Schmitt, Karl (1989). *Konfession und Wahlverhalten in der Bundesrepublik Deutschland*. Berlin: Duncker & Humblot.

——(1990). 'Religious Cleavages in the West German Party System: Persistence and Change, 1949–1987', in Karl Rohe (ed.), *Elections, Parties and Political Traditions: Social Foundations of German Parties and Party Systems*. New York: Berg.

Schröder, Wilhelm Heinz (1995). *Sozialdemokratische Parlamentarier in den deutschen Reichs- und Landtagen 1867–1933: Ein Handbuch*. Düsseldorf: Droste.

Schumpeter, Joseph A. (1943). *Capitalism, Socialism and Democracy*. London: Allen & Unwin.

Sheehan, James (1978). *German Liberalism in the Nineteenth Century*. London: Methuen.

Squire, Peverill (1988). 'Career Opportunities and Membership Stability in Legislatures'. *Legislative Studies Quarterly*, 13: 65–82.

Steinmetz, George (1997). 'German Exceptionalism and the Origines of Nazism: The Career of a Concept', in Ian Kershaw and Moshe Lewin (eds.), *Stalinism and Nazism: Dictatorships in Comparison*. Cambridge: Cambridge University Press, 251–84.

Ullmann, Hans-Peter (1988). *Interessenverbände in Deutschland*. Frankfurt am Main: Suhrkamp.

——(1995). *Das Deutsche Kaiserreich 1871–1918*. Frankfurt am Main: Suhrkamp.

Urwin, Derek (1974). 'Germany: Continuity and Change in Electoral Politics', in Richard Rose (ed.), *Electoral Behaviour: A Comparative Handbook*. New York: Free Press, 109–70.

Vogel, Bernhard, Nohlen, Dieter, and Schultze, Rainer-Olaf (1971). *Wahlen in Deutschland: Theorie- Geschichte-Dokumente 1848–1970*. Berlin: de Gruyter.

——and Schultze, Rainer-Olaf (1969). 'Deutschland', in Dolf Sternberger and Bernhard Vogel (eds.), *Die Wahl der Parlamente und anderer Staatsorgane*, i, part 1. Berlin: de Gruyter, 189–411.

Weber, Max (1947; orig. 1919). 'Politics as a Vocation', in H. H. Gerth and C. W. Mills (eds.), *From Max Weber: Essays in Sociology*. London: Kegan Paul.

——(1971). 'Wahlrecht und Demokratie in Deutschland' (orig. 1917) and 'Parlament und Regierung im neugeordneten Deutschland' (orig. 1918) in *Gesammelte politische Schriften*, 3rd edn. Tübingen: Mohr, 245–91 and 306–443.

Wehler, Hans-Ulrich (1987; 1995). *Deutsche Gesellschaftsgeschichte*, ii and iii. Vol. ii: Von der Reformära bis zur industriellen und politischen 'Deutschen Doppelrevolution' 1815–1845/49; iii: Von der 'Deutschen Doppelrevolution' zum Beginn des Ersten Weltkrieges 1849–1914. Munich: C. H. Beck.

Wessels, Bernhard (1997). 'Germany', in Pippa Norris (ed.), *Passages to Power*. Cambridge: Cambridge University Press, 76–97.

Westphalen, Raban Graf von (ed.) (1993). *Parlamentslehre: Das parlamentarische Regierungssystem im technischen Zeitalter*. Munich: Oldenbourg.

Zapf, Wolfgang (1965). *Wandlungen der deutschen Elite*. Munich: Piper.

6

Belated Professionalization of Parliamentary Elites: Hungary 1848–1999

GABRIELLA ILONSZKI

1. PERIODS OF PARLIAMENTARY DEVELOPMENT

Hungarian parliamentary tradition begins in 1848 and in the following 150 years its parliament has existed virtually uninterrupted: that is, throughout the long liberal period up to 1918; in the interwar authoritarian system, with its façade of democratic institutions; in the diverse Communist periods; not to mention the intermezzos of 1918 and 1945 when attempts were made to establish democratic parliamentary government. Nevertheless, despite its long existence, the Hungarian parliament could only rarely act as an agent of modernization and democratization and parliamentary elites show clear trends of professionalization only in the last two legislative terms, that is, after the collapse of Communism in 1990.

In this long process and among the several abrupt changes, it is not easy to describe the major tendencies of parliamentary elite circulation and to connect parliamentary elite changes to the national political scene. Up to 1945, parliamentary elites reflected the otherwise prevalent characteristics in the wider national elite. Thus, when we examine the characteristics of parliamentary elites, we see that their features result from the social, economic, and political characteristics of the entire elite; moreover, conflicts within the national elite are also reflected in the parliamentary elite framework. In the first 100 years of parliamentary politics, the Hungarian parliament did not mirror society but rather reflected the developments within the national elite.

During those 100 years, two main political movements strove to extend the representative dimension of parliament by advocating broader voting rights and thus hoping to bring in new elites into parliament. One was the usual left approach, embodied by the Social Democrats and some minor Liberal parties, which were pursuing aims of democratization. The other, starting in the 1930s, was the radical right, which was seeking a nationalistic mass mobilization and sought to challenge the old, traditional elites in the parliamentary arena and elsewhere. Eventually, both failed to transform parliamentary elites, so that during this long period, representation of larger social groups appeared only at the margins of this parliamentary elite.[1] The consequence was that, on the one hand, the parliamentary elite had problems defining the interest of 'the people' or of the nation and in pursuing policies accordingly, and on the other hand, large social groups were virtually excluded from parliament in terms of personal representation.

Apart from the left and right groups struggling to change the configuration of the parliamentary elite, some leading political figures were also aware that the social background of members of parliament matter. In the face of the relative immobility of the parliamentary elite, some prime ministers, and/or leaders of the largest parties, occasionally attempted to introduce changes in this area in order to strengthen their own political line, or to establish the basis for new initiatives. They wanted to change the parliamentary elite, and thus the dynamics of parliamentary politics, by increasing the significance of party organization, either through new candidate selection procedures, or simply through personnel politics. For example, the dominant prime minister of the liberal period, Kálmán Tisza (1875–90), tried to give more prominence to state bureaucracy in parliamentary politics; in the interwar years, Prime Minister Count István Bethlen (1921–31) sought to stabilize parliamentary politics against the radical right by selecting more (including young) aristocrats for the parliamentary benches; as a response, in the middle of the 1930s, the new prime minister, Gyula Gömbös, brought the new middle class into parliament in opposition to the traditional elite.

We can rightly conclude that, in these periods, parliamentary elite features were a dependent variable in Hungary (Cotta and Verzichelli 1995), but not in a simplified sociological mirroring sense of the term. The parliamentary elite did not mirror society but was dependent on the general elite framework, and on the institutional, organizational, and personnel decisions and concepts of the top political elite. At the same time, it is obvious that they were also an independent variable: it seemed to matter who sits in parliament. This explains why top leaders sought to manage policy changes by attracting new political elite groups into parliament. An elite-centred understanding of parliamentary politics is justified by the fact that mass electoral linkages were weak. As Table 6.1 shows, in the liberal period before World War I, a mere 6% of the population was eligible to vote, and even between the two world wars the figure was below 30%, with the exception of the 1920 elections.

The end of World War II constitutes a clear dividing line regarding the parliamentary elite. In 1944, the old parliamentary elite was first

---

[1] Larger, i.e. as Birch (1964:16) put it, both 'by virtue of their activities . . . or by virtue of their personal characteristics'.

Table 6.1. Elections in Hungary between 1848 and 1994

Year	Population (millions)	Population eligible to vote (millions)		Electoral system	Number of MPs	Number of parties in the legislature
		n	%			
1848	11.2	0.8	7.1	majoritarian	411	—
1861	9.5	0.7	7.3	majoritarian	322	—
1865	12.5	0.85	5.8	majoritarian	395	—
1869	13.2	0.9	6.8	majoritarian	395	—
1872	13.4	0.9	6.7	majoritarian	413	5
1875	13.5	0.85	6.5	majoritarian	413	4
1878	13.7	0.82	6.0	majoritarian	413	4
1881	13.8	0.82	6.0	majoritarian	413	4
1884	14.3	0.84	5.9	majoritarian	413	5
1887	14.6	0.85	5.8	majoritarian	413	5
1892	15.3	0.87	5.7	majoritarian	413	5
1896	15.9	0.89	5.6	majoritarian	413	4
1901	16.8	1.02	6.1	majoritarian	413	7
1905	17.6	1.05	6.0	majoritarian	413	9
1906	18.0	1.08	6.2	majoritarian	413	7
1910	18.2	1.16	6.4	majoritarian	413	7
1920	8.0	3.13	39.7	majoritarian	208	8
1922	8.0	2.38	29.5	mixed	245	11
1926	8.5	2.23	26.6	mixed	245	8
1931	8.7	2.6	29.4	mixed	245	8
1935	8.9	3.0	30.0	mixed	245	15
1939	9.2	2.76	30.0	mixed	260	12
1945	9.0	5.2	60.0	proportional	421	5
1947	9.1	5.4	60.0	proportional	411	10
1949	9.3	6.05	65.5	proportional	402	1
1953	9.6	6.5	68.0	proportional	298	1
1958	9.8	6.6	67.0	proportional	338	1
1963	10.1	7.1	71.0	proportional	340	1
1967	10.2	7.2	70.7	majoritarian	349	1
1971	10.3	7.4	71.8	majoritarian	352	1
1975	10.5	7.7	73.0	majoritarian	352	1
1980	10.7	7.8	73.0	majoritarian	352	1
1985	10.6	7.7	72.5	majoritarian	386	1
1990	10.6	7.9	73.4	mixed	386	6
1994	10.3	7.96	74.5	mixed	386	6

Note: Between 1848 and 1920, the electoral system was a plurality system with single-member constituencies. Mixed electoral systems in the interwar years combined a proportional list system with a single-member majoritarian system and two types of districts: in the majority of them an open ballot and in the minority a secret ballot was taking place. After 1945, a proportional list system was introduced and used until 1963—quite ironically in a one-party system. Then single-member districts were re-established. Since 1990, 176 seats are filled from single-member districts with a run-off majority ballot and the remainder either from regional party lists or a national compensation list.

spontaneously, and then consciously replaced, but in the short democratic period a truly democratic parliamentary elite could not be consolidated. The Communist take-over in 1948 meant that although parliament was to mirror—and thus, according to the Communist propaganda, represent society—it became even further removed from the notion of a modern parliament than its predecessors. We cannot even talk of a real parliamentary elite in that period; a Communist Party elite, which also sat in parliament among an always changing group of 'representatives of the people' ruled instead.

After the first fully democratic election in 1990, but particularly after the second in 1994, several emerging features of the parliamentary elite suggest that the consolidation and professionalization of a truly parliamentary elite is gathering ground. While the rise of the professional parliamentary politician is neither a virtue in itself (Riddell 1995) nor an undebated issue, and even though the formation of a 'class apart' (in terms of a professional elite rather than a pre-1945 traditional elite) has its critiques, the chapter will examine in what sense we can consider the new developments as a significant step forward as compared to previous periods.

Even though a systematic calculation has not been completed for all the parliamentary cycles, pre-1945 statistics and different analyses made at that time may help us understand the major trends. While these analyses differ somewhat from the structure and methodology of the CUBE project, they are embedded in sound historical knowledge about the Hungarian political scene and, although sometimes with different indicators, they will reveal the realities of parliamentary elite politics. For the Communist period, perspective data acquisition is discouraging because it is hard even to identify the always changing group of grey members who had been picked by the Communist Party apparatus for 'representative purposes'. A more complete collection of data is available for the last three parliaments; that is, the final Communist one of 1985 and the democratic ones of 1990 and 1994. Their comparison will help to evaluate the directions of change. On these grounds, the main thesis of the chapter will be that—despite substantial changes in the parliamentary elite configuration in the past 150 years and the sometimes turbulent history of parliament itself—the professionalization of parliamentary elites has been taking place only recently, that is, after the democratic transition of 1989–90. This chapter, therefore, will examine in turn the major parliamentary periods (1848–67; 1868–1918; 1920–43; 1944–7; 1949–85; 1990 up to the present) to prove this argument.

2. 1848–1867: PRELUDE AND U-TURNS IN THE PARLIAMENTARY ELITE

Similar to several European democracies, the history of the modern Hungarian parliament began with the 1848 revolution, which was headed by liberal nobility and young radical intelligentsia. The Habsburg court was forced to accept for Hungary the nomination of a prime minister (Lajos Batthyány) and a government responsible to parliament. In April 1848, the parliament accepted a package of laws which—beside abolishing several feudal privileges—also laid down the foundations of a liberal constitution. The popular election of the members of parliament (to be held every third year) was decided (Article V of the April laws). Thus the old parliament of estates gave way to a modern parliament, which was to have regular yearly sessions in Pest (Article IV), as opposed to previously irregular sessions in Pozsony. An independent government responsible to the Hungarian parliament (Article III) was created, while the central administrative offices dependent on the Viennese court which had previously handled Hungarian affairs were eliminated.

The first liberal parliament was formed in June 1848 after the elections. In addition to the nobility (*c*.200,000 persons) about 600,000 people received the right to vote on the basis of property and educational requirements: 7.1% of the population was thus enfranchised.[2] This first liberal parliament understandably reflected the influence of the nobility, the majority of whom advocated the cause of liberal transformation in Hungary. These reforms did not have an impact upon the Upper Chamber.

After the repression of the revolution, its achievements were erased and the Habsburg court ruled by dictatorial measures. In 1860, the 'Diploma of October' promised to reinstate the Hungarian national assembly but only with limited powers, and decisions on election rules were left to a council to be convened later. The 'Patent of February' of 1861, which subordinated the prospective Hungarian assembly to the Assembly of the Habsburg Empire, was in many respects another step backward. Nevertheless, the growing weakness of the Habsburgs on the international scene and internal tensions forced new elections in 1861, virtually according to the 1848 electoral law. The political as well as the personal continuity in the parliament was striking. About two-fifths of the representatives elected in 1861 had also been members in 1848, and about one-seventh suffered imprisonment after the suppression of the revolution. They came largely from the land-owning nobility and demanded a return to the achievements of the 1848 liberal revolution. But since the emperor did not accept 1848 as a basis

---

[2] In Hungary, the aristocracy, the nobility, and the clergy had been the three estates. The aristocracy and the clergy had their place in the Upper House while the nobility sent representatives to the Lower House. The aristocracy (a few families) and the nobility (about 200,000 members) largely differed in property size, lifestyles, and political orientations, although overlaps (intermarriages or political co-operation) occasionally occurred. In the liberal period, the nobility became more and more divided internally: many lost their landed property and only a minority was able to adapt to the capitalist forms of agricultural production. Large groups among them began to occupy positions in the state bureaucracy. The landed nobility or '*bene possessionati*' were more closely connected to their land than the aristocrats (who might not have visited their property for years); they were 'less international'; and they were more tied to their local environment, i.e. the county with its distinct political functions and separate political apparatus. Occasionally the landowning classes were connected to this apparatus in person, or more often through economic interests and family ties.

of discussion, the new parliament was eventually disrupted by force some months later.

Both in Vienna and Budapest it was obvious, however, that sooner or later a compromise should be worked out between the two largest nations of the Habsburg Empire. When the emperor again convened the parliament at the end of 1865, the elections resulted in a landslide: only about half of the members of the 1861 parliament were re-elected. Due to the growing internal demand for compromise, many of the radical reformers of 1848 were left out. About 180 members constituted the largest (centre-right) group, the leader of which, Ferenc Deák, the 'wise man of Hungary' as he was called, hammered out the Compromise of 1867, that is, the dualist reconstruction of the Habsburg Empire. The new framework was advantageous for Hungary in economic terms but proved to be disastrous at least from two perspectives. First, it placed the constitutional issue, that is, the issue of independence, into the centre of political discourse for the next fifty years, and as a result inhibited the development of other political cleavages and representative linkages. Secondly, although the majority of the population of the dualist monarchy belonged to 'minority' groups, it did not handle this problem, which soon became an obstacle to the introduction or extension of liberal freedoms because of fears of ethnic revolt.

The 1865 parliament was not only new with respect to its members, but structurally somewhat different as well. The share of aristocrats rose to 16.5% (in contrast to 6% in 1848 and 13.3% in 1861). They represented more conservative attitudes and replaced the more radical wing of the nobility. The weight of land-owning nobility decreased but was still very high (62.4%). Another 20% belonged to the intelligentsia and the middle classes. Members of ethnic minorities represented about 10%. A substantial group (about 150 members) had bureaucratic positions in the counties, but they were rooted in and connected to the land-owning nobility.

The first period of modern parliamentarism, which began in 1848, concluded with ambiguous results. After a temporary period when the extension of franchise and more radical parliamentary politics were on the agenda, the old aristocracy and the more established nobility groups regained control of the parliamentary arena.

3. 1868–1918: A LIBERAL PARLIAMENT WITH LIMITATIONS AND APPARENT HOMOGENEITY OF ELITE POLITICS

Within the framework of the Austro-Hungarian dualist monarchy, the liberal period brought about economic success for Hungary. Nevertheless, from the perspective of elite circulation and elite characteristics, we must note that limited franchise, the predominant party system, and the virtual lack (with the exception of one election) of government change, cemented the old parliamentary elite in its positions, that is, the parliamentarians still largely came from the old ruling classes. This period became infamous because, although parliamentary politics had become a widely reported public matter for the first time in Hungary, and debates seemed significant, the world of *mameluks* (those who only nod), paternalism, and corruption prevailed on the parliamentary benches.

The party system reflected mainly constitutional issues, that is, relations with the monarchy and Vienna, with parties being divided accordingly.[3] As a result, the cleavage structure that began to develop in Western Europe in this period did not take shape or at least was not transformed into the realm of Hungarian politics. From the middle of the 1870s and after the initial stage of consolidation following the Compromise, two large parties—both within the liberal stream and differing mainly for their attitude *vis-à-vis* the Compromise—represented the major political orientations. The Liberal Party, which supported the Compromise, was in power uninterruptedly between 1875 and 1906 when its opponent, the Party of Independence, took over as the head of a coalition. The coalition period was short, however, and in 1910 the Liberals were back in power. It is important to note here that, with the exception of the short intermezzo between 1906 and 1910, the government party was always large enough to form the government by itself and to feel safe in its position. Consequently, although there were several other parties in parliament, they could not challenge this framework[4] and Hungary remained a predominant party system throughout the entire pre-1945 period. Indeed, the huge government parliamentary parties incorporated different groups of the elite and embodied the elite compromises or pacts that were to protect the regime from challengers.

Both the lower or the non-traditional strata of Hungarian society and the ethnic groups were considered as challengers. The efforts to ensure further liberalization—not to mention democratization—were first of all halted by

---

[3] For an analysis of this period, see László (1984: 86–165), János (1982: chs. 3–6). For the interwar years, Rotschild (1990: 137–99) gives an overview. A small but interesting segment of interwar politics is discussed in Nagy (1983).

[4] The constitutional orientation of the two large parties: the pro-Compromise Liberal Party and the pro-1848 Party of Independence did not change in the period, although some leading figures occasionally left these parties and tried to establish new elite organizations. Party policies in the liberal period concentrated around party leaderships and influential political personalities. The Liberal Party changed its name to National Working Party in 1910. Minor parties were also and often embodied by an influential political personality. Many among them did not last long. An exception was the People's Party representing protectionist agrarian interests with the conservative aristocracy and Catholic clergy in its background. After the turn of the century, new and more lasting political orientations appeared: the Radical Democratic Party sought to represent the middle classes and the intelligentsia, the Agrarian Party the interests of the well-to-do peasantry. The Social Democratic Party was very active but could not send an MP to parliament before 1920.

Table 6.2. Age groups of MPs 1887–1931 (%)

Age group	1887	1892	1896	1901	1905	1906	1910	1920	1922	1927	1931
Under 40	36.6	30.0	19.1	28.6	27.1	36.1	28.1	34.8	29.4	12.2	9.8
41–60	49.1	56.9	56.9	55.7	57.9	53.2	56.7	58.0	62.4	77.6	78.0
Above 61	14.3	13.1	14.0	15.7	15.0	10.7	15.2	7.2	8.2	10.2	12.2

Source: Rudai (1936: 227).

the recurring reference to the ethnic issue. For example, several initiatives failed to introduce electoral reform, particularly between 1905 and 1912, when in the Austrian part of the Empire the extension of the franchise took place. We can conclude that prevalence of both the constitutional issue and ethnic problems inhibited the modernization of parliament and the parliamentary elite.

As we have seen, by the end of the previous period, the radical nobility—generally with middle-sized land property and with the counties' self-government organization as its political basis—lost ground in favour of the aristocracy. The reform of the Upper House contributed after 1885 to pushing the aristocracy towards the House of Representatives (although its members had already been allowed to run for seats in the Lower House since 1848).[5] The share of the aristocracy, both in the government and opposition parties, was between 10% and 15% throughout the whole period (10.6% in 1869, 8.6% in 1872, 10.8% in 1875, 11% in 1878, 12.4% in 1881, 12.8% in 1884, 13.3% in 1887, 16.4% in 1892, 13.4% in 1896, 13.6% in 1901, 14.4% in 1905, 11.1% in 1906, and 15.7% in 1910) (Lakatos 1942: 28 and 28–30).

The aristocracy was overrepresented in the dominant Liberal Party, but the leading force of the more radical coalition government between 1906 and 1910, the Party of Independence, also had a substantial share of aristocrats among its ranks (7.2% in that period). Being an aristocrat—as happened in many other European liberal democracies at that time—was an entrance ticket to parliamentary politics. They were influential and most often well-to-do, thus, in harmony with the liberal approach to parliamentary politics, they were thought to be capable of pursuing politics in a 'proper' way. The meaning of aristocracy began to change, however,

---

[5] Previously, all the male members of the aristocracy had been members of the Upper House (in addition to Catholic and Greek-Catholic clergy and the leaders of the counties). After 1885, only the largest tax-paying aristocrats remained while the Protestant clergy became represented and highest rank judges entered the scene. The monarch could nominate 50 members to the Upper House, which he did to honour special services to the Court and the country. The aristocratic majority in the Upper House had not been challenged throughout the entire period, however.

particularly after the turn of the century. In addition to the 'old' aristocracy, based on heritage and landed property, new aristocrats appeared. Among the three aristocratic ranks (duke, count, and baron) the number and the share of the lowest (i.e. barons) increased. They were sometimes of foreign origin and mostly connected to the new industrial interests.

Table 6.3 concentrates on the economic and social background of MPs rather than on their social status; for example, aristocracy will mainly appear among the group of landowners, but this group will also include the owners of middle-sized properties. Landowners, lawyers, and bureaucrats constituted the three largest groups among MPs and the majority of the representatives. Throughout the entire period, landowners were the largest socio-economic group—always above the 30% level. Indeed, their share only decreased substantially after 1930, which already represents a different period in the political development of Hungary. The position of the landowning interests was unchallenged in both of the two main parties (see Table 6.4).

Lawyers were the second largest group, close to or above the 20% level, but in larger numbers among the opposition than on the government benches (see Tables 6.3 and 6.4), like the intelligentsia and the clergy. In contrast, MPs with commerce and industry as their background were in larger numbers in the governing party. It seems, that the rich, rather the 'nouveaux riches', preferred the Liberal Party to opposition forces. This was in accordance with their economic interest—built on the economic prosperity of the Compromise—and also served their aim to assimilate.

The third largest group were the bureaucrats, but with huge differences between the various levels of origin. Central (ministerial), regional (county), and local (town) bureaucracy all served as channels of interest representation for the ruling classes, with many parliamentary careers beginning at the county level. Bureaucrats from the county level outnumbered those from the ministerial level, while the share from the town level was minimal. Bureaucracy in the counties was closely attached to (or overlapped with) the nobility and the governing Liberal Party, which had the greatest number of bureaucrats as representatives, consciously sought to attract this group, relying on them as a political base. A change in this trend can be seen in the exceptional coalition period of 1906 to 1910, and is even more pronounced after 1920 when the more traditional county bureaucrats lost ground in favour of those from ministerial level. The growing number of ministerial bureaucrats after World War I clearly shows a different power base and represents a more centralizing force among the parliamentary elites.

Modern social groups or modern middle classes appear in relatively small numbers, like those coming from industry and commerce, or professions such as engineering, education, medicine, and so on. The latter group either

Table 6.3. Professional background of MPs 1887–1931

Year	Landowners	Lawyers	Bureaucracy in the counties	Bureaucracy on the ministerial level	Bureaucracy on the town level	Clergy	Industry, commerce, and trade	Writers, journalists, teachers, artists, scientists	Medical profession, soldiers	Workers, freelancers
1887	31.3	18.9	17.9	7.8	0.3	3.5	5.8	12.1	2.4	0
1892	37.5	24.2	10.4	6.0	1.7	3.6	5.8	9.3	1.5	0
1896	31.7	18.4	17.9	10.2	1.2	3.6	5.8	9.7	1.5	0
1901	34.8	23.0	11.1	6.3	3.1	4.1	5.8	9.9	1.6	0.3
1905	31.7	26.8	9.7	6.3	2.2	4.9	3.9	11.1	2.2	1.2
1906	33.7	28.6	4.8	4.1	1.9	8.0	5.3	10.2	2.2	1.2
1910	36.8	21.1	8.5	8.2	1.6	3.1	6.8	10.4	2.4	1.1
1920	30.0	11.2	4.3	9.1	2.4	12.1	7.7	15.0	4.8	3.4
1922	26.9	14.3	11.0	9.4	1.6	6.1	7.8	9.0	4.1	9.8
1927	26.6	15.1	9.4	12.7	2.0	6.1	6.9	9.4	6.1	5.7
1931	22.5	17.1	11.4	13.5	1.2	3.7	8.6	9.0	6.1	6.9

Source: Rudai (1936: 218).

Table 6.4. Professional background of government and opposition MPs 1887–1931

Year	Landowners		Lawyers		Bureaucracy in the counties		Writers, journalists, teachers, artists,		Bureaucracy on the ministerial level scientists		Clergymen		Workers, freelancers		Industry, commerce, and trade		Medical profession, soldiers		Bureaucracy on the town level	
	Gov.	Opp.	Gov.	Opp.	Gov.	Opp.	Gov.	Opp.	Gov.	Opp.	Gov.	Opp.	Gov.	Opp.	Gov.	Opp.	Gov.	Opp.	Gov.	Opp.
1887	31.9	30.2	16.7	22.8	19.0	15.4	11.0	14.1	10.3	3.4	2.3	5.4	—	—	6.5	4.7	2.3	3.4	—	0.6
1892	37.9	37.7	19.7	30.3	14.3	5.2	8.0	10.8	9.2	1.7	0.3	7.4	—	—	7.2	4.0	1.7	1.2	1.7	1.7
1896	28.6	39.0	17.5	21.1	22.4	6.5	9.3	10.6	13.1	3.3	0.7	10.6	—	—	6.2	4.9	1.1	2.4	1.1	1.6
1901	36.6	31.8	18.1	31.8	16.2	2.0	10.1	9.5	8.3	2.7	0.8	10.1	1.2	0.7	6.1	5.4	1.5	2.0	2.3	4.0
1905	30.2	32.7	20.1	31.2	20.1	3.1	9.5	12.2	11.3	3.1	0.6	7.5	1.2	1.2	3.2	4.3	0.6	3.1	3.2	1.6
1906	35.2	31.2	32.0	22.9	2.3	8.9	11.3	8.3	2.3	7.0	6.7	10.2	—	1.3	5.5	5.1	1.2	3.8	2.3	1.3
1910	31.3	44.9	21.1	20.9	12.5	1.9	9.8	12.1	11.8	2.5	1.5	6.3	—	2.5	8.6	3.8	1.5	3.8	1.9	1.3
1920	34.1	19.3	9.3	15.8	4.0	5.2	14.7	15.8	6.7	15.8	13.3	8.8	3.3	3.5	7.3	8.8	5.3	3.5	2.0	3.5
1922	33.3	17.3	15.0	13.3	15.6	4.1	6.1	13.3	10.9	7.1	4.1	9.2	0.7	23.4	8.8	6.1	4.8	6.1	0.7	3.1
1927	29.7	18.8	16.4	12.2	12.9	1.4	4.7	16.2	14.0	9.5	3.5	12.2	1.2	13.5	9.4	8.1	6.4	5.4	1.8	2.7
1931	23.7	20.4	19.8	12.9	15.8	4.3	7.2	11.8	15.1	10.8	1.3	7.5	0.7	17.2	9.2	7.5	5.9	6.5	1.3	1.1

Source: Rudai (1936: 221).

came from impoverished noble families or from the well-to-do peasantry who managed to finance the education of their sons. The largest group in the middle classes was the intelligentsia (writers, journalists, teachers, artists, and so on), which constituted about 10% of the members with a slightly higher share among the opposition than among the government ranks.

In principle, lawyers and bureaucrats embody modernity or professionalism in parliaments, as opposed to the classical old ruling classes, which tend to embody amateurism and tradition. Yet we must note several paradoxes regarding the Hungarian scene in this respect. First of all, as previously mentioned, bureaucrats were largely linked to the old land-owning interests—both because of personal connections and/or because of territorial location in the counties that embodied provincialism and agricultural interests opposing urban and industrial interests. Thus, we cannot expect its members to be the forerunners of modernization and parliamentary professionalization. Bureaucracy in the counties and ministerial level was the bastion of the governing party—the Liberals—and MPs were given positions there as patronage from the party.

Secondly, many lawyers were so-called 'one case' lawyers, that is, they served only the interest of a single concern, such as a big estate or a firm, and consequently were dependent on one particular (rich) person or family. Thus, in the background of these seemingly modern groups we find the most hated features of the liberal period in Hungary: clientelism, patronage, corruption.

The ethnic diversity of the country also contributed to these phenomena. Most 'ethnic' districts (i.e. where a non-Hungarian population prevailed) were dominated by the Liberal Party, while the Party of Independence had more 'Hungarian seats'. The usual explanation emphasizes that the Hungarian electorate was more independence oriented than the ethnic electorate, and thus in the Hungarian constituencies the (opposition) Party of Independence was more successful. Another reason is that in the ethnic constituencies the candidate had to rely more on party support than in the Hungarian constituencies because the electorate had to be persuaded to vote for a Hungarian party. Persuasion was either through force, or through food and drink!—both of which were more available to the Liberal Party in power. As a result, representatives of the Liberal Party who had been nominated in these seats became very much dependent on party support: they became representatives of the party hierarchy and of their 'patron' rather than of the wider public. This explains the vague representative linkage between parliament and electorate in terms of policies, and also reveals characteristics of the parliamentary elite. Many MPs could not at all be called independent: they were dependent both on persons having leading positions in the party and on the party itself, which—being cemented in power—was able to guarantee them positions. This is well demonstrated by the characteristics of the coalition intermezzo: the number of bureaucrats decreased substantially—although the number of lawyers did not.

Thirdly, data demonstrate that both county and ministerial bureaucracies were much more strongly represented in the government party. For example, in 1887 the share of county bureaucrats was 19% in the governing party and 15.4% in the opposition. This difference actually grew with time: the figures are 14.3% versus 5.2% for 1892, 22.4% versus 6.5% for 1896, and 16.2% versus 2% in 1901. The tendency changed when in 1906 the opposition party achieved power: then the share of county bureaucracy in the new governing party was very low (2.3%—see Table 6.4).

The impact of change in electoral fortune is shown by variations in the mean age of representation. In 1906, the new government party brought in a substantially younger group of MPs. Between 1887 and 1905, there was the first 'long cycle' of parliamentary elites whereby parliamentary turnover rates were low and the share of the younger generations decreased. In the coalition period between 1906 and 1910, this trend reversed and representatives were younger. However, after 1920, the number of young representatives again greatly declined (see Table 6.2).

Concerning the second period of the Hungarian parliamentary government, we can conclude that up to the end of World War I the Hungarian parliament remained an institution of limited liberalism. Although parliament was an important decision-making forum of the period, it was controlled not by the electorate, however, but by a domineering government party, and by the old ruling classes who tended to block any attempt at modernization by the opposition. Even if we do not have complete information about personal continuity patterns in this period, on the whole continuity seems to have been the prevalent tendency: no significant changes in the background of MPs could be found, except for the exceptional and only government change in 1906. In the two large parties, the post-Compromise generations remained dominant. New MPs tended to appear in some newly formed minor parties (see footnote 4), but this development did not have a significant impact on the qualitative outlook of the entire parliamentary membership as far as social background is concerned.

4. 1920–1944: OLD AND NEW PARLIAMENTARY ELITES

World War I and the breakdown of the dualist monarchy, which followed in the wake of the military collapse, resulted in two revolutions in Hungary. The democratic revolution of October 1918 could not fulfil its aims to democratize and modernize the country due to international circumstances.

The Communist revolution in March 1919 rejected the idea of parliament-arism, and in the short time span of its existence, established a soviet system where legislative and executive power were exercised by the same body. Nevertheless, by January 1920, although still under military and interna-tional pressure, a temporary government convened elections in the occu-pied country.

In the period which began with these dramatic events, several important questions which exceed the pure issue of parliamentary elite circulation have at least to be briefly dealt with. For example, there is the need to clarify what kind of continuity prevailed between the pre-1918 and the post-1919 political regimes with respect to the constitutional framework, the party system, and general elite configuration. The previous period had been char-acterized by stable political patterns and by continuity in the elite configu-ration—except for one major blow in 1906. Between the wars, institutional developments were more complex. Although the regional and ethnic dimension, and the constitutional issue, virtually disappeared from political life, in other respects the political landscape became more varied.

As in the pre-1918 period, in the interwar years Hungary had a predominant party system. Under different names (Party of Christian National Unity, Party of Unity, Party of National Unity), the same govern-ment party had no serious challengers and held more than 60% of the seats throughout the whole period. The new dominant party was a conglomera-tion of different orientations: representatives of the traditional elites and the new and old middle classes could be found in its ranks. While before World War I the MPs of the governing party largely advocated national liberalism, after 1920 the dominant political orientation became national conservatism. The traditional national conservative elite groups (which included aristocrats and large landowners) were joined by middle-class groups generally sharing more radical political orientations.

In contrast to the relative homogeneity of elite politics around the turn of the century, in the new period, the party scene became more fragmented with the number of parties in parliament often exceeding ten. One can also see diverse political orientations in parliament at this time, including the Social Democratic Party on the left (Communists were illegal up to 1944), small conservative-Christian groups, liberals, smallholder-agricultural parties, and right-wing groups, including extreme right. Some minor royal-ist groups also participated in parliamentary politics, although the take-over of Admiral Horthy, and his election as governor in 1921, put an end to extensive debates on this matter. This meant that, although Hungary remained a kingdom, the throne was vacant and the governor entitled to play the role of monarch.

The electoral system was more open than before but still had serious limitations. The 1920 elections were indeed the most democratic. But afterwards, the franchise was again restricted on the basis of economic and educational requirements. Until 1939, the majority of mandates came from open districts and only a minority of mandates came from districts with a secret ballot. The open districts were dominated by the government party (and the candidates here often won unopposed), while the Liberal and Social Democratic opposition mainly won seats in secret constituencies (i.e. in Budapest and other city areas; see footnote to Table 6.1).

The elections in 1920 (the first after the war) represented a break with the past in several respects. The new parliament was called the 'parliament in boots' because a large share of MPs represented the landowning peasantry: a relatively open electoral law, and international surveillance, not unexpectedly, combined to open the doors of parliament to this new social group. The influential members of the old elites had not managed to establish new parties by that time and the old party framework was lying in ruins. The break with the past is demonstrated by the increased share of the clergy and the intelligentsia and the decreased share of the traditional state bureaucracy (see Table 6.3).

This was an exceptionally middle-class parliament as compared to the previous and following ones. The democratization of mass and elite politics proved, however, to be short-lived. Not only were more restrictions put on the franchise but already in early 1922, Count Bethlen managed to unite the winning party of 1920, the Smallholders, with his own groups under the name of Unity Party (*Egységes Párt*). As a result, a large governing party, dominated by members of the old elite, was established and a new parliamentary cycle began, which lasted almost until 1944. This long cycle was similar to the pre-1918 patterns, albeit with some substantial differences: that is, the influence of landowners decreased while groups from industry and commerce, medical and military professions, from self-employed or comparable situations (that is, independent existences, mainly from middle and lower middle-class groups, as diverse as pensioners and shareholders) became stronger. The lawyers' group also increased, again approaching pre-World War I levels, with the important difference that among the opposition parties their share remained low. This is due to differences in the nature of the opposition in the two periods: while they were part of the ruling classes in pre-World War I decades, in the interwar years they became not only more fragmented but comprised mainly outsiders (like the Social Democrats or the liberal National Democrats) or challengers of the old elite (like the radical racist Race Protectionist Party). The overall share of bureaucrats, primarily those at ministerial level, regained the level at the end of the last century. With their specific expertise and knowledge of the central state apparatus, they can be considered a more modern segment of the parliamentary elite than those of the pre-1918 period. Representatives from the intelligentsia, workers, self-employed, and the clergy were clearly more numerous in the ranks of the opposition parties.

Nevertheless, the outlook of the parliamentary elite was shaped to a great extent by the characteristics of the members of the large governing party who were the most numerous and the most influential in parliament. The stability of this segment of the parliamentary elite is striking. Throughout the three legislative terms following the 1922, 1926, and 1931 elections, altogether 263 members occupied the parliamentary benches of the Unity Party and a substantial group among them served more than one legislative term: 65 politicians served in all the three terms, 100 in two, and, although 98 served only one term, almost half of these were elected in 1931, which marked the beginning of changes in the elite and in parliamentary politics anyway (Barta 1995). The Unity Party included different groups, but until that point the most influential members of the party belonged to the circle of the prime minister (I. Bethlen) and were aristocrats themselves (27 members), or came from the old political families of the pre-war years (49 members) and also had good contacts with the new economic elite. Nevertheless, there were more than two dozen MPs in the Unity Party who really came 'from below', that is, mainly from the peasantry (Barta 1995). The Unity Party reflected the religious division of the country: 140 Catholics, and 89 Protestants (of whom 24 were Calvinists), just to mention the largest groups. In addition, more of its representatives came from Budapest and the lost territories of the old monarchy than from the other regions (the prime minister himself had lost landed property in Transylvania). Except for the smallholder-peasant segment, the Unity Party MPs were highly educated: about half of them had a doctoral degree and many had attended elite grammar schools in Hungary or/and had international educational experience.

Intra-elite developments from the 1930s began to challenge the hegemony of the old elite and its compromise with the old and new middle classes. Already in the 1931 elections and even more so in those of 1935, new and radical members were elected in larger numbers. As I have tried to show elsewhere (Ilonszki 2000), the elite framework of the inter-war years can be understood as a struggle between the conservative traditional elites and the old middle-class groups, whereby ideologically disunified elite groups sought to establish their power base (Higley and Burton 1989). The old middle-class groups, with their roots in the military, in the gentry, and in middle-level bureaucracy had previously belonged to the privileged elite. After the collapse of the old regime, the old middle-class groups, deprived of their military and bureaucratic positions, felt themselves to be losers and joined similar groups elsewhere, particularly in Germany and Italy.

Thus, the challenging groups were not connected to modernizing trends but rather to those of the extreme right of the period. A leading and characteristic figure of this group was Gyula Gömbös, prime minister in the 1930s and a rival of the 'traditionalist' Bethlen. Gömbös sought to transform the large government party in the interest of his followers (placing his companions as candidates) in the same way as Bethlen had done more than a decade before. In his attempt to transform elite politics into mass politics, he flirted with wide-ranging electoral reforms and wanted to change the government party into a mass party with proper mass membership. Although the particular coalition politics of the Hungarian system—when coalitions are formed within the government party—continued until the end of World War II, the new elite group became more dominant in parliament as a result of Gömbös's policy. Eventually, Bethlen and several others from the old elite left the government party and the previous unity of the elites was never again established. The government party remained dominated by newcomers and the more radical saloon-fascist middle classes, which had a catastrophic impact on the country's international performance and record during World War II.

It is interesting to note that the parliamentary elite reflected the major controversies between large social groups much better than before World War I because members of the parliamentary elite were drawn from wider groups than before. The new groups mainly sat on the opposition benches, but some entered the government party ranks. Opposition representatives were really diverse: among them can be found the party and trade union cadres of the Social Democratic Party (they mainly appear in the worker or freelance group of Tables 6.3 and 6.4); members of the intelligentsia in the National Liberal Party, in the National Democratic Party, and the Radical Party (although some of their members will appear in the lawyers' group); many self-employed, both in the liberal and on the extreme right spectrum of the party and parliament. The old elite, however, was not seriously challenged by the opposition representatives but rather by peripheral groups of the elite itself. The controversies between the elites embodied political alternatives and led to policy choices, which proved to be consequential for the entire country. Here again, parliamentary elites were reflections and initiators, that is, dependent and independent variable at the same time.

5. 1944–1947: DEMOCRATIC PARLIAMENTS— ELITES UNDER PRESSURE

The Hungarian fascists took over—with German support—in October 1944, when Governor Horthy was forced to resign. This was an unhappy ending for the Hungarian parliamentary institutions, which, in any case, had always been limited in their freedom, and were often only a façade. An extremist segment of the governing party accepted the fascist Arrow Cross as leader and the regime as legitimate. The fascist-oriented parliament was moved to Sopron in the western part of the country, while Soviet troops gradually occupied the eastern part of the country where democratic parties were soon re-established and emigrant communist groups returned. As early as December 1944, five parties and the trade unions declared a programme in which they advocated a constitutional national assembly. In Moscow, another solution was supported: instead of a common initiative of the democratic parties to begin constitutionalization and form a government on this basis, Moscow advocated immediate popular elections in the occupied parts of the country. They hoped that the parliament (the national assembly, as we shall call it here)[6]—elected by popular vote—would be a counterbalance to the party system, in which conservative democrats were also present.[7]

Elections took place in December 1944, but only in the eastern part of the country, where about 1.5 million people participated (Feitl 1991). The temporary national assembly (TNA) obviously showed little continuity with the previous period. Only six members had been in parliament before (four Smallholders, one Social Democrat, and one non-affiliated) and the new assembly was predominantly left-oriented (the three left-wing parties—Communists, Social Democrats, and the Peasant Party—held 65% of the seats).

The TNA held its first, very short session in December 1944 and ruled on some important constitutional issues (e.g. sovereignty), elected the executive (whose members were nominated in Moscow), and also established the Political Committee of the TNA, which was entitled to control the executive. However, it was soon obvious that it was neither in the interest of the left nor of the right to have elections in the newly liberated parts of the country. The conservative and liberal groups were satisfied with their executive positions, while the left felt safe having Moscow in the background. Thus, inter-party agreements and bargains decided the party division of the new members who were co-opted into the TNA. Co-option, which resulted in 19 former MPs gaining seats, occurred in two stages, first with respect to Budapest and then to western Hungary. Table 6.5 demonstrates the differences in the social background of the small and the extended TNA, but it is important to note that the left proved to be more successful not only in the original 'elections' but in the bargaining process as well. The Social

---

[6] In Hungarian, there are several words that cannot be translated into English. The major difficulty lies in the distinction between *országgyûlés* and *nemzetgyûlés*, the former being the country's assembly (the closest equivalent of parliament) and the latter the national assembly, indicating that some issues relating to important state affairs are still open to discussion. One explanation certainly is that the state and the nation historically did not overlap.

[7] The parties were: Communist Party, Social Democratic Party, Peasant Party, Smallholders' Party, Civic Democratic Party.

Table 6.5. Occupational background 1944–1947

Occupation	Small TNA		TNA		NA (1945)		Parliament (1947)	
	n	%	n	%	n	%	n	%
Peasantry, farmers	74	32	117	23	121	29	112	27
Small businesses	24	10	31	6	28	7	14	3
Industrial workers	54	23	135	27	61	15	73	18
Intellectuals and teachers	41	18	114	23	112	27	110	27
Employees	20	9	65	13	57	14	83	20
Factory owners	3	1	6	1	11	3	5	1
Other (clergy, soldiers)	14	6	30	6	31	7	13	3
Total	230	100	498	100	421	100	410	100

Notes: Small TNA: Temporary National Assembly only for the eastern part of the country, elected in December 1944.
TNA: Temporary National Assembly for the territory of the whole country, consisting of the originally elected members as well as co-opted ones.
NA: National Assembly after the first proper elections in November 1945.
Parliament: formed after the elections in August 1947.

Source: Hubai and Tombor (1991: appendix, 255).

Democrats increased their share from 18.7% to 25.3% and the Communists remained the largest party, although their share of 40% in the small TNA decreased to 33.5% in the enlarged TNA. The second session of the TNA, held in September 1945, before the first regular election, enacted some important laws, including the electoral law.

The November 1945 elections were the first fully democratic elections in Hungary, somewhat paradoxically considering the international political status of the country and the obvious impact of the Communists. From the 498 members of the TNA, 216 were re-elected (89 smallholders, 54 communists, 52 Social Democrats, 13 peasant party representatives, one civic democratic party representative, and seven non-affiliated); thus from the 421[8] members of the national assembly, 51% had served in the previous term. Understandably, continuity with pre-war parliaments remained at a low level: altogether 27 politicians had previously been MPs (16 Smallholders, eight Social Democrats, one Civic Democratic Party, and two non-affiliated; Hubai 1991).

Although the largest party—the Independent Smallholders Party—had an absolute majority, it established a coalition government with the Communists, the Social Democrats, and the Peasant Party. This was again the assembly of the 'people', and the social background of the representatives of the different parties is typical: in the ranks of the Smallholders Party the

---

[8] The number of elected members was only 409, but afterwards a group of 12 honourable persons were co-opted.

Table 6.6. Educational background of the national assembly (1945) and the first Parliament (June 1948)*

Education	National Assembly		Parliament	
	n	%	n	%
Elementary	157	37.3	136	37.9
Middle school	63	15.0	41	11.4
Grammar school	60	14.2	37	10.3
Teacher-training college			13	3.6
Higher education	141	33.5	117	32.6
Other	—	—	15	4.2
Total	421	100.0	359	100.0

Note: *By this time the number of MPs had been reduced to 359 due to parliamentary expulsions and purges.

Source: Hubai and Tombor (1991: appendix, 259–60).

peasantry, intellectuals, factory owners, and those listed as 'other' were over-represented; among the Communists, workers were overrepresented (with nearly 50% of all seats); as were employees and workers among the Social Democrats.

This did not prove to be a period of parliamentary consolidation at all. Very soon the largest party began to melt away because it was the main target for the Soviet authorities and the Communist secret police alike. The 1947 elections had already occurred under extreme political pressure. The Smallholders disintegrated, and in 1947, the anti-Communist opposition became fragmented and organized in six parties. They could not halt the Communist take-over. By various ways and means, in the following year, the Communists first eliminated the democratic opposition and then their own coalition partners. These developments had nothing to do with parliamentary realities. Although the Smallholders had the highest level of parliamentary continuity, and thus possibly expertise (81% of the 1947 parliament members had seats in the 1945 national assembly (NA) as well, while the Communists had only a 52% continuity) and although the Communist MPs were the least educated (50% in 1947 had only four elementary school years, while on average their share was 37%), parliamentary change did not depend on elections nor on the level of parliamentary expertise but rather on power politics.

Unfortunately, the 1944–7 years, despite the efforts and good faith of large electoral and political elite groups, produced only weak or façade parliaments. In the background of democratic institutions, the influence of the Soviet Union and the Communist Party became more and more obvious and eventually led to the elimination of large parliamentary elite groups and of democratic parliamentary institutions themselves.

6. 1949–1985: COMMUNIST PARLIAMENTS AND PARLIAMENTARY ELITES—A MISCONCEPTION

It is a misconception to deal with the assemblies of the Communist period as if they were true parliaments. In fact, parliament again became just a façade. Nevertheless, some parliamentary developments reflected political changes demonstrating that even in a Communist regime the parliamentary arena may respond to transformations in the political system. In the following pages, I will discuss those features of the Communist period that show the inter-relatedness of parliamentary and non-parliamentary politics or those which still have some impact on the parliamentary framework under democratic conditions today.

The Communist parliaments were always conceived as mirrors of society: in fact, there was a deliberate ideologically guided programme to have the working classes or other groups, for example women, represented according to their respective share in the population at large. We cannot neglect the fact, however, that in this respect the Communist period can be divided into at least two stages. The totalitarian phase before 1956 adhered to this ideal more directly, while post-totalitarianism, particularly its mature phase in the 1970s and 1980s, meant a decrease in the number of peasants and an increase in the number of professionals. These were signs that the political leadership handled the notion of representation more pragmatically and did not particularly want to hide the existence of a new political class of party *apparatchiks* (see Table 6.7).

Although the share of Communist Party members remained surprisingly stable, at around 70% between 1949 and 1985 (with the only exception of 1958 when the 82% share had a demonstrative message function and probably also reflected the power elite's decision to play safe after the 1956 revolution), it is more revealing to look at the connections between leading party functions (Politburo and Central Committee membership) and parliamentary positions (see Table 6.8). After 1962, the party hierarchy no

Table 6.7. Distribution of MPs according to their original occupation 1949–1985

Period	Workers	%	Peasants	%	Professionals	%	Employees	%
1949–53	174	43.3	114	28.4	92	22.9	22	5.5
1953–8	129	43.3	90	30.2	79	26.5	—	—
1958–63	169	50.0	75	22.2	78	23.1	16	4.7
1963–7	142	41.8	64	18.8	123	36.2	11	3.2
1967–71	136	39.0	76	21.8	129	37.0	8	2.3
1971–5	137	38.9	60	17.0	131	37.2	24	6.8
1975–80	157	44.6	48	13.6	146	41.5	1	0.3
1980–5	158	44.9	46	13.1	130	36.9	18	5.1

Source: *Almanach* 1990 (1994: 597).

Table 6.8. Connections between Communist Party hierarchy and parliamentary membership

Year of party congress	Members of party Central Committe	Number of MPs in Central Committee	Percentage of MPs among Central Committee Members	Members of Politburo	Number of MPs in Politburo	Percentage of MPs among Politburo Members
1948	66	58	87.8	14	14	100
1954	70	52	74.2	9	9	100
1959	71	55	77.4	12	11	93.3
1962	81	55	67.9	13	12	92.3
1966	101	38	37.6	11	8	72.7
1970	105	35	33.3	13	9	69.2
1975	125	34	27.2	13	9	69.2
1980	127	33	25.9	13	11	84.6
1985	105	30	28.6	13	12	92.3

Source: Kukorelli (1988: 87).

longer saw the need to win its legitimacy through parliament so that it was no longer a requirement to have all high-ranking political functionaries in parliament. Consequently, the share of the Communist Party's Central Committee members in parliament decreased from about 68% in 1962 to 28.6% in 1985. In fact, two hidden agendas replaced the representative function that democratic elections should have ensured. On the one hand, representation of diverse interests was taking place through the Communist Party hierarchy because the party absorbed and accepted the latent pluralism of the society. On the other hand, particularly after the electoral system change in 1967 when single-member constituencies, as opposed to party lists, were re-established, the MPs became more closely tied to their constituents and began to lobby for them openly within the party or in the ministries.

The share of ministers with a parliamentary seat also decreased, reaching its lowest point in 1985 (all 18 ministers were MPs in 1949, 17 MPs out of 19 in 1953, 19 out of 23 in 1958, 17 out of 24 in 1963, four out of 22 in 1967, five in 1971, seven in 1975, four in 1980, and three in 1985). The major change occurred in 1967 when, due to expectations regarding economic and partial political reform, government functions were assumed to be less political, and more based on expertise. Although reform was blocked, there was no return to the previous period when party hierarchy, executive positions, and parliamentary membership were inseparably intertwined. After 1967, the number of *apparatchiks* from the party and from societal organizations declined significantly (see Table 6.9).

Despite these changes and the occasional case-work of influential MPs, the Communist parliaments did not acquire any significance until 1985.

Table 6.9. Professional background of MPs 1967–1985 (%)

Professional background	1967	1971	1975	1980	1985
Industry and tertiary sector	23.5	26.8	33.6	33.9	33.9
Agriculture	18.1	15.9	13.6	14.2	18.4
Party apparatus	14.3	12.8	10.8	11.6	7.8
State apparatus[1]	10.9	11.9	9.4	9.2	10.9
Apparatus of societal organizations	10.6	8.2	7.6	6.5	6.8
Public sector employees (health, education)[2]	17.8	19.3	17.9	15.9	18.4
Churches	1.7	1.7	1.7	1.9	2.0
Others	3.2	3.4	5.4	6.8	1.8
Total	100	100	100	100	100

Notes: [1] The state apparatus included highly politicized positions.
[2] Teachers, members of the medical profession, officials in public sector are included here.

Source: Kukorelli (1988: 85).

They sat for only a couple of days per year and were simply the rubber-stamps of the Party's political decisions. One-term members, peasants, women, or miners were only picked to hide the lack of legitimacy. The 1983 electoral law was a real turning-point in the history of the Communist parliaments. Based on political decisions and in line with liberalization attempts, the law made multi-candidacy compulsory. In the single-member districts, two or more candidates had to be nominated—under Communist Party control, naturally. Previously, there had been only one candidate to 'choose from'. To make the system more 'representative', a separate list, with leading figures of the cultural, political, religious elites, was also incorporated into the electoral system (Ilonszki 1993).

The 1985 elections held on this basis led to some unexpected results. The number of new MPs became exceptionally high—63%—as opposed to the regular one-third turnover (exceeded only once in 1967 when it was due both to the 'individualization' of the electoral system and the gentle wind of reform preceding the introduction of the new economic mechanism in 1968; see Table 6.10). In 1985, many from among the 'no-name' MPs and even from the old guard were not re-elected, while a few independent MPs managed to get into the House, and parliament again became a focus of interest for the public. This was the first term when MPs publicly discussed political and policy alternatives, and where it was broadcast on television. This was also the first time when concrete questions regarding the functions of parliament were raised (e.g. its role in legislation and in executive scrutiny), and when the institutional requirements to fulfil these functions were put forward. Consequently, after by-elections in which new MPs were elected from openly opposing platforms, parliamentary party groups were officially formed and began to operate in 1988. Overall, it can be seen that democratic transition was not due to changes in the parliamentary elite but

Table 6.10. Parliamentary turnover

Beginning of the parliamentary term	Number of MPs	New MPs in %	
June 1949	402	213	53
July 1953	298	166	56
Nov. 1958	338	157	46
Mar. 1963	340	116	34
Apr. 1967	349	163	47
May 1971	352	118	34
July 1975	352	131	37
June 1980	352	124	35
June 1985	386	244	63

Source: Kukorelli (1988: 81).

rather that parliament was a partner in the transition. After all, although it was the last Communist parliament that enacted the fundamental laws which established systemic change, the majority of parliament had no other option and only a minority full-heartedly supported the transition.

7. 1990–1998: PROFESSIONALIZATION TRENDS IN THE NEW DEMOCRATIC PARLIAMENTS

In Hungary, the introduction of democratic parliamentary institutions in 1989–90 has often been compared to the introduction of modern parliamentary government in 1848–9 (Deák 1983). Although the outcomes are obviously different—parliamentary and democratic stability versus a quick return to the methods of absolute government—similarities are worth noting. In both cases, internal developments—closely related to international affairs—resulted in an elite compromise which concluded in the establishment of a new constitutional framework. Both frameworks were based on the notion that legislative power resides with the parliament elected by (a more or less limited group of) the people, and that executive power is embedded in the government, which is responsible to parliament. The most obvious similarity, however, is that in both cases, the new institutional setting was enacted by the 'old' parliament, that is, the parliament of the estates in 1848, and the last Communist parliament in 1989. Moreover, after both transformations, the new parliamentary elites were substantially different, although after the 1848 revolution a U-turn followed, while after 1989 we can see the first signs of professionalization trends among the parliamentary elite.

The two parliaments of 1990 and 1994 have been the only ones in the past 150 years that have established substantial and potentially long-term

Table 6.11. Division of seats in the first, second, and third democratic parliaments 1990–1998 No. and % of mandates

Party	1990		1994		1998	
	n	%	n	%	n	%
MDF	164	42.5	38	9.8	17	4.7
SZDSZ	92	23.8	69	17.8	24	6.2
FKGP	44	11.4	26	6.7	48	12.4
MSZP	33	8.5	209	54.1	134	34.7
Fidesz–MPP	21	5.4	20	5.1	147	38.1
KDNP	21	5.4	22	5.7	—	—
MIÉP	—	—	—	—	14	3.6
Other	10	2.8	2	0.5	1	0.2
Total	386	100.0	386	100.0	386	100.0

democratic changes concerning parliament, and which have also resulted in a trend towards professionalization. This is so despite the prevalence of high levels of discontinuity in the parliamentary membership. In the first democratic parliament, elected in 1990, only 7% of the MPs had previous parliamentary experience, and in 1994, due to the electoral landslide, the share of new members was again high (64%; see Table 6.11 for party strengths in the two parliaments). This is an interesting phenomenon, particularly in view of the elite pact between the Reform Communists and the new opposition forces, the smoothness of the transition, and the general environment of mature post-totalitarianism (Linz and Stepan 1996).

It seems that, despite the elite agreement, anti-Communist sentiments peaked and turned voters against the post-communist party at the first elections. The first elite group was substantially different from all previous elite groups: they represented intellectuals from the human sciences in large numbers and replaced the elite of the last Communist parliaments who had been leaders of large agricultural co-operatives, directors of big firms, engineers, and agricultural engineers (see Tables 6.12 and 6.13 for the social profile of MPs). In 1990, historians, sociologists, and poets ruled the scene. Many of them were, and wanted to remain, free intellectuals and thus decided to quit after the first legislative term, but another group decided to stay in politics and become professional politicians. Personal decisions of this type and voters' volatility equally explain the large turnover rate at the second democratic elections. Large groups in society seemingly lost the representation they 'enjoyed' in the Communist period, for example, women and those employed in agriculture. The share of women dropped from 21% in 1985 to 7.3% in 1990, while manual workers virtually disappeared from the parliamentary scene. The notion of representation as mirroring society was replaced by the legitimacy of parliament rooted in democratic elections and responsible government.

Table 6.12. Age and education of MPs 1990, 1994, 1998 (%)

Age and education	MDF			SZDSZ			FKGP			MSZP			Fidesz–MPP			KDNP			MIÉP			Total		
	1990	1994	1998	1990	1994	1998	1990	1994	1998	1990	1994	1998	1990	1994	1998	1990	1994	1998	1990	1994	1998	1990	1994	1998
Average age in years	44.7	49.6	46.8	42.4	45.4	47.5	58.6	56.4	50.8	52.0	45.3	48.5	27.8	35.2	41.3	54.7	54.1	—			52.9	46.0	46.5	46.1
Education																								
Elementary	0	0.6	0	0	0	0	4.9	7.7	2.1	6.1	0.5	0	0	0	0	4.8	0	—			0	1.6	0.8	0.3
Middle ed.	4.8	0	6.7	10.6	8.6	4.2	19.5	34.6	19.1	9.1	8.1	7.5	27.3	0	5.4	14.3	9.1	—			7.1	9.9	8.8	8.0
Higher ed.	94.5	100	93.3	89.4	91.4	95.8	75.6	57.7	78.1	84.8	91.4	92.5	72.7	100	94.3	81.6	91.0	—			92.9	88.5	90.4	91.7
Type of degree																								
Law	14.7	28.9	21.4	26.2	28.1	39.1	25.8	46.7	36.1	7.1	10.7	15.4	37.5	35.0	26.3	58.8	40.0	—			0	20.9	20.4	23.8
Humanities	41.9	42.1	21.4	46.4	46.9	39.1	29.0	26.7	19.4	67.9	41.4	40.7	56.3	45.0	30.5	23.5	15.0	—			61.5	43.1	40.5	34.6
Engineeing, natural sciences	14.9	28.9	57.1	27.4	25.0	21.7	45.2	26.7	44.4	25.0	48.4	43.9	6.3	20.0	41.2	17.6	45.0	—			38.5	36.0	39.1	41.6

Table 6.13. Professional background of MPs 1990, 1994, 1998 (%)

Professional background	MDF			SZDSZ			FKGP			MSZP			Fidesz–MPP			KDN			MIÉP			Total		
	1990	1994	1998	1990	1994	1998	1990	1994	1998	1990	1994	1998	1990	1994	1998	1990	1994	1998	1990	1994	1998	1990	1994	1998
Teachers, professors	21.8	18.4	0	16.0	14.3	4.2	2.0	4.0	9.3	12.1	13.5	8.5	18.2	15.0	11.0	4.8	18.2	—			21.4	16.1	13.8	9.4
Writers, journalists	3.6	0	0	1.1	1.4	0	1	0	0	6.1	1.9	0.8	4.5	5.0	0	9.5	4.5	—			0	3.6	1.8	0.3
Lawyers	7.3	13.2	14.3	12.7	12.9	12.5	3.0	12.0	9.3	0	4.3	3.1	0	0	7.4	14.3	13.6	—			7.1	7.5	7.4	6.6
Managers, businessmen	10.9	10.9	0	14.9	18.6	4.2	8.0	4.0	16.3	6.1	24.0	21.7	9.0	15.0	16.9	9.5	9.1	—			0	11.4	18.8	16.6
Politicians	0	5.3	42.9	0	4.3	70.8	1	12.0	23.3	21.2	16.3	35.7	4.5	35.0	27.9	0	9.1	—			21.4	2.5	13.3	33.2

If the stabilization of careers is still to be achieved, there are other characteristics which might reveal professionalization trends and the direction
of changes in parliament (see Table 6.14 for some relevant aspects). Differences among parties are particularly revealing. In the first electoral term,
MPs of the new parties had either limited or no background in local politics, but the same applied to the post-communists—not surprisingly since
members of the party hierarchy were nominated as candidates for elections.
At the second election, the picture is somewhat changed: parties consciously
sought candidates with local political experience. The Socialist Party has a
particularly large proportion of MPs with a background in local (town and
country) government. One can even draw conclusions about the failure (as
in the case of the MDF, the large governing party and the leading umbrella
organization of the transition) or success (as in the case of the FKGP, the
party of smallholders) of some parties in this respect. The variable 'leading
party position' suggests that in the first election some parties were forced
to place all their leaders in the parliamentary arena (as was the case of
Fidesz and of the KDNP), while in the second term there is a more balanced distribution between MPs with a party position and those without.
Government experience shows again the particularity of the Socialists, and
the seemingly more favourable position of the parliamentarians of the
MDF. The variable, 'parliamentary experience' provides information about
the different continuity patterns of individual parties. All these variables
taken together indicate that the majority of MPs in each party now have
had some kind of political background. Thus, Hungarian MPs would seem
to be on the way to becoming professional politicians, even if electoral
results might bring some surprises.

Institutional developments within parliament, and attitudes and the
behaviour of MPs, provide further evidence about the process of professionalization. The institutionalization of parliamentary party groups, committees, and the Standing Orders concerning the formation of MPs'
perceptions about their roles and the functions of parliament all confirm this
tendency, although this cannot be examined here in detail. MPs obviously
now want, and tend to adopt, a professional attitude to parliamentary work.

Differences between the two parliamentary terms also prove support for
the thesis of professionalization. In the first term, the member of parliament
as an individual was still the focus of attention, and parliamentary institutions worked accordingly. For example, individual MPs' motions dominated
the parliamentary timetable, MPs often changed parliamentary benches
and advocated their personal independence (a phenomenon that cannot be
separated of course from their intellectual background). In the second term,
one can see more efficiency- and expertise-oriented behaviour by MPs. Of
course, this is also related to growing party discipline and to the dependence
of MPs on their party (Ilonszki 1995).

Table 6.14. Some dimensions of professionalization of MPs 1990, 1994, 1998 (%)

Political experience	MDF			SZDSZ			FKGP			MSZP			Fidesz–MPP			KDNP			MIÉP			Total		
	1990	1994	1998	1990	1994	1998	1990	1994	1998	1990	1994	1998	1990	1994	1998	1990	1994	1998	1990	1994	1998	1990	1994	1998
(%) of new MPs*	95.2	31.6	52.9	97.9	22.9	12.5	100	73.1	64.6	81.8	81.8	15.7	100	30.0	77.0	100	50.0	—	—	—	64.3	93.5	61.1	47.9
Local politics background	10.5	7.9	41.2	5.6	11.4	8.3	5.6	23.1	25.0	0	35.3	9.7	0	10.0	50.7	0	27.3	—	—	—	14.3	4.6	27.5	29.0
Party position	68.4	39.5	29.4	88.9	32.9	45.8	94.4	42.3	18.8	58.6	15.3	9.7	100	35.0	18.9	100	42.5	—	—	—	42.9	77.5	27.5	18.7
Government position	0	36.8	0	0	0	41.7	0	0	0	20.7	0	11.2	0	0	0	0	2.7	—	—	—	0	4.6	6.4	6.5
Parliamentary experience*	4.8	68.4	35.3	2.1	75.7	83.3	0	26.9	33.3	20.7	15.3	83.6	0	70.0	18.9	0	36.4	—	—	—	7.1	5.2	36.3	47.4
No political position	78.7	7.9	23.5	62.8	14.3	0	61.4	26.9	39.6	36.4	43.5	12.7	40.9	20.0	28.4	42.9	13.6	—	—	—	35.7	64.4	30.6	22.5

Note: * New MPs are those who did not have a mandate at the end of the previous parliamentary term while those with parliamentary experience are incumbents. The two figures do not necessarily add up to 100% because there is a growing number of 'returners', that is, MPs who return to parliamentary benches after a shorter or longer pause. Sometimes the interval is long indeed, for example, one returned in 1998 who was a sitting MP in 1945–7. The share of returners in totals is 1.3% in 1990, 2.6% in 1994, and 4.7% in 1998.

As a preliminary statement, one can conclude that, although in personnel continuity uncertainties still prevail, among the sitting members professionalization trends are obvious. Institutional developments within the parliament provide the basis for these changes and trends, which will clearly continue in the process of stabilization. The past two democratic parliaments belonged to the 'most educated' parliaments in Europe and added to the members' high level of education has been political expertise, rooted in either local or parliamentary politics (particularly in the second term). It seems that those from the group of the 'transition elites' who remained in party and parliamentary politics decided that they would devote their prospective careers to politics. They could become the hard core of the first really professional and modern political elite in Hungary.

Appendix: Abbreviations

Fidez–MPP	Alliance of Young Democrats–Hungarian Civic Party
FKGP	Independent Smallholders Party
KDNP	Christian Democratic People's Party
MDF	Hungarian Democratic Forum
MIÉP	Party of Hungarian Justice and Life
MSZP	Hungarian Socialist Party
SZDSZ	Alliance of Free Democrats

References

Almanach 1990 (1994). Az 1990-ben Megválasztott országgyűlés Almanachja. Budapest: Magyar parlament.

Barta, Róbert (1995). 'Az Egységes Párt parlamenti képviselőinek társadalmi összetétele az 1920-as években' (Social background of the representatives of the Unity Party in the 1920s), in Tibor Valuch (ed.), *Hatalom és társadalom a XX. századi magyar történelemben*. Budapest: Osíris Kiadó, 407–18.

Beér, János (1949). 'Választási rendszerek a felszabadulás elötti Magyarországon' (Electoral systems in pre-war Hungary). *Jogtudományi Közlöny*, 9–10.

Birch, A. H. (1964*). Representative and Responsible Government: An Essay on the British Constitution*. London: George Allen and Unwin Ltd.

Cotta, Maurizio, and Verzichelli, Luca (1995). 'European Parliamentary Elites: Long-Term Patterns of Change in Comparative Perspective'. Bordeaux ECPR Joint Sessions.

Deák, István (1983). *Kossuth és a magyarok 1848-9-ben*. Budapest: Gondolat (1st pub. (1979). *Lawful Revolution: Louis Kossuth and the Hungarians, 1848–1849*. New York: Columbia University Press.

Feitl, István (1991). 'Az Ideiglenes Nemzetgyűlés létrejötte és jogalkotása' (The establishment of the Temporary National Assembly and its legislative activities), in, Hubai, László and Tombor, Lajos (eds.), *A magyar parlament 1944–1949*. Budapest: Gulliver, 7–44.

Földes, György, and Hubai, László (eds.) (1994). *Parlamenti képviselőválasztások 1920–1990* (Parliamentary Elections 1920–1990). Budapest: Politikatörténeti Alapítvány.

Higley, John, and Burton, Michael G. (1989). 'The Elite Variable in Democratic Transitions and Breakdowns'. *American Sociological Review*, 54/1: 15–28.

Hubai, László (1991). 'A parlament politikai és társadalmi összetétele' (Political and social division in the parliament), in Hubai, László and Tombor, Lajos (eds.), *A magyar parlament 1944–1949*. Budapest: Gulliver, 225–52.

——and Tombor, Lajos (eds.) (1991). *A magyar parlament 1944–1949*. Budapest: Gulliver.

Ilonszki, Gabriella (2000). 'Hungary: Crisis and Pseudo-Democratic Compromise', in D. Berg-Schlosser (ed.), *Conditions of Democracy in Europe 1919–1939*. London: Routledge, 242–62.

——(1993). 'Tradition and Innovation in the History of Parliamentary Government in Hungary'. *Journal of Theoretical Politics*, 5/2: 253–65.

——(1995). 'Institutionalisation and Professionalisation in the First Parliament', in Attila Ágh and Sándor Kurtán (eds.), *The First Parliament: Democratisation and Europeanisation in Hungary*. Budapest: Hungarian Centre for Democracy Studies, 191–201.

János, A. C. (1982). *The Politics of Backwardness in Hungary 1825–1945*. Princeton: Princeton University Press.

Kovács, Alajos (1925). *A magyar választójogi reformok számszerű hatása* (Numerical impact of Hungarian electoral reforms). Budapest.

Kukorelli, István (1988). *Így választottunk* (The way we voted). Budapest: ELTE.

Lakatos, Ernő (1942). *A magyar politikai vezetőréteg 1848–1918* (The Hungarian political elite 1848–1918). Budapest.

László, P. (1984). 'The Dualist Character of the 1867 Hungarian Settlement', in G. Ránki (ed.), *Hungarian History—World History*. Budapest: Akadémia, 86–165.

Linz, Juan, and Stepan, Alfred (1996). *Problems of Democratic Transition and Consolidation: Southern Europe, South America and Post-Communist Europe*. Baltimore: Johns Hopkins University Press.

Nagy, L. Zsuzsa (1983). *The Liberal Opposition in Hungary 1919–1945*. Budapest: Akadémia.

Riddell, Peter (1995). 'The Impact of the Rise of the Career Politician'. *The Journal of Legislative Studies*, 1/2: 186–91.

Rotschild, J. (1990). *East Central Europe between the Two World Wars*. Seattle: University of Washington Press.

Rudai, Rözs (1936). *Adalék a magyar képviselőház szociológiájához 1861–1935* (Notes to the sociology of the Hungarian parliament 1861–1935). Budapest.

Sipos, Péter, Stier, I., and Vida, I. (1967). 'Változások a kormánypárt parlamenti képviseletének összetételében 1931–1939' (Changes in the parliamentary representation of the government party 1931–1939). *Századok*, 2–4: 601–23.

7

Parliamentary Elite Transformations along the Discontinuous Road of Democratization: Italy 1861–1999

MAURIZIO COTTA, ALFIO MASTROPAOLO, AND LUCA VERZICHELLI

1. INTRODUCTION

The beginnings of Italian parliamentary history must be traced, as in a number of other European countries, to the fateful year of 1848, that is to say, thirteen years before the creation of the kingdom of Italy. In that year, the constitution granted by the King of Sardinia to the north-western regional states covering Piedmont, Savoy, Genoa, and the island of Sardinia established the first durable elected parliament on the Italian peninsula. In 1861, as a consequence of the process of Italian unification, which had been successfully engineered under the leadership of the Piedmontese state, this constitution and this Parliament became the constitution and parliament of the new Italian state and were extended in the following decades to the other regions as they were integrated. The *Statuto Albertino*, which was effective until the new republican constitution of 1948, provided for a bicameral parliament with an elected Chamber of Deputies and a Senate nominated by the King. In 1860, with the annexation of Lombardy, Emilia-Romagna, and Tuscany, the original Chamber of 204 deputies of the Piedmontese state was expanded to 387 members. In 1861 when Marche, Umbria, and Southern

Mastropaolo is particularly responsible for paragraphs one and two, Cotta for three, four and seven, Verzichelli for five and six and the preparation of the data. The data used for building the Italian data set were collected by the three authors from different sources. The collection of the data for the period before World War I was begun by Farneti (1971 and 1989) and completed by Mastropaolo. For the parliaments of 1919–24, data have been collected by Luca Verzichelli on the basis of official biographical sources (*Deputati al Parlamento. Biografie e Ritratti*). Data for the period after the World War II coming from the directories published at every new parliament (*Deputati e senatori del Parlamento repubblicano*, the so-called *Navicella*) were integrated with rounds of questionnaires repeatedly submitted to members of parliament by G. Sartori in the 1960s (Sartori 1963) and later by M. Cotta and L. Verzichelli. We wish here to thank all the Italian parliamentarians who have responded to our requests for information. Support for the creation of the data set was provided by the Italian National Research Council (Contract no. 97.00650.CT09) and by the University of Siena (local projects fund for 1997).

Italy were acquired, it expanded further to 443 (but at the same time the 30 constituencies of Savoy and Nice were lost to France), to 493 in 1866 when Veneto joined Italy, to 508 in 1870 when Rome was conquered, and finally to 535 in 1921 after the new expansion to the regions of Trento and Trieste following World War I. The Republican constitution of 1948, written by an elected Constituent Assembly of 556 members, then established a system of two chambers (*Camera dei Deputati* and *Senato*), both directly elected and with the same powers. Only limited aspects—age of voting and eligibility, size of the constituencies, and the absence of the preference vote in the Senate—differentiated the two chambers, since all the initial proposals aiming to create two really different chambers had finally failed to win a majority in the Constituent Assembly.

The two constitutions define the two main periods of Italian parliamentary history, but a more accurate periodization also needs to take some important changes in the electoral laws and the extensions of suffrage into account. From 1861 to 1919, the Italian electoral system followed that of the Piedmontese: a majority system with run-offs in single-member constituencies.[1] In 1919, the proportional list system with multimember constituencies (and preference vote) was reintroduced but was bound to last for only two elections (1919 and 1921). In the transition period between democracy and fascism a new electoral system was adopted with the deliberate purpose of stifling opposition to the new authoritarian rule; it was based on a national constituency and assigned two-thirds of the seats to the strongest list on the condition that it had reached at least 25% of the votes, while the remaining seats were distributed proportionally among the other lists. This system was used only once (1924) in what can be termed the last competitive election (albeit heavily distorted by significant use of violence) before the dictatorship. After the fall of fascism, the proportional representation (PR) system was reintroduced for both chambers and survived until the reform of 1993 when a mixed plurality and PR system (for 75% and 25% of the seats respectively) was adopted (D'Alimonte and Chiaramonte 1993).

The franchise was at first quite restricted. Only males over 25 years who were paying a substantial level of tax contribution or had special qualifications (such as a university degree, or that of being a state employee) had the right to vote. This enfranchised approximately 2% of the total population (about 7.5% of adult males; Ballini 1988: 54). By lowering the voting age to 21 and extending the franchise to all those who had completed primary education (independently of their income), the reform of 1882 increased the size of the electorate to about 7% of the population or 28% of adult males. In 1912, the great extension of suffrage occurred (Ballini 1988: 158) to include

---

[1] A proportional list system with multi-member constituencies was adopted only for the three elections of 1882, 1886, and 1890.

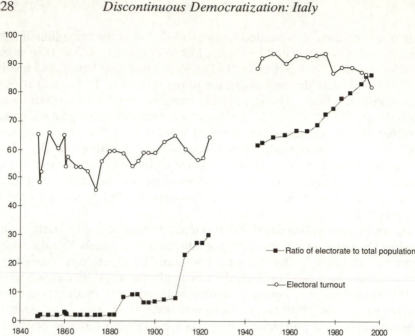

Graph 7.1. Turnout rates and share of voters in Italy 1848–1998

almost all adult males, that is, those of 21 years and over.[2] In addition the first limited allowances for members of parliaments were introduced at this time. In 1919, the remaining limitations to universal male suffrage were abolished, but the proposal to grant the vote to women was not carried until 1946. In 1946, voting was also made compulsory, which had a significant impact on turnout rates (Graph 7.1). Concerning eligibility, 30 was the minimum age required until 1946 when it was lowered to 25 for the Chamber of Deputies. Positions in the civil service, as well as ecclesiastical offices, were incompatible with a parliamentary seat.

Combining constitutional and electoral elements, we have thus four main periods:

1. the period of restricted suffrage and, except for a short interruption, of a majoritarian electoral system (1861–1912);
2. the period of universal male suffrage (and low turnout) with changing electoral systems (1913–1924);
3. the period of universal male and female suffrage (and high turnout) under a PR electoral system (1946–1993)—commonly referred to now as the First Republic;

---

[2] Only limited exceptions survived: for instance, for illiterates who had not done military service, the right to vote was set at 30 years of age.

4. from 1994 onwards—as for period 3—but with a predominantly plurality system.

From a more political point of view, we can add that the formal organization of parties only begins at the end of the nineteenth century. Before this time, parliament had been divided mainly between Right (*Destra storica*) and Left (*Sinistra storica*).[3] These parliamentary groupings, which strictly speaking do not qualify as true parties, had lost much of their meaning by the end of the 1870s and the *trasformismo* (this word was coined to indicate the increasing proximity between the two sides) of the 1880s more or less put an end to this cleavage, giving the hegemony over parliamentary life to a broad 'liberal area', with internal factions but without a clear party structure. This began to emerge within the 'extreme left' of republicans and (after 1882) socialists, but it was only after the elections of 1919 that parliament can be said to have been predominantly structured along party lines with formally recognized parliamentary groups.

2. PARLIAMENTARY ELITES IN THE EARLY STAGES OF LIMITED DEMOCRACY

Although the *Statuto Albertino* had opted for a 'constitutional monarchy' rather than a fully parliamentary form of government, the responsibility of the cabinet *vis-à-vis* parliament was already established in the kingdom of Sardinia. The alliance of monarchy and parliament in promoting the unification process reinforced the parliamentary character of the new Italian state from its very beginning, so that it was not merely a symbolic act that Victor Emanuel II was given the title of King of Italy by parliament. While the King maintained a significant influence in the fields of external affairs and defence and in the nomination of the ministers responsible for these domains, for some time, parliament became the effective centre of political life so that the parliamentary class gained a dominant role in the process of state- and nation-building. It is not the case that Gaetano Mosca developed his theories of the political class—which in spite of their universalistic ambitions had as their starting-point the new parliamentary elites—from his observations of the Italian situation (Mosca 1884). The central role of parliamentary elites in Italy was also linked to the fact that the new Italian state could not count upon a strong and common aristocratic or military or bureaucratic elite (in that each of the former regional

---

[3] According to the coding rules of this project, both groups of MPs need to be coded as *Right Liberals*. However, because of the importance of the historical distinction between *Destra* and *Sinistra storica*, we have maintained two separate trends in the figures until the first decade of the twentieth century (from 1919 onwards, the trace line for Right Liberals will summarize the two groups). Thus, we have coded the Radicals and Republicans as *Left Liberals* at this time.

states had its own elites) and even the authority of the monarchy was far from unchallenged. In addition, the Piedmontese state, in spite of its crucial role in promoting the unification process, was too small for effective domination of the new Italian polity. Parliament, on the other hand, provided an institutional arena where regional elites could become progressively unified. Although not completely disassociated from geographical cleavages (the Right being stronger in the North and the Left in the South), it was the need to sustain the cabinet, and the political division between Right (the government) and Left (the democratic opposition) which dominated political life in the first two decades of the new state that played the major role in pushing political elites beyond regional borders and promoting larger aggregations.

As could be expected, given the severely limited franchise, the Italian parliament was dominated from its beginning by the *notabili*—something which did not change significantly until the aftermath of World War I and the subsequent political transformations. However, before the new set-up could become consolidated, the crisis of the democratic regime rapidly unravelled (Farneti 1978). A widely accepted interpretation is that the traditional liberal elite of the notables was not capable of adapting to the conditions of mass politics which rather abruptly came into being. According to a well-known paradox of the twentieth century, it was the antidemocratic elites who proved much more adaptable to the era of mass democracy, thereby gaining control of the democratization process, only to destroy it.

Given the very limited extension of the franchise, there are good reasons to expect that the social profile of the parliaments that inaugurated the political history of a unified Italy should be highly skewed when compared to the total population. At the same time, we might expect a high level of correspondence between the (few) electors and the elected. On the basis of franchise criteria, we can assume that the voters were at this time landowners, rentiers, free professionals, professors and teachers, civil servants, officers, businessmen, tradesmen, and the richest stratum of artisans. And, with few exceptions, they would be literate. If we look at the profile of the first representative elites of the new state, to a great extent we do indeed find these categories. Yet, even under these special conditions, the members of parliament cannot be seen as a faithful statistical facsimile of the enfranchised society. There are social groups which are clearly overrepresented and others that are indeed rather weaker.

Given that these early parliamentary institutions had been granted by the monarchy rather than won against it, it is to be expected that, in the first years at least (before the mobilization of the oppositions could take off), elites linked to the monarchy and the traditional leading social stratum would have a disproportionate weight in the parliament. The fact that about a third of the deputies in the first parliaments can be ascribed to the nobility

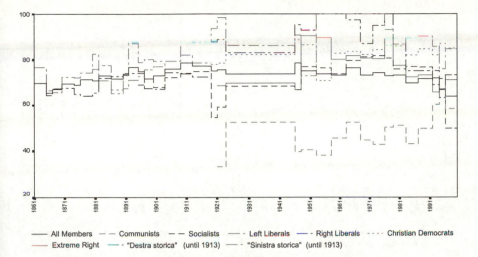

Fig. 7.1. Italy 1861–1999: university degree

Note: In all Figures, the trend lines during the Fascist interruption of the democratic regime (1925–1943) indicate the levels of each variable after the last free election.

(Fig. 7.7) and that at least a fifth were representatives of the primary sector (which under those franchise conditions meant being a landowner; Fig. 7.9), confirms this expectation.

Yet the importance of this group does not amount to a clear predominance of the traditional sociopolitical 'establishment'. About a half of the members of the first parliaments had a background in the free professions, among whom lawyers were absolutely dominant (45–50% and 35–40% respectively) (Fig. 7.11). Even in the context of limited suffrage, the specific resources of the lawyers—their clientele, the ability to solve problems and to fight for interests, the flexibility of their job—plus the social prestige that they typically enjoyed at the local level, proved to be a match for the resources of more traditional elites in the competition for electoral support.

The next significant group of representatives was made up of those with a 'state background'. The categories from the public sector (especially teachers, officers, judges, and other civil servants) accounted for about a quarter of the members of parliament (Fig. 7.13). On the contrary, business representatives, entrepreneurs, and journalists were only a tiny proportion of the Chamber of Deputies.

The analysis of educational levels can be brought in to complete this picture: 70% of the deputies had a university degree (Fig. 7.1) and in seven out of ten cases this meant a degree in law (Fig. 7.2).

The original profile of the parliamentary elite we have briefly sketched

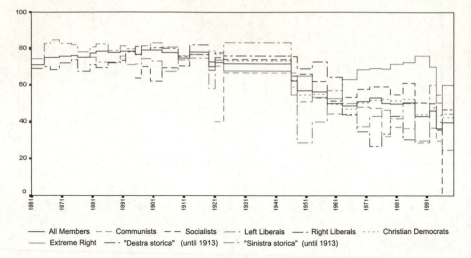

Fig. 7.2. Italy 1861–1999: law degree

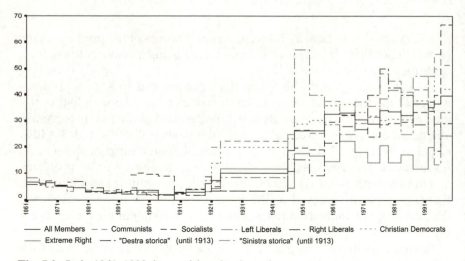

Fig. 7.3. Italy 1861–1999: humanities, theology degree

proved fairly stable in the following years. This again should not come as a surprise given the institutional success of the new parliament and the slow pace of transformations prevailing until World War I. In fact, no serious institutional disruption of the electoral–parliamentary process took place until that event and the overall turnover rates remained law, oscillating between 20% and 35% and declining throughout the nineteenth century

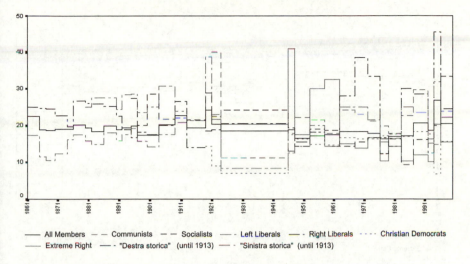

Fig. 7.4. Italy 1861–1999: engineering, sciences, medicine degree

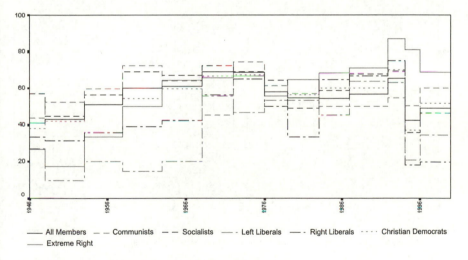

Fig. 7.5. Italy 1946–1999: local politics background

(Fig. 7.22). During the same period, the mean age of deputies rose slowly for the whole period (Fig. 7.20). All in all, within the narrow boundaries of an elitist democracy, the process of institutional entrenchment of the representative elite was on its way.

The most evident change during this period was the slow but sure decline of the nobility. Deputies with a nobility title remained a significant group

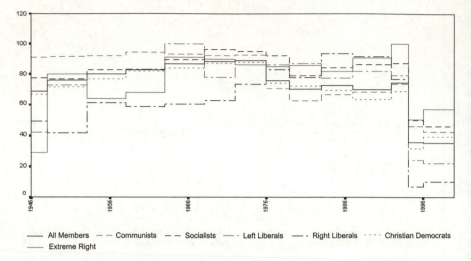

Fig. 7.6. Italy 1946–1990: leading party position

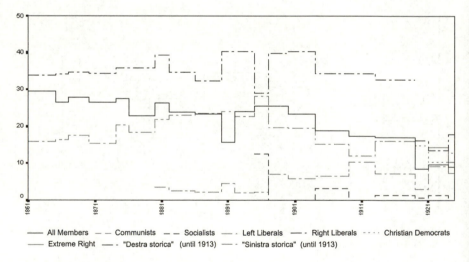

Fig. 7.7. Italy 1861–1924: nobility

throughout the whole period, but by the time of World War I they accounted
for only 18% and were clearly a minority. A similar trend can be detected
for deputies with a background in the primary sector. Interestingly enough,
a steady decline can also be seen for a third important group, that of MPs
with a background in the public sector: between 1861 and 1900 the size of
this group was almost halved (from 26.6% in 1861 to 14.7% in 1897). This

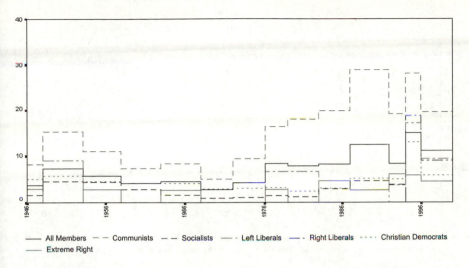

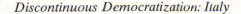

Fig. 7.8. Italy 1946–1999: female legislators

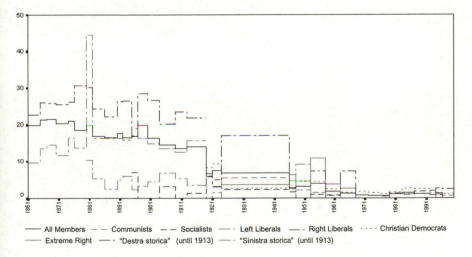

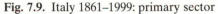

Fig. 7.9. Italy 1861–1999: primary sector

decline touched more or less all its subcategories, but it was particularly striking for military officers who, having started as one of the more signific-ant groups, had practically disappeared by the turn of the century. This, however, is not so surprising: as the glorious memories of independence wars faded into the past, so did the symbolic appeal of the officers. The decline, however, even if less dramatic, also touched all the other groups,

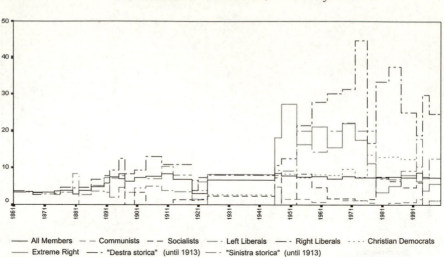

Fig. 7.10. Italy 1861–1999: managers, businessmen

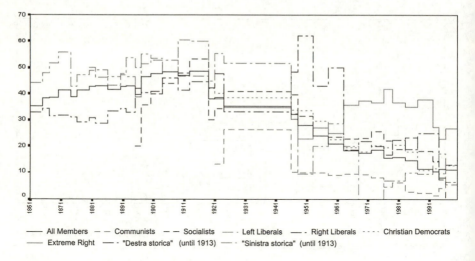

Fig. 7.11. Italy 1861–1999: practising lawyers

such as teachers, judges, and high civil servants (Figs. 7.14–7.16). We can perhaps interpret this as an indication that bureaucracy was challenged in its ability to perform the representative function by a new political class that had its roots more in civil society, and that the process of political mobilization made society (or at least its enfranchised strata) less dependent on the tutelage of the bureaucratic state.

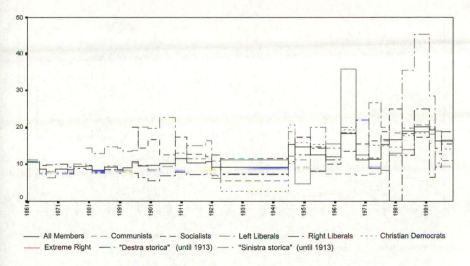

Fig. 7.12. Italy 1861–1999: professions other than the law

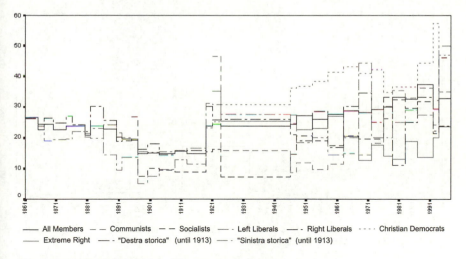

Fig. 7.13. Italy 1861–1999: public sector employees

Which groups gained from the decline of the traditional upper classes and of the 'state class'? We can find, especially from the 1880s onwards, some growth in the number of managers and businessmen who entered parliament. This tendency to some extent matches the country's industrial take-off during this period (Romeo 1972). Yet this category never won great prominence in Italy. Rather, the group that most clearly gained during this

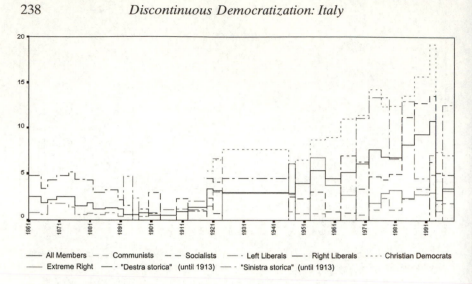

Fig. 7.14. Italy 1861–1999: higher civil servants

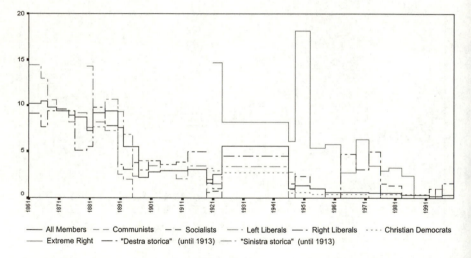

Fig. 7.15. Italy 1861–1999: military persons

period was that of lawyers, and by the beginning of the new century nearly half of the chamber was made up of deputies with some background in this profession (Fig. 7.11). In a parallel trend, university education (in most cases a law degree) showed constant growth (Fig. 7.1).

It is not difficult to interpret the picture offered by this first group of data. The different elements converge in suggesting the emergence of what we

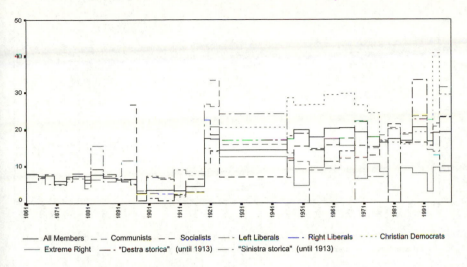

Fig. 7.16. Italy 1861–1999: teachers and professors

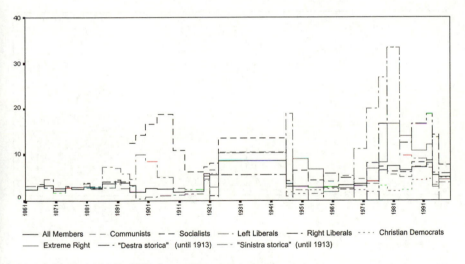

Fig. 7.17. Italy 1861–1999: journalists and writers

might call a 'proto-professional' parliamentary elite, the backbone of which were lawyers. These were educated people who were able to deal with other people and with their conflicting interests and who asserted their political authority through repeated elections, that is to say, through the ability to win and re-win 'popular' support. In Burkean language, they were the typical trustees. Next to them there was a substantial but declining group

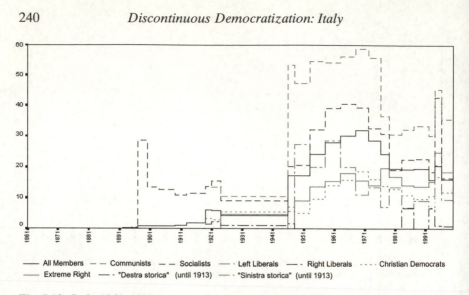

Fig. 7.18. Italy 1861–1999: party and pressure group officials

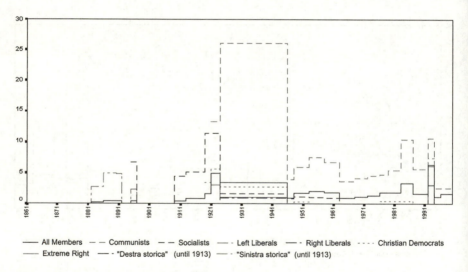

Fig. 7.19. Italy 1861–1999: blue-collar workers

of politicians who could count upon sources of authority that were more independent from the electoral process (a nobility title, land-ownership, linkages with the state or industry) and who in some way expressed older or newer forms of corporatist representation by peers.

We must now look at the internal articulation of the political elite. As we have said, the main distinction during this period was that between Right

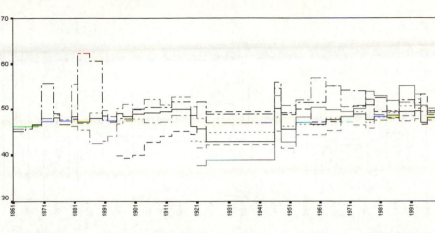

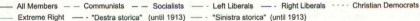

Fig. 7.20. Italy 1861–1999: mean age

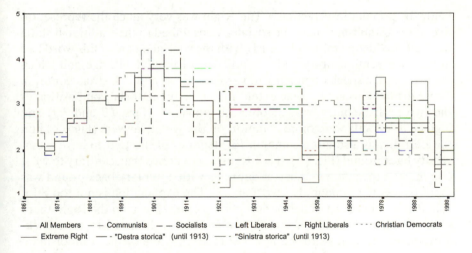

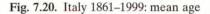

Fig. 7.21. Italy 1861–1999: mean number of elections

(*Destia storica*) and Left (*Siuistra storica*). This division between the two wings had to do with a mix of attitudes towards the monarchy (the Right being staunchly royalist and the Left originally more republican) and towards the process of unification (the Right having supported a more prudent process of expansion led by the Piedmontese dynasty, while the Left had put their hopes in a more 'revolutionary' process pushed from

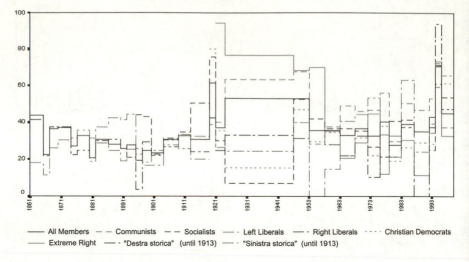

Fig. 7.22. Italy 1861–1999: newcomers

below by popular insurrections). The Right was very much the representative of the establishment, of the social groups linked to the traditional state;
the Left was 'democratic' (obviously with the special meaning this word had
in the nineteenth century under conditions of limited suffrage and which
did not entail a special sympathy towards peasants and industrial workers).
These distinctions are to some extent matched by the social composition of
the two parliamentary wings. Nobles, landowners[4] (Figs. 7.7 and 7.9) and
high civil servants were more common on the Right; lawyers (Fig. 7.11) on
the Left. It was also more common for deputies of the Left to have a university background (Fig. 7.1). It is interesting to notice that, contrary to what
one might expect, the number of deputies with a military background was
more or less the same in the two 'parties'. The explanation is not too difficult; there were in fact in this period two types of officer: on the Right there
were the career officers of the old state, often with an aristocratic background; on the Left were the new voluntary officers of the wars of independence with a middle-class background and democratic sympathies.
Another difference is that the Right typically had a more urban outlook,
while the Left was more rural and provincial. An analysis of the size of the
place of birth of deputies supports this view (Farneti 1989).

Differences between the profiles of the two political groupings were to
some extent blurred because of the partial overlapping of the political and
geographical cleavage. In the South, because of the unhappiness of the

---

[4] This figure is surely underestimated because it is highly probable that other deputies, who
were coded as officers, lawyers, etc., were also and often primarily landowners.

liberal elites of these regions with the process of unification dominated by the Piedmontese monarchy, the Left was relatively stronger, which meant that it recruited a good number of the more progressive aristocrats and landowners of those regions into its ranks. In the North, where the Right was stronger, and being an area of greater economic development, a number of politicians with a background in the free professions were recruited. Yet, on the whole, the Left remained more middle class than the Right.

The parliamentary and then the electoral victory of 1876 brought the Left to power and in a few years the political differences between the two fronts declined. The so-called *trasformismo* made the borderline between government and opposition often uncertain and the crucial division became increasingly one between the extreme Left (radicals, republicans, and then socialists) and the rest of parliament (Cotta 1992: 148–53). That said, the differences that we have noted in the personal characteristics of the deputies were little changed.

Geographical differences warrant a closer look. The existence of significant economic, social, and cultural differences between the North, Centre, and South of Italy is well known; but to these we must also add the important political differences linked to the specific histories of the regional states and to the style of political life that had developed within their borders. The profile of the members of parliament indeed shows significant variations along geographical lines: in the more advanced North, lawyers were more frequent as were entrepreneurs, managers, and engineers. In addition, since the new state 'came from the North', there were also more high-ranking civil servants. In the Centre and South, landowners were initially more frequent but with the passing of time the number of lawyers grew significantly.

3. FROM ELITE TO MASS REPRESENTATION: THE FAILURE OF THE FIRST ATTEMPT

The partial extension of the franchise in 1882, which went along with a temporary change of the electoral system, did not produce any dramatic alteration in the trends we have described. Indeed, none of the variables discussed shows an extraordinary 'jump' in the elections of this period, indicating that the political system was able to absorb a shock which in any case was a limited one. In addition, data about parliamentary turnover show that the 'normal' pace of renewal was not significantly affected by those changes.

We must wait for the last years of the nineteenth century and the first decade of the twentieth century to see a more substantial transformation in the political landscape. The extreme Left made up of Radicals, Republicans, and, since 1892, Socialists, started to grow (it rose from a 12% share of the seats in the elections of 1895 to about 20% in 1904 and 1909; Ballini 1988: 125) and with it increased the number of deputies linked to relatively more well-defined party organizations. Of the new groups, the Radicals were characterized by the strong importance of the free professions—first of all lawyers (Fig. 7.11), but also doctors, who embodied the progressive positivist culture of the natural sciences—and teachers and journalists (Figs. 7.4, 7.12, and 7.17). Journalists won an even bigger share among the Socialist ranks, where their number reached about a third of the parliamentary group. Most of them were indeed professional politicians in a sense that comes very near to the contemporary one. The absence of blue-collar workers among Socialist deputies was conspicuous.

In 1913, the first elections after the introduction of what can be termed (in spite of some persisting exceptions) male universal suffrage produced an acceleration in the transformation of political equilibria but what happened was far from an earthquake. This is clearly shown by the percentage of newcomers which, at about 30%, was almost the same as in previous elections (Fig. 7.22). The traditional elite was thus able to retain a large majority in the elective chamber despite the substantial progress made by the parties of what used to be called the Extreme Left (Radicals, Republicans, and Socialists).[5] With 169 deputies, they reached approximately a third of the Chamber of Deputies. Some workers made their first entrance in the parliament in the Socialist ranks; yet even the party of the working classes was still predominantly represented in parliament by deputies with a middle-class background (Farneti 1989), of which lawyers were by far the largest occupational group. The difficult relationship of the Socialist Party with the state is well evidenced by the smaller number of public employees in its ranks than in those of any other party. Only the subcategory of teachers was near to the percentages that could be found in the traditional political establishment.[6]

It was with the elections in 1919 that change became much more substantial: universal suffrage coupled with a new electoral system (PR with multimember districts), the founding of the new Catholic party, the *Partito popolare* (PPI), and the political consequences of World War I combined to produce a turnover in the parliamentary class which was twice as high as

---

[5] The main explanation for the lack of a greater political transformation was that the traditional political elite was able, on that occasion, to win through an explicit pact (the so-called '*Patto Gentiloni*') the support of Catholic voters by capitalizing on their fear of a Socialist victory. However, that support had no stable basis and was not to be available again in future elections (Cotta 1992: 157–8).

[6] At the moment of the formation of a large Socialist group in parliament (1919), the proportion of MPs with a public sector background stood at 15.6%. Within the Catholic party, the rate was 23.2% and higher than 30% among the liberal groups.

in the previous three elections. Not surprisingly, some more significant changes in the features of MPs began to emerge. A very substantial change in the age of deputies can be noticed. Thanks to the influx of the two 'new parties', the mean age dropped by four to five years reaching the lowest levels since 1861 (Fig. 7.20). But in the elections of 1924, the Fascist triumph was bound to produce a new record.

The next point to be underlined is the decline of the traditional upper classes, which is well exemplified by the substantial decrease of the nobility and also of the landowners. Significantly enough this phenomenon was not compensated for, as it had been to some extent in the past, by an increase in the newer upper classes (businessmen, managers, and professionals; Fig. 7.10); in fact, their share declined or, at most, remained constant. The next important feature is that the legal profession, which had become the dominant background of the parliamentary class in the age of limited suffrage, suffered a very clear setback for the first time, marking the beginning of a steady decline that continued throughout the century (Fig. 7.11). For blue-collar workers, journalists, party and trade union officials, as well as public employees, a significant rise can be detected (Cotta 1979; Mastropaolo 1990, 1993). Notably from among the public sector employees, teachers were the group most clearly on the rise (Fig. 7.16). The first professional groups mentioned suggest the rise of a new form of political professionalization, linked to the growing party organizations. Workers and journalists (and obviously full-time politicians) who entered parliament were typically individuals involved in the organizational life of the parties or of trade unions which had strong links with them (Figs. 7.17 and 7.18). Probably many teachers were also representatives of an 'intellectual class' which were often at the forefront of local party organizations.

The transformation of the old parliamentary class of notables was, however, far from complete in the elections of 1919 and 1921. A clear evaluation of this fact can be derived from the analysis of members of parliament along party and regional lines. With regard to party differences, we can easily draw a line between old parties and parties of the 'new type'—that is, the Socialists (and from 1921, also the Communists) and the Christian Democrats of the Popular Party (PPI). The great parliamentary renewal of 1919 was primarily due to the parties of the second group, for which the percentages of newcomers were particularly high (Cotta 1983). Among the Liberals of different orientations, the renewal rate, even if greater than in the past, was much lower than for the former (about 42% against 82%). This means that, while in the old parties the continuity of the political elite was more or less preserved, after the war, the other parties brought a fundamentally new and inexperienced elite into parliament (Fig. 7.22). If we look at the background of parliamentarians, the most significant changes from the traditional model can be found among Socialist parliamentarians. The number of MPs with a university degree was lower compared to the rest of parliament but also when compared to the Socialist Party before the war. Blue-collar workers did not cease being a minority but became a somewhat more significant group. Full-time politicians also had some weight in this party. On the contrary, the MPs of the PPI were much less different *vis-à-vis* their liberal colleagues, except for their links with the Catholic Church and its organizations, and for their younger age.

Regional differences, linked as they were to party differences, also became significant. The old parties had retained their influence in Southern Italy, while the new parties had won their greatest successes in the North and Centre. Thus, because of the stronger political differentiation between the two parts of Italy, the historical difference between politicians of the South and those of the rest of Italy increased.

4. THE RISE OF THE PARTY PROFESSIONALS AFTER WORLD WAR II

4.1. The Making of a New Political Elite after the Regime Discontinuity

The failure of liberal elites to adapt to the conditions of universal franchise in the crucial years between 1912 and 1922 contributed to making a controlled incorporation of the parties representing the newly enfranchised groups within a mutually accepted framework of mass democracy impossible. As a result of this failure, the transformation of parliamentarians from notables to party professionals (a crucial step in the building of mass democracies) did not succeed. This opened the way to a completely different restructuring of political elites under an authoritarian leadership and according to a non-democratic project. From our point of view, an important consequence of the democratic breakdown (the main result of this failure) was the interruption of elite continuity: the parliamentary elites of the first democracy were to a great extent displaced.

The destructive action of the non-democratic regime was manifold. On one side, there was repressive action against the leaders of the leftist parties: the means adopted were in a few cases severe physical injuries and even assassination, more commonly jail or exile. *Vis-à-vis* Catholic politicians or Liberal opponents, Fascist repression was generally less severe provided that there was a readiness on behalf of the politicians to retire to private life. Co-option into the new fascist elite was the instrument adopted for another important section of the old parliamentary elites and had played an important role in the semi-competitive elections of 1924. These elections were fought with a new electoral system which encouraged broad coalitions. Mussolini promoted a National List which made the Fascist component somewhat less visible and more palatable to moderate and conservative voters. A significant number of the members of the Liberal parliamentary groups were offered (and accepted) the chance to survive politically by providing support to the rising Fascist regime. Their survival, however, was on a strictly individual basis and not as an organized group. This meant that their weight in the new regime was bound to be limited. Moreover, their political honour was damaged and the possibility for many of them to make a come-back after the fall of fascism was seriously weakened.

One should add that the interruption of democratic life for almost twenty years also interrupted the regular process of recruitment of young politicians capable of replacing the old ones. This effect was particularly serious in the case of the political groups that lacked a true extra-parliamentary organization (as was the case with the Left and Right Liberals). Parties with a stronger organizational mould (such as the Communist Party) could to some extent preserve at least a limited continuity, either in exile or in clandestinity, and thus recruit some younger politicians into their ranks even during the non-democratic period (or especially during the transition to democracy). A similar effect also occurred for the Christian Democratic Party, which was to be the successor of the Popular Party; it could count for its recruitment upon religious organizations which, because of their non-political character, had a better chance of survival under the authoritarian regime (Moro 1979).

Given the differential impact of the non-democratic regime upon the old parliamentary elites, we should expect significant variations across the political spectrum at the time of the rebuilding of a democratic elite after the fall of fascism. Age profiles and the political experience of the parliamentarians of the newly established regime should reflect the impact of the factors mentioned above. More specifically, one would expect that, with the liberalization of political life, those parties which had managed to preserve some vestige of their older organization or had been able to restore a new organization more quickly, would be able to produce a more balanced elite where survivors of the past would be matched with a greater number of younger recruits. The opposite would happen with those parties that, because of their weaker organization, had been more affected by the regime interruption. They would prove less successful in recruiting new politicians, and they would have to rely more heavily on those among the older politicians who had managed to survive from pre-Fascist democracy.

This is, in fact, what can be seen with the first representative assembly elected after the fall of fascism, that is, the Constituent Assembly. Age profiles and pre-fascist parliamentary background of the members indeed

Table 7.1. Continuity and renewal among members of the Constituent Assembly 1946–1948 (%)

Members	PCI	DC	Right[a]	PSI	All
Born before 1899	42	51	66	74	57
With a parliamentary background in pre-fascist legislature	6	14	32	24	15

Note: [a] The Right includes Liberals, Monarchists, and other minor parties.
Source: Cotta (1979).

show significant differences across the parties (Table 7.1). The parties of the Right, and the Socialist Party (which had been seriously weakened by internal splits), had a much higher proportion of older MPs and a smaller proportion of young recruits than the Communist Party (PCI) and the Christian Democratic Party (DC). In a similar fashion, the percentage of MPs with a parliamentary background dating back to the pre-Fascist democracy was higher in the Socialist Party and in the parties of the Right than in the PCI and DC.

Thus, rather than a Left/Right difference, what we find is a difference linked to the ability of the parties to counteract the negative effects of the non-democratic interruption upon elite recruitment. The Communist Party and Christian Democrats, because of their organizational resources, were better placed from this point of view compared to the Socialist Party and to the small parties of the Right (the heirs of the pre-fascist Liberals).

4.2. The Consolidation of the New Parliamentary Elites

With the third round of elections taking place in 1953,[7] the stabilization of the new parliamentary class becomes increasingly evident. If we use the percentage of newcomers[8] as a gross measure of stabilization, it is quite clear that, starting with 1953, renewal rates had gone down again to a 'normal' level, that is, to one which can be compared to that of the years before the earthquake of World War I. At each election, a large majority of MPs were re-elected so that, until the crisis of the 1990s, fluctuations in renewal rates remained fairly limited (see Fig. 7.22). This suggests that the recruitment process had acquired a relatively stable pattern. We would therefore expect that the qualitative features of the parliamentary elites would also change only gradually.

As soon as we adopt a breakdown of the data by party, however, this

[7] The elections of 1946 for the Constitutent Assembly are counted here as the first election of postwar democracy.
[8] It should be remembered that turnover rates are the combined effect of different inter-party and intra-party factors.

global picture requires some important qualifications. There are in fact significant differences in the renewal rates of the three largest parties. Differences between the largest opposition party (the PCI) and the largest governing party (DC) were especially clear during the whole period from 1963 until 1992. With the only exception of the election of 1979, the rate of newcomers in the DC parliamentary group was substantially lower than that of the PCI (differences oscillate between 15 and 27 percentage points). As for the Socialist Party (PSI), it shows a profile of parliamentary renewal that is (except for the elections of 1979) remarkably more similar to that of the DC than of the PCI.

An inspection of these data suggests that the Left/Right dimension is not the best predictor of differences in parliamentary turnover. The PSI, one of the two main parties of the Left, shows greater similarity to the DC than to the other party of the left. We are left, therefore, with two other possible explanatory factors: (1) the governing or opposition role of the parties; (2) the organizational model. Both factors suggest the need to explore the incentives to seek re-election that are available for members of parliament. In a situation with a 'permanent' division of the governing and opposition roles, the incentives to prolong their stay in parliament in parliament should be greater for those members of parliament belonging to the parties that have a chance to participate in the allocation of cabinet positions than for those belonging to parties that are excluded from them. But the incentives to stay in parliament could also vary significantly in connection with different organizational models of parties. Where the party has a weaker extra-parliamentary organization, the incentives to prolong the parliamentary career are greater because no alternative (paid) political position is available. On the contrary, if a strong extra-parliamentary organization exists, members of parliament can also find a satisfactory position outside the legislature. Incentives are just one aspect of the question. The allocation of the authority to select the candidates for re-election is another. Different power structures within parties may increase or decrease the possibility of ensuring a higher turnover. The more concentrated the power, the more it is feasible to impose a higher turnover; the more dispersed the power, the greater the odds in favour of the incumbents. Since during the period under examination both Christian Democracy and the Socialist Party belonged to the permanent governing parties, and since both had a weaker extra-parliamentary organization when compared to the PCI, we are in a situation of uncertainty regarding the choice of the explanatory factor. In order to provide a satisfactory answer to this question, it would be useful to explore a wider section of political elites, including party leaders who are not members of parliament, and to analyse the concrete mechanisms of candidate selection in some detail (Cotta 1979; Di Palma and Cotta 1986; Wertman 1988).

   After having documented the stabilization of the parliamentary personnel, it is time to look at its qualitative profile. To what extent have the post-
fascist members of parliament changed (*vis-à-vis* their pre-fascist
predecessors) and to what extent has their profile evolved during the forty
years of continuous development under the First Republic?

   As we have seen, the democratic transformation of the years after World
War I produced a divided parliament. More or less two-thirds of the total
membership had fundamentally kept the features of the old parliamentary
notables for whom social and professional qualifications provided the
crucial resources for sustaining a political career; on the contrary, about a
third had begun to be affected by the transformations connected with the
age of organized parties. These differences had probably played a significant part in the difficulties encountered by Italian democracy during the
postwar years: for instance, building coalitions between parties of the old
and the new type proved far from easy. Given the post-World War II development of organized parties in all sectors of the political spectrum, we
should expect a significant transformation in the background of members
of parliament and a substantial increase in the level of political professionalization based on the organizational resources provided by the parties.
At the same time, the data concerning renewal rates, which show substantial cross-party differences in the degree of parliamentary entrenchment of
the new political elites, provide some reasons for expecting significant variations in the qualitative profiles of MPs of different parties.

   Social prestige and professional achievement, which were crucial
resources for the building of a political career in the age of the *notabili,*
should give way to different resources in the age of organized parties.
Among our variables, education and professional background are the first
indicators to be considered for assessing to what extent this process has
taken place. Data about university education do not show major variations
over the years. The number of MPs with a university degree was high
throughout the period examined (Fig. 7.1). However, it has been generally
a bit lower than it was in the parliaments of the early twentieth century
before fascism and we can detect a weak downward trend. If one adds the
fact that the social 'weight' of a university degree has decreased with the
progressive broadening of access to universities, we can already derive from
this variable some (limited) signs of the decreasing weight of a 'strong'
social background as a resource for political careers.

   Even more significant is the change in the type of university education.
The dominance of law degrees has increasingly given way to a much
broader mix. Humanities and social sciences have grown spectacularly so
that by the 1980s they are almost equal to the share of those with a background in law (Fig. 7.3). If we consider the fact that such degrees generally
do not entail a very strong professional element, we probably have another

sign of the diminished importance of university education in political careers.

But university education is still a relatively 'light' indicator of social prestige and professional achievement. To substantiate this finding, we must turn to the occupational background of MPs and see what has happened to the groups which had a greater weight in the past. Starting from the most traditional category, that of landowners (more than a 'profession', this was a 'social condition'), the data indicate that this group, which had already suffered a serious setback in the elections after World War I, virtually disappears from the republican parliament. Even more significant are variations in the weight of the free professions. In the parliament of 1919, nearly half of the MPs still had such a background (38.3% lawyers and 11% other free professionals). After World War II, their number was already lower and between 1946 and the 1970s their aggregate weight had nearly halved (Fig. 7.11). This transformation is essentially due to the dramatic decline of the legal profession which ceased to be a major recruiting ground for a parliamentary career. Variations were less significant for other types of 'high' professional or social backgrounds; for instance, the percentage of managers and businessmen did not show any real change in spite of the tremendous economic growth of postwar Italy. The low global weight of this category remained more or less the same as in the first years of the century.

Which occupational groups profited then during this period from the decline of the free professions? Two phenomena deserve to be mentioned here. The first one is the steady rise of the whole group of public sector employees, according to a trend that had already started with the first legislatures after World War I. Teachers at different levels are the largest component of this professional group, but higher civil servants seem to be the subcategory with the highest rate of growth (Figs. 7.13, 7.14, and 7.16). The second is the dramatic growth of full-time professional politicians and trade unionists (Fig. 7.18). Among the 'non-phenomena', we must underline the extremely limited share of members of parliament with a background as a blue-collar or agricultural worker or of those with a small business background of some kind (shopkeeper, craftsman, and so on).

A joint reading of these figures provides a preliminary but at the same time sufficiently clear and consistent picture of the transformation that took place during the post-fascist Republic. The importance for the building of political careers of a personal and independently based social prestige, which was linked in the past mainly with the autonomous professions (or, though decreasingly so, with land ownership) has declined significantly. The rise of less 'rich' occupational backgrounds (in terms of social prestige), and of more strictly political professions, suggests that other resources have increasingly taken the place of social prestige in the recruitment of

Table 7.2. Class background of MPs' family (%)

Class	Parliaments						
	1946	1948	1953	1958	1963	1968	1972
Upper class	9	6	6	5	4	3	3
Upper middle class	42	39	36	33	34	28	29
Lower middle class	33	36	38	39	42	42	42
Working class	13	13	14	16	15	19	19
Peasant	3	6	5	7	6	7	7

Source: Cotta (1979).

parliamentarians. The finding is in accordance with what could be expected given the strongly enhanced role of organized parties in the political life of Italy after World War II. In an earlier study, an attempt was made to evaluate the social background of MPs' families more precisely (Cotta 1979: 139). On the basis of the occupation and level of education of MPs' fathers, the analysis covering the years from 1946 to 1972 provided the results shown in Table 7.2.

We can easily see a very steady decline in the share of MPs with an upper- or upper-middle-class background (which, taken together, at the beginning of this period accounted for more than the majority of the MPs), and a rise in MPs from less privileged social backgrounds. Those with lower-middle-class backgrounds had reached a dominant share in the 1960s and there was also a significant rise of members from a working-class background. In a graphical representation of social background, the inverted pyramid has given way to a lozenge-shaped distribution.[9]

The other aspect of this process of change should emerge from a more detailed analysis of the political dimension of the recruitment and careers of parliamentarians, and the substitution of social prestige with political (party) professionalization should become apparent from the variables that are more specifically linked to this dimension. This is indeed the case. The increased importance of a party background is easily and consistently documented throughout the 1970s by a number of different variables.

The first variable that can be used is party affiliation. Data until the 1970s indicate that almost all the parliamentarians were formally affiliated to their party prior to their first election to parliament. The number of 'independ-

[9] A footnote must be added to this analysis. The data about working-class background seem inconsistent: they represent a significant percentage when we analyse family background, but a very small one when we look into the personal history of MPs. Apart from the phenomenon of upward intergenerational mobility, which surely plays some role here, the explanation must be found in the category of professional politicians and trade unionists. In this group, a good number of MPs with a working-class background are included.

Table 7.3. Percentage of newly elected MPs affiliated to their party before the age of 25

Party	Parliaments						
	1946	1948	1953	1958	1963	1968	1972
PCI	83	79	69	65	91	82	85
PSI	74	57	33	72	62	70	73
DC	33	32	40	43	75	77	88
All MPs	50	50	40	53	76	73	80

Source: Cotta (1979).

ents' was extremely low (2–4%) and for an increasingly large number of parliamentarians, party affiliation had occurred at a young age (Table 7.3). Yet, in order to substantiate the importance of party background, the simple affiliation to a party does not reveal very much. Rather, it is more helpful to use indicators of active involvement in the organizational life of parties, such as the offices held at different levels of party organization. If one counts all leadership positions from the local to the national level, a very large majority of MPs have, in fact, had such political experience before coming into parliament and until the 1970s, there is very clear growth of this variable (Figs. 7.5, 7.6).

In order to evaluate more precisely the meaning of this experience, both as a factor of socialization and as a resource, the level of party offices attained before entering into parliament would seem to be a good indicator for this purpose. The higher the party office, the greater should be the time spent in participating in party life, as should be the political resources thereby accumulated that can be used for building a parliamentary career. Our data show, in fact, that for a substantial number of MPs, a party career did not simply mean an obscure party office but rather some important and often national position. The picture can be completed by adding that this was the result, in most of the cases, of an elaborate career within the party organization, starting at a young age with low-level offices and then developing through the years until reaching the higher level (Cotta 1979). The increasing substitution of independent social prestige by a party career is thus a plausible interpretation of the transformation starting after World War II and developing until the 1970s.

In any case, a party career was not the only aspect of the political background of MPs. Elective positions at the local level—in municipalities, provinces, and regions—have become with the passing of time more and more common for a great majority of deputies. So much so, that by the 1970s, about three-quarters of the parliamentarians had had such an experience before entering into parliament (Fig. 7.5).

4.3. Party Variations within a Common Trend?

We have already seen that data about parliamentary renewal suggest that the recruitment of Italian deputies was affected by constraints and incentives which varied significantly from party to party. However, it is also necessary to examine the extent to which the social and political background of MPs also varied along party lines.

The first question to be answered concerns the degree to which social prestige and professional achievement were substituted by political professionalization. For reasons of simplicity, we will concentrate our attention upon the three largest parties (DC, PCI, and Socialists) leaving aside the smaller parties of the centre—Social Democrats (PSDI), Republicans (PRI), and Liberals (PLI)—and of the extreme right and left. It is immediately clear from many indicators that the differences in the social background of parliamentarians of these parties were substantial. The number of Communist MPs with a university education was significantly lower that that of the Christian Democratic MPs throughout the whole period of the First Republic (Cotta and Verzichelli 1996). And the opposite was true for the proportion of MPs with only a basic education. The gap between the two parties declined slightly over time, but only very slowly. Since it is plausible to assume an association between lower levels of education and a lower social background, these data suggest rather clearly that MPs with a working-class background must have been a rather more substantial group in the Communist Party than in the DC. The analysis of the social status of the parents of MPs gave, in fact, a corresponding picture (Cotta 1979: 142–3). During the 1946–76 period, a working-class family background could be found among between 30% to 40% of the Communist MPs, against only approximately 10% of Christian Democrats. With regard to the Christian Democratic party, however, it is noticeable that the frequency of an upper-class or upper-middle-class family background has declined significantly with time. While the two groups added together were at first larger than any other, their place was soon taken by parliamentarians coming from lower-middle-class families. Social status as a resource in political careers had obviously also lost importance for the DC.

When we look at the Socialist Party, findings are also contrary to our expectations. Education levels and family status consistently show a much greater similarity of Socialist MPs to Christian Democratic rather than to Communist MPs. As we had found with turnover rates, the dividing line was not between Left and Right, and these data suggest that the organizational variable must have been the crucial one. The Socialist Party, because of a weak organizational structure, could not effectively recruit representatives from the lower classes but rather had to rely upon individuals who, thanks to their higher status, had stronger personal resources.

The data concerning the occupational background of parliamentarians show important differences between the three parties but also some similarities in the developmental trends. The legal profession is a case in point. The number of lawyers was significantly higher at the beginning of the period examined among Christian Democratic and Socialist MPs than among Communist MPs. But the decline over the years of this professional group, while affecting all the parties, was particularly significant in the two where the weight of this profession had been stronger. The profiles of the three main parties have thus become somewhat more similar (Fig. 7.11). The same can be said of the weight of professional politicians: the very clear advantage the Communist Party enjoyed at the beginning of this period declined somewhat thanks to a growth of the proportion of professional politicians in the Socialist Party and in the Christian Democratic Party (Fig. 7.18).

We can now add to the social variables the ones pertaining to the party career and, as might be expected, the degree of partyness was generally higher among parliamentarians of the Communist Party than among those of the other two parties. Many indicators consistently confirm this picture. Higher numbers of Communist MPs had held a party office of some type in their career; and typically their affiliation to the party had taken place at a young age (Table 7.3): the same can be said for the first party office (Cotta 1979: 175–6). Finally, their party career had developed more frequently through the full range of levels: from the offices at the bottom to those at the top. In the DC, and also in the PSI, affiliation to the party took place at a more advanced age, and the proportion of MPs without a party office in their c.v. was higher than among their Communist colleagues; moreover, those who had held a party office had done so at an older age.

However, if we look at these variables from a developmental perspective, differences among the parties tend to lose some of their strength over time. All indicators show a growing degree of partyness for the Christian Democrats (and generally also for the Socialists) who tended to become more and more similar from this point of view to their colleagues of the opposition party. By the 1970s, the number of Christian Democratic and Socialist MPs who had held a party office before their first parliamentary election was more or less the same as for the Communist MPs (Fig. 7.6). This also holds for precocity in party affiliation (Table 7.3).

Summing up, we can say that, with the 1970s, the process of standardization of recruitment along a party-centred model had probably reached its highest point. The wave had started from the (Communist) left but had increasingly touched the other parties and undoubtedly the Christian Democractic Party. Duverger's (1976; orig. 1951) model of 'the contagion from the Left' for the interpretation of this period, fits quite well with our data. The challenge coming from the highly developed organization of the main opposition party has been accepted and the leading party of government has followed along the same lines. To say, however, that this has produced a fully homogeneous parliamentary elite would be going too far. In spite of the significant similarities that have developed with time, some differences between political groups have not disappeared, two aspects of which deserve to be stressed here. The first concerns social and occupational background; the second some features of political careers. With regard to the first aspect, we must stress that, in spite of all changes, the number of MPs with a higher social status and professional background retained a significantly more substantial size in the DC and in the PSI than in the Communist group. This suggests that in the two governing parties there were a larger number of MPs who individually 'owned' social resources that could be used for their political career. The second aspect concerns turnover and its variations across parties. The data we discussed earlier indicate the existence of differences in what we may call the 'institutional entrenchment' of the politicians. For the two governing parties, the weight of parliamentary incumbency has been significantly greater than for the main opposition party. From our data (Cotta and Verzichelli 1996), it is clear that this was not the effect of a greater ability of their candidates, compared to those of the opposition, to succeed at elections; quite the contrary: in opposition most incumbent Communist candidates were re-elected. The crucial factor was candidacy. More Socialist and Christian Democratic than Communist incumbents (were allowed to? were willing to?) run for re-election, so that consequently, a larger number were returned to parliament (Table 7.4). This

Table 7.4. Percentage of the incumbents of the outgoing parliament running at each new election

Party	Parliaments											
	1953	1958	1963	1968	1972	1976	1979	1983	1987	1992	1994	1996
DC	82.0	83.0	89.3	84.9	86.5	78.4	79.5	85.8	92.1	83.8	37.7	
PPI												79.3
PCI	88.3	77.9	69.8	64.0	60.1	62.6	70.1	52.6	58.1	50.7		
PDS											63.0	80.4
PSI	82.1	85.9	81.4	79.1	96.0	78.7	52.4	81.3	95.0	84.3	24.8	
FI												71.4
LN											74.6	59.3
AN												84.0
All MPs	83.3	82.8	82.8	76.2	80.0	74.3	68.4	76.1	79.7	65.9	49.8	73.9

Source: Cotta (1979) and data collected by L. Verzichelli.

situation suggests that a greater number of Socialist and Christian Democratic parliamentarians probably had relatively more autonomous control
of electoral resources and were less strictly dependent on the party as such.
This helps to explain the difficulty experienced by the governing parties
in enforcing a strong discipline in the law-making process among their
parliamentarians.

The data concerning the two different aspects point in the same direction. They suggest the need to differentiate within the common model of
the party professional at least two sub-models (Cotta 1979: 197–206;
Panebianco 1988). The first model is what we might call the 'party organ-
ization-centred party professional'. In this case, the centre of political
activity is predominantly the extra-parliamentary party organization and
it is within that realm that the most important political resources are
distributed and have to be won by politicians. Other arenas of career
are less relevant. The second model is what we might call the 'electorally
oriented party professional'. In this case, the resources provided by a career
in the party apparatus are still very important but probably somewhat less
dominant. Politicians also play their career game with the help of other
resources that can be used in the electoral competition (which in their
cases is not completely controlled by the party apparatus). Frequent
re-elections contribute significantly to accruing the weight of such
parliamentarians.

4.4. Something Changes in the 1980s?

With regard to the aspects of recruitment discussed so far, we can now raise
the question of whether something had already begun to change in the
1980s (i.e. before the crisis of the early 1990s, which will be discussed in the
next paragraph). Some data indeed seem to suggest a positive answer to
this question. Indicators, such as the number of full-time party politicians
and the proportion of MPs with experience in party offices, show some
decline in the degree of partyness (Figs. 7.6 and 7.18). In particular, this
seems to affect the Communist Party more substantially. We may ask then
whether this reduction in the role of the party organization is compensated
for by some other element. The growth of a public sector background could
perhaps be an answer: here the state bureaucracy, thanks to an increased
party penetration, can be used as a substitute for party organization.

The data available seem to confirm this interpretation. Between the end
of the 1970s and the end of the 1980s, there is a very substantial increase
of parliamentarians with a public sector background (Fig. 7.13). This picture
becomes even clearer if we look at inter-party variations. As expected, the
DC—the permanent (and dominant) party in government—had always
recruited heavily from the public sector (more than a third of its MPs)

whereas the two Left parties had, on the contrary, been much weaker in this respect. The case of the PCI is easily explained by its permanent role in opposition while the PSI, starting in the 1960s, had become a quasi-permanent government party (although it was only a junior partner in the cabinets and its ability to gain an influence in the state apparatus was smaller that that of the DC). The growth of this variable in both parties, but particularly in the PCI, in the 1970s is striking. In fact, during these years, the quasi-monopoly of influence of the DC in public administration gave way to a much more pluralistic pattern of party penetration, from which both parties of the Left could profit. It is understandable that this new situation would appear also in the profile of the representative elite.

This growing *étatisme* of the political class is quite in line with the observations made by some recent studies concerning the transformation of European parties (Katz and Mair 1995). In the Italian case, however, as will be shown later in this chapter, this process will not go unchallenged. With the crisis of the 1990s, a reaction of 'civil society' against the traditional party politics defied that breed of politicians with some success. On the whole, however, one could say that the 1980s were years of incremental adjustments of the elite profile, but that the fundamental patterns of parliamentary recruitment remained unchanged (Verzichelli 1998). Till the beginning of the 1990s, the *ceto politico* was mainly composed of party-trained professional politicians whose careers before election to parliament had developed through party offices and local elective positions (Mastropaolo 1993).

5. OTHER ASPECTS

Two aspects, so far left out of this analysis of parliamentary elites after World War II, deserve specific discussion: gender representation and regional variations.

5.1. Gender

The enfranchisement of women had been discussed at some length in parliament for the first time in 1912 at the time of the universalization of male suffrage, but its adoption was postponed to a 'later stage' (Ballini 1988: 159). After World War I, new bills were introduced for this purpose, but a final agreement could not be reached before the fascist take-over and women had to wait the fall of the authoritarian regime to win the right to vote. Even then, for a long time, the vote of women has brought very few women into the Italian parliament and this can be rightly considered one of the most extreme cases of 'sociological distance' between voters and representatives (Fig. 7.8). Within this general picture, which has begun to change slowly only at the end of the 1970s, some minor variations need to be noted. First, the election which, before the more recent changes, sent the highest number of women into parliament was that of 1948. Secondly, the Communist Party has typically elected slightly more female legislators than any other party; here too 1948 represents a peak, followed by a decline. Only in the 1970s does a substantial change begin to take place; from that point, the Communist Party substantially increased its recruitment of women, thus becoming the strongest vehicle of their global growth in parliament.

A few comments can be suggested by these data. The first is that the party which initially profited most from the vote of women—that is to say, the DC—did not have to include in its lists many female candidates in order to win their electoral support. Quite obviously, the mechanisms of representation that have been at work here were different from those of 'sociological representation'. The main opposition party, on the contrary, has probably felt a somewhat greater need to use this instrument in order to overcome its electoral disadvantage among women. The second is that the very competitive election of 1948[10] induced the two major parties to make an extra effort in order to win the vote of women. Once the great battle was over and it was clear where the majority of women's votes would go, the parties lost interest in recruiting women into parliament. Only in the 1970s, with the beginning of the process of female mobilization, did the main opposition party make an attempt to ride on top of this new wave by giving more space to the recruitment of women. The other parties followed, but at some distance. Two factors probably concurred to explain inter-party differences. The first is that, in the Christian Democratic and Socialist Party, the much fiercer internal competition for a position in the electoral lists and then for the preference votes made the recruitment of women legislators much more difficult than in a party such as the PCI where the centre had greater control over the recruiting process and could implement more easily a 'new policy' of openings for women. The second is that the more militant women groups and their leaders tended to choose the opposition party as their political partner. The PCI could therefore count upon a greater supply of potential female politicians than the other parties.

5.2. Regional Variations

The persistence of important political differences between the different parts of Italy throughout the First Republic is a well-known fact. This has

---

[10] These elections were fought head on by two irreconcilable fronts (the Left under the banners of the Popular Front, the Centre and Right under the leadership of the DC) and during the campaign forecasts about the results had been extremely uncertain.

meant first of all that the electoral strength of parties has displayed substantial territorial variations; but also that the style of political life, the level
of electoral participation, and the quality of party organizations have varied
significantly between North, Centre, and South (Cartocci 1990).[11] It would
naturally be surprising if this phenomenon did not have some effect upon
the recruitment of political elites.

As expected, when comparing parliamentarians elected in the three parts
of Italy, we find significant differences in many aspects of their social
and political profile. A number of indicators suggest that in the South the
weight of social prestige has kept a bigger role, even during the age of party
professionalization. Deputies elected in southern regions have more frequently had a university education (and in some cases also an academic
career) than their colleagues of the North and Centre, and a larger proportion of them also have a lawyer's background. Differences between
North and Centre concerning these aspects have been minor. In the South,
a position in the public sector has also been a rather more important
resource than in the North and Centre. The other side of the picture is
offered by a direct measure of political professionalization. Greater
numbers of MPs coming from a paid party or trade union job have represented the North and the Centre than the South. However, here we find
also a North–Centre difference, whereby deputies of Central Italy very
clearly lead in this field.

In spite of some oscillations these differences have been fairly constant
over the years, suggesting that recruiting patterns must have been anchored
to stable variations in the structure of the political market existing among
Italian regions. The main difference seems to be the one between the South
on the one hand and the North and Centre on the other. Yet some differences also exist between the latter areas, suggesting the existence of two
sub-types within that recruitment pattern. But to what extent are such differences really due to a regional effect or rather to a party effect? Since we
know that the electoral and parliamentary strength of parties is not the
same throughout Italy, and that there are important differences in their
recruiting models, the question arises whether differences between Southern Italy and the rest of the country or between North and Centre are due
to the direct impact of specific regional variables or, on the contrary, to
variations in the weight of parties (which adopt different models in the
recruitment of parliamentarians).

In order to answer this question, we need to control for the party vari-

[11] There is among Italian political sociologists a lively debate about the most appropriate
way of defining the parts of Italy. For the sake of simplicity, we have adopted here the traditional division into North (Piedmont, Aosta Valley, Lombardy, Liguria, Veneto, Trentino-Alto
Adige; Friuli-Venezia Giulia), Centre (Emilia-Romagna, Tuscany, Marche, Umbria, and Lazio)
and South (all the other regions).

able, which can be done by analysing differences between parliamentarians of the three areas within each party group. Starting with the DC, the most national of the big parties, it is easily noticeable that the North/South variation is well reproduced within its parliamentary group. The North/ South difference in the proportion of university trained (and also of academic) MPs is practically the same as for the whole parliament. The same can be said for the background as a lawyer or in the public sector. The picture is a bit more blurred when we look at the Centre. For some variables, the Centre appears more similar to the South (university education and, until the end of the 1960s, public sector); for other variables, the Centre is more similar to the North (percentage of lawyers). The explanatory hypothesis could be that where the party is weaker, as in the Centre, its recruiting patterns become less distinctive and acquire some of the features of the South.

If we look at the PCI, we find more or less the same differences between South and Centre and North, yet such differences generally decline from the 1970s onwards. It would seem that after some time (required for the build up of its organization?), the Communist Party has became capable of reproducing a more homogeneous recruiting model than the DC, which on the contrary seems more dependent on (or more adaptable to) regional variations (Table 7.5).

Summing up briefly, we can say that the often-mentioned predominance in the politics of Southern Italy of personalized exchanges versus more impersonal organizational structures is confirmed by our data. In order to become a member of parliament, personal resources were relatively more important compared to collective resources in a constituency of southern Italy than in other parts of Italy. The main opposition party was able to counteract, at least in part, this territorial conditioning. More difficult to understand is whether such ability, probably linked at least in part to its more coherent organizational structure, was not also due to the relatively marginal role of the party in that area of Italy. Being smaller, was it easier for the PCI to avoid environmental influences?

6. THE 1990S: THE (TEMPORARY?) FALL OF THE PARTY PROFESSIONALS

At the beginning of the 1990s, after forty years of prevailing continuity, a combination of long- and short-term factors have brought about an unprecedented transformation of the Italian political system. Without attempting here a detailed discussion of this event (McCharty 1995; Morlino 1996; Cotta and Isernia 1996; Mastropaolo 1996), we must mention at least four crucial phenomena that developed between the end of the

Discontinuous Democratization: Italy

Table 7.5. Territorial differences in some of the characteristics of MPs*

a. University background (%)

Party	1948	1953	1958	1963	1968	1972	1976	1979	1983	1987
DC	22.3	21.9	28.0	22.9	28.1	21.3	17.8	13.4	18.6	12.3
PCI	26.8	50.3	21.7	44.2	36.5	19.3	4.3	6.0	13.1	16.3
All MPs	21.5	17.7	24.5	16.3	21.9	15.6	6.9	8.7	10.2	12.5

b. Lawyers (%)

Party	1948	1953	1958	1963	1968	1972	1976	1979	1983	1987
DC	9.8	11.2	19.7	19.7	19.6	16.0	17.8	20.8	16.1	13.1
PCI	6.9	9.7	11.9	8.8	−4.4	1.4	5.2	8.7	0.5	2.5
All MPs	14.6	10.0	17.0	15.7	12.6	13.0	11.3	15.4	14.1	11.8

c. Public sector (%)

Party	1948	1953	1958	1963	1968	1972	1976	1979	1983	1987
DC	10.1	10.9	8.5	8.9	8.8	4.8	−2.7	−7.4	−1.9	1
PCI	11.5	10.9	7.0	10.6	12.0	15.7	0.4	−7.8	−8.9	2.3
All MPs	5.5	9.3	6.8	6.4	7.3	7.8	2.5	−4.3	1	7.3

d. Paid politicians (%)

Party	1948	1953	1958	1963	1968	1972	1976	1979	1983	1987
DC	−5.7	−7.2	−10.6	−9.1	−9.0	−4.0	0.3	5.3	7.9	2.3
PCI	19.6	−4.3	1.8	−14.1	7.4	4.7	7.6	14.9	7.5	−8.5
All MPs	−3.7	−6.1	−6.7	−6.6	−6.5	−3.2	1.2	3.1	0.7	−2.8

Notes: * The data in these tables are the differences between the percentages calculated for the two sub-groups of MPs of each party elected in the Southern regions (Abruzzo, Molise, Campania, Puglia, Basilicata, Calabria, Sicilia, Sardegna) and Northern regions (Valle d'Aosta, Piemonte, Lombardia, Trentino Alto Adige, Veneto, Friuli-Venezia Giulia) of Italy. In the case of the PCI differences were calculated between Southern and Centre regions (Emilia-Romagna, Tuscany, Umbria, Marche, Lazio) because they are more significant. A positive sign means that the percentage of the South is higher than that of the North or Centre; a negative sign the opposite.

Source: CUBE.

1980s and the beginning of the 1990s, and which contributed significantly to that transformation and have had significant implications for political recruitment. The first is the birth of the Venetian and Lombard Leagues (later fused and renamed the Northern League) and their spectacular growth, beginning with the regional elections of 1990[12] in the northern part of the country. The second is the transformation of the traditional Communist Party, which was renamed the Democratic Party of the Left in 1991,

[12] The Lombard League reached in 1990 4.8% of the whole national electorate, but it became the second party in Lombardy (19.9%). In 1992, the national share of the Northern League was around 6%, and in 1994 it increased to 8.6%.

and from which the die-hards split, creating the Communist Refoundation Party. The third is the popular movement in favour of a majoritarian democracy, which promoted two successful referenda (in 1991 and 1993), thus leading to a deep change in the electoral system (from a PR system based on multimember constituencies to a predominantly plurality system with single-member constituencies; D'Alimonte and Chiaramonte 1993). The fourth is the 'clean hands' judicial campaign against political corruption, which between 1992 and 1993 put a large proportion of the politicians of the governing parties on trial.[13] Closely paralleled by the crisis of the party system, which had started to emerge in the elections of 1992 and became fully evident in 1994, there is an unprecedented rate of parliamentary renewal: the percentage of newcomers, already relatively high in 1992 by Italian standards (about 40%), reaches the extraordinary level of 70% in 1994 and falls somewhat back (but still to a rather high level of 50%) in 1996 (Fig. 7.22).

What is the impact of this dramatic break of continuity upon the features of parliamentary elites? The elections of 1992 did not produce any very significant changes. If we leave aside the exception of the Northern League, the reliance upon the traditional system of political recruitment based on the strong role of party experience is for the other parties still fundamentally unshattered. In fact, some of the new parties (such as Communist Refoundation) also reproduce rather than change the old pattern. Far more significant are the transformations brought about by the elections of 1994 which coincide with a dramatic crisis of the traditional governing parties (DC, PSI, PSDI, PRI, and PLI) and with the success of new parties (*Lega* and *Forza Italia*) or of old parties that have managed through a restyling of their identity to overcome their traditional marginality (as in the case of the MSI turned into National Alliance).

If we look at the general picture, we can find some clear indicators of a 'political deprofessionalization' of the parliamentary elite: mean age (Fig. 7.20) and mean number of elections (Fig. 7.21) are down.[14] Elective experience at the local level (Fig. 7.5) and party offices before the first election to parliament (Fig. 7.6) also show a very substantial decline compared to previous periods. In addition, as previously mentioned, the public sector is reduced to a more limited role. On the other hand, there are signs of a stronger weight of independent resources mainly linked to the private sector of the economy: leaders of small businesses, managers, entrepreneurs,

---

[13] Only one year after the election of 1992, judiciary proceedings were initiated against more than 50% of all MPs and the percentage was even higher among MPs from the governmental majority and members of the cabinet (Ricolfi 1993).

[14] The rate of seniority (mean number of re-elections) decreases from an average of approximately 2.5 terms, attained after 1968, to 1.5 in 1994 and to 2.0 in 1996. A discussion of the dynamic of the renewal of MPs in the nineties can be found in Lanza (1995) and Verzichelli (1998).

and free professionals all gain a greater share in parliament. The overall picture, however, conceals greater inter-party variations than in the past, with the dividing line running more or less between the 'old' parties (PRC, PDS, PPI, AN) and the new 'challengers', that is, the Northern League and Berlusconi's *Forza Italia* (Cotta and Verzichelli 1996). As could be expected, given the larger number of incumbents they have managed to re-elect, the old parties (or their successors in case of splits or 'face-lifts') have brought a political elite into parliament that is not so different from the past. The challengers, on the contrary, are characterized by a much more substantial degree of innovation. The representatives of these parties show a very low degree of political professionalization and strong links with the productive sectors of society. But important differences are also to be found between them (Verzichelli 1995). In particular, it is easy to notice that parliamentarians of the Northern League frequently had experience as 'grass-roots party activists' in the new movement since its recent beginning. With regard to their professional background, they typically come from the middle class of the rich northern regions. Free professions (other than that of law) on the one hand, trade and small businesses on the other are the two most common recruiting grounds for the *Leghisti*. These occupational groups taken together constitute 50% of this parliamentary group. Another distinguishing feature of the League is the younger age of those elected: five years below the parliamentary mean. With few exceptions, the deputies of *Forza Italia* cannot count upon a political experience in their own party, first, because the party itself was born just a few months before the elections, secondly, because it has only a very ephemeral structure. Typically, they come from a somewhat higher social milieu than their colleagues of the *Lega*. Managers and entrepreneurs from the private (Fig. 7.10) sector are taken together (with more than 32% of the total) the largest professional group. This level, which is absolutely unprecedented in the whole of Italian history for a large party, reveals a lot about the transformations in relations between politics and the economy that have taken place during the last few years. The free professions are (with 25%) the next important group for the new party of the centre-right (Fig. 7.12). None of the other parties equals the *Lega* and *Forza Italia* in their specific recruiting domains. Only the National Alliance displays a partial similarity because of the strong weight of the free professions, but even so, its parliamentarians come much more frequently from a long political career inside the old neo-fascist party (Verzichelli 1995; Lanza 1995).[15]

[15] The mean tenure for all the MPs of *Alleanza Nazionale* is relatively low (1.4 terms) because of the great expansion of the parliamentary group; but if we take into account only the incumbents, the mean goes up to 2.6. The value for the main post-Communist Party (PDS) is 1.8 (2.1 for the incumbents) and for the PPI 1.9 (2.1).

The instability of political alliances after the earthquake of 1994 (Caciagli and Kertzer 1996) leads us rapidly to a new election which is fought by two large coalitions of centre-left and centre-right plus the League which prefers to run alone (Di Virgilio 1998). The election of 1996 has been interpreted as a partial step towards the consolidation of the new party system (Cartocci 1996) and the same can be said with regard to the parliamentary elite. Turnover was significantly reduced compared to 1994, yet the level still remains higher than that of the elections of the first republic. Part of this phenomenon is due to the relatively high proportion (26%) of incumbents that (voluntarily or not) drop out of the electoral race. The rate of dropouts is strongest in the new parties (*Lega* and *Forza Italia*) and lowest in the older ones (PDS and AN; Verzichelli 1998), indicating that the consolidation of the new elites is taking place at different speeds.

With regard to the profiles of different party groups, the results of 1996 basically confirm those of 1994. The strongest level of political professionalization can be found inside the two successor parties of the PCI, followed by the National Alliance. The weight of the public sector is highest among the deputies of the two 'post-Christian Democratic parties' (notwithstanding their location in the two opposite coalitions), immediately followed by the 'post-communist' representatives, while *Forza Italia* and the League confirm themselves as the parties of the private sector. Age and education differences are also fairly stable: the League is again by far the youngest party and, together with Communist Refoundation, the one with the lowest level of university education.

If we analyse in some detail the political backgrounds of parliamentarians, the data for 1994 indicate a visible decrease of local elective experience and, even more so, of party experience. Understandably, it was the brand new party of Silvio Berlusconi that showed the greatest lack of political experience both at the party level and in local elective offices. The old parties were at the other extreme of the continuum, yet, even among their ranks, the number of experienced politicians had generally declined compared to the past. The election of 1996 corrected this trend somewhat, bringing back into parliament a larger number of politicians with some background in party organization or in the elective bodies of municipalities, provinces, and regions. Even if the average is still significantly lower than in the age of *partitocrazia*, the decline of political professionalization seems to have stopped. After the great crisis, we sense the beginning of a rebuilding of 'political careers', but this does not erase the significant differences existing among party groups. *Forza Italia* in particular, where the weight of *homines novi* without political experience is predominant, persists in being markedly different from the other parties. However, the deputies of the League, at least from this point of view, have become rather similar to those of the other parties. In addition, the number of those who, before the first election to parliament, had gone through another success- ful electoral experience at the local level has increased substantially.

In every sector of the political spectrum, the effort to select candidates from 'civil society' in order to fill the vacuum created by the crisis of the 1990s and to face the strong anti-party feelings of the voters (Morlino and Tarchi 1996) is still evident, although the countervailing force of incum- bency is beginning to make itself felt (see Table 7.3). Somewhat paradox- ically, rather than helping to consolidate the party system, this may create some problems for relatively weak external party organizations that have limited control over electorally entrenched members of parliament (Bartolini and D'Alimonte 1998).

7. CONCLUSIONS

At the end of this discussion of the Italian case, a few points can be high- lighted. The first point to be underlined is that, during the history of the Italian parliamentary regime, there have been fundamentally 'two' fairly stable and distinctive parliamentary elites: the one of the *notabili,* covering more or less the period from Italian unification to World War I, and that of 'party professionals', from the World War II to the beginning of the 1990s. It is true that, within each of these two elites, it was possible to find some significant internal differences (Old Right versus Old Left in the first; Chris- tian Democrats and Socialists versus Communists in the second), but the broader outlook has been similar.

During both periods, there have been incremental changes which, however, have not amounted to a fundamental transformation of the basic features of the parliamentary elite. Yet, in both cases, this process of gradual adaptation has been interrupted at some point by a more dramatic crisis which has caused the exit of the dominant component of the old elite (the Liberal Right in one instance, the Christian Democrats in the other). In both cases, the elite crisis has taken place in conjunction with a peculiar combination of internal and external events: suffrage extension, change of the electoral system, birth of new parties, and World War I in the first case; birth of new parties, change of the electoral system, institutional referen- dums, action of the judiciary, plus the crisis of European Communism and the dawning of the 'Maastricht era' in the second case. In both cases, the crisis coincided with new waves of political mobilization. It is also worth noticing that, in both cases, the crisis of the old elite has erupted with greater speed in the North of Italy, while in the South the pace of change has been slower. As a result of this, the traditional regional differences existing within the elite have been enhanced, producing a more distinctive territorial gap.

This peculiar developmental pattern (long cycles of incremental stability followed by deep and temporally concentrated crises) stimulates the obvious question: why was a more continuous transformation of the old elites not possible? This is not the place, however, to attempt a detailed answer, yet a suggestion might be that, in some way, a continuous process of adaptation was made more difficult because of the peculiar relationship between the governing elite and the opposition. The lack of alternation in power which gave to the governing elites the feeling of being 'irreplaceable' and left the opposition 'frozen' in a sort of Indian reserve probably contributed a great deal to producing a Paretian type of elite circulation, whereby at some point the old 'foxes' were challenged by new 'lions'. Fortunately, in the 1990s, the challenge did not have the ruinous results for democracy that it had in the 1920s (Cotta and Verzichelli 1996: 373–5).

Abbreviations

AN (since 1994)	*Alleanza Nazionale*	National Alliance (formerly MSI)
DC (1946–94)	*Democrazia Cristiana*	Christian Democracy
DS (since 1998)	*Democratici di Sinistra*	Left Democrats (formerly PDS and PCI)
FI (since 1994)	*Forza Italia*	Italy ahead! the centre-right party, founded by Silvio Berlusconi
LN (since 1992)	*Lega Nord*	Northern League
MSI (1948–94)	*Movimento Sociale Italiano*	Italian Social Movement (later AN)
PCI (1946–92)	*Partito Comunista Italiano*	Italian Communist Party (later PDS and DS)
PDS (1992–8)	*Partito Democratico della Sinistra*	Democratic Party of the Left
PLI (1946–94)	*Partito Liberale Italiano*	Italian Liberal Party
PPI (1919–24) (1994–)	*Partito Popolare Italiano*	Italian People's Party (at the same time the name of the predecessor of the DC between 1919 and 1924, and of one of the successors of the DC after 1994)
PRI (1882–94)	*Partito Repubblicano Italiano*	Italian Republican Party

PSDI (1948–94)	*Partito Socialista Democratico Italiano*	Italian Social Democratic Party
PSI (1892–94)	*Partito Socialista Italiano*	Italian Socialist Party
RC (since 1992)	*Partito della Rifondazione Comunista*	Refounded Communist Party (a splinter of the PCI)

References

Ballini, P. (1988). *Le elezioni nella storia d'Italia dall'Unità al Fascismo*. Bologna: Il Mulino.

Bartolini, S., and D'Alimonte, R. (1998). 'Majoritarian Miracles and the Question of Party System Change'. *European Journal of Political Research*, 34: 151–69.

Caciagli, M., and Kertzer, D. I. (eds.) (1996). *Italian Politics: 1996*. Boulder, Colo.: Westview Press.

Cartocci, R. (1990). *Elettori in Italia*. Bologna: Il Mulino.

——(1996). 'Indizi di un inverno precoce: il voto proporzionale tra equilibrio e continuità'. *Rivista Italiana di Scienza Politica*, 26: 609–54.

Cotta, M. (1979). *Classe politica e parlamento in Italia: 1946–1976*. Bologna: Il Mulino.

——(1983). 'The Italian Political Class in the Twentieth Century: Continuities and Discontinuities', in M. M. Czudnowski (ed.), *International Yearbook for Studies of Leaders and Leadership*, i: *Does Who Governs Matters? Elite Circulation in Contemporary Societies*. Dekalb, Ill.: Northern Illinois University Press, 154–87.

——(1992). 'Elite Unification and Democratic Consolidation in Italy: An Historical Overview', in J. Higley and R. Gunther (eds.), *Elites and Democratic Consolidation in Latin America and Southern Europe*. Cambridge: Cambridge University Press, 146–77.

——and Isernia, P. (eds.) (1996). *Il gigante dai piedi di argilla. La crisi del regime partitocratico in Italia*. Bologna: Il Mulino.

——and Verzichelli, L. (1996). 'La classe politica italiana: Cronaca di una morte annunciata?' in Cotta and Isernia (1996), 373–408.

D'Alimonte, R., and Chiaramonte, A. (1993). 'Il nuovo sistema elettorale italiano. Quali opportunità?' *Rivista Italiana di Scienza Politica*, 23: 513–47.

——and Nelken, D. (eds.) (1997). *Italian Politics: 1997*. Boulder, Colo.: Westview Press.

Deputati al Parlamento per la XXV legislatura. Biografie e ritratti (1919). Milano: Fratelli Treves (a similar publication is also available for the 1921 and 1924 parliaments).

Deputati e senatori del primo Parlamento republicano (1948). Roma: La Navicella (a similar publication is available for all the parliaments elected since then).

Di Palma, G., and Cotta, M. (1986). 'Cadres, *Peones* and Entrepreneurs: Professional Identities in a Divided Parliament', in E. N. Suleiman (ed.), *Parliaments and Parliamentarians in Democratic Politics*. New York: Holmes & Meier, 41–78.

Di Virgilio, A. (1998). 'Electoral Alliances: Party Identities and Coalition Games'. *European Journal of Political Research*, 34: 5–33.

Duverger, M. (1976; orig. 1951). *Les Partis politiques*. Paris: Armand Colin.

Farneti, P. (1971). *Sistema politico e società civile*. Turin: Giappichelli.

——(1978). 'Social Conflict, Parliamentary Fragmentation, Institutional Shift, and the Rise of Fascism: Italy', in J. Linz and A. Stepan (eds.), *The Breakdown of Democratic Regimes: Europe*. Baltimore: The Johns Hopkins University Press, 3–33.

——(1989). *La classe politica italiana dal liberalismo alla democrazia*. Genoa: ECIG.

Katz, R. S., and Mair, P. (1995). 'Changing Models of Party Organization and Party Democracy: The Emergence of the Cartel Party'. *Party Politics*, 1: 5–28.

Lanza, O. (1995). 'Gli eletti: il ricambio dei parlamentari', in G. Pasquino (ed.), *L'alternanza inattesa. Le elezioni del 27 marzo 1994 in Italia*. Soveria Mannelli: Rubettino, 209–56.

McCharty, P. (1995). *The Crisis of the Italian State*. New York: St Martin's Press.

Mastropaolo, A. (1990). 'Parlamenti e parlamentari negli anni ottanta'. *Rivista Italiana di Scienza Politica*, 20: 29–71.

——(1993). *Il ceto politico. Teoria e Pratica*. Rome: NIS.

——(1996). *La repubblica dai destini incrociati*. Florence: La Nuova Italia.

Morlino, L. (1996). 'Crisis of Parties and Change of Party System in Italy'. *Party Politics*, 2: 5–30.

——and Tarchi, M. (1996). 'The Dissatisfied Society: The Roots of the Political Change in Italy'. *European Journal of Political Research*, 3: 351–87.

Moro, R. (1979). *La formazione della classe dirigente cattolica*. Bologna: Il Mulino.

Mosca, G. (1884). *Teorica dei governi e governo parlamentare*. Turin: Loescher.

Panebianco, A. (1988). *Models of Party*. Cambridge: Cambridge University Press.

Ricolfi, L. (1993). *L'ultimo parlamento*. Rome: NIS.

Romeo, R. (1972). *Breve storia della grande industria in Italia*. Bologna: Cappelli.

Sartori, G. (1963). 'Dove va il Parlamento?' in G. Sartori (ed.), *Il Parlamento Italiano: 1946–1963*. Naples: Edizioni Scientifiche Italiane, 281–386.

Verzichelli, L. (1995). 'The New Members of Parliament' in R. S. Katz and P. Ignazi (eds.), *Italian Politics 1995. The Year of the Tycoon*. Boulder, Colo.: Westview Press, 115–33.

——(1998). 'The Parliamentary Elite in Transition'. *European Journal of Political Research*, 34: 121–50.

Wertman, D. (1988). 'Italy: Local Involvement: Party Control', in M. Gallagher and M. Marsh (eds.), *Candidate Selection in Comparative Perspective*. London: Sage, 145–68.

8

Representatives of the Dutch People: The Smooth Transformation of the Parliamentary Elite in a Consociational Democracy 1849–1998

INEKE SECKER

1. INTRODUCTION

On 23 February 1996, the President of the Dutch Lower House, the Second Chamber, opened a debate on 'Representation of the People'. In his remarks, he referred not only to his contemporary fellow MPs, but also to those elected some centuries earlier, in 1896 and 1796. This discussion took place in the Hague on the very spot where, on 1 March 1796, the first elected National Assembly had met in the former ballroom of the *Stadhouder*, the Prince of Orange. This continued to be used until 1992, when a new building was inaugurated as the meeting-place of the Second Chamber.

Can we seriously consider this first National Assembly in 1796 to be a true predecessor of the current Second Chamber? Certainly, the Assembly of 1796 (the *Staten-Generaal*), had some modern features. It had been democratically elected, albeit indirectly, by a large percentage of the male population aged 20 or over, and representatives were authorized to pass resolutions without the mandate of their electorate. This truly modern parliament, however, did not last long. Under the influence (and intimidation) of the French occupying forces, several constitutional changes were introduced between 1796 and 1810, which led to a radical reduction of the once-applauded idea of the sovereignty of the people. Even the pretence of the Netherlands remaining an independent centralized state did not last when in 1810 it was absorbed into the French Empire. After Napoleon's defeat, a new era began in 1813 with the return to the Netherlands of the Prince of Orange, now invested with monarchical power. In the Constitution of 1815, as he had promised, a Second House was added to the traditional *Staten-Generaal*. From then on, the States-General have consisted of the

I want to express my gratitude to Mr. N. R. M. N. Cramer and Dr B. H. van den Braak, from the Parliamentary Documentation Centre, for their help in providing all data.

(politically most important) Second Chamber and the First Chamber or Senate.

Why then not take 1813 or 1815 as the starting-point for a review of 'the Dutch legislator'? The main reason lies in the electoral rules of that time, whereby the Second Chamber was elected in a very complicated, and indirect way, with the final result coming from the Provincial Councils. This remained the case until 1848, although in the 1830s a minority of progressive Liberals had already insisted on changes in the electoral system, especially on the introduction of direct suffrage. These changes were finally realized in 1848, when a liberal constitution introduced direct suffrage and ministerial responsibility. In addition, prior to the introduction of these reforms, parliamentary power had been heavily curtailed by the exercise of the royal prerogative. The period between 1815 and 1848, therefore, can be characterized by the struggle between an autocratic, dominant King and a Second Chamber striving for a more powerful position. However, in 1848, the second King, William II, yielded to demands for major constitutional reforms and it is for this reason that 1848 is known as the start of true parliamentary government. It is logical, therefore, that 1848 should also serve as the beginning for our analysis of the recruitment of Representatives of the People.[1]

2. THE CONSTITUTIONAL SETTING

Fear of revolutionary outbursts, similar to those in several European countries in 1848, had persuaded the Dutch King to give way to a rather small group of reform-minded Liberals by signing the progressive constitution. Many of the MPs were taken by surprise by the unexpected royal conversion and the King even had to persuade the majority of the First Chamber to get its approval. However, William II died within a year and his son, William III, found it extremely difficult to live with his father's constitutional heritage. Due to the absence of political parties, and hence the lack of a clear parliamentary majority, the new King frequently succeeded in imposing his will upon his ministers. However, in a heavy clash at the end of the 1860s, the Second Chamber gained absolute control over government, since when the principle of ministerial responsibility has been uncontested.

The principle of direct suffrage, the second major feature of the 1848 Constitution, was never seriously challenged, though the electoral law was adapted several times. One of the most important of these changes concerned the electoral system itself. A system of geographical representation

---

[1] The new electoral rules were actually used for the first time in 1849.

was used until 1917 when it was replaced by proportional representation. Although suffrage had also been expanded gradually over this period, the constitutional reform of 1917 was also of extreme importance because it introduced universal male suffrage, female suffrage being introduced two years later (Tables 8.1 and 8.2).

2.1. Electoral System

According to the Constitution of 1848, the first electoral law was passed in 1850. This law maintained a system of geographical representation (as was already known in some sense before 1848) whereby the country was divided into mainly plural-member and some single-member constituencies. Those qualified to vote could do so only for the election of candidates within the borders of their electoral district. The winning candidate was whomsoever received an absolute majority of the votes in a district. In order to arrive at a majority, a second run-off between the top two candidates was often necessary. Candidates were not bound by any rule of residence. For forty years, the number of representatives was linked to population density: one seat per 45,000 persons. Thus, an increase in the population required a change in the number of seats in the Second Chamber and, consequently, of the borders of the constituencies. This meant that by the 1880s, the number of representatives had risen from 68 in 1848 to 86. Finally, in 1887, complaints about gerrymandering, that is, electoral-geographical manipulation, because of the frequent revision of the constituency borders, led to the number of seats being fixed at 100. When proportional representation was introduced in 1917, this number did not change until 1956 when it was raised to 150. Although, since 1848, parliamentary tenure has been four years, up to 1888 elections actually took place every two years, allowing the electorate to renew half of the representatives. The number of elections was also increased as a result of interim dissolutions of the Chamber, such as when constitutional reforms were implemented, or during conflicts between the Cabinet and Second Chamber. Such conflicts, which were much more common in the nineteenth century than in the first half of the twentieth century, have tended to recur during the last three decades.[2]

2.2. Suffrage

Before the introduction of universal suffrage, the franchise was limited under the criteria of property and income. Under the electoral law of 1850, people were only qualified to vote if they were a 'Dutchman, of age,

---

[2] Between 1848 and 1888: six times; between 1888 and 1918: one, between 1918 and 1946: zero times; between 1946 and 1967: once; between 1967 and 1994: three times.

Table 8.1. The Development of the Dutch Electoral System since 1848

Year	Right to vote — Gender	Age	Other conditions	No. of seats (1:45,000 inhabitants)	No. of districts	Single districts	Plural districts — 2 seats	Plural districts — 3 or more
1848	Male	23	Liable to min. fl. 20 tax					
1850				68	38	11	26	1
1858				72	38	9	27	2
1864				75	39	8	29	2
1869				80	41	8	30	3
1878				86	43	8	32	3
				Fixed no.:				
1888			Liable to min. fl. 10 tax	100				
1896		25	Liable to min. fl. 1 tax or some other criteria		100			
1917[1]		23	No conditions / Compulsory voting		No districts:	Prop. repr.		
1919	Male and Female							
1922		25						
1946		23						
1956				150				
1963[2]		21						
1970			No more compulsion					
1972		18						

Notes: [1] 1917: no conditions; no districts; proportional representation.
[2] After 1963.

Table 8.2. The Extension of the Dutch Electorate

Year	Max. votes	Percentage of population	Percentage of male	Percentage actual voters
1853	83,561	2.7	10.7	
1860	89,153	2.8	10.9	
1870	103,538	2.9	11.3	
1880	122,481	3.1	12.3	
1887	134,987	3.1		
1888	292,613	6.6		
1890	295,570	7.4	26.8	
1891	299,416	6.6		
1894	298,479	6.1		
1897	577,059	11.7		
1901	609,511	11.8	51.8	
1905	750,550	13.4		
1909	843,550	14.3	63.2	
1913	960,676	15.5	68.0	
1917	1,079,475	16.1	70.8	
1918	1,517,380			
1922	3,299,672			
1925	3,543,085	97.2		91.4
1929	3,821,612	97.1		92.7
1933	4,126,430	96.3		94.5
1937	4,468,852	97.1		94.4
1946	5,275,888	97.1		93.1
1948	5,433,663	96.6		93.7
1952	5,792,679	96.8		95.0
1956	6,125,210	97.5		95.5
1959	6,427,864	98.5		95.6
1963	6,748,611	98.6		95.1
1967	7,452,776	97.9		94.9
1971	8,038,726	97.9		79.1
1972	8,916,947	97.8		83.5
1977	9,506,318	97.7		88.0
1981	10,040,121	97.3		87.0
1982	10,216,634	97.0		81.0
1986	10,727,701			85.8
1989	11,112,189			80.3
1994	11,455,924			78.7
1998	11,755,132			73.3

inhabitant of the kingdom and fully enjoying all civic rights'.[3] Moreover, the law required voters to be liable to a certain degree of taxation. Under this *census régime* a mere 11% of the male adults were qualified to vote, something which remained unchanged until constitutional reforms were

---

[3] 1848 Constitution, art. 76.

introduced in 1887, which resulted in the electorate doubling by 1888. When, in 1896, the new electoral law lowered the electoral threshold even further by reducing the minimum fiscal requirements, and by introducing some alternative criteria, suffrage was extended to almost half of the adult male population. However, it is interesting to note that on the eve of the introduction of universal suffrage, due to economic growth, two-thirds of the male population were already qualified to vote under the old criteria. The expansion of suffrage to all adult males in 1917 was matched two years later by the enfranchisement of all adult females. Thereafter, the extension of suffrage was reached by lowering the voting age, which had been fixed at 23 years in 1848. However, when the reforms of 1887 enlarged the socio-economic criteria for the right to vote, the age qualification was raised to 25 years. In 1946,[4] after World War II, 23 year olds regained the right to vote. Since then, the minimum age gradually declined to 21 in 1963 (first applied in the 1967 election) and finally to 18 in 1972.

2.3. Eligibility and Incompatibilities

For a long time it seemed easier to be able to stand for elections to the Second Chamber than to be able to vote. In some respects, similar qualifications were required: one had to be a 'Dutchman and enjoy all civic rights'. Obviously there was a minimum age (30 in 1848) which was higher than that required of voters. This minimum age rule remained unchanged for over a century and was not lowered to 25 until 1963. It took a further 20 years before constitutional reforms granted 18 year olds the right to stand for elections and, even so, they had to wait until this change in the age of majority was recognized by law in 1988. In the interim, all 21 year olds were declared qualified to stand for an election. Women have been accepted as candidates since 1917, two years before they were actually admitted as voters. It is also striking that the exclusion of women as voters and Representatives was not mentioned before the Constitution of 1887.[5] Besides nationality, age, and gender, no other conditions stood in the way of becoming a Member of Parliament. However, from 1848 to 1917 the constitution stipulated that a Member of Parliament who was subsequently appointed to a public office, or promoted to a higher one, military forces included, had to resign and stand for re-election when appropriate.[6] The following public offices were declared incompatible with the membership of the Second

---

[4] During a short period only, from 1917 to 1922, adults of 23 regained the right to vote.

[5] The explicit exclusion of women in 1887 was due to the preceding unexpected attempt of the first Dutch female physician, Aletta Jacobs, to be listed as a voter.

[6] In any case, members of the armed forces were put on half pay during their parliamentary mandate.

Chamber: membership of the First Chamber, Attorney-General or member of the Supreme Court, membership of the Government Audit Office, Provincial Governors (till 1983), clergymen and other religious ministers (till 1887). The constitutional reform in 1887 introduced a new incompatibility: membership of the Council of State. In 1938, the office of Cabinet Minister was formally declared incompatible with membership of the House. However, from 1848, an unwritten rule had dictated that a Cabinet Minister should give up membership of Parliament and in only a few cases was this ignored.

2.4. Financial Compensation

At the end of the eighteenth century, opinions about the status of Representatives of the People underwent the influence of Enlightenment and they came to be held in much higher esteem. This led to them being granted the considerable sum of fl. 4,000 a year in 1798. Occasionally, however, this amount was reduced, until the 1848 Constitution set the so-called parliamentary 'compensation' at fl. 2,000 a year.[7] The fear of profiteering candidates was always present but this fear often worked in the members' favour because the view was that members, in order to keep their independence, needed to be paid properly. The fact that, in pre-Napoleonic times, members had been paid by the Provincial Estates, who had then dictated how their deputies should vote, was not lost in this debate. The financial compensation of fl. 2,000 lasted for more than half a century, that is, up to 1917 when the parliamentary salary amounted to fl. 3,000. From then on, parliamentary pay was more closely linked to the financial conditions offered by other occupations,[8] although some right-wing Liberals insisted on maintaining the tradition of considering representative functions as merely honorary. The amelioration of the financial compensation to MPs in 1917 was connected to the rather strongly decreasing purchasing power, on the one hand, and pressure from the growing Socialist Party to enable less well-off candidates to stand for elections, on the other. Some years later, the compensation was raised considerably, to fl. 5,000. However, in the 'miserable 1930s' it was cut to fl. 4,500, and was restored to fl. 5,000 again after World War II. From then on, the parliamentary salary was amended regularly:[9] from fl. 10,000 in 1958, fl. 15,000 in 1962, fl. 17,500 in 1964, to fl. 20,000 in 1965. In 1968, a new Parliamentary Financial Compensation Act was passed. The compen-

---

[7] In 1805: fl. 3,000; in 1815: fl. 2,500.

[8] From 1917 also dated the introduction of a first pension claim to resigning or not re-elected Members. Moreover, some financial support was guaranteed to the relatives of a MP in the event of his death.

[9] To amend the parliamentary salary, a constitutional revision was needed until 1956. Since then, this could be done by law, with a qualified majority of two-thirds of the votes.

sation was fixed at fl. 25,000, to be raised to fl. 40,000 the following year. Since then, parliamentary salary has been connected to the salaries of other officials. In the 1980s, it rose to over fl. 90,000; in 1997, it was about fl. 150,000.[10]

3. POLITICAL DEVELOPMENTS AND PERIODIZATION

In recruitment of MPs, political parties are of vital importance. A longitudinal study, however, as in the present case, can have some problems in this regard. Strictly speaking, political parties in the modern sense did not exist before the end of the nineteenth century. Prior to this, individuals contested a seat, supported by relatives and friends. Gradually, local electoral associations were established to promote the appointment of favourite local candidates or other persons willing to devote their energy to some specific theme or interest. These political associations and their associated Representatives, began to be given labels. Those who aimed at constitutional and other reforms were referred to as liberals, radicals, or progressives. Politicians who opposed such reforms were named conservatives, a name they did not use themselves. Religion was not a decisive factor in political life at that time and the dominant groups in society were non-fundamentalist or belonged to the less militant orthodox-Protestant groups within the Dutch Reformed Church.

In 1879, the first mass party, the orthodox-protestant Anti-Revolutionary Party (ARP), was formed in protest against the new liberal School Act.[11] Catholics, who shared the anti-revolutionary objections against the neutral character of public schools, did not, however, establish a formally centralized organization before 1926 (Roman-Catholic State Party, RKSP). Like the Roman-Catholics, Liberals were far from eager to organize themselves. However, confronted with the strong appeal of the denominational groups at the polls, they attempted reluctantly to come to a union in 1885, but did not succeed in establishing a strong organization. Only half of the Liberal electoral associations and their favoured MPs joined the Liberal Union. The more radical Members in particular kept their independence. Thus, at the turn of the century, there were three distinct Liberal party groups in Parliament. The first Socialist Member of Parliament, leader of the Social Democratic Party, established in 1882, made his appearance in 1888, but

---

[10] The amounts mentioned exclude all kinds of allowances regarding travel and lodging expenses and so on.
[11] Founding father was clergyman Abraham Kuyper. The word 'revolutionary' expressed opposition to the ideas of the French Revolution concerning the sovereignty of the people rather than of God.

lasted only until the next election. In 1894, a new Socialist party (Social Democratic Worker's Party, SDAP) was founded. Due to the limited suffrage in those years, the party remained very weak for some time. After the election of 1897, the first based on the new electoral law, three SDAP candidates entered the Second Chamber. Their number rose gradually. And, on the eve of the introduction of universal suffrage, 15% of parliamentary seats were occupied by Socialists.

At the end of the nineteenth century, the oldest party, the Protestant ARP, had, just like the Liberals, fallen apart into politically more progressive and more conservative factions. The latter, more conservative particularly in matters of suffrage expansion, later became the Christian-Historical Union (CHU). The two Protestant groups were also different in some other respects. The ARP became more and more the party for the orthodox (*gereformeerde*) 'man in the street', while the CHU attracted the more well-to-do, less orthodox (*hervormde*) Protestants. In spite of the split in the Protestant group, the political scene at the turn of the century was dominated by a rather rigid *antithesis* between Right (denominational parties) and Left (Liberals), based on two major issues: extension of the suffrage and the financial position of private, that is, religious schools. For approximately 30 years, the polls led to alternating majorities of one of the groups until the slowly growing appeal of the Socialists intervened. After 1900, the Liberals never again won an absolute majority and the introduction of both proportional representation and universal suffrage in 1918 only caused them further electoral damage. In the interwar years, all the Liberal parties put together rarely managed to win more than 10% to 15% of the votes. Social Democrats, although occupying a quarter of the parliamentary seats from 1918 onwards, were not admitted to the Cabinet until the last pre-war 'emergency' Cabinet in 1939. All elections between the two world wars confirmed the solid position of the three major religious parties, which thus dictated the formation of all Cabinet coalitions.

This comfortable position has not been seriously threatened until the 1990s. However, in those first postwar years it was thought wiser to share responsibilities with the second major party, the Social Democrats, (now the Labour Party, PvdA).[12] Most postwar Cabinets were based on a broader basis of three or four parties. Besides the inevitable denominational parties that continued to be the pivot on which everything turned, either Liberals or Social Democrats participated. Changing voting patterns in the 1960s caused electoral damage mostly to the denominational parties. Growing numbers of floating voters made each election result, and hence the following Cabinet coalition, more difficult to predict. For a long time, joint

---

[12] The Labour Party was the merger of the pre-war SDAP, the progressive-liberal VDB, and some individual denominational party supporters.

action by the Liberals and Social Democrats was thought 'a mission impossible'. The pivotal role of the three Christian Democratic parties, in 1980 merged into one party (Christian Democratic Appeal, CDA), therefore lasted, notwithstanding rather heavy electoral losses after the 1960s. After the elections of 1994, which resulted in four parliamentary groups of more or less equal size, the Christian Democrats were kept out of the Cabinet for the first time since 1918. The right-wing Liberals (identified by the colour blue), the Social Democrats (red), together with the progressive-liberal D66 (established in 1966) joined forces: a brand-new coalition was born, named Purple, that was repeated after the elections of 1998.

While the constitutional reforms of 1848, 1887, and 1917 are considered the natural *caesurae* in many studies on parliamentary history, less unanimity exists with respect to the periodization of the time span after 1917. Concerning the Electoral Law, no significant changes, age excluded, have taken place since then, but political culture, and the relative strength of the political parties, have changed. Opinions about the role of World War II as a vehicle for change differ, and the postwar parliamentary period has often been described as simply a return to pre-war times, particularly after the failure of the political leaders to alter parliamentary and political institutions. Generally uncontested is the definition of the 1960s as a watershed, mainly because of the renewed interest in or criticism at that time of the existing system, and when various reform proposals concentrated on the relationship between elections and government formation—'the Achilles' heel of the Dutch political system' (Andeweg 1989: 49). Voters manifested this criticism and caused a landslide at the 1967 polls so that the political and cultural landscape underwent enough changes to represent a new era.

In sum, the following periods can be distinguished in Dutch parliamentary history:

1848–88	responsible government; highly limited franchise; no or weak party organization;
1888–1918	from limited to universal male suffrage; increasing party organization;
1918–46	stabilization of party forces; rapidly increasing social segmentation;
1946–67	integration of Social Democrats;
1967–94	from polarization to 'Purple'; floating voters; new perspectives?

These periods are also useful when reviewing the personal characteristics of the Dutch Parliament.

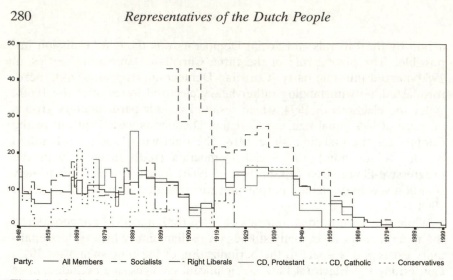

Party: —— All Members — — Socialists —— Right Liberals - - - - CD, Protestant · · · · CD, Catholic - · - · Conservatives

Fig. 8.1. Netherlands 1849–1998: basic education

4. MPS PORTRAYED: FROM NOTABLES TO POLITICIANS

In the historical development of the social composition of the Second Chamber, several class- and status-related aspects of the background of the MPs are of vital importance. Remnants of the Dutch Republican past, in matters of recruitment of members of the political elite, were still present in the nineteenth century. Traditionally, the social position of the family played a major role, affecting also the educational level or occupational positions. Membership of the Dutch Reformed Church was almost taken for granted.

4.1. Nobility and Patriciate

From a comparative perspective, it may be interesting to focus on nobility as an historical recruiting channel *par excellence*. In the Dutch case, though, one has to bear in mind that a considerable proportion of the noble families has not had the highly distinguished position associated with aristocracy in many other European countries. Two centuries of republican régime had thinned out ancient nobility considerably. When, after the French occupation, the Vienna Congress decided to unite the Southern Netherlands (Belgium) and the former Republic of the Seven United Dutch Provinces into a monarchy, nobility attained a new position. To fill the

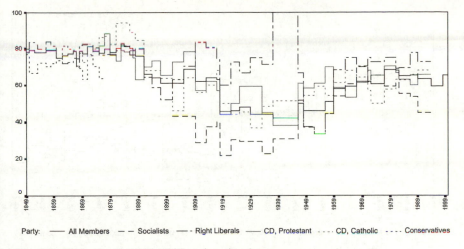

Party: —— All Members — — Socialists ——· Right Liberals —— CD, Protestant ···· CD, Catholic ---- Conservatives

Fig. 8.2. Netherlands 1849–1998: university degree

gap,[13] the first King of the House of Orange, William I (1813–1840) ennobled many Dutch *regenten*. *Regenten* were the descendants of families
who had gained wealth and power from successful commerce, finance, and
city government during the centuries and whose descendants had obtained
the exclusive right to occupy the important city government posts. Due to
this dominant position, members of these *haute bourgeoisie* or patrician
families, came very close, at least socially, to nobility.[14]

Even after the introduction of direct voting in 1848, noblemen and *regenten* obviously succeeded in maintaining a powerful position in Parliament
for a long time (Fig. 8.7).[15] Before political parties were established, well-
known family names offered a certain guarantee of political expertise to
many voters. Until 1900, it sometimes happened that several members of

[13] The ennoblement of numerous Dutch prominent families served to keep pace with the
numerical strength of the Belgian nobility. The new constitution stipulated that the new First
Chamber should be composed of noblemen and other prominent persons, appointed by the
King.

[14] Most members of *regenten* families who had not been ennobled were registered in the
Yearbook of the Dutch Patriciate, a series started in 1910 in imitation of a similar series, *Yearbook of the Dutch Nobility* (1903). Socially, there was not a great distance between the new
ennobled families and their not ennobled 'patrician' relatives. In many Dutch publications
about elites, the word 'aristocracy' therefore refers to the conglomerate of both social groups,
nobility and patriciate. In this contribution, however, 'nobility' or 'aristocracy' exclusively
relates to formally registered noblemen, both of ancient and more recent origins.

[15] See Van den Berg (1983: 45–52). In his study, percentages of nobility and patriciate are
given separately. In our description, we used some of his data. In the adapted CUBE data,
only officially registered noblemen are included, the same category Van den Berg used to indicate nobility.

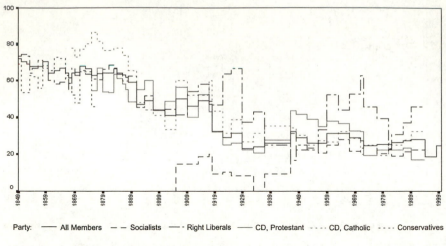

Party: —— All Members — — Socialists —— · Right Liberals —— CD, Protestant · · · · CD, Catholic · · · · Conservatives

Fig. 8.3. Netherlands 1849–1998: law degree

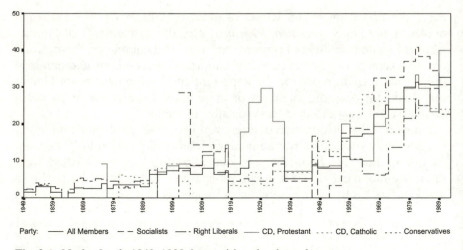

Party: —— All Members — — Socialists —— · Right Liberals —— CD, Protestant · · · · CD, Catholic · · · · Conservatives

Fig. 8.4. Netherlands 1849–1998: humanities, theology degree

one family occupied political positions, whether in succession or, in some cases, at the same time. Mainly these were the offspring of noble and patrician families. As a consequence, from 1848, the appearance of Dutch national political life as a stately, distinguished society was maintained for more than half a century. Indeed, nobility and patriciate together accounted for over 60% of the MPs during this period. The beginning of a slight decline could be observed in the last twenty years of the nineteenth century.

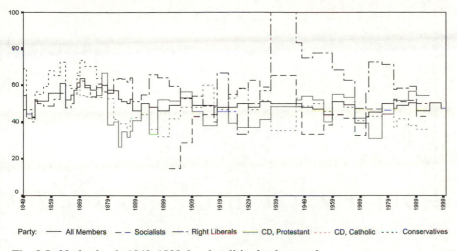

Fig. 8.5. Netherlands 1849–1998: local politics background

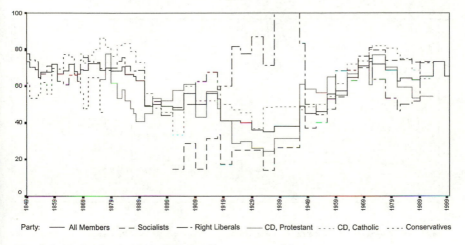

Fig. 8.6. Netherlands 1849–1998: leading party position

However, it was not until the elections of 1913 that a majority from more humble origins was returned to the Second Chamber. From then on, the decline of these highest milieus as an important recruiting channel was irreversible.

When we focus on the role of the nobility in particular, a similar development is visible. In the first directly elected Second Chamber in 1849, one in five members belonged to a noble family. This increased as a result of

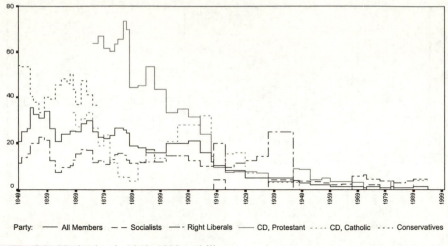

Fig. 8.7. Netherlands 1849–1998: nobility

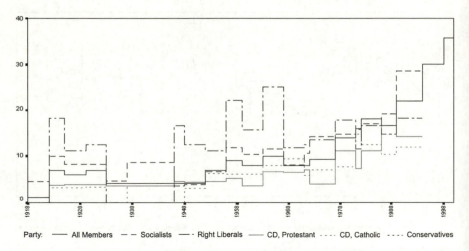

Fig. 8.8. Netherlands 1918–1998: female legislators

following elections, as if illustrating the reluctance of the electorate to accept the too rapidly developing modernization of political life. Even after the fall of the first progressive-liberal Thorbecke ministry in 1853, 35% of noblemen were elected. On average, between 1848 and 1888, about 25% of MPs had noble titles. From the moment the census threshold was lowered, fewer nobles were elected, although some of them survived politically for

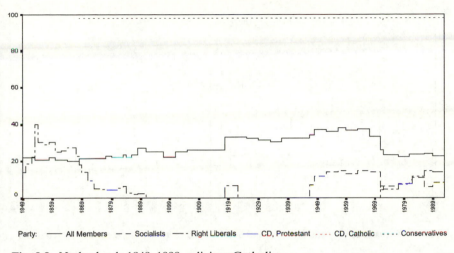

Fig. 8.9. Netherlands 1849–1998: religion: Catholic

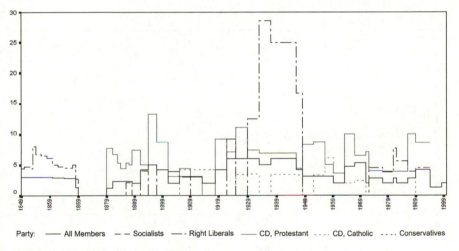

Fig. 8.10. Netherlands 1849–1998: primary sector

some time. The growth of the denominational parties, together with the rise of the number of Socialist Members, was decisive in the gradual disappearance of nobility. In 1888, the percentage of noble Members dropped below 20 for the first time. Certainly, the nobility had not profited from the expansion of the number of parliamentary seats from 86 to 100 in that year. It was initially the new Members of the growing Anti-Revolutionary Party who gave the Second Chamber a more bourgeois appearance. Their leader,

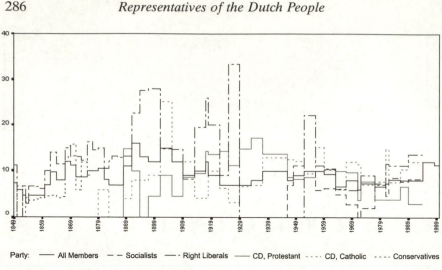

Fig. 8.11. Netherlands 1849–1998: managers, businessmen

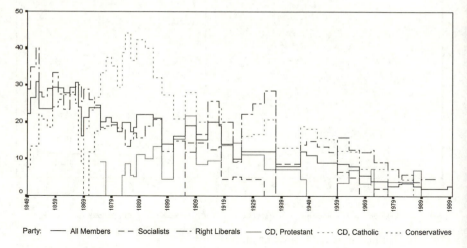

Fig. 8.12. Netherlands 1849–1998: practising lawyers

Abraham Kuyper, a man of the people himself, appealed in particular to ordinary people, who strongly welcomed his struggle for the financial support of private schools. While in the preceding years the first orthodox-Protestant Members of the House came almost exclusively from prominent families, the party led by Kuyper attracted more and more 'ordinary' candidates. This change was even one of the reasons for the separation of the

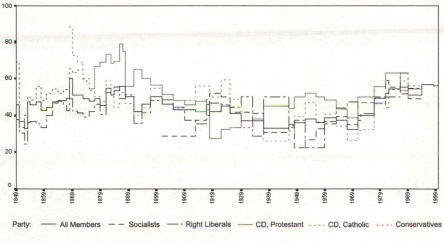

Party: —— All Members – – Socialists —— Right Liberals —— CD, Protestant ···· CD, Catholic ···· Conservatives

Fig. 8.13. Netherlands 1849–1998: public sector employees

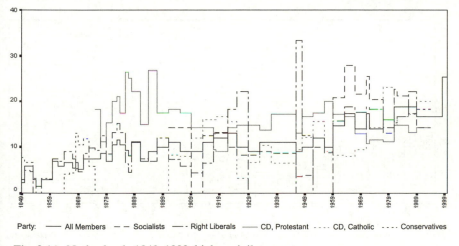

Party: —— All Members – – Socialists —— Right Liberals —— CD, Protestant ···· CD, Catholic ···· Conservatives

Fig. 8.14. Netherlands 1849–1998: higher civil servants

Christian Historicals in the 1890s. Among Liberals and Roman-Catholics, the proportion of noble Members did not diminish accordingly. A new Electoral Law, seven elections, and twenty years later, the Second Chamber still comprised 12% aristocratic MPs. The introduction of universal male suffrage in 1917, however, dealt a death-blow to the political position of the nobility. At each subsequent election, it was clear that

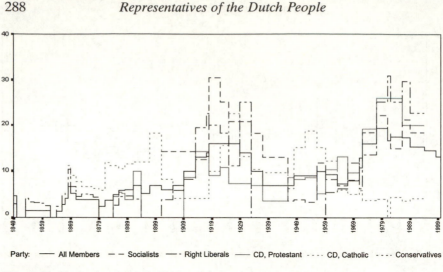

Fig. 8.15. Netherlands 1849–1998: teachers and professors

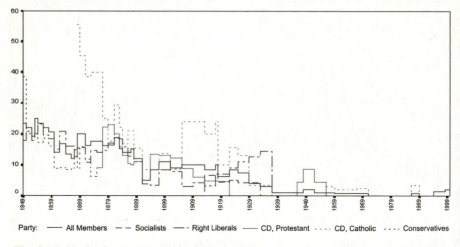

Fig. 8.16. Netherlands 1849–1998: judges

the nobility was no longer a major recruiting channel. Obviously the growing number of Socialist Members in particular was conducive to this process. In the interwar period, the proportion of nobility in Parliament sank from 10% to 5%, and after 1945 this declined even further. Today the presence in the House of an MP with a noble title seems to be purely incidental.

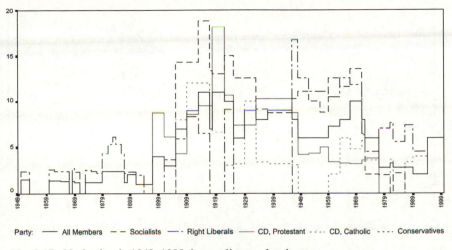

Party: —— All Members – – Socialists —— Right Liberals —— CD, Protestant ···· CD, Catholic ·-·- Conservatives

Fig. 8.17. Netherlands 1849–1998: journalists and writers

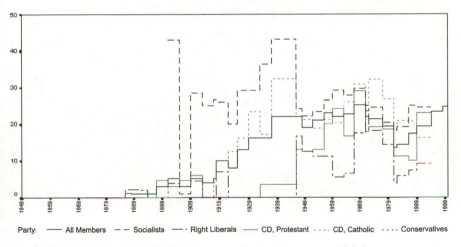

Party: —— All Members – – Socialists —— Right Liberals —— CD, Protestant ···· CD, Catholic ·-·- Conservatives

Fig. 8.18. Netherlands 1849–1998: party and pressure group officials

4.2. *Professional Inheritance*

For a long time political functions were thought to be the almost exclusive right of aristocrats and patricians, which is well illustrated by the proportion of MPs coming from those high circles. The persistence of some kind of professional inheritance in the public sector can also be demonstrated by analysing data about the recruitment of MPs from families with a public

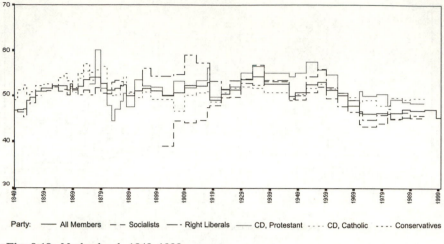

Party: —— All Members — — Socialists —— · Right Liberals —— CD, Protestant · · · · CD, Catholic · · · · Conservatives

Fig. 8.19. Netherlands 1849–1998: mean age

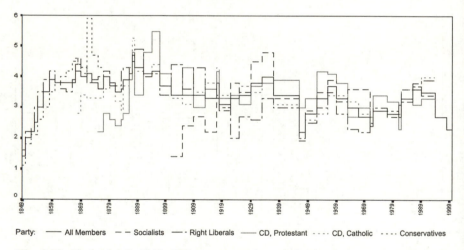

Party: —— All Members — — Socialists —— · Right Liberals —— CD, Protestant · · · · CD, Catholic · · · · Conservatives

Fig. 8.20. Netherlands 1849–1998: mean number of elections

office record (Van den Berg 1983: 62–70). It is striking to see that over 50% of the Members in the second half of the nineteenth century had promin-ent fathers who had held high-level political, governmental, or other public positions. Van den Berg pointed out that in all legislatures between 1848 and 1970, at least one Member of Parliament was the son or grandson of a former member of the highest public offices such as the Cabinet, Parlia-ment, or the Council of State. Even in the nineteenth century, a majority of

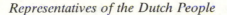

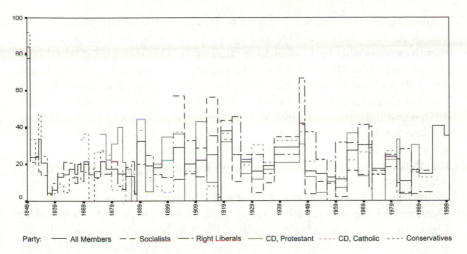

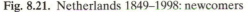

Party: ——— All Members — — Socialists ——· Right Liberals ——— CD, Protestant ---- CD, Catholic ·---· Conservatives

Fig. 8.21. Netherlands 1849–1998: newcomers

Members had fathers who had served in higher civil or military offices. From the turn of the century, an increasing proportion of MPs were sons of fathers who had no public service record whatsoever. Nevertheless, in the 1930s, one in five MPs still came from a civil service family. In addition, a large number of Members had fathers who had served in representative offices, mostly in a local political institution. However, their share shrank from a quarter in the second half of the nineteenth century to a mere 11% in the interwar period, rising slightly again after World War II. The last pre-war election, held in 1937, appears to have returned the maximum number of *homines novi*, in other words, Representatives without any political, hereditary backing, to the Second Chamber.

4.3. Education

The effect of education, regarding both level and discipline, is not contested in elite studies. More than other data, information regarding the educational background of MPs tells us about the practical qualities of politicians on the one hand, and about general developments in society on the other. Two developments in the educational field itself partly predict the outcome of this part of the investigation. With time, education became more diversified and the threshold to participate in higher education was lowered. Inevitably, such developments had their impact on the recruitment process of the Representatives. In addition, education is apparently not a political neutral factor, as inter-party differences tend to show (Figs. 8.1.–8.4.).[16]

---

[16] Van den Berg (1983: 275 n. 5) refers to a number of writers from Max Weber to E. A. Shills and T. B. Bottomore, who dealt with this very subject.

Initially, the proportion of university graduates among the Members was extremely high, between 75% and 80%. However, by the end of the nineteenth century, this had fallen to around 60%. This downward trend continued until 1918 when universal male suffrage was applied for the first time and only 44% of Members had a traditional university education. The proportion of academics in the House stabilized at between 40% and 50% until 1956 when it again rose above 50%, reaching over 60% after 1967. Thus, in the last three decades of the twentieth century, the proportion of MPs with a university education reached the same level as that at the end of the nineteenth century.[17] The lower proportion in the interwar period corresponded with an increasing number of Members with an intermediate level of education, but MPs without any real formal education were never numerous. However, in the nineteenth century, 10% of Members had not received higher or even middle-level education. This can be explained partly by the fact that it was not unusual for sons from well-to-do families to be taken into the family business or that of friends at a young age and without any formal schooling. Secondly, undoubtedly, several Members without public qualifications had been privately educated. From 1888 onwards, the proportion of Members with only basic education rose slowly to between 12% and 14%, but was reduced to half this by 1910. Among the MPs elected after universal suffrage had been introduced, again 12% or more had only received basic education. The maximum of 16% of MPs from this modest educational level was reached in the 1930s.

Almost all studies on recruitment of political elites refer to Max Weber who wrote about the convergence of some professions with political functions. Lawyers in particular ranked highly, often because of qualities such as capability and availability. The Dutch case is no exception and for some time, the overwhelming majority of university-trained politicians were graduates in law. During the *ancien régime*, sons from the class of *regenten* used to study law to prepare for their future offices. On the other hand, among the new, progressive Liberals of the 1850s, former law students were no exception either. Thus, until 1888, an average of two-thirds of the Second Chamber consisted of Members who had been trained in law. After this time, the presence of jurists declined slowly and after 1918, the proportion was reduced to 25%. However, despite this decline, the first ranking of jurists among MPs with degrees did not change before the elections of 1967. What is also striking, especially from a comparative perspective, is the fact that among MPs from non-law disciplines, former students of theology were predominant (Van den Berg 1983: 134, Table 4.4; 142, Fig. 4.4). Their presence in the House, which was rather modest in the nineteenth century, rose

---

[17] This rise in the proportion of academic Members after the 1960s can be particularly attributed to the Left Liberals (D66) and Social Democrats.

to between 5% and 7% at the turn of the century and peaked at just under 20% in the interwar period. Also remarkable is the fact that theology-trained MPs are not only to be found in religious parties but across the whole political spectrum.

Other fields of study, which are common today, such as the political sciences and economics, only date from the twentieth century. This growing diversification of academic disciplines at the beginning of this century is illustrated partly in the recruitment of more MPs who had studied areas other than law or related fields. Scientists became more prominent after 1918, their presence being most noticeable in the 1930s when they represented one in five MPs with degrees. This strong presence during two legislatures matched that of theologians, but after World War II, the share of both categories of academics was reduced, though less so for the scientists than for the theologians. The proportion of this latter group of Members shrank to a negligible 1% in 1963. In those same postwar years, a new type of academic MP made an appearance, the economist. From an 11% share in 1946, the proportion more than doubled at the 1967 elections. Since the 1950s, economists surpassed the second group of scientists. Undoubtedly, the decline in MPs trained in law to below 50% is due to this new category of Members. Economists are found particularly among the representatives of parties on the Left, although several can also be found in the Catholic party, both of which political currents had been very critical about governmental economic policy in the 1930s.[18]

4.4. Religion

The Dutch political scene is renowned for its historical division along religious lines. Indeed, formal discrimination against Roman Catholics and dissident Protestants, such as Lutherans, Anabaptists, and Mennonites, only ceased at the end of the eighteenth century. Religious discrimination had a particularly significant effect on the political participation of Catholic citizens who constituted the largest minority among the population (*c.*35–40%) and for Jews who had also long been excluded from civil rights.[19]

The main religious cleavage that dominated the nineteenth century, however, was between Catholics and Protestants.[20] Until the 1870s, three-

---

[18] See Van den Berg (1983: 136).

[19] In this study, we have classified as Jewish only those MPs who were definitely known for their adherence to the Jewish faith. They hardly ever outnumbered 1 or 2% in the House. Sometimes this proportion grew to 4% (1891, 1913), once even to 5% (1937). Jewish Members were to be found among the Liberals and Radicals.

[20] For that reason, in this study Protestants of the different denominations have been taken together. The other Protestant denominations had far fewer members than the Reformed Church.

quarters of the House consisted of Protestants, most of whom were closely associated with the Dutch Reformed Church. This was the old, main church of Holland, membership of which gave almost exclusive entry into public office for over two centuries. Only between 5% and 10% were dissenters. In the 1870s, the proportion of Protestant MPs dropped below 70%, so that by 1888 it was below 60% and had declined to just over 50% in 1918. The decline continued even more rapidly after World War II when Protestant members only accounted for 40% of MPs. Throughout, a stable 8% to 11% of these Protestant Members belonged to the *gereformeerden*, the more orthodox Protestants.

During the period between the two constitutional reforms of 1848 and 1888, the number of Catholic MPs was quite stable, between 20% and 22% (Fig. 8.9). This was, however, far below the 35% to 40% Catholic share of the population, at that time. One of the main reasons for this discrepancy was the electoral system which favoured the upper classes. However, after the constitutional reforms of 1888, a quarter of the members of the newly elected House were of Catholic origin. This rose further in 1918 and the following years due to the extension of suffrage and the introduction of proportional representation. For some time now, every third MP has been a Catholic, which mirrors the proportion of Catholics in the population. At the end of the nineteenth century, we see a slight rise in the number of non-denominational members. This increased gradually so that it was over 10% in the interwar period, and between 25% and 30% after World War II. Data concerning the religious background of MPs after the 1960s, however, have to be treated with caution. For a considerable portion of the House, data about religious affiliation are simply missing. The enormous increase of unaffiliated MPs, however, seems to match data taken from the general population in 1986.[21] Other similar indications also point to the phenomenon, which is significant in itself, that denomination has lost much of its meaning in national politics.[22]

4.5. Geographical Representation

In the present Dutch electoral system, although the country is treated as a single electoral district, there are in fact nineteen districts mainly for administrative purposes. These allow parties to submit different lists of candidates to attract as many votes as possible, without any legal requirement for a

---

[21] The proportion of non-denominational MPs is in accordance with similar data for the entire population. Data published by H. Knippenberg in 1992, based on population censuses taken until 1971 and a sample in 1986, mention the following percentages of unaffiliated among the entire population: in 1947: 17.1%, in 1960: 18.3%, in 1971: 23.6%, and in 1986: 48.6%.

[22] The need for a merger of the three major denominational parties, to stop further electoral losses, was another indication of the decreasing stability of religious strength.

relationship between the candidate and the electoral district. As a matter of course, the major parties are pressed to put the names of local candidates on their lists. The Labour Party is particularly known both for strong influence from regional branch organizations and for promoting relations between MPs and their administrative districts. However, as Andeweg and Irwin have stated, these are internal party matters and not a part of the electoral system (Andeweg and Irwin 1993: 87).

There was a time when regional elements did play a predominant and legal role in the representation in the Dutch *Staten-Generaal*. During the two centuries following independence from the Spanish Habsburg House, the Dutch Republic had consisted of a confederation of seven united provinces, each of which sent its own deputies to the States-General. Inhabitants of the Dutch Republic identified themselves with their provinces or cities in the first place, so that they were first and foremost inhabitants of Zealand, Utrecht, Frisia, or Amsterdam, and 'Dutch' second. Although the unitary state had been introduced under French control by the end of the eighteenth century, when the House of Orange was reinstated in 1813, the twenty years of French influence and domination had not erased all traces of the previous confederal existence. Consequently, although the first post-Napoleon constitution explicitly confirmed the unitary character of the state, remnants of the provincial influence were also present. In this way, the provincial councils maintained a powerful position, particularly through their right to elect the Members of the Second Chamber.[23] From 1849 until 1918, the Members of the Second Chamber were elected by direct vote, in plural (until 1896) or single-member constituencies. It therefore is for this seventy-year period only that it is worthwhile to examine connections between electoral districts and parliamentary candidates.

For the last thirty years, the desirability of returning to some kind of geographical representation has been under discussion. Geographical representation is supposed to reinforce the political affiliation between the electorate and the elected, and under such a system MPs are supposed to keep in close contact with their electoral district. They are, however, not required to have any natural ties to the area by birth, residence, or otherwise. Advocates of this idea have in mind the electoral system of the second half of the nineteenth century, when the Members of the Second Chamber were elected in plural or single-member constituencies. Indeed, when this system was in operation, it was the traditional local connections between voters and MPs that adherents of the existing system gave as a reason for their opposition to the proposed system of proportional representation.

---

[23] The provincial councils had the right to elect the Members of the Second Chamber from 1814 to 1848. Since 1848, they have been exercising the same right as to the election of the Members of the First Chamber. The elected Members, however, had to declare that they would act as *national* Representatives and not as Representatives for specific provinces.

Today, the inference is still that such a system of representation automatically ensures strong geographical ties between constituency and elected Member of Parliament. However, it has to be questioned whether such strong ties ever did exist when such an electoral system was in operation, especially as a residency rule has never been mooted. In light of all this, it would be interesting to examine relations between electoral district and the local roots of candidates. However, such detailed data are not available. Rather, we can provide information which shows links between the province of MPs' birth and the district in which they were first elected.[24]

From 1848, until the elections in the 1880s, about 60% of representatives were born in the same province in which their first constituency was situated. From the 1881 election onwards, this proportion declines slowly, from 50% during the 1880s to below 40% at the last three elections under this system. For an explanation of this data we refer again to the results of the Van den Berg study, which provides more detail (1983: 80–98). His analysis of the regional origin of MPs revealed a strong coincidence between place of birth and region of domicile in the first three decades after 1848, whereby MPs and their families had strong local roots.[25] They did not change residence very often and fulfilled many political and other functions in the same place or within the borders of the same province. Consequently, these local notables were well known by the, albeit restricted, electorate of that time.

Information on the geographical representation of MPs between 1848 and 1888 has also been confirmed by data concerning their previous local political experience (Fig. 8.5).[26] Most Members who were elected between 1848 and 1888 had served a political function in local or provincial institutions, which can easily be interpreted as the continuation of a tradition from the confederal Republic. This changed slightly after 1888 when the number of MPs with local political experience decreased somewhat. After the 1880s, however, the proportion of Members experienced in local politics stabilized between 40% and 50%. Universal suffrage and the introduction of proportional representation did not stop the recruitment of numerous MPs from local politics. Therefore local politics can be considered as a permanent attractive recruitment channel, and a training-ground for numerous national politicians.

---

[24] The eleven provinces were each divided into several electoral districts, the number of which varied over time. See Sect. 2.1.

[25] For this study, we do not pay attention to the role of cities as places of birth, which, as has been demonstrated by Van den Berg, was overwhelming in the first decades following 1848. In the next phase, at the turn of the century, the role of the cities as predominant places of birth of the political elite generally decreased due to the extension of the electorate and the increase of representatives of new parties.

[26] For more detailed information of this kind concerning all Dutch Members since 1888, see Secker (1995).

The first extension of the suffrage in the 1880s to the less well-to-do also marked the end of local support for many traditional political families. The improved travel facilities at this time also seem to be linked to a weakening of geographical affiliation, as demonstrated in this respect. Analysing this fact, Van den Berg pointed to 'a process of political modernisation: a combination of nationalisation, politicisation and democratisation' (1983: 88), that led to a weaker regional affiliation between voter and candidates. Overall, regional affiliation was not able to persist against the growing move towards *Weltanschauung*, or political affiliation. The declining importance of geographical affiliation is most clearly demonstrated by the Liberals, the developments in all other parties, both Protestant and Catholic, being more capricious. In particular, irregularities are evident in the 1850s and 1860s. In subsequent elections, links between provincial nativity and electoral district of Members from all parties showed the same rate of decline.

4.6. Occupational Background

Ever since the development of parliamentary democracy, strong connections have existed between Parliament and the public sector, as can be seen in the considerable number of Dutch MPs recruited from the civil service (Figs. 8.13–8.16). In the nineteenth century, almost half of the House consisted of former state employees, and although this dropped to 30% in 1853, it continued to rise in following electoral years, so that between the elections of 1868 and 1887, the majority of the MPs had held public office. This declined somewhat after this period, and even more so after 1918. However, even during the postwar period, one-third of all Members had had a public sector career prior to joining the House. After the 1970s, the percentage of Members with a background of public office was the same as, or even higher then, that of the 1850s. Thus, the public sector as recruitment channel appears to be a permanent feature in Dutch parliamentary history but, as Daalder and Van den Berg have stressed, the connection between MPs and the civil service has undergone important changes over time. Nineteenth-century politicians had been predominantly office holders (*ambtsdragers*), whereas their twentieth-century colleagues have been recruited from the civil service in general (*ambtenaren*).

In the nineteenth century, the juridical sector constituted the second major recruiting sector and a quarter to a third of MPs in the first decades of the period under study had practised as lawyers. However, after the 1860s, this proportion declined to 20% and sank even further after 1900 (Fig. 8.12). This decline continued so that after the 1950s, their share was less than 10%, and in most recent years not even one MP in thirty has practised as a lawyer. The recruitment of MPs coming from the judiciary, which includes Public Prosecutors, followed a similar path at a somewhat lower level (Fig. 8.16). However, dating back to the nineteenth century, Dutch constitutional law has rejected any political role for the judiciary. For a long time, the independence of judges was protected by appointment for life. Even today they are strictly separated from public administration while the Public Prosecutors and their substitutes are under the direct control of the Minister of Justice. The excessive number of law courts which existed until the end of the nineteenth century undoubtedly accounted for the large number of their members in Parliament.[27]

Since the end of the nineteenth century, the occupational background of MPs has changed considerably and new occupational categories such as educational professions and political and trade union officials are to be found. During the nineteenth century, only a handful of MPs (never more than 5%) came from teaching institutions (Fig. 8.15). All were university professors, the most famous among them being Johan Rudolf Thorbecke, writer of the 1848 Constitution. After the beginning of this century, more former teachers were returned to the House (10% in 1909, rising, temporarily, to 14% in 1917). Recently, there has been an increase of MPs in this category and, after the 1977 elections, their share rose to an all-time high of about 20%.

Although the role of the press became of major importance in the 1870s, journalists did not immediately enter the Second Chamber in any great number, although full-time, professional journalists did play a role of some importance between 1900 and 1967 (Fig. 8.17). However, their share seldom exceeded 10%.[28] The number of MPs recruited from the world of trade or business was also never extensive, and as the Netherlands is renowned for its outstanding role in this sector, this may seem curious (Fig. 8.11). However, as mentioned earlier, the nineteenth-century political elite were mainly the offspring of the former *regenten*, the caste of city rulers that owed their privileged position to their families' business prosperity. They themselves, therefore, tended to live on the means collected in earlier times. Interestingly, a deviating pattern emerged after the elections of 1994 and 1998, when the percentage of Representatives with a business background rose above 10%.

The primary sector never played an important role in supplying representatives to the House, and only between 3% and 5% (6% between 1925 and 1929) of MPs ever came from this sector (Fig. 8.10). Even more weakly represented were the blue-collar workers. The first Member of Parliament recruited from this sector entered the House in 1897. However, for a correct

---

[27] In the 1850s there were 11 Provincial Courts, 34 other courts of justice, and 150 lower magistrates' courts. Each time this excessive (and expensive) judicial system was questioned, MPs who represented the constituency concerned opposed the reduction. Reorganization and reduction in this field succeeded partially in 1877 for the first time.

[28] Their number may be somewhat underestimated. Among the MPs who have been described as coming from trade unions or other social organizations, some had journalistic experience as well.

analysis of these occupational background data, one has to bear in mind that candidates from both sectors had climbed the social ladder long before standing for an election. A career in political organizations or trade unions was especially useful in bringing former workers into parliament, and MPs from such organizations were no longer considered to belong to the primary sector or industry. Indeed, professional politicians with such backgrounds formed a considerable proportion of the first Social Democrat MPs. Together with leading party officials, they belonged to the new category of full-time politicians which took off in 1918 (Fig. 8.18). At first, one in ten MPs belonged to this category but between the 1930s and the 1960s, nearly one-quarter of MPs were recruited from this group. Roman Catholics started to contribute more substantially to this high percentage after the 1920s, while Protestant MPs with a similar occupational background appeared in greater numbers after 1945. It was the denominational parties in particular that ascribed a paramount importance to all kinds of inter-mediate organizations between the pure public and private domains. These organizations, which particularly prospered in the *Verzuilings* period, were an outstanding breeding-ground for future Christian and Socialist politi-cians. When the *Verzuiling* had passed its peak, the importance of this cat-egory of professionals also declined in Parliament, although they still ranked second after MPs with public office backgrounds.

4.7. Political Experience

No specific education or formal examination are required to enter the House. Nevertheless, Members are expected to possess certain abilities or qualifications which enable them to be good representatives. Of particular importance, naturally, are those abilities directly linked to activities in the political field, and for this reason, we are interested in the past political experience of MPs. At some time before being elected, many MPs had acquired some kind of practical training in other political institutions, at either local or national level. In fact, as has been discussed earlier, Dutch national political life has shown a strong affiliation between local politicians and national politics, going back to the era of the confederal Republic of the Seven United Provinces (see Sect. 4.5 and Fig. 8.5). Much less numer-ous were MPs who prior to their entrance in the Second Chamber had acquired some political expertise while occupying a seat 'on the other side of the *Binnenhof*', that is, in the First Chamber. Indeed, there were hardly ever more than 5% of the Members of the Second Chamber who had been a Senator before being elected to the Second Chamber. Only after two elec-tions, in 1948 and 1952, did the proportion of ex-Senators in the Second Chamber rise above this to between 10% and 12%, respectively. It is not without justification that the Senate has often been depicted as a gentle-men's club for elder statesmen *after* a successful political career!

From a comparative point of view, it may be more significant to see to what degree former Cabinet Ministers returned to Parliament. The absence in Dutch parliamentary history of the tradition of a transition from Cabinet Minister to MP has often been explained by referring to the incompatibility of the two positions. Irrespective of whether incompatibility was a constitutional rule or not, on average, no more MPs were recruited from the Cabinet than from the Senate. In the mid-1850s, one in ten new MPs had previously occupied a ministerial seat, and after the next elections, this proportion was reduced further to a mere 5%. The short-lived rise of ex-Senators, elected to the Second Chamber in some postwar elections, was accompanied by a slight increase of ex-Ministers in the House. A similar synchronism was absent when the proportion of ex-Ministers in the Second Chamber rose again, at the end of the 1970s. This was because, when the expected second Den Uyl Cabinet did not take place, several former Socialist Ministers returned to the House. However, ex-Cabinet Ministers, instead of accepting parliamentary membership, usually prefer to wait for an appropriate appointment somewhere else.

Prior to their election or appointment in one or other political institutional job, many MPs had been involved with their parties at national or local levels (Fig. 8.6). The number of MPs in the nineteenth century (two-thirds), who had participated in local electoral groups that can be considered as forerunners of the political parties, was particularly high. Paradoxically, however, as more national political parties increased, fewer party politicians entered the House. While in the 1890s, over half of MPs had had no previous party political function, recruitment from party political organizations actually sank to its lowest in the interwar years. This lower party political preoccupation was particularly marked for MPs affiliated to denominational parties. However, after the 1950s, it was these same parties that accounted for the rise to over 70% in the 1970s, of Members who had been active in political parties. Generally, as in the last six elections over 60% of the MPs were recruited from party political circles, membership of Parliament can be seen as a definite reward for former party political activities.[29]

5. THE TRANSFORMATION OF THE SECOND CHAMBER RECONSIDERED

Having considered several background characteristics of all Dutch MPs over one and a half centuries, it is time for an overall view. To what extent did the successive institutional changes and party political developments

---

[29] Recent studies on candidates' nomination affirm this tendency; see Hillebrand (1992).

affect the personal composition of the Second Chamber? In particular, it is important to note the turnover and incumbency rate of individual MPs before proceeding to our conclusions. This is also necessary because the first condition leading to a transformation in the composition of Parliament is related to the degree of turnover of candidates and the proportion of individual new Members.

5.1. Turnover and Incumbency

As previously mentioned, during the time of geographical representation, and possibly because of it, rather strong ties existed between candidates and their electorate. There is no doubt that this was partly accounted for by the limited size of the electorate and the fact that candidates and voters belonged to the same upper and middle classes. Does this time, when no political parties dictated candidacy, imply longer tenures and more re-elections of the MPs?

When, in 1849, the first direct elections were organized according to the newly written constitutional rule, over 80% of Members returned to the Second Chamber were new, so that the average number of elections in which these MPs had stood was only 1.4 (Figs. 8.20, 8.21). This extremely high level of turnover, and such a low level of parliamentary expertise, has never been surpassed. With each subsequent election, the average personal number of elections rose, so that by the end of the 1860s, when there were several elections within a short time, it had reached an average of 4.0. In the 1880s, the average rate rose again, this time reaching 4.7 and remaining above for some time. This is all the more remarkable because during this period the number of parliamentary seats also rose (by 14). After this time, the average personal number of elections fell from 4.7 to 4.3.[30] Further analysis of the average elections rate of the various political families shows some inter-party differences. The average election rate of about 4.0 between the 1860s and 1900 is predominantly due to the Liberals and their contemporary colleagues of the Catholic group. This is because, in 1864, a new policy condemning liberalism, which was more or less dictated by 'Rome',[31] put an end to the political career of many Catholic MPs. In the southern provinces in particular, new candidates were put forward and elected who, mindful of the papal directives, declared themselves opponents of the, until then, mainly liberal policy. Protestants too, albeit less numerous, replaced their 'first generation' parliamentary delegates in the House in the 1860s

---

[30] The situation in 1956 was almost identical notwithstanding the even stronger extension of the House in that year by 50 seats. The average number of elections of the Members fell from 3.7 to 3.3.

[31] The encyclical letter *Quanta cura* (1864) condemned liberalism as such, liberal school policy in particular.

and 1870s. The lower re-election rate after the 1890s may be ascribed to the rise of political parties, the expansion of the electorate, and changes in the electoral system. In addition, notable families and local groups no longer played a major role in the electoral procedure. From the 1890s to 1918, when the introduction of proportional representation caused drastic changes in the political scene, the re-election rate fell below 4.0, although it did remain above 3.0 until World War II. After 1918, a pattern emerges which can be seen in all political parties, and suggests that there are 'generations' of MPs. At crucial times, part of the House is renewed and a new generation starts its parliamentary career which lasts for three to four legislatures on average. Deviations are mainly accounted for by parties' electoral fortunes.

One should expect an increasing average of the re-election rate to be matched by a decreasing proportion of turnover. However, this has not always been the case. Elections which led to the highest degree of renewal, which was, in the Dutch case, several times over 30%, were not always identical to those that reduced the average number of elections. Turnover was extremely high in 1853, when the Second Chamber was dissolved because of a conflict between King and Cabinet. After the following elections, the voters returned relatively more conservative candidates to the House, who consolidated the King's position. Another very high turnover took place in 1888, after new electoral rules had been introduced. This renewal was, as has been said before, not strongly expressed in the consequent re-election rate. Even higher was the turnover in 1918, after universal male suffrage had been introduced. The average number of elections fell, albeit not dramatically, from 3.8 to 3.1. Most impressive was the renewal of the House in the first election after World War II: in 1946, 42% entered the House for the first time. At the same time, the re-election rate fell from 3.4 to 2.2. Here the rate of renewal and of re-election kept step. In two more election years that brought a rather high degree of renewal again (1967, 1971), the average number of elections was rather low. These two cases of high turnover rates were repeated in the two last elections, in 1994 and 1998, when over 40% and 35% of the MPs respectively entered the House for the first time. Occasionally the polls brought extremely few new Members into the House. In 1887 and 1917, elections were linked to constitutional reforms, and a time when parties, after years of struggle, had finally reached a compromise. In fact, in 1917, the parties actually collectively agreed to renounce new nominations in order to safeguard the important compromise.

5.2. Expansion of the Suffrage

As we have seen, suffrage was extended gradually from 1848 onwards, ending with full suffrage in 1919. What is interesting is, whether the new voters, and changes in the electoral system over time, resulted in a new type of Representative being elected. Without detailed information about the Representatives prior to 1848, this is hard to demonstrate. However, the analysis of the recruitment of the MPs in the 1850s does not point to a pure reflection of the composition of the electorate. Without doubt, the proportion of nobles, academics, and employees among the voters did not match the corresponding number among the elected parliamentarians. Over several decades, the average MP, irrespective of political background, was typically male, from a well-to-do family, well-educated, with a career in public office, a bureaucrat, or similar.

Changes in recruitment patterns did occur each time the electorate was considerably extended; however, the composition of the House never mirrored the electorate to any real extent, and MPs coming from the lower social strata have never been present in any substantial numbers. Therefore, in what way did recruitment change in the various periods under review? The first major change to be seen came after the doubling of the electorate in 1888. In the following elections, fewer academics, hence fewer jurists, and fewer nobles, gained parliamentary seats. Social milieu, as such, lost its impact and hereditary traditions weakened. After the expansion of suffrage came the entrance of the first full-time politician into the House. In 1918, one in ten MPs belonged to this category. In short, recruitment patterns did indeed change after the 1887 constitutional reform, but it is between 1888 and 1918 that real transformation can be observed. Transformation did not take place radically from the very beginning but somewhat erratically, and perhaps rather in anticipation of the drastic reforms introduced in 1917.

The constitutional revision in 1917 with the introduction of universal suffrage and proportional representation, indeed radically affected the composition of the House. It is, in fact, difficult to measure which of the two simultaneous reforms most affected the recruitment of Members, all the more so because of simultaneous developments in the political parties. However, there is no doubt that it was not only the new parties that introduced new types of Representatives: Representatives from all parties demonstrated the new 'rules' of democratization. Overall, differences emerged gradually. The decrease in the number of Members from aristocratic background and of university-graduated Members, especially in law, continued, as did the advance of full-time politicians, whereby in 1937, one in five Members came from this sector. The interwar years can be characterized as the epoch of the 'organized society', mirrored in the House by the presence of numerous Representatives, especially of the religious and Socialist parties, who were recruited from all kinds of political and social-economic organizations. Regional recruitment was hardly affected by the rather radical change of electoral system and, from the beginning of the nineteenth century, taking their province of birth into account, MPs have come from across the entire country. Although World War II has not been a clear watershed as far as the recruitment of MPs is concerned, the postwar Second Chamber is marked by the growing number of MPs who are full-time politicians and who do not continue their former career once elected.

5.3. Impact of the (New) Parties

In 1848, the Dutch Parliament was a more or less non-partisan constitutional institution and Thorbecke's Constitution emphasized the dualistic character of the relationship between Parliament and the government. However, over the years Parliament has developed towards a political arena. This was expressed first in the establishment of nation-wide political parties, which of course also influenced the recruitment of Members, although no sudden break with traditional recruitment took place. At first, the emancipatory parties who were established in opposition to the dominating liberal majority were represented by gentlemen figures similar to the traditional conservative and liberal candidates, except that they differed in religious background. More fundamentalist MPs, Protestants as well as Catholics, entered the House. Catholics, of old, had weak connections with public office (with the exclusion of the judiciary), nobility, and the like. Not even the election of the first Social Democrats caused any major social transformation of the House.[32] Thus, in the years following the 1887 constitutional reform, recruitment patterns changed only slowly.

Evidently, new recruitment sources were tapped after 1918. The relative strength of the parties caused by the newly introduced proportional electoral system certainly played an important role in these developments. The electoral results for the various parties not only affected the political composition of the Second Chamber, but the social and religious composition as well. Success for the Liberals was followed by a higher proportion of lawyers, of academics in general, and of non-fundamentalists. When the orthodox-Protestants were successful, it was easier for some former clergymen to find their way into Parliament. In the interwar period, 'democratization' of the House reached its peak. Representation of the people was never more broadly mirrored in terms of social background and education. The major religious parties and the Social Democrats (who had dominated all elections since 1918 at the cost of the Liberals) introduced new types of MPs. It is also striking that a similar 'democratization' in the liberal parties lagged behind in this period, which is all the more remarkable because it was the Liberals in the nineteenth century who had been the first to recognize the need for constitutional reform, electoral in par-

---

[32] In fact, the first representative from artisan background did not even belong to the Social Democratic family, but was a Liberal.

ticular. One might conclude that they did not keep step with developments in other parties in opposition to the rising Labour Party, which has, from the very beginning, contrasted most with other parties in terms of recruitment patterns. More conformity with other parties, due primarily to the merger of Social Democrats and left-wing Liberals with the new Labour Party, was reached after World War II.

6. CONCLUSION

'Members of Parliament represent the entire Dutch people.' This formulation, stipulated in the first constitution in Dutch monarchal history has been maintained since 1814, but at the beginning of the nineteenth century it expressed a new principle. The new constitution did not return to the days of the old Republic, when the States-General represented primarily and exclusively the sovereign Provincial Councils. It was formally stated, once and for all, that sovereignty lay in hands of the centralized state, at the expense of previous autonomous provinces. To a certain degree, geographical ties between representatives and their electorate continued by way of the electoral district system, and the traditional, locally rooted affiliation of upper-class families persisted until the end of the nineteenth century. In another way, the formulation regarding the representation of the entire people may be interpreted as directed against a monopoly position of various ideological, interest, or social groups in society. Notwithstanding this originally neutral, blank interpretation of Parliament as a true representation of society, MPs have turned into people who primarily represent the respective political parties that supported their nomination, and which undeniably represent a mixture of classes, social organizations, interest groups, ideologies, even regional or local interests.

Taking several data together, we see various aspects related to the social milieu emerge as characteristic recruitment patterns. Dutch representatives in the nineteenth, as well as at the beginning of the twentieth, century are mainly recruited from higher—noble or bourgeois—families. A considerable number among them came from families where the fathers played important roles in governmental or representative institutions. It is mainly due to the absence of political parties at that time that hereditary factors, such as family traditions in the political or public sector, continued to play such an important role, even after the turn of the century. Sons of political families (nobility and patriciate) declined after the turn of the century. However, their presence did not stop as abruptly as one might assume, after the introduction of universal suffrage. Part of the explanation for the persistent importance of traditional families, as far as the recruitment procedure is concerned, is their flexibility and their adaptability to new movements. Thus, the first representatives of new political movements were often members of traditional families who over the years had adapted new political views. However, like some descendants of traditional political families who participated in the breakthrough of progressive Liberals after 1848, they only survived the rise of new, religious political parties to a certain degree. From the beginning of the present century, the decline of recruitment from traditional milieus was irreversible. Party organizations, as well as other social syndicates, offered new recruitment channels to representatives without a traditional political inheritance. The rise of these institutions caused the slow retreat of the hereditary political class.

6.1. Democratization

One of the most interesting findings of the recruitment analysis, as Van den Berg has already stated, was that the interwar period was the period of greatest democratization. Once franchise extension was complete, representatives from different, new sectors of society entered the House: less exclusively recruited from the upper classes or a university background, they came from new occupations like teachers, political party officials, and the like. From a geographical point of view, the role of cities diminished, while a broad variety of traditional geographic recruitment seems to have survived even under proportional representation. Certainly, representatives from the religious parties primarily came from rural areas. In one respect, recruitment patterns did not change, that is, the public sector remained a substantial recruiting channel, although, as Daalder and Van den Berg observed, there has been a definite lag, first for the Catholics and later for the Socialists.

It is remarkable to see that this interwar democratization in recruitment was not continued after 1945. We see no further increase of MPs with only primary or secondary education, and the level of academics among the Members rises again. This occurred along with a sharp rise in the number of persons with experience in various political and social organizations. Representatives from the public sector were also returned to the House in great numbers, against a further decline of Members with a traditional—free profession—background. From the world of commerce and industry, the number of representatives was not of any real significance until the 1990s. Manual workers, who for a long time were also absent, made up for this shortfall from 1918 onwards, by way of representatives from trade unions and other interest groups. In fact, the category of representatives from specialized social and interest organizations, including party bureaucracies, the media, welfare, and cultural organizations, grew fastest and even became the largest after World War II.

Has the once elite-dominated regional pluralism been replaced by

representation via the party-election channel in the world of corporate pluralism, as Stein Rokkan stated? Daalder points to a paradox: the links
between parties and organizations have long since been loosened, while, at
the same time, the job of a Member of Parliament has become a full-time
profession. Most striking indeed in the postwar period is the growing transformation of MPs into full-time professional functionaries. The much
improved salary conditions, as fixed in 1968, certainly contributed to this
comparatively common fact.

6.2. *Changes in Elite Profiles in*
Recent Times

In his analysis of changes in the composition of the Second Chamber, Van
den Berg (1989: 191–200) wrote that the cultural changes were very obvious
in the newly elected House of 1973. Taking the last election, and that of the
previous year together, more than half of the Members were newcomers,
coming not only from the many new 'splinter' parties, but also from traditional ones (Fig. 8.21). Of the new parties, some have succeeded in surviv-
ing. Among the traditional parties, the merger of the three denominational
parties, inevitable since the continued election losses, was most striking.
Notwithstanding this merger, the predominant role of religion lost much of
its meaning. This phenomenon is one of the most obvious changes the
House underwent in the postwar period. Both the Liberals and, although
to a lesser degree, the Socialists have also profited by de-confessionalization. The rather sharp rise of university graduates among MPs since 1945
constituted a second major development, which has continued in the most
recent period. Together with some 20% of MPs who received other high-
level schooling, the number of highly educated Members has regained the
same high level as was the case in the mid-nineteenth century (Figs. 8.1,
8.2).

In the occupational field, some remarkable developments can also be
observed. Generally speaking, the dominant position of the MPs from the
'quartair' sector continued. In other words: experience in public offices,
social organizations, and education holds for more than half of the
Members. Within this field, the emphasis shifted from the organizations in
the 1950s and 1960s to the educational professions in the 1970s and 1980s
(Fig. 8.15). In the meantime, the bulk of MPs from this sector was—as
always—recruited directly from the public service. Both elections of the
seventies, in 1971 and 1972, also led to a lower mean age of the MPs, which
obviously means less previous experience in other sectors in society (Fig.
8.19). Consequently, in 1972, Members had on average served a mere
4.5 years. This very low tenure, however, appeared to be incidental, not

structural. Subsequent elections brought the mean tenure of the House back to the length of nearly two mandates.

Unmistakably new was the development in the recruiting process that Van den Berg (1989: 202–3) described as the *feminization* process. From less than 10% until the 1960s, the percentage of female representatives had more than doubled by the 1980s. Feminist movements finally saw their persistent efforts since the 1960s rewarded. In particular, parties on the Left returned a high proportion of female Members to the Second Chamber. Two of the three Communist Members in 1982, half to two-thirds of the Green Left members in the 1980s were women. The Left-Liberal D66 shows a rather capricious policy in this respect: a high female representation (50% in 1982) followed by a steep fall to 10% in 1986. The electoral results, being just as capricious in those years, may account for the disappearance of so many female MPs. In fact, this fits in perfectly with Van den Berg's observation in 1989. He drew attention to the fact that many women only entered the House in the second instance, replacing MPs who left the House midterm. This very phenomenon, moreover, often led to rather short tenure, when the polls brought negative results for their party. Gradually, however, it looks as if women are being successful in gaining a more stable, less hazardous position on the list of candidates. In 1994, for the first time, one-third of Members were women. Nor has this process stopped: as a result of the elections in May 1998, 36% of MPs are female. Again, most women can be found on the Left.[33]

One of the most outspoken findings of the analysis of the recruitment study was the conclusion that inter-party differences on social background criteria have been decreasing since the 1950s. The increasing professionalization of the parliamentary job converted Members of all parties into persons of a more or less homogeneous type. This process of more and more homogeneity in the recruiting process reached its peak in the 1970s, since when it has not seriously changed. Political parties lost much of their diverse recruiting criteria, so that it has become hard to distinguish between the candidates of the various parties. Or, in the words of Van den Berg (1989): they have become 'Prefab-MPs'.

References

Andeweg, Rudy B. (1989). 'Institutional Conservatism in the Netherlands: Proposals for and Resistance to Change', in Hans Daalder and Galen A. Irwin (eds.), *Politics in the Netherlands: How much Change?* London: Frank Cass.

[33] Almost one in two Socialists, Left-Liberals and New Left, one in three Liberals, and one in four to five Christian Democrats are women.

Andeweg, Rudy B. and Irwin, Galen A. (1993). *Dutch Government and Politics*. London: Macmillan.

Daalder, Hans (1981). 'Consociationalism, Center and Periphery in the Netherlands', in Per Torsvik (ed.), *Mobilization Center-Periphery Structures and Nation-Building*. Bergen: Univ.-Fort, 181–240.

——(1995). *Van oude en nieuwe regenten. Politiek in Nederland*. Amsterdam: Bert Bakker.

——and J. T. J. van den Berg (1983). 'Members of the Dutch Lower House: Pluralism and Democratisation, 1848–1967', in Moshe M. Czudnowski (ed.), *Does Who Governs Matter? Elite Circulation in Contemporary Societies*. DeKalb, Ill.: Northern Illinois University Press, 214–42.

——and Irwin, Galen A.(1989). *Politics in the Netherlands: How Much Change?* London: Frank Cass.

Elzinga, D. J. (1985). *De financiële positie van de leden der Staten-Generaal*. Groningen: Wolters-Noordhoff.

Hillebrand, R. (1992). *De antichambre van het parlement: Kandidaatstelling in Nederlandse politieke partijen*. Leiden: DSWO Press.

Kennedy, James C. (1995). *Nieuw Babylon in aanbouw: Nederland in de jaren zestig*. Amsterdam: Boom.

Knippenberg, Hans (1992). *De Religieuze Kaart van Nederland: Omvang en geografische spreiding van de godsdienstige gezindten vanaf de Reformatie tot heden*. Assen: Van Gorcum & Comp. BV.

Secker, W. P. (1995). 'Personal Circulation in the Dutch Second Chamber 1888–1993: Towards Institutionalisation and Professionalisation and then?' *Historical Social Research*, 20/1: 3–32.

Van den Berg, J. T. J. (1983). *De toegang tot het Binnenhof. De maatschappelijke herkomst van de Tweede-Kamerleden tussen 1849 en 1970*. Weesp: Van Holkema & Warendorf.

——(1989). 'Het 'prefab-kamerlid'. De gewijzigde recrutering van de Tweede kamerleden sinds 1971–1972', in J. T. J. Van den Berg, H. M. Bleich, A. van Gameren, W. P. Secker, and G. Visscher (eds.), *Tussen Nieuwspoort & Binnenhof. De jaren 60 als breuklijn in de naoorlogse ontwikkelingen in politiek en journalistiek*. Den Haag: SDU, 191–210.

Van Tijn, T. (1971). 'The Party Structure of Holland and the Outer Provinces in the Nineteenth Century', in J. S. Bromley and E. H. Kossmann (eds.), *Britain and the Netherlands IV: Metropolis, Dominion and Province*. Den Haag, 176–207.

9

Democratization and Parliamentary Elite Recruitment in Norway 1848–1996

KJELL A. ELIASSEN AND MARIT SJØVAAG MARINO

1. THE NORWEGIAN POLITICAL SYSTEM IN TRANSITION

1.1. The Liberal Constitution of 1814

Modern parliamentary representation in Norway dates back to the Constitution of 1814, which established a parliament based upon popular election. At the time of construction, the Norwegian Constitution was highly advanced with respect to giving formal rights of citizen participation in national elections. It created a comparatively open access to the electoral channel. In 1815, it was estimated that because of the dominance of a free peasantry in Norway, about 45% of all men above the age of 25 were given the right to vote and to be elected into parliament (Kuhnle 1975). In practice, however, this liberal suffrage was restricted by registration requirements and indirect elections, and the enfranchised population was only gradually mobilized to take part in elections. Shifts in the composition of the parliamentary elite happened even more slowly.

From 1814 onwards, there was little change in the effective electorate until 1884. The threshold of inclusion was, however, substantially lowered during the next twenty years (Rokkan 1970: 183–4).[1] Universal suffrage was eventually achieved in 1913. Rights of participation at the local level existed from 1840 and conformed to those at national level. The electoral system remained an indirect absolute majority system from 1814 until 1906. At this time, it was transformed into a single-member absolute majority system that lasted until 1919, when a system of proportional representation was introduced. Particular to the Norwegian system, and of special interest to this chapter, was the requirement for close ties between the constituency and its representatives, which was taken so far as to demand that the

[1] The Constitution of 1814 restricted the franchise to officials, freeholders, and leaseholders in the countryside, owners of real estate and holders of merchant's artisan's licences in the cities. From 1884, the franchise was extended to residents qualifying as taxpayers on the basis of their income. In 1898, all accountable men over 25 were given the right to vote.

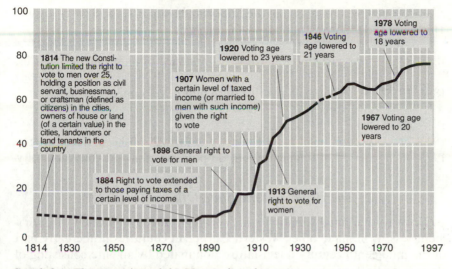

Graph 9.1. The extension of the Norwegian electorate

Note: Dotted line is an estimate.

representative should live in the constituency (*bostadsbånd*). This arrangement lasted until 1952, and is one explanation for the high proportion of MPs with political experience derived from local politics. These developments in suffrage extension and the electoral system are illustrated in Graph 9.1.

Norwegian political history from 1814 until the 1960s can roughly be divided into three periods: the *regime of the officials* from 1814 until 1884, with centralized bureaucratic rule (referred to by Seip and Rokkan as the 'pre-party' period); the *multiparty regime* of 1885 to 1945, characterized by rapidly changing governments and frequent shifts in parliamentary constellations and alignments; and the *one-party regime* after 1945, with the Labour Party continuously in power until 1965 (Seip 1963). These three periods, albeit an oversimplified classification, point to three crucial elements in the political development in Norway: the centralized bureaucratic rule; the territorial and cultural opposition to the governing officials and the urban elite; and the intensification of class contrasts which paralleled the development of a market economy and industry across the country (Rokkan 1967).

In our analysis, we will divide Norwegian history into five periods. Taking the three main periods as given above, we think it helpful to divide the second period (of territorial and cultural opposition) further into one period of mass mobilization (1884–1918) and one of politicized rule-making (1918–40), and the third period (intensification of class contrasts) is again divided into the bureaucratic state up to 1972, with a final period characterized by a reduction in the importance of parties and party loyalty. This gives the following periods in the analysis:

1848–84   'pre-party' period, with a dominance of high state officials in the political elite;

1884–1918   period of mass mobilization and development of the party structure;

1918–40   'rule of the politicians';

1945–72   predominant party regime and growth of the welfare state;

1973–96   period of fragmentation, de-politicization and voter volatility.

1.2. The Regime of the State Officials 1848–1884

In Norway, the initial situation with regard to the composition of parliament was, as in many other Western European countries in the early part of the nineteenth century, a legislature dominated by an elite consisting of state officials, large landowners, and merchants. The creation of elected national assemblies had not brought about any fundamental change in their position, primarily because they had been able to expand their formal power positions to include the newly created legislative institution. The exact composition of the incumbents in each country was, however, determined by historical tradition and overall social composition. Norway had no powerful landed aristocracy dominate the early legislatures, as was the case in other countries such as Prussia and Great Britain. The major force in the elite was *embetsmennene*, that is, higher state officials, who controlled both the parliament and the cabinet.

The bases of legitimacy for the incumbent elite were that they belonged to the controlling section of the population themselves and had an 'understanding' of the mutual set of rights and obligations. Their qualifications were derived from experience, first from their own function as mediators between state and society, and secondly from their position as owners, which gave insight into how the economic and political system functioned. The recruitment process was mainly based on this ascriptive social status.

1.3. Mass Mobilization and Political Parties 1884–1918

Mass mobilization in Norway was a long and slow process and started with gradual social, cultural, and religious mobilization in the wake of the newly gained independence from Danish rule in 1814. It took, however, until 1884 for the principle of parliamentarism to be applied. This was the culmination of a power struggle between the Liberals (*Venstre*—the Left Party) and the Conservatives (*Høyre*—the Right Party) during the establishment period of their respective parliamentary parties. As Rokkan states:

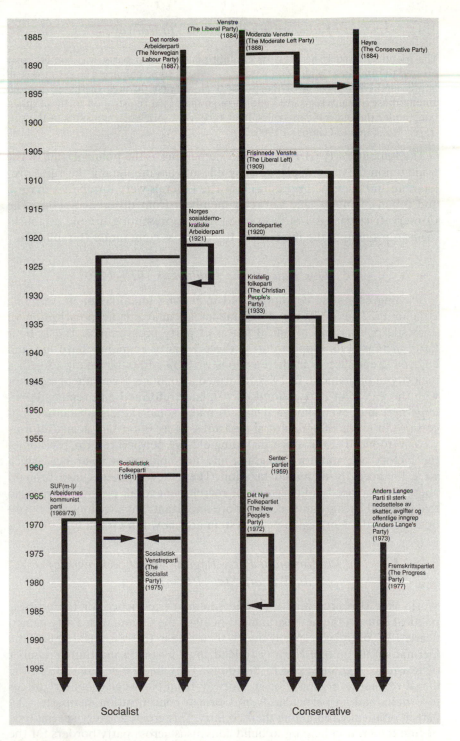

Graph 9.2. The development of the Norwegian party system

The [political] system had lost its equilibrium, and each party was continuously pressed to bring in new allies on its side to achieve some balance. The result was an unprecedented expansion of the political arena: first through increased turnout among those already registered and through increased registration of those qualifying under the old franchise rules, later through a series of extensions of the suffrage. (Rokkan and Campbell 1966: 76)

The Labour Party (*Arbeiderpartiet*), emerging as the political wing of the trade union movement, played a significant role in aligning the rural proletariate and the urban working class. The Liberals were torn between rural and urban members, and between members from different regions. The Conservatives changed in this period from representing the old establishment to promoting the interests of the business community (Graph 9.2).

1.4. The 'Rule' of the Politicians 1918–1940

Worsening economic conditions and increasing unemployment, reaching 20% in 1927 and 33% by 1933, meant an unavoidable polarization of domestic politics and a radicalization of party programmes. The Labour Party increased its support during these years of economic hardship, and enjoyed great success in the elections of 1933, although failing to gain a majority in parliament. In 1935, it formed a coalition government together with the Agrarian Party (*Bondepartiet*, later reformed and renamed *Senterpartiet*) and, even though it had to make some rather substantial concessions in terms of agricultural measures, many important social reforms were introduced at this stage, including old-age pension reform, revision of the factory act, statutory holidays, and unemployment insurance, which were financed by increased taxation. These developments also brought about an increased politicization of recruitment to all political parties, so that political background became more important. The divisions and developments of the Norwegian party system are shown in Graph 9.2.

1.5. The Predominant Party Regime and the Growth of the Welfare State 1945–1972

World War II represented a unique common experience for the postwar political elite. In the new parliament of 1945, the Communist Party gained nearly 12% of the vote, partly due to their role in the resistance against the German occupation of Norway. Indeed, in all parties, a substantial number of resistance fighters were to be found. They had come home from the illegal resistance organization in Norway, from Norwegian military forces in Britain, and, in particular, from German concentration camps, to take part in politically rebuilding their country. This created a very special type of elite integration helping to build consensus across party borders for the next ten to fifteen years.

The Labour Party dominated Norwegian politics from 1945 until 1961, either with a single overall majority in parliament or, as in 1945, in coalition with the Communist Party. The beginning of the postwar period was characterized by very little political conflict, mainly due to the common experience of the war and to the integration of the political elite. Although, in the electoral campaign of 1949, there was a substantial repoliticization of the parties, probably in order for them to attract voters, the period that followed was dominated by depoliticization and a narrowing of political conflict between parties (Torgersen 1967). Indeed, the reduction of political conflict became so extreme that the lack of opposition in some political areas, such as foreign policy and defence, meant that they were effectively removed from the political process. This also led to a concentration of political parties in the middle of the political spectrum, implying fierce competition for the 'median voter' and a general development of consensus in the political landscape.

In the fifty-two years after 1945 there were thirteen legislatures, during which the Labour Party governed for more than forty years. Postwar Norway had, however, with the establishment of the Christian Peoples' Party (*Kristelig Folkeparti*) in 1933, six political parties: the Communists and the Labour Party on the Socialist wing of the spectrum, the Liberal Party, the Agrarians, and the Christians in the political Centre, and the Conservatives on the Right. This situation remained stable until 1961, when there was a split-off from the Labour Party to form the Socialist People's Party (*Sosialistisk Folkeparti*).

The overriding issue in 1961 was Norway's possible entry into the European Common Market (the predecessor of the European Union), an issue which created deep divides within the political landscape. The Labour Party and the trade union movement, together with the Conservative Party, advocated entry, while the Socialists and Agrarians were strongly against Norwegian membership, and the Left and the Christians were split. Old regional contrasts remanifested themselves. 'The Southerners and Westerners again stood out as the defenders of the cultural autonomy of the provinces against the encroachments of the centre. This time the enemy was not just in Oslo, but, what made it much worse, in the distant bureaucratic centres on the European continent' (Rokkan 1967: 402).

1.6. Fragmentation, Depoliticization, and Voter Volatility 1973–1996

The 1970s were marked by the growth and increased importance of the oil industry to the Norwegian economy. The first Norwegian oil was shipped ashore in 1971, and a decade later one-quarter of the state's income stemmed from the oil industry. Public expenditure had an average growth rate of 7% per annum between 1974 and 1980. Norwegian economy increased its reliance on raw materials and products for further refinement, and the rights of sea and natural resources became a political issue. Public ownership of the oil company, *Statoil*, turned the state into the largest and most influential capitalist in society (Furre 1992).

The turbulence in the economy and shifting societal structures and values might explain some of the political development in this decade. Growth in the public sector meant an increase in the number of lower-rank public officials and civil servants, who were targeted as potential voters by the Conservative Party. Furthermore, general economic growth resulted in more well-paid young voters with a propensity to vote with the right wing. The Labour Party, on the other hand, had difficulties meeting demands from all the various groups that it had formerly accommodated. The parliamentary outcome of this was that, throughout the 1970s, the Conservatives (*Høyre*) and the Progress Party (*Anders Langes Parti*, later *Framskrittspartiet*, the first populist party in Norway, emerging in the first half of the 1970s) both increased their representation.

Another aspect that deserves attention in this period is the issue of influential decision-making power in the public apparatus, that is, who makes the decisions? The shift from a politician-dominated parliament in the 1960s to a bureaucrat-driven decision-making system in the 1970s had inherent difficulties with legitimacy in a country so proud of its openness and democratic, egalitarian traditions.

The 1972 referendum and fight over Norway's proposed entry into the EEC had a large and destructive impact on the party structure in Norway. After the general elections in 1973, an alliance of left-wing opponents to EEC membership (Socialistic Left—*Sosialistisk Venstreparti*) gained a large proportion of the votes, and the Christian People's Party also became more popular. However, the Conservatives and the Liberals suffered heavy losses, with the Labour Party having its worst electoral results in the postwar period (Furre 1992: 320–50).

What remains of this change in the relevant weighting between the different parties is not so much the pattern from 1973, but rather the phenomenon of voter fluctuations and a decreased loyalty to any one political party. Moreover, non-party organizations have gained an important role in the policy-making process generally, resulting in a shift in both the importance and the role of the traditional democratic structures.

At the end of the 1970s it became clear that the social democratic order was in a deep crisis. The belief in a strong state, capable of managing the economic and social development towards high social welfare goals, faded. Values like equal distribution and solidarity were weakened. The ideological hegemony was lost. (Furre 1992: 417)

The 'wind from the right' increased in power, and at the beginning of the 1980s the social-democratic idea of social solidarity was transformed into a grouping of special interests. Differences between the 'haves' and the 'have-nots' increased.

The 1980s were the decade of liberal ideologies, deregulation, and electoral volatility. Any clear patterns of parliamentary representation were shattered, and pragmatism and new cleavages resulted in fragmentation. In 1981, for the first time since the war, the country returned a non-Socialist government. The incoming Conservative/non-Socialist government retained power until 1986, and again, although only for a brief period, at the end of the decade. However, with the existence of the Progress Party, the Conservatives (*Høyre*) had a competitor for conservative voters and, because they needed to build alliances with (at least some of) the centre parties in order to form a government, the Conservatives had a rather difficult task in positioning themselves. Political parties saw a decline in the number of members. This might signify some dissatisfaction with the actual policies pursued by the parties, but a more significant factor is the general depoliticisation of society. Trade unions had taken on a role as service providers for their members rather than interest mediators, and were run by professionals in line with modern management principles.

Ties with other countries continued to grow in importance and complexity, maybe best illustrated by the Norwegian relationship to the EU. In November 1994, the European issue provoked the second referendum in twenty-two years. The battle for and against membership was not less fierce in the 1990s than it had been in the 1970s, and it revealed that, some twenty years later, many of the old divisions were still very much alive. Due to the recent signing of the Treaty on European Union, which had the word 'union' in the title, the no-voters had yet another emotional card to play. Norway had been in a union with Sweden until 1905, an experience which had left scars on the Norwegian population. Furthermore, the old centre–periphery conflict was still evident. The Norwegian rejection of EU membership in 1994 was also made possible by the very strong and stable economic situation, due mainly to the wealth produced by oil and gas resources. The country could afford to stay out of the European Union, especially with a well-functioning European Economic Area (EEA) in place (Eliassen 1996).

The parliamentary situation after the last referendum has been much more stable and not as dramatic as in 1972. However, although this time the government did not resign, and the return to normal political life was much more rapid than twenty-two years earlier, the same political conflict pattern can still be seen reflected in the 'No to the EU' vote. That said, despite the same cleavage lines remaining in the population as in the post-1972 period, this is not reflected in recruitment to parliament. We believe this can be ascribed to two main factors: first, to the general depoliticization of society where the legitimacy of the system as problem-solver has been shattered; secondly, to the increased importance of issues such as environmental concerns, the future of the welfare state, how to handle increased interdependency in the global environment, which cut across the traditional Left–Right alignment of parties. Thus, we can see significant growth of NGOs (non-governmental organizations) and narrow interest groups as mediators of political interest, and the traditional political parties losing out in the competition.

2. FEATURES OF PARLIAMENTARY ELITES— PATTERNS OF INTERLOCKINGNESS BETWEEN SOCIETY AND POLITY

The democratic ideal of a legislature whose composition mirrors the representation of various societal groups has spurred much of the existing research on elected assemblies. Many of these investigations have focused on the demographic and social background of the political elites, operationalized in terms of gender, age, occupation, and education, and based on the assumption that background has an impact on attitudes and actions. Investigation shows that the Norwegian parliament, like many others, has never been an exact mirror image of the population.

At the beginning of the nineteenth century, Norway possessed a legislature dominated by a traditional elite of state officials, large landowners, and merchants, whose position had been little affected by the creation of elected national assemblies (Figs. 9.7, 9.8, 9.10). The basis of legitimacy

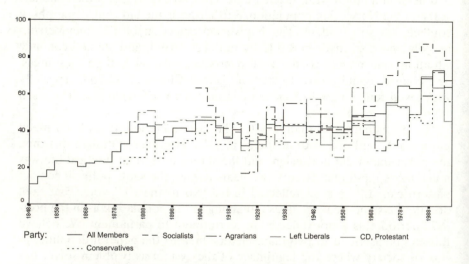

Fig. 9.1. Norway 1848–1996: intermediate education

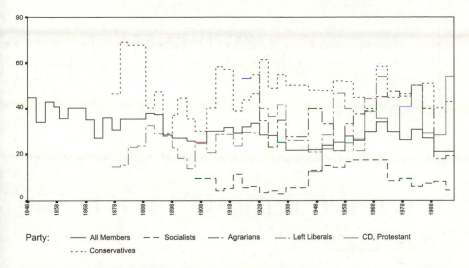

Fig. 9.2. Norway 1848–1996: university degree

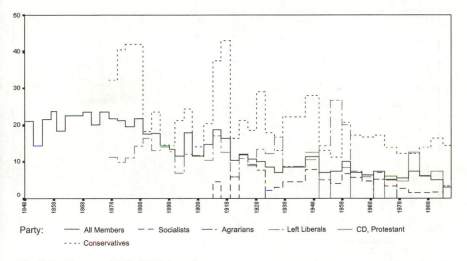

Fig. 9.3. Norway 1848–1996: law degree

for the incumbent elite was that they belonged to the leading part of the population and understood the mutual set of rights and obligations, which existed for both citizens and the state. Indeed, the system of recruitment was closely linked to the basic idea behind the creation of national parliaments and more generally to the concept of the nation state. Citizens were those who were *involved* with the state, either because they owned some property, paid taxes, or were public officials. Their rights were the right to

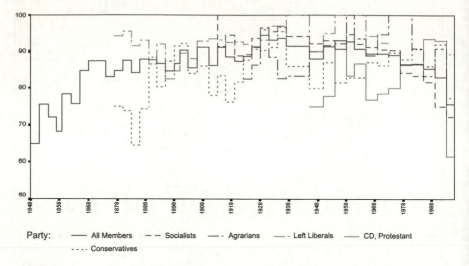

Fig. 9.4. Norway 1848–1996: local politics background

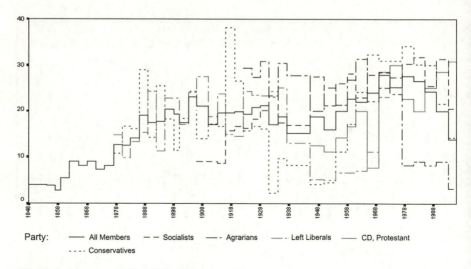

Fig. 9.5. Norway 1848–1996: cabinet positions

vote and to stand for election. Their duties were to serve the state in their various occupations and positions in society and to obey the rules of the state as laid down by their fellow citizens in parliament.

Thus recruitment was mainly based on ascriptive status and few of the enfranchised peasants and smaller property holders in the towns questioned this established view of who were the natural leaders in society. Most

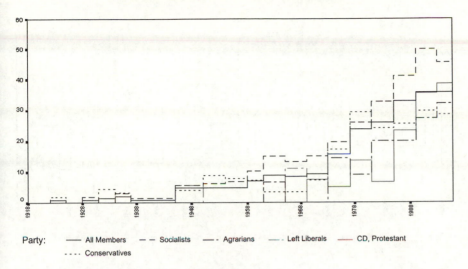

Party: —— All Members – – Socialists —–· Agrarians —–· Left Liberals —— CD, Protestant
····· Conservatives

Fig. 9.6. Norway 1918–1996: female legislators

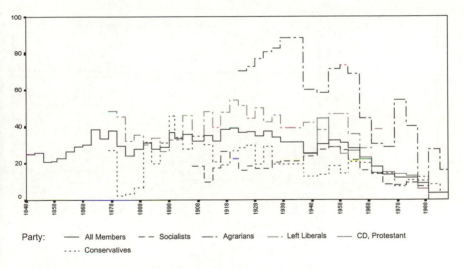

Party: —— All Members – – Socialists —–· Agrarians —–· Left Liberals —— CD, Protestant
····· Conservatives

Fig. 9.7. Norway 1848–1996: primary sector

rural areas elected local staff officials or large landowners as their representatives, so that the proportion of peasant members of parliament was far less than their share of the electorate.

Certain professions then, particularly high status ones, have always been dominant in parliament. The composition of the dominant group has, however, changed with general social development. Even just after the turn

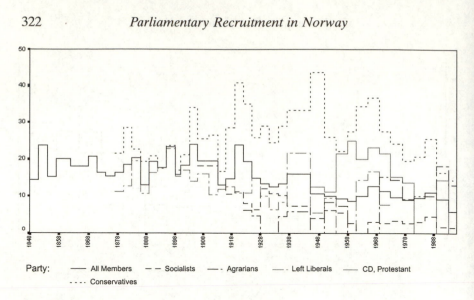

Fig. 9.8. Norway 1848–1996: managers, businessmen

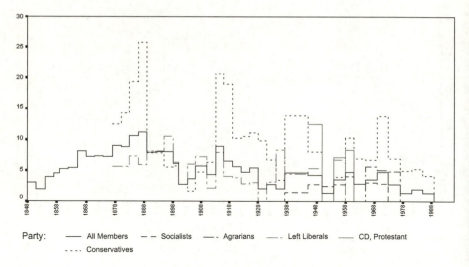

Fig. 9.9. Norway 1848–1996: practising lawyers

of the century, the lower level civil servants increased their relative import-ance, taking over the dominant position from state officials. This tendency has been strengthened, and teachers from various levels of educational institutions, persons in various free professions, civil servants, organizational employees and farmers became the most important professions in Parlia-ment (Figs. 9.7, 9.10, 9.15). In this regard, an examination of the data also

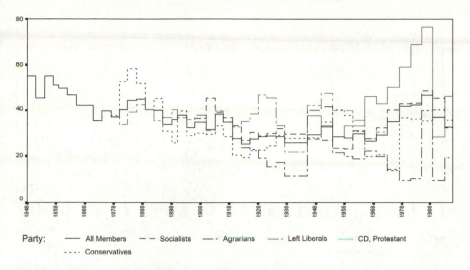

Party: —— All Members – – Socialists —·— Agrarians —·— Left Liberals —— CD, Protestant
···· Conservatives

Fig. 9.10. Norway 1848–1996: public sector employees

suggests that, although the current parliamentary assembly is still skewed compared to the general population regarding professional and gender parameters, this skew towards high social status professions is weaker than that found in other countries.

2.1. The Low Status Groups

Measured in terms of occupational and status categories, the pattern of recruitment changed only marginally in the first fifty years of parliamentary rule. In the 1830s, the number of farmer newcomers to parliament, initially about 15%, increased slightly as a result of their political mobilization, but fluctuated between 10% and 20% thereafter until 1860. The number of state officials was somewhat reduced, but the major shift away from the dominance of the incumbent elite happened only gradually after this time. Figure 9.7 illustrates the further development of the recruitment pattern from 1840 onwards.[2]

The data show that MPs from the primary sector were particularly numerous during the 1870s, and seemed to retain a high representation from the turn of the century until about 1930. From then onwards, there is a gradual but clear decrease (with the exception of the first decade after

---

[2] The figure shows the share of MPs with primary sector background, a broader category than 'peasant newcomers'. Primary sector background also includes fishermen and combined fishermen/peasants, as well as a minor proportion of forest owners, which is why the initial level shown is higher than 10–20%.

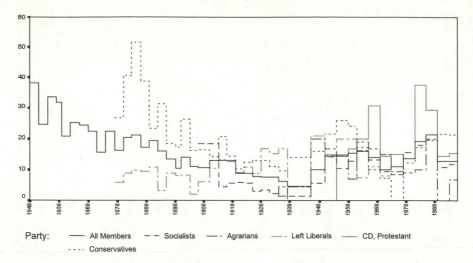

Party: —— All Members — — Socialists ——·— Agrarians ·······— Left Liberals ——— CD, Protestant
- - - - Conservatives

Fig. 9.11. Norway 1848–1996: higher civil servants

1945) in the number of MPs from this sector. However, compared with the population at large, the primary sector is still overrepresented in parliament and seems more able than other areas to retain a higher parliamentary representation, even when their relative share of the population rapidly decreases.

In Norway, however, this overrepresentation has been stronger and has lasted longer than in most other European countries. Reasons for this can be found in at least two factors. First, the free peasantry in Norway goes back to the Middle Ages. In contrast to most other European countries, Norway had no feudal structure, so that Norwegian farmers were landowners in their own right and largely independent. They were therefore also free to organize themselves, which resulted in a strong self-consciousness among the peasants, and they achieved a very special status in society. This well-functioning organizational structure, with strong formal and moral ties between this segment of the population and its representatives, enhanced the possibilities for electoral success. The strong feeling of loyalty towards the Agrarian Party from the 1920s onwards, and the role of farmers' organizations and parties, are also possible contributory factors. Secondly, primary sector overrepresentation in Norway is related to the importance of one particular social cleavage, namely the centre–periphery division. This has historically been very strong in Norway and constitutes perhaps the most important basis for the development of both the party system and the system of interest groups and interest organizations (Rokkan and Campbell 1966). Urbanization in Norway has also been somewhat slower

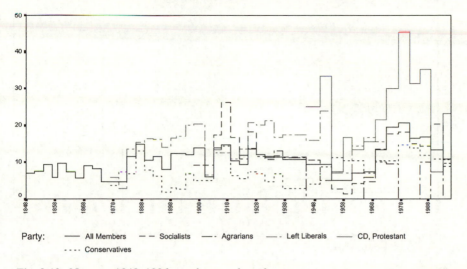

Fig. 9.12. Norway 1848–1996: teachers and professors

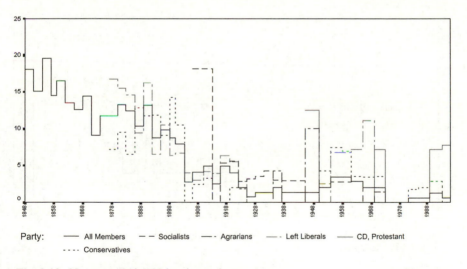

Fig. 9.13. Norway 1848–1996: priests, clergymen

than in other European countries, and even when people moved to urban areas they retained strong affiliations to rural communities. This rural dimension in politics constituted one of the most important reasons for the Norwegian rejections of membership in the European Union in 1972 and 1994 (Eliassen 1996).

As would be expected, representatives with a primary sector background

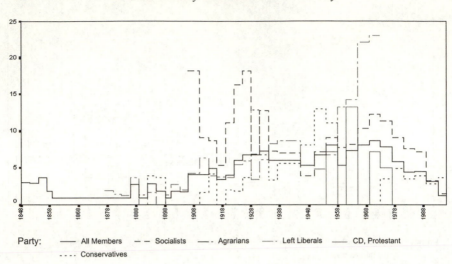

Party: —— All Members – – Socialists —– · Agrarians —···· Left Liberals —— CD, Protestant
···· Conservatives

Fig. 9.14. Norway 1848–1996: journalists and writers

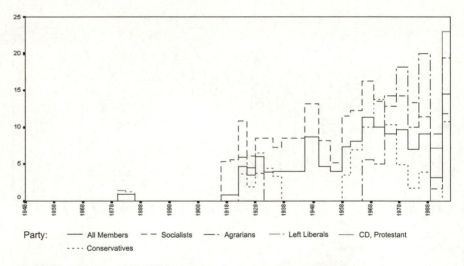

Party: —— All Members – – Socialists —– · Agrarians —··· Left Liberals —— CD, Protestant
···· Conservatives

Fig. 9.15. Norway 1848–1996: party and pressure group officials

have been much more significant in the Agrarian Party than among the other parties and, from the 1920s, when the party was established, until the mid-1960s, more than half of the Agrarian Party's parliamentary members came from the primary sector. The sharp decline which can be seen after the late 1970s must be ascribed to new channels of recruitment and the fact that the party's overall representation in parliament declined from 13.5%

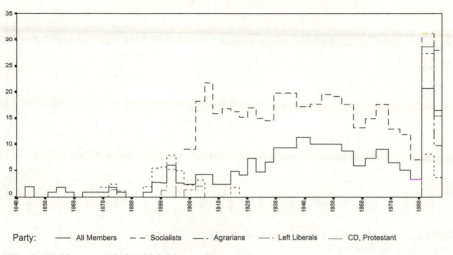

Party: —— All Members — — Socialists ——· Agrarians —— · Left Liberals ········ CD, Protestant

Fig. 9.16. Norway 1848–1996: blue-collar workers

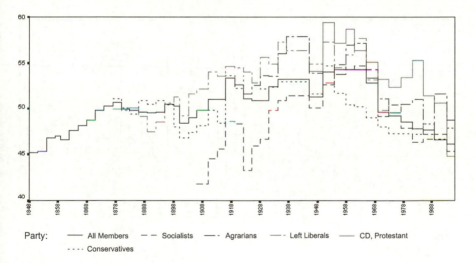

Party: —— All Members — — Socialists ——· Agrarians —— · Left Liberals ········ CD, Protestant
- - - - Conservatives

Fig. 9.17. Norway 1848–1996: mean age

of the vote (21 representatives) in 1973 to almost half, 7.7% (11 representatives), in 1981.

We also see that, whereas the Conservatives had a higher proportion of
MPs with primary sector backgrounds than the Labour Party until the
1930s, after this period, the Socialists and the Labour Party score relatively
highly on this variable. The Labour Party, which had emerged as the

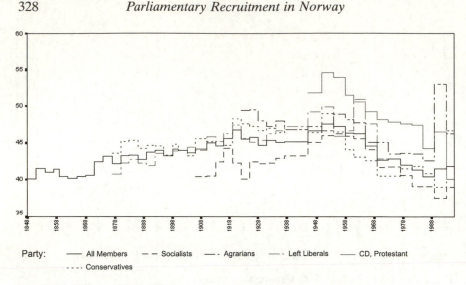

Party: —— All Members   – – Socialists   —— · Agrarians   —— · Left Liberals   —— CD, Protestant
· · · · Conservatives

Fig. 9.18. Norway 1848–1996: mean age of newcomers

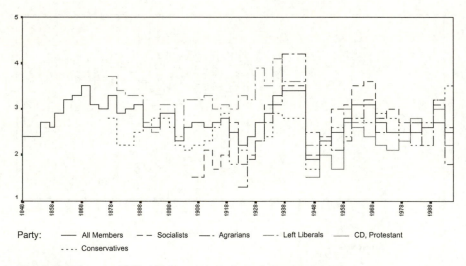

Party: —— All Members   – – Socialists   —— · Agrarians   —— · Left Liberals   ······· CD, Protestant
· · · · Conservatives

Fig. 9.19. Norway 1848–1996: mean number of elections

political wing of the trade union movement and sent its first representatives to parliament in 1903, played a significant part in aligning the rural proletariate and the urban working class. Its earliest Members of Parliament were voted in from the extreme north of Norway in response to an immense mobilization of the coastal population against the dominating class and the established system. But even in the period of bureaucratic politics after

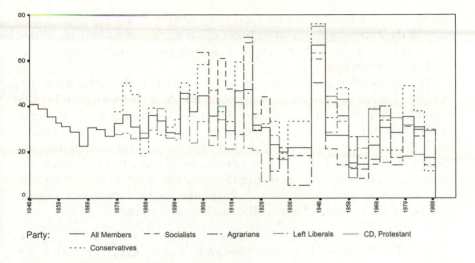

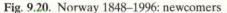

Fig. 9.20. Norway 1848–1996: newcomers

1945, we find that the Labour Party still held a large number of farmers and others from the primary sector. One reason for this is the continued importance of holding top local political offices before entering into parliamentary positions.

Figure 9.16 shows the representation of blue-collar workers in the period 1840–1993. As we can see, the representation from this group remains relatively low until the late 1980s. Up to the 1920s, the group had less than 5% of all MPs, climbing to between 5% and 10% in the period up to the late 1980s, but remaining far below the number of blue-collar workers in the population. While this tendency for workers to be underrepresented in parliament is also a general European phenomenon, two comments have to be made with particular reference to Norway. First, the Labour Party, although defining itself as 'the working class party', had a tendency to recruit as parliamentarians people with a background either in the trade unions or as party officials. This has to do partly with the party organizational structure, but also with the general professionalization of politics.

Secondly, the representation of blue-collar workers is relatively low because of the special Norwegian feature of parliamentary recruitment via local politics. The reasons for this phenomenon are obviously varied, ranging from societal structures, where Norway lacks a clear academic or politically professional elite as, for example, in Britain or France, to reasons of legitimacy, reflecting the deep centre–periphery cleavage in the nation. When the local political leaders are recruited to parliament, they have often had a long paid political career as, for example, mayors, or they had been able to get a new job through local political activity. This might either be in the municipality itself or within local state administration or in organizations in the Labour movement or other interest organizations. Thus, when recruited to parliament, their occupational backgrounds are no longer those of blue-collar workers.

The classification and definition of our data set also influences the outcome. Instead of showing the last occupation of parliamentarians before becoming full-time politicians, the 'occupational background' variable refers to the MP's occupation immediately prior to their entry into parliament. Thus, the Norwegian peculiarity of high recruitment of MPs through local politics, and the Labour Party's procedure of recruitment through the party system, does not do full justice to the actual numbers of MPs having backgrounds as blue-collar workers (nor other occupational categories). This skews the number of blue-collar workers downwards.

2.2. Business Representatives and Public Employees

Figure 9.8 illustrates the development of managers and people with business backgrounds elected to parliament. As previously mentioned, only the occupation directly preceding first election to parliament is counted. However, despite the twists and turns of the curve during the whole period, there is a clear trend from the 1920s onwards for the percentage of managers and business representatives to decrease. We believe that this can be explained by two factors: time and money. MPs' wages are considerably lower than those of business people in the private sector, so there is no economic incentive, especially for private sector managers, to become professional politicians. Consequently, for young, newly graduated Norwegians, with the possibility of working in the private sector, professional politics is usually a less attractive career.

An additional contributing factor to the decline of managers and people with business backgrounds in parliament, is likely to be their general low status and regard within the general population, so that willingness to accept them as political representatives has been rather limited. Norway is perhaps the country in Europe with the lowest status for business skills, competence, and background. A good illustration of this is that as late as 1980, Norway had only one recognized institution for higher business management education, with only a few hundred students. Both workers' and farmers' movements have expressed historically a deep scepticism for business and its values.

The proportion of MPs with backgrounds in management or business is much higher within the Conservative Party than within other parties. Data from Svåsand (1985) has shown that business's preference for the Conservative Party has increased significantly in the postwar period, which would explain why many Conservative MPs have managerial or business backgrounds. It is interesting to note, however, that even through the period of the bureaucrats' rule (postwar to mid-1970s) more than 20% of Conservative MPs came into parliament directly from their business occupation. The curve also reflects the upswing of Conservative votes in the 1980s, when new MPs entered the scene. Another remarkable feature in this graph is the considerable presence of MPs with business backgrounds in the Labour Party group. Throughout the post-World War I era, this share has been up to 8%. This group consists mainly of managers from the co-operative movement.

2.3. Public Sector Background

Figures 9.10 to 9.12 show the parliamentary representation of public sector employees, higher civil servants, and teachers, respectively. As the proportion of teachers in society is generally lower than 3% or 4%, and as their level in parliament remains between 5% and 15% throughout the entire period under review (climbing as high as 20% in the late 1970s), it is clear that this group has always been significantly overrepresented.

Our general hypothesis is that the Norwegian parliament and political system were dominated by public sector employees from 1884 until the 1930s when we see a politicization and radicalization due to social problems, particularly unemployment and economic hardship. Apart from two elections (1897 and 1910), the level of teachers as MPs was higher than 10% until after World War II, that is, at least three times the proportion in the general population. This implies that the teachers 'survived' in parliamentarian elections during the change from the 'civil servants' state' to the 'politicians' state'.

One reason for their continued membership could be their high social standing, combined with firm local affiliations bridging the centre–periphery cleavage. Teachers also represent the rather small section of the population, in both rural communities and small cities, with higher levels of education. Also, they have often been active both in cultural and political organizations at the local level. However, in the postwar period up to the 1970s, as can be seen in Figure 9.12, there was a temporary drop in their representation, which strengthens our hypothesis of a postwar 'bureaucrats' rule'. But, despite this decrease, teachers still held on to their strong representation relative to the population at large. After the 1970s, they became one of the most important groups defending the interests of the growing number of public employees and of the welfare state.

Generally, with regard to party membership, teachers have traditionally constituted an important part of the socialist and centre parties. However, the formation of new parties caused by the radicalization in politics after the referendum on Norway's proposed entry into the EEC, seems to have offered additional routes into parliament for teachers, and it is likely that the upsurge in the proportion of teachers in the post-1972 period can also be explained by these new parties gaining popularity.

From our hypothesis we would expect to see a high level of representation from higher civil servants during the pre-1930s period and in the postwar-to-1972 period. This expectation is born out relatively well by Figure 9.11, although the representation of higher civil servants shows a gradual decline from the 1850s to World War II. The decline after 1884 can be explained by the introduction of parliamentarism and by the newly established political parties' need to broaden their electoral support to new groups of the population. The introduction of direct election to parliament in 1909 further increased the chances for representatives of the new groups to become MPs and hence reduced the relative number of civil servants. The propensity for higher civil servants to align themselves with the Conservative Party, together with the increased politicization of society and the strengthening of the Labour Party from 1927 to 1930, further decreased recruitment from this group. After the war, and as we would expect from our hypothesis, there was an increase in the percentage of higher civil servants during the 'bureaucrats' rule'. Their high representation in 1981 and 1985, when more than 20% of MPs came from this group, must, however, be explained by the Conservative Party's good results in these elections.

If we look at the overall category 'MPs with public sector background' (Fig. 9.10), we observe the same tendencies, albeit smoothed out by the broader category. Generally we can conclude that public sector MPs had their lowest representation during the most politicized period, but that they maintained a high representation in all elections. This is likely to be because of Norway's (at least since World War II) very large public sector and the relatively low legitimacy of the business community and the private sector.

When public sector background is categorized according to political party affiliation, a persistently high level of public sector employees among the Christian Democrats can be seen, although it is difficult to find a convincing explanation for this. In addition, there are never fewer than 22% of public sector employees in the Labour Party ranks, but this we believe, at least in the period after the mid-1960s, can be largely explained by the strong representation of women. Furthermore, after World War II, the Labour Party became known as the party for public employees. However, from the late 1970s, the Left Socialists took over this role.

2.4. Gender

Women were given the right to vote in Norway in 1913 and, since the 1960s, Norway has had a reputation for being relatively progressive regarding women's rights. An illustration of this is the Labour Government of 1979, under Gro Harlem Brundtland, where nearly 40% of ministers were women. This was the culmination of a long process, whereby the proportion of women in parliament (see Fig. 9.6) increased from 6% in the 1940s and 1950s to 35% in the parliamentary assembly of 1996. Correspondingly, the proportion of female ministers has also increased, from 6% to 22%, and is today approaching 40%. However, even though the increase has been substantial, perfect proportional representation of the population has still not been obtained. Nevertheless, compared to other European states, the proportion of female MPs is high.

The large representation of female MPs in Norway can be linked to the strong economic growth starting in the 1970s, due to the development of the oil economy, and the size of the public sector, which is by far the biggest employer of women. The 1970s in Norway (as in many other Western European countries) saw a fundamental change of roles in society. More women became economically independent, more people chose to live without marrying, fewer children were born, all of which have meant a change in the role of the family unit. The new female role included a higher and broader degree of participation in society, first at the local level, but increasingly also at higher political levels, and in parliament.

Women have increased their representation significantly in all political parties, especially during the postwar period. This increase, however, was somewhat slower in the Agrarian and Christian Democratic parties, where traditional family values and social roles have the highest standing. Nevertheless, in 1990, all four main parties had female party leaders. The flattening out of the curve in the 1980s could be temporary but it might also be a sign that a further increase in female MPs is dependent upon further changes in the home sphere and in the male role. Our periodization does not seem to play a major role in the picture concerning women's representation. However, it is interesting to note that their very strong participation corresponds with the post-1972 period in which we have hypothesized that the normal channels for recruitment declined rapidly and new ones emerged. This would seem to have been to the advantage of female representation.

3. POLITICAL PROFESSIONALIZATION OF PARLIAMENTARY RECRUITMENT

3.1. The Concept of Professionalization

Political professionalization is a response to growth in political interest and activity among the masses. Mass mobilization creates a demand for new

qualifications, new kinds of political leaders, and implies an opening of possibilities for participation and an increase in their use. As electoral participation grows, and as mass parties and interest organizations are established
and developed, the pressure upon the legislature increases; political professionalization is part of the response (Eliassen and Pedersen 1978).

The term 'professionalization' has been widely used in political sociology
and political science in general. Max Weber was probably the first to use it
in his classical analysis of political career (Weber 1947; orig. 1919) and subsequent research has dealt with the same topic in much the same terms. This
study of changes in elite recruitment, and the professionalization of Western
European parliaments, is thus a useful continuation of these earlier studies.
The concept has, however, been used in so many different ways that it is
not useful unless given an unequivocal definition. In trying to develop an
operational definition on the basis of the data presented in this book, we
will follow the definition developed in Eliassen and Pedersen (1978) as far
as the empirical evidence permits.

The general statement that the legislative elite becomes more and more
professionalized as time passes lends itself to at least two major interpretations, both of which have been used as a point of departure for this definition. First, professionalization may be interpreted as an aspect of the
increased workload of legislators. This is in line with Max Weber's famous
distinction between politics as a vocation and politics as a profession,
whereby the 'occasional' politician is replaced by the 'professional' who not
only lives for politics, but also lives from politics (Weber 1947; orig. 1919).

The basic argument has tended to imply that professionalization is a
deplorable phenomenon, a change from a 'golden age' in which politicians
were mainly drawn from independent individuals characterized by personal
wealth and substantial achievement in the world outside politics, towards
an era in which politicians tend to be recruited from party activists. Party
loyalty, political experience, and power positions in the political hierarchy
become major assets for the prospective legislator (Eliassen and Pedersen
1978: 291). Put another way, political professionalization is a process
whereby social status gives way to political status as the basic criterion for
political recruitment.

A second main dimension of the professionalization of the recruitment patterns to parliamentary positions has been the growing number of
legislators drawn from the professional-intellectual strata. Intellectual
knowledge and qualifications based on higher education, as well as expert
knowledge, are aspects of the professionalization syndrome that would
seem to be complimentary to political experience as relevant factors in
recruitment to parliamentary and government positions. This is supported
by the conclusion of Eliassen and Pedersen (1978) that development in the
routines, demands, and increased workload of legislators results in a pro-

fessionalization along two major dimensions: namely, those of political and intellectual expertise.

3.2. MPs' Political Background

Indicators related to political background and careers open an access to an analysis of the process of political professionalization, whereby the most striking indication of political background in Norway is local political experience (Fig. 9.4). From the end of the nineteenth century until today, almost all representatives have had a background of serving on local council boards, either as leader or as member. After 1870, the level of MPs with experience from local politics never falls below 80%, and in some postwar parliaments, this has risen as high as 88%.[3] With such high figures, there is not much variation among the parties. For all parties, the share has in most periods since 1900, or since the creation of the party, stayed above 80%. However, in the 1970s, the Labour Party, which traditionally has always had the largest proportion of representatives with local political backgrounds, started to drop below the other parties and was down to 70% in the 1993 election.

Additionally, throughout the whole period from 1850 until the 1980s, there is an increasing proportion of MPs with backgrounds from cabinet positions, and a decreasing number of parliamentary members without any political function preceding their MP status. In fact, after 1900, the proportion of 'absolute novices' in parliament never exceeds 10%. Both these parameters underpin the downward move towards a party-bureaucratic legislature. The increase in the number of full-time party and trade union officials also supports this development (Fig. 9.15). At the same time, there is a clear tendency in the post-World War II period, both in parliament and in the government, for an increasing proportion of members to have had either local or national party leadership positions before election or appointment. In the period 1973–85, as previously stated, as many as 80% of the representatives had had local political leadership positions, and 37% had held key national party positions, either as leader or member of central national boards. Within these indicators, we find the greatest variation among the political parties. The Labour Party has clearly had the highest number of full-time paid politicians more or less throughout the entire period. The proportion of representatives with cabinet position experience varies according to the periods when the different parties have been in government. With regard to representatives with experience of leading party positions, we generally find a higher proportion in the non-Socialist parties. In sum, the growing importance of party political leadership positions

---

[3] There was, however, a drop in the last parliament of 1996.

indicates that there are new, more administrative or knowledge-related qualifications that are increasingly requested in the complex society after World War II. It appears that the point is not whether it is political experience or knowledge-related experience that is required, but increasingly that it is both.

3.3. Intellectual Professionalization

Education is an important part of the concept of intellectual professionalization and, in Norway, as in many other countries, it has been linked, historically, to the incumbent elite. This is illustrated when we look at MPs with higher levels of education (see Fig. 9.2). Education is also, together with gender and profession, one of the central variables in investigations of political elites, both regarding questions of qualifications and bases of legitimacy. Higher education gives knowledge, experience in analytical work, and a professional identity. These are all qualifications central to the work of the modern politician. At the same time, education has always been a significant part of the basis for the status-related cleavages in society. Higher education tends to give social status. Both these aspects of education have in Norway, as in many other countries, contributed to an overrepresentation of those with higher education in the political elite.[4]

The level of higher education in the Norwegian parliament is, however, low compared to other European countries. This is particularly true for the last part of the last century and for the period after World War II. In the first part of the nineteenth century, however, the level of recruitment of MPs with higher education was almost 60%, decreasing to around 40% in the 1850s. In order to explain this comparatively low percentage of MPs with university education, the social value and status of education in Norway must be considered. Generally, this has never been very high. This could be linked partly to the importance of the centre–periphery dimension in Norwegian politics and to the fact that the legitimacy of high social status and higher education for recruitment to parliamentary positions was limited. The strong, periphery-based, mass mobilization process around the turn of the century further reduced the importance of higher education.

In the period after World War I, the major increase in the recruitment of different educational groups is found in the proportion of MPs with middle-track education, that is, teachers, social workers, and other public servants whose higher education, although three to four years in length, is not university-based but in regional colleges of education (Fig. 9.1). If we add

---

[4] For the entire period of 1945–85, an average of 26% of parliamentary members had had a university education. This number increases from 24% in the period 1946–61, to 28% in the period 1981–5.

this type of education to the university level, then the Norwegian pattern is, at least for the period after World War II, somewhat similar to that of other European countries. However, the differences of the nineteenth century persist. Educational differences among the parties also vary a good deal, with the Labour Party and the other Socialist parties constantly having the lowest proportion of members with higher education.

4. SENIORITY AND CAREER STABILITY

Professionalization of politics means that Members of Parliament tend to have an increasing need for a solid basis of legitimacy drawn from sources other than their personal characteristics. As we have argued, there are two lines along which this legitimacy is based. First, political experience through political activity over a number of years will help in the role of MP. Secondly, higher education and professional experience give legitimacy (in the sense of trust) in a society where outcomes of the political process tend to mean more to system stability than the actual representative decision-making process. Both of these factors could be expected to raise the mean age of parliamentary members, but this is even more likely when experience is deemed necessary for a satisfactory level of legitimacy to be achieved, and when it is remembered that experience only comes with time.

The development of the mean age of parliamentary members and mean age of newcomers follow each other to some extent, the mean age of parliamentary members being generally higher than that of newcomers (see Figs. 9.17–9.18).[5] For the period before 1900, when politics was the preserve of the old establishment, through to the time when political parties came into being, the mean age for MPs remains about four years higher than that of the newcomers. As approximately 30% of the parliament were newcomers in that period, the implication is that the age at which people entered parliament decreased at this time. We link this to the formation of the political parties and the growth of mass politics, giving room for new channels of recruitment and a change in the pattern of the political elite.

Between 1900 and 1930, there is an age difference of five to seven years between MPs in general and newcomers. This is almost twice that of the period before 1900 and corresponds with an increased level of professionalization of politics. Furthermore, it underpins our hypothesis of this period being the rule of the politicians. With regard to the mean age of

---

[5] It is noticeable that the difference between the two curves is largest in the period 1860–1900, and that it again increases from 1960 onwards.

newcomers for each of the main parties in this period, the Labour Party representatives were generally younger than those of the Conservatives. In the postwar period, there is a substantial drop of about six years in the mean age of newcomers. Our data show that bureaucrats dominated the postwar years up to the mid-1970s and it seems to be plausible to correlate these two to account for this decrease. After World War II, the economy grew much more complex with the consequence that requirements for higher levels of education among politicians increased. Governing was no longer only about questions of how to distribute the nation's resources in society, but also about handling the nation's economic and political bonds with other countries, and the increasing economic complexities resulting from increased international trade.

We have already seen that the level of education among parliamentarians increased during this period. We suggest that the decrease in mean age relates to the above-mentioned factors in that those with education—and hence with the necessary basis for trust in the constituencies—simply were younger than those previously elected. If we look at the differences between the parties in this period, the relatively high mean age of the Christian Democrats is clearly visible and can be linked to the fact that they have received their most substantial support from the older age groups. The Labour Party, meanwhile, experienced a significant drop in the mean age of their newcomers from 1960 onwards. It is clear from other studies that this period saw a fundamental change in recruitment patterns, from one where parliamentary status was achieved through loyalty to the party organization for many years, to one where highly educated persons became MPs. The number of representatives with backgrounds of activity in the party's youth organization (the *Arbeidernes Ungdomsfylking* (AUF)) dropped substantially at this time.

If we look at Figure 9.20, two points should be made: first, the peak in 1945 was caused by the return of Norwegian resistance fighters after World War II, which explains why almost 70% of the parliament were newcomers. Secondly, the relative importance of the political parties shifted substantially, with the Communists returning eleven MPs to parliament, and the Labour Party increasing their representation, while representation from the bourgeoisie parties decreased.

5. CONCLUSION

In this chapter we have described recruitment to the parliamentary elite in Norway over 150 years. The main changes in the recruitment pattern can be summed up by focusing on five main periods where changes in the political climate were significant: the period before 1884, dominated by high state officials; a period of mass mobilization and development of the party structure up to World War I; the politicized period from the 1920s until World War II; the significant influence of bureaucrats in the postwar era up to the mid-1970s; succeeded by the period of fragmentation and voter volatility still visible today.

Different social cleavages and political issues presented themselves during the 150 years we have discussed, changing both the composition and the characteristics of MPs. Generally, we have shown that before 1930, parliament was dominated by MPs with backgrounds as high state officials. The politicization preceding World War I is illustrated by the increased level of full-time party and pressure group officials. The postwar period was dominated by public sector employees as we have seen in Figure 9.10, whereby the levels reached after World War II approach those before the turn of the century.

Some cleavage lines persist over time, particularly the centre–periphery conflict, but even this seems to be less relevant for parliamentary representation after the mid-1970s. The growth of non-governmental organizations and narrow interest groups as mediators of political interest has undoubtedly had a significant impact on recruitment patterns. After the mid-1970s, almost all parameters show a marked turn, with the exception of the proportion of female legislators. Even the share of novices to politics shows an upswing for this period, underpinning the argument that recruitment to parliamentarian elites went through drastic changes at this point in time.

References

Eliassen, K. A. (1996). 'Norway and the EU: The No-Vote, the EEA and the Future'. *Journal of European Studies* (Chulalongkorn University), 21–40.

——and Pedersen, M. N. (1978). 'Professionalisation of Legislatures: Long Term Change in the Political Recruitment in Denmark and Norway'. *Comparative Studies in Society and History*, 20: 286–318.

Furre, B. (1992). *Norsk historie 1905–1990: vårt hundreår*. Oslo: Samlaget.

Kuhnle, S. (1975). *Patterns of Social and Political Mobilisation: A Historical Analysis of the Nordic Countries* (Sage Professional Papers, Contemporary Political Sociology Series, 06.005). Beverly Hills, Calif.: Sage Publications.

Rokkan, S. (1967). 'Geography, Religion and Social Class: Crosscutting Cleavages in Norwegian Politics', in S. M. Lipset and S. Rokkan (eds.), *Party Systems and Voter Alignments*. New York: Free Press.

——(1970). *Citizens, Elections, Parties: Approaches to the Comparative Study of the Processes of Development*. Oslo: Universitetsforlaget.

——and Campbell, A. (1966). 'Citizen Participation in Political life: A Comparison of Data for Norway and the United States of America'. *International Social Science Journal*, 12: 1–99.

Seip, J. A. (1963). *Fra embedsmannsstat til ettpartistat og andre essays*. Oslo: Universitetsforlaget.

Svåsand, L. (1985). *Politiske Partier*. Oslo: Tiden.

Torgersen, U. (1967). 'The Formation of Parties in Norway'. *Scandinavian Political Studies*, 2: 43–68.

Weber, M. (1947; orig. 1919). 'Politics as a Vocation', in H. H. Gerth and C. W. Mills (eds.), *From Max Weber: Essays in Sociology*. London: Routledge and Kegan Paul Ltd., 396–450.

10

Political Recruitment and Elite Transformation in Modern Portugal 1870–1999: The Late Arrival of Mass Representation

JOSÉ M. MAGONE

1. INTRODUCTION

While the first forms of parliamentary institutions in Portugal can be traced back to the early thirteenth century, a modern form of parliamentary representation based on universal suffrage and full party competition was only established in 1975. Most of the history of Portuguese parliamentarism is characterized by regime discontinuity, patrimonial forms of representation, and last, but not least, lack of professionalization and routinization (Magone 1997*a*). The executive, thanks to its dominance over the parliamentary institution, played a major role in the control of access to parliamentary institutions until the Revolution of Carnations on 25 April 1974. The methods of control varied from the establishment of a sophisticated electoral machine, as happened in the nineteenth and early twentieth century, and to violent means of coercion, as in Salazar's authoritarian regime. The composition of Portuguese parliaments between 1822 and 1975 was heavily influenced or even fully defined by the respective ruling executive. Clientelism and patronage, together with nepotism and frequent cases of family inheritance, led to a high level of continuity of parliamentary personnel under the constitutional monarchy between 1870 and 1910. During the First Republic (1910–26), parliamentary elites were, on the contrary, to experience a greater discontinuity due to the high levels of political violence and governmental instability leading repeatedly to early elections. This prevented the stabilization of the parliamentary elite, and this effect was further reinforced by the growing factionalism and personalism within parties. For these reasons, it is appropriate to define the elections of 25 April 1975 as the starting-point of modern parliamentarism: the

I want to thank Manuel Braga da Cruz, Pedro Tavares de Almeida, and Luis Vidigal for making their published data available. Any gaps or shortcomings in the text are entirely mine.

period before that being characterized as the 'prehistory' of modern parliamentary representation.

The chapter starts with an historical overview of parliamentary elites between 1870 and 1974, followed by sections dealing with the period between 1974 and 1995 in greater detail. The great transformation from elite to mass representation will be the central focus of Section 3. Other questions related to the emergence of new parties as agents of elite transformation, the growth of party professionalization, and changes of elite profiles will also be addressed, as will the need to take into account the fact that modern (or perhaps should we say post-modern) political parties arrived quite late in Portugal in comparison to party developments in other Western European countries. I will then deal with the problems of professionalization and routinization of the members of parliament after 1975, and assess more thoroughly the impact of regime discontinuities on parliamentary elites. The chapter will close with some conclusions on the Portuguese case.

2. PARLIAMENTARY ELITES IN THE AGE OF LIMITED SUFFRAGE

While other Western European countries experienced continuous development towards parliamentary democracy, Portuguese parliamentarianism was shaped by discontinuity of regimes and, consequently, of parliamentary elites. In order to examine the long road towards modern parliamentary representation, which started in the mid-nineteenth century and ended with the founding elections of 25 April 1975 during the Revolution of Carnations, I will delineate the elite configurations as follows: that of the Constitutional Monarchy (1852–1910); the First Republic (1910–26); the dictatorship of Antonio Oliveira Salazar (1926–68), and that of Marcelo Caetano (1968–74).

2.1. *Political Recruitment and Elite Transformation during the Constitutional Monarchy*

In the second half of the nineteenth century the Portuguese Constitutional Monarchy[1] was dominated by a political arrangement called *rotativismo*.

[1] The amended constitution of 1852 represented a compromise between the liberals who had a more radical view of democracy in Portugal and the conservatives who tended to think in more oligarchical terms. The outcome was a bicameral parliament. The members of the Chamber of Peers were nominated by the government and the Chamber of the Deputies was directly elected by the population under a system of restricted suffrage based on social and economic criteria. Between 1852 and 1910, there were 42 elections. Before 1852, Portugal was

Under this system, in an attempt to follow the English model of a two-party system, the two main parties, the Progressive Party (*Partido do Progresso*) and the Regenerator Party (*Partido Regenerador*) agreed on a regular alternance in power. The clientelistic system of *caciquismo* based on local dignitaries (*caciques*) influenced heavily the outcome of elections and patterns of elite recruitment. The *cacique* was able to offer to the government a supply of votes in return for which favours were granted to him and his followers. Throughout the period of *rotativismo,* beside a limited franchise (see Table 10.1), the number of eligible persons was also very restricted and did not exceed 100,000 (about 2% of the total population and 7% of the male adult population). The government controlled the territory and the electorate through an 'electoral machine' based on clientelism and patronage, thus preserving the status quo and preventing any real change of the ruling elite (Sobral and Almeida 1982: 661–9). Parliament was characterized by high longevity of mandates, and the importance of relations of consanguinity among parliamentarians indicates the closed character and autoreproduction of political elites (Almeida 1991: 182).

The two chambers of the Portuguese parliament were dominated by the middle classes (particularly by the liberal professions) and by members of the aristocracy (Almeida 1991: 188). After 1885, the second chamber came even more under the influence of the executive, which had the right to appoint members. This practice was abused by the government, so that in the first decade of the century the number of appointed members became larger than the number of hereditary peers and clergymen (Table 10.2).[2] Most of these members were university and school teachers, diplomats, judges, civil governors, to the point that after 1887 public servants who were closely linked to the government formed a majority. By the turn of the century, the Chamber of Peers had lost credibility with the Chamber of the Deputies because of its complete dependency on the government.

Results of elections were agreed between the parties beforehand, so that there was no real competition and the manipulation of electoral processes led to a fundamental stability of the parliamentary elite (except for a significant decline in the weight of landowners). The parties had local networks which assured that the elections produced predictable outcomes. In this context, one has to differentiate between the local (or regional) and the national elites. Local elites consisted of *caciques* (influential persons such as priests, lawyers, landowners) who, in return for favours, were able to

engulfed in a civil war between constitutionalists and absolutists. There were 13 elections between 1820 and 1852. *Rotativismo* was basically the agreed alternance in government of two parties through a system of clientelism. This was possible because suffrage was restricted to a small number of voters.

[2] This practice of appointment by the government after consultation with the King was called *fornada* (Monica 1994: 141–4).

Table 10.1. Electoral systems in Portugal 1852–1998

Extension of suffrage	Voting age (years)	Form of scrutiny
1852–77: restricted suffrage (income criteria) (1864–77: 9–10% of population)	25	1852–83: two-ballots plurality system with plurinominal constituencies
1878–94: enlarged suffrage, combining literacy and social criteria (family heads) (approx. 18–19% of population)	21	1884–94: plurality system in plurinominal constituencies
1895–1910: new restrictions based on income and literacy (1910: approx. 12% of population)	21	1895: simple plurality system in uninominal constituencies
	21	1897–1910: simple plurality system (Lisbon and Porto with plurinominal constituencies)
	21	1901–10: limited vote
1911–12: enlarged suffrage, literacy, and social criteria (family heads) (approx. 14.2% of population)	21	1911–15: limited vote plus PR (D'Hondt method) in Lisbon and Porto constituencies
1913–17: restricted suffrage; literacy criteria (1915: approx. 8% of population)	21	1915–26: limited vote plus PR
1918: universal male suffrage	21	PR
1919–26: restricted suffrage (literacy criteria)	21	PR
1926: restricted suffrage (literacy plus heads of family) extended later to women with higher education	21	PR
1975: universal secret suffrage	18	PR: 22 multimember constituencies
		1997: electoral reform including more single-member constituencies beside the existing multimember constituencies

Note: The terms related to the electoral systems follow the typology developed by Bernard Grofman and Arend Lijphart (1986) and Lijphart (1984).

Source: Almeida (1991: 213–15).

Table 10.2. The members of the Chamber of Peers (*Câmara dos Pares*)

	1842		1905	
	n	%	n	%
Peers	62	76	37	25
Clergymen	4	5	12	8
Appointed members	16	19	98	67
Total	82		147	

Source: Marques (1981: 66).

provide national MPs with the necessary support to become elected to the Chamber of Deputies. The national parliamentary elites had in most cases almost no contact with the constituency in which they were elected. In this sense, the parliamentary political elite was mainly urban, while their election was organized by the two main parties in contact with local dignitaries (Sobral and Almeida 1982: 664–5; Vidigal 1988: 61–8).[3] The urban central and the rural regional elites were completely detached from each other. In the last phase of the constitutional monarchy, legislatures were very short due to the lack of a strong majority for the governmental party. Elections had to be rerun to enable the government parties to produce the majority of seats required to stay in power. This, however, became more and more difficult by the turn of the century because of the growing success of the Portuguese Republican Party and other radical parties. Moreover, the Freemason secret organizations tended to undermine, with their propaganda for the Republic, the ideological legitimacy of the Constitutional Monarchy.

The social composition of the Chamber of Deputies shows a very clear predominance of three main groups: aristocracy and landed interests, state bureaucracy (essentially, higher civil servants, teachers of different levels, and military officers), and liberal professions (Table 10.3). The first group is clearly dominant until the 1880s but the other two groups increase their weight progressively so that by the end of the century they form the majority. Thus following the election of 1902, the three groups of civil servants, military officers, and liberal professions provide more than 80% of the MPs. This means also that parliament was dominated by a rather well-educated political elite: university and school teachers, high- and middle-ranking bureaucrats, lawyers, doctors, engineers, writers, and journalists.

On the whole, one can assert that the majority of the MPs were related to the government in some way. Even the clergy were dependent on the Ministry of Justice and Church Affairs. The executive dominated the

---

[3] The etymological origin of the word *cacique* is explained quite well by Kern (1974): 'Although the word *cacique* was not associated with liberalism until 1878, the stereotype had existed for some time and the term had been a part of the Spanish language for even longer. Originally, *cacique*, with its derivatives *cacicato* and *caciquil*, were words of Amerindian origin encountered by Spaniards in Santo Domingo early in the conquest of the Americas.' A *cacique* was a chief owner of serfs in the New World, but in Spain the word quickly came to refer to royal agents. In subsequent decades, its meaning broadened to include people with more than normal power or independence, although *consejero o ministro del Rey* continued to remain the standard definition. This usage increased during the reign of Carlos III in the eighteenth century, when royal ministers were appointed in larger numbers and with greater powers. The modern stereotype of *cacique*, however, began in the period of disentailment. Although records of this process were not well kept, an estimated 189,092 ecclesiastical properties valued at 2,300,134,116 *reales* changed hands. Similar phenomena can be found in other Southern European countries as well (Magone 1998: 221–2). Sapelli (1995) suggests that the present Southern European political systems still have features of what can be called 'neocaciquism', a more sophisticated bureaucratic form of the original.

Table 10.3. Social and professional composition of the Chamber of Deputies

Social and professional categories	1861 n	1861 %	1872 n	1872 %	1880 n	1880 %	1890 n	1890 %	1902 n	1902 %
Aristocracy	19	12	24	25	16	13	34	25		
High	7		7		6		13			
Medium	12		17		10		21			
Landowners	72	46	23	24	31	24	15	11		
Civil servants[1]	13	8	10	10	11	9	17	12	41	30
Teachers	13	8	11	11	17	13	9	7		
University	13		10		15		8			
School	—		1		2		1			
Officers	16	10	14	14	13	10	21	15	37	27
Army	16		12		13		18			
Navy	—		2		—		3			
Clergy	1	1	2	2	8	6	2	1	8	6
Liberal professions	19	12	9	9	26	20	33	24	33	24
Lawyers	12		3		17		15			
Doctors	7		5		8		17			
Journalists	—		1		1		1			
Businessmen[2]	4	2	4	4	5	4	5	4	16	12
Total with data	157	100	97	100	127	100	136	100	135	100
Total MPs[3]	165		100		137		152		155	

Notes:
[1] General-directors, general-inspectors, engineers, diplomats, and other incumbents of higher public offices.
[2] Businessmen, industrialists, and bankers.
[3] MPs elected in the continental and insular constituencies.

Sources: Almeida (1991: 185); for 1902, Sobral and Almeida (1982: 649–71).

Table 10.4. Registered voters during *rotativismo* (1870–1910) and the Republic (1910–26)

Year	Number of voters (thousands)	Population (millions)
1864	350	3,829
1875	455	4,160[1] (1878)
1880	845	4,660
1901	598	5,016
1910	700	5,547[2]
1911	850	5,547
1913	400	5,547
1915	471	5,547
1918	900	5,547
1919	471	6,032[3]
1925	574	6,032

Notes: [1] 1878 figure.
[2] 1911 figure.
[3] 1920 figure.

Source: Marques (1981).

recruitment of the legislative and could thus preserve the status quo of the political system. On average, most MPs were elected for four legislatures, but some served in as many as twenty legislatures, while one-fifth of them were newcomers. Moreover, consanguinity was a major factor determining the succession of MPs and often sons 'inherited' their father's seat. The status quo was preserved by a very restricted electoral system, which was changed during this period of *rotativismo* several times (Table 10.1). In sum, the patterns of elite recruitment were quite closed and dominated by the executive. The political elite was predominantly urban and well educated in its outlook. The restrictive electoral law reinforced by *caciquismo*, 70% illiteracy, and the urban-rural cleavage gave passive and active voting rights only to a minority of the population. In the first decade of the twentieth century, political instability increased and the radical Portuguese Republican Party began to gain support inside the government and among the population.

2.2. The Republican Elite 1910–1926

On 5 October 1910, the Republican Revolution took place which ended the degenerated system of *rotativismo*. However hopes turned very quickly into disenchantment: the Republican elite could not agree upon a common programme, rural *caciquismo* was replaced by an urban one, and the new restrictive electoral law[4] was ever more biased towards the urban centres. Political, economic, and social instability, violence, and stagnating public policies prevented the implementation of the radical change announced by the Republican elite. The Republican elite saw the control of the electoral process by rural *caciques* as a major obstacle to the development of democracy in Portugal and believed that this problem could be overcome only by excluding the rural masses from the political system. Widespread illiteracy and a lack of political information reinforced this exclusion. In fact, the state apparatus of the monarchy remained almost intact and the former personnel was not changed by a Republican one. In the end, the practices of the monarchy were largely reproduced by the Republicans, so that the Republic was soon confronted with the same dysfunctional features as the previous political culture (Vidigal 1988: 63–7). Political violence and instability were caused by unwillingness to extend the electorate and change the composition of the political class and eventually the former structural obstacles to democratic development began to reappear.

As was argued by Lawrence Wheeler, elections were increasingly discredited. Because of their election monopoly based upon an organized

---

[4] There were seven elections between 1910 and 1926: in 1911, 1915, 1918, 1919, 1921, 1922, and 1925. During the First Republic, the regime was interrupted by short military dictatorships, such as the one by Sidonio Pais in 1917–18.

election machine and the loyalty of a core of the bureaucracy, the PRP won every election except that of June 1921. Rather than providing the electorate with real choices, most elections served only to consolidate the hold of the party already in power, a tendency which had been institutionalized under the monarchy. Because of their core of loyal supporters in the military, for a long while the PRP could neutralize or co-opt coup attempts. Or, if they lost in the streets as occurred in 1915, 1917–18, and briefly 1921, they could organize a comeback by means of a counter-coup (Wheeler 1978: 160). In sum, the restriction of the electorate to the urban centres and on the basis of literacy requirement excluded workers and peasants and incorporated only the upper and middle classes into the political system. The nature of elections continued to produce a strong dependency of the legislative on the government and many MPs simultaneously held governmental positions as ministers.

A major impediment to elite transformation was the lack of a consistent education policy during the whole Republican period. The high level of illiteracy was regarded by the Republicans as the major obstacle to the inclusion of the masses. Literacy was in fact seen as a necessary precondition to exercising the passive and active right of vote. The Republican elite feared that the rural masses—a large majority of which was almost completely illiterate—would tilt the balance of forces in favour of monarchy again. Education was regarded also, by the strongly anti-clerical Republicans, as an instrument with which to fight against the church. Education would enable the population to make more conscious decisions about their political choice, thus undermining the power of the church in rural communities. However, although the Republican elite emphasized in principle the necessity to improve the education system in Portugal, in practice, governmental instability led to very inconsistent policy implementation. In the field of secondary and higher education, the Portuguese Republican elite was quite successful in improving and expanding infrastructures and human resources, but in primary education—the crucial level to integrate the masses politically, socially, culturally, and economically—little was done.[5] This meant that the masses were neither integrated through democratic participation nor through socialization. The rising working classes had therefore to turn to more radical groups such as the anarcho-syndicalists in the 1920s (Oliveira 1974).

The restriction of the electorate and the high rate of illiteracy confined the recruitment pool of the political elite to the urban well-educated citizens so that a very small circle of politicians with no connection whatsoever to the masses dominated politics. At the beginning of republicanism,

---

[5] In fact, the persistence of illiteracy remains a problem even today and still prevents a significant part of the population from being fully integrated in the political system (Marques 1980: 83–8).

however, things had been different. Most of the leaders between 1870 and 1910, the challengers to the dominant *haute bourgeoisie* during the monarchy, came from the middle classes, both from urban centres and rural areas. Many were lawyers from the University of Coimbra, doctors, pharmacists, engineers, teachers, or journalists. Even soldiers could be found in this group. Here, also, the role of the Freemasonry cannot be underestimated. It provided a forum for joining forces against the monarchy and for creating a Republican ideology. Both the working class and rural labourers supported the Republican Revolution initially and the emergence of the Republic was regarded as the beginning of a new age (Wheeler 1978: 32–3). However, just over one year later, the Republican government began to suppress all demonstrations by the land labourers and the working class, thus alienating two quite important allies for the implementation of its programme (Pereira 1982: 21–76; Oliveira 1974).

In the Portuguese parliament of the First Republic, although the upper classes were still important, a considerable increase in the middle classes was obvious (Table 10.5). Broadly speaking, the Republic came to be dominated by the middle classes, who occupied the state apparatus. To a significant extent also, the lower middle classes and the petty urban bourgeoisie gained access to government offices. The allocation of such governmental posts via clientelistic practices and patronage was confirmed by parliament bypassing competitive procedures (Vidigal 1988: 85) so that the system was increasingly discredited. More than that, the fragmentation of the Republican party, due to personal likes and dislikes (the so-called

Table 10.5. Class origins, educational background, and economic sector of origin of the Members of Parliament in the constituent National Assembly of 1911

Social background	%
Class origins	
Aristocracy	15
Upper middle classes	35
Lower middle classes	19
Petty urban bourgeoisie	31
Education	
Higher education degree	65
High school	30
Basic education	4
Economic sector	
Primary Sector	5
Secondary Sector	3
Tertiary Sector	92

Source: Estimations of the 234 members made by Vidigal (1988).

personalismo), reinforced the erosion of the Republican political system's legitimacy.

That literacy was the main form of capital held by these groups is clearly shown by the data concerning MPs' educational backgrounds, which show that a large majority held higher education degrees (Table 10.5). With respect to the three economic sectors, most MPs came from the tertiary sector and, concerning regional background, most MPs had urban origins with only sporadic links to their constituencies. In addition, most MPs were very young (between 31 and 45), characterizing the nature of this revolutionary movement.

2.3. The Elites of the Estado Novo 1926–1974

The First Portuguese Republic ended on 28 May 1926 through a military *coup d'état* under the leadership of General Gomes da Costa. Subsequently, the military dictatorship was transformed into a civilian authoritarian dictatorship led by Antonio de Oliveira Salazar, considered by the military to be the ideal person to solve the economic crisis. Salazar took absolute financial powers over all other ministries and was able to build up his power within the government. In 1933, a new corporatist constitution was adopted in a dubious referendum, in which the large number of abstentions were added to the yes votes. In the revolutionary spirit of the 1930s, the new regime was seen as an instrument for overcoming the deficits of the First Republic. The First Republic was portrayed by Salazar as being chaotic because of its adherence to political liberalism and the leeway it gave to revolutionary ideologies such as socialism. In contrast to the previous regime, the two words used to characterize the new one were order and tranquillity. Salazar tried very much to avoid his authoritarian regime having the same profile as that of Italian fascism or Nazi Germany. He wanted to preserve the status quo and to prevent any change to the social structure, which would have endangered his regime (Figueiredo 1976; Georgel 1985).

The *União Nacional* (National Union) was the only party represented in the new parliament called the National Assembly (which was composed of two chambers: the Legislative Chamber and the Corporatist Chamber). This single-party system obviously affected patterns of recruitment but, in many respects, the new political elite did not differ very much from previous ones. At most, one can recognize a further increase of the middle classes in comparison with the legislatures of the Constitutional Monarchy and of the First Republic. Between 1933 and 1935, all radical right-wing opposition groups, such as the National syndicalists of Rolao Preto and Count Monsaraz, were banned from political life (Costa Pinto 1985: 36) so that, when the first elections to the legislative chamber of the new National Assembly took place on 16 December 1934, one was able for the first time to know who the MPs of the new political elite were.

The composition of the Legislative Chamber tells us that, in reality, the government was still, as in the past, dominating parliament. About 41% of MPs were dependent on the state, a proportion which rises to 48.7% if the military is added. Lawyers were the second largest group with about 24.4%, followed by engineers with 10%; landowners were also very well represented (Table 10.6). As for educational profile, we find that nearly all MPs had a higher degree (94.5%) with only 5.5% having lower levels of education. This kind of profile suggests that cultural capital was an important factor in recruitment (Rosas 1985: 48). Another factor in recruitment, however, was the loyalty to the new political regime. Many of the new MPs were related to the personal political and academic career of Salazar, having been involved in the political fights in the University of Coimbra, in the *Centro Académico de Democracia Cristã* (Academic Centre of Christian Democracy), and in the *Centro Católico* (Catholic Centre), or coming from the Faculty of Law of Coimbra. The younger members were integrated directly by Salazar into the new political regime and more than half of the new MPs were between 35 and 49 years old (Rosas 1985: 53–5). Thus the new parliamentary elite was in general quite young. On the whole, one can say that the new parliamentary elite reinforced the trend towards the middle classes and the dominance of the state upon the legislative assembly. Recruitment seems to have been even more controlled by the government, or rather by António Oliveira Salazar himself, which was part of the ideology of Salazarism, to preserve the status quo and prevent the political participation of the masses. Therefore, the exclusion of the rural masses and of the working class continued, and was even strengthened, under the new regime.

In the first legislative elections, most MPs originated from Lisbon and the provinces of Beira Alta and Beira Litoral, Salazar's political, educational, and professional trajectory having passed through all three regions. A large part of the political elite was therefore very close to Salazar and influenced by the ideological assumptions of a corporatist state based on family, fatherland, and religion. The fundamental unit of the new political system was to be not the individual, but the paternalist family. In elections, women and illiterates could only vote if they fulfilled some prerequisites such as education and income levels, respectively. The ideology emphasized also the unity of the nation. Opposition parties were only allowed after World War II, but election results were still controlled by the government so that, as with former Portuguese political regimes, parliaments were 'made'. A kind of 'political economy of repression' was used to disband the opposition groups after elections. This meant that repression was used only against certain groups of the opposition such as the Communists, while other

Table 10.6. Socio-professional structure of members of the legislative chamber

Legislature: Social groups and professions	1934–8 %	1938–42 %	1942–5 %	1945–9 %	1949–53 %	1953–7 %	1957–61 %	1961–5 %	1965–9 %	1969–73 %	1973–4 %
Landowners, industrialists	14.4	8.9	10.4	9.2		11.7	6.7	10.0	26.9	16.9	13.3
Liberal professions	28.9	27.8	34.4	35.8		25.0	53.3	53.8	33.1	38.5	28.7
Civil administration	34.4	34.4	28.9	20.8		32.5	17.5	20.8	23.8	30.0	48.0
University members	8.9	13.3	12.2	12.5		10.8	7.5	5.4	5.4	8.0	56.0
Army members	12.2	12.2	12.2	15.8	15.8	15.8	11.7	8.5	6.1	14.6	13.3
Church	1.1	1.1	1.1	0.8	2.5	2.5	2.5	1.5	1.5		
Journalists	2.2	1.1	2.5			1.7	0.8	2.3	0.7		
Technicians			0.8						1.5		
Unknown			0.8								
Total (n)	90	90	90	120	120	120	120	130	130	130	130

Note: There are some gaps in the data.

Sources: Rosas (1985: 48); Cruz (1988a: 209).

opponents of the semi-legal opposition could escape with a warning. A kind of differentiated repressive system targeting working-class opposition more heavily and middle-class opposition more softly occurred throughout the authoritarian regime.

The main values of the paternalistic family model were 'peace', 'tranquillity', and 'order'. Political concepts were reduced to the order of family relationships, conflicts were suppressed, and the idea of liberal individualism was regarded as a danger to the status quo. This kind of idealized paternalistic family was in fact not completely utopian. It was to some extent the reality, sustained by a high level of illiteracy, of rural Portugal. The corporatist model propagated the idea of harmony between labour and capital, although trade unions were suppressed and capital dominated the whole corporatist structure of the political regime. One could speak of a sort of symbiosis between state administrative structures and entrepreneurs. The Legislative Chamber of the National Assembly was less affected by it, but the Corporatist Chamber embodied very clearly this bias of the authoritarian regime (Scotti-Rosin 1982; Kay 1971; Lucena 1979; Wiarda 1979).

The major trend that can be recognized in the formation of the 'parliamentary elite' of the authoritarian regime is the very high number of civil servants in the elected national assembly (Table 10.6). This process was defined by Philippe Schmitter and Manuel Braga da Cruz as 'political incest'. Due to the restrictive rules and the oppressive way in which elections were conducted, civil servants tended to elect civil servants. Such a process of governamentalization of the National Assembly was so strong that it could not be stopped by the reform attempts of the successor of António Salazar, Marcelo Caetano (Cruz 1998*a*). Although the authoritarian regime pursued its model of politics well into the 1950s, it was forced to make a U-turn in the 1960s. The increasing necessity to be involved in global trade, and the emerging unification of Western Europe had a spillover effect on public policies in Portugal. While the system of representation seemed to be stagnating and self-reproducing, the economic and social system began to change rapidly. Emigration, tourism, the colonial wars in Angola, Mozambique, and Guinea-Bissau, and the growing left-wing *Zeitgeist* at world level changed the conditions under which the authoritarian system could survive. It had to abandon its policy of splendid isolation and become more integrated in the world system. In this period, illiteracy fell to 30.1% (1970), the working class became a major force in the larger urban centres, and, in the late 1960s, the new middle classes of high-technology professionals emerged as an additional category in the class system. For these reasons, the original composition of the Salazarist conservative political elite comprising landowners and classic middle classes was under pressure to integrate the new social groups. Although in the late 1960s the successor of Salazar, Marcelo Caetano, intended to reform the system, he had to realize that the authoritarian political regime was not able to cope with the growing complexity of a modern society. The political structure could no longer hold to the ideology of the static 'paternalistic family'. The mobility and flexibility of social and economic life demanded a democratic political system which would integrate the new social groups that had emerged in the 1960s (Passos 1987; Graham 1975; Schmitter 1975).

3. THE GREAT TRANSFORMATION FROM ELITE TO MASS REPRESENTATION

3.1. *The Portuguese Revolution of Carnations 1974–1975: The Rise of the Military*

The authoritarian regime was overthrown on 25 April 1974 when a group of middle-ranking officers staged a *coup d'état* which, with the mobilization of the population, turned into a revolution. The whole revolutionary process lasted until 25 November 1975, during which time conflicting models of representation were proposed by different political actors: the Western democratic system of representation being only one among many. Thanks to the fact that, until the elections of 25 April 1975, political parties had no democratic legitimacy, the Movement of Armed Forces (*Movimento das Forças Armadas* (MFA)) under the leadership of Prime Minister Vasco Gonçalves tried to push the revolutionary process in the direction of a Soviet-style model. However this attempt, which was regarded even by the Communist leader Álvaro Cunhal as too radical, was destined to fail. Vasco Gonçalves became isolated in the 'hot summer' of 1975 and was replaced by a moderate provisional government, including all major parties, under the leadership of Admiral Pinheiro de Azevedo (Ferreira 1983; Harvey 1978).

The elite of the transition was composed both by military and civilians but, before looking at the social profile of the Constituent Assembly, it is worthwhile to discuss briefly the composition of the MFA (Movimento das Forças Armadas). While most of the higher ranking officers originated from the upper middle classes, the members of the MFA had their origins in the urban lower middle classes and in the rural middle classes. About 41.5% originated from the urban centres, while 50.5% came from rural areas. A study of the socio-professional background of their parents shows that most of the officers were from lower-middle or middle-class origin (Table 10.7). The main motivation behind the birth of MFA was the desire to put an end to Portugal's colonial wars and the acknowledgement that they could not

Table 10.7. Professions of the parents of MFA officers 1974–1975

Profession	%
Civil servants	22
Military	17
Landowners and businessmen	12
Workers and artisans	10
Qualified employees	8
Shopkeepers	8
Employees	6
Self-employed	5
Farmers	5
Not classified	7

Note: The survey was done among 703 officers of the army.

Source: Aniceto and Costa (1985: 97–122).

be won militarily and a political solution was required. Beneath the surface there was also a conflict between the higher and middle-ranking officers. The latter were personally involved in the wars, while the former rarely went to the fighting fields. Moreover, the higher-ranking officers felt that the integration of new officers with higher education degrees would jeopardize the seniority principle of promotion (Porch 1977: 85).

The military were quite dominant until April 1975, but afterwards the Constituent Assembly and political parties took over and succeeded in promoting the Western model of democracy. The elections of 1975 were based on universal suffrage, even though 30% of the population was still illiterate.[6] For the first time in the history of Portugal, full democracy and the political incorporation of the masses were achieved. Before that, there had been proposals to postpone elections until the whole population was 'mature' enough to vote—something which was refused by the civilian political elite.

An analysis by party and occupation of the candidates elected to the Constituent Assembly on 25 April 1975 shows an essentially similar pattern of recruitment among the two main parties (Table 10.8), that is, professional and managerial occupations predominate (66% and 74% in the case of the Socialist Party and of the People's Democratic Party, respectively). The third largest party, the Communist Party, is quite different with only 20% from this category. On the other hand, its parliamentary group comprised of 50% workers, 20% white-collar workers, and 10% farmers, land

---

[6] Five parties were elected to the Constituent Assembly. The Socialist Party got 38% (116 seats), the People's Democratic Party 26% (81 seats), the Communist Party 13% (30 seats), the Democratic Social Centre 8% (16 seats), the Democratic People's Movement/ Democratic Electoral Commission 4% (5 seats), and the Democratic People's Union 0.8% (1 seat).

Table 10.8. Occupational background of the members of the Constituent Assembly 1975–1976

	Communist Party		Socialist Party		People's Democratic Party	
	n	%	n	%	n	%
Lawyers	2	7	32	28	27	33
Teachers and lecturers	3	10	17	15	11	13
Doctors	—		5	4	3	4
Engineers	1	3	6	5	3	4
Journalists and writers	—		8	7	1	1
Businessmen and managers	—		3	3	6	8
Other professions (including students)	—		5	4	9	11
Subtotal: professional and managerial occupations	6	20	77	66	60	74
White-collar workers	6	20	20	17	8	10
Blue-collar workers	15	50	13	11	3	4
Agriculture workers and fishermen	3	10	6	5	2	3
Non-classified	—		1	1	7	9
Total	30	100	116	100	81	100

Source: Gallagher (1983: 215).

labourers, and fishermen. These groups account for only 34% of the Socialist MPs and 26% of the People's Democratic Party. Most of the new civilian politicians, particularly those from the Socialist and Communist Parties, had been in exile. Some MPs of the People's Democratic Party had been active in the previous National Assembly, trying to change the system from within. They had been elected in 1969 to the legislative chamber, but had given up shortly afterwards. They were involved in the study group called SEDES (*Sociedade de Estudos para o Desenvolvimento Económico e Social*) which attempted to influence the former regime towards modernization of the country.

The new unicameral parliament, which originally comprised 265 members, was reduced to 230 in 1991. Overall, it seems that the socio-professional structure had not changed very much compared to that of the former authoritarian regime. Most of the new democratic politicians had started their careers in parliament. Only with the progressive ageing of the new democratic regime have patterns of recruitment become more differentiated. In other words, the turbulence of the transition period continued during the early consolidation period but eventually the increasing necessity to achieve a higher level of professionalization had an impact on patterns of recruitment and the call for specialists in corresponding fields led to the inclusion of more professionalized parliamentarians.

3.2. The Portuguese Second Republic 1976–1998

Between 1976 and 1995, Portugal experienced eight elections with parliament often being dissolved before the regular end of its normal mandate. This made it difficult to increase the routinization and professionalization of the new parliament. Moreover, until 1987, the legislatures were quite fragmented; no party was able to gain an absolute majority, which was quite destabilizing for a young democracy still learning to create and comply with the rules of the new political game. Between 1976 and 1979, the Socialist minority government, and later the caretaker governments, were not able to foster governmental stability. The fragmentation of the parties required complicated strategies to build coalitions. This was the case in 1979–80 with the Democratic Alliance, a coalition between the People's Democratic Party/Social Democratic Party (PPD/PSD), the Social Democratic Centre (CDS), and the Monarchic People's Party (PPM), and in 1983 with the Central Block coalition between PS and PSD, both of which helped to reduce the ideological rigidity between left and right within the party system (Bruneau 1984; Bruneau and Macleod 1986). Finally, in 1985, the PSD formed a minority government which was able to bring some governmental and parliamentary stability into the political system.

The year 1987, however, can be considered the turning-point in the development of Portuguese democracy. The absolute majority gained by the PSD in 1987, and again in 1991, was an important factor in promoting the stabilization, routinization, and professionalization of the Portuguese Assembly of the Republic. For the first time in the history of the new democracy, legislatures were not interrupted by early elections. On the contrary, the Cavaco Silva governments completed the regular four-year term of the legislature. This enabled some long-term planning and the reorganization of the structures of the Assembly of the Republic (Aguiar 1994).

3.2.1. The Late Arrival of Modern Political Parties

The new parties born after 25 April 1974 were to a significant extent shaped by external influences and followed party models adopted in other countries. The Socialist Party, which became the dominant party in the early phase of the political system, was founded in Bad Münstereiffel (Germany) in 1973 and was strongly supported by the Friedrich Ebert Foundation, which was close to the German Social Democratic Party (Eisfeld 1984). It never changed its character as a party of cadres and can be defined today as a cartel party. The Communist Party (*Partido Comunista Português* (PCP)) was by far the best organized force in the political system. Founded in 1921, it can be characterized as the only true membership party in terms of organization and active membership. On the right, the Social

Democratic Party (*Partido Social-Democrata* (PSD)) is a highly factional-ized party consisting of the so-called *baronatos* (the political fiefdoms of regional bosses), requiring a strong leader to keep the different factions together, as could be observed during the leadership of Francisco Sá Carneiro in the 1970s and Anibal Cavaco Silva from 1985 to 1995. The Democratic Social Centre/People's Party (*Centro Democrático Social/Partido Popular* (CDS/PP)) consisted (and still does) of notables. Like the PSD, the party is dominated by personalism, which means that disputes between leaders tend to dominate the inner life of the party. These new parties had to be created shortly before or after the Revolution of 25 April 1974, to accommodate the changed conditions of political representation. The uncertainty of the outcomes of the transition was a major problem in the early stage of the establishment of the political parties, and it was only on 25 April 1975, with the founding elections of the new democracy, that the parties were confronted with the new phenomenon of electoral competition under universal suffrage conditions.

A study of the social background of MPs today shows that the present Portuguese parliament is dominated by the middle classes while the other social groups are underrepresented (Table 10.9). Looking at the profes-sional composition of the sixth and seventh legislatures in the 1990s, lawyers have increased their share in the Assembly of the Republic, which may indi-cate the need to have more legal expertise for the job of MP. In terms of social background, Portuguese MPs are more heterogeneous compared to the first legislatures of the new democracy. In the category 'others' are included businessmen, economists, engineers, doctors, art traders, students, administrators, nurses, and banking employees. Until the sixth legislature, we see a steady decline of MPs with this background. Nevertheless, in the last legislature (1995–99), the heterogeneity of the social background of MPs has increased again, due to the shift in power from the PSD to the PS. More people with a secondary education or a technical education were able to gain access to the Assembly, although the structure is more diversified among MPs with higher education. However, in spite of all this, the main groups represented in the Assembly of the Republic continued to be uni-versity and school teachers (with 20–22% of the total seats in each legisla-ture since 1987), civil servants (6–10%), and lawyers (20–24%). In fact, those three groups comprise about 40–50% of total MPs in each legislature since 1987, which can be contrasted to the first three legislatures, where the weight of the first two categories was lower.

As one can see, the middle classes are the dominant element in the polit-ical elite. The trend indicates an increase in the number of representatives from the middle classes and a decrease of the number of working-class MPs. One of the main reasons was the necessity, because of the growth in the

Table 10.9. Occupational background of MPs 1976–1999 (%)

Occupation	Legislatures				
	I 1976–9	Interim 1979–80	II 1980–3	III 1983–5	IV[1] 1985–7
University/school teachers	9.9	10.0	11.4	14.8	14.0
Journalists and writers	2.9	1.9	1.2	2.3	—
Civil servants	2.5	3.4	3.8	5.1	3.2
Lawyers and jurists	23.9	31.0	31.6	22.3	9.6
Employees	12.6	8.0	9.9	15.6	2.8
Blue-collar workers	11.6	7.2	7.6	7.1	2.0
Agricultural workers	1.4	1.5	1.1	—	1.6
Other	35.2	37.0	33.4	32.8	19.6

Occupation	V 1987–91		VI 1991–5		VII 1995–9	
	n	%	n	%	n	%
Teachers	57	22.8	50	21.3	51	22.2
Journalists	3	1.2	3	1.3	5	2.2
Civil servants	16	6.4	23	10.0	19	8.3
Lawyers	55	21.6	53	23.0	56	24.3
Political employees	13	5.2	6	2.6	7	3.0
Blue-collar workers	6	2.4	20	9.0	—	
Military	1	0.4	2	0.9	—	
Other	79	31.6	73	31.9	92	40.0

Note: [1] I was not able to find out the occupational background of 118 (47.2%) MPs in the Fourth Legislature.

Sources: Sousa (n.d.), xerocopied paper, kindly supplied by Prof. Manuel Braga da Cruz (1995: 216); data from 1987 to 1997 are a compilation from Azevedo (1989); Assembleia da Republica (1993 and 1996).

complexity of the topics dealt with in the legislative process, to integrate MPs with a specialist knowledge. Parliamentarians with higher education degrees represented 60 to 80% of the whole Assembly of the Republic in the last three legislatures (Table 10.10). Among them, those with a law degree were the dominant group. This kind of necessity also led the Communist Party to recruit more middle-class representatives in their parliamentary group. In contrast, blue-collar workers lost importance after the Revolution (Cruz and Antunes 1990, 1989: 355). In the 1990s, the MPs of the Assembly of the Republic were also older than in the first three legislatures (Table 10.11). More MPs over 50 years were elected in the sixth and seventh legislatures, reflecting the increasing number of MPs with previous parliamentary experience, and indicating a growing routinization and professionalization of the Assembly of the Republic.

The growing number of MPs originating from small towns or rural areas

Table 10.10. Educational background of MPs 1987–1995

Educational level	Legislature							
	IV 1985–7		V 1987–91		VI 1991–5		VII 1995–9	
	n	%	n	%	n	%	n	%
Doctorate	4	1.6	3	1.2	13	5.7	8	3.5
Master			2	0.8	8	3.4	10	4.3
Licenciatura	40	16.0	125	50.0	55	23.9	89	38.7
Licenciatura in law	45	18.0	69	27.6	110	47.8	58	25.2
Polytechnic	17	6.8	21	8.4	20	8.7	11	4.8
BA	3	1.2	3	1.2	4	1.7	2	0.9
Military degree	1	0.4	2		1	0.4	2	0.9
High School degree	24	9.6	24	9.6	14	6.1	47	20.4
Basic education	1	10.4	1	0.4	1	0.4		
Unknown	115	46.0			4	1.7	3	1.3

Source: Compilation based on Azevedo (1989); Assembleia da Republica (1993 and 1996). This informa-tion can be only an estimation due to the number of substitutes during the two legislature periods.

Table 10.11. Age of Portuguese MPs 1987–1999

Age category	Legislature							
	IV 1985–7		V 1987–91		VI 1991–5		VII 1995–9	
	n	%	n	%	n	%	n	%
20–30	16	6.4	7	2.8	1	0.4	12	5.2
31–40	44	17.6	41	16.4	33	14.3	46	20.0
41–50	47	18.8	85	34	76	33.0	83	36.1
51–60	17	6.8	62	26	81	35.2	64	27.8
61–70	6	2.4	26	10.4	16	6.9	11	4.8
71–80	4	1.6	11	4.4	13	5.6	2	0.9
81–90	—		2	8	1	0.4	1	0.4
Unknown	116	46.4	36	14.4	8	3.4	11	4.8

Source: Compilation based on Azevedo (1989); Assembleia da Republica (1993 and 1996).

is also challenging the dominance of MPs coming from the main urban centres—Lisbon, Porto, and Coimbra—which occurred in the first four leg-islatures (Cruz 1988*b*: 112). In the 1990s, the distribution of MPs is clearly more even still (Table 10.12). Finally, with regard to gender, we can see that the Portuguese Assembly of the Republic is still largely dominated by male MPs but, as Table 10.13 shows, the last elections witnessed what is likely to be the beginning of an increase in the share of female MPs in the Assembly.

Table 10.12. Regional background of Portuguese MPs 1987–1999

Regional background	Legislature							
	IV 1985–7		V 1987–91		VI 1991–5		VII 1995–9	
	n	%	n	%	n	%	n	%
Urban	51	20.4	112	44.8	77	33.5	92	40
Rural	61	24.4	104	41.6	132	57.4	111	48.3
Africa/Asia	12	4.8	17	6.8	5	2.2	8	3.5
USA							1	0.4
Brazil	1	0.4	1	0.4			1	0.4
Unknown	125	50.0	16	6.4	16	6.9		

Source: Compilation based on Azevedo (1989); Assembleia da Republica (1993 and 1996).

3.2.2. *The Political Professionalization of Members of Parliament*

Portuguese parties were created late and did not have much time to build up mass organizations, such as those of the former Italian Communist Party, or of the Austrian Socialist Party or the Swedish Social Democratic Party. Portuguese parties are parties of cadres, or perhaps we should say, along the lines of Klaus von Beyme's assertion with respect to Southern and Eastern European parties, that they were cartel parties from the beginning. This fact affects the profile of the parliamentary elite. As we have seen, the members of the elite are coming predominantly from the new middle classes and the academic profession. This reflects the importance of cultural capital for recruitment. Moreover, it is a small elite, made up of politicians elected more than once to the Assembly of the Republic. Overwhelmingly they had occupied elective or other positions at local, regional, or national level (Table 10.14). In the sixth and seventh legislatures, between one-third and a half of MPs had had previous experience in local government or other local institutions and one-fifth were incumbents of central government offices. If we look at the data concerning party offices, a large minority of parliamentarians are incumbents of offices at the national level in their respective parties; if we add to these the incumbents of local offices, we find that a majority of MPs have been or are incumbents of party offices (Table 10.15).

This seems at first to contradict what was previously said about the weak organization of Portuguese parties, but in reality one can assert that the strong presence of party officers is not matched by a corresponding grass-roots attachment to the parties. All four main parties together have no more than 300,000 members, which is less than 5% of all eligible voters. This says much about the 'partyocratic' nature of democracy in the Portuguese parliament. The accumulation of different political positions has always been

Table 10.13. Gender of MPs 1987–1999

Gender	Legislature															
	I 1976–9		Int. 1979–80		II 1980–3		III 1983–5		IV 1985–7		V 1987–91		VI 1991–95		VII 1995–9	
	n	%	n	%	n	%	n	%	n	%	n	%	n	%	n	%
Female	15	5.3	20	8	21	8	19	7.4	12	4.8	14	6	25	11	28	12
Male	248	94.7	230	92	229	92	231	92.6	238	95.2	236	94	205	89	202	88

Source: Compilation based on Azevedo (1989); Assembleia da Republica (1993 and 1996).

Table 10.14. Incumbents of local and governmental offices 1987–1999

Office	Legislature							
	IV[1] 1985–7		V 1987–91		VI 1991–5		VII 1995–9	
	n	%	n	%	n	%	n	%
Local executive	26	10.4	89	35.6	31	13.5	47	20.4
Local assembly	27	10.8	31	12.4	50	21.7	51	22.8
Minister	14	5.6	18	7.2	12	5.2	15	6.5
State Secretary	9	3.6	20	8	28	12.2	14	6.1
Civil Governor	—	—	8	3.2	4	1.7	6	2.6

Note: [1] I was not able to trace the data of 118 (46%) of MPs for the fourth legislature.

Source: Compilation based on Azevedo (1989); Assembleia da Republica (1993 and 1996). There are double counts included in the figures.

Table 10.15. Incumbents of party offices among Portuguese MPs 1987–1999

Party offices	Legislature							
	IV[1] 1985–7		V 1987–91		VI 1991–5		VII 1995–9	
	n	%	n	%	n	%	n	%
Central Party Office	48	19.2	125	50	85	37	88	38.3
Local Party Office	83	33.2	63	25.2	43	18.7	41	17.8

Note: [1] I was not able to trace the data of 118 (46%) of MPs for the fourth legislature.

Source: Compilation based on Azevedo (1989); Assembleia da Republica (1993 and 1996).

quite a normal practice in Portuguese politics. MPs who want to return to their work are allowed to appoint substitutes to represent them in parliament. This practice is, in fact, quite common and the offices of the Portuguese parliament have lost track of the exact number of substitutes. This indicates that recruitment patterns have not changed entirely since the beginning of the century. The persistence of patrimonialism in the form of accumulation of political offices, the substitute system, and the still low level of professionalization are serious obstacles to the modernization of the political system. The predominance of the executive over the legislative body is a further factor preventing a stronger professionalization of the political elite. This has been demonstrated quite thoroughly by recent studies which came to the conclusion that a culture of parliamentarism is still in the making, while one of anti-parliamentarianism seems to prevail (Bandeira and Magalhães 1993: 161–2; Magalhães 1995; Bandeira 1995). One could say, however, that after integration into the European

Community, the level of professionalization of Portuguese elites has increased considerably. The integration into external networks and the contact with parliamentary colleagues from other EU member states has led to a kind of political spillover effect (Magone 1995) and the thrusts of modernization imposed by the European Union may lead to yet further professionalization. Indeed, this can already be measured by the improvement of the work done in the committees of the Assembly of the Republic in recent years. Furthermore, parliamentary groups seem to adapt very quickly to the changing environment and the information services of the Socialist and Communist Parties may be mentioned in this respect.

3.2.3. *The Impact of Regime Discontinuities on Parliamentary Elites*

The Portuguese path towards democracy was characterized by many major regime discontinuities. In fact, the pool of those eligible for parliamentary recruitment was severely restricted until 1974. This obviously means that cross-temporal comparisons of data about parliamentary elites are extremely problematic. In contrast to other European countries, regime discontinuities were not related to external factors, such as the two world wars. On the contrary, domestic upheavals, such as revolutions or *coups d'Etat*, were responsible for the lack of continuity of parliamentarism and parliamentarian elites. On the whole, one can say that the Portuguese case has many similarities with the pattern found in other Southern, Central, and Eastern European countries. In the past twenty-five years, the parliamentary elite became less and less discontinuous. After nearly a generation of democracy, the number of MPs who had grown up after the Revolution of Carnations has increased steadily. Also, both government and parliament have become more stable over time. All this has created the conditions to make the present Portuguese democracy more sustainable and resistant against authoritarian and totalitarian dangers. The inclusion in the European Union has been a powerful factor in reinforcing the democratic commitment of the country. Turnover rates since 1976 show a steadily growing number of MPs being re-elected to the Assembly, often after having served many terms in previous legislatures (Table 10.16).

4. CONCLUSIONS: POLITICAL INCLUSION, DEMOCRATIZATION AND CHANGING PATTERNS OF ELITE RECRUITMENT

The Portuguese case shows that one cannot compare patterns of recruitment and elite transformation without taking a diachronic perspective into consideration. The purpose of this chapter was to show the relationship

Table 10.16. Turnover of MPs between 1976 and 1999

Turnover	Legistature												
	Int. 1979–80		II 1980–3		III 1983–5		IV 1985–7		V 1987–91		VI 1991–5		VII 1995–9
	n	%	n	%	n	%	n	%	n	%	n	%	n	%
I (1976–9)	120	48	109	44	67	26.8	55	22	31	12.4	23	10	19	8.2
Int. (1979–80)			175	70	95	38	75	30	38	15.2	—		—	
II (1980–3)					118	47	93	37.2	47	18.8	48	20.9	22	9.6
III (1983–5)							132	52.8	65	26	63	27.4	31	13.5
IV (1985–7)									101	40	82	35.6	34	14.8
V (1987–91)											92	44.3	43	18.7
VI (1991–5)													133	57.8

Note: * Data for 1979–80 are unreliable and therefore not included.

Source: Cruz (1988: 114) completed by data compiled from Assembleia da Republica (1993 and 1996).

between structural impediments and the democratization of political elites. The quality of a democracy will depend on the ability of these elites to achieve a strong endogenous culture of democracy, which creates genuine democratic socialization structures to achieve this aim. Gradually, the democratic structures will not only shape the citizens, but also flux representations. One will then be able to speak of a strong self-sustained democracy based upon an active civil society (Barber 1984: 151). We have seen that in Portugal the distance between the elites and the socially disadvantaged groups of the population has been traditionally quite large. The main element in this gap has been education. This lack of education was also used as an argument to exclude the population from passive and active voting rights until 1975. Patterns of recruitment have been circular and closed, with the executive having always had a strong influence upon the legislative. This small elite was not able to incorporate new social demands.

The present changes at world level have given emphasis to the emergence of a knowledge-based society so that, more than ever, the main cross-cutting cleavage today is education. In this respect, the Portuguese population is divided very roughly into three different cultural worlds: the world of informatics and cyberspace, the world of written culture, and the world of illiteracy, including structural illiteracy. In spite of these differences, the Portuguese parliamentary elite resembles, at least in terms of its social composition, regional background, party and parliamentary professionalization, its counterparts in other Western European countries. Nevertheless, a place in the Assembly of the Republic is still not highly valued by the political class, so that many elected MPs tend to choose substitutes to represent them as has been practised for years in Portugal. MPs are not very well paid and in general the salaries of Portuguese politicians are much lower than those of the other European democracies. But the latest developments in Portugal suggest that the process of democratic accountability and participation will increase in the near future. If there is a particularity in the development of parliamentary elites in Portugal, then it is the fact that the discontinuous process of elite replacement, which had prevailed since the early nineteenth century, ended after the revolutionary process of 25 April 1974. For twenty-five years one has witnessed a steady process towards the institutionalization of a parliamentary elite with a correspondingly strong parliamentary culture.

Abbreviations

CDS   *Centro Democrático Social* (Social Democratic Centre)
MFA   *Movimento das Forças Armadas* (Movement of the Armed Forces)
PCP   *Partido Comunista Português* (Portuguese Communist Party)
PPD   *Partido Popular Democrático* (People's Democratic Party)
PPM   *Partido Popular Monárquico* (Monarchic People's Party)
PRP   *Partido Republicano Português* (Republican Portuguese Party)
PS   *Partido Socialista* (Socialist Party)
PSD   *Partido Social-Democrata* (Social Democratic Party)
SEDES *Sociedade de Estudos para o Deseurolvimento Económico e Social* (Association far the Study of Economic and Social Development)
UDP   *União Democrática Popular* (People's Democratic Union)
UN/ANP *União Nacional-Acçao Nacional Popular* (National Union–People's National Action)

References

Aguiar, Joaquim (1994). 'Partidos, eleições, dinámica politica'. *Análise Social*, 29: 171–236.
Almeida, Pedro Tavares de (1991). *Caciquismo e Eleições no Portugal Oitocentista.* Lisbon: Difel.
Aniceto, Henrique Afonso, and Costa, Manuel Braz da (1985). 'Subsidios para a caracterização sociologica do movimento dos capitães (exército)'. *Revista Critica de Ciências Sociais*, 15–17: 97–122.
Antunes, Miguel Lobo (1988). 'A Assembleia da República e a Consolidação da Democracia em Portugal'. *Análise Social*, 24: 77–95.
Assembleia da República (1993). *Biografias dos Deputados. VI Legislatura (1991–95).* Lisbon: Assembleia da República.
——(1996). *Biografias dos Deputados. VII Legislatura (1995–99).* Lisbon: Assembleia da República.

Azevedo, Cândido de (1989). *A Classe Política Portuguesa. Estes politicos que nos governam.* Lisbon: Ediçao.

Bandeira, Cristina Leston, and Magalhães, Pedro Coutinho (1993). 'As relações Parlamento/Governo nas IV e V Legislaturas', Tese de Licenciatura (unpublished). Lisbon: ISCTE.

——(1995). 'O Controlo do Governo pela Assembleia da República na IV e V Legislatura'. *Cadernos de Ciência da Legislação*, 12: 121–52.

Barber, Benjamin (1984). *Strong Democracy: Participatory Politics for a New Age.* Berkeley: University of California Press.

Biezen, Ingrid van (1998). 'Building Party Organisations and the Relevance of Past Models: The Communist and Socialist Parties in Spain and Portugal'. *West European Politics*, 21/2: 32–62.

Borish, Steven (1991). *The Land of the Living: The Danish Non-Violent Path to Democracy.* New York: Dolphin Press.

Bourdieu, Pierre (1984a). 'Sozialer Raum und "Klasse"', in Pierre Bourdieu, *Sozialer Raum und 'Klassen', Leçon sur la leçon. Zwei Vorlesungen.* Frankfurt am Main: Suhrkamp.

——(1984b). *Distinction: A Social Critique of the Judgement of Taste.* London: Routledge & Kegan Paul Ltd.

Bruneau, Thomas (1984). *Politics and Nationhood: Post-Revolutionary Portugal.* New York and Philadelphia: Praeger.

——(1997). 'Introduction', in Thomas Bruneau (ed.), *Political Parties and Democracy in Portugal: Organisations, Elections, and Public Opinions.* Boulder, Colo.: Westview Press, 1–22.

—— and Macleod, Alex (1986). *Politics in Contemporary Portugal: Parties and the Consolidation of Democracy.* Boulder, Colo.: Lynne Rienner.

Cortesao, Luiza (1988). *Escola, Sociedade: Que Relação?* Porto: Afrontamento.

Cunha, Carlos (1997). 'The Portuguese Communist Party', in Thomas Bruneau (ed.), *Political Parties and Democracy in Portugal: Organisations, Elections, and Public Opinions.* Boulder, Colo.: Westview Press, 23–54.

Cruz, Manuel Braga da (1988a). *O Partido e o Estado no Salazarismo.* Lisbon: Editorial Presença.

——(1988b). 'Sobre o Parlamento Português: Partidarização Parlamentar, Parlamentarização Partidária'. *Análise Social*, 24 (100).

——(1995). *Instituições Políticas e Processos Sociais.* Lisbon: Bertrand.

—— and Antunes, Miguel Lobo (1989). 'Parlamento, Partidos e Governo-acerca da institucionalização politica', in Mário Baptista Coelho (ed.), *Portugal: O Sistema Político e Constitucional 1974–1987.* Lisbon: Instituto de Ciências Sociais-Universidade de Lisboa, 351–68.

————(1990). 'Revolutionary Transition and Problems of Parliamentary Institutionalisation: the Case of the Portuguese National Assembly', in Ulrike Liebert and Maurizio Cotta (eds.), *Parliament and Democratic Consolidation in Southern Europe.* London: Pinter, 154–83.

Czudnowski, Moshe (1972). 'Sociocultural Variables and Legislative Recruitment'. *Comparative Politics*, 561–87.

Eaton, Martin (1994). 'Regional Development Funding in Portugal'. *Journal of the Association for Contemporary Iberian Studies*, 7/2: 36–46.

Esping-Andersen, Gosta (1990). *Politics Against Markets*. Cambridge: Cambridge University Press.

——(1993). 'Post-Industrial Class Structures: An Analytical Framework', in Gosta Esping-Andersen, *Changing Classes: Stratification and Mobility in Post-Industrial Societies*. London: Sage, 7–31.

Eisfeld, Rainer (1984). *Sozialistischer Pluralismus in Europa. Ansätze and Scheitern am Beispiel Portugal*. Cologne: Verlag Wissenschaft und Politik.

Ferreira, José Medeiros (1983). *Ensaio Histórico sobre a Revolução do 25 de Abril: O Periodo Pré-Constitucional*. Lisbon: Imprensa Nacional-Casa da Moeda.

Figueiredo, António de (1976). *Portugal: Cinquenta Anos de Ditadura*. Lisbon: Publicaçoes Dom Quixote.

Frain, Maritheresa (1997). 'The Right in Portugal: The PSD and the CDS/PP', in Thomas Bruneau (ed.), *Political Parties and Democracy in Portugal. Organisations, Elections, and Public Opinion*. Boulder, Colo.: Westview Press, 77–111.

Gallagher, Tom (1983). *Portugal: A Twentieth Century Interpretation*. Manchester: Manchester University Press.

Georgel, Jacques (1985). *O Salazarismo*. Lisbon: Publiçoes Dom Quixote.

Graham, Lawrence (1975). *Portugal: The Decline and Collapse of an Authoritarian Order*. London and Beverly Hills, Calif.: Sage.

Graziano, Luigi (1975). '*A Conceptual Framework for the Study of Clientelism*', Western Societies Program. Cornell University: Occasional Paper 2/4.

Grofman, Bernard, and Lijphart, Arend (1986). 'Introduction', in Bernard Grofman and Arend Lijphart (eds.), *Electoral Laws and their Political Consequences*. New York: Agathon Press, 1–5.

Harvey, Robert (1978). *Portugal: Birth of a Democracy*. London: Macmillan Press.

Heimer, Franz Wilhelm (1988). 'A cultura politica da classe politica: saliências e omissões. Uma nota de pesquisa'. I Congresso de Sociologia; policopied paper.

Janos, Andrew (1988). 'The Politics of Backwardness in Continental Europe: 1780–1945'. *World Politics*, 325–58.

Kay, Hugh (1971). *Die Zeit steht still in Portugal. Hintergrund eines politischen Systems*. Bergisch-Gladbach: Gustav Luebbe Verlag.

Kern, Robert W. (1974). *Liberals, Reformers and Caciques in Restoration Spain, 1875–1909*. Albuquerque N. Mex.: University of New Mexico Press.

Knudsen, Tim, and Rothstein, Bo (1994). 'State Building in Scandinavia'. *Comparative Politics*, Jan., 203–20.

Lane, Jan-Erik, and Ersson, Svante (1994). *Comparative Politics: An Introduction and New Approach*. Cambridge: Polity Press.

Lewis, Paul H. (1978). 'Salazar's Ministerial Elite, 1932–1968'. *Journal of Politics*, 40: 622–47.

Lijphart, Arend (1984). *Patterns of Majoritarian and Consensus Government in Twenty-One Countries*. New Haven: Yale University Press.

Lobo, Marina Costa (1996). 'A evolução do sistema partidário portugués á luz de mudanças económicas e políticas (1976–1991)'. *Análise Social*, 31: 1085–116.

Lopes, Fernando Farelo (1994). *Eleições e Caciquismo na Primeira República*. Lisbon: Teorema.

Lucena, Manuel de (1979). 'The Evolution of Portuguese Corporatism under Salazar and Caetano', in Lawrence S. Graham and Harry M. Makler (eds.), *Contemporary Portugal: The Revolution and its Antecedents*. Austin, Tex. and London: University of Texas Press, 47–88.

Magalhães, Pedro (1995). 'A actividade legislativa da Assembleia da República e o seu papel no sistema politico', in *Cadernos de Ciência Legislação*, 12, Jan.–Mar.: 87–119.

Magone, José M. (1995). 'The Portuguese Assembleia da República: Discovering Europe'. *Journal of Legislative Studies*, 1/3: 151–65.

——(1996). *The Changing Architecture of Iberian Politics: An Investigation on the Structuring of Democratic Political Systemic Culture in Semiperipheral Southern European Societies*. Lewiston, NY: Mellen University Press.

——(1997a). 'The Portuguese Assembleia da República', in *World Encyclopaedia of Parliaments*. Washington: G. Kurian Publisher.

——(1997b). *European Portugal: The Difficult Road to Sustainable Democracy*. Basingstoke and New York: Macmillan and St Martin's Press.

——(1998). 'The Logics of Party System Change in Southern Europe', in Paul Pennings and Jan Erik Lane (eds.), *Comparing Party System Change*. London: Routledge & Kegan Paul Ltd., 217–40.

Makler, Harry M. (1979). 'The Portuguese Industrial Elite and its Corporative Relations: A Study of Compartmentalisation in an Authoritarian Regime', in Lawrence S. Graham and Harry M. Makler (eds.), *Contemporary Portugal: The Revolution and its Antecedents*. Austin, Tex. and London: University of Texas Press, 123–65.

Marques, A. H. Oliveira (1980). *A Primeira República Portuguesa*. Lisbon: Livros Horizonte.

——(1981). *História de Portugal*, iii: *Das Revoluções Liberais aos Nossos Dias*. Lisbon: Palas Editores.

Monica, Maria Filomena (1994). 'A lenta morte da Camâra dos Pares (1878–1896)'. *Análise Social*, 29: 121–52.

Mouzelis, Nicos (1978). *Modern Greece—Facets of Underdevelopment*. London: Macmillan.

——(1986). *Politics in the Semiperiphery: Early Parliamentarianism and Late Industrialisation in the Balkans and Latin America*. London: Macmillan.

Oliveira, César (1974). *O Operariado e a República Democrática*. Lisbon: Seara Nova.

Pedersen, Mogens (1976). *Political Development and Elite Transformation in Denmark*. London: Sage.

Passos, Marcelino (1987). *Der Niedergang des Faschismus in Portugal. Zum Verhältnis von Ökonomie, Gesellschaft und Staat/Politik im einem europäischen Schwellenland*. Marburg: Verlag für Arbeiterbewegung und Gesellschaftswissenschaft.

Pereira, José Pacheco (1982). *Conflitos Sociais Nos Campos do Sul de Portugal*. Lisbon: Publicações Europa América.

Porch, Douglas (1977). *The Portuguese Armed Forces and the Revolution*. London: Croom Helm.

Putnam, D. Robert (1976). *The Comparative Study of Political Elites*. Englewood Cliffs, NJ: Prentice-Hall.

Rae, Douglas W. (1967). *The Political Consequences of Electoral Laws*. New Haven and London: Yale University Press.

Rosas, Fernando (1985). *As primeiras eleições legislativas sob o Estado Novo. 16 de Dezembro de 1934*. Lisbon: Cadernos 'O Jornal'.

Sablovsky, Juliet Antunes (1997). 'The Portuguese Socialist Party', in Thomas Bruneau (ed.), *Political Parties and Democracy in Portugal: Organisations, Elections, and Public Opinion*. Boulder, Colo.: 55–76.

Sapelli, Giulio (1995). *Southern Europe since 1945: Tradition and Modernity in Portugal, Spain, Italy, Greece and Turkey*. Harlow: Longman.

Schmitter, Philippe (1975). *Corporatism and Public Policy in Authoritarian Portugal*. London and Beverly Hills, Calif.: Sage.

Schwartzman, Kathleen (1987). 'Instabilidade Democrática Nos Países Semiperiiféricos: A Primeira República Portuguesa', in *O Estado Novo. Das Origens ao Fim da Autarcia 1926–1959*, i. Lisbon: Fragmentos.

—— (1989). *The Social Origins of Democratic Collapse: The First Portuguese Republic in the Global Economy*. Lawrence, Kan.: University Press of Kansas.

Scotti-Rosin, Michael (1982). *Die Sprache der Falange und des Salazarismus. Eine vergleichende Untersuchung zur politischen Lexikologie des Spanischen und Portugiesischen* (Europaeische Hochschulschriften: Ibero-roman. Sprachen und Literaturen. vol. 24). Frankfurt am Main: Peter Lang.

Sobral, José Manuel, and Almeida, Pedro Ginesta Tavares de (1982). 'Caciquismo e poder politico. Reflexões em torno das eleições de 1901'. *Análise Social*, 18: 649–71.

Sousa, Vinicio Alves da Costa e (n.d.). 'Caracterização da Classe Política Portuguesa', policopied manuscript.

Stieffel, Matthias, and Wolfe, Marshall (1994). *A Voice for the Excluded: Popular Participation in Development: Utopia or Necessity?* London and New Jersey: Zed Books.

Stoer, Stephen R. (1986). *Educação e Mudança Social em Portugal 1970–1980: Uma década de transição*. Porto: Edicões Afrontamento.

—— and Arayujo, Helena G. (1992). *Escola e Aprendizagem para o Trabalho: Educaçao e Democracia num País da (Semi) Periferia Europeia*. Lisbon: Escher.

Vidigal, Luis (1988). *Cidadania, Caciquismo e Poder: Portugal, 1890–1916*. Lisbon: Livros Horizonte.

Wheeler, Douglas L. (1978). *Republican Portugal: A Political History 1910–1926*. Madison: University of Wisconsin Press.

Wiarda, Howard J. (1979). 'The Corporatist Tradition and the Corporative System in Portugal: Structured, Evolving, Transcended, Persistent', in Lawrence S. Graham and Harry M. Makler (eds.), *Contemporary Portugal: The Revolution and its Antecedents*. Austin, Tex. and London: University of Texas Press, 89–122.

Wolf, Eric R. (1977). 'Kinship, Friendship, and Patron-Client Relations in Complex Societies', in Steffen W. Schmidt, Laura Guasti, Carl H. Landé, and James Scott (eds.), *Friends, Followers and Factions: A Reader in Political Clientelism*. Berkeley: University of California Press.

11

Spanish *Diputados*: From the 1876 Restoration to Consolidated Democracy

JUAN J. LINZ, PILAR GANGAS, AND
MIGUEL JEREZ MIR

1. INTRODUCTION

The 1812 liberal constitution of Cadiz[1] did away with the remnants of estate representation in Spain and established equal citizenship and universal suffrage by a complex procedure of indirect suffrage at three levels with one representative for 70,000 inhabitants, leading to a chamber of 149 *diputados*. On his return from France, King Ferdinand VII refused to accept the constitution and established absolute rule. In 1820, a *pronunciamiento* by the army forced him to swear the constitution but soon, with the help of the Holy Alliance, he would re-establish absolute rule. The death of the king led to a succession war between his brother, Don Carlos, and the partisans of his daughter, Isabel II, that was also an ideological war between the defenders of absolutism, of the special role of the Church and traditional institutions, and those of liberalism. The re-establishment of the 1812 constitution was only temporary and in 1834 the *Estatuto Real* with a bicameral legislature was granted by the Queen Regent. The government and the Cortes (the Spanish parliament) elaborated a new electoral law based on census restrictions and in 1836 convoked new elections.[2] The Queen Regent in 1836 enacted the re-establishment of the constitution of 1812 and a new constitutional text was approved in 1837, which separated electoral law from the constitutional text. The new law extended the suffrage to 2.2% of the population and in 1843, 4.3% were eligible voters.

Sections 1–3 of this chapter were written by J. J. Linz. Pilar Gangas has written Section 4. Miguel Jerez Mir has co-operated in the control of the data and the revision of the texts. The part written by Linz grows at least in part out of papers presented at a meeting in Bellagio in 1970, organized by Mattei Dogan, and at a session of the IPSA Congress in Brussells. A longer version has appeared as an Occasional Paper of the Centre for the Study of Political Change of the University of Siena (2000). Linz also wants to acknowledge the collaboration of Rocío de Terán and of Maurizio Cotta in shortening a much longer paper.

[1] For the constitutional history of Spain, see Sánchez Agesta (1964) and Sáinz de Varanda (1957).

[2] 4.6% of the population had the right to vote: 50,141 property holders and 14,926 on the basis of professional and educational qualifications.

The Carlist War, which had started at the death of Ferdinand VII in 1833, ended with the Treaty of Vergara between the military commanders of both sides. Not long afterwards, the Queen Regent abdicated and General Espartero became Regent until 1843. Between 1843 and 1854, there was a period of the moderates, then the revolution of 1854, and in 1858 the Liberal Union assumed power, followed by a period of ultra-conservative rule which ended with the revolution of 1868 and Queen Isabel II leaving Spain.

As a result of the electoral law of November 1868 granting universal male suffrage, the number of eligible voters increased from 395,000 in the 1866 election to 3,801,000. The Cortes elected at that time approved the 1869 constitution and after considerable manoeuvring and international tension in November 1870, Amadeus of Savoy was elected King. Not long afterwards, in February 1873, he abdicated, frustrated, and the Federal Republic was proclaimed. The new regime, in the course of one year, had four presidents and had to confront a Carlist uprising, a rebellion of extremist Federal Republicans, and was finally overthrown in January 1874 by the occupation of the Chamber by a general, leading to a provisional government which, in turn, was overthrown by the end of the year by a *pronunciamiento* that proclaimed Alphonse XII, son of Isabel II, as King. The leading Alphonsine politician, Canovas, set out to construct a new liberal constitutional monarchy and after an election with universal suffrage, the 1876 constitution that would rule Spain until 1923 was enacted. In 1878, a more restricted suffrage was reintroduced. After the death of the King, the liberal leader, Sagasta, was called to form the government and reintroduced in June 1890 male universal suffrage. The Regency would last until the assumption of power in 1902 by Alphonse XIII who, after the dictatorship established in 1923 and a period of uncertainty in 1930–1, would leave the country following the proclamation of the Republic on 14 April 1931. It is to this period of relative political stability and civilian government, based on two dynastic parties and their factions alternating in power, which allowed the political participation of opponents willing to take part peacefully in the political process, with the exclusion of overt military *pronunciamientos*, that we will turn our attention.

Spaniards have been called to elect parliaments that would write constitutions in 1810, 1854, 1868, 1875, 1931, and 1977. From the first enactment of male universal suffrage in 1868 until 1977, they went to the polls 29 times, although four times (1879, 1881, 1884, 1886) the suffrage was restricted and only since 1933 have women had the vote (Artola 1975, 1993; Martínez Cuadrado 1969). The reported participation fluctuated considerably after the granting of universal male suffrage, from 70% in 1868 to 46% in the election of 1872. In the period of restricted suffrage after the Restoration (1878–90), it ranged between 68% and 72%. With the re-enactment of universal male suffrage in 1890[3] participation dropped to 50%, increasing later to a maximum of 67%. After the Law of 1907, which provided for automatic election when there were no candidates competing (art. 29), turnout in the remaining districts was 54% in 1910, reaching a maximum of 59% in 1920 to drop in the three subsequent elections to 42%. During the Republic, turnout was 70% in 1931, 67% in 1933—when women voted for the first time, and in 1936, in the heated political atmosphere and with some of the anarchists, who generally abstained in principle, turning out to vote, 72%.

2. POLITICS AND ELITES OF RESTORATION SPAIN
(1876–1923)

After a period of rapid political democratization, turmoil, localism encouraged by a Federal Republican ideology, and a revival of Carlist insurgency, the Restoration represents a period of peace, relative stability, considerable civil liberties, significant but insufficient economic progress, formal democracy despite the survival of oligarchic structures, a centre-right compromise between clericalism and the anti-clerical tendencies so dominant at the time in Europe. It was a period in which the legislature was able to enact much of the basic legal framework of Spanish government and administration, though not to solve many of the basic political problems, particularly the regional and social questions. It was also a period in which, at least initially, the army withdrew from active interference in politics. In the intention of its framers, it was a compromise that slowed down the process of revolutionary mobilization without, however, rejecting European modern political institutions. The last efforts to retain control of Cuba and the Philippines and the war with the United States, ending in defeat in 1898, led to a profound crisis reflected not so much in the parties and political elites but in the rise of peripheral nationalisms and the intellectual critique of the system. It was a time when the two major parties, their leaders, and followers in the provinces, exercised power, sharing it with the landowning classes, the traditional institutions—Church, army, and King—even when indirectly, and the professional middle classes and, to a lesser extent, with the emerging big business bourgeoisie of the industrial regions. In its early stages, the workers were not yet organized to share in power or to challenge the system seriously, but after 1911, and particularly after World War I, they became a threat to it, although not at the electoral level. The intelligentsia remained largely outside, even when the Liberal Party established interesting links with some sectors of the intellectual community.

[3] Which expanded the electorate from 807,000 in 1886 to 4,100,000 in 1890.

The compromise between the moderate right, that isolated the more reactionary Catholics supporting the Carlists, integrated slowly the collaborationists among them, the 'mestizos' of the *Unión Católica*, and the old progressives turned reasonable under the leadership of Sagasta, perhaps narrowed the political spectrum too much. The great question to which our data might contribute some answer is how different were the two great parties of Cánovas and Sagasta, Conservatives and Liberals, at the *fin de siècle*? Historians hostile to their performance tend to stress the lack of real differentiation and the underlying *caciquismo*—a mixture between notable, committee, machine, and government-controlled politics—as a unifying factor. Our feeling is that the two main parties were more different in social composition and their policies than has been generally assumed, but certainly less so than Conservatives and Liberals in other nineteenth century two-party systems, particularly in the United Kingdom. Several reasons might account for this: the less differentiated social structure of Spain, a much less economically developed country, the link established around the turn of the century between the Catalan manufacturers and a regionalist autonomy movement outside the two-party system, the presence of a large number of bourgeois landowners resulting from the land reforms of the nineteenth century that made a conflict between a landed aristocracy and an urban liberal party less likely in Spain than other countries, the decision after the religious conflicts in the nineteenth century to accept a *modus vivendi* by the Liberals, the defensive foreign policy of Spain that excluded great debates on such issues, except for some disagreement about the position to take in World War I.

The Restoration was a period of rule of the politicians, skilled in parliamentary life, many of them great orators, linked to more prosaic interests through their law offices, experts in electioneering and election manipulation both in the Ministry of Interior and in the provinces. Organized interest groups were few, even though some were already powerful and linked with the political elite. The trade unions, at an early stage, were illegal or semi-legal, turning later to political action through the Socialist Party or the syndicalist movement. However, the presence of the PSOE (*Partido Socialista Obrero Español*) in the legislatures before 1923 was small compared with the Italian Socialists. Even in municipal government, the Radical Party, a republican party, played a more important role than the PSOE.

With the constitution of 1876 the legislature was composed of the Senate and the *Congreso de los Diputados*, with equal powers. The House was elected for five years, until 1890 by all males paying annually 25 pesetas in real estate taxes and 50 in business taxes, civil servants with a minimum income, army officers, professionals, and all those teaching who were paid by the state. The number of eligible voters in 1881 was 846,961, compared to 3,989,612 in the 1876 election which was still conducted under universal male suffrage. After universal male suffrage was reintroduced in 1890, the number of eligible voters increased to 4,800,000.[4] The change in the electoral law represented an increase in the electorate from 4.8% of the population to 27%. The Senate was to be composed of senators in their own right, life senators appointed by the crown, and as many elective senators as of the above-mentioned categories.[5]

2.1. The Parliamentary Elite of 1879

For a collective portrait of the political elite of the Restoration, we have a collection of biographies of the members of the first legislature elected, according to the 1876 constitution, in 1879 under the Prime Ministership of General Martínez Campos and consequently dominated by the Conservative Party (De Tebar and De Olmedo 1879). This should be kept in mind in analysing the data since those for a later period suggest that the parliamentary representation for a dominant party is somewhat different from that of the same party in a lean year. The biographical data available have many gaps, despite the fact that we have combined some information on the same individuals from a volume of biographies of those elected in 1886. Therefore, the data have to be considered only indicative, but they allow us to contrast the two parties of the Restoration in its early phase, shortly after the compromise that established the regime. We will limit our analysis to the composition of the lower house.

The very incomplete information available on regional origin points towards a greater Liberal strength in Catalonia, Levante, and also Old Castile. The democratic opposition to the two-party system came apparently mainly from Andalusia and Valencia. The information on the education of the deputies is only slightly better. It is impossible to know whether the lack of information in the short biographical sketches is due to lack of information or the lack of any formal education of the members worth reporting. We suspect both. The outstanding fact is that in all political groups those with legal training outstrip those with any other training (Table 11.1). Relatively speaking, the democratic opposition has fewer lawyers and more university graduates in other disciplines.[6] Some readers

---

[4] The population census of 1877—rectified in 1883—gave a population of 16,634,345 inhabitants.

[5] The senators in their own right were the holders of certain high military commands, the archbishops, the five heads of high tribunals and advisory councils, and the *grandes de España*—the top rank of the titled nobility—with a certain level of income. The life senators could only be appointed from among those having occupied or occupying certain elite positions in politics, administration, the church, and cultural life, and some social categories as long as they could prove a certain level of income. The elective senators were to be renewed by halves every five years or in their totality, should the King dissolve that part of the chamber.

[6] It is not surprising, if we remember the characters of the novels of the Spanish Balzac,

Table 11.1. Education of the *diputados* of the Cortes elected in 1879 by party tendencies (%)

Education	Liberals	Conservatives	Traditionalists	Democratic parties	Independents	No Information	Total
Commerce school	—	—	—	7.1	—	—	0.3
Other middle school	—	0.9	—	—	—	—	0.5
Higher technical	5.6	4.6	6.2	—	—	14.6	5.9
Law	42.3	38.1	37.5	57.1	37.5	27.1	38.1
Law incomplete	—	0.9	—	—	—	—	0.5
Other university	7.0	4.6	—	21.4	25.0	6.2	6.1
Military	12.7	9.6	6.2	—	—	10.4	9.6
Ecclesiastical	1.4	—	—	—	—	—	0.3
Other	1.4	0.9	—	—	—	—	0.8
No information	35.2	44.0	50.0	21.4	50.0	45.8	42.1
Total (n)	(71)	(218)	(16)	(14)	(8)	(48)	(375)

Source: De Tebar and De Olmedo (1879).

might find it surprising that those with military education should be found somewhat more often on the Liberal side of the Chamber, but for anyone familiar with the long liberal tradition of the Spanish army in the nineteenth century, the finding is less unexpected. The larger number with a technical and military education among those not clearly identified with either of the two major parties nor with the right or left dissidents may point towards a type of non-partisan professional presence in Spanish politics, leaning to one or the other party, while among them the number of lawyers is surprisingly small. The greater lack of information on the Conservatives might be explained by the majority character of their representation, normally with more unknown men elected than the minority Liberals, but it might also be a reflection of the less urban, less intellectual and progressive character of the party.

The information on occupation (Table 11.2) allows us to nuance our portrait further: for example, among the lawyers on the Liberal benches, more seem to practise as attorneys, while more Conservatives are landowners with a law degree or inactive at the bar, and the same is true for those few identifying themselves as independents. The overwhelming number of lawyers in the democratic opposition are active as attorneys, indicating the tendency towards more professional practice as we move leftward. The greater link between Liberals and the intellectual community is reflected in the larger number of university professors among them.[7] Significantly, we also find an important minority of university professors in the democratic opposition. Professional army officers are represented in both parties but their number, irrespective of rank, seems slightly larger on the Liberal side. The world of business is represented in both dynastic parties and absent in the democratic opposition, while it constitutes an important contingent among those with no clear information on party identity. The impact of the revolutionary experiences of past decades explains the slightly greater presence on the Conservative side, probably reinforced by the move away from free trade by the Spanish business community.[8] Neither of the two parties can be called the party of manufacturers or bankers.[9] Agrarian interests, particularly the large owners, by comparison seem to have made a clear choice to run on the Conservative slate.

In all parties, we find some representatives of the nobility, but by German standards their number is low. While one cannot characterize the

Benito Pérez Galdós, that the engineers should be slightly more represented on the Liberal benches under the leadership of Sagasta, himself an engineer.

[7] Though the proportion of law school professors in both major parties is identical, as is the number of secondary school teachers and journalists.

[8] Only the shipowners, probably mostly Basques from the liberal city of Bilbao, stand out among the Liberal businessmen.

[9] As Vicens Vives (1959) has shown for Barcelona, just as there was a two-party system, there were also two great banking houses (Girona and Arnus) linked with the two parties.

Table 11.2. Occupation of the *diputados* of the Cortes elected in 1879 by party tendencies (%)

Occupation	Liberals	Conservatives	Traditionalists	Democratic parties	Independents	No information	Total
Lawyers (practising)	23.9	17.9	31.3	42.9	12.5	18.8	20.5
Lawyers (no information on practice)	7.0	8.3	6.2	7.1	12.5	4.2	7.5
Lawyers and owners	4.2	5.5	—	7.1	12.5	2.1	4.8
Other legal professions	—	0.5	—	—	—	—	0.3
Law School professors	2.8	2.8	—	—	12.5	2.1	2.4
Diplomats	—	1.4	—	—	—	—	1.1
Judges	1.4	0.9	—	—	—	—	0.8
Pharmacists	1.4	—	—	—	—	—	0.3
Secondary school professors	2.8	—	—	—	12.3	4.2	1.3
University professors (other than law) or at technical schools	1.4	0.5	—	7.1	—	—	0.8
Architects and engineers	5.6	4.1	—	—	—	10.4	5.3
Journalists	7.0	3.2	—	—	—	8.3	4.3
Writers	5.6	4.1	6.2	7.1	—	12.5	5.6
High civil servants	4.2	4.1	6.2	—	12.5	2.1	4.0
Middle civil servants	—	2.3	7.1	—	—	—	1.6
Military (general rank)	5.6	3.2	—	—	—	6.2	3.7
Military (colonel rank)	5.6	2.8	—	—	—	—	2.7
Other military	1.4	1.4	—	—	—	—	1.1
Navy admiral rank	—	—	—	—	—	2.1	0.3
Military justice	—	0.9	—	—	—	—	0.5
Financiers, bankers	5.6	7.3	6.2	—	—	4.2	6.1
Important manufacturers	1.4	3.2	—	—	—	14.6	4.0
Other manufacturers	1.4	0.5	—	—	—	—	0.5
Managers	1.4	—	—	—	—	—	0.3
Merchants	—	2.8	—	—	37.5	2.1	2.7
Shipowners	1.4	0.5	—	—	—	2.1	0.8
Farmers (large)	7.0	18.3	6.2	7.1	12.5	10.4	14.1
Farmers (small)	—	1.4	6.2	7.1	—	—	1.3
Total (n)	(71)	(218)	(16)	(14)	(8)	(48)	(375)

Source: See Table 11.1.

Conservatives as the party of the nobility and the Liberals as a bourgeois opposition, the difference between both parties in this respect is marked (25.4% versus 7.5%) (Table 11.3). Many of those sitting on the Conservative benches are not grandees of Spain and quite a few (6.2%) owe their titles to the Popes rather than to the Spanish kings. This reflects the greater identification of the Conservatives with the clerical cause, but probably also the feudalization of some sectors of the business bourgeoisie by acquiring, through generous contributions to the Church, a pseudo-aristocratic rank. When we turn to the date of concession of the titles, we find the old nobility more represented on the Conservative benches, with the Liberal title holders owing their status to the nineteenth-century monarchs. The small Traditionalist representation includes a large proportion of aristocrats whose titles date from before 1700 (12.4% versus 6.4% among the Conservatives and none among the Liberals) or at least before the Napoleonic invasion. These figures run counter to the image of a Liberal inclination on the part of the high nobility in the early nineteenth century.

The 1879 legislature does not represent a change of regime or dominant party, since it is the second one to sit after the Fall of the Republic, but it is the first one elected according to the restricted suffrage reintroduced by Cánovas del Castillo, and therefore represents a discontinuity with the democratic period initiated after the 1868 revolution. This discontinuity is reflected in the relatively small number of deputies on the Conservative benches with parliamentary experience before the Restoration, which contrasts with the political background of the Liberals, but also of the minority dissidents, who had accumulated parliamentary experience before the return of Alphone XII, particularly in the National Assembly (1873–4). In this respect, the Restoration, in its first period, despite a change of regime, represents less discontinuity in the political class than twentieth-century regime changes we will analyse later (Table 11.4).

2.2. Politics in the Reign of Alphonse XIII

After the death of the great leaders Cánovas and Sagasta, the two-party system experiences a crisis, since first the Liberals and later the Conservatives divide into factions, sometimes defining themselves as parties. Those tensions made the King an arbiter, allowing him to choose among the leaders a Prime Minister and to prevent others—even those, such as the Conservative Maura, with parliamentary support—to accede to power. This reinforced the factionalism of the parties after the assassination of Canalejas (1912) and the withdrawal of Maura from the leadership of the Conservatives. The ambiguity of the 1876 constitution with the 'dual confidence' of the Crown and the Chamber and the incapacity to achieve constitutional reform in 1917 ultimately provoked a stalemate, government instability,

Table 11.3. Nobility titles among the *diputados* elected in 1879 by party tendencies (%)

Title	Liberals	Conservatives	Traditionalists	Democratic parties	Independents	No information	Total
Duke	2.8	0.5	6.2	—	—	—	1.1
Marquis with *grandeza*	—	1.8	6.2	—	—	—	1.3
Marquis without *grandeza*	2.8	8.7	25.0	7.1	12.5	6.2	8.0
Count with *grandeza*	—	1.8	—	—	—	—	1.1
Count without *grandeza*	1.4	5.5	—	—	—	—	3.5
Viscount without *grandeza*	—	0.9	—	14.3	—	—	1.1
Barons and seigneurs without *grandeza*	—	—	6.2	—	—	—	0.3
Papal titles	0.5	6.2	—	—	—	—	0.5
Total (n)	(71)	(218)	(16)	(14)	(8)	(48)	(375)

Source: See Table 11.1.

Table 11.4. Previous parliamentary experiences of *diputados* elected in 1879 by party tendencies (%)

First election	Liberals	Conservatives	Traditionalists	Democratic parties	Independents	No information	Total
Cortes according to the 1845 constitution							
12. 1846 to 8. 1850	—	—	—	—	—	—	—
10. 1850 to 4. 1851	—	0.5	—	—	—	—	0.3
11. 1851 to 12. 1852	—	—	—	—	—	—	—
3. 1853 to 12. 1853	—	0.5	—	—	—	—	0.3
Constituent Cortes							
11. 1854 to 9. 1856	4.2	0.5	—	—	—	—	1.1
Cortes according to the 1845 constitution							
12. 1857 to 9. 1858	—	1.8	—	—	—	—	1.1
11. 1863 to 9. 1864	5.6	3.7	—	—	—	—	3.2
12. 1864 to 10. 1865	4.2	4.1	6.2	7.2	—	2.1	4.0
12. 1865 to 11. 1866	5.6	5.5	—	—	—	2.1	4.5
3. 1867 to 5. 1868	1.4	3.7	6.2	—	—	2.1	2.9
Constituent Cortes after 1868 revolution							
2. 1869 to 1. 1871	15.5	1.8	—	50.5	12.5	8.3	7.2
Cortes according to the 1869 constitution							
4. 1871 to 1. 1872	16.9	2.3	—	25.7	—	2.1	6.1
4. 1872 to 6. 1872	12.7	1.4	—	14.3	—	2.1	4.0
9. 1872 to 2. 1873	2.8	1.4	—	21.4	—	2.1	2.4
2. 1873 to 4. 1873	1.4	0.5	—	14.3	—	2.1	1.3
National Assembly							
6. 1873 to 1. 1874	4.2	2.3	6.2	57.1	—	4.2	5.1
Constituent Cortes of the restoration							
2. 1876 to 3. 1879	45.1	40.4	31.3	14.3	12.5	16.7	36.3
No previous parliamentary experience	12.7	48.1	50.0	28.5	62.5	62.5	40.8
Total (n)	(71)	(218)	(16)	(14)	(8)	(48)	(375)

Source: See Table 11.1.

suspension of legislative sessions, and emergency rule in the face of public protest, together with a loss of legitimacy for the system that opened the door to the Primo de Rivera dictatorship.

The resignation of the Prime Ministers was a consequence of their defeat on particular issues, the disintegration of support in the party, a hostile climate of public opinion, the feeling that they were incapable of tackling difficult problems. The result was the transfer of power by the Crown to the leader of the other party who proceeded to organize new elections. Those elections did not lead to a free competitive decision by the electorate but to the 'rigging' of the election using the *encasillado* which assured a majority for the party in power.[10]

The electoral laws—the restricted versus universal suffrage and the allocation of seats to single-member districts and multimember *circunscripciones*—are not sufficient to understand the mechanisms of elite recruitment. Electoral practice, changing under the same laws, accounts for some of the outcomes as does the nature of oligarchic politics which does not fit into the model of 'notable' politics in some other European countries (Ranzato 1989). Many, if not most, 'notables' of the Spanish parties are not notables with roots in safe districts where they own land or enjoy influence based on their wealth or professional activities. These men have been professional politicians for many years, occupying seats in parliament, many through political offices mostly under the control of the administration, linked by personal ties to other successful politicians until the time came to succeed them or to organize a dissident faction, whose support made them eligible to form or enter a government. Many lived for politics and indirectly from politics (although until 1922 they received no parliamentary per diem) by holding office, from professional activities close to politics like journalism and the bar, and as lawyers for economic interests. Many of them were of humble origins, without wealth (except perhaps by marriage), personally honest, and left no fortunes. Their reward was power, influence, and prestige.

The system of the *turno pacífico*, invented by Cánovas and Sagasta, assured for a large number of politicians and hangers-on down to village level, and even for outsiders to the dynastic regime who supported parties,

---

[10] Maura, the Conservative leader, described the system in these terms: 'The real electoral competition took place in the ministry at the Puerta del Sol to appear as a candidate of the government in one of the boxes of the chart of districts, *circunscripciones* (multimember districts) and senatorships to be elected. The Minister of Interior set up the *encasillado* with the names of all the parties, taking care to reserve to the oppositions and attribute to them the number of seats that the political situation (convenience) would suggest, to assign to those recommended by influential persons the free districts, that is those where the *caciques* only obeyed the provincial governor, whoever he would be, and to assure the head of the government, in the majority the largest possible number of unconditional supporters' (Martínez Cuadrado 1969: 316).

regular access to power, without the need to call on the support of *golpista pronunciamiento*-prone officers or the urban mob. This assured a peaceful political order, based on all the basic freedoms of the press, opinion, assembly, and so on (increasingly even for those anti-system groups which did not turn to violence). The paradox, in view of other similar systems in nineteenth-century Europe, was that none of the system parties succeeded in or attempted to mobilize the electorate (except in the first decades of the twentieth century, although unsuccessfully) and that those opposing the system and willing to participate in electoral politics were not able to mobilize much support to challenge the system (with the exception of the Catalans of the *Lliga*, the Radicals in Barcelona, and the Socialists in a few districts). The distorted system did not allow victors to claim to represent the demos; neither the *adictos* (loyal to the government) nor the opposition had the legitimacy to do so and to demand constitutional change—formally or in practice—thus eliminating the role of the Crown. Collective economic interests normally mobilized opinion and organized pressure groups, but they did not enter the political sphere directly and create a third party. They worked with one or other faction or politician in the system, which did not become dependent on them since their electoral success was assured by other mechanisms and the opportunity to use them depended on the Crown.

How was all this possible? Ultimately, it was the consequence of the apathy of the citizens (except the few committed to revolutionary change), reflected in large proportions of non-voters, and the willingness to vote as told—the result of a rural society with a low level of literacy,[11] composed in part by landless labourers and poor farmers in latifundia Spain, and large numbers of minifundia farmers. This apathy was in part rewarded by a myriad of small favours for those who supported a politician and minor sanctions, with those gains or losses not being permanent in many places due to the turnover at the top and with it of the administrative-judicial machinery. It could be added that the desire for stability and peace after the civil wars with the Carlists, the constant *pronunciamientos*, and the turmoil after 1868 and with the Republic had an impact. Peace, relative order, political freedoms for the upper and middle classes, mainly aristocratic and professional elites, and probably periods of economic development, contributed to that apathy.

Shortly before or after World War I, a number of European monarchies

---

[11] The *Anuario Estadistico de España* of 1915 (p. 274) gives data on the number of eligible votes by province and the electorate the proportion of able to read and write by province. Of the 4,753,699 eligible voters, 2,858,929 were literate (60.1%); (there was no information on 4.2%). The literate ranged from 33.0% in the Canary Islands, to 93.2% in Burgos, with 84.2% in Madrid, and 76.1% in Barcelona. In 12 provinces, literacy was over 80% and in 12 under 50%.

experienced a process of democratization in the sense that the electorate assumed a greater autonomy and protagonism—often coinciding with an expansion of suffrage. Moreover, monarchs gave up their more direct intervention in politics in favour of parliament or were displaced by republics. Spain had, after 1876, under the Regency and powerful leaders, in many respects been a parliamentary regime. But, paradoxically, in the second decade of the century, rather than parliament asserting itself and the parties becoming more powerful actors, King Alphonse XIII would exercise growing influence, obtain a direct relation with the armed forces, support and veto political leaders, generating distrust and conflict among them. One consequence of the distortion of the electoral process, the fractionalization of the parliamentary parties, and the growing role of the monarch in the process of cabinet formation, was that the forces on the margin or outside the 'two-party system' came to play a more important role. Their leaders had considerable prestige and support in 'public opinion' and could on occasion work together advocating constitutional reform—as in the case of the *Asamblea de Parlamentarios* in 1917—and three of their members (Cambó, Ventosa, Pedregal) were appointed to cabinet posts. The small size of their parliamentary representation should not lead us to neglect this aspect.

Risking being 'politically-intellectually' incorrect, it could be argued that the parliamentary and government elite of this period had a legitimacy, even if weak: neither derived from the electoral process, tainted as it was, nor from a traditional-monarchical legitimacy (eroded by the 1808–15 crisis, the Carlist succession war, the 1868 revolution with its sequels—an elective monarchy and a Republic). In this, it would contrast with Prussia and even Imperial Germany. Even more outrageously, one could claim that the system showed considerable efficacy, guaranteeing peace, a reasonable level of order, considerable institution-building and economic development, a lively intellectual life, and so on.

Only when confronted with new problems in the first quarter of the century did the efficacy become questionable. First, the 1898 defeat by the United States, then Catalanist demands, labour unrest linked with the anarcho-syndicalists, a costly war in Morocco. With limited legitimacy, the crisis of efficacy led to the passive (and by a minority, sympathetic) acceptance of the Primo de Rivera dictatorship. That regime destroyed the legal-rational component of the 1876 compromise constitution, led to a questioning of the Crown even by members of the old party elite, and in the end to an inevitable turn to the people that brought the Republic overnight.

One distinctive factor in the recruitment of parliamentary elites from 1910 to 1923 was the application of article 29 of the 1907 electoral law which stipulated that if a seat was not contested, the unopposed candidate (or candidates in multimember constituencies) would immediately be declared elected. This meant that a significant number of voters—between 11.3% in 1918 and 35.7% in 1916—did not have a chance to vote. The number of seats covered in this way ranged from 61 (in 1918) to 146 (in 1923) out of 409. The 1918 election, a moment of crisis in Europe, was the most competitive, with 88.7% of the electorate having a chance to vote (and a participation rate of 70.4%). In the three subsequent elections, the number of seats covered by article 29 increased dramatically, and where an election was held, abstention was 36% in 1919, 40% in 1920, and 35.5% in 1923. The rule worked in favour of candidates whom their opponents considered unbeatable, given their strength in a district and the resources at their disposed. However, it did not benefit only the *caciques* of the dynastic parties but also the Carlists and some Reformists (originally Republicans) who were in opposition to them.

2.3. The Political Elite of the Constitutional Period of the Reign of Alphonse XIII

The information available on the *diputados*, elected in 1907, 1910, and 1914 (for a total of 741 deputies), allows us to study the political elite in the early decades of this century (Sánchez de los Santos 1908; Sánchez de los Santos and De la Redondela 1910; 1914). Among them, 395 were elected to the 1907 Cortes, dominated by the Conservatives, of whom 47% would continue in the 1910 Cortes and 42% in the Cortes of 1914. Another 391 constitute the 1910 Cortes, dominated by the Liberal Party which, after years of crisis, was ready to govern with considerable authority under the new leadership of Canalejas. Of those deputies, 208 would also sit in the Conservative chamber of 1914. These continuities between the three consecutive legislatures reduce the 1,173 theoretical chances of being a member of the *Congreso de los Diputados* to 741 incumbents.[12] For these 741 men (no woman was elected), we will analyse the main features: their age, place of origin, education, professions or activities, ties with the aristocratic tradition.

Physical age is one of the basic categories of social life, defining status; sociologically, age groups stand also for generations: groups of contemporaries who have lived through the same historical crises, particularly in their formative years. Among those sitting in parliament between 1907 and 1916, only one-quarter were born before 1860, so that most of them grew up after the Restoration in 1874, in a period of stability and without personal memory of the civil wars, the revolutions of earlier decades, or even of the

---

[12] These figures are not exact since there are always vacant seats, voided elections, etc., so that the number of deputies over the period covered might have been slightly larger.

1873 Republic. About one-third lived through the loss of Cuba and the 1898 crisis as young adults, and quite a few served in the war preceding it. In this respect, they were part of the 'regenerationist' generation who could not be happy with the Cánovas–Sagasta Restoration system, whose advantages, after years of civil strife, probably appeared pallid compared to its failures. It is important to note that this group of politicians includes a fair number of men in the prime of life: the late thirties and early forties and even a sprinkling of younger ones in their late twenties and early thirties. This should be kept in mind when we consider the consequences for Spain of the almost complete displacement of this political elite by the Primo de Rivera dictatorship and the sudden establishment of a Republic in which few of these men continued in politics at the national level. In terms of age, a significant part of a political generation was lost.

The data on party tendencies also have some surprises for us (Table 11.5). It is generally assumed that the Conservative parties are led by older men, and that the more radical parties are those of youth. Even taking into account the fact that the Left is represented to a greater extent in the later legislatures among those studied, it is significant that the number of older men in the Republican ranks is as large, if not larger, as on the benches of the dynastic parties. In fact, there are more young men among the Liberals. One explanation would be that minority parties can only win seats for their leaders and offer few chances for the election of young men. However, we are not convinced that this is the only explanation, and that the 'historical' and somewhat nostalgic character of Republicanism after 1874, with its revered but ineffective former presidents leading the different factions over many years, did not contribute to it. In fact, under the Second Republic (1931–6), the leftist leaders reaching the cabinet were also older than their centre-right colleagues, and the youngest prime minister then was to

Table 11.5. Decade of birth of the *diputados* elected in 1907, 1910, and 1914 by party tendencies (%)

Decade of birth	Conservatives	Liberals	Right	Regionalists	Left
1820–30	—	*	—	—	—
1830–40	*	1	—	4	—
1840–50	3	5	9	—	11
1850–60	14	16	18	20	18
1860–70	24	26	14	36	26
1870–80	27	23	36	28	28
1880–90	7	15	—	—	9
No information	24	12	23	12	9
Total (n)	(357)	(258)	(22)	(25)	(57)

Note: * less than 1%.

Source: Sánchez de los Santos (1908); Sánchez de los Santos and De la Redondela (1910, 1914).

be the Catholic leader of the CEDA, José M. Gil Robles. The importance of the *fin de siècle* and the generation of 1898 for the Catalans is reflected in the predominance of the middle-aged among the Regionalists, as well as the relative impermeability of the *Lliga* to the very young men who, a few years later, would contribute so decisively to the split of *Acció Catalana*. The greater opportunity for a party to elect younger men in the good years is reflected in the data on each of the three legislatures for Conservatives and Liberals (Table 11.6).

How far did any of the non-regionalist parties represent Catalonia and the Basque country, not in terms of deputies elected there, but in terms of men of that regional background? The Catalans who, in 1910, were 10.5% of the national population (somewhat less if one were to discount the immigrants into Catalonia from Castilian-speaking Spain) contributed only 2% to the Conservative parliamentary group (Table 11.7). Not surprisingly, given the positions of both the Right (mainly the Carlists) and the Left (mainly the Republicans) on decentralization, both have a disproportionate number of Catalans in their ranks. The alienation of Catalonia from the system shows clearly in these figures. Obviously, practically all the Regionalist deputies for whom we have information were born in Catalonia.

The pattern of estrangement of the Basque country and Navarre from Restoration Spain, a combination of cultural-regional-religious cleavages, is also manifest in the figures. The importance of industrial Spain for the Left, for example, Asturias and a developed agricultural region like Valencia, is apparent in the regional origin of its deputies. It is noteworthy that Andalusia, despite the traditional elements in its social structure (or perhaps on account of them) is the birthplace of a significant number of Left deputies. Apart from their weakness in Catalonia, the Basque country, and Navarre, the two dynastic parties recruit almost equally in most of the country. The success of the Liberals in León, Castile, and Aragón is reflected somewhat in the figures. Neither of the two dynastic parties can be considered a sectional party, nor is the sectional representation in any of them as important as that of the South in the Democratic Party in the United States, or East Elbia in the German (really Prussian) Conservative Party, or even Wales among British Liberals.

Turning to the data on regional origin of the system parties in the three legislatures, we find considerable fluctuations depending on the changing fortune of the party at the polls and the decisions made at the Ministry of the Interior. The difficulty of the comparisons is increased by the different proportions of 'no information' for each legislature and each party. There is some difference between 1907 and subsequent elections in the number of Catalans, easy to account for in view of the resounding victory of the *Solidaritat Catalana* in 1907. If we look at the data for all legislatures

Table 11.6. Decade of birth of the *diputados* elected in 1907, 1910, and 1914 by party tendencies (%)

	1907			1910			1914		
	Conservative	Liberal	Total	Conservative	Liberal	Total	Conservative	Liberal	Total
1820	—	1	1	—	1	*	—	1	*
1830	*	1	1	—	3	5	—	3	2
1840	4	13	6	5	16	18	1	11	12
1850	19	30	22	19	29	28	8	30	26
1860	22	24	23	30	23	27	25	32	36
1870	25	19	24	30	15	11	37	16	13
1880	2	6	3	6	—	—	11	—	—
1890	—	—	1	—	—	—	—	—	—
No information	27	4	20	10	10	10	14	7	11
Total (n)	(231)	(67)	(395)	(109)	(201)	(391)	(195)	(117)	(387)

Notes: Totals include all other parties in addition to the dynastic parties.
* less than 1%.

Source: See Table 11.5.

Table 11.7. Regional origin of *diputados* elected in 1907, 1910, and 1914 by party tendencies (%)

Region of birth	Conservatives	Liberals	Right	Regionalists	Left
Madrid	11	13	—	—	5
New Castile	2	2	—	—	—
Old Castile	6	7	5	—	2
Albacete	1	1	—	—	—
León	1	4	—	—	2
Galicia	4	4	5	—	4
Asturias	3	2	5	—	11
Navarra	1	1	5	—	—
Basque Country	2	1	5	—	5
Catalonia	2	5	23	80	25
Baleares	1	*	—	—	—
Aragón	1	3	—	—	5
Valencia	6	10	—	—	7
Murcia	3	2	—	—	—
Eastern Andalucia	6	6	—	4	9
Western Andalucia	11	9	5	—	9
Extremadura	3	3	—	—	—
Canary Islands	1	2	—	—	2
No information	35	24	41	16	16
Total (n)	(357)	(258)	(22)	(25)	(57)

Note: *less than 1%.

Source: See Table 11.5.

irrespective of party, there is, over time, a slight tendency towards greater representation of Madrid.

The information on birthplace can give us some indication of the milieu from which the legislators come, the ties they might still have through family and friends. Do they come from cities or from smaller communities? In Spain, the provincial capitals, somewhat irrespective of their size, represent 'urban' ways of life and almost all cities of some importance were also provincial capitals. In view of this, we tabulated the proportion born in provincial capitals and outside them. A very large number of legislators of all tendencies, with the exception of the Right (and this may be a statistical artefact given the large number without information among them), were born in the capital of one of the fifty provinces of Spain (Table 11.8). Even if all those without information had been born in smaller places, it would be a high proportion—considering that the 1887 Census, close to the median birth year of these men, reports 13.5% of the population living in the 49 provincial capitals. The number of those born in the place which gives its name to the electoral district they represent is not large. The number born in places of less importance is larger than those born in the capital of an election district they do not represent. Consonant with the urban-bourgeois

Table 11.8. Place of birth of *diputados* elected in 1907, 1910, and 1914 by party tendencies (%)

Place of birth	Conservatives	Liberals	Right	Regionalists	Left
Provincial capital	40	45	27	52	46
Capital of electoral district (represented in any of the legislatures by the deputy)	7	10	9	8	9
Other places that give name to a district (not represented by the deputy)	2	3	—	4	2
Other places	14	19	18	20	26
Overseas or Morocco	1	1	—	4	—
Foreign countries	1	1	—	—	2
No information	34	22	45	12	16
Total (n)	(357)	(258)	(22)	(25)	(57)

Source: See Table 11.5.

character of Catalan regionalism, its deputies are overwhelmingly urban born (in the provincial capitals), but there is also a contingent from smaller places, which do not give their name to any election district. The more urban character of the Liberal Party is visible in the data for each legislature by party.

Unfortunately, we do not have information on education for one-quarter of the legislators, though it is likely that those for whom we have no data would be among the less educated. Even assuming that all those for whom there is no information on education would have had little formal schooling, the proportion of legislators with higher education received in the universities or technical institutions is very high in all parties (Table 11.9). The number of Conservatives for whom we have no information is certainly not due to a high representation of the working class excluded from educational opportunities, but probably to the number of rural representatives and other traditional groups of considerable status and wealth but with little interest in education. On the Liberal Party benches, we find more men with higher education, something that is confirmed by the closer ties of that party with the *Institución Libre de Enseñanza* which served as ferment for educational reform and intellectual innovation through its influence on the scholarship programme administered by the *Junta de Ampliación de Estudios*. The most salient fact is that in all tendencies an absolute majority had legal training. These were chambers dominated by men trained in the law, and making laws rather than policies was probably their main skill and at the same time their weakness.[13]

---

[13] We should not forget that the Restoration legislatures created most of the modern legal system of Spain—starting with the *Código Civil*—and that important laws enacted then are still on the books.

Table 11.9. Education of *diputados* elected in 1907, 1910, and 1914 by party (%)

Education	Conservatives	Liberals	Right	Regionalists	Left
Commerce	*	2	—	—	4
Teacher training	—	1	—	—	2
Other middle school	1	—	—	—	—
Higher technical	4	5	—	12	2
Other university incomplete	*	—	—	—	2
Law	52	57	59	52	60
Other university education	6	12	14	20	14
Military	6	6	5	4	—
Other	2	4	—	—	4
No information	31	20	22	24	23
Total (n)	(357)	(258)	(22)	(25)	(57)

Note: *less than 1%.

Source: See Table 11.5.

Perhaps more revealing than the total number with higher education, or with university education, in each of the dynastic parties, is the larger proportion among the Liberals of those who studied subjects other than law. This is also characteristic of the Left and even more of the Regionalists. Higher technical education is not found too often among the legislators, but consonant with the bourgeois industrial character of the party, it is more frequent among the Regionalists. The number of those with only a secondary or middle-level education is minimal in all tendencies, but, not surprisingly, it is higher among the Left where we find some deputies with business school and teacher's college training.

The high level of education, the importance of the men with a legal training, and the absence of men admitting publicly a lack of education, contrasts with the large number of illiterates (40% of eligible voters according to the 1915 electoral census) that had the right to elect these men. If we turn to the data on the dynastic parties in the three elections, we find the basic patterns persist, as we might expect, given the continuity of the membership of the House and the absence of decisive changes in the nature of the parties. However, one minor finding demands our attention: both in 1907 and in 1910, the party most highly underrepresented (Liberals in 1907 and Conservatives in 1910) seems to have more men with a legal background on its benches. This might be another indication of the pre-eminent position of lawyers in the leadership of the parties, since the likelihood of election of the powerful men in a party must have been higher than that of junior men.

No other quality is more likely to shape a man's personality and mentality than his occupation. We encounter difficulties in knowing the extent to which the occupation reported (Table 11.10) is really a former activity, with politics having become a full-time occupation. The men we are studying, unless permanently in the highest offices of the government (and even then!) were busy in their own professions, or at least minding their interests. There were a number of leading politicians with successful law practices during this period. Occupation therefore for these men is not a past experience as it would be for many labour leaders in parliament, nor is it part of their 'public image' as it would become in our age of mass media

Table 11.10. Occupation of the *diputados* elected in 1907, 1910, and 1914 by party tendencies (%)

Occupation	Conservatives	Liberals	Right	Regionalists	Left
Lawyers (practising)	16	20	—	20	19
Lawyers (no information on practice)	26	28	36	20	30
Lawyers and owners	2	2	5	—	2
Notaries, property registrars	1	2	5	4	—
Law school professors	2	2	5	—	5
Judges	1	1	5	—	2
Physicians	1	3	—	—	—
Pharmacists	1	2	—	—	—
Veterinarians	*	—	—	—	2
Degree in natural science (probably middle-level teaching)	*	1	—	4	—
Degree in humanities (probably middle-level teaching)	*	*	—	—	2
Secondary school professors	1	2	—	—	—
University professors (other than law) or at technical schools	3	4	5	—	11
Architects or engineers	5	3	—	12	—
Journalists	6	16	14	28	21
Writers	8	16	5	12	21
Artists	*	—	—	—	—
Diplomats	1	*	—	—	—
High civil servants	7	11	—	—	5
Middle level civil servants	—	*	5	—	—
Army officers	4	4	—	4	—
Navy officers	1	1	—	—	—
Military justice	1	—	—	—	—
Financiers, bankers	4	5	5	4	2
Important manufacturers	4	3	5	12	4
Managers	1	1	—	—	—
Merchants, wholesalers	1	1	—	8	4
Shipowners	*	—	—	4	—
Farmers large	18	12	18	12	4
Manual labourers	—	—	—	—	4
Total (n)	(357)	(258)	(22)	(25)	(57)

Note: * less than 1%.

Source: See Table 11.5.

and electorates conscious of group interests and images. Only the claim to be a writer or a journalist by many of these men could not always stand the test of 'professionalism', even when without doubt many of them devoted considerable time to these activities successfully and—this is significant—prided themselves on doing so. The one-sidedness of the occupational background and the consequent limitation of experience and horizon is not a problem discovered by the contemporary social scientist. Even at the time when these men were in office, one of their colleagues, Santiago Alba, member of many cabinets and later Liberal Party leader, had raised the issue. In a remarkable little book, he compared the composition of Spanish parliaments with that of the French and noted the absence of many productive activities and the dominance of lawyers and persons deriving their income from the state in one way or another (Alba 1916).

The data for all deputies of the period 1907–16 grouped by political tendencies show the dominance of lawyers in all of them. The Left—in which we included the Reformists, Radicals, Republicans of other shades, Catalan Republicans, and even the few Socialists elected on the *Conjunción Republicano Socialista* ticket—has as many as the dynastic parties. The practising lawyers seem to be more numerous among the Liberals, while those entitled to do so but apparently not doing so among the Conservatives are slightly more numerous. If we add to the lawyers notaries, property registrars, professors of law schools, judges, and military justice officers, the proportion of those in the legal professions is certainly close to or over 50% in all tendencies, with the exception of the Catalan Regionalists. To these we have to add a number of higher and middle-level civil servants and the few diplomats.

In contrast, other liberal professions are poorly represented. The health professions, so important in the French Chambers dominated by the Radicals, are not prominent in the Cortes. However, there are a few more physicians and pharmacists in the Liberal ranks than in those of the Conservatives. The engineers—an occupation of considerable social prestige in Spain—were already almost as numerous, apparently more so on the Conservative benches. In addition to law school professors, institutions of higher learning were represented, much more so than those of the secondary level who would enter in considerable numbers in the elite of the Second Republic, but already disproportionately represented on the benches of the Left (11% of its deputies). They are outstanding in their absence from the Regionalist parliamentary group. After law, journalism and writing are heavily represented, to a large extent as a second occupation or an avocation. Significantly, the number of both is greater among the Liberals than the Conservatives and, in turn, among the Left parties than the Liberals. It is more surprising that among the Regionalists this activity is also reported with considerable frequency. This may help to account for the ideological character the regional issue was about to take and for the importance of the language question. Army and navy officers constitute another important contingent of the House, but perhaps less than we would expect, given the role of the army in politics. There is no visible difference in the number of officers sitting for either of the dynastic parties, a fact congruent with the position of the parties on military issues and the history of liberalism of the army in the nineteenth century and its slow turn towards a more conservative position in this century.

Business, either large or small, is not heavily represented as compared with the professions and the civil service and even with academic intellectuals. Its representation in the two major parties is quite comparable, and as expected, smaller on the Left except for a few more merchants. Only one party stands out as representative of the business bourgeoisie: the Catalan Regionalists. Financiers, manufacturers, merchants and wholesalers, and shipowners are all found more often in its ranks than in any of the dynastic parties. They constitute one-quarter of its parliamentary elite. Obviously, business interests were not without representation in parliament: the outstanding lawyers, who were often among the most powerful political figures, were also frequently the legal advisers of important companies like the railways and utilities, and sat on the boards of the growing business corporations. Yet the Spanish bourgeoisie was not personally—with some outstanding exceptions—represented in the Cortes; and only the Catalans found in the *Lliga* a party ready to defend its interests.

In a predominantly agrarian country, we would have expected a significant number of large landowners and even farmers, but even adding lawyers who do not appear to practise and who are reported as important *propietarios*, their representation is not proportional to their weight in the economy and society. Many of the professionals, particularly the lawyers, who were often local notables, were also large landowners and to them we have to add the influence through the Senate of some of the great aristocratic landowning families with seats in the House of Lords because they were Grandees of the kingdom. Rural representation is naturally weakest on the Left, but, surprisingly, not so weak among the Regionalists. Undoubtedly, the agricultural capitalism of the *Instituto Agrícola de San Isidro* was one of the pillars of conservative Catalanism.

The comparison between Conservatives and Liberals shows that in each of the three legislatures the agrarian representation was significantly larger among the Conservatives. The rural background of the Conservatives is a constant phenomenon, increasing somewhat over time. However, it needs to be stressed that the conflict between the two great parties was not one between city and countryside, that both had strong ties with agrarian interests, and that, at most, they were differentiated somewhat along regional lines. Certainly, the Spanish Conservatives cannot be equated with the Prussian Conservatives or the *Reichspartei*, nor the Liberals with the National-Liberals, as a comparison of the rural represen- tation in those parties would prove. The British Conservatives and Liber- als were also more differentiated along rural–urban lines of cleavage at this time.

Let us not forget that we are studying the political elite of a constitutional—some would say a semi-constitutional—monarchy. This, together with the economic power of the large landowners, among whom the nobility still occupied an important place, in a basically agricultural country, makes further study of the role of the aristocracy inevitable. We think that our data, particularly when put in comparative perspective, will run counter to the image of a traditional agrarian-feudal society, though this does not imply that it was a modern industrial-bourgeois society in the normal sense of these terms. The data raise important and interesting prob- lems that deserve research, particularly in view of the latent hostility to aris- tocratic values found in recent studies of social prestige both of the population and of local elites, and the strong feeling against the aristocracy under the Republic.

The weight of the titled nobility in the lower house, even when constant over the years following the Restoration, was relatively modest. The Senate naturally and by law had an important aristocratic contingent. These data on the parliament acquire more significance if we turn to those for the *gobernadores civiles* of the provinces—the prefects of the Napoleonic system—where the aristocratic contingent is smaller. Given their power, their influence on elections, and so on, this fact deserves considerable atten- tion. At the level of local office, where prestige is a more important vari- able and social functions are part of the activity, as with the mayors of provincial capitals, only a minority are title holders. The weak representa- tion of the nobility in the army is even more striking and contrasts blatantly with Prussia (Preradovich 1955).[14]

But let us turn to our data on the legislators. Not only is the aristocratic representation in the lower chamber numerically reduced, but most of it is constituted by men ennobled in the nineteenth century in the course of the civil wars, thanks to political achievement in a semi-democratic context or to exploits in business (especially under Amadeus of Savoy and after the Restoration) (Table 11.11). Already at the beginning of the period, the titles dating from the Middle Ages and the Habsburg dynasty constitute only one-third and their share decreases throughout the period. The old nobil- ity in the reign of Alphonse XII and the first years of the Regency is still one-half of the aristocrats in the House, but close to the end of the period

---

[14] If we were to give the date of ennoblement of these officers, the loss of a continued aristocratic tradition in the army in the nineteenth century would become even more apparent.

Table 11.11. Nobility titles among the *diputados* elected in 1907, 1910, and 1914 by party tendencies (%)

Titles	Conservatives	Liberals	Right	Regionalists	Left
Duke	1	1	—	—	—
Marquis with *grandeza*	2	1	—	—	—
Marquis without *grandeza*	7	3	5	4	—
Count with *grandeza*	2	1	—	—	—
Count without *grandeza*	4	2	9	—	—
Viscount without *grandeza*	1	*	—	—	—
Total nobility titles	17	8	14	4	—
Total (n)	(357)	(258)	(22)	(25)	(57)

Note: * less than 1%.

Source: See Table 11.5.

only one-third.[15] If we turn to the titles of deputies elected by different political tendencies, we consistently find no aristocrats on the Left. The 17% of titled deputies among Conservatives contrasts with the 8% among the Liberals. The rank of the Conservative title holders is higher than that of their Liberal counterparts. The Right, made up of the supporters of the dynasty defeated in the Carlist wars by the liberal monarchy, has few aristocrats in its ranks.[16] This absence may be because of the opposition of the Right to the ruling house. Among the Regionalists, we find one title holder, and he received his title after 1885.

The more aristocratic character of the Conservative Party is confirmed by the data by party for each of the three elections. The information of the date of concession of the titles of the nobles sitting on the benches of each party confirms our impressions even further. In each of the Cortes, more than half of the Liberal deputies had received their titles from kings in the nineteenth century, specifically from the Regency and the Alphonses. They were ennobled bourgeois. Among the Conservatives, we find over one-third in that situation, but in each Cortes the holders of titles conferred before 1700 were much more numerous among them than among the Liberals.

2.4. How Representative were the Representatives?

In view of the distortion of the electoral process by the practices of *caciquismo*—real but also exaggerated in the critical literature of the time— one can ask the question: how representative were those elected between

---

[15] In the reigns of Isabel II and Amadeus of Savoy, many nobility titles were granted to officers, politicians, bankers, and industrialists. The Regency and Alfonse XIII created 214 marquis, 167 counts, 30 viscounts, and 28 barons, a total of 439 new titles of nobility.

[16] A marquis and a count without *grandeza* but granted before the Bourbons.

1869 and 1923, or whom did they represent? First of all, it should be noted that the degree to which that different elections were corrupted varied considerably. In particular, elections in the larger urban districts and probably in some rural areas were truly competitive. Strong and well-organized ideological minority parties were able to gain representation: from early on, this was the case for the Carlists, Traditionalists, Integrists—the anti-system Right—in the Basque Country and Navarre. Only full proportional representation (PR) could have given them a larger representation. The different Republican factions were also able to gain representation in urban areas and some areas in the countryside. Again, only PR could have given them a stronger representation. Proof of their limits is that the coming of the Republic did not lead in many parts of Spain to the victory of 'historical republicanism' but of new parties constituted in 1930 under a new leadership. The regional-nationalists in the twentieth century, particularly due to their organisational skills, could gain representation. *Caciquismo* probably did not affect decisively their capacity to gain representation. The question becomes more complicated in the case of the PSOE. Was its meagre success—by comparison with Italy—due mainly to the *caciquista* pressures? Certainly its weakness in the areas dominated by the agricultural proletariat, which would give them so many votes in the 1930s, would argue for this, but the remaining strength of republicanism, the growing appeal of anarcho-syndicalism, and the data we have on membership of the party and the UGT would not lead us to expect great electoral successes. Even in the cities, in local elections, the Socialists failed to gain considerable strength and the greatest success in 1918 was made possible only in the *Conjunción Republicana* coalition.

If the representation of minorities—anti-system parties of the extreme right, Republicans, Regionalists, nationalists, and Socialists—could not have been much larger even with a more honest electoral practice, given their social bases, organizational strength, and, in many cases, ideological appeal, plus the split of the working class into two movements, the question becomes: how far did the dynastic parties, and their increasingly differentiated factions after 1910, represent their voters? The answer depends largely on what we mean by representation. Certainly not a mirror of the social composition of the electorate. Largely not of the interests of the people in deep reforms of the economy, the agricultural property structure, class relations, large expansion of social services, reform of the armed forces, that academic observers and even some of the politicians perceived as necessary. It is more doubtful whether the radical anticlericalism of the Republicans in 1931 was representative of many of those voters. Whose interests did those elected then represent? Obviously their own in their careers and power. But not only that: protectionism and free trade divided them, particular industries like shipbuilding, above all, the railway expansion, specific

agricultural interests, and last but not least those of their voters in the building of a road, the location of a school, army barracks, telegraph service,
harbour improvement, and so on. The classic benefits of pork-barrel politics. No one would deny that this was in their interest, obviously more so
of the owners, that it changed provincial life, and distributed territorially
the meagre resources of the budget. Without the limited, distorted democracy, the coverage of the country with those 'benefits' would probably not
have taken place and the modernization of the country would have been
slower and more uneven. To gain votes, the *caciques* of the dynastic parties
had to do something in addition to discouraging opponents and stuffing
ballot boxes. At the same time, those representatives at the centre represented alternative responses to broader issues, more than they are credited
as doing by their critics.

2.5. Continuity and Renewal in the Parliamentary Elite

The problem of continuity and renewal in the parliamentary elite is of
central interest in any study of elections and parties, and it affects the style
of a parliament and the political elite. Parliaments, in order to work, require
a certain continuity of membership, and some have provided for this by the
mechanism of partial renewal. However, oligarchic tendencies preventing
the entry of new men would be a serious obstacle to social change, and ultimately endanger the survival of parties following such a policy.

We can present some data on the three legislatures studied. In each of
them, new entrants make up approximately 30%, with a slightly higher rate
(37%) in 1910, a fact that makes sense considering the crisis and change
associated with that year, the new role of the Liberal Party, and the entry
of the first Socialist into parliament. Some of the members in each legislature trace their election back through a large number of Cortes, and some
cohorts are more heavily represented than others, indicating moments in
which the political elite must have been renewed. So, in 1907, we find more
deputies initially elected in 1903 and 1891 than in some of the intermediate years. In the 1914 legislature, we find a similar bump in the distribution
for initial entrants from 1899, the date when Silvela took over the leadership of the Conservative Party and made his bid for national regeneration
and broke with the Cánovas system. In the Liberal-dominated 1910 legislature, we find fewer such overrepresented cohorts but a somewhat larger
number of recent entrants.

The change of the electoral system in 1907 and the relative cutting point
that 1910 represents have led us to study more intensively the deputies
elected between that date and the dismissal of the parliamentary system by
Primo de Rivera in 1923, that is, over seven legislative periods. Taking the
total number of seats up for election (with some margin of error given the

void elections, by-elections, and so on), we calculated how many of the incumbents had been elected only once or more times up to seven, both in the country and each of the great historical regions (except Canarias, where a reapportionment made calculations difficult) (Table 11.12). The total number of seats to be filled was 2,765, while the number of persons elected over the period was 1,338, counting a few persons twice if they were re-elected but not by the same district. This means that a number of men had to be elected more than once. In fact, 49 were elected all seven times, among them equal numbers of Conservatives and Liberals; another 42, six times; 52, five; 77, four; 115, three; 234, two; and 870, only once. The 870 elected only once by their district seems a high figure (65% of all those elected), suggesting considerable turnover in the political personnel in this period. Obviously, some might have retired from political life after years in office in previous periods and others were newcomers in 1923 who had no chance to continue being re-elected after the *coup d'état* frustrated their incipient political careers. If we were to distinguish continuous and discontinuous sittings, we might find more analogy with the United Kingdom with members leaving the Chamber after one election but returning to the next one. Our data show this for the Conservatives between1907 and 1914—two Conservative years.

If we consider the Primo de Rivera dictatorship and the Republic we find that of the 741 men sitting in the semicircle from 1907 till 1916, only 15 (2%) return to the *Asamblea Nacional* created by Primo de Rivera. Few of them would return elected after the change of regime in 1931 (Table 11.13). The political discontinuity could not be greater. Spain might not have experienced a change in the social and economic ruling class, but certainly she suffered a gigantic discontinuity in her political class. In fact, we suspect that it was not only a discontinuity in the political but in the ruling class—or sectors of it—in general. If that hypothesis were proven, we would have to look for the sources of rigidity in the institutions of the society rather than in the men, or even families, holding power. While there are societies, like the British, with much continuity in the ruling elite but considerable social and political change, Spain might be the case of considerable discontinuity in the elites but considerable resistances to change coming from elsewhere. Here we can only retain these data on instability and discontinuity in the political class, as we noted before the lack of a continuous role of the old aristocracy in key elites.

The *golpe* in September 1923 by General Primo de Rivera and the establishment of the dictatorship suspended the legislature elected in 1923. The dictator created an *Asamblea Nacional Consultiva* in 1927 with appointed, ex-officio and indirectly elected members (Ben-Ami 1983; Linz 1987). The number of persons occupying seats was changing. Of a total of 359 seats and 429 persons, 56 (15.6% and 13.0%) were ex-deputies or elective

Table 11.12. Deputies elected more than once in the same district, by region 1910–1923 (%)

Region:	Number of times elected							Total number of seats in the seven elections	Proportion of seats included in the analysis
	Seven	Six	Five	Four	Three	Two	Once		
Catalonia	2	1	1	2.9	4.4	11.3	30.5	301	97
Basque country	1	—	2	2	5	14.1	28.5	98	98.2
Levante	1.3	0.9	1.8	2.7	4.5	4.9	40.5	220	96
Murcia	2.6	2.6	1.3	5.2	2.6	5.2	18.2	77	97.4
Albacete	—	2.9	—	—	2.9	14.3	42.9	35	97.1
New Castile	1.1	1.7	1.1	1.7	4	12.6	26.8	175	91.4
Eastern Andalusia	1.1	1.5	3.9	0.8	2.7	8.9	31.5	258	97.3
Western Andalusia	1.4	0.7	2.2	4.0	4.8	7.8	2.8	273	97.8
Extremadura	—	3.4	2.5	1.7	5.9	4.2	29.4	119	94.9
Old Castile and León	2.6	1.3	0.9	3.2	2.8	10.1	26.9	532	99.4
Aragón	1.3	1.9	2.5	1.3	3.7	7.5	39.1	161	97.5
Navarra	—	2.1	—	4.1	8.1	8.1	18.4	49	87.7
Austrias	3.1	2.1	3.1	1	3.1	5.1	28.5	98	97
Galicia	1.9	1.9	2.2	3.5	5.7	3.5	19.6	315	93.7
Baleares	6.1	—	—	4.1	4.1	6.1	10.2	49	93.8
Canaries	—	—	—	—	—	—	—	—	—
Total	1.7	1.5	1.9	2.8	4.2	8.4	31.5	2,765	98.8

Source: Calculations of the author (see footnote 17).

Table 11.13. Deputies of the Republic having been elected in the nineteenth legislature 1920–1923

Party affiliation in the Republican legislature	Republican legislature		
	1931	1933	1936
PSOE	3	3	2
Izquierda Republicana	—	2	2
Esquerra	2	—	1
Reformists	—	2	2
Radicals	3	4	1
Progressives	—	—	—
Centre	2	1	1
Agrarians	—	3	3
Lliga	1	3	2
CEDA	—	2	2
Traditionalists	—	1	—
Independents	—	1	1
Independent monarchists	1	1	1
Unidentified	16	11	2
Total	28	34	20

Source: Calculations of the author (see footnote 17).

ex-senators (in the period 1916 to 1923). Of those 56, four came from the extreme right, 10 were Mauristas and 23 others Conservatives, 10 were Liberals, four were from other groups, and two were without party identification.

There was some continuity between the political elite of the 1916–23 period and that of the Republic. Although in 1931 only 64 (13.8%) had occupied a seat in the 468-member Cortes, in 1933, there were 70 (14.9%), and 59 (12.4%) in 1936. This represents a total of 116 of the 992 elected (11.7%) occupying 193 of the 1,384 seats (13.8%). Some were deputies of the parties which were in opposition to the monarchy, a few were also political leaders of the monarchy who had come to favour of the Republic, most prominently Niceto Alcalá Zamora, a Liberal Party faction leader and cabinet member, who became head of the provisional government and first President of the Republic. Given the small representation of the Republican and Socialists in the legislatures of the monarchy, we find few of them in the ranks of the parties of the majority in 1931: nine Socialists, 16 Republicans (10 of them Radicals), and 16 Catalan nationalists. The Reformists contribute six, mostly to the center-right republicanism. The dynastic parties contributed 50 members to the Republican legislatures, 33 coming from the Liberals, 16 from the Conservatives, and 10 from the Mauristas. Contrary to what is said by those who saw no real differences between parties before 1923, they aligned quite differently: four Mauristas with the extreme right, compared with only one of the Conservatives; none of the Liberals would join the CEDA compared to seven of the 16 Conservatives. A non-clerical, non-authoritarian, socially conservative party like the Agrarians would attract 16 former legislators. Of the 13 Agrarian deputies in the Republic, six had been Liberals, five Conservatives, and two Mauristas.

3. THE REPUBLIC 1931–36[17]

3.1. *The Republic and its Political Problems*

On 14 April 1931 the Republic was proclaimed and power assumed by a provisional government of bourgeois republican leaders and, for the first time in Spanish history, three Socialist ministers. The new regime faced many difficult problems: to create new institutions, secularize the state, reduce the power of the army, carry out basic social reforms, most specifi-

[17] We have based our analysis on the deputies listed in Cortes (1932, 1935, 1936). These are handy small booklets published officially, listing deputies in alphabetical order, giving district represented and address, as well as information on parliamentary office and committee membership. The 1936 issue also gives information about party groups in parliament and number of deputies in each (with some errors). These lists do not include names that other sources report as elected. We decided to ignore those not included. The party identification in 1933 has been taken from *Boletín de Información Bibliográfica y Parlamentaria de España y del Extranjero*, 1/6 Nov.–Dec. 1933: 1054–71. The publication includes the occupation officially declared by MPs in 1936 and decisions on incompatibilities. To complete the information on occupation we consulted the newspaper ABC for 20 Dec. 1933. Our analysis is based on the data of the *Lista*. For 1933, the *Lista* includes 451 names; the *Boletín de Información* lists an additional 10, who, for a variety of reasons, did not occupy their seats. Therefore, our count differs: instead of 101 Radicals we have 97, of 115 CEDA we have 114, of 31 Agrarios 30, of 12 PNV 10, of 27 other parties 25. Besides, there were eight vacant seats in Dec. 1933. Therefore, we deal with 451 deputies rather than 469 in 1933. In 1936, of 473 seats, the official list mentions 3 vacant seats. In the case of *Izquierda Republicana* (IR), we have not counted Azaña who had become President of the Republic before June 1936.

An example of the difficulty in establishing the lists of members by party is the PSOE delegation in 1936. The June 1936 listing published by the Chamber includes the name and address of Eduardo Castillo Blasco, deputy for Zaragoza, whose name does not appear in the listing of the members of the PSOE group. This list includes Eduardo Castellano Blanco and Amando Viance Pampin, who do not appear in the first list with names, addresses and districts represented. No other sources include these two names and therefore we have not counted them in our analysis. In the same publication, a figure of 99 PSOE deputies is given, but counting the names in the list, there are 100. Ignoring the 2 just mentioned, there would be 98, to whom we have to add Castillo Blasco, resulting in a total of 99 (but different names).

No two sources agree on the party composition of the Cortes. Only the official list for June 1936 gives party identification. Even in that list there is an error since it counts 39 members of UR but actually lists only 38 names. It lists 87 IR members although 88 were elected since Manuel Azaña became President of the Republic. We have used the Mar. 1935 official list for the legislature elected in 1933 and the party identification at the time of election in the *Boletin Informativo* of Dec. 1933. This explains why the data on occupation in Table 18 refer to fewer members since two did not occupy a seat in 1935, for example, Luis Companys of *Esquerra*, who had become the head of the Catalan regional government. The Radicals elected 101 or 102 deputies (depending on the sources) but our analysis is based on 97 in 1935. One CEDA deputy elected in 1933 does not appear in the 1935 list.

cally an agrarian reform, solve the problem of the relation between the central government and the regions with autonomistic aspirations. It had to face these issues just when the years of prosperity that coincided with the Primo de Rivera dictatorship had come to an end, in the context of a Europe in which rising Fascist movements were questioning parliamentary democracy (Payne 1993; Linz 1967, 1978; Varela 1978).

The men who created the new regime were probably more interested in political and cultural problems than in strictly economic ones and gave priority to questions of religious and military policy over those of economic development. Although more or less committed to agrarian reform, they tended to assume that it was largely a problem of aristocratic latifundia. In attempting to secularize the state and society and fighting the militaristic traditions, they probably went overboard and antagonized deeply the Church and the army, two key institutions. The immediate gains the new regime could offer the working classes of city, and even more, the countryside, could probably never—even under more favourable circumstances—have satisfied the raised expectations of a rapidly mobilized working class. Besides, a large part of that working class gave its allegiance to the CNT—a trade union federation ideologically oriented towards anarchosyndicalism—rather than parliamentary democracy. So it is not surprising that the regime found many difficulties during its brief existence.

The provisional government enacted a new electoral law by a decree of 8 May 1931. The single-member districts of the monarchy, which favoured *caciquismo* and the election of notables, were deliberately substituted by the 50 provinces as districts, to which the cities with over 100,000 inhabitants were added as separate districts as well as Ceuta and Melilla in North Africa. There was to be one deputy for 50,000 inhabitants. Article 29 of 1907 was abolished. The voting age was changed from 25 to 23 years, but women, while eligible, were not granted the vote. Each voter could cast his vote for a certain number of candidates on the list, a rule that favoured the majority. If there were candidates with less than 20% of the votes, there would be a second round. The reform of that law in 1933 established that if no candidate or list obtained 40% of the votes there would have to be a run-off.[18] This led some parties to instruct their voters to vote for a leading candidate of the opposition so that there would be no run-off and their party would be assured the minority seats.[19]

[18] The voters could cast a certain number of votes from two to 16 to elect between three and 20 members, fewer than the number of candidates to be elected, but not all made use of that opportunity since some voted for a smaller number. Blank and void votes are not always reported. The number of votes cast therefore does not correspond to the number of voters, after dividing them by the number that voters could cast in each district. The voters were also free to vote for candidates of different lists, sometimes those of a party on a coalition list and some not included in the list.

[19] In a few cases, parties sure of a large plurality would play the game of going '*al copo*'—

The overall result of the law was a very majoritarian electoral system that forced parties to make broad coalitions before the election, including extremists who presumably had few votes, but who could make a great difference in obtaining a majority.[20]

The party system of the Republic was highly fragmented, particularly in the Constituent Assembly since many small Republican factions, based on regional, personality, and ideological differences, had sprung up in the short period of freedom after the fall of the dictatorship and the monarchy (Tusell 1982) (Table 11.14). Some time had to pass until the Right could create a new mass party, the CEDA—we would perhaps call them conservative democrats Christian[21]—besides the presence of the regional bourgeois Right, particularly the *Lliga*. The Radicals, who could have been a large and powerful centre party given their tradition and electoral strength, had to face the competition and the pull towards the bourgeois anticlerical Left, particularly when they had to govern with the support of the CEDA after the 1933 election. The bourgeois left of centre in turn, when faced with socio-economic issues, like agrarian reform and collaboration with the Socialists, also splintered (Table 11.15). In the years 1931 to 1936, the extremist movements—Anarcho-syndicalists (not a party but an ideological and trade union mass movement), Communists, Fascists, Monarchist-authoritarians, Traditionalists—did not participate in government. Only after the polarization that crystallized in the Civil War had destroyed the regime, did extremists enter the governments of each of the two Spains in combat.

Two of the large mass parties of the 1930s, the Socialists (PSOE) and the CEDA, were not represented in government in proportion to their representation in the Chamber, nor in the electorate, and even less so in terms of the organized institutional strength behind them: the trade unions of the UGT and the Catholic Church. They were, particularly the Socialists after 1933, divided between those wanting to operate within the legality of the system, pressing for its reform to suit their ideology, and those maximalists

that is, obtaining the seats of the majority and those of the minority by running two sets of candidates or distributing the votes in their list.

[20] The lack of agreement between the PSOE and the Left Republicans in 1933 led to the victory of the Centre Right and Right. In 1936, both sides, aware of the stakes, formed two major broad coalitions which contributed to the polarization. It meant the crushing defeat of centre parties not in coalitions and the oversized representation of the majority of the Popular Front in the legislature. At the same time as the system had majoritarian results, the pattern of heterogeneous coalitions of large numbers of different parties retaining their identity led to a highly fractionalized polarized multiparty system. The majoritarianism is reflected in the great swings in the party composition of the three legislatures of the Republic and the high rate of discontinuity, while the 'proportionality' in the composition of the coalition lists and the freedom of the voter to choose candidates led to party fractionalization. It would probably have been difficult to design a more perverse electoral system.

[21] But the old divisions persisted between *Carlists* and *Alfonsinos*—a dynastic, ideological split.

Table 11.14. Party affiliation of members of the Constituent Cortes (at the time of election) and vote for different parties in June 1931 (first election round)

Party affiliation	Seats		Vote %
	n	%	
PCE	—		0.8
BOC	—		0.1
Other extreme left	3	0.7	—
PSOE 1	116	24.9	21.2
Total Left	119	25.6	22.1
RDS	57	12.2	12.0
Federal	15	3.2	3.8
Federal Agrario	4	0.9	—
AR (Azaña)	18	3.9	3.5
AISR	6	1.3	1.3
Alianza Republicana	8	1.7	1.8
RD (Lerroux)	65	13.9	13.1
PURA	9	1.9	
Independent Republicans	15	3.2	4.2
Autonomous Republicans	8	1.7	2.1
DLR	24	5.1	8.8
Progresistas	2	0.4	—
LD	2	0.4	1.2
Other Republicans	8	1.7	2.0
Independents	4	0.9	—
Total bourgeois Left and Centre	245	52.6	53.9
Agrarios	15	3.3	2.8
AN	5	1.1	1.9
Right	6	1.3	—
Other Right 'Católicos'	3	0.6	0.9
Fueristas	—		
Católicos	3	0.6	
Independent monarchists	1	0.2	0.2
Others	—	—	1.6
Total Right	33	7.1	5.8
Extreme Right			
Unión Monárquica	1	0.2	—
Traditionalists	4	0.9	1.1
Total Extreme Right	5	1.1	1.1
Regionalists			
ERC	29	6.2	6.7
USC	1	0.2	0.4
PCR and Republican Catalanists			
PRDF, RAD	6	1.3	0.5
Lliga	3	0.6	1.7
PNV	6	1.3	1.5
ANV	—	—	0.2
FRG	14	3.0	2.2
Galleguistas	2	0.4	0.3
Regionalist	1	0.2	—
Total Regionalists	62	13.3	13.6
Vacant seats	2	0.4	
Others	—	—	1.3
Total Cortes	466	100	100

Source: Calculations of the author (see footnote 17).

Table 11.15. Seats held by the parties in the 1933 and 1936 legislatures of the Second Republic

Party	1933 Seats		1936 (June) Seats		Vote in first election round %
	N	%	N	%	
PCE	1	0.2	17	3.6	2.5
Other extreme left	—	—	2	0.4	0.3
PSOE	59	12.4	99	21.1	16.4
AR	5	1.1	87	18.5	13.7
ORGA	3	0.6	—	—	—
RSI	2	0.4	—	—	—
RS	1	0.2	—	—	—
UR	—	—	38	8.1	5.9
Fed.	1	0.2	—	—	—
Progresistas	3	0.6	6	1.3	0.9
Centre	—	—	16	3.4	5.1
Republican Conservatives	16	3.4	3	0.6	0.8
PLD	10	2.1	1	0.2	0.8
Radicals	102	21.5	4	0.8	3.6
Agrarians	32	6.7	11	2.3	2.6
CEDA	115	24.3	88	18.8	23.2
Independent Right	13	2.7	11	2.3	3.1
Renovacion Española	15	3.2	13	2.8	3.8
Traditionalists	21	4.4	9	1.9	3.4
PNE, FE	2	0.4	—	—	0.8
Esquerra	22	4.6	36	7.7	4.1
Lliga	26	5.5	12	2.6	2.8
PNV	12	2.5	10	2.1	1.4
No party identity	5	1.1	3	0.6	—
Vacant seats	8	1.7	3	0.6	—
Vote for parties without representation					5.6
Total	474	100	469	100	100

Source: The calculation of the vote was done with the help of J. Colomer on data provided by J. Tusell (see footnote 17).

who felt that the system did not deserve their loyalty and who were eager to collaborate with the disloyal opposition: the Socialists with the Communists and many of the CEDA with the Monarchists of Calvo Sotelo. The ambivalent position of the PSOE and the CEDA at one point or another, also led their partners to divide about the desirability of a coalition with them, and in the case of the CEDA, to a prolonged veto by the President of the Republic on their entry into the cabinet or any growth in their influence. This accounts for the fact that most cabinets were formed by the main Centre Left or Centre Right parties (*Izquierda Republicana* and Radicals), often by adding as partners small parties, or personalities with no party identification, or even by forming minority cabinets with nonparliamentarians. If we consider as major parties the PSOE, *Acción Repub-*

licana (on account of Azaña's leadership, rather than its parliamentary strength in 1931), *Izquierda Republicana* in 1936, the *Esquerra* (due to its regional dominant position), the Radical-Socialists (only on account of their seats in 1931), the Radicals, and the CEDA, they only provide 50 of the 88 cabinet members and fill only 160 incumbencies.

Despite the political fragmentation, the many small centre parties, and the regional parties, the dividing line between Right and Left was clearly drawn. Only four men served in Republican-Socialist governments of the first two years or in Left-bourgeois Popular Front-supported cabinets in the spring of 1936, *and* in Radical Party-dominated ones between 1933 and 1936.[22] None of the parties in the centre after 1933, or at the latest the autumn of 1934, had the *Allgemeinkoalitionsfähigkeit* (general ability to enter coalitions) of the French Radical Party in the Third and Fourth Republics or some Christian Democratic parties in postwar Europe. One reason must have been the electoral system that forced minor parties to enter one or other of the major electoral coalitions, except in a few districts; another reason, the ideological character of politics and the ambivalence towards the two great mass parties—PSOE and CEDA—perceived as semi-loyal oppositions by the other side and sometimes acting or at least talking as such (Linz 1978).

The change of regime after the dictatorial period, without a process of *Machtübergabe* (transfer of power) by the old elite, as a result of rupture rather than reform, led to an elite change which was incomparably greater than the one brought about by the Weimar Republic, where the leading parties represented considerable continuity with the last Imperial *Reichstag* (Linz 1972). At the same time, the ideological ambivalence in the Republican parties, the effects of the electoral law, and the extra-parliamentary pressures led to a fractionalization of the elite and considerable discontinuity. The Primo de Rivera dictatorship had pushed aside the political class of the Restoration monarchy and dismantled the *cacique* political network which linked it with local life; with a few exceptions, this could not be reconstructed after the installation of the Republicans in power. In considering the election of 1931, we should bear in mind that it was a 'transitional election' (Tusell 1982). There were 1,015 candidates put forward by 24 groups, but only 4 groups competed nation-wide.

3.2. The 1931 Constituent Cortes

The Cortes of 1931 represents a great change, not only on account of the discontinuity of the political class, but in terms of the social background of

[22] One of them, the old Mr Republican, the Radical party leader Lerroux; another, one of his followers, who split from him in a rightwards direction: Martínez Barrio; the third, a Radical who followed Martínez Barrio out of the party into *Unión Republicana*, and the fourth an army general serving on a professional basis.

its members (Table 11.16). For the first time, a significant contingent of manual workers enters the halls of the palace on the Carrera de San Jerónimo (9.3%). They are mostly PSOE deputies with leadership positions in the trade union movement: the UGT. Undoubtedly, their number is still small, particularly considering the high level of trade union and political mobilization of the working class. This is largely due to the split between UGT and CNT followers, between a Socialist working class willing to enter the parliamentary arena and an anarcho-syndicalist mass rejecting it. However, even in the PSOE, the workers constitute only one-third of the parliamentary group that, in this respect, is not dominated by the trade union leadership, compared to other labour parties. The number of workers in the parliamentary representation of other parties is very small, with the Radicals claiming more than some of the more leftist bourgeois parties. The *Esquerra*, despite benefiting from working-class votes in Catalonia, counts few workers among its members. The Catalan workers were deprived of direct representation in the legislature.[23]

Another basic shift is the increased presence of the lower middle class: white collar-employees, middle-level professionals and civil servants, small businessmen. They constitute an important part of the parliamentary representation of the Left bourgeois parties but even more of the Radicals, among whom the more intellectual middle class, particularly the university professors, have a much weaker representation. While the academics have always constituted an important element in the Spanish political elite, their presence and weight in the first legislature of the regime stands out. However, it would be dangerous to accept the stereotype of a professors' Republic, fostered by the anti-intellectual Right and the foreign sympathizers of the new regime, ignoring the strong petty bourgeois and professional component of the founding group.

One continuity with the past is the weak representation of the business community, particularly big business. The defeat of the *Lliga* by the *Esquerra* is one contributing factor, even when some of the few businessmen sit on the benches of the Left-Catalan party. Surprisingly, the Right of the Constituent Assembly—Agrarians and *Minoría Vasco-Navarra* (MVN)—count few men identifying themselves as businessmen, even when a number of them had close ties as professionals and probably as owners to business. Significantly, the only party in whose ranks we find men identified just as businessmen is the Radicals, a fact that makes the rapid shift towards the Right of this traditional republican party more understandable. The absence of men identifying themselves as landowners or farmers from Spanish politics, despite the agrarian character of the economy, becomes even more salient in 1931.

[23] Curiously enough, the rightist *Minoría Vasco-Navarra* (MVN) claims to have one worker, a PNV member.

Table 11.16. Occupation of deputies in the Republican Cortes elected in 1931, by political parties* and all deputies (%)

	PSOE	AR	Esquerra	RS	Radicals	RC (M)	ASR	Agrarians	MVN	Total
Farmers	0.9	3.2	2.9	—	1.1	—	—	—	6.7	1.7
Workers	32.5	3.2	2.9	3.6	7.7	—	—	4.2	6.7	9.4
White-collar employees	4.4	—	5.9	3.6	1.1	—	7.7	—	—	2.8
Merchants and small business	2.7	6.5	2.9	1.8	13.5	7.1	—	—	—	4.3
Larger business and managers (also public entreprise and finance)	—	—	2.9	—	—	—	—	—	—	1.0
Middle-level professions	14.9	9.7	17.6	14.5	2.2	—	—	—	6.7	12.0
Lawyers	7.9	—	38.2	40.0	47.2	71.4	30.8	45.8	46.7	34.9
Teaching except elementary	7.9	3.2	5.9	1.8	6.7	—	—	—	—	4.3
Medicine	12.3	9.7	14.7	10.9	6.7	7.1	15.4	—	—	10.3
Other free professions	1.8	9.7	—	5.5	2.2	—	—	—	—	2.3
Engineering and architecture	3.6	3.2	5.9	3.6	5.6	7.1	15.4	12.5	26.7	5.4
Military	3.5	3.2	5.9	—	2.2	14.2	—	4.2	—	3.0
University professors	12.3	29.0	—	10.9	10.1	7.1	30.8	20.8	—	13.6
Civil servants (university degree)	—	—	—	1.8	3.4	—	7.7	4.2	—	1.8
Clergy	—	—	—	1.8	1.1	—	—	16.7	6.7	1.7
Other	—	—	—	1.8	—	—	—	—	—	0.2
No information	—	—	—	—	—	—	—	—	—	0.2
Total (n)	(114)	(31)	(34)	(55)	(89)	(14)	(13)	(24)	(15)	(464)

Note: * The information is given only for the most important parties.

The proportion of lawyers is reduced in comparison to the legislatures of the first two decades of the century, but over one-third are still identified as attorneys, ignoring those who are also law school professors or civil servants who might well have also practised law. Turning to the representation of lawyers in the parliamentary groups, only the PSOE stands out with less than one in ten (7.9%), followed by its closest ally in the first *bienio*, the followers of Azaña in *Acción Republicana* (AR) (with 29.0%) and the *Agrupación al Servicio de la República* (ASR), a short-lived grouping of intellectuals that, in some ways, resembles the Italian *Partito d'Azione* of the post World War II period. The *Esquerra* and the Radical Socialists (RS) which, on the political spectrum also occupy an intermediary position, are also in between the new intellectual bourgeois Left and a politicians' party, like the Radicals and the parties of the Right. Should we place parties on a Left–Right continuum by the proportion of lawyers in their fraction in parliament, in 1931 the Radicals would already be on the Right rather than on the side of the Left-bourgeois-socialist coalition they initially supported. There is only one important exception to such a correlation between a Left–Right continuum and the proportion of lawyers: the Conservative Republicans, the party of the politicians of the monarchy alienated from the King and his co-operation with the dictatorship, of the Catholics rallying to the Republic, among whom lawyers constitute the overwhelming majority. It is not by chance that this party attempted, together with the Liberal Democrats, to be the bridge between the past and the new regime.

Physicians, as well as other free professionals and secondary-level teachers, occupy an opposite position to lawyers on the political spectrum. They constitute an important contingent of the PSOE—in its ranks alone do we find more doctors than lawyers—but also in the Left-bourgeois parties one in ten or more of the deputies are MDs. A number of factors account for this orientation of the medical profession: a nineteenth-century tradition of anticlericalism, a greater contact with social problems, and perhaps the relatively low income, social prestige, and social origin of a large number of doctors in Spain. However, the presence of some outstanding medical personalities among the deputies, the fact that they constitute one of the largest contingents in the ASR—in comparison to all other parties—suggest the importance of the professional climate of opinion as a major factor. In this respect, once more the Radicals already appear as different from the bourgeois-Left Republicans.

Engineering and architecture, occupations that had acquired high social prestige in Spain, and for which the policy of *numerus clausus* in the technical schools assured that their higher social origin and professional activities brought them into contact with the business community, were found on the Right, among the Agrarians and particularly the MVN. However, they also constitute an important minority among the 'elitist' party of the bourgeois Left: the ASR. Academics—university professors—are found in almost all parties, except the extreme Right, and constitute an important contingent of the PSOE, but it is no accident that almost one-third of the ASR should be made up of by professors, with AR—the party led by the intellectual Manuel Azaña—following close behind (Espín 1980).

If we take the social composition of the parliamentary group, we can speak of only one class party: the PSOE, representing the workers, while in no party is a single occupational group overwhelmingly represented. The Agrarians do not appear—in terms of social composition—as an agrarian party in the European sense, showing clearly that name was a matter of convenience for a sector of the Right. Only two parties, in terms of heterogeneity of occupational backgrounds of their deputies, appear as *Volksparteien*, parties of democratic integration to use Sigmund Neumann's terminology: the *Esquerra* and, to a lesser extent, the Radicals, even when, among the latter, the large number of lawyers points towards a party led by professional politicians: notables or men of a machine. The *Esquerra*'s dominant position in Catalonia as a regional movement appealing to all classes, except the upper bourgeoisie, fits well with this social composition of its parliamentary representation (Iverni Salvà 1988).

Looking at a table of the regions represented by different parties, we discover a considerable degree of 'localization' even of the non-regional parties, with the exception of the PSOE, the Radicals, and Radical Socialists (Table 11.17). The *Minoría Vasco-Navarra* represents the Basque-Navarrese region, even when it also acted as the representive of clerical interests; the *Esquerra* is a strictly Catalan party, but not much less regionally localized are the Agrarians with 91.7% of their deputies representing either of the two Castiles or León and over half Old Castile. The contrast between the areas of strength of the two Left-bourgeois parties *Acción Republicana* and the stronger, but more poorly led, Radical Socialists, is revealing: the more Castilian base of the former, the broader national base of the second, which is far from pointing towards the different success of both in the future. The parallelism, but also the differences in areas of strength of Radical Socialists and Radicals following Lerroux, is interesting. The Radical Socialists tend to be weaker in the periphery: Galicia, Levante, Canary Islands, Balearics, even Aragón, but above all in Andalusia, most of them areas of traditional republicanism, while the new and successful dissidents seem to be stronger in the Castilian heartland, León, Extremadura, regions where the non-bourgeois middle classes dominate. The style of the two parties, pragmatic if not opportunistic in the case of the Radicals, principled and ideological and prone to factionalism in that of the Radical Socialists, as well as the differences in social composition of their parliamentary representation, are not unrelated to their different

Table 11.17. Occupation of the 71 *diputados* elected in the three legislatures of the republic (1931, 1933, 1936) compared to those elected in 1931

Occupation	Deputies elected in the three legislatures		All deputies 1931 %
	n	%	
Farmers	1	1	1.7
Large business	1	1	1.0
Small business	2	3	4.3
Journalists, writers, and middle-level occupations	10	14	12.0
Lawyers	28	39	34.9
Teaching	2	3	4.3
Medicine	3	4	10.3
Humanities	1	1	2.3
Pharmacy, veterinary	1	1	
Architecture, engineering	8	11	5.4
Army officers	3	4	3.0
Elite civil servants (including university professors)	9	13	13.6
Other university-educated civil servants	1	1	1.8
Clergy	1	1	1.7
Other	1	1	0.2
Manual workers	8	11	9.4
White-collar employees	—	—	2.8
Total (n)	(71)	(100)	(464)

ecological basis. To understand Spanish socialism, we should never forget that 43.8% of its deputies have been elected in Andalusia and Extremadura, two regions in which the agrarian problem, particularly the dominance of latifundia and rural overpopulation and unemployment, were salient, and that the two main industrial regions, Catalonia and the Basque country, contributed fewer deputies to the PSOE than their share in the Spanish population.

We will provide first of all an overview of the main features of the parliamentary elite in the 1933 and 1936 elections and of variations across parties. Then we will discuss in a comprehensive way the profiles of each party or party family.

3.3. Professions and Occupations in the 1933–1936 Cortes

The liberal professions constitute a large contingent of the legislatures, 245 in 1931, 270 in 1933, and 196 in 1936 (52.9%, 57%, and 41.3% respectively). In the Left-dominated legislature of 1936, they are fewer, but still the largest professional category (Tables 11.18 and 11.19). Among the professionals,

Table 11.18. Occupation of the *diputados* in the 1933 Cortes by party

Occupation	PCE n	PSOE n	PSOE %	Left Republicans n	Republicans Conservatives n	Republicans Conservatives %	Liberal Democrats n	Liberal Democrats %	Agrarians n	Agrarians %	Radicals n	Radicals %	CEDA n	CEDA %
Lawyers	—	3	5.1	3	8	50.0	6	60.0	17	56.6	41	42.3	43	37.7
Medical doctors	1	2	3.4	1	1	6.3	3	30.0	1	3.3	7	7.2	4	3.5
Pharmacists, veterinarians	—	—	—	—	—	—	—	—	—	—	3	3.1	—	—
Architects or engineers	—	2	3.4	2	1	6.3	—	—	3	10.0	5	5.1	17	14.9
Journalists, writers	—	9	15.3	1	—	—	—	—	—	—	7	7.21	2	1.7
Elite civil servants	—	2	3.4	1	2	12.5	—	—	2	6.7	4	4.12	5	4.4
Other civil servants	—	5	8.5	—	—	—	—	—	—	—	2	2.1	—	—
Military officers	—	—	—	1	—	—	—	—	—	—	—	—	3	2.6
Notarios, registradores	—	—	—	—	1	6.3	—	—	—	—	3	3.0	3	2.6
University professors	—	5	8.5	2	1	6.3	—	—	1	3.3	—	—	7	6.1
High school professors	—	3	5.1	—	1	6.3	—	—	1	3.3	7	7.2	3	2.6
Schoolteachers	—	4	6.8	—	—	—	—	—	—	—	—	—	—	—
Priests	—	—	—	—	—	—	1	10.0	—	—	1	1.0	4	3.5
Merchants	—	—	—	—	—	—	—	—	—	—	7	7.2	—	—
Businessmen, bankers	—	1	1.7	—	—	—	—	—	3	10.0	5	5.1	5	4.4
Farmers	—	—	—	—	—	—	—	—	2	6.7	2	2.1	4	3.5
Owners	—	—	—	—	—	—	—	—	—	—	1	1.0	7	6.1
Minor professions	—	2	3.4	—	—	—	—	—	—	—	1	1.0	—	—
Employees	—	7	11.9	—	—	—	—	—	—	—	1	1.0	1	0.9
Manual workers	—	13	22.0	—	—	—	—	—	—	—	—	—	2	1.7
No information	—	1	1.7	—	1	6.3	—	—	—	—	—	—	—	—
Total	1	59	100	11	16	100	10	100	30	100	97	100	114	100

Table 11.18. (*cont.*)

	REN	Traditionalists		Esquerra		Lliga		PNV		Others		All	
	n	n	%	n	%	n	%	n	%	n	%	n	%
Lawyers	7	10	47.6	4	23.5	12	46.1	6	60.0	12	48	172	38.1
Medical doctors	—	—	—	3	17.6	—	—	—	—	1	4.0	24	5.3
Pharmacists, veterinarians	—	2	9.5	—	—	—	—	—	—	1	4.0	6	1.3
Architects or engineers	1	3	14.3	—	—	1	3.9	1	10.0	2	8.0	37	8.2
Journalists, writers	2	1	4.8	—	—	2	7.7	—	—	1	4.0	26	5.8
Elite civil servants	2	—	—	—	—	3	11.5	—	—	1	4.0	22	4.8
Other civil servants	—	—	—	1	5.8	—	—	—	—	—	—	8	1.8
Military officers	—	—	—	—	—	2	7.7	—	—	—	—	4	0.8
Notarios, registradores	1	—	—	1	5.8	2	7.7	—	—	—	—	10	2.2
University professors	—	—	—	—	—	—	—	—	—	—	—	19	4.2
High school professors	—	—	—	1	5.8	—	—	—	—	—	—	16	3.5
Schoolteachers	—	—	—	1	5.8	—	—	—	—	—	—	5	1.1
Priests	—	—	—	—	—	—	—	—	—	1	4.0	6	1.3
Merchants	—	—	—	—	—	—	—	—	—	—	—	8	1.8
Businessmen, bankers	—	2	9.5	1	5.8	3	11.5	—	—	3	12.0	20	4.4
Farmers	1	—	—	1	5.8	—	—	—	—	—	—	11	2.4
Owners	—	2	9.5	—	—	—	—	1	10.0	2	8.0	15	3.3
Minor professions	—	—	—	2	11.7	—	—	—	—	—	—	5	1.1
Employees	—	—	—	—	—	—	—	1	10.0	—	—	10	2.2
Manual workers	—	1	4.8	2	11.7	—	—	1	10.0	—	—	19	4.2
No information	—	—	—	—	—	1	3.9	—	—	1	4.0	8	1.8
Total	14	21	100	17	100	26	100	10	100	25	100	451	100

Source: See footnote 17.

Table 11.19. Occupation of *diputados* in the 1936 Cortes by party

Occupation	PCE, Extreme Left		PSOE		Izquierda Republicana		Unión Republicana		Agrarios		Centre		CEDA	
	n	%	n	%	n	%	n	%	n	%	n	%	n	%
Lawyers	1	5.3	13	13.3	25	28.7	12	31.6	7	63.3	4	25.0	34	39.1
Medical doctors	2	10.5	6	6.1	8	9.2	6	15.8	—	—	4	25.0	3	3.4
Pharmacists, veterinarians	—	—	—	—	2	2.3	2	5.3	—	—	1	6.2	1	1.1
Architects, engineers	—	—	4	4.1	6	6.9	2	5.3	—	—	1	6.2	11	12.6
Journalists, writers	2	10.5	10	10.2	6	6.9	3	7.9	—	—	—	—	2	2.3
Elite civil servants	—	—	3	3.1	2	2.3	1	2.6	3	27.3	2	12.5	6	6.8
Other civil servants	—	—	3	3.1	4	4.6	2	5.3	—	—	1	6.2	—	—
Military officers	—	—	—	—	1	1.1	—	—	—	—	—	—	2	2.3
Notarios, registradores	—	—	—	—	3	3.5	1	2.6	—	—	—	—	4	4.6
University professors	—	—	9	9.2	12	13.8	2	5.3	—	—	—	—	7	8.0
High school professors	—	—	6	6.1	5	5.7	—	—	—	—	1	6.2	—	—
Schoolteachers	1	5.3	2	2.0	—	—	—	—	—	—	—	—	3	3.5
Priests	—	—	—	—	—	—	—	—	—	—	—	—	—	—
Merchants	—	—	—	—	9	10.3	3	7.9	—	—	1	6.2	—	—
Businessmen, bankers	—	—	2	2.0	—	—	1	2.6	—	—	1	6.2	6	6.9
Farmers	—	—	4	4.1	—	—	—	—	—	—	—	—	2	2.3
Owners	—	—	—	—	—	—	1	2.6	1	9.1	—	—	4	4.6
Minor professions	—	—	5	5.1	—	—	1	2.6	—	—	—	—	—	—
Employees	2	10.5	6	6.1	2	2.3	—	—	—	—	—	—	1	1.1
Manual workers	11	57.9	23	23.2	2	2.3	1	2.6	—	—	—	—	1	1.1
No information	—	—	2	2.0	—	—	1	2.6	—	—	—	—	—	—
Total	19	100	98	100	87	100	38	100	11	100	16	100	87	100

Table 11.19. (*cont.*)

	Renovación n	Renovación %	Traditionalistas n	Traditionalistas %	Esquerra n	Esquerra %	Lliga n	PNV n	Independents n	Others n	Others %	All n	All %
Lawyers	6	46.1	5	55.5	10	27.8	6	7	8	8	38.1	146	31.0
Medical doctors	2	15.4	—	—	4	11.1	—	—	—	—	—	35	7.4
Pharmacists, veterinarians	—	—	1	11.1	—	—	—	—	—	1	4.8	7	1.5
Architects, engineers	—	—	—	—	5	13.8	1	—	2	4	19.0	31	6.6
Journalists, writers	—	—	—	—	1	2.8	2	1	—	2	9.5	32	6.8
Elite civil servants	2	15.4	—	—	—	—	—	—	3	3	14.3	28	5.9
Other civil servants	—	—	—	—	—	—	—	—	—	—	—	10	2.1
Military officers	—	—	—	—	1	2.8	—	—	—	—	—	3	0.1
Notarios, registradores	—	—	1	11.1	1	2.8	1	—	—	1	4.8	11	2.3
University professors	1	7.7	—	—	1	2.8	1	—	—	—	—	32	6.8
High school professors	—	—	—	—	—	—	—	—	—	—	—	15	3.2
Schoolteachers	—	—	—	—	1	2.8	—	—	—	1	4.8	5	1.1
Priests	—	—	—	—	—	—	—	—	—	—	—	3	0.1
Merchants	—	—	—	—	2	5.6	1	—	—	—	—	1	0.2
Businessmen, bankers	2	15.4	—	—	2	5.6	—	—	—	—	—	13	2.8
Farmers	—	—	1	11.1	1	2.8	—	—	1	1	4.8	11	2.3
Owners	—	—	—	—	2	5.6	—	—	—	—	—	9	1.9
Minor professions	—	—	—	—	1	2.8	—	—	—	—	—	8	1.7
Employees	—	—	1	11.1	1	2.8	—	1	—	—	—	14	3.0
Manual workers	—	—	—	—	3	8.3	—	1	—	—	—	42	8.9
No information	—	—	—	—	1	2.8	—	—	—	—	—	4	0.8
Total	13	100	9	100	36	100	12	10	14	21	100	471	100

Source: See footnote 17.

the lawyers, 162 in 1931, 207 in 1933 and 128 in 1936 (respectively 34.8%, 38.1%, 31%), are the largest single professional group. The difference between the legislatures again reflects the dominance of the Left in 1936. The proportion of lawyers in the conservative CEDA in 1933 (37.7%), and in 1936 (37.5%), compared to that in the ranks of the PSOE (respectively 5.1% and 13.1%) could not be more significant. Lawyers were often closely linked to banking and industry, and probably some should have been classified as business executives or managers. A significant number of large landowners also were practising attorneys. The number of deputies who in the three legislatures identified themselves as lawyers was large. It is not possible to say how many of them practised law but probably a large proportion, to which one would have to add those who, while declaring other occupations, were also practising lawyers. The proportion of lawyers is very small in the PCE (5.8%) and the PSOE (5.1%) in 1933 to grow considerably among the Left Republicans (IR 28.7% and UR 31.6%). It is already over one-third among the Right Republicans: the Radicals in 1933 (42.3%) and the two minor Centre parties, the Republican Conservatives (50%), and the Liberal Democrats (60%). In 1933, they are a majority or almost so among the parties of the Right: the *Agrarios* (56.6%), *Renovación* (50%), and the Traditionalists (47.6%). The same is true for the Catalan Right, the *Lliga*: 46.1% in 1933 and 50% in 1936, in contrast to the *Esquerra*: 23.5% in 1933 and 27.8% in 1936. In calculating the proportion of lawyers, we have, in principle, not counted as lawyers those who gave another profession like university professor, civil servant, landowner, although some most probably also practised law. On the other hand, many who reported being lawyers were also landowners, financiers, or business owners. To give one example, Cambó, the leader of the *Lliga*, declared himself a lawyer, but this Spanish peer of Rathenau, head of Spanish General Electric, writer, art collector, and lifetime politician, was not just a lawyer. In some cases, we did not code such persons as lawyers.

Medical doctors made up 5.1% in 1933 and 6.5% in 1936. They were around 5% in the ranks of the CEDA and a similar proportion among the PSOE deputies. Engineers and architects made up 8.2% in 1933 and 6.6% in 1936. They constitute an important contingent (14.9% in 1933 and 10.2% in 1936) of the CEDA delegation, compared to that of the PSOE (3.4% and 1.0%). This different proportion indicates the social status of the engineering profession; due to the *numerus clausus* and competitive selection, engineers had strong ties to the business world and a lesser 'social consciousness' than the doctors.

Even in the nineteenth century and the *Restauración*, many politicians owed their prestige, influence, and power to their journalistic activities, often not only as writers but as owners of newspapers. Many of them prided themselves on being writers. This would continue to be the case in the

Republic, but probably those identifying themselves as journalists in their statement on occupation for the Cortes were a different type of journalist, some writing for party newspapers. It is hard to know how many made a living as journalists or writers and how many declaring other occupations were prominent writers. We have to think only of Unamuno, Ortega y Gasset, Marañón, who were university professors in the 1931 Cortes. In 1936, the only representative of the *Bloque de Unidad Marxista* was a writer and one of the PCE deputies. The PSOE delegation had 10 (10.1%) members declaring themselves to be journalists to which we should perhaps add the 'stenographer' Indalecio Prieto, long associated with journalistic activities. In the two left bourgeois parties, IR and UR, journalists formed close to 10% of MPs and the same would be true of the Left-Catalan *Esquerra Republicana de Cataluña* (ERC) with five deputies (13.9%).

The teaching professions are a major component of the parliamentary elite of many parties. While high school professors and schoolteachers play an important role in the bourgeois Left and Socialist Parties in many countries, proportionally in Spain in the 1930s they very much take second place compared to university professors. University professors might have been more 'dispensable', able to devote time to politics, and in the case of law professors, particularly qualified for legislative tasks. They also, probably even before the Primo de Rivera dictatorship, enjoyed more freedom than high school and elementary school teachers, who were more constrained by the local context. In 1933, the teaching professions were represented by 39 persons (8.2%) and by 42 (8.9%) in 1936. There was a smaller number among the CEDA (6.1% in 1933 and 4.5% in 1936) than among the PSOE, where, not only were university and engineering school professors twice as numerous (10.2% in 1933 and 8.1% in 1936), but schoolteachers also occupied some seats.

The Republic has often been characterized as a professors' republic. Therefore, it is of special interest to study the presence of academics in the Cortes. In the Constituent Cortes, 37 of the 464 deputies are professors, but almost one-half will never return after the 1933 dissolution, some will continue through all three legislatures and only a small minority will return with the Popular Front victory. In the 1933 legislature, dominated by the Radicals and the Right, the number of professors diminishes by one-third and only eight are newcomers, two of them staying only for one legislative period. In 1936, only 14 of the original 37 university professors from the Constituent Assembly will meet again; most of their former colleagues must have been disillusioned or lost the favour of the party committees who arranged the candidacies or of the voters, most probably the first. The honeymoon of the intellectuals with the Republic was relatively short, and it is not just the leading intellectuals, like Ortega y Gasset and Unamuno (both deputies only in 1931) who must have become critical (Tusell and Queipo de Llano 1990). Many did not have to wait until the Civil War to take the decision to stand aside as a third Spain. Of the 51 professors who used some of the 84 chances to be *diputados*, a large plurality (18) were law school professors, only four were scientists, and a good number (13) humanists. They and the 12 professors of medicine were the new component of the presence of the academy in the legislature.

One group of civil servants is clearly overrepresented in the political elite: the *abogados del Estado*. Their function is to defend the interests of the state in different conflicts—except in criminal cases—and legality in the administration. They have been recruited by highly competitive examinations among lawyers. They also often act as attorneys. Other civil servants are not very well represented, and the judiciary and prosecutors are practically absent. The lower civil servants, posts and telegraphs, for example, occupy seats on the benches of the Left-bourgeois parties. A problem in counting the number of public employees is the fact that the graduates of several *Escuelas Especiales* of Engineers (civil engineering, mining, forestry, agronomists) are automatically members of a *cuerpo* with opportunity for public employment (although they could opt for an *excedencia* or leave to devote themselves to private employment). Their position between the public and the private sector makes it doubtful that they should be added the public employment figures and we have considered them part of the liberal professions. Also with an ambiguous status are two legal professions represented mainly in the conservative parties: the notaries and the *registradores de la propiedad*. Though not public employees, they were recruited by highly competitive and regulated examination, their careers were dependent on those examinations, and the positions available and their fees were regulated by the state, creating for them a privileged social and often economic status. Since their functions in other countries are exercised by lawyers, we could also add this group to the legal profession, which they also exercised simultaneously. As much or more than other civil servants, the notaries and *registradores* enjoyed 'dispensability' since they could hold on to their position while elected and charge a substitute (to whom they paid part of their salary) with their work while in office.

In contrast to the post-1978 democracy, during the Republic army officers could seek elective office. In the Constituent Assembly, a general sat on the benches of the *Agrarios*, another on those of the Radicals, a captain in those of AR, a major among the PRS, the brother of Franco, an air-force major, as a revolutionary Left member. In 1933, there were eight officers in the Cortes. Many of those elected, like the Radical general Cabanellas and the Agrarian general Fanjul, would not be listed in the official list of MPs because, on account of incompatibility or resignation, they would later not occupy their seats.

The Republic in 1931 abolished the incompatibility between clerical status and eligibility and as a result a small number of priests were elected: eight in 1931, six in 1933 (four of them by the CEDA, one Radical, and one independent who sympathized with the extreme Right), and two in 1936, both by the CEDA. None of them played in the CEDA a role comparable to Sturzo in the Italian PPI, Kaas in the German *Zentrum*, or Seipel in the ÖVP.

There is an underrepresentation in the Republican Cortes of businessmen, from owners and managers of large enterprises to small shopkeepers, if we rely on the declaration of the legislators. In addition, the terminology used at the time—*industrial*—covered both industry and commerce; *propietario* (owner) most likely refers to landowners but may include some business owners. Most of the executives would identify as lawyers, a more prestigious activity and one more congruent with being a legislator, and which they exercised simultaneously. Even taking this into account, few leading businessmen sat in the Cortes: a financier like March, two prominent leaders of the *Lliga*, a ship-owner for *Renovación*. On the other end of the spectrum, some workers would be self-employed small businessmen. One liberal profession, with a university degree, could also be counted as commerce: the pharmacists. If there is a party in which businessmen, industrialists, and financiers assumed for themselves the representation of their interests in parliament rather than leaving it to lawyers or elite civil servants, it is the *Lliga*. Catalonia was the only region with a self-conscious and proud bourgeoisie which saw itself as different from the *clases medias*—the professional middle classes dominating Spanish politics.

To explain the relatively small number of declared landowners or farmers in the elite, we have to remember that large landowners in Spain were not gentlemen farmers living on their estates, like *Junker Gutsherrn*, but more often than not, holders of a university degree, generally in law, living in Madrid or a provincial capital. They were absentee owners, leaving management to others. Although in touch with their farms and agrarian interest groups, the profession they were proud of was the law and politics, even though their income might have come from the land.

With the Republic and the electoral success of the PSOE, the proportion of manual workers in the *Congreso* increased significantly: 9.4% in 1931, 3.9% in 1933, 8.9% in 1936. Those giving working-class jobs as their occupation had, for a long time, held positions in the *Unión General de Trabajadores* (UGT) as leaders of the mining, railway, and metalworkers trade unions, a disproportionate number were typesetters, and only three gave as occupation farm labourer (despite the large number of landless labourers and their weight in the UGT after 1931). As we move from Left to Right, the proportion diminishes: 58.8% in the PCE in 1936; 32.5% in 1931, 22.0%

in 1933, 23.2% in 1936 in the PSOE; 2.3% in IR, 5.7% among the Radical
Party ranks in 1933; 2.3% in the CEDA in 1936, and 4.8% among the *Tradicionalistas*. In the Catalan *Esquerra*, 8.3% in 1936 compared to none among
the *Lliga* delegation and one in the PNV. The presence of one or two
workers in parliamentary groups outside the PSOE and the extreme Left
is purely symbolic since they played no significant role and generally sat
only once in parliament.

The PSOE was characterized by its critics as a bureaucratic-professional
party, but the actual number of paid employees was small and even the
number of paid trade union leaders was probably also modest. Even so,
many of its deputies can be considered full-time professional politicians.
The CEDA was also a mass membership party, a character reinforced by
its links with Catholic lay organizations. We know less about its paid officials, but given the enthusiasm generated by its cause and the leadership of
Gil Robles, it could rely on a large number of volunteers. Its MPs did not
depend on the party financially since the majority had stable and successful professional positions. Probably, except for a few top leaders, politics
was not a full-time activity. This would be even more true for the parties of
the extreme Right, although the Carlists had a committed membership,
some of whom were even involved in a paramilitary organization. The *Lliga*
was also a membership party but many of its leaders were notables, successful professionals such as bankers and businessmen economically independent from the party.

It is much more difficult to characterize the Left and Right bourgeois
republican parties. Probably the Radicals included a larger number of
leaders living off rather than for politics, dependent on patronage and positions in local politics. *Acción Republicana*—later *Izquierda Republicana*—
was closer to being an electoral party led by professionals and academics
living for politics rather than of politics. We know much less about the PRS
(*Partido Radical Socialista*) which, at the start of the Republic, had considerable membership but no bureaucratic organization and whose leaders
again did not live off politics, except for some patronage opportunities at
the local level.

3.4. Education of the Legislators

We do not have direct information on the level of education attained but
indirectly we can give a reasonable estimate of the studies of members of
the Cortes. All those who report a liberal profession and higher civil service
positions have a university degree of *licenciado*—the normal conclusion of
university studies—or a degree from the highly selective engineering and
architecture schools. We can add the career officers of the armed forces and
the clergy who are their equivalent. In addition, a number of those with

university degrees have more than one degree and a doctorate (at least the university professors).

Those with university degrees, or those even more esteemed and difficult to attain from the *Escuelas Especiales* for engineers and architects, dominated the parliamentary elite. Only among the PCE were they totally underrepresented: 17.5% in 1936. In the PSOE, they were at least 33.8% in 1933 and 41.4% in 1936. In IR they were 66.7%, in UR 63.7%, and among the PLD 90.0% in 1936. In 1933, in the *Partido Radical* they were 74.3% and among the *Agrarios* 83.3%. The CEDA had 72.8% in 1933 and 68.9% in 1936. In 1933 *Renovación* had 78.6%, the *Tradicionalistas* 71.4%, *Esquerra* 52.9%, the *Lliga* 69.2% (but probably more), and the PNV 50% in 1933 and 70% in 1936. All these figures underestimate the proportion with university or higher technical education, since we have not identified the education of journalists and writers, nor considered the education of those declaring themselves to be businessmen (with some obvious exceptions), landowners, or 'farmers'.

Those with only elementary education (or even less) would be the manual workers, a few white-collar workers, and small business owners, which leaves us with a significant but not large number of persons with various middle-level professional degrees like the *peritos*, or with a commercial school diploma or teacher training college quallification. We cannot identify those with only a secondary school education—the *bachillerato*— and no further education. Some of those in agriculture and small business would fit into this category.

3.5. Other Aspects

Religion, militant secularism and traditional catholicism, anticlericalism and clericalism, would be one of the deep divides in politics in the 1930s, in support of, or opposition to, the secularizing 1931 Constitution and its supplementary laws. However, it is almost certain that practically all deputies were baptized Catholics. It is not possible to identify the few that might not have been. There are therefore no identifying characteristics except the positions of the parties and perhaps some roll-call votes. One indicator would be a masonic affiliation, but there is some controversy about who was a mason. Ferrer Benimeli (1980: 218–22) estimates that some 183 of the Constituent Cortes had masonic connections, Arbeloa (1981) gives a figure of 129, and Gómez Molleda (1986) analyses the party affiliation of 151 deputies who were presumably masons. The numbers given for 1931 are 30 (57%) of the PRS, seven (58%) of the *Federales*, 12 (53%) of AR, 43 (49%) of the *Radicales*, 11 (37%) of the *Esquerra*, three (23%) of the ASR, three (21%) of the FRG, and 35 (30%) of the PSOE. Clearly the masons sat mainly on the benches of the Left-bourgeois parties. At the other end of the spectrum, we have affiliation to Catholic Action, particularly the elitist *Asociación Católica Nacional de Propagandistas* (ACNdP), but this leaves the 'religiosity' of other members undefined.

Gender is another aspect to be mentioned. Women were granted the suffrage for the first time by the Primo de Rivera dictatorship, which also appointed 13 women to the *Asamblea Nacional*. In the 1931 election, women were eligible but did not have the vote. Women's suffrage was granted in 1931 by a vote of 161 in favour, 121 against, and 188 absent (Capel 1975). It expanded the electorate from 6.2 million to 12.9 million in 1933, and participation from 4.3 million (70%) in 1931 to 8.7 million (67%) in 1933. In the 1931 Constituent Cortes there were three women, representing the PSOE, the *Partido Radical Socialista*, and the Radical Party. Irwin (1991: 265–6) has listed the 52 women running in 1933 (several in more than one district): 20 for the PCE, 15 for the PSOE, five for the RS, two Radicals, two for the CEDA, one *Renovación*, one Traditionalist, and six for different parties. Five women would be elected: four Socialists (only one re-elected from 1931), and one Agrarian. Many on the left, however, blamed the electoral victory of the Right on the fact that women had been granted the suffrage. However, that same electorate voted for a chamber dominated by the Popular Front where there would be three Socialist women, one for the *Izquierda Republicana* and Dolores Ibarruri— la *Pasionaria* of Civil War fame—representing the Communist Party. Women would not enter the cabinet until after the start of the civil war when an anarchist leader—not a member of parliament—would join the government.

3.6. Party Profiles

In the 1931 election, party identifications were largely undefined. The disorganized Right had obtained seats for a heterogeneous coalition: the *Minoría Vasco-Navarra* (MVN), in which future CEDA, Traditionalists, and PNV Basque nationalists sat together. Two important parties in 1931 would practically disappear in 1933: the ASR dissolved and the Radical Socialists disintegrated. In 1933, the party system crystallized into major groups, whose number would be even smaller in 1936. It has therefore made more sense to characterize the party representations in 1933 and 1936. Some of the most interesting differences are between parties that in a simplified classification would be grouped together. In some cases—the Radical Party in 1933, *Unión Republicana* (UR), the *Centro*, and the Communists in 1936— it was not possible to establish trends, since they had a significant representation in only one of the two legislatures.

In our analysis of the extreme Left legislators, we have combined all those elected by the PCE, the BOC (*Bloque Obrero i Camperol*), the POUM

(*Partido Obrero de Unificación Marxista*), a lonely representative of a Syndicalist party (a former CNT leader), and two 'revolutionary candidates' in 1931. The extreme Left had few elected members: two self-styled revolutionaries and one communist (a medical doctor) in 1931, one (again a medical doctor) in 1933, and 17 Communists (PCE) elected on the Popular Front ticket, one deputy of the *Bloque Unificación Marxista*, and one Syndicalist in 1936: incomparably fewer than in Germany and France in the 1930s and in Italy before Fascism. In 1931, the PCE obtained 190,605 votes, mainly in Andalusia, Vizcaya, and Zaragoza. Persecution, splits, and factionalism are not the only explanation for the weakness of the party in comparative perspective. The main reason was probably the competition of the revolutionary syndicalists of the CNT and, in 1936, the radicalized PSOE. In the PCE delegation, after the Stalinist purges, we find no leaders coming from the division between Socialists and Communists in the 1920s, and few of the leaders of the PCE in the early 1930s. Except for one leader of the *Bloque de Unificación Marxista*, there are no leaders of intellectual or professional significance. Of the 17 PCE deputies in 1936, 10 (59%) were manual workers, two white-collar employees, one journalist, three liberal professionals (one lawyer and two medical doctors), and one schoolteacher.

Five of the deputies of the *Esquerra* parliamentary group were members of two minor left parties, *Unió Socialista de Catalunya* and *Partit Català Proletari*, which would fuse during the Civil War with the Communists to constitute the PSUC, the Catalan affiliate of the PCE. Another MP, listed officially as 'independent', who ran on the Popular Front ticket in Zaragoza capital, was the labour lawyer Benito Pabón. In his campaign, he stressed that he was fully identified with the CNT, its ideology and organization, and that he was ready to take a seat in the Cortes only under the exceptional circumstances of the 1936 election. Taking into account the radical Left and the MPs of the *Esquerra* and the CNT supporter, the extreme Left representation was probably closer to 26 (5.4%) members than the 19 we have counted: even so, a small number that in no way mirrored the extreme Left mobilization in the country.

The PSOE, as its name indicates, was the party of the working class, and its parliamentary representation included more workers than any party to its right: 32.5% in 1931, 22.0% in 1933, 23.2% in 1936. If we add to these the white-collar workers—4.4% in 1931, 11.9% in 1933, and 6.1% in 1936— the lower-class component was very important indeed. However, there was also a significant contingent of free professionals: 25.6% in 1931, 13.6% in 1933, 23.2% in 1936. Lawyers, though, made up only 7.9% in 1931, 5.14% in 1933, and 13.1% in 1936. As in other social democratic parties, the teaching professions played an important role: 21.3% in 1931, 20.3% in 1933, and 17.1% in 1936. Among them, university professors were particularly important (12.3% in 1931, 8.5% in 1933, and 9.7% in 1936). Surprisingly, or perhaps not so surprisingly, the radicalization of the party, accompanied by a great renewal of the parliamentary elite, occurred alongside a drop in the number of workers, presumably most of them trade union leaders, and an increase in the number of professionals.

Izquierda Republicana, the party led by Manuel Azaña,[24] had 11 deputies in 1933 and 88 deputies (18.6%) in 1936. It was formed by AR (*Acción Republicana*) as a core, minor parties joining and attracting politicians from other parties. Lawyers constituted the largest occupational group (27% in 1933 and 28.7% in 1936), but there were fewer than in all parties to its right. Free professionals (27% in 1933 and 18.4% in 1936) and journalists and writers (6.9% in 1936) would be an almost equally important group. However, the most significant fact was the presence of university professors (two in 1933 and twelve or 13.7% in 1936), more than in any other party, to which we could add another five deputies in teaching professions. Civil servants (6.9%) in comparison were much less well represented, certainly less than in the ranks of the parties of the Centre and the Right. Businessmen and commercial activities (10.3%) were present but not prominent. The two workers and two employees were a token representation.

Unión Republicana formed by the fusion of the *Partido Radical Demócrata* (PRD) and the PRS in 1934, was the 'right-wing' of the Popular Front (Ramírez Jiménez 1977: 127–69). The PRD was the schism of the Radicals under the leadership of Martínez Barrio, disturbed by the rightward shift of the Radicals. Before 1936, the PRD attracted a few MPs of other parties. In 1936, as part of the Popular Front, the UR gained 38 seats, constituting the fourth largest parliamentary group. The UR parliamentary delegation in 1936 (8% of the Chamber), was formed largely by liberal professionals (57.9%), many of them lawyers (31.6%), and relatively few civil servants (7.9%) and teaching professionals (7.9%). In contrast to the Radical Party, the number of businessmen, farmers, and owners was small and, consonant with its bourgeois character, there were no manual workers. In the Left-bourgeois UR, located to the right of IR, the number of lawyers was slightly larger than in IR; free professionals, mainly doctors, writers, and journalists had a significant presence (34.2%). Perhaps the most salient difference with IR was that only one university professor and two other persons in the teaching professions sat on its benches. Certainly IR had a greater attractiveness for the intellectual elite than UR, with its more 'mesocratic' tone, closer to the old Radical Party from which some of its leaders came, although without the presence of business we found among the Radicals.

It is difficult to place some minor republican parties on the Left/Right

---

[24] The leader of the Left, Prime Minister in the first two years of the Republic, and briefly in 1936 before becoming President.

dimension. The leaders of some, like the *Progresistas* and the *Partido Republicano Conservador* (PRC), were among the founders of the Republic, but by 1933 could be considered part of the right, although the PRC in 1934 opposed the entry of the CEDA in the government. For broad international comparisons, we can include them among the Right Liberals with the Radicals they vehemently rejected on moral grounds. The Republican Conservatives, 16 (3.4%) in 1933, were mostly lawyers (50%); to these should be added two free professionals, one university professor and one high school professor, two high civil servants, and one notary. The party that wanted to be the right of a non-clerical but not anticlerical bourgeois republic, was ultimately a small party of educated upper-middle-class elites.

The PLD (*Partido Liberal Demócrata*), led by Melquiades Alvarez, the Republican founder of the *Reformista* party under the monarchy can, after 1931, clearly be placed on the Right as a conservative party, however fully committed to democracy and the Republic, together with the CEDA with its ambivalences on both counts. Its deputies, 10 (2.1%) in 1933, were mostly lawyers (six) and medical doctors (three), with one merchant.

The President of the Republic, hostile to the Popular Front and to the Right, in December 1935 formed a cabinet of 'personalities', some of them not members of the legislature, mostly personal friends, who dissolved parliament and called for the February 1936 election. His hope was that Portela, a Liberal politician of the monarchy and Galician *cacique*, could organize a candidacy of the Centre. In the polarized political atmosphere of February 1936 only 16 (3.4%) *Centro* deputies were elected: four lawyers, four doctors, one engineer, one pharmacist (that means 62.5% liberal professionals), two *abogados del Estado*, one civil servant, one financier, one businessman, and one professor of the School of Commercial Studies. One-half of these men had been deputies in 1933 of Centre parties.

The Radical Party, led by Alejandro Lerroux, presents a difficulty when we try to place it on a Left/Right spectrum (Ruíz Manjón 1976). In 1931, many of its candidates ran on lists of the *Conjunción Republicano-Socialista*, the regime-founding coalition. Lerroux was a cabinet member in the provisional government and the first governments of Azaña, and therefore the Radicals could be considered a party of the Left. After leaving the government, the party shifted towards the Right and in the 1933 election in many districts, particularly in the South, it reached an understanding with the CEDA that assured the election of its candidates, and formed governments with the support of the Right, finally entering a coalition government with it. Should the Radical deputies between 1933 and 1936 be classified as Right, or should we divide them between Right and Left Republicans on the basis of the split? We are inclined to do the latter but have ended up doing the former.

In 1933, the Radicals were the second largest parliamentary group, with 97 deputies (20.5%), and would provide a large number of cabinet members. In 1936, after the schism of the *Partido Radical Demócrata* to form the UR, only four deputies (0.8%) would return under the party label. The party, a Right-bourgeois-liberal party, was represented by a disproportionate number of lawyers (42.3%) and other liberal professionals (11.7%), among them a large number of doctors and pharmacists—as was the case among the French Radicals. Notaries and property registrars (3.1%), and a minority of civil servants, were also represented. Journalists and writers constitute another significant group. However, the most distinctive group compared to CEDA is the number of those in commerce (7.2%), and industry (5.1%), a total of 12, mostly lower middle class. Self-identified farmers and landowners did not constitute a significant group but were probably present among the lawyers and free professionals. Summarizing, the Radicals were not a party of the social nor of the intellectual elite but a cross-section of the middle classes, a number of them professional politicians. In 1936, the Radical Party had practically disappeared from the Cortes. Most (19) of the 21 (21.6%) that left the leadership of Lerroux to follow Martínez Barrio to form the *Partido Radical Demócrata* returned to San Jerónimo under the banner of UR. Only four were re-elected as *Radicales* and the historical leader Lerroux did not gain a seat.

In contrast to Northern and Eastern Europe and to a lesser extent Central Europe, in Spain there were no farmer or peasant parties with a distinctive programme or ideology. In the Republic, there was only a small Agrarian Party that initially served to represent the disorganized Catholic right and was led by wealthier landowners of north-central Spain. The class structure of the countryside, the anticlerical–clerical conflict, the regional nationalism in Catalonia and the Basque country and to a lesser extent in Galicia, the strength of *caciquismo* politics in the interior of Galicia, all occupy the political space that in other countries is taken by farmer or peasant parties. The *Partido Agrario* in 1933 had a significant representation of 30 deputies (6.3%), reduced to 11 (2.3%) after the defeat of the Right in 1936. Only three identified themselves as farmers and two as landowners, mirroring the fact that it was a conservative party rather than a Northern European farmers' or Eastern European peasant party. More than half of its 1933 delegation (17 or 56.7%) and seven of its 11 members (63.6%) in 1936 were lawyers, to which we can add four free professionals in 1933. Its social elite character was illustrated by the presence of two *abogados del Estado* in 1933 and three in 1936. Many of the lawyers were also landowners or spokesmen for their interests.

A difficult decision was the location of the CEDA (*Confederación Española de Derechas Autónomas*) in the political families as defined in this book. Good arguments could be made to consider it a Catholic party, some would even say Christian Democratic, but an equally strong case can be made to consider it centre right or conservative, and there would be those who would group it with the extreme Right. The strong conservatism, the absence of a Christian trade union movement, the authoritarian proclivities of some of its leaders, would certainly make defining the CEDA as Christian Democratic questionable, although some of its deputies came from a minor party founded in 1923 with the name *Partido Popular* which wanted to be Christian Democratic (Montero 1977). Although the CEDA is considered (for the purpose of this book) as a party of the Right, a number of its legislators can be considered part of the extreme Right. They published in the intellectual organ of the monarchist right, *Acción Española*, and participated in meetings it organized. A few seceded from the party before 1936 and then in February ran under *Renovación Española* (*Bloque Nacional*) and Traditionalist labels. Those CEDA politicians would be prominent in the Franco regime while others, like Giménez Fernández and Luis Lucía, would suffer persecution. Giménez Fernández, Minister of Agriculture of the CEDA, estimated in 1935 that 70 of the MPs were loyalists to the 'leader' Gil Robles with no distinctive opinion, some 30 were Christian Democrats (15 publicly defined as Republicans), and 15 hard-liners ('*Conservaduros*'), not all monarchists.

The social composition of the parliamentary group—the largest in 1933 with 115 (24.2%), and the second largest in 1936 with 87 (18.3%)—confirms our decision to consider it a party of the Right, without denying a Christian Democratic component. The elite of the CEDA in 1933, when it was the largest parliamentary group, and in 1936, when it was the main opposition party, mirrors its conservative character and (with only two workers and one white-collar employee among its ranks) it is not a Christian-Democratic *Volkspartei*. The strong links with the Church are reflected in the close ties a large proportion (27.8% in 1933 and 29.5% in 1936) of its deputies had with an elite organization of Catholic Action (*Acción Católica Nacional de Propagandistas*). The largest occupational group was that of practising lawyers (35.1% in 1933 and 39.1% in 1936), although many of them were also landowners, businessmen, and a few professors. The other liberal professions were the next largest group (18.4% in 1933 and 17.2% in 1936), disproportionately engineers and architects (elite occupations in Spain), and few medical doctors (four in 1933 and three in 1936), particularly in comparison with other parties. Civil servants, particularly of elite corps, constituted another significant contingent. The teaching professions, mostly university professors, were represented but in proportionately smaller numbers than in the parties of the bourgeois Left and the Socialists. Although many of the deputies were landowners and occupied leadership positions in agricultural interest groups, when declaring their occupation to the Cortes, few stated explicitly landowner (7.9%) or farmer (4.5%) in 1936 (on the basis of other sources of information, we were able to classify as landowners some of those identified as professors or lawyers). As in other Spanish legislatures and parties, with the exception of the *Lliga*, few identified themselves as businessmen, although a number of those in other occupations had close ties to financial institutions and industry. Congruent with its conservative character, there were only two workers and two employees on the CEDA benches. The party, therefore, was one of elite liberal professionals, mainly lawyers with close ties to different economic interests, significantly to agrarian interests. The other salient characteristic was their membership in lay Catholic organizations.

The parliamentary representation of the anti-democratic extreme Right in comparison with other European countries was small: four members in 1931, 38 in 1933, 22 in 1936. It was composed by ultra-conservatives linking with nineteenth-century resistance to Liberalism, the Traditionalists, and the authoritarian monarchists of *Renovación Española*, led by Calvo Sotelo, a former cabinet member of the Primo de Rivera dictatorship inspired by *Action Française* (Gil Pecharromán 1994). The incorporation of fascist themes, a fascisticized rhetoric, symbolism, particularly by the CEDA youth organization, limited the appeal of the small Falangist party. One could say the same about the PCE, in which case the maximalist radicalization of the PSOE helps to explain the PCE's limited success: only 17 MPs in 1936. One of the consequences of the unbelievable electoral weakness of Spanish fascism, whose candidates in 1936 received 0.08% of the vote, was that the only MP was José Antonio Primo de Rivera, founder of *Falange Española*, son of the dictator, professionally a lawyer, elected in 1933 on a conservative ticket in a district where his family had influence (Payne 1993). The absence of a true fascist party meant that the extreme Right benches were not occupied by young activists of more or less plebeian or petty bourgeois origin, but by members of the establishment: Carlists and fascistized authoritarian monarchists.

Renovación Española, the party of the alphonsine monarchists, led by Calvo Sotelo (an *abogado del Estado*), in 1933 had 14 deputies, half of them lawyers, two *abogados del Estado*, one university professor, one engineer, two writers, and one wealthy landowner, a group of high status with no populist concessions. Three of them would be cabinet members under Franco. There were 13 in 1936, three of them coming from the CEDA delegation in 1933. Of the eight Carlists elected in 1931, only one was under 50 years of age, and most were in their late fifties. Three of those elected in 1931 were successful lawyers, another was an engineer, another an architect. One was a member of a business dynasty of bankers and industrialists in the Basque Country. Three were large landowners, playing a leadership role in agrarian interest groups, while another was a priest. In 1933, on a wave right-wing popularity, 21 Carlists were elected, among them 15 new-comers: four in their thirties and two in their twenties; 10 were lawyers, three successful businessmen, one an engineer, another a journalist, and one a worker.

To the extreme Right in 1933, we would have to add the leader of the *Partido Nacionalista Español* (PNE), founded in April 1930 by José Albiñana, a physician with a fascist programme, rhetoric and organization, and militia. The PNE was even more unsuccessful than other Spanish Fascist parties. Albiñana was elected in 1933 in the second round in the Castillian city of Burgos. In 1936, he was elected on the ticket of the *Frente Con-trarevolucionario de Unión de Derechas* and joined the *Renovación* parliamentary group.

In most countries, the nationalist opposition in the periphery to the central government and the dominant nationality is formed by a single party. This was true in the Basque Country during the Republic—in contrast to the present fragmentation into three parties—when the PNV (*Partido Nacionalista Vasco*) was the only nationalist party with representation, but not in Catalonia where, from the early decades of the century, the conservative *Lliga* was challenged by various Centre and Left Republican parties. In the 1930s, two parliamentary groups, the *Lliga* and the *Esquerra Republicana de Cataluña* (ERC) were bitterly opposed. In 1933, ERC was represented by 17 deputies (3.5%) compared to the 26 of the right-wing *Lliga* (5.5%). In 1936, with the shift of the country to the Left, their delegations were respectively 36 (7.6%) and 12 (2.5%). The two Catalan parties could not be more different in the social sectors they represented, the social composition of their leadership, and their parliamentary representation. The *Esquerra*—literally the 'Left'—was a populist party with a heterogeneous social base including radical leftist candidates identified with minor Left parties and lower middle-class occupations, while the *Lliga* was the party of the upper bourgeoisie of a rich and industrial region. Among the 17 ERC deputies in 1933, we find one manual worker, a school-teacher, an insurance salesman, and in 1936 three workers (8.3%), occupations absent among *Lliga* deputies. There were four lawyers (23.5%) in ERC in 1933 and 10 (27.8%) in 1936, compared to 12 (46.1%) in 1933 and six (50%) in 1936 among *Lliga* deputies. There was no university professor among ERC MPs but two in 1933 and one in 1936 on the benches of the *Lliga*. As in other Spanish Left-bourgeois parties, MDs are a significant group: three in 1933 (17.6%) and four in 1936 (11.1%) and none in the ranks of the *Lliga*.[25]

Basque nationalism was represented in the Cortes only by the *Partido*

[25] The *Esquerra* lists and parliamentary group in addition included five deputies of the extreme left, one of them future leader of the PSUC (*Partit Socialista Unificat de Cataluña*), the Catalan affiliate of the Communist Party.

Nacionalista Vasco (PNV) and its 12 (2.5%) deputies in 1933 and 10 (2.1%) in 1936. Of the 12, six were lawyers (although one, the future head of the Basque government, was a successful soccer player and the family had a prosperous business). A deputy elected in 1931, 1933, and 1936 was a journalist and writer, another an office employee, and one elected in 1931 and 1936 was a typesetter. In addition, in 1933 there was a landowner who would return to politics after Franco. The image the party provided was clearly one of catch-all people's party.

3.7. Continuity and Discontinuity in the Three Legislatures of the Republic

In studying the parliamentary elite of the Republic, one of the most striking facts is the discontinuity in its personnel. The official lists of deputies of the Cortes for the three legislatures we have used in our analysis—from which some vacant seats on account of death or resignation are missing—include 1,384 incumbencies, rather than a theoretical total of 1,419. Limiting ourselves to the 1,384, we find a total of 995 persons occupying those seats. Of those members, only 71, that is, 7.3%, served in all three legislatures. Another 246, that is, 24.6%, served twice, while the immense majority (678 or 68.1%), were elected only once. Among those elected, 179, that is, 18.0%, sat in successive legislatures, while another 67 (6.6%) served in 1931 and 1936 but not in 1933. These figures have grave political implications: only a small number of legislators could develop the informal relations across party lines that continuous contacts in the halls and lobbies of a parliament can provide. It also means that few members had a chance to become fully acquainted with the legislative process, interest groups, and so on, particularly if we keep in mind the premature dissolution of the first two legislatures.

A number of circumstances account for this pattern of discontinuity. The rapid shift in the climate of opinion after the first *bienio* from a Centre Left to a Centre Right or Right in the 1933 elections and the even more marked process of radicalization of the electorate in early 1936. The electoral system, with its advantages for the majority, its large districts which prevented—intentionally—candidates with local roots favoured by small districts, the complex process of electoral coalition making it incumbent on the parties to assure electoral victory, all contributed to exaggerate the impact of those shifts in opinion and of that radicalization. Moreover, many of those elected to the Constituent Assembly represented small parties without tradition and organization, who soon became disillusioned with politics, which explains that of the first 464 deputies, 260 would never return to the Cortes. Among the members of the 1933 Cortes, despite an even greater swing of the electoral pendulum, the more defined political calling of many legislators assured the re-election of a larger proportion than of those elected in 1931.

Disintegration due to fractionalization or internal crisis by a number of parties was another factor, particularly the deep crisis in the Radical Party which contributed to a fall from 100 seats in 1933 to four in 1936, even when a number of its deputies returned, as members of a dissidence on the Left, as deputies of *Unión Republicana*. To all this, we have to add that even major parties, after a lean year in 1933, at the time of victory in 1936 elected a large number of persons who had not been *diputados* in 1931. We suspect, but without an analysis of the candidacies cannot affirm, that the internal cleavages and shifts in leadership and ideological orientation account for such changes in their parliamentary group at least as much as the vagaries of the electorate. We underline this discontinuity in parliamentary personnel because we feel that it is one key—obviously among others—to the ineffectiveness of parliament, to the tense atmosphere of many of its sessions, to the difficulties of forming stable governments and coalitions, that contributed so much to the breakdown of Spanish democracy.

To what extent is there a continuity in the parliamentary personnel of the different parties in the three legislatures of the Republic? The answer reflects the electoral fortunes of the parties, exaggerated by the electoral system, but also the continuity in the leadership and orientation of the major parties. The 1933 election represented, particularly at the parliamentary level, a great defeat, and therefore it is more interesting to see to what extent the deputies elected in 1931 returned in 1936 with the victory of a coalition that included many of the parties and leaders of the first two years of the regime. When we turn to the data, we find to our surprise that, despite the very different parliamentary strength of the PSOE in 1933 and 1936, the proportion of its 1931 parliamentary group returning in both legislatures—without necessarily being the same individuals in both years—is almost identical (Table 11.20). Even in the most organized mass party, we find therefore a great discontinuity in parliamentary personnel, which, in this case, must reflect (though we have no data to prove it), the shift from reformism to maximalism in the PSOE. Similarly, the *Esquerra* seems to have undergone considerable change between 1931 and 1936 since, in that year only, one-quarter of its 1931 contingent returned to the Cortes in Madrid, a proportion identical to the 'lean' year 1933. Only one party on the Left shows considerable continuity between 1931 and 1936 after being thrown out into the wilderness more than any other in 1933: *Acción Republicana*, called in 1936 *Izquierda Republicana*. The ORGA— Galician Regional Party—and the Radical Socialists, maintained a lower level of continuity, with 40% of their parliamentary group in 1931 returning in 1936.

The much smaller minorities of the Centre Right and Right of 1931 did

Table 11.20. Continuities in parliamentary representation in subsequent legislatures of deputies elected in 1931 by different parties

Party	Legislatures		Total
	1933	1936	
PSOE.	27.2	28.1	114
Catalan Socialists	20.0	—	5
Acción Republicana	9.7	54.8	31
Federación Republicana Gallega	25.0	40.0	20
Esquerra	23.5	23.5	34
Acción Catalana	—	100.0	1
Radical Socialista	5.5	40.0	55
Dissident Radical Socialists	—	—	2
Federalists	7.7	23.1	13
Radicals	42.7	14.6	89
Republicano Conservador	35.7	21.4	14
Progresista	37.5	25.0	8
Agrupación de Intelectuales al			
Servicio de la República	23.1	15.4	13
Liberal Demócrata	100.0	50.0	2
Lliga	50.0	50.0	4
Agrario	83.3	45.8	24
Minoría Vasco Navarra	46.7	53.3	15
Independents	23.5	17.6	17
Monárquico Liberal	100.0	100.0	1
Others	50.0	50.0	2
All deputies	29.7	29.7	464

not return massively with the 1933 victory, with the exceptions of the so-called Agrarians. One of the most surprising and interesting findings, worthy of further exploration in electoral sociology, is the discontinuity in the parliamentary representation of the Radicals between 1931 and 1933—even ignoring the subsequent split between Lerroux and Martínez Barrios and the formation of the Radical Democratic Party. It would be important to know to what extent that discontinuity is a reflection of the electoral result or of the process of candidacy formation and the beginnings of crisis in that party, a crisis that culminated dramatically in its virtual disappearance in the 1936 legislature. This discontinuity in a party so central to the Latin Democracies, might be one of the key differences between the Spanish Republic and the Third French Republic, despite many similarities in the party system. The different fate of the two original parliamentary groups, the Left-bourgeois-reformist *Acción Republicana* and the ASR, in many sociological aspects so similar, reveals the importance of personal leadership in politics: of Azaña versus a group of individual personalities.

If we turn to the continuities between 1933 and 1936, we discover that the party system had crystallized considerably: more deputies (41.1%)

continued in the 1936 legislature. The continuity was greater in the victorious parties, with the notable exception of the PSOE, probably as a result of the crisis in that party and the opportunity to give preference to one or another candidate on the Popular Front ticket. From the data, the PNV benefited most from safe seats and few changes in leadership. Few of the men of the Right had been deputies in 1931 and one-half or less would return to the legislature in 1936. Nothing could better illustrate the difficulties in transforming the CEDA into an integrated and experienced parliamentary party than the fact that only 7.6% of its deputies had been parliamentarians in 1931, even when it was able to return 46% of its 1933 members again in 1936.

3.8. The Core Parliamentary Elite of the Republic

The data on the 71 parliamentarians who sat continuously in the Cortes highlight the occupational composition of the political leadership of the Republic, particularly when compared with those elected only once or even twice (Table 11.21). The dominance of the liberal professions is common to the three groups (49.3% among those elected once, 58.6% among those elected twice, and 56.3% among those elected three times). The lawyers make up respectively 32%, 45%, and 39.5%, while the physicians are less likely to be elected more than once. The larger representation of journalists and writers (respectively 6.7%, 9.6%, and 12.7%) stands out. The teaching professions constitute the next largest group, with 16.8% among those elected three times, 14.4% among those elected twice, and 9.8 among those elected once. The proportions of university or higher technical school-teachers were respectively 11.2%, 7.2%, and 4%. Civil servants and the military are most represented among those elected twice (14.4%), largely because the higher civil service was more represented on the benches of the Right in 1933, although they still constituted a significant group of the core elite, 9.8%. More surprising is the continuous presence (11.2%) of manual workers, which, however, is easily explained by the continuous trade union leadership representation in the ranks of the PSOE (in interpreting these figures, one should not forget the somewhat larger number for whom there is no information among those elected once or twice and the somewhat greater number reporting more than one occupation, among the 'Core' members).

3.9. Continuities after the Civil War

Although the electorate of the Right provided the civilian support for the Franco regime, not many of the legislators of the right would return to the Cortes created by Franco in 1943. Only 3.1% of the 992 elected to one of

Table 11.21. Occupation of legislators of the Second Republic elected once, twice, and three times

Occupation	Elected once		Elected twice		Elected three times	
	n	%	n	%	n	%
Lawyers	215	32.0	112	45.0	28	39.5
Medical Doctors	66	9.8	17	6.8	3	4.2
Engineers or architects	38	5.6	13	5.2	8	11.2
Other liberal professions	16	2.4	4	1.6	1	1.4
Journalists or writers	46	6.7	24	9.6	9	12.7
Total liberal professions		56.5		68.2		69.0
Schoolteachers	10	1.5	2	0.8	—	—
Other Teachers	17	2.5	6	2.4	2	2.8
Professors (high school)	13	1.9	9	3.6	2	2.8
Professors (university or technical school)	27	4.0	18	7.2	8	11.2
Total teaching		9.9		14.0		16.8
Clergymen	7	1.0	3	1.2	1	1.4
Elite civil service corps.	12	1.8	14	5.6	2	2.8
Civil service (university degree)	14	2.1	7	2.8	1	1.4
Lower-level civil service	9	1.3	6	2.4	—	—
Property registrars, *notarios*	16	2.4	4	1.6	1	1.4
Military officers	15	2.2	5	2.0	3	4.2
Total administrative sector		9.8		14.4		9.8
Businessmen	7	1.0	4	1.6	—	—
Merchants	22	3.3	3	1.2	2	1.4
Total entrepreneurs		4.3		2.8		2.8
Farmers	20	3.0	7	2.8	1	1.4
Owners	9	1.3	6	2.1	—	—
Farm labourers	3	0.4	—	—	—	—
Manual workers	51	7.6	20	8.0	8	11.2
Total working class		8.0				11.2
Middle-level technicians, white collar	25	3.7	9	3.6	—	—
No information	56	8.3	10	4.0	—	—
Total	671	100	250	100	71	100

Source: Calculations of the author based on official publications (see footnote 18).

the three Republican legislatures, most of them elected in 1933, sat in the non-democratic Cortes. The deputies that became *procuradores* were four *Tradicionalistas*, three from *Renovación*, and 17 from the CEDA—a small proportion considering the 153 that had sat on the CEDA benches and the 1979 *procuradores* between 1943 and 1967. Only three (Count Romanones, an independent monarchist, Count Rodezno, a Traditionalist, and Aizpun of the CEDA) had been members of the three legislatures. Of the 992 deputies, nine were ministers under Franco, four came from the CEDA, two from the *Traditionalistas*, and three from *Renovación*. The great toll of executions and assassinations of politicians on both sides of the political

spectrum and the exile of those of the left and some peripheral nationalists means that in 1977 few would return to political life and to the benches
of the first freely elected legislature after more than forty years. The time
elapsed was much longer than in Germany between 1932 and 1949 and even
Italy between the advent of Fascism and 1946.

4. THE NEW DEMOCRATIC PARLIAMENT OF POST-FRANCO SPAIN 1977–1996[26]

4.1. Transition to Democracy

Democracy returned to Spain in June 1977, with the celebration of free parliamentary elections for the first time since those held in February 1936
during the Second Republic. Franco had died in November 1975 and had
been succeeded by King Juan Carlos as Head of State. The transition to
democracy was basically completed between 15 December 1976 and 6
December 1978, dates of the two referendums for the *Ley para la Reforma
Política* (Law for the Political Reform) and for the present constitution.
Popular support for a democratic regime, after forty years of dictatorship,
had already been made clear in the first referendum called by Adolfo
Suárez, the young Head of Government appointed by the King scarcely five
months earlier. Turnout was over 75%, and 94% of votes were favourable.
The Law for the Political Reform—the draft of which had previously been
approved with a large majority by the old corporative Cortes of the
Francoist regime—defined the procedures and institutions for the installation of the new democracy. The new institutional design was meant to create
the conditions for political stability, by favouring a low fragmentation and
polarization of the party system and of the parliament (Gunther *et al.* 1986;
Linz and Montero 1986). Behind this also lay the fact that memories of the
tensions and instabilities of the one-chamber parliament of the Second
Republic and of its dramatic end were still very vivid (Carr and Fusi 1979;
Aguilar 1996).

The period since 1977 has been one of exceptional stability in the history
of Spanish democracy. The previous sections have reviewed the difficulties
faced by former attempts to democratize Spain, all of which ended in new
eras of repression, but in the last twenty-five years a full democracy has
finally developed. Civil liberties expanded in the mid-1970s and early 1980s,
guaranteeing for the first time in many decades basic democratic rights such
as freedom of speech and of assembly, or the rights to associate freely politi-

[26] The following analysis is restricted to the *Congreso de los Diputados*, the Lower Chamber.
The data have been gathered from the official publications of the Parliament for each legislature and confronted with the official data in their archives.

cally and to compete in open, contested political elections. This new democratic period involved the entrance of new people into the political arena. A new, younger generation took over and remained in power, first, under UCD (*Unión de Centro Democrático*) goverment, then with the PSOE (*Partido Socialista Obrero Español*).

In the new bicameral parliament, the electoral system chosen for the *Congreso de los Diputados* is a straightforward PR.[27] The number of seats for every district is in proportion to the district's population. The candidates have to present themselves in blocked and closed lists, including as many names as there are seats in the electoral district. Seats are assigned using the d'Hondt formula. This has a strong majoritarian effect in the small rural districts, while resulting in more proportional representation in the big urban districts.[28] As a result, large parties gain significantly more seats than their proportional share of the votes (see Table 11.22). Learning from the past, the laws passed during the Spanish transition were designed to favour the consolidation of a small number of strong, stable, highly developed party organizations at the national level, but also to enable the representation of regional parties in the national parliament. The result was in fact the emergence of two large national parties, one or two smaller ones, and several regional parties. Since 1977, seven general elections have taken place. The first two were won by a 'centrist' party, the UCD; the PSOE won the next four and remained in office from 1982 until 1996, when it was replaced by the Conservative Party, the PP (*Partido Popular*) (Liuz and Montero 2000).

4.2. General Profile of Deputies

In the last quarter of the twentieth century, Spanish deputies typically have been male, in their mid-forties, and usually lawyers, professors, teachers, or civil servants. Consequently, as some of the lawyers and most of the professors and teachers work for the state, the weight of the public sector among deputies is considerable. Many have had previous political and

[27] The Spanish electoral system has the strongest majoritarian effects of all proportional ones (Rae and Ramírez 1993). The proportionality of the 1977 electoral law is corrected given the relatively small size of the electoral districts, the closed and blocked lists, and the 3% threshold for obtaining representation in parliament.

[28] There is an overrepresentation of the large parties: this has benefited especially the two largest national parties and some of the regional parties. Besides the effects of the electoral system, there are other regulations that reinforce the stability of the largest parties of the party system. The laws on party funding provide public funds—at present the main source of party income—to the central party organization in accordance with its electoral results and seats, so that central co-ordination and discipline are favoured (Del Castillo 1985). It is also worth mentioning the early development of a 'sophisticated vote': Spaniards soon learnt to make their vote useful, i.e., to vote for the parties that had a greater chance of forming the government or of exerting direct opposition (Gunther *et al.* 1986). This has also helped greatly to promote the stability of the party system.

Table 11.22. The Spanish parties 1977–1996

Party	1977		1979		1982		1986		1989		1993		1996	
	Votes %	Seats % (n)	Votes %	Seats % (n)	Votes %	Seats % (n)	Votes %	Seats % (n)	Votes %	Seats % (n)	Votes %	Seats % (n)	Votes %	Seats % (n)
PCE/IU[1]	9.3	5.3 (20)	10.8	6.6 (23)	4.0	1.1 (4)	4.7	4.3 (7)	9.1	4.8 (17)	9.5	5.1 (18)	10.5	6.0 (21)
PSOE	29.3	33.7 (118)	30.4	34.6 (121)	48.1	57.7 (202)	44.1	52.6 (184)	39.6	50 (175)	38.8	45.4 (159)	37.3	40.3 (141)
AP/CP/PP[2]	8.8	4.6 (16)	6.0	2.6 (9)	26.4	30.6 (106)	26.0	30 (105)	25.8	30.6 (107)	34.8	40.3 (141)	38.6	44.6 (156)
UCD/CDS[3]	34.4	47.4 (166)	34.8	48 (168)	6.8	3.1 (14)	9.2	5.4 (19)	7.9	4 (14)	1.8	0	—	—
UDC/CIU[4]	0.9	0.3 (2)	2.7	2.3 (8)	3.7	3.4 (12)	5.0	5.1 (18)	5.0	5.1 (18)	4.9	4.8 (17)	4.6	4.6 (16)
PNV	1.6	2.3 (8)	1.6	2 (7)	1.9	2.3 (8)	1.5	1.7 (6)	1.2	1.4 (5)	1.2	1.4 (5)	1.3	1.4 (5)
Others	15.9	6.0 (21)	13.3	4 (14)	5.8	1.1 (4)	9.0	3.1 (11)	10.7	4 (14)	8.2	2.6 (9)	4.9	3.1 (11)
Total	100.0	(350)	100.0	(350)	100.0	(350)	100.0	(350)	100.0	(350)	100.0	(350)	100.0	(350)

Notes: [1] The Communist Party ran from 1986 together with other leftist parties under the *Izquierda Unida* label.
[2] *Alianza Popular* ran in coalition with Christian Democrats and liberals in 1979, 1982, and 1986. The party changed its name to *Partido Popular* in 1989.
[3] After the breakdown of UCD (*Unión de Centro Democrático*) its leader, Adolfo Suarez, created the *Centro Democratico y Social* (CDS) which took part in elections from 1986 until 1993.
[4] In 1977, there were only two deputies elected under the UDC label. In fact there was a a larger Catalan parliamentary group—13 deputies—most of them members of the *Pacte Democratic de Catalunya*. In the following elections, they were elected under the label of *Convergencia y Unió*.
Source: Heras (1997).

representative experience, mainly in the new democratic institutions but a considerable number also on different levels of the previous regime. Most have arrived in parliament after a career, both in the party ranks and at the local and regional elective levels. However, despite those similarities, there are significant variations over time and across parties.

A crucial feature of any parliament is the degree of stability of its membership. We have already stated in former sections of this chapter that a certain degree of continuity is a prerequisite for a fully functioning democracy. A certain degree of continuity allows legislators to 'develop the informal relations across party lines so that the continuous contacts in the halls and lobbies of a parliament can provide the chance to become fully acquainted with the legislative process' (Linz 1972: 394). Too little renovation is, on the contrary, a sign of oligarchic tendencies inside political parties and also of the closeness of their political elites to social change (ibid).

One of the possible measures of continuity of the parliamentary personnel is to count the percentage of parliamentarians that survive from one legislature to the next. In five out of six elections, the percentage of re-election for Spanish deputies was over 50% (Table 11.23). The only exception was 1982, when only around one-third of the outgoing deputies were re-elected. As we will see in the sections devoted to individual party profiles, this low rate was due to the collapse of one of the major parties and to the success of others. The dramatic crisis of the UCD, which brought it directly from government to destruction, produced a major discontinuity in the recent democratic history of Spain and induced the low survival of 1982 deputies (Morán 1989, 1996).

It has been said previously in this chapter that Spanish deputies are predominantly male. However, it must be noticed that, especially since 1989, a remarkable growth in the presence of women in the Spanish Parliament has taken place. The percentage of women among MPs has increased more than threefold since the beginning of democracy (from 5.9% in 1977, to 21.6% in 1996; Table 11.23).[29] This increase, starting in 1986, could be considered as a natural consequence of the changing role of Spanish women in society as a whole, and of their growing integration in the labour market. However, other cases, such as the United Kingdom, France, or the United States, which have even larger percentages of female workers but at the same time a comparatively low presence of women in the parliamentary arena, indicate that an increase in the percentage of women in politics is not an automatic outcome of the evolution of the economic role of women.[30] Why, then,

---

[29] The percentage of women politicians has also increased at regional and local level (López Nieto 1994; Uriarte and Elizondo 1997).

[30] The world average percentage of women in Parliament was 10.10% in 1994 (data from the Interparliamentary Union). In Great Britain, the figure for women MPs was only 12% in

Table 11.23. Survival rates, percentages of women, and age 1977–1996

Features	1977		1979		1982		1986		1989		1993		1996	
	%	n	%	n	%	n	%	n	%	n	%	n	%	n
Survival rates			52.8		36.4		70.9		51.1		64.5		53.3	
Females	5.9	21	5.4	19	5.6	21	8.4	33	14.0	49	15.6	55	21.6	75
Age groups														
Up to 29	6.2	22	4.3	15	2.4	8	3.0	10	0.6	2	0.3	1	1.4	5
30–9	33.5	119	40.4	141	34.9	114	29.0	98	26.3	92	17.6	62	19.0	66
40–9	31.5	112	34.4	120	32.1	105	42.9	145	47.7	167	48.9	172	45.1	157
50–9	18.6	66	13.2	46	22.6	74	21.0	71	22.3	78	27.8	98	27	94
60–9	8.5	30	5.4	19	6.7	22	3.0	10	2.3	8	5.1	18	7.5	26
70 or more	1.7	6	2.3	8	1.2	4	1.2	4	0.9	3	0.3	1	0.0	0
Mean age (years)	44.1		43.0		44.7		44.1		44.7		46.6		46.6	

Source: Own calculations on data published by the Chamber.

this sharp increase in Spain? Recent research on recruitment patterns in Spanish political parties points to selection at local level and at the effects of multimember districts as the factors favouring these changes in parliamentary recruitment (Uriarte and Elizondo 1997). Spanish women have become a strategic sector of the electorate that parties are trying to attract. Feminist lobbies have developed in the main political parties, ensuring the inclusion of female issues on their political agendas. Their gradualist strategy is proving successful. The inclusion of a greater number of women in the lists of candidates, the introduction in the late 1980s of gender quotas—formally in the PSOE and *Izquierda Unida* (IU), informally in AP/PP—as well as the increasing visibility of women during electoral campaigns—are symptoms of the new strategies by Spanish political parties aimed at attracting the female vote.

With regard to the age of deputies, there has been very little variation in the mean (approximately 46 years) over time, but there have been significant changes in the distribution of age groups. In the first two legislatures, around three-quarters of deputies were younger than 50 years and in the last two legislatures the same proportion applies to the age group between 40 and 59.The politicians who led the transition to democracy and its consolidation were in comparative terms very young, most of them being in their thirties and forties. However, as in the Restoration, young did not equal radical; young Spanish politicians, from both the Right and the Left, have proved to be responsible leaders. By the end of the 1990s, most deputies were in their forties and fifties, thus becoming more akin to the parliamentarians of other European countries. The transition from Francoism to democracy had also involved a generational replacement, bringing a group of young politicians from the UCD and the PSOE to govern the country. The electoral victory of the conservative PP in 1996 involved another generational change: the Felipe González generation, in its mid-fifties, was replaced by the Aznar generation, a decade younger.

We have seen the dominance of the juridical professions in Spanish parliaments throughout the century, with civil servants being the second most represented category during the Restoration period and that in 1916 the two groups combined accounted for up to half of the Chamber. During the Second Republic, lawyers continued to be the most represented group, with an average share of the Chamber of 34.8 from 1931 to 1936, although there were fewer civil servants (only 6.9%) than before. In the new democracy, the importance of lawyers, and of university professors and school-teachers, is quite evident (Table 11.24). The third main group is that of civil servants: the importance of the public sector is even more evident when we consider that professors and teachers are, with few exceptions, state

1997, in France even lower: 8.6%. Spain's figures are also above the EU average of 17.1% (European Commission 1998).

Table 11.24. Occupation 1977–1996

Occupation	1977		1979		1982		1986		1989		1993		1996	
	%	n	%	n	%	n	%	n	%	n	%	n	%	n
Lawyers	28.2	97	20.8	71	17.5	42	21.5	68	14.6	47	16.5	50	19.0	57
Other professions	13.7	47	11.4	39	12.4	39	13.9	44	12.1	39	10.9	33	9.3	28
High civil servants	5.8	20	15.0	51	12.4	39	7.3	23	5.9	19	6.9	21	15.7	47
Other civil servants	2.3	8	2.6	9	2.5	8	3.8	12	8.4	27	9.6	29	9.7	29
University professors	10.2	35	18.5	63	18.5	58	17.4	55	14.9	48	17.2	52	15.0	45
Other teachers	6.4	22	7.0	24	9.6	30	12.0	38	13.7	44	13.9	42	17.0	51
Managers	1.7	6	5.9	20	9.2	29	7.9	25	1.9	6	3.6	11	3.0	9
Entrepreneurs	3.8	13	1.5	5	3.5	11	2.5	8	2.5	8	1.7	5	2.0	6
White-collar workers	5.8	20	4.7	16	2.5	8	0.9	3	1.9	6	2.3	7	0.7	2
Blue-collar workers	10.2	35	5.0	17	3.8	12	6.0	19	7.1	23	4.0	12	5.0	15
Primary sector	2.3	8	2.1	7	1.9	6	2.2	7	3.1	10	3.0	9	1.0	3
Others	9.6	33	5.6	19	6.1	19	4.4	14	14.0	45	10.6	32	2.7	8

Note: Percentages are based on known cases.

Source: Own calculations on data published by the *Congreso de los Diputados*.

employees. Another significant group among deputies is that of professionals with a non-juridical education, such as doctors, engineers, and so on. All these groups taken together account for between two-thirds and three-quarters of the chamber. Although still significant, the legal profession, which we have seen to be the predominant occupation throughout the nineteenth and twentieth centuries, is in this period at its historical lowest. The main new feature to be noticed in this democratic period is the constant growth in the share of school teachers; in twenty years, their weight has almost tripled. The strong presence of lawyers, civil servants, teachers, and professors is linked to the compatibility of their occupations with a parliamentary mandate, particularly the possibility of their rejoining their profession after their time in parliament (Linz 1972). The suitability of their skills to the parliamentary job is another factor. On the other hand, the percentage of entrepreneurs, blue- and white-collar workers,[31] and primary sector workers has been small during the whole period under study; moreover, the weight of these groups taken together has gradually but substantially declined (from 22.1% in 1977 to only 8.7% in 1996).

4.3. Parliamentary Groups and Parties

Underneath the general picture traced above, major differences can be found when we compare the deputies of the main parliamentary groups from the beginning of the new democracy; namely: UCD, PSOE, PP, and PCE/IU and of the two most important regional parties, CiU (*Convergencia i Unió*) of Catalunia and the PNV (*Partido Nacionalista Vasco*) of the Basque region. The main differences between them are concerned with the renewal rates of the parliamentary groups (electoral successes and failures have had an obvious impact here) and with the occupational background of the parliamentarians.[32]

The UCD is quite a unique case of a party that went directly from government to destruction. It was founded in 1977, shortly before the general elections, by the leaders of several small parties of different ideologies (Christian Democrats, Liberals, Social Democrats, Regionalists) who agreed to join forces under the banner of the UCD and the leadership of the Prime Minister Adolfo Suárez.[33] Among the leaders of these heterogeneous groups, some had been on the side of the democratic opposition to

---

[31] The reduction in the percentage of workers is linked to an internal rule of the Spanish Trade Unions, making it incompatible since the III Legislature (1986–1989) to hold a representative mandate in a Union and in Parliament simultaneously.

[32] The unit of analysis is the parliamentary group. The number of deputies is in some of the tables larger than the number of deputies in the parliamentary groups because substitutes (taking the place of a retired or dead MP) have been included when possible.

[33] Adolfo Suárez had been Minister Secretary of the *Movimiento* in the first Cabinet after the death of Franco.

the dictatorship, while others on the contrary had occupied administrative or political positions in the Franco regime.[34] The prestige of the Head of Government and the image of his party as a 'centrist' formation, connected well with the basic moderation and apathy of a large part of the electorate. The initial platform of the UCD had as its central point the means by which Spain should achieve democracy, that is, by gradual reform negotiated among the leaders of the different political parties,[35] and also the institutional design for the new regime. The UCD was in government between 1977 and 1982.

From the very beginning, the UCD suffered from internal conflicts, mainly between the group supporting Adolfo Suárez and the rest of the party, and particularly concerning the preparation of electoral lists whereby quotas of candidates were assigned to each of the internal groups. These quotas were always a cause of serious conflict, especially as there continued to be a strong presence of the 'independents', the group of MPs that supported Adolfo Suárez: for example, in 1977 they represented 54% of the UCD candidates for the *Congreso* (Huneeus 1985). The party managed to remain united only until the second legislature. After it had led a successful transition to democracy and the basic goals which had been agreed upon had been achieved, the UCD was dissolved, victim of its internal struggles and the several splits which had taken place in 1980. The collapse of the UCD, and the disappearance of most of its deputies in 1982, resulted in a major discontinuity for the young Spanish democracy. In 1979, more than half of the UCD deputies had been re-elected (94 out of 170); but in 1982, only 10 (5.6%) of the original deputies survived. In 1986, of the UCD deputies elected in 1977, only two remained in the CP parliamentary group. In this or following elections, some of the original deputies of the UCD returned to the *Congreso*, either in the ranks of the Conservative Party (eight in 1986 and 1989, nine in 1993, and eight in 1996) or in those of the CDS (*Centro Democrático y Social*)[36]—three in 1986 and one in 1989. Thus, the politicians from the party that had led the transition process to democracy largely disappeared from the political arena after 1982.

Among UCD deputies, the share of women was quite close to the average for the Chamber as a whole in 1977 and 1979, but was reduced to zero in 1982 when the size of the parliamentary group was drastically reduced

---

[34] For a detailed analysis of the party families, see Hopkin (1995). Other sources for the UCD are De Esteban and López Guerra (1982), Huneeus (1985), Gunther *et al.* (1986), and Linz and Montero (1986).

[35] The leaders of the parties that formed the UCD had agreed on the ideas advanced in the former few years by a group of moderate opposition to the Francoist regime called Tácito. This group gathered regularly and published several articles offering their views about the road to and the general features of the new democratic regime (Tácito 1975).

[36] The CDS, which was the Centrist party founded before the 1982 elections by Adolfo Suárez once he had resigned from office, obtained good electoral results in the 1986 and 1989 general elections, but disappeared from parliament in 1993.

Table 11.25. General features of UCD MPs 1977–1982

Features	1977		1979		1982	
	%	n	%	n	%	n
Survival rates		170	55.3	94	5.6	10
Females	4.2	7	6.0	10	0.0	
Age groups						
Up to 29	2.4	4	1.8	3	—	—
30–9	33.3	55	35.1	59	*	1
40–9	39.4	65	45.2	76	*	4
50–9	19.4	32	13.7	23	*	4
60–9	5.5	9	2.4	4	*	2
70 or more	—	—	1.8	3	—	—
Occupation						
Lawyers	35.0	56	22.2	37	*	2
Other professions	14.4	23	9.6	16	*	1
High civil servants	7.5	12	22.8	38	*	5
Other civil servants	3.1	5	3.0	5	—	—
University professors	8.1	13	15.0	25	*	1
Other teachers	4.4	7	6.0	10	—	—
Managers	3.1	5	9.0	15	*	2
Entrepreneurs	5.0	8	1.8	3	—	—
White-collar workers	0.6	1	—	—	—	—
Blue-collar workers	8.1	13	3.0	5	—	—
Primary sector	1.3	2	1.2	2	—	—
Others	9.4	15	6.6	11	—	—

Note: * Total n too low to calculate percentages. Percentages are based on known cases.

Source: Own calculations on data published by the *Congreso de los Diputados.*

(Table 11.25). The party ceased to exist before the general increase of women deputies in parliament took place. In 1977 and 1979, approximately three-quarters of the Centrist deputies were below the age of 50, while in 1982 the mean age of the few survivors, obviously those candidates placed first on the lists, was somewhat greater. The UCD deputies of 1977 and 1979 were professionally more experienced than the average for the Chamber. In the first two legislatures, the UCD had the highest percentage of lawyers (35% in 1977 and 22.2% in 1979), and twice the average percentage of high civil servants (in 1979, 22.8%). This figure would be even larger if we took into account the fact that some of the deputies coded as lawyers were *abogados del Estado*, that is, also civil servants. In total, lawyers, civil servants, and members of the teaching professions accounted for more than two-thirds of the Centrist parliamentary group. These figures are higher than for any other parliamentary group at any time, confirming the profile of UCD deputies as young, but well qualified in the field of state and legal affairs.

The Socialist Party[37] is an interesting example of a successful party that has experienced a significant degree of continuity in its political leadership since 1977, but also some relevant changes in the profile of its parliamentary group. When the transition to democracy started, by European standards, the PSOE was still a rather radical Socialist Party, defending Marxist ideals. Just a few years earlier, a group of young politicians under Felipe González had gained control of the party, which until then had remained in the hands of the exiled leaders of the 1940s. This group, to date, has remained in control of the party.

The PSOE was the main opposition party after the first two general elections, was in office between 1982 and 1996, and returned to being the principal opposition party in 1996. During this period, continuity in the parliamentary group prevailed with more than half of the Socialist deputies maintaining their seats. The highest figure (70.6%) occurred in 1982, when, in an election marked by high political discontinuity for the chamber as a whole, the PSOE gained office (Table 11.26). The basic continuity of the PSOE parliamentary group has been the result of the stability of the leading core of the party since the beginning of the 1970s. This is supported by the fact that, despite the passage of time, as many as 22.5% of the Socialist deputies elected in 1989, and 18.3% of those elected in 1993, had already been members of the 1977 legislature. Only when the party lost the general elections in 1996 did the size of the original cohort drop to 10.8%.

The increase in the mean age of the Socialist parliamentarians during this period is striking. In the 1970s, the youth of the leaders of PSOE was reflected in the overall parliamentary group: in 1977, 57% of the deputies were younger than 40 and in 1979 the share of this age group was even larger (64%). In addition, the mean age of PSOE deputies was considerably lower than that of the chamber. By 1996, however, less than 15% of the Socialist deputies were younger than 40, while most were between 40 and 60, thus approaching the average for the whole chamber and also coming closer in terms of age to the representatives of the other European countries. Here we have a very clear and strong cohort effect: thanks to the substantial continuity of the parliamentary personnel, the ageing of the whole parliamentary group is to a great extent the consequence of the ageing of the politicians of the 'democratic transition cohort'.

Regarding gender, the percentage of women in the PSOE has been lower than the average, being 4.2% in 1979 and 7.1% in 1986. In the second half of the 1980s, a policy of positive discrimination was adopted by PSOE. This was initially an informal agreement but soon became a formal internal rule. The first quota, although never totally respected, was that 25% of

[37] For the sources for the history of PSOE, see Martín Najera (1991), Tezanos (1983, 1992).

Table 11.26. General features of Socialist MPs 1977–1996

Features	1977 %	1977 n	1979 %	1979 n	1982 %	1982 n	1986 %	1986 n	1989 %	1989 n	1993 %	1993 n	1996 %	1996 n
Survival rates			61		70.6		59		57.4		67.1		51.8	
Females	8.5	10	4.2	5	6.9	14	7.1	13	17.7	31	17.6	28	27.0	38
Age groups														
Up to 29	12.0	14	8.3	10	3.3	6	2.8	5	1.1	2	0.0	—	1.4	2
30–9	41.9	49	55.0	66	45.7	84	33.1	59	26.3	46	13.2	21	12.8	18
40–9	21.4	25	23.3	28	39.7	73	51.7	92	57.1	100	59.7	95	51.1	72
50–9	12.0	9	8.3	10	9.8	18	10.1	18	13.1	23	23.3	37	30.5	43
60–9	11.0	12	3.3	4	1.1	2	1.1	2	1.1	2	3.1	5	4.3	6
70 or more	1.8	2	1.7	2	0.5	1	1.1	2	1.1	2	0.6	1	0.0	—
Occupation														
Lawyers	21.1	24	20.0	23	15.3	27	13.5	23	9.4	15	8.9	12	11.7	14
Professions	11.4	13	16.5	19	12.5	22	16.3	28	10.6	17	10.4	14	10.0	12
High civil servants	2.6	3	5.2	6	9.1	16	7.6	13	3.1	5	5.9	8	11.7	14
Other civil servants	1.8	2	3.5	4	3.4	6	5.9	10	8.8	14	10.4	14	13.3	16
University professors	14.9	17	21.7	25	23.3	41	21.8	37	18.8	30	23.7	32	23.3	28
Other teachers	7.0	8	9.6	11	15.3	27	16.3	28	17.5	28	18.5	25	20.0	24
Managers	0.9	1	1.7	2	3.4	6	4.1	7	1.9	3	2.2	3	0.8	1
Entrepreneurs	1.8	2	0.0	—	0.0	—	0.0	—	0.0	—	0.0	—	0.0	—
White-collar workers	12.3	14	7.8	9	3.4	6	1.2	2	3.8	6	4.4	6	0.8	1
Blue-collar workers	14.9	17	8.7	10	5.7	10	8.8	15	8.8	6	4.4	6	6.7	8
Primary	2.6	3	2.6	3	2.8	5	1.2	2	0.6	2	1.5	2	0.0	—
Others	8.8	10	2.6	3	5.7	10	2.9	5	16.9	13	9.6	13	1.7	2

Note: Percentages are based on known cases.

Source: Own calculations on data published by the *Congreso de los Diputados*.

candidates should be female. Thus there was a sharp increase in 1989, when the 17.7% level was reached. That figure has been increasing slowly over time, resulting in a growth in the percentage of women in parliament. By 1996, it had reached 27.0%.

Socialist deputies, besides having grown older, have also changed from the point of view of their occupational profile, and if their occupations in 1977 and 1979 are compared with the rest of the Chamber, some clear differences become evident. Among Socialist deputies, consistent with the leftist character of the party, there were significantly more workers, both white and blue collar, than the average. There were also fewer lawyers, high civil servants, managers, and entrepreneurs. With the passage of time, the percentage of blue-collar workers has substantially declined, while the teaching professions have experienced a spectacular increase, attaining more than 40% of the parliamentary group in 1996. The share of civil servants has also grown. Overall, one can say that the occupational profile of the Socialist group has gradually become much more similar to that of the parliament as a whole.

The current *Partido Popular* (PP) was formerly named *Alianza Popular* (AP)[38] and competed as an electoral coalition of *Coalición Democrática* (CD) and *Coalición Popular* (CP) in the general elections before 1989. Two different moments can be seen as turning-points in AP's history. In 1982, after the collapse of the UCD, AP became the largest opposition party in Spain. While in the first two democratic elections, AP had won little support (8.3% of the votes in 1977 and 6.0% in 1979), the party made spectacular progress in 1982 (obtaining 26.5% of the votes, and 105 seats), thereby becoming the second most voted for party. By 1986, despite this upward trend, there was a widespread belief that the leadership of Manuel Fraga Iribarne, formerly a minister and diplomat during the dictatorship, imposed an 'electoral ceiling' on AP, which prevented it from winning elections (Montero 1989). To solve this impasse, in 1986 AP embarked on a renovation of its top leadership that was only successfully completed by 1989, when Manuel Fraga suggested José María Aznar to the party's Congress as candidate for Prime Minister. At the same time, AP changed its name to PP and entered the European Popular Party. Once it was confirmed that Aznar, a young but experienced politician as a regional President—and also without links with Francoism—was able to maintain at least the previous electoral results, he was elected President of the PP at the Seville Congress in 1990, while Fraga chose to devote himself to Galician politics.

José María Aznar heightened the renovation of the PP's political elites, by integrating younger politicians into the party, and by conclusively breaking with the PP's former identification with Francoism. He and his team

---

[38] For the history of AP/PP, see López Nieto (1988; 1994), also Montero (1989).

were also able to put an end to the constant internal struggles that had characterized the earlier history of this party. Finally, under his leadership, after having defeated the PSOE in the 1994 European elections and in the local and regional elections of 1995, the PP won the 1996 general election. These changes had a major impact on the conservative deputies, as is amply revealed by their age (Table 11.27). In 1977 and 1979, in a chamber filled with the young politicians of the other parties, AP's small parliamentary group was mainly formed by people of more mature years (14 out of 16 in 1977, and all in 1979 were older than 50). By 1982, the enlarged parliamentary group had some deputies younger than 40, and more than one-third under 50, although the largest cohort was still between 50 and 59 years. By 1989, the largest single group was of deputies between 40 and 49 years, but overall 65% of deputies were younger than 50, evidencing a new parliamentary profile in tune with that of the new party leaders. As of 1996, the PP has the youngest parliamentary group among the parties studied, with nearly a quarter of the deputies younger than 40.

The survival rate of AP deputies was also affected by the important elite renewals that took place in the 1980s. In 1989, only 15.8% of the deputies elected in 1982 remained and only 7% of the 1982 deputies are currently in the PP group in the *Congreso* which was elected in 1996. A large turnover of AP deputies took place in 1986; in an election when the survival rate for the chamber was 70.9 per cent, only 39.9 of the 1982 deputies of AP managed to maintain their seat. After this deep renewal, in the 1990s there has been a much more stable parliamentary group, with rates of survival above the average (71% in 1993 and 64.4% in 1996). The representation of women has followed the general trend of growth but has lagged somewhat behind the average for the *Congreso* as a whole. This party did not introduce formal quotas for women candidates, which might account for the comparatively lower figures of female deputies. However, women have gained a higher visibility in the electoral campaigns and the governments of the 1990s. The distribution of occupational backgrounds has remained rather stable over time. More or less one-third of the deputies come from the legal and other independent professions. The civil service, and especially its top echelons, provide another significant recruiting ground. The teaching professions play a less important role than in the other main parties, as one would expect for a party that does not show any particular sympathy for intellectuals. Consistent with the party ideology, there has been very little representation of primary sector, blue-collar, or white-collar workers. It is interesting to note that managers and entrepreneurs had a rather significant role in the 1980s; but since then their importance has declined. Can we interpret this as a sign that the broader appeal developed by its new leadership has entailed some distancing from an originally more 'classist' connotation of the party?

Table 11.27. General features of AP/PP MPs 1977–1996

Features	1977 %	n	1979 %	n	1982 %	n	1986 %	n	1989 %	n	1993 %	n	1996 %	n
Survival rates			67.7		58.7		39.9		42.9		71		64.4	
Females	6.3	1	11.1	1	1.9	2	7.6	8	9.4	10	14.9	21	14.7	23
Age groups														
Up to 29			—				2.9	3	0.0	—	0.7	1	1.9	3
30–9	12.5	2	*	1	15.1	13	25.2	26	24.5	26	21.3	30	23.7	37
40–9	87.5	14	*	6	20.9	18	31.4	32	40.6	43	41.1	58	37.8	59
50–9					44.2	38	32.4	33	30.2	32	28.4	40	26.9	42
60–9			*	2	19.8	17	6.9	7	4.7	5	8.5	12	9.6	15
70 or more					0.0	—	1.0	1	0.0	—	0.0	—	0.0	—
Occupation														
Lawyers	26.7	4	—	—	20.7	18	28.7	27	19.0	19	25.2	31	24.8	34
Professions	13.3	2	—	—	12.6	11	10.6	10	14.0	14	10.6	13	9.5	13
High civil servants	20.0	3	*	4	17.2	15	10.6	10	12.0	12	8.9	11	19.7	27
Other civil servants	—		—		1.1	1	1.1	1	8.0	8	9.8	12	7.3	10
University professors	20.0	3	*	2	13.8	12	10.6	10	13.0	13	12.2	15	10.2	14
Other teachers	6.7	1	*	1	2.3	2	7.4	7	10.0	10	8.1	10	9.5	13
Managers	—	—	—		14.9	13	14.9	14	1.0	1	5.7	7	5.8	8
Entrepreneurs	—	—	*	1	11.5	10	8.5	8	6.0	6	3.3	4	2.9	4
White-collar workers	—	—	—		—		—		—		0.8	1	—	
Blue-collar workers	—		0.0	—	0.0	—	1.1	1	5.0	5	2.4	3	4.4	6
Primary	—		0.0	—	1.1	1	1.1	1	5.0	5	3.3	4	2.2	3
Others	13.3	2	0.0	—	4.6	4	5.3	5	7.0	7	9.8	12	3.6	5

Note: *Total n too low to calculate percentages. Percentages are based on known cases.

Source: Own calculations on data published by the *Congreso de los Diputados*.

The Spanish Communist Party (PCE), now integrated as part of United Left (*Izquierda Unida*: IU), had been severely repressed during Francoism because of its active role of opposition to the dictatorship.[39] Because of this activism under Franco and in the final stage of the dictatorship and their moderation during the transition, the leaders of the PCE had great hopes of winning second place in the 1977 elections. The results in the first and second general elections (9.4% and 10.8% of the votes, respectively) dashed any such hopes, and plunged the party into a long period of internal crisis. The turning-point for the PCE came in the early 1980s; in 1982, the party obtained the lowest result of the period (4.0% of the vote, and only four deputies) and in 1983 the party's historical leader, Santiago Carrillo, left the formal direction of the party to his young supporter Gerardo Iglesias, a former mineworker. Iglesias reacted against the personalization of leadership and the excesses of discipline of the former period, which had resulted in frequent internal turmoils. Between 1983 and 1985, the PCE went through new internal struggles between the factions, supporting the former and new leaders. A second turning-point came in 1986. For the parliamentary elections of that year, the PCE had joined an electoral coalition with other leftist groups which, after the improved electoral result (seven deputies and 4.6% of the vote) became the new party of *Izquierda Unida* (IU). In 1988, Julio Anguita, a successful politician in Andalusia, was elected Secretary General of the PCE and 'General Coordinator' of IU. These internal changes have had an impact upon continuity within the Communist parliamentary group. The most dramatic example of this can be seen in 1986, when none of the 1982 deputies survived to sit in the new *Congreso* (Table 11.28). IU has in fact proved more stable. The survival rate since 1989 is slightly higher than average; yet a gradual renewal has been ensured by the internal rule limiting the number of representative mandates to two.

The PCE was originally led by old, exiled politicians, but in the 1980s a new political generation came to the fore. Indeed, the age structure of the parliamentary group reflects very vividly the changes undergone by the party. While in 1977 and 1979 about 40% of the deputies were over 60, by 1986 only one of this age group was left, and by 1996, 75% were younger than 50. Concerning the representation of women in parliament, after a rather strong beginning in 1977 there is a decline, linked probably to the internal problems of the party. However, after 1986 there is a very strong growth which has led IU to the forefront in this field: 33.3% in 1996 is the historical peak of female deputies in Spain. IU was also the first party formally to introduce an internal rule that prohibited the representation of either gender being lower than 35%, and has gradually increased this quota over

---

[39] For the PCE history, see Mujal-León (1983), Hermet (1972), Claudín (1983).

Table 11.28. General features of PCE/IU MPs 1977–1996

Features	1977 %	1977 n	1979 %	1979 n	1982 %	1982 n	1986 %	1986 n	1989 %	1989 n	1993 %	1993 n	1996 %	1996 n
Survival rates	77.7		—		10.0		0.0		42.8		52.9		42.8	
Females	15.8	3	9.1	2	0.0	—	0.0	—	11.8	2	22.2	4	33.3	7
Age groups														
Up to 29	10.5	2	4.5	1	—	—	—	—	—	—	—	—	—	—
30–9	21.1	4	22.7	5	—	—	16.7	1	29.4	5	16.7	3	19.0	4
40–9	10.5	2	18.2	4	—	—	50.0	3	47.1	8	50.0	9	57.1	12
50–9	15.8	3	18.2	4	*	1	16.7	1	23.5	4	33.3	6	19.0	4
60–9	36.8	7	36.4	8	*	2	—	—	—	—	—	—	4.8	1
70 or more	5.3	1	—	—	—	—	16.7	1	—	—	—	—	—	—
Occupation														
Lawyers	5.6	1	4.8	1	—	—	*	1	20.0	3	12.5	2	22.2	4
Professions	16.7	3	4.8	1	—	—	—	—	20.0	3	18.8	3	5.6	1
High civil servants	—	—	9.5	2	—	—	—	—	—	—	6.3	1	11.1	2
Other civil servants	5.6	1	—	—	—	—	—	—	*	1	6.3	1	11.1	2
University professors	5.6	1	19.0	4	—	—	*	2	—	—	18.8	3	5.6	1
Other teachers	—	—	9.5	2	—	—	*	1	*	4	25.0	4	27.8	5
Managers	—	—	—	—	—	—	*	—	—	—	—	—	—	—
Entrepreneurs	5.6	1	4.8	1	*	1	*	—	—	—	—	—	—	—
White-collar workers	5.6	1	23.8	5	—	—	—	—	—	—	6.3	1	5.6	1
Blue-collar workers	22.2	4	4.8	1	—	—	20.0	1	—	—	—	—	5.6	1
Primary	11.1	2	19.0	4	0.0	—	0.0	—	*	1	6.3	1	5.6	1
Others	27.8	5	—	—	0.0	2	0.0	—	*	3	—	—	—	—

Note: *Total n too low to calculate percentages. Percentages are based on known cases.

Source: Own calculations on data published by the *Congreso de los Diputados*.

time. With regard to occupational background, some significant transformations have to be underlined. While in the first two parliamentary terms, the weight of white- and blue-collar workers and of agricultural labourers was substantial, in more recent years they have practically disappeared. On the contrary, teachers, civil servants, and, which is more striking, lawyers too, have been on the rise. The strong working-class associations of the past have faded away.

The *Convergencia i Unió* (CiU) and the *Partido Nacionalista Vasco* (PNV)[40] are the two most important regional parties as far as the national party system is concerned. Both, besides obtaining large electoral successes in their own Autonomous Communities, have also gained enough seats in the national parliament to become important strategic players in the national arena. Their support has guaranteed the stability, first of UCD governments, then of those of the PSOE and PP when these parties could not gain an absolute majority at general elections.[41]

CiU is the nationalist, moderate centre-right coalition that has dominated political life in Catalonia (Molas 1998). It was formed by two parties, the *Convergència Democràtica de Catalunya* and the *Unió Democrática de Catalunya*, that agreed in 1978 to form an electoral coalition which has proved to be very successful (Marcet 1987). CiU has been the dominant party in regional elections (Pallarés and Font 1995)[42] and its leader, Jordi Pujol, has been the President of the *Generalitat*—the Catalonian government—continuously since 1980. CiU has been able to form its own parliamentary groups in the national parliament since 1979.[43] In 1993 and 1996 when the PSOE and the PP, respectively, lacked an absolute majority in parliament, the parliamentarians of CiU provided the support required to form a government. In return, Jordi Pujol successfully negotiated special concessions for Catalonia regarding the development of regional autonomy and of financial resources (Pallarés and Font 1995).

PNV, a nationalist, Centre-Right party, received the most votes in the first regional parliamentary elections in 1980, since then becoming the party in government of the Basque Autonomous Community. However, given the well-known polarized pluralism of the Basque party system, the PNV has had to form coalitions with other nationalist parties or with the PSOE to form the regional government (Llera 1994). At national level, the PNV, after

[40] For CiU, see Marcet (1987) and Molas (1988). For the PNV, see Llera (1994, 1999).

[41] The PSOE gained an absolute majority of votes in the general elections of 1982, 1986, and 1989. It was necessary to pact with the nationalist parties in all the other legislatures in order to assure a stable parliamentary support for the government policies.

[42] Since the 1984 regional elections, Catalan voters have largely practised a 'dual vote'. Almost one out of six voters has alternated his or her vote for a national party in the general elections and for a nationalist party in the autonomous elections (Pallarés and Font 1995). The electoral competition is based on getting the vote of the central part of the electorate (Molas 1992).

[43] For 1977, the deputies in Congress ran under the *Pacte Democratic per Catalunya* (PDC).

Table 11.29. General features of CIU MPs 1977–1996

Features	1977 %	1977 n	1979 %	1979 n	1982 %	1982 n	1986 %	1986 n	1989 %	1989 n	1993 %	1993 n	1996 %	1996 n
Survival rates	—	—	62.5	5	25.0	3	38.8	7	50.0	9	64.7	11	31.3	5
Females	—	—	12.5	1	—	—	5.6	1	5.6	1	5.9	1	25.0	4
Age groups														
Up to 29	*	1	—	—	—	—	5.0	1	—	—	—	—	—	—
30–9	*	2	*	2	*	4	17.6	3	33.3	6	17.6	3	25.0	3
40–9	*	7	*	6	*	3	41.2	7	33.3	6	35.3	6	50.0	6
50–9	*	2	—	—	*	4	35.3	6	33.3	6	47.1	8	12.5	2
60–9	*	1	—	—	—	—	—	—	—	—	—	—	12.5	2
70 or more	—	—	—	—	—	—	—	—	—	—	—	—	—	—
Occupation														
Lawyers	*	5	*	1	*	4	37.5	6	33.3	6	28.6	4	15.4	2
Other professions	*	2	*	1	*	1	6.3	1	5.6	1	14.3	2	15.4	2
High civil servants	—	—	—	—	—	—	—	—	—	—	—	—	7.7	1
Other civil servants	—	—	—	—	—	—	6.3	1	5.6	1	—	—	7.7	1
University professors	*	3	*	3	*	1	12.5	2	11.1	2	7.1	1	15.4	2
Other teachers	*	1	—	—	—	—	6.3	1	5.6	1	14.3	2	30.8	4
Managers	—	—	*	2	*	2	12.5	2	5.6	1	—	—	7.7	1
Entrepreneurs	*	1	*	1	*	1	18.8	3	16.7	3	14.3	2	—	—
White-collar workers	*	2	—	—	—	—	—	—	—	—	—	—	—	—
Blue-collars	*	1	—	—	—	—	—	—	—	—	—	—	—	—
Primary	—	—	—	—	—	—	—	—	—	—	—	—	—	—
Other	—	—	—	—	18.2	2	—	—	16.7	3	21.4	3	—	—

Note: * Total n too low to calculate percentages. Percentages are based on known cases.

Source: Own calculations on data published by the *Congreso de los Diputados*.

Table 11.30. General features of PNV MPs 1977–1996

Features	1977 %	1977 n	1979 %	1979 n	1982 %	1982 n	1986 %	1986 n	1989 %	1989 n	1993 %	1993 n	1996 %	1996 n
Survival rates	—	—	71.4	5	37.5	3	33.3	2	40.0	2	40.0	2	40.0	2
Females	—	—	—	—	25.0	2	—	—	—	—	—	—	20.0	1
Age groups														
Up to 29	*	—	*	1	—	—	—	—	—	—	—	—	—	—
30–9	*	3	*	4	*	3	*	3	*	1	*	3	*	4
40–9	*	2	—	—	*	1	*	2	*	2	*	1	*	1
50–9	*	1	*	1	—	—	—	—	—	—	—	—	—	—
60–9	—	—	—	—	—	—	—	—	—	—	—	—	—	—
70 or more	*	1	*	1	—	—	—	—	—	—	—	—	*	1
Occupation														
Lawyers	*	3	*	2	*	1	—	—	*	1	—	—	*	1
Other professions	*	2	*	1	*	1	—	—	—	—	—	—	—	—
High civil servants	—	—	—	—	—	—	—	—	*	1	*	1	*	2
Other civil servants	—	—	—	—	—	—	—	—	—	—	—	—	—	—
University professors	*	2	*	2	*	1	*	2	*	1	*	1	—	—
Other teachers	—	—	*	1	*	1	—	—	—	—	*	1	*	1
Managers	*	1	*	1	*	1	—	—	*	1	—	—	—	—
Entrepreneurs	—	—	—	—	—	—	—	—	*	1	—	—	—	—
White collar	*	1	—	—	—	—	*	2	*	1	—	—	—	—
Others	—	—	*	1	—	—	*	1	*	1	*	1	—	—

Note: *Total n too low to calculate percentages. Percentages are based on known cases.

Source: Own calculations on data published by the *Congreso de los Diputados*.

a very promising result in terms of electoral support in 1977 when it was able to win eight deputies, has suffered a gradual decline, and in 1996 was left with only five deputies.

The two parties have presented a greater instability in their compositions than the average for the whole parliament. We can see that there has been a high renewal of these parliamentary groups, especially for the PNV. None of the deputies of the PNV that were in parliament in 1977 or in 1982 were still there in 1996, and only two of the CiU deputies of 1977 have survived. Typically, the leaders of these parties are engaged in the regional parliaments and governments. The national deputies of these parties have often had previous experience in regional representative positions and often return to regional politics after having served for some time in the national parliament. They are also slightly younger than the average[44] and, especially in the PNV parliamentary group, the presence of women is clearly less than the average. The number of lawyers in the Catalan group is rather high, while civil servants, teachers, and professors are less represented than in the general profile of the chamber. Given the low numbers involved, it is less easy to find a clear pattern for the PNV.

5. CONCLUSION

This chapter highlights the great discontinuities in Spanish political history over the last one and a quarter centuries. The effects of regime changes upon parliamentary elites, with two dictatorships interrupting democratic development during the twentieth century (one of them for more than forty years), were further reinforced by discontinuities in the party system, not only between different democratic periods but sometimes also within the same period. Worth mentioning are, for instance, the collapse of the Radical Party in the 1930s and that of the UCD in the 1980s, and the consequences this had for the entire party system. All this has not only prevented the slow and cumulative change in political elites typical of stable democracies but has not even allowed the more limited phenomenon of the return of some prominent leaders from previous democratic experiences, as was possible in Germany and Italy despite their regime interruptions. Each phase of Spanish democratic development has had, therefore, to face anew the task of building a parliamentary class and a democratic leadership.

In spite of all this, our data do also show some elements of continuity, namely in the qualitative outlook of members of parliament. When we look at the professional background of parliamentarians it is rather clear that

[44] The mean age for CiU deputies has been 44.7 in 1977; 44.2 in 1979; 41.2 in 1982; 43 in 1986; 45.5 in 1989; 47.6 in 1993; 45.2 in 1996. Regarding the PNV, the mean age has been 43.4 in 1977; 38.6 in 1979; 37.3 in 1982; 35.3 in 1986; 44.6 in 1989; 41 in 1993; 45.6 in 1996.

the liberal professions, especially the legal one, have had a prominent role throughout the three democratic periods. Although no other group has ever been of greater importance, the teaching and intellectual professions have also been significant. What is equally noticeable is the lack of importance of some other categories. For example, the nobility, i.e., titled parliamentarians, have been few. The weight of landowners, even during the early democratic period, has also not been particularly strong. Moreover, although our data may, to some extent, underestimate the frequency of this background, which is often associated with other types of professions, it seems likely that this important social group has tended to delegate its political representation to the lawyers, the first 'professional politicians' of democratic life. The same probably applies to the business sector.

On the other side of the social spectrum, it is noticeable that the number of representatives from either a peasant or a working class background has never reached a significant level. This, however, should not come as too much of a surprise, seeing that the typical period for the development of the organised mass parties of the lower classes and of a new pattern of recruitment of parliamentary members in most of Europe was predominantly a period of non democratic regimes in the case of Spain. The only period when a Socialist party could develop a strong and stable position in the party system was in the post-Franco democracy, in the age of television politics and catch-all parties, when even left wing-parties have tended to recruit their personnel much more from the middle classes than from the workers.

The last period of the history of the Spanish Parliament between 1977 and 1996 has seen two developments similar to that of many other European parliaments. The first is the great increase of the weight of civil servants of different levels and of the teaching professions among parliamentarians. This has meant that the public sector as a whole has acquired a dominant role to an extent it never had before. To this should be added the steady growth in the number of women representatives, which has put Spain ahead of the other southern European democracies.

ABBREVIATIONS

ACNdP	Associación Católica Nacional de Propagandistas/ National Catholic Association of Propagandists.
ANU	Acción Nacionalista Vasca/ Basque Nationalist Action
APAN	Alianza Popular Acción Nacional/ Popular Alliance National Action
AR	Acción Republicana/ Republican Action
ASR	Agrupación al Servicio de la Republica/ Association Serving the Republic

BOC	Bloque Obrero i Camperol/ Worker and Peasant Block
CEDA	Confederación Española de Derechas Autónomas/ Spanish Confederation of Autonomous Rightists
CiU	Convergència i Unió/ Convergency and Unity
CNT	Confederación Nacional del Trabajo/ National Confederation of Work Convergència Democràtica de Catalunya-Unió Democratica de Catalunya/ Democratic Convergency of Catalonia-Democratic Union of Catalonia
ERC	Esquerra Republicana de Cataluña/ Republican Left of Catalonia
FRG	Federación Regional Gallega/ Galician Regional Federation
FE	Falange Española/ Spanish Phalanx
IR	Izquierda Republicana/ Republican Left
IU	Izquierda Unida/ United Left
MVN	Minoría Vasco-Navarra/ Navarre-Basque Minority
ORGA	Organización Republicana Gallega Autónoma/ Autonomous Galician Republican Organization
PCE	Partido Comunista de España/ Spanish Communist Party
PLD	Partido Liberal Demócrata/ Democratic Liberal Party
PNE	Partido Nacionalista Español/ Spanish Nationalist Party
PNV	Partido Nacionalista Vasco/ Basque Nationalist Party
POUM	Partido Obrero de Unificación Marxista/ Worker Party of Marxist Unification
PP	Partido Popular/ Popular Party
PR	Partido Radical/ Radical Party
PRC	Partido Republicano Conservador/ Conservative Republican Party
PRD	Partido Radical Demócrata/ Democratic Radical Party
PRS	Partido Radical Socialista/ Socialist Radical Party
PSOE	Partido Socialista Obrero Español/ Spanish Worker Socialist Party
PSUC	Partit Socialista Unificat de Cataluña/ Unified Socialist Party of Catalonia
RS	Radical-socialistas/ Radical-Socialists
RSI	Radical Socialistas Independientes/ Independent Radical Socialists
UCD	Unión de Centro Democrático/ Democratic Center Union
UGT	Unión General de Trabajadores/ General Union of Workers
UR	Unión Republicana/ Republican Union

References

Aguilar, P. (1996). *Memoria y Olvido de la Guerra Civil Española*. Madrid: Alianza Editorial.

Alba, S. (1916). *Problemas de España*. Madrid.

Alvarez Junco, J. (1990). *El Emperador del Paralelo. Lerroux y la demagogia populista*. Madrid: Alianza Editorial.

Arbeloa, V. M. (1981). 'La masonería y la legislación de la Segunda República'. *Revista Española de Derecho Canonico*, 363–9.

Artola, M. (1975). *Partidos y Programas Políticos 1808–1936*. Madrid: Aguilar.

——(1979). *El modelo constitucional español del siglo XIX*. Madrid: Fundación Juan March.

——(ed.) (1993). 'Cronología, Mapas, Estadísticas', in *Enciclopedia de Historia de España*, vi. Madrid: Alianza Editorial.

Ben-Ami, S. (1983). *Fascism from Above: The Dictatorship of Primo de Rivera in Spain 1923–1930*. Oxford: Clarendon Press.

Boletín de Información Bibliográfica y Parlamentaria de España y del Extranjero (1933), 1: 1054–71.

Capel, R. M. (1975). *El sufragio femenino en la segunda república española*. Granada: Universidad de Granada.

Carr, R., and Fusi, J. P. (1979). *Spain: From Dictatorship to Democracy*. London: Allen and Unwin.

Claudín, F. (1983). *Santiago Carrillo: Crónica de un secretario general*. Madrid: Planeta.

Colomé, G. (1993). 'The Catalan Party System', in E. Fossas and G. Colomé (eds.), *Political Parties and Institutions in Catalonia*. Barcelona: Institut de Ciències Polítiques y Socials.

Cortes (1932). *Cortes Constituyentes de 1931, Lista de los Señores Diputados*. Madrid.

——(1935). *Cortes de 1933: Lista de los Señores Diputados*. Madrid.

——(1936). *Cortes de 1936: Lista de los Señores Diputados*. Madrid.

De Esteban, J. and López Guerra, L. (eds.) (1982). *Los Partidos Políticos en la España Actual*. Barcelona: Editorial Planeta.

De Tebar, P., and De Olmedo, J. (1879). *Las Segundas Cortes de la Restauración*. Madrid: Imprenta de Manuel G. Hernández.

Del Castillo, Pilar (1985). *La Financiación de Partidos y Candidatos en las Democracias Occidentales*. Madrid: Centro de Investigaciones Sociológicas.

Espín, E. (1980). *Azaña en el poder: El partido de Acción Republicana*. Madrid: Centro de Investigaciones Sociológicas.

Ferrer Benimeli, José A. (1980). *Masonería española contemporánea*. Madrid: Siglo Veintiuno de España Ed.

Gil Pecharromán, J. (1994). *Conservadores subversivos: La derecha autoritaria alfonsina, (1913–1936)*. Madrid: Eudema.

Gómez Molleda, M. D. (1986). *La masoneria en la crisis española del siglo XX*. Madrid: Taurus.

Guía Oficial de España (yearly publication).

Gunther, R., Sani, G., and Shabad, G. (1986). *Spain after Franco: The Making of a Competitive Party System*. Berkeley: University of California Press.

Heras, R. (1997). *Enciclopedia Política y Atlas Electoral de la Democracia Española*. Madrid: Ediciones Temas de Hoy.

Hermet, G. (1972). *Los Comunistas en España*. Paris: Ruedo Ibérico.

Hopkin, J. (1995). *Party Development and Party Collapse: the Case of Unión de Centro Democrático in Post-Franco Spain*. Florence: PhD. dissertation European University Institute.

Huneeus, C. (1985). *La Unión de Centro Democrático y la Transición a la Democracia en España*. Madrid: Centro de Investigaciones Sociológicas.

Irwin, W. J. (1991). *The 1933 Cortes Elections*. New York: Garland Publishing.

Ivern i Salvà, M. D. (1988). *Esquerra Republicana de Catalunya (1931–1936)*. Montserrat: Publicacions de l'Abadia de Montserrat.

Linz, J. J. (1967). 'The Party System of Spain: Past and Future', in S. M. Lipset and S. Rokkan (eds.), *Party Systems and Voter Alignments*. New York: Free Press, 197–282.

——(1972). 'Continuidad y discontinuidad en la élite política española: De la Restauración al régimen actual', in *Libro-Homenaje al Prof. Carlos Ollero. Estudios de Ciencia Política y Sociología*. Madrid: Gráficas Carlavilla 361–423.

——(1978). 'From Great Hopes to Civil War: The Breakdown of Democracy in Spain', in J. J. Linz and A. Stepan (eds.), *The Breakdown of Democratic Regimes: Europe*. Baltimore: The Johns Hopkins University Press, 142–215.

——(1987). 'La Asamblea Nacional de Primo de Rivera', in *Política y Sociedad. Estudios en Homenaje a Francisco Murillo Ferrol*, ii. Madrid: Centro de Investigaciones Sociologícas and Centro de Estudios Constitucionales, 559–82.

——and de Miguel, J. M. (1977). 'Hacia un análisis regional de las elecciones de 1936 en España'. *Revista Española de la Opinión Pública*, 48: 27–67.

——and Montero, J. R. (eds.) (1986). *Crisis y Cambio: Electores y Partidos en la España de los años Ochenta*. Madrid: Centro de Estudios Constitucionales.

——(2000) 'The party system of Spain: old cleavages and new challenges', in L. Karromen and S. Kuhule. London: Routledge.

Llera, Franciso José (1994). *Los vascos y la política: el proceso político vasco: elecciones, partidos, opinión pública y legitimación en el País Vasco, 1977–1992*. Bilbao: Universidad del País Vasco.

——(1999). *The Construction of the Basque Polarized Pluralism*. Barcelona: Institut de Ciencies Polítiques y Socials.

López Nieto, L. (1988). *Alianza Popular: Estructura y Evolución Electoral de un Partido Conservador*. Madrid: Centro de Investigaciones Sociológicas.

——(1994). 'Innovación Urbana Española: Una Nueva Clase Política?' *Revista de Estudios Políticos*, 86.

Marcet, J. (1987). *Convergencia Democrática de Cataluña. El partido y el Movimiento Político*. Madrid: Centro de Investigaciones Sociológicas.

Martín Najera, A. (1991). *Fuentes para la Historia del PSOE y de las Juventudes Socialistas de España. 1879–1990*. Madrid: Editorial Pablo Iglesias.

Martínez Cuadrado, M. (1969). *Elecciones y Partidos Políticos de España (1868–1931)*. Madrid: Taurus.

Molas, I. (1988). 'Estructura de la Competència Política a Catalunya' (Working Papers). Barcelona: Institut de Ciències Polítiques i Socials.

——(1992). 'Electores, Simpatizantes y Partidos Políticos: el Caso de Cataluña', in *Revista de Estudios Constitucionales,* 12: 145–79.

Montero, J. R. (1977). *La CEDA: El Catolicismo Social y Político en la II República.* Madrid: Ediciones de la Revista de Trabajo.

——(1989). 'Los Fracasos Políticos y Electorales de la Derecha Española: Alianza Popular, 1976–1987', in J. F. Tezanos, R. Cotarelo, and A. de Blas (eds.) (1989). *La Transición Democrática Española.* Madrid: Sistema.

Morán, M. L. (1989). 'Un Intento de Análisis de la "Clase Parlamentaria" española: Elementos de Renovación y de Permanencia (1977–1986)'. *Revista Española de Investigaciones Sociológicas,* 45.

——(1996). 'Renewal and Permanency of the Spanish Members of Parliament (1977–1993): Reflections on the Institutionalisation of the Spanish Parliament', *Working Paper* No. 81. Madrid: Instituto Juan March de Estudios e Investigaciones.

Mujal-León, E. (1983). *Communism and Political Change in Spain.* Bloomington, Ind.: Indiana University Press.

Pallarés, F., and Font, J. (1995). *The Autonomous Elections in Catalonia (1980–1992).* Barcelona: Institut de Ciències Polítiques i Socials.

Payne, S. G. (1993). *Spain's First Democracy: The Second Republic, 1931–1936.* Madison: University of Wisconsin Press.

Preradovich, N. von (1955). *Die Führungsschichten in Österreich und Preußen (1804–1918)—mit einem Ausblick zum Jahr 1945.* Wiesbaden: Steiner.

Rae, D., and Ramírez, V. (1993). *El Sistema Electoral Español.* Madrid: McGraw-Hill.

Ramírez Jiménez, M. (1977). *Las reformas de la II República.* Madrid: Tucar.

Ranzato, G. (1989). 'Natura e funzionamento di un sistema pseudo-rappresentativo: la Spagna liberal democratica. 1875–1923', in *Suffragio, rappresentanza, interessi.* Istituzioni e società fra '800 e '900, *Annali della Fondazione Lelio e Lisli Basso-Issoco, 9.* Rome, 167–253.

Ruíz Manjón, O. (1976). *El Partido Republicano Radical 1908–1936.* Madrid: Tebas.

Sáinz de Varanda, R. (1957). *Colección de Leyes Fundamentales.* Zaragoza: Acribia.

Sánchez Agesta, L. (1964). *Historia del constitucionalismo español,* 2nd edn. Madrid: Editora Nacional.

Sánchez de los Santos, M. (1908). *Las Cortes Españolas. Las de 1907.* Madrid: Antonio Marzo.

——and De la Redondela, S. (1910). *Las Cortes Españolas. Las de 1910.* Madrid: Antonio Marzo.

————(1914). *Las Cortes Españolas. Las de 1914.* Madrid: Antonio Marzo.

Tácito (1975). *Tácito.* Madrid: Ibérica Europea de Ediciones.

Tezanos, J. F. (1983). *Sociología del Socialismo Español.* Madrid: Editorial Tecnos.

——(1992). 'El Papel Social y Político del PSOE en la España de los años Ochenta: Una Década de Progreso y Democracia', in A. Guerra and J. F. Tezanos, *La Década del Cambio. Diez Años de Gobierno Socialista.* Madrid: Editorial Sistema, 21–56.

Tusell, J. (1971). *Las elecciones del Frente Popular.* Madrid: Editorial Cuadernos para el Diálogo (EDICUSA).

Tusell, J. (1974). *Historia de la Democracia Cristiana en España*. Madrid: Editorial Cuadernos para el Dialogo (EDICUSA).

——(1982). *Las Constituyentes de 1931: Unas elecciones de transición*. Madrid: Centro de Investigaciones Sociológicas.

——and Garcia Queipo de Llano, G. (1990). *Los intelectuales y la República*. Madrid: Nerea.

Uriarte, E., and Elizondo, A. (eds.) (1997). *Mujeres en Política*. Barcelona: Ariel.

Varela Ortega, J. (1977). *Los amígos politicos: Partidos, elecciones y caciquismo en la Restauración (1875–1900)*. Madrid: Alianza.

Varela, S. (1978). *Partidos y Parlamento en la Segunda República*. Madrid: Fundación Juan March-Editorial Ariel.

Vicens Vives, J. (1959). *Historia social y económica de España y America*, iv. 2. Barcelona: Teide.

12

Continuity and Change: Legislative Recruitment in the United Kingdom 1868–1999

MICHAEL RUSH AND VALERIE CROMWELL

1. CONTINUITY AND CHANGE

The British political system has been characterized by enormous historical continuity. The Norman Conquest apart, English history has not been marked by sociopolitical disjunctions which substantially remoulded the political system. To be sure, the English Revolution, with its earliest stirrings in the reign of Elizabeth I (1558–1603) and its culmination in the 'Revolution Settlement' of 1701, constituted a major social and political upheaval, but the pre-revolutionary political institutions were adapted and developed rather than replaced. Later significant changes, such as the extension of the franchise and the development of the party system, were similarly adaptive and developmental. This is not to argue that all was inevitable, but to stress the strength of the thread of continuity.

Political recruitment has been as much part of that continuity as other institutions and processes: the Parliaments elected immediately before and after each of the Reform Acts of 1832, 1867, and 1884 were not radically different in socio-economic composition one from another, although 1884 is a partial exception.[1] Political recruitment, like many other developments, was inevitably subject to a time lag in both the machinery of recruitment and even more the personnel recruited. Of course, some elections were marked by a significant turnover in the membership of the House of Commons, but these reflected changes in party fortunes and resulted in more or fewer new Conservatives or Liberals with a largely similar socio-economic background to that of their re-elected colleagues. Even the dramatic socio-economic transformation of the Labour Party, from an almost exclusively working-class group of MPs before 1922 to one with a growing middle-class element, was largely the consequence of a major shift in the

---

[1] This was because the agricultural depression of the 1880s and the redrawing of constituency boundaries in 1885 reduced the proportions of landowners, members of the aristocracy, and primary producers.

party system. Institutional stability has always been greater than socio-economic stability and there were significant shifts in the latter in 1885, 1918, and 1945, but not to the extent that they undermined the norm of gradual rather than sudden socio-economic change.

For political recruitment, the strongest continuity of all is the maintenance of a high degree of local autonomy in the selection process, in spite of the development of a powerful and significantly centralized party system and, indeed, political system. In the nineteenth century, the persistence of 'pocket boroughs' (where the nomination was in the hands of an individual or small group of individuals) ensured effectively until the 1880s the continuance of electoral 'influence' which had developed in the eighteenth century. This might be local or it might not. Even in borough constituencies with larger electorates, local landed or business interests might control the selection of candidates. In short, historically, British politics has been nationalized, but political recruitment remains strongly localized.

2. OPPORTUNITY STRUCTURES

2.1. The Party System and the 'Selectorate'

Historically, arguments continue over how long Britain has had an essentially two-party system, but in the sense that the overwhelming majority of MPs have been drawn from two parties and that the government of the day is usually drawn exclusively from whichever of the two parties has a majority in the House of Commons, it is clear that a modern two-party system has existed at least since 1868. Furthermore, it can be argued that the modern party system involving a parliamentary party, a national party organization, and local party organization in virtually every constituency dates from the same period. But, just as 1868 can be pinpointed as marking the clear emergence of the modern two-party system (notwithstanding the replacement of the Liberals by the Labour Party), so it can be said to mark the emergence of the modern British system of government. From 1868, a government drawn from a single party with majority support in the House of Commons, using that majority to secure parliamentary approval for its policies and increasingly coming to dominate parliamentary time and business, became the norm. The primacy of Parliament as the clearly defined political career path goes back much further than 1868, however, and the growing dominance of the House of Commons from the seventeenth century onwards has resulted in MPs becoming the recruitment pool for all but a few of the highest political offices.

Much has been written about the development of parties and the party system in Britain (Shaw 1985; Stewart 1989; Hill 1976 and 1985) and a scholarly dispute continues as to how far back the concept of party can properly be pushed. Suffice it to say that before and after 1832 there were groups of like-minded individuals who regularly acted together and behaved in a way that today is encompassed by the term 'party'.[2] Where such groups differed from modern parties is that for the most part they lacked any significant extra-parliamentary organization.

A major stimulus in the development of party organization was growth of the electorate as a result of the passing of the Representation of the People Acts of 1832, 1867, 1884, 1918, and 1928. In 1831, the estimated electorate was 515,920 (2.1% of the *total* population) (Cook and Keith 1975: 115);[3] in 1832, the number of registered electors was 812,938 (3.4%), in 1868, 2,484,713 (7.9%), in 1885, 5,708,030 (16.4%), in 1918, 21,392,322 (49.6%), and 1929, 28,952,361 (63.4%) (Craig 1989: 66–9). The increases in 1918 and 1929 were mainly the result of enfranchising women and changes in the registration system of 1918. Although the size of the electorate also reflects the doubling of the population between 1821 and 1901, it reflects much more the establishment of universal suffrage. The increase in the size of the electorate was an important factor in the reduction and elimination of corruption: the traditional methods of bribery, treating, jobs, housing, and so on simply could not cope with such a massive increase, but the increased electorate was also largely responsible for stimulating the growth of extra-parliamentary organization. A major spur to the increasing sophistication of local party organization was the introduction in the Reform Act of 1832 of a statutory requirement for voters to be registered. Although between 1832 and 1867 many borough constituencies still had electorates small enough to permit the persistence of older forms of electoral corruption, the requirement to register voters stimulated the formation of local registration associations which quickly devised methods to exploit the new procedure to party advantage. These methods were to be crucial in both general parliamentary and also local government elections. The Conservative Party had a national party agent from 1832 (with a gap between 1846 and 1853)

[2] It is worth noting that Edmund Burke defined 'party' as 'a body of men united for promoting by their joint endeavour the national interest, upon some particular principle on which they are all agreed' (Burke 1883: i. 375).

[3] In the nineteenth century, the proportion of adult males who had the vote varied in different parts of the UK because of variations in the franchise, but it has been calculated that the ratios were as follows:

Date	England and Wales	Scotland	Ireland
1833	1 in 5	1 in 8	1 in 20
1869	1 in 3	1 in 3	1 in 6
1886	2 in 3	3 in 5	1 in 2

Source: Cook and Keith (1975: 116).

to co-ordinate electoral registration and the Liberals from the 1840s, but national party organization in the modern sense, bringing local parties under the aegis of a national body and holding an annual conference, came later. The first Conservative Party annual conference took place in 1867 and the first Liberal Party conference in 1877. The first moves were thus being made towards greater formalization in any two-way channel of communication of political opinions and local pressures. Party organization was more highly developed in Parliament, with both major parties appointing chief whips in the House of Commons from the 1830s onwards, although the Conservatives had a chief whip from about 1802 until 1832 before appointing a successor in 1835. As the electorate expanded, however, the chief whip acted as a liaison between the party in Parliament and local party associations, in due course becoming involved in distributing party funds to those associations lacking wealthy patrons or unable to find a candidate able to meet his own election and other expenses. To that extent, the national party organization, usually in the person of the chief whip or the national party agent or organizer, became involved in political recruitment, but that involvement should not be exaggerated and in no meaningful sense amounted to central control of recruitment. Local autonomy remained the order of the day. Indeed, it was strengthened by the impact of the redrawing of constituency boundaries in 1885, made necessary by the further extension of the franchise in 1884. In particular, the division of most counties into a number of smaller, separate constituencies, each with one Member (replacing larger, two-Member divisions) combined with the agricultural depression of the 1880s to loosen the grip of the landed interests and strengthen the hand of local party organization in political recruitment.

The Labour Party provides an interesting comparison. In his study, *British Political Parties* (1955), Robert McKenzie argues that, although the Labour Party began its life outside Parliament, being established specifically to secure the representation of working-class interests in Parliament, it fairly rapidly succumbed to the pressures of the political system. In particular, following the tradition of Michels, he asserted that under its constitution the Labour Party was dominated by its extra-parliamentary organization— notably the annual conference, but that in practice the party leadership soon came to dominate its operation.[4] McKenzie was concerned with the distribution of power within the Conservative and Labour Parties, but there is a also clear parallel between the older parties and Labour in political

---

[4] McKenzie also argued that the Conservative Party become more responsive to its extra-parliamentary organization as a result of the same pressures. He ignored the Liberal Party since, by the time he came to conduct his research, it had clearly been pushed into third-party status.

recruitment. In its early days, the Labour Party sought to impose a degree of central control over candidate selection and, as relatively recently as the 1930s, the party's National Executive Committee (NEC) decided which seats it would contest at general and by-elections. The purpose was to ensure that the party's resources, particularly financial, were used wisely: thus, where the local party was weak and local support limited, it might be denied the opportunity to fight the seat.

This was one of a number of provisions, most of which can still be found in the Labour Party's constitution, allowing the national party organization—effectively the leadership—substantial control over the recruitment process. For example, the nomination of short-listed candidates is subject to NEC approval—usually a formality, ensuring bona fide membership of the party and so on, and the final choice of the local party is subject to the endorsement of the NEC. The choice of the local party is normally respected, but from time to time the NEC has used and continues to use its powers for other than formal reasons. Moreover, the NEC may, in certain circumstances, impose a candidate on a local party and from time to time still does so in by-elections.[5] The reality, however, is very much closer to the situation found in the Conservative Party to the point that central intervention in the selection process is the exception to the general rule of local autonomy.

In the period since 1945 in particular, the role of national party organizations in candidate selection has been threefold—laying down the rules by which local parties choose candidates, exercising a degree of 'quality control' by maintaining lists of possible candidates, and, in the last resort, retaining a right to veto the local choice. The latter power is in practice used infrequently and together these powers do not normally allow the party leadership to impose candidates on local parties, let alone establish central control over political recruitment. Of course, there are less formal means by which local parties can be encouraged to select a candidate favoured by the national party leadership, but more often than not such 'encouragement' tends to be counter-productive: local autonomy is jealously guarded (Rush 1969 and 1987; Norris and Lovenduski 1995). However, there are signs that the centre is becoming more dirigiste in that national party organizations are exerting greater influence over candidates for the European Parliament and for the new, sub-national legislatures in Scotland and Wales, especially in the Labour Party.

---

[5] Under Neil Kinnock and John Smith, the party leadership began to take a more active role in candidate selection, but only in a minority of cases and mostly at by-elections. This has continued under Tony Blair, but a much more interventionist approach has been adopted in the selection of Labour candidates for the European Parliament and for the newly created Scottish Parliament and Welsh National Assembly.

2.2. Legal and Financial Constraints

Although there have historically been restrictions on who may be elected to the House of Commons, few now remain. In medieval times, a residential requirement was introduced, but by the seventeenth century was no longer enforced. Similarly, religious restrictions were introduced, particularly during the Reformation, but now apply only to Anglican clergy and Catholic priests (see Fig. 12.11). Property qualifications were removed in 1858, but women did not become eligible until 1918. Serving but not retired military personnel (or those on the reserve) were also excluded.[6] Bankrupts and convicted criminals remain excluded, but the most important remaining restriction is that civil servants may not be parliamentary *candidates* unless they first resign. This restriction was extended to all civil servants in 1884, but some restrictions date back to the Act of Settlement, 1701. With the establishment of a constitutional monarchy, following the replacement of James II by William III under the authority of a Convention Parliament, Parliament sought to impose its hegemony by limiting the ability of the monarch to control the House of Commons through MPs financially dependent on the Crown. It did this by making holders of 'offices of profit under the Crown' ineligible to be MPs and any Member accepting such an office had to resign. This excluded not only civil servants (most judges were already excluded) but also ministers. Members of the House of Lords may not stand for election to the Commons and, incidentally, are not entitled to vote in parliamentary elections. In effect, a partial separation of powers was introduced—partial because members of the House of Lords could still be ministers. However, the restriction proved politically inconvenient, with the result that it was repealed in 1706 and re-enacted in a modified form in 1708. This was done by requiring ministers to submit themselves to re-election through by-elections, effectively forcing them to secure the approval of their constituents.[7] In practice, this still allowed a substantial number of public appointments to be held by MPs—as many as 200 in the mid-eighteenth century, until all civil servants were made ineligible in 1884 (Parris 1969: 33–6; Plucknett 1960: 564–7). Thus the separation of politicians from civil servants is a long-established practice in British politics and the civil service does not provide a significant career path for would-be politicians. Making comparisons with continental European practice, however, is complicated by the fact that neither teachers nor local government officials (with the exception of mayors) have ever been categorized as civil servants and so they have always been eligible for election. However, in the nineteenth century and earlier, neither teachers nor local government officials were an important source of parliamentary recruitment, but increasingly in

---

[6] This did not apply under emergency legislation during the two world wars.
[7] This requirement remained in a more limited form until 1926.

the twentieth century, teachers, particularly in higher and further education, have become an important source of MPs. The number of local government officials remains low. In general, as the suffrage was extended, so the range of those eligible to stand for Parliament increased, but there was an inevitable time lag between the two.

The swift retreat from a significant element of the separation of powers ironically gave, not the monarch, but the government of the day a powerful means of exerting control over the House of Commons. MPs ambitious for ministerial office increasingly had a strong incentive to support their parties, with many government backbenchers hopeful of office at the next ministerial reshuffle and would-be ministers on the opposition benches hopeful of office after the next election. This 'payroll vote', as it is often called, is thus matched by a would-be 'payroll vote' on the opposition benches. As governmental responsibilities expanded, particularly during the twentieth century, the number of ministerial posts increased and the part played in maintaining party cohesion by ministerial ambition encouraged rather than discouraged the expansion of governments. In April 1999, the Labour government elected in 1997 had 115 ministers of whom no fewer than 90 were MPs, the remainder, with one exception, being members of the House of Lords.

The most significant socio-economic change since the middle of the last century is that the House of Commons is no longer the preserve of the wealthy or those with access to the funds necessary to fight elections and sustain membership of the Commons. H. J. Hanham has pointed out that the Reform Act of 1867

created mass working class constituencies in the cities, but it had provided no simple and cheap way of electioneering in them, so that most of the biggest constituencies could only be contested by rich men or those who had the support of such men ... After 1867 the ... counties became the strongholds of the old order. (Hanham 1978: pp. xii and xxv)

This was put more dramatically by a contemporary commentator: 'the House of Commons ... is only open to those who can pay the tariff' (Holyoake 1868: 8–9). This 'tariff' was a major restricting factor on the opportunity structures for would-be MPs, much more so in the nineteenth century and earlier, but extending significantly into the twentieth century. These financial constraints were the cost of fighting elections and, once elected, of meeting most of the costs of being a Member of Parliament.

Elections are a costly business, all the more so if corruption plays any part. At this point, a distinction needs to be drawn between the costs of administering an election and those arising from a corrupt electoral process. From the seventeenth century onwards, electoral officials began charging fees and election expenses to candidates and this practice was given some statutory force in 1712. However, the universal practice of making the administrative costs of elections a charge on candidates was primarily a matter of usage and custom. The practice of charging candidates remained until such costs became a charge on the public purse in 1918. But the same legislation introduced a further potential cost—an election deposit of £150, which was forfeited by any candidate who failed to secure more than an eighth of the votes cast. The deposit was increased to £500 in 1985, but the proportion of votes required was lowered to a twentieth. Its purpose was and remains to deter so-called frivolous candidates.

At the General Election of 1832, the returning officer's expenses averaged £141 per constituency, a not inconsiderable sum at the time and distorted by the fact that a significant number of candidates were unopposed—28.7%, whose expenses would have been low. At the general election of December 1910, the last before that of 1918, the average was £280, with 24.3% of candidates unopposed (Craig 1989: 64–5). Before 1832, the overwhelming majority of constituencies were uncontested at elections. This was particularly true of English county seats, which tended to have larger electorates and therefore greater electoral costs (Sedgwick 1970: i, App. 1; Namier and Brooke 1964: i, App. 1; Thorne 1986: i, App. 1; Coates and Dalton 1992).

In addition to the administrative costs of elections, there were other legitimate costs—the employment of an election agent and other staff, printing, the hire of rooms, and so on—which also fell on the candidate, but which are now almost entirely borne by parties. There was no limit to such expenditure before 1885 and candidates were not required to submit information about it until 1857. At the general election of that year, the average costs per candidate were £493, a figure again distorted by the number of unopposed returns (Craig 1989: 60).

The cost of fighting an election could also be substantially increased if the result was legally challenged. Between 1832 and 1885, no fewer than 979 individual elections were the subject of election petitions. It is some measure of the costs involved that two-fifths of these petitions were withdrawn, but more than a quarter of these challenges were successful and, successful or not, the costs incurred could be considerable. From 1885, however, the number of petitions fell markedly and between 1885 and 1910 there were only 74; since 1910 there have only been 10 (Craig 1989: 173–4), although, in March 1999 a Labour MP was found guilty of exceeding the legal limits on election expenses in the 1997 general election and disqualified from membership of the Commons as a result, but the conviction was overturned on appeal and the Member was reinstated. The reason is not difficult to discern: before 1832, British elections were notoriously corrupt; after 1832, corruption gradually lessened, especially with the staged elimination of a large number of 'rotten' and nomination boroughs, but it remained a significant factor until the introduction of the secret ballot in 1872 and, much more importantly, the passing of the Corrupt and Illegal Practices Act, 1883. The 1880 general election had proved the most expensive ever, despite the introduction of the secret ballot in 1872: even then 109 seats remained uncontested The 1883 Act not only established more effective machinery for monitoring election expenditure, but defined legitimate expenses and placed strict limits on the amount of money that could be spent. Until then, corruption added very considerably to the costs incurred by many candidates.

The cost of maintaining membership once elected was another problem. In medieval times, the wages and travelling expenses of MPs were met by their constituents, but the practice fell into disuse by the sixteenth century, although isolated cases have been identified in 1641, 1643, and, most well known, the poet Andrew Marvell, MP for Hull, in 1678 (Porritt 1909: i. 153). MPs were not paid until 1911 and it was not until 1972 that a clear distinction was drawn between the parliamentary salary and the expenses incurred in carrying out parliamentary duties.

The cost of fighting elections and of being a Member of Parliament was a particular problem for the Labour Party and the problem was addressed by a system of financial support or sponsorship, mainly by trade unions. In 1906, for example, 47 (94.0%) of the 50 Labour candidates and 28 (96.5%) of the 29 Labour MPs were sponsored. Of these, 70.0% and 72.4% respectively were union-sponsored. After the introduction of pay for MPs in 1912[8] and as Labour began to contest most parliamentary seats, the proportion of sponsored candidates and MPs fell, since the unions mainly supported candidates in Labour-held or marginal seats the party was likely to win with a favourable electoral swing. Thus the proportion of union-sponsored MPs fell from 86.0% in 1918 to less than 40% for the most of the period after 1945, although the proportion has risen in recent elections to more than half (Craig 1989: 91–2; Rush 1969: 165–204; Harrison 1960).[9]

3. THE SOCIO-ECONOMIC TRANSFORMATION OF THE HOUSE OF COMMONS[10]

The evolutionary nature of the British political system has meant that the effects of specific changes, such as the successive extensions of the franchise,

---

[8] The salary in 1911 was £400, the equivalent of £23,624 in 1996.

[9] Following the First Report of the Committee on Standards in Public Life (Cmnd. 2855-I, May 1995), the Labour Party has abandoned the sponsorship of candidates and introduced a system by which organizations affiliated to the party may sponsor particular constituency parties. The operation and significance of this change awaits further research.

[10] There is a variety of published data sources on the socio-economic background and career patterns of British MPs, but none provides systematic data covering membership of the House

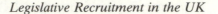
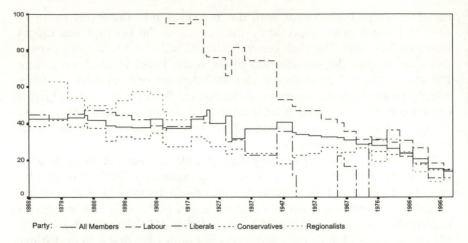

Fig. 12.1. United Kingdom 1868–1997: basic education

the payment of MPs, and making women eligible for election to Parliament, have taken time—often a considerable time—to have a marked impact on the composition of the House of Commons. The most obvious case is the number and proportion of women MPs (see Fig. 12.6): it was not until 1987, nearly seventy years after women became eligible to stand for Parliament and the first woman MP took her seat, that the proportion exceeded 5%. It was still less than 10% in 1992, although it rose to 18.2% in 1997. The absence of a system of proportional representation with multimember constituencies undoubtedly militates against the election of more women, but the cause and remedy is ultimately in the hands of the parties: if they do not select more women candidates, the electorate cannot elect more women MPs.[11] It would, of course, be surprising in most instances if changing the *legal* opportunity structures had an immediate and dramatic effect on the socio-economic composition of the Commons. Clearly, if a legal requirement that 50% of the candidates supported by each party had to be women was introduced, the effect would be dramatic, but thus far no party has

of Commons since its inception. The volumes produced by the History of Parliament Trust come nearest to this, but the data are not always absolutely comparable and the series is not yet complete. Other sources cover particular periods, but inevitably define variables differently and do not always cover the same variables. The authors of this chapter have data sets covering 1868 to the present, but they are part of ongoing research and are not yet available in published form. However, they form a crucial basis for this chapter, importantly supplemented by other sources. The most important of the latter are Thomas (1939; 1958), Rush (1969), Ross (1948; 1955), Mellors (1978), the Nuffield Election Series (1945–97), Stannage (1980), Guttsman (1963), Stenton (1976), and Stenton and Lees (1978–81).

[11] A major part of the explanation, however, lies in the supply side of the recruitment equation.

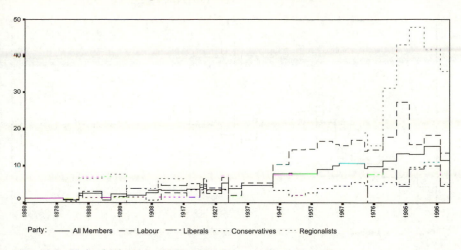

Fig. 12.2. United Kingdom 1868–1997: intermediate education

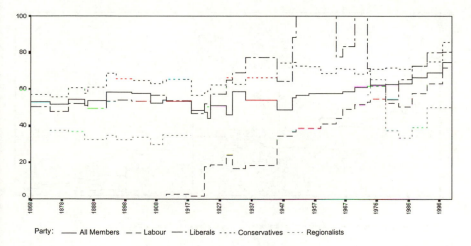

Fig. 12.3. United Kingdom 1868–1997: university degree

advocated such a requirement, although the Labour Party has engaged in positive discrimination and the Liberal Democrats in affirmative action. In Labour's case this consisted initially of requiring that at least one woman should be included on the short-list of possible candidates drawn up by local parties, but later required particular constituencies to draw up all-women short-lists. Both requirements significantly increased the number of women

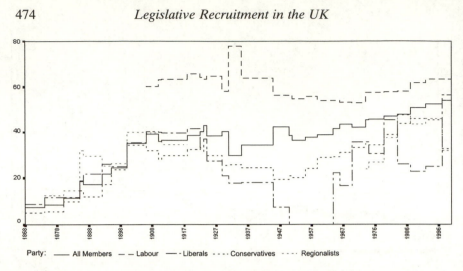

Fig. 12.4. United Kingdom 1868–1997: local politics background

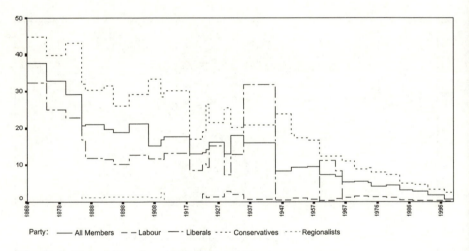

Fig. 12.5. United Kingdom 1868–1997: nobility

candidates selected, but all-women short-lists were subsequently declared illegal by an industrial tribunal on grounds of sex discrimination!

  Dramatic or relatively dramatic changes in the socio-economic composition of the Commons, or of one or other of the parties represented in the House, is much more likely to result from *political* changes. The obvious case is that of a lasting party split, such as the Peelite split in the Conservative Party in 1846 and the split in the Liberal Party over Home Rule for

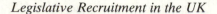

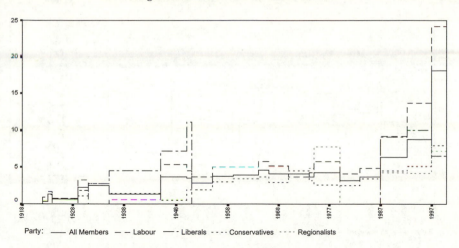

Fig. 12.6. United Kingdom 1918–1997: female legislators

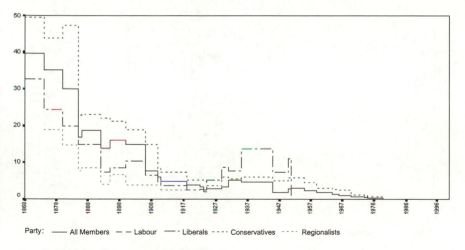

Fig. 12.7. United Kingdom 1868–1997: primary sector

Ireland in 1886. In both instances, fairly distinctive socio-economic groups broke away from the party and joined their rivals: the splits simply meant a redistribution between the parties in the Commons. Thus, in socio-economic terms, the Peelites and the Liberal Unionists had more in common with their new Liberal and Conservative allies respectively than they did with their former Conservative or Liberal colleagues.

A less dramatic but similar process took place with the rise of the Labour

Party: —— All Members — — Labour ——· Liberals ···· Conservatives ---- Regionalists

Fig. 12.8. United Kingdom 1868–1997: managers, businessmen

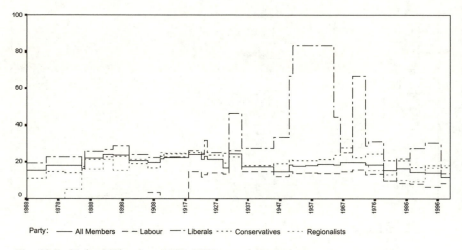

Party: —— All Members — — Labour ——· Liberals ···· Conservatives ---- Regionalists

Fig. 12.9. United Kingdom 1868–1997: practising lawyers

Party. The first two clearly working-class MPs were elected in 1874 as Liberal-Labour (Lib-Lab) candidates and the Liberal Party continued to encourage working-class candidates under the Lib-Lab label, but their number declined under the impact of the challenge from the Labour Party (Fig. 12.14). Ironically, just when Labour was establishing a significant foothold in the House of Commons, with the election of 29 MPs in 1906, the number of Lib-Labs reached its highest—24, declining to eight in the

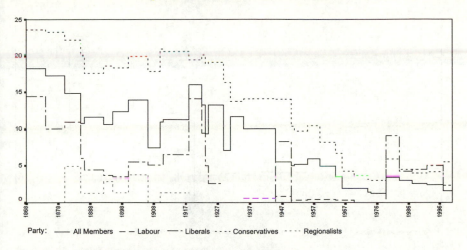

Fig. 12.10. United Kingdom 1868–1997: military persons

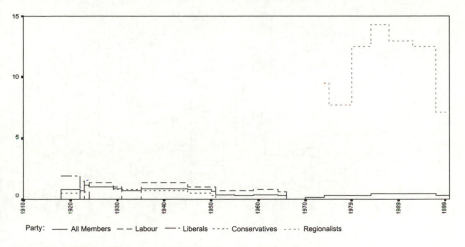

Fig. 12.11. United Kingdom 1910–1997: priests, clergymen

election of December 1910. Indeed, until the General Election of 1922, nine out ten Labour MPs were working class, but the decline of the Liberals and rise in support for Labour resulted in a growing number of middle-class Labour Members. Even in 1945—Labour's greatest electoral triumph before that of 1997—only just over two-fifths of Labour MPs were working class.

In 1832, more than half the members of the House of Commons

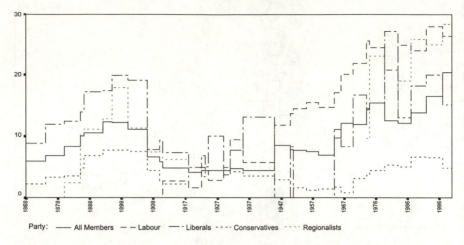

Fig. 12.12. United Kingdom 1868–1997: teachers and professors

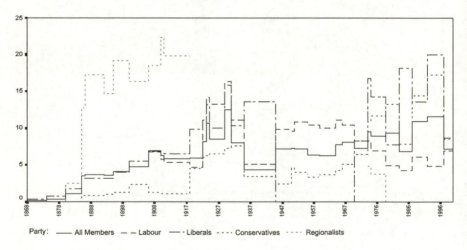

Fig. 12.13. United Kingdom 1868–1997: journalists and writers

represented landed interests; in 1900 only a sixth represented such interests (Fig. 12.7). Conversely, industrial, commercial, and financial interests increased from rather more than a quarter in 1832 to more than half in 1900, almost a complete reversal (Fig. 12.8). As might be expected, professional interests increased and the beginnings of working-class representation were also apparent. It would be an error, however, to assume that the Tory/Conservative Party was the principal repository of landed interests

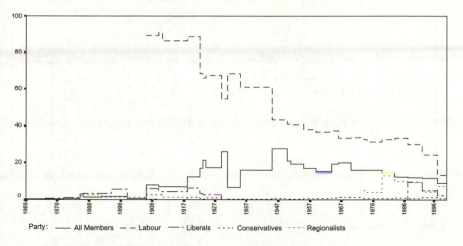

Party: —— All Members — — Labour ——· Liberals ···· Conservatives ···· Regionalists

Fig. 12.14. United Kingdom 1868–1997: blue-collar workers

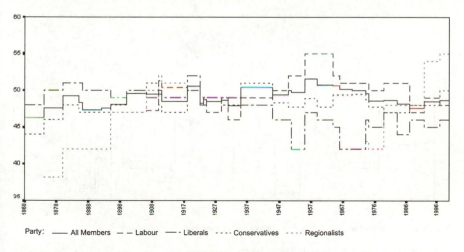

Party: —— All Members — — Labour ——· Liberals ····Conservatives ···· Regionalists

Fig. 12.15. United Kingdom 1868–1997: mean age

and the Whig/Liberal Party of industrial interests: both parties were remarkably similar in 1832 and 1900; it was in 1868 that the greater contrast existed, when landed interests comprise nearly half the Conservative interests and industrial interests nearly half of those represented by Liberals. In short, the nineteenth century saw the House of Commons reflect the socio-economic changes brought about by the agricultural and industrial revolutions (Thomas 1939). As early as 1841, the proportion of the work-

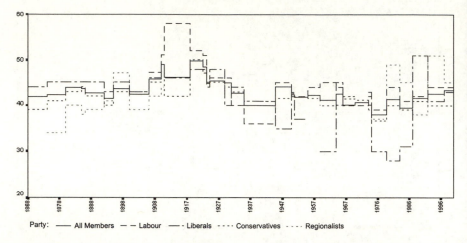

Party: ── All Members ── Labour ──· Liberals ···· Conservatives ···· Regionalists

Fig. 12.16. United Kingdom 1868–1997: mean age of newcomers

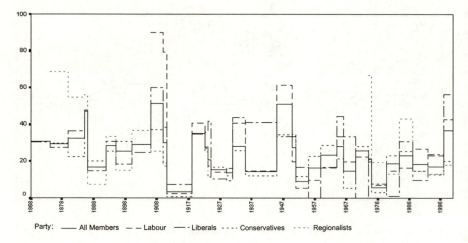

Party: ── All Members ── Labour ──· Liberals ···· Conservatives ···· Regionalists

Fig. 12.17. United Kingdom 1868–1997: newcomers

force engaged in manufacturing exceeded that in agriculture, forestry, and fishing—35.7% compared with 28.6%. By 1881, the proportions were 33.5% and 17.6% and by 1901, 35.2% and 12.0%. This contrasted with much lower manufacturing and higher agricultural workforces in Germany, France, and Italy.[12]

[12] The data refers to Great Britain only, thus excluding Ireland, where the agricultural work-force was 68.5% in 1841, 55.2% in 1881, and 54.0% in 1911. In 1882, the proportion of the

The importance of landed interests, however, did not mean that the Commons was a largely aristocratic body (Fig. 12.5). By no means all those with landed interests were members of the nobility or aristocracy in that they held hereditary titles. In any case, most holders of peerages had seats by right in the House of Lords and were consequently ineligible for election to the Commons. MPs with aristocratic connections were therefore sons of living peers or otherwise related to peers. However, many with landed interests were the descendants of wealthy but untitled families, while others were *nouveaux riches* who had bought estates with their industrial or commercial wealth. True, in 1868, 44.9% of Conservatives had aristocratic connections and the figure was still 43.4% in 1880, compared with 32.2% of Liberals in 1868 and 22.8% in 1880 (Cromwell 1992).[13] However, the agricultural depression of the 1880s, with its attendant fall in the price of land, and the loosening of the grip of the landed interests through the electoral reorganization following the Reform Act of 1884, accelerated the decline of the aristocracy (Cannadine 1992). As a result, in 1885, Conservatives with aristocratic connections had declined to 32.0% and Liberals to 16.9% and, by 1918, only 17.0% of Conservatives and 8.6% of Liberals had aristocratic connections. The Conservatives retain a small aristocratic element—still 8.0% as recently as 1974, but this had shrunk to a mere 2.4% by 1997 and is of no real significance. The election of 1885 also saw an associated decline in those representing the primary sector, again particularly marked among the Conservatives (Fig. 12.7).

The impacts of economic changes, particularly industrialization, are reflected in an analysis of the occupational backgrounds of MPs, who have increasingly come to represent a wider range of occupations than was the case in the middle of the nineteenth century. In 1868, the professions were largely dominated by the law (Fig. 12.9) and the military (Fig. 12.10); today the Commons has representatives of most major professions. Until 1992, lawyers remained the largest single group, but they were then overtaken by teachers and lecturers (Fig. 12.12). Lawyers are, however, more commonly found among Conservatives and teachers and lecturers in the Labour Party. The military now constitute less than 5%, almost exclusively Conservative. The commercial and financial interests represented in the nineteenth century have been replaced in the twentieth by a broader range of business

workforce in Germany engaged in manufacturing was 27.8% and in agriculture, forestry, and fishing 42.6%; in France the proportions in 1896 were 23.1% and 45.7%; and in Italy in 1881, 14.2% and 54.0% (Mitchell 1978, Table B1).

[13] Aristocratic connections are defined as the son, grandson, or nephew of the holder of a peerage or baronetcy (i.e. an hereditary knighthood). Until the right of hereditary peers to sit in the House of Lords was abolished in 1999, the House of Lords was, of course, largely an aristocratic body by definition, since membership depended on holding a peerage, except for the 26 bishops of the Anglican Church. Until the passing of the Life Peerages Act, 1958, all peerages, apart from a small number of judicial titles, were hereditary.

interests (Fig. 12.8). This persistence of business interests contrasts significantly with most continental European legislatures and originally stemmed
from industrial and commercial interests seeking to have a direct impact on
policy through Parliament, especially during the industrial revolution. Business interests, however, continued to remain important in response to the
rise of the Labour Party, with its perceived anti-business stance, and such
interests are therefore now largely concentrated in the Conservative Party,
although nearly 10% of Labour MPs have business backgrounds. Journalists have become more numerous, once more common in the Liberal
and Labour Parties, but recent elections have produced more Conservative journalists (Fig. 12.13).

But the most significant changes in the twentieth century have been the
rise and later decline of working-class representation (Fig. 12.14). Initially
the Labour Party was and for many years remained a vehicle for working-
class representation: from its inception in 1900 to 1918, the party was overwhelmingly working class, its MPs coming either directly from the factory
floor or the mine or having been trade union officials recruited via factory
and mine; middle-class trade union officials in the first half of the century
were rare. From 1922, however, a process of embourgeoisement of the
Labour Party began and, although working-class MPs remained in a substantial majority during the interwar period, in 1945 the proportion fell to
43.4% and then slowly declined to 12.7% in 1997. Simultaneously, the proportion of Labour MPs from the professions and from other occupations
increased dramatically in 1922 and rose steadily after 1945. This process was
triggered by a split in the Liberal Party. This occurred initially in 1916, in
the middle of World War I, when Lloyd George ousted Asquith as Prime
Minister and in 1918 Coalition Liberals fought anti-Coalition Liberals,
leaving Labour as the second largest party and the official opposition in
Parliament. By the time the Liberals reunited in 1923, it was too late: their
position as one of the two major parties had been usurped by Labour and
in 1924 Labour formed its first government and the Liberals were reduced
to 40 seats in the Commons. Some Liberals joined the Labour Party and
contributed to its embourgeoisement, but Labour's growing strength also
meant that left of centre politicians who wished to continue their political
careers and those who wished to embark on such careers became increasingly drawn to the Labour Party. This was also reflected in the types of candidates sponsored by the unions: until the 1970s, the great majority of such
candidates and MPs were manual workers (with some lower-level white-
collar workers), but more recently an increasing proportion of sponsored
MPs have been middle class and had no occupational connection with the
unions sponsoring them.

The industrialization of Britain was inevitably accompanied by the extension of educational opportunities (Figs. 12.1–12.3). Compulsory schooling
was introduced in 1870 and later the opportunities for further and higher

education increased substantially, especially in the twentieth century. This too was reflected among members of the House of Commons, although even in 1868 56.9% of Conservatives and 50.4% of Liberals had had a university or equivalent education. The advent of the Labour Party, however, with its strong emphasis on working-class representation, interrupted the rising educational qualifications of MPs. Until 1918, nine out of ten Labour Members had had only an elementary education and this remained the case with more than half in the interwar period. But the expansion of educational opportunities increased upward social mobility and this in turn contributed to the decline of working-class representation. Traditional working-class candidates found it increasingly difficult to compete with better-educated, largely middle-class candidates, all the more so because a significant proportion of the latter had working-class antecedents. The proportion of university-educated Labour MPs jumped from less than a fifth in 1935 to more than a third in 1945 and increased steadily thereafter, reaching 71.8 % in 1997. This compares with 85.4 % of Conservatives in 1997.

However, important educational differences between the parties continue to exist (see Table 12.1). Conservative MPs have always been

Table 12.1. Elitist educational background of MPs 1868–1997 (%)

Educational background	Elected at general elections between			
	1868–95	1900–10	1918–35	1945–97
Conservative				
All public schools	57.4	70.2	63.8	70.1
Clarendon schools[1]	46.9	50.8	35.8	30.6
Oxford	27.7	31.1	22.7	26.2
Cambridge	18.5	17.7	16.6	21.0
Total Oxbridge	46.2	48.8	39.3	47.2
Other (UK and overseas)	11.9	8.5	10.6	25.4
Liberal				
All public schools	30.5	47.4	38.8	42.9
Clarendon schools	22.4	20.5	14.6	8.3
Oxford	14.4	16.3	12.6	21.4
Cambridge	15.6	17.3	11.2	14.3
Total Oxbridge	30.0	33.6	23.8	35.7
Other (UK and overseas)	20.0	18.6	22.5	39.3
Labour				
All public schools	—	1.2	10.1	17.5
Clarendon schools	—	—	4.5	3.6
Oxford	—	—	3.3	11.1
Cambridge	—	—	4.8	5.7
Total Oxbridge	—	—	8.1	16.8
Other (UK and overseas)	—	—	12.8	33.4

Note: [1] The 'Clarendon' schools were those named in the Royal Commission on Public Schools, 1864—Eton, Harrow, Winchester, Charterhouse, Shrewsbury, Rugby, Westminster, St Paul's, and Merchant Taylors'.

disproportionately drawn from fee-paying public schools, particularly the exclusive 'Clarendon' schools, and from Oxford and Cambridge, Liberal MPs in the nineteenth and early twentieth centuries less so. But only a small proportion of Labour Members were and are public school products, although since 1922 the proportion has always been above the national average. Moreover, Labour MPs are now far more commonly the products of further education and of non-Oxbridge universities, including the former polytechnics.

There has thus been a socio-economic convergence in that the House of Commons has been recruited increasingly from the middle class, but this convergence should not be exaggerated. Although Conservative and Liberal MPs in the nineteenth century had much in common socio-economically, to a significant degree they were drawn from different sectors of society. Similarly, and much more sharply, Conservative and Labour MPs are drawn largely from different sectors of the middle class—lawyers and businessmen among the Conservatives and teachers and other public sector professionals for Labour—and this is clearly reflected in their educational and occupational backgrounds.

4. THE CHANGING POLITICAL CAREER PATTERNS

Members of Parliament in the nineteenth century and earlier, especially those representing county or rural constituencies, commonly came from or near the area they represented. In 1868, 66.7% of Conservative MPs and 48.2% of Liberals had direct connections[14] with their constituencies before first being elected, while the proportions of MPs with not even regional connections were as low as 13.0% and 20.9% respectively. Geographical and social mobility gradually reduced the incidence of constituency connections, although they remain important in both the Conservative and Labour Parties. Indeed, recent elections have shown a marked increase in direct constituency connections among Labour MPs and in 1997 as many as 56.9% had such connections.

For MPs generally and Labour MPs in particular, one of the most frequent forms of constituency connection is as a local councillor (Fig. 12.4), with pre-election local government experience increasing among Conservatives from between a third and a quarter to 45.5% in 1992, though

---

[14] Direct connections include being born, living, or working in the immediate locality, a member of the local party, and being an elected member of a local government body within the constituency or within which the constituency lies. The decline of the representation of landed interests in 1885 inevitably contributed to decline in those with direct local connections, falling from 52.2% in 1880 to 44.1% in 1885, with a dramatic fall of 60.7 to 47.6% among Conservatives.

falling again to 32.7% in 1997. Among Labour MPs, the figures are much higher, often as high as two-thirds, never less than half, and applying to 63.2% in 1997. Pre-election local government service became more common as the elective local government system developed, largely in the latter part of the nineteenth century: in 1868, only 5.1% of Conservatives and 8.5% of Liberals had held local elective office before first being elected, but increasingly local government became one of the pathways to Parliament, particularly in the Labour Party.

There is also substantial evidence to support the view that the competition for election to Parliament has increased markedly. Uncontested seats were common throughout the nineteenth century and earlier, as already noted, and in the earlier part of the twentieth, but since 1955 all seats have been contested. It is now also the norm for a majority of newly elected Conservative MPs and a substantial minority of Labour MPs to have had previous electoral experience in one or more parliamentary contests. In 1997, 65.2% of all Conservative and 38.5% of all Labour MPs had fought parliamentary elections before first being elected.

Nineteenth-century political careers were quite often fragmented, sometimes by electoral defeat, but at least as often by voluntary retirement followed by subsequent re-election. Being a Member of Parliament was widely seen as performing a public service and in some constituencies it was a duty shared by members of the same family. It was also, again as already noted, an expensive business, electorally and subsequently, and a long purse was a prerequisite and continuing necessity. None the less, there is a remarkable degree of continuity in the length of parliamentary careers and the age structures of successive Parliaments (see Table 12.2 and Figs. 12.15–12.16).

The mean length of service of MPs between 1715 and 1754 was 15 years (Sedgwick 1970: 137), even longer in the second half of the eighteenth century, and the proportion of new Members in each parliament averaged a fifth. After 1832, however, the length of service fell and it dropped dramatically to less then ten years, rising slowly in the nineteenth century, but not returning to pre-1832 levels again until after 1945: it now averages 18 years. Turnover was also greater and more varied between 1832 and 1935, averaging from a quarter to a third in the nineteenth century and two-fifths from 1900 to 1935, but with massive fluctuations. In 1885, for example, it was 46%, in 1906 60%, 1918 65%, and 1945 a dramatic 74%, although the last two figures in part reflect the absence of a general election for eight and ten years respectively. Since 1950, the average has been about a fifth. The turnover in 1997 was 40%,[15] more than double the postwar

---

[15] Turnover in the UK tends to be increased by the simple plurality electoral system, which translates relatively small movements in electoral support for the various parties into much larger numbers of seats changing hands.

Table 12.2. Length of parliamentary service 1868–1997 (%)

Length of parliamentary service	Period left Parliament			
	1868–99	1900–17	1918–44	1945–97
Conservative				
Less than 5 years	8.0	6.5	22.0	6.6
5–9 years	27.5	19.0	19.5	19.9
10–14 years	24.2	29.0	23.6	18.3
15–19 years	14.9	15.0	11.5	18.8
20–24 years	10.4	12.4	11.5	15.4
25 or more years	10.5	18.1	11.9	21.0
Liberal				
Less than 5 years	14.9	20.0	3.8	10.2
5–9 years	28.2	15.1	15.2	25.6
10–14 years	18.8	26.1	15.7	23.1
15–19 years	14.3	16.7	14.6	12.8
20–24 years	10.3	11.3	7.6	12.8
25 or more years	13.5	10.7	8.1	15.4
Labour				
Less than 5 years	—	13.0	29.2	7.3
5–9 years	—	19.6	17.8	23.9
10–14 years	—	17.4	14.2	16.4
15–19 years	—	26.1	16.4	18.7
20–24 years	—	8.7	9.4	13.6
25 or more years	—	15.2	13.0	20.0

Table 12.3. Achieved ministerial or parliamentary office[1] (%)

Party	Period left Parliament			
	1868–99	1900–17	1918–44	1945–97
Conservative	14.3	17.9	19.1	39.0
Liberal	14.6	23.2	23.6	9.6
Labour	—	32.6	28.2	31.3

Note: [1] Parliamentary offices consist of Speaker or Deputy Speaker of the House of Commons.

mean and the consequence of the massive electoral swing to Labour (Fig. 12.17).

Being a Member of Parliament also offers the possibility of realizing ministerial ambitions (see Table 12.3) and the opportunities for ministerial office have increased markedly since 1868, when the government totalled 57. Even in 1900, there were only 60 ministers compared with the 1999 total of 115. Moreover, in 1868, a significant proportion were members of the House of Lords, but nowadays about 90 MPs are ministers at any one time.

Table 12.4. Age at which MPs entered and left Parliament 1868–1997 (%)

A. Age at which first elected	Period first elected			
	1868–99	1900–17	1918–44	1945–97
Conservative				
Under 30	20.6	16.1	12.3	7.5
30–49	55.7	60.7	56.5	80.7
50 or over	23.7	23.2	31.2	11.8
Liberal				
Under 30	15.8	9.6	8.5	7.1
30–49	54.2	64.6	60.7	73.8
50 or over	29.9	25.8	30.8	19.0
Labour				
Under 30	—	—	2.7	3.2
30–49	—	69.6	60.4	74.1
50 or over	—	30.4	36.9	22.7

B. Age on leaving Parliament	Period left Parliament			
	1868–99	1900–17	1918–44	1945–97
Conservative				
Under 30	1.2	0.4	0.2	0.1
30–49	26.3	22.4	24.2	20.4
50 or over	72.5	77.2	75.6	79.5
Liberal				
Under 30	1.2	0.6	1.1	—
30–49	22.7	23.5	27.1	41.0
50 or over	76.1	75.9	71.8	59.0
Labour				
Under 30	—	—	—	0.2
30–49	—	13.0	21.0	18.4
50 or over	—	87.0	79.0	81.3

Of course, an important factor is how often a Member's party itself holds office and the Conservatives have been in government more frequently than any other party since 1868. In addition, no Liberal MP has held office since the wartime coalition of 1940–5.

The average age of MPs has long been in the 40 to 50 range, nearer the lower end in the eighteenth century and the upper end in the nineteenth century and later. Conservative MPs have tended to be marginally younger than Liberals and, more particularly, Labour MPs older. First election under the age of 30 was more common in the eighteenth and nineteenth centuries and, although more MPs now serve beyond the age of 50, most retiring MPs leave at or near a normal retirement age of 65. Furthermore, although electoral defeat accounts for the ending of about a quarter of political careers, voluntary retirement is the commonest cause, accounting for more than two-fifths.

The extensive continuity in the career patterns of MPs, notably length of service, laid the foundation for the next stage in that pattern—the professionalization of the Member of Parliament.

5. THE PROFESSIONALIZATION OF THE MEMBER OF PARLIAMENT

The fact that MPs received no remuneration until 1912 meant that being a Member of Parliament required a private income, a professional or other career, personal wealth, or, from the later nineteenth century, financial sponsorship by a trade union, the latter being crucial to the Labour Party. Before 1912 and for many years after, most MPs had private wealth or were able to continue to earn a sufficient income from business or professional activities. It is hardly surprising, therefore, to find that in 1868, 49.6% of Conservative MPs and 38.6% of Liberals had relied on private means, most of the rest having business or professional incomes, or were former military personnel. By 1900, the proportion of Conservatives reliant on private means was 18.9% and by 1918, only 5%; the corresponding figures for the Liberals were 10.4% and 2.6%. Indeed, the immediate reason why the payment of Members was introduced by the Liberal government was to help its Labour allies, whose MPs relied mainly on payments by their trade unions. Such payments had been undermined by a court judgement in 1909 ruling that unions could not use their funds for political purposes. The government subsequently changed the law, but it is clear that the payment of Members was the logical solution.

None the less, even after 1912, Conservative and Liberal MPs needed additional wealth or income to maintain their pre-election standard of living. Furthermore, apart from the introduction of the travel allowance in 1924, it was not until 1972 that a proper distinction was drawn between the salary paid to a Member and the expenses incurred in carrying out parliamentary duties, although a proportion of the salary was regarded as a tax-free element to meet expenses. In fact, in the 1950s and 1960s, a number of MPs, mostly but not exclusively Conservative, were legitimately claiming the whole of their parliamentary salaries against tax to meet the cost of secretarial and other expenses. Nor was there a pension scheme before 1964. In the late 1960s, however, a secretarial allowance and free telephone calls and postage were introduced. This was followed in 1972 by a subsistence allowance and thereafter both salary and allowances have been subject to periodic review and, in the case of allowances, linked to appropriate civil service rates (Rush and Shaw 1974; Rush 1989).

All this was part of the professionalization of the Member of Parliament.

In the middle of the nineteenth century, most legislation still consisted of private bills, that is, bills applicable to limited localities or named persons. As the two-party system become more firmly entrenched, single-party majority government became the norm and, in response to the needs of an increasingly industrialized society, governments became more interventionist. In Parliament, government business came to take precedence and by the turn of the century the government dominated the parliamentary timetable. Legislative output increased: most of the bills that passed were initiated by the government and were public bills, that is, legislation applicable to the country as a whole and all members of the public. In addition, these public bills increasingly came to require delegated legislation which only rarely received scrutiny by Members.

The demands upon MPs increased, not merely from their parties—one intent on implementing its programme, the other in offering itself as an alternative government—but from constituents. MPs had long sought to help their constituents collectively by seeking to advance their economic interests, but during the twentieth century the demands of individual constituents increased enormously, especially with the development of the welfare state. In addition, it was Gladstone who, in 1855, told MPs, 'Your business is not to govern the country, but it is to call to account . . . those who do govern it'.[16] Thus to the partisan and constituency roles can be added the scrutiny role. Both the constituency and scrutiny roles demand adequate resources to pit against those of the executive. However, the demand for such resources and, therefore, the latest stage in professionalization are recent developments.

Until the late 1950s and early 1960s, the two major parties each had a block of MPs on whom they could rely for largely unquestioning support. For the Conservatives, it was the 'knights of the shire'—Members representing safe Conservative seats in rural areas for whom a political career was a form of public service and who were rewarded with knighthoods; for Labour, it was the trade union MPs, mostly from safe seats in industrial areas, whose selection was often seen as a reward for long and faithful service as a union official. These MPs were increasingly replaced by Members who were not prepared to accept a largely passive role; they demanded a positive role and in support of that role demanded better pay, service, and facilities. In 1971, a review body on MPs' pay concluded that 'by any reasonable standard . . . most Members must be considered as working on a full-time basis' (TSRB 1971, para. 25; see also King 1972 and Riddell 1993) and this view was supported by survey evidence of how

---

[16] Gladstone was responding to a motion to set up a select committee to investigate the conduct of the Crimean War. The motion was carried and the government resigned (HC Debates, 3rd series, vol. 136, 29 Jan. 1855, c. 1202).

much time MPs spent on their parliamentary duties. That picture has been confirmed in subsequent surveys (TSRB 1976, 1979, 1983, and SSRB 1996).

Once elected, MPs are now professional politicians in the sense that they are and expect to be full-time Members of Parliament and that they are provided with substantial resources to enable them to perform their various roles. Whether they are fully professionalized in the way they go about their performing their duties and, therefore, whether the House of Commons could be said to a professionalized legislature remains a matter of dispute.

6. CONCLUSIONS

Parliamentary recruitment in the UK is marked by a considerable degree of continuity. The selection process has long been and remains largely in local rather than national hands, historically involving local notables and, since the rise of modern parties, local party organizations. The role of the national party organization is to maintain a watching brief over recruitment and, in the last resort, reject the local choice, a rare outcome in practice. Opportunity structures have been extended and adapted so that, for example, as the local government system developed, so local government became an increasingly important part of those opportunity structures. Socio-economic changes in the composition of the House of Commons have reflected changes in British society at large, but slowly over time rather than with dramatic suddenness. Occasional splits in one of the major parties have produced more rapid change, but most relatively dramatic shifts have been the result of electoral fortunes not so much transforming as modifying the socio-economic composition of the Commons in favour of one major party at the expense of the other. Such shifts are made more dramatic by the simple plurality electoral system, which translates modest movements in opinion into disproportionate changes in the distribution of seats. Overall, the House of Commons has become increasingly middle class in its composition, marking a clear socio-economic convergence between the Conservative and Labour Parties, but they tend to draw their MPs from significantly different sections of the middle class. MPs have also become increasingly professionalized in terms of pay, services, and facilities and, above all, in the extent to which being a Member of Parliament is a full-time job.

The UK thus provides a major example of great institutional stability, but it is an institutional framework which has shown great adaptability, capable of absorbing and reflecting significant socio-economic changes in society.

References

Burke, Edmund (1883). *The Works of Edmund Burke* (ed. George Bell), i. London: George Bell.

Cannadine, David (1992). *The Decline and Fall of the British Aristocracy*. London: Macmillan.

Coates, R. Morris, and Dalton, Thomas R. (1992). 'A Note on the Cost of Standing for the British Parliament: 1852–1880'. *Legislative Studies Quarterly*, 17: 585–93.

Cook, Chris, and Keith, Brendan (1975). *British Political Facts, 1830–1900*. London: Macmillan.

Craig, F. S. (ed.) (1989). *British Electoral Facts, 1832–1987*. Chichester: Parliamentary Research Services.

Cromwell, Valerie (1992). 'Peers and Personal Networks: Links between the Two Houses of Parliament since the Mid-nineteenth Century', in H. W. Blom, W. P. Blockmans, and H. de Schepper (eds.), *Bicameralism: Tweekkamerstel vroeger en nu*. Gravenhage: Sdu Uitgeverij Koninginnegracht, 383–94.

Guttsman, W. L. (1963). *The British Political Elite*. London: MacGibbon & Kee.

Hanham, H. J. (1978). *Elections and Party Management: Politics in the Age of Disraeli and Gladstone*, 2nd edn. Harvester Press.

Harrison, Martin (1960). *The Trade Unions and the Labor Party since 1945*. London: Allen & Unwin.

Hill, B. W. (1976). *The Growth of Parliamentary Parties, 1689–1742*. London: Allen & Unwin.

——(1985). *British Parliamentary Parties, 1742–1832*. London: Allen & Unwin.

Holyoake, G. J. (1868). *Working Class Representation*. Birmingham: Guest.

King, Anthony (1972). 'The Rise of the Career Politician—and its Consequences', *British Journal of Political Science*, 2: 249–85.

McKenzie, Robert T. (1955). *British Political Parties: The Distribution of Power within the Conservative and Labour Parties*. London: Heinemann.

Mellors, Colin (1978). *The British MP: A Socio-economic Study of the House of Commons*. Farnborough, Hants: Saxon House.

Mitchell, B. R. (1978). *European Historical Statistics 1750–1970*. London: Macmillan.

Namier, Sir Lewis, and Brooke, John (1964). *History of Parliament: The House of Commons 1754–1790*. London: HMSO.

Norris, Pippa, and Lovenduski, Joni (1995). *Political Recruitment: Gender, Race and Class in the British Parliament* (Nuffield General Election Series, 1945–97). Cambridge: Cambridge University Press.

Parris, Henry (1969). *Constitutional Bureaucracy: The Development of British Central Administration since the Eighteenth Century*. London: Allen & Unwin.

Plucknett, T. F. T. (1960). *Taswell Langmead's English Constitutional History*, 11th edn. London: Sweet & Maxwell.

Porritt, Edward (1909). *The Unreformed House of Commons: Political Representation before 1832*. Cambridge: Cambridge University Press.

Riddell, Peter (1993). *Honest Opportunism: The Rise of the Career Politician*. London: Hamish Hamilton.

Ross, J. F. S. (1948). *Parliamentary Representation*. London: Eyre & Spottiswoode.

Ross, J. F. S. (1955). *Elections and Electors: Studies in Democratic Representation.* London: Eyre & Spottiswoode.

Rush, Michael (1969). *The Selection of Parliamentary Candidates.* London: Nelson.

—— (1987). 'The "Selectorate" Revisited: The Selection of Parliamentary Candidates in the 1980s', in Lynton Robins (ed.), *Political Institutions in Britain: Development and Change.* London: Longman, 151–65.

—— (1989). 'The Professionalisation of the British Member of Parliament'. *Papers in Political Science: Department of Politics*, University of Exeter.

—— and Shaw, Malcolm (eds.) (1974). *The House of Commons: Service and Facilities.* London: Allen & Unwin.

Sedgwick, Romney (1970). *History of Parliament: The House of Commons 1715–1754.* London: HMSO.

Shaw, Eric J. (1985). *Political Parties in Britain, 1783–1867.* London: Methuen.

SSRB (Senior Salaries Review Body). (1996). *Report No. 38*, Cmnd. 3330-II, July, Sect. 2: Survey of MPs.

Stannage, Tom (1980). *The British General Election of 1935.* London: Croom Helm.

Stenton, Michael (ed.) (1976). *Who's Who of British Members of Parliament*, i: *1832–1885.* Brighton: Harvester Press.

—— and Lees, Stephen (eds.) (1978, 1979, 1981). *Who's Who of British Members of Parliament*, ii: *1886–1918*, iii: *1919–1945*, and iv: *1945–1979.* Brighton: Harvester Press.

Stewart, Robert (1989). *Party and Politics, 1830–1852.* London: Macmillan.

Thomas, J. A. (1939). *The House of Commons, 1832–1901: A Study of its Economic and Functional Character.* Cardiff: University of Wales Press.

—— (1958). *The House of Commons: An Analysis of its Economic and Social Character.* Cardiff: University of Wales Press.

Thorne, R. G. (1986). *History of Parliament: The House of Commons 1790–1820.* London: Secker & Warburg.

TSRB (Top Salaries Review Body) (1971). *First Report: Ministers of the Grown and Members of Parliament*, Cmnd. 4836, Para. 25.

—— (1976). *Report No. 8*, Cmnd. 6574, July, App. A: Survey of MPs.

—— (1979). *Report No. 12*, Cmnd. 7598, June, App. C: Survey of MPs.

—— (1983). *Report No. 20*, Cmnd. 8881-II, May, Sect. 1: Survey of MPs.

13

Between Professionalization and Democratization: A Synoptic View on the Making of the European Representative

MAURIZIO COTTA AND HEINRICH BEST

1. THE CONSOLIDATION AND SPREAD OF REPRESENTATIVE DEMOCRACY IN EUROPE

At the end of the twentieth century, a large majority of European countries have achieved consolidated democratic regimes and others have at least undertaken the first crucial steps in the process of democratization. If in the gloomy years between the two world wars the future of democracy in Europe seemed in dire straights, and if for several decades after World War II it was challenged by totalitarian and authoritarian regimes, the twentieth century has closed on a definitely more optimistic note. Democracy is no longer an endangered species but is rather the winner (Linz 1995). Further, despite oft-voiced complaints about the decline of parliaments, one of the most obvious results of these political developments has been the diffusion of parliamentary institutions. Indeed, parliaments appear to be a *sine qua non* of democracy, something which is well attested to by the fact that parliamentary elections are considered a crucial political test in all European countries, and that parliaments themselves remain the main channel for a career in government (Blondel and Thiébault 1991).

Modern democracy has at its centre the idea of representation: those who govern are the representatives of the people. As is well known, this revolutionary idea is both at once simplistic—all people cannot themselves govern and thus need someone to represent them—and extremely complicated: What is meant by 'the people', are they isolated individuals, territorial or functional groups, or an organic whole referred to as 'the Nation' (Sartori 1987)? What is to be represented—the personal properties of individuals (gender, age, profession, class), their opinions, short- or long-term interests, or the common good? Also, how should the representatives 'represent'—as delegates bound by strict mandates or as trustees free from specific instructions? Finally, is representation the result of specific actions or concerned with specific qualities of the representatives themselves? Parliaments may not have the monopoly of representation (parties, interest groups, or the executive may also have an important part in this process), yet, thanks to their institutional design, they can put their members in the position to play multiple roles in this political game. Parliamentarians may represent local and sectional groups, but they can also be the promoters of broad interpretations of the public good; they may transmit into the heart of government the petty desiderata of the represented but also act with great freedom in shaping wide-ranging 'representative platforms'; they may in some cases reproduce the personal features of the represented and share intimately their specific interests and preoccupations, but otherwise they may act as 'professional' representatives who do not need to mirror the represented in order to represent them. Thus, within the same parliament, different levels, modes, and styles of representation can be found to coexist. This is even more evident when the scope of observation is extended to eleven countries over 150 years.

The comparative study of parliamentarians, therefore, offers an access to a fuller understanding of their function and performance in modern democracy. In this book, which is the result of the first phase of a broader research project, the recruitment patterns of legislators in eleven European countries (Denmark, Finland, France, Germany, Hungary, Italy, the Netherlands, Norway, Portugal, Spain, and the United Kingdom) have been systematically surveyed. Although, for historical reasons, the data available in these countries do not have the same degree of completeness, this book provides a first comprehensive overview of variations in the profile of parliamentary elites, across countries and across time, in a significant portion of Europe. Even if some important countries are still missing at this stage of the project, the variety of European states is well represented in our sample. We not only have Northern and Southern, Western and Eastern, insular and continental, large and small countries, but also those where democratic development was gradual and continuous (Denmark, Finland, the Netherlands, Norway, the United Kingdom), and those where regime crises and breakdowns interrupted the path of democratization, and parliamentary development (France, Germany, Hungary, Italy, Portugal, Spain).

2. DIRECTIONS AND PATTERNS OF CHANGE

In the introductory chapter, we developed a conceptual framework for the long-term study of legislative recruitment which blended a supply and demand model of the recruitment process with assumptions about fundamental changes of the parameters determining the 'recruitment function' during the past 150 years. The key concepts used in this dynamic model were the inherently contradictory processes of 'democratization' and 'professionalization': Contradictory because, while democratization refers to an opening of the channels for political participation and legislative recruitment to more social groups, professionalization refers to the process whereby those recruited tend to establish area-specific standards and routines which increase their own control over legislative careers, income, legal status, and social standing, thus restricting access to the parliamentary arena. It was assumed that the developments we would find would indicate increasing levels of both democratization and professionalization across all countries studied.

The processes of democratization and that of professionalization can be fitted into the wider conceptual framework of modernization theory which has been routinely used as a basis for explorations of the changes in European societies and polities since the eighteenth century. Although modernization theory has never been developed into a codified set of testable hypotheses, it can be used as a starting-point for a deductive argument from which further propositions can be derived. In our project, we made a heuristic use of the concept, like a philosopher who introduces the idea of the 'creator' in a certain line of argument without actually believing in God. Empirical evidence can be then confronted with what is to be expected according to the benchmarks set by the theoretical model.

In a very broad sense, modernization can be understood to be a profound transformation of societies and polities which involves their different levels and functional areas. It is expected to be a configuration of progressive, irreversible, and global processes in which less developed societies acquire the characteristics of more developed ones. Within a given society, less advanced sectors should catch up with the development of more progressive ones (Huntington 1971). If we have a set of time series which are supposed to depict 'modernization', their trace lines should be linear, progressive, and convergent. Regression, stagnation, divergence, and cycles should not occur, at least not as persistent and enduring patterns. Partial modernization, which leaves important areas of societies untouched and produces an incoherent structure of progress and stagnation, is considered to be a source of societal tension and conflict. These are strong assumptions and it will be shown to what extent our data have conformed to such a model. However, before we can enter into a final synoptic inspection of the data, it has to be clarified what modernization actually means with regard to parliamentary recruitment, and which indicators can offer themselves as measures.

Some propositions can be drawn from the concept of 'political development' which was introduced to the sphere of politics in the late 1960s as a focused adaptation of modernization theory. It was Samuel Huntington (1968) in particular who amalgamated some pivotal elements of established political theory and turned them into a comprehensive developmental concept, which postulates the nature and direction of institutional and attitudinal change in the order of political life. Although it might have developed a somewhat deep patina by now, this should not necessarily be considered a disadvantage where comparative and cumulative political research over a wide time span is concerned. According to Huntington, a central feature of political modernization is the replacement of rural and agrarian elites, often from aristocratic backgrounds, by a political elite recruited from the urban middle classes. Thus, the centre of gravity of the power structure shifts from rural to urban elites and to middle-class standards and values. This process is complemented by an extension of participation—namely, by a transfer of suffrage and eligibility to formerly disenfranchised categories of the population. The abolition of property requirements and gender barriers furthers the democratization of society. A third feature of political modernization is the differentiation of structures, which can be associated with the establishment of a centralized and functionally differentiated power structure. The development of the modern state, the separation of powers, and the emergence of the professional politician can be subsumed under this heading. Finally, Huntington includes the rationalization of authority in the dimensions of political modernization. *Inter alia*, this refers to the replacement of the 'divine right' by more secular principles for the legitimization of authority. The shift from ascriptive to more achievement-based criteria for elite recruitment and subsequent access to power, can also be included here.

Such developments change the basis of the power structure of polities and societies and, therefore, should be particularly well reflected at the level of political elites. Thus, the emergence of specialized political roles, such as the professional politician, the declining significance of a prestigious family background as a criterion for political recruitment, the shifting presence of interest groups in representative bodies, the opening of political careers for previously disadvantaged categories of the population, such as women, are directly connected to these four lines of political development and can be taken as indictors of political modernization.

3. OUTCOMES AND THEIR VARIATIONS

In the presentation of the main results of this book it is useful to start at the end, that is, with the outcomes of the long developmental processes that have been examined in the country chapters. The picture which can be drawn from the data concerning the decades between 1970 and 1990 (a

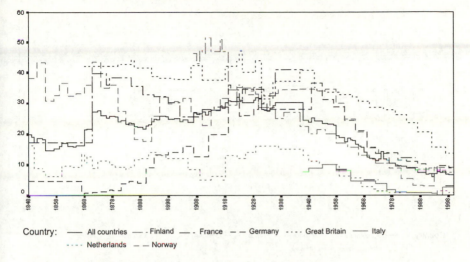

Fig. 13.1. European Parliaments 1848–1999: basic education

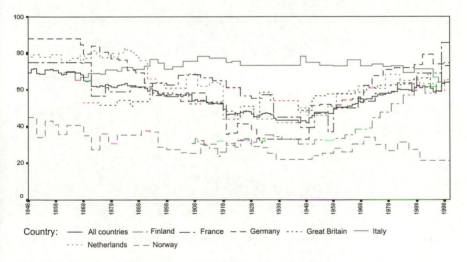

Fig. 13.2. European Parliaments 1848–1999: university degree

period when, having finally overcome the effects of World War II, European societies enjoyed a long phase of prosperity and stability) shows important common elements but still some significant discrepancies.

The first clear aspect to emerge is that the typical European representative is very middle class. This can be revealed using both the education and professional background of the MPs. In all countries (with the striking

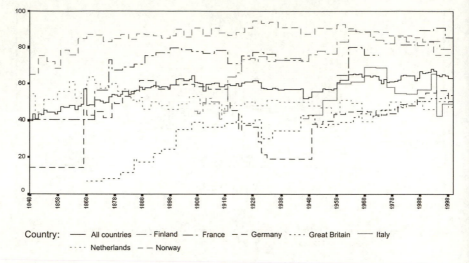

Fig. 13.3. European Parliaments 1848–1999: local politics background

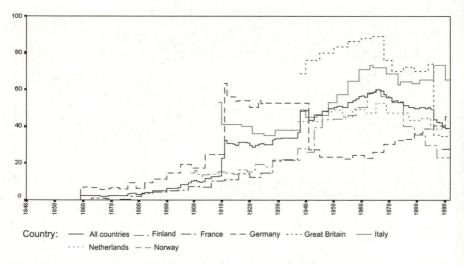

Fig. 13.4. European Parliaments 1848–1999: leading party position

exception of Norway) a large majority of representatives has a university degree, while the proportion of MPs with the lowest levels of education (the typical stigma of the working classes) has significantly declined (generally under 15%; Figs. 13.1 and 13.2). Analysing the type of university degrees can help the role of education to be better understood. The postwar years

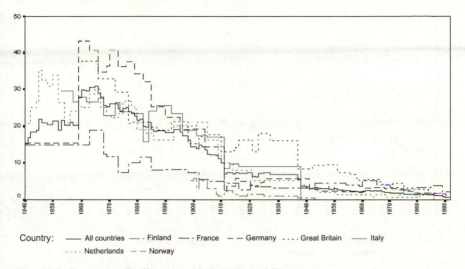

Country: —— All countries ——·Finland ——·France —— Germany ····Great Britain —— Italy
···· Netherlands —— Norway

Fig. 13.5. European Parliaments 1848–1999: nobility

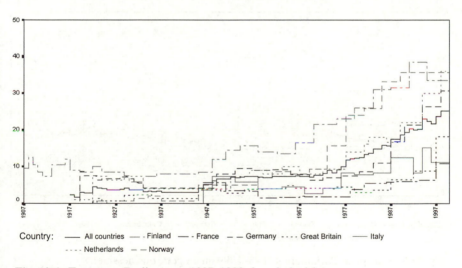

Country: —— All countries ——·Finland ——·France —— Germany ····Great Britain —— Italy
···· Netherlands —— Norway

Fig. 13.6. European Parliaments 1907–1999: female legislators

have seen a decline of the formerly predominant law degrees and a very significant increase of more general degrees, such as those from the humanities or social sciences, which are not associated with automatic access to highly paid professions. Rather they are a sign of the diffusion of a basic university education which has ceased to be associated with higher social

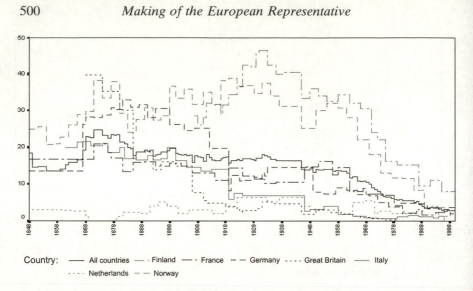

Fig. 13.7. European Parliaments 1848–1999: primary sector

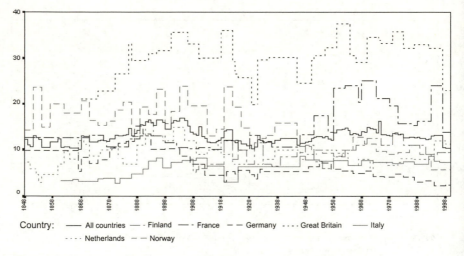

Fig. 13.8. European Parliaments 1848–1999: managers, businessmen

status and has become a typical attribute of the greatly expanded middle classes.

The available data about professional background confirm this picture: the two extremes of the social spectrum provide a relatively minor proportion of MPs. Blue-collar workers are a small and clearly declining minority in all countries (Fig. 13.13). At the other extreme (with the exception of

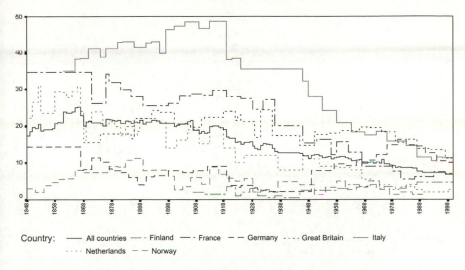

Country: —— All countries —— - Finland —— - France — — Germany ···· Great Britain —— Italy
···· Netherlands — — Norway

Fig. 13.9. European Parliaments 1848–1999: practising lawyers

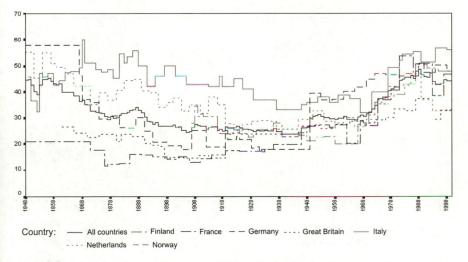

Country: —— All countries —— - Finland —— - France — — Germany ···· Great Britain —— Italy
···· Netherlands — — Norway

Fig. 13.10. European Parliaments 1848–1999: public sector employees

France and the United Kingdom) managers and business leaders, and the free professions, particular lawyers, are also a minority or show a marked decline (Figs. 13.8 and 13.9). In most countries, employees in the service sector dominate the parliamentary arena, particularly various categories of public sector employees, and of those, primarily teachers (Figs. 13.10 and 13.11). To this we should add the substantial group of party organization or

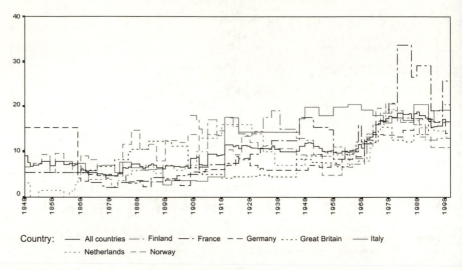

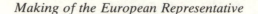

Fig. 13.11. European Parliaments 1848–1999: teachers and professors

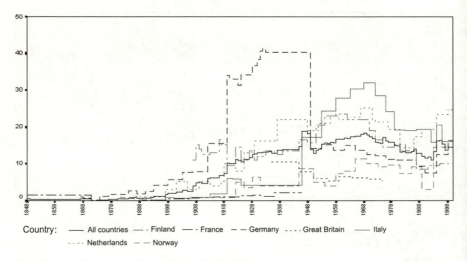

Fig. 13.12. European Parliaments 1848–1999: party and pressure group officials

trade union officials (the size of which is probably somewhat underestimated by our data; Fig. 13.12).

A reading of these data also indicates that, in this period, not only has a high social status ceased to be a crucial resource for a political career, but the demand for direct representation by the disadvantaged classes has also

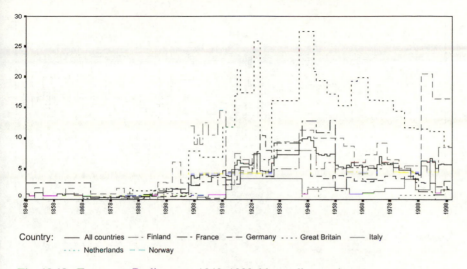

Country: —— All countries — · Finland —— · France — — Germany · · · · Great Britain —— Italy
· · · · Netherlands — — Norway

Fig. 13.13. European Parliaments 1848–1999: blue-collar workers

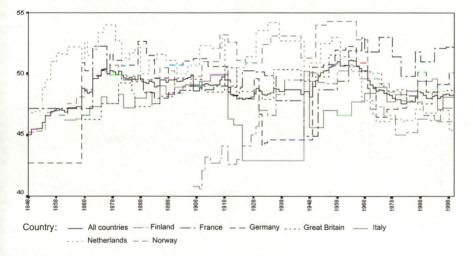

Country: —— All countries — · Finland —— · France — — Germany · · · · Great Britain —— Italy
· · · · Netherlands — — Norway

Fig. 13.14. European Parliaments 1848–1999: mean age

declined, giving way to more mediated forms of representation. The large bulk of elected politicians have not derived a particular benefit from their previous professional experience, except for some rather broad and general skills. Their professional background is usually more connected to the public and state sphere than that of the market, which comes as no

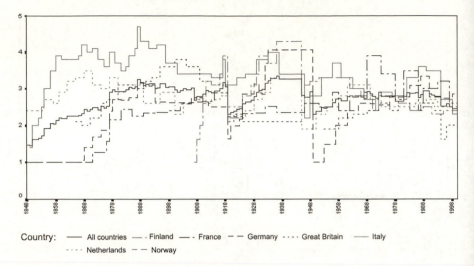

Fig. 13.15. European Parliaments 1848–1999: mean number of elections

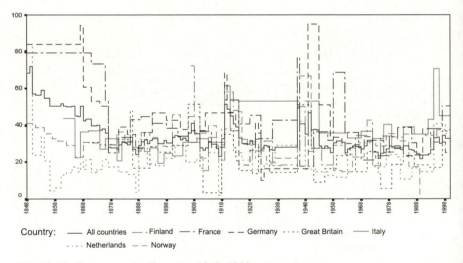

Fig. 13.16. European Parliaments 1848–1999: newcomers

surprise in a period which has seen a surge towards the welfare state and general state intervention in the economies of all European countries. Thus, when politics is primarily about public administration of society, it is understandable that the public sector will provide a privileged recruiting ground for political representatives. There, the necessary skills are readily available, as are interests that will push to be heard.

For a more complete picture, we must add to the MPs' occupational backgrounds some indicators concerning the political career that has preceded their first election to parliament. A survey of the positions in the party organizations and of the elective offices at the local level (such as in municipalities, provinces, and regions) held by MPs before their election to Parliament provides us with a better sense of what type of personnel occupies parliamentary seats (Figs. 13.3 and 13.4). The fact that becoming an MP is not an isolated political experience but a position that follows some sort of political career is well borne out by the observation that a very large proportion of MPs (from 40% upwards) had an elective or governing position at local or regional level before entering into the national representative body. The other significant component of a political career is obviously party experience. Generally, more than 30% of MPs (up to around 80% in some countries) can be seen to have held a leading party position at a local or national level before their first election to Parliament.

The mean age of newcomers, which is typically around the early forties, is another indicator that a parliamentary career is generally neither for inexperienced youngsters nor for people who are very advanced in some other career (Fig. 13.14). Data concerning turnover and tenure of MPs show that the parliamentary career is typically well established (Figs. 13.15 and 13.16). Turnover rates of MPs indicate that, while European Parliaments undergo a regular process of renewal (20–30% of new members at every normal election), the chances for incumbents to be re-elected are quite favourable. In addition, the mean number of elections an MP has successfully survived (around 2.5) shows that a substantial proportion of parliamentarians remain in office for three or more terms, thus having the opportunity to gain substantial experience which helps them to retain their position.

The overall picture delineated by these data is the clear predominance among European representatives of a professional politician with a middle-class background, medium to high levels of education, significant political experience, and the likelihood of extended parliamentary service. Political representation now appears to be a profession in itself, requiring much more than a simple mirroring of the features of those who are to be represented in order to be elected and act as representative.

If this is the common picture, we must now turn to variations across the countries. In fact, the Parliaments of Europe show significant differences in a number of aspects, one of which is education. Here, the three Nordic countries included in our study, particularly Norway, differ from the rest of Europe: there, a university education is (or was until recently, as in Finland and Denmark) much less important for a political career (Figs. 13.1 and 13.2). Yet even in Norway, a declining minority of MPs has only a basic education. With regard to the type of university education, Nordic countries differ again in that law degrees seem less important compared to the other countries.

Two other cases of deviation from the general European trend are evident when we consider social background indicators. There was (again until recently) a Nordic difference in the proportion of MPs with a primary sector background: here the much higher share was a clear reflection of the political mobilization of this section of the population, and of the particular importance of the agrarian parties (Fig. 13.7). This is probably one of the most important examples where representation entailed a strong similarity of social background between representatives and those represented. With regard to occupational background, the United Kingdom and France are atypical in that the proportion of managers and entrepreneurs has been far more significant than that in all other cases (although the Hungarian parliaments of the post-communist period come close; Fig. 13.8). In the United Kingdom, this suggests that one of its two main parties has a more direct linkage with business interests than is the case with any other party on the continent. Interestingly, the British case also displayed the highest proportion of MPs with a working-class background (confirmed by the relatively high levels of parliamentarians with a low education level), which indicates that the other party also maintains some direct representative link with 'its' side of the class struggle (Fig. 13.13). In the French case, the representational relationship between polity and economy might be reversed since we have here a strong tradition of state interventionism and a close interlockingness between careers in the state sector and managerial positions in the economy.

In sum, these data indicate that, if on the one hand, the relative homogeneity in the contemporary configuration of European parliamentary elites can be taken as the result of convergent processes of democratization and professionalization of political representation that have indeed made Europe homogeneous from the point of view of the political personnel, then on the other hand, some persistent differences can be linked to the specific developmental paths followed by each country to reach this goal.

4. DEVELOPMENTAL PATHS AND THEIR VARIATIONS

The developmental paths towards stable mass democracy followed by the European countries included in our data set have been quite different, with varying starting-points and diverse time schedules. Moreover, the incremental transformations of some countries contrast with the dramatic discontinuities of others. Therefore, it comes as no surprise that developmental paths pertaining to elite recruitment patterns are also dissimilar. However, before proceeding to a survey of these findings it is important to discuss the starting-points of these processes.

4.1. The First Parliamentary Establishment from the Middle of the Nineteenth Century until the 1880s

First of all, the characteristics of the political elites at the outset of the parliamentary experience we are describing need to be clarified. How similar were the first parliamentary establishments in the different countries? Who were the dignitaries generally assumed to have been the fundamental component of that establishment, and were they of the same type everywhere? Answering these questions is complicated by the fact that it is not always easy to define a precise starting-point. In most of the countries we were able to include, modern elected parliaments did not begin from scratch but were either the result of a continuous transformation of pre-modern representative assemblies (e.g. in the United Kingdom), or followed experiences of indirectly elected parliaments (e.g. in the Netherlands and Spain), or had been preceded by one or more short-lived 'failed starts' (e.g. in France, Germany, Hungary, Portugal, Spain). Since the starting-points differ, when we follow a strategy of chronologically synchronic comparison we must remember that we are in fact comparing systems with a different 'institutional age'. Conversely, if our focus is on institutional age, we have to compare political systems at different time points.

As in most cases, suffrage was initially granted only to the upper strata of society, the obvious expectation is that initial parliamentary representation would reflect the traditional power structure of societies and thus perpetuate many features of the *ancien régime*. In the countries where an extended franchise was granted from the outset, we could, on the other hand, expect a less clear dominance of the upper strata of society, although an 'independent' mobilization of the lower strata might have proved to be difficult and lengthy. An inspection of different indicators, such as level of education, aristocratic status, professional background, and economic sector of origin of MPs can help us to define the profile of the first parliamentary elites and to detect some significant cross-country variations.

The importance of the traditional upper classes in the period under observation is confirmed by the high proportion of members with an aristocratic background (Fig. 13.5). The most traditional basis of authority—hereditary transmission—was, in fact, quite successful in passing the 'legitimacy test' of elections. This is not surprising in countries where suffrage was initially severely restricted (like Hungary, Italy, the Netherlands, Portugal, the United Kingdom), but the findings are unexpected in countries where the franchise was much wider (or even universal, for males), as in the cases of Imperial Germany, the French Second and Third Republics or Restoration Spain. On the basis of a simple mirroring model of representation, we could expect a much lower share of this category. Yet our cases do not support this decisively. Rather, the picture they provide is one of diversity. For example, data for Imperial Germany show that, until the 1880s, well over a third of Parliamentarians were titled—a level which is significantly higher than that of Italy and the Netherlands, comparing more closely to the British case (where MPs belonging to aristocratic families were assigned to this category). On the other hand, Norway does not comply with the model of deferential recruitment, in that titled MPs were almost totally absent from its Parliament. As for the French Third Republic, after a somewhat exceptional result in the first election, the share of nobility is relatively minor. Restoration Spain begins with levels similar to those in France but proves to be more stable. Therefore, the extent of the franchise alone cannot explain the importance of ascriptive social qualification among representatives, so that other factors need to be examined. The most obvious is the share of nobility in society, which differs significantly, ranging from the large share in Germany, to a somewhat intermediate level in France to a near absence in Norway. The existence of a monarchy with which the nobility had a relationship of allegiance and co-operation, may be part of this explanation. Probably both the supply of contenders and the demand by the selectorates contribute to the differing share of this category.

In a period, such as the one examined here, where higher education was accessible only to very limited groups of the population, education levels can be used as another indicator of social status (although one should remember that education also entails an element of achievement, which is mostly absent in the previous indicator, and may point to the upward mobility of intermediate social strata). The highest level of education, a university degree, very clearly dominates the early landscape of parliamentary life in Germany, Italy, and the Netherlands, followed (although at a distance) by France, Spain, and the United Kingdom (Fig. 13.2). Denmark and Norway are very clearly the outliers of the group, in that less than half of their parliamentarians held an academic degree at this time. Finland shows a very similar pattern in its first modern parliament of 1907. This indicator reinforces the image conveyed by the previous one whereby the Nordic countries appeared the least elitist in this period.

Economic and professional background is the third element that can provide us with some information about the characteristics and resources of the parliamentarians, their linkages with the interests in society, and the recruitment process. We will use here three main indicators: the percentage of parliamentarians with a background in the primary sector, those with a background in the public sector, and the percentage of lawyers (Figs. 13.7, 13.9, and 13.10). A background in the primary sector indicates a direct linkage with a component of economic life, to which (with the exception of the United Kingdom) until the last third of the nineteenth century a majority of the population was still attached, and one which was generally the most traditional sector of society. A background in the public sector can indicate the extent to which the bureaucratic state had extended its influence upon polity and society. Finally, the legal profession points to the development of a special type of representative, one who, thanks to professional ability and independent standing, can engage in the representation of different interests and can, to some extent, be seen as an early form of professional politician.

The importance of the primary sector in the first stages of parliamentary representation is well documented. In all the countries examined, this sector produces a very significant group of parliamentarians ranging from one-fifth (France, Italy) to the peaks of around 40% (Denmark, Norway, Portugal, and the United Kingdom). These figures might even be somewhat underestimated as a number of parliamentarians who fall under other headings (military officers, judges, lawyers, and so on) were often also land-owners. The only exception among the countries analysed is the Netherlands, where the primary sector is hardly represented. The markedly urban character of Dutch society (and even of its nobility) provides the most likely explanation for this deviation. However, the level of economic development and industrialization of a country seems to have a very limited impact on this indicator, since the United Kingdom and Portugal—countries at the extremes of this scale—have more or less the same level of representation of the primary sector. The same can be said about levels of electoral democratization. We have similarly high levels of primary sector representation in countries with limited suffrage (Portugal, the United Kingdom) and in some with a much wider franchise (such as Germany).

The importance of the primary sector is matched or even exceeded by the public sector, which represents at the opening of the parliamentary era a very substantial group (from 20% upwards). In some countries (such as Germany, the Netherlands, and Norway), it is the dominant group with percentages oscillating around the 40–50% mark. Such data suggest the need for a reassessment of the political meaning of representation in the early stages of parliamentarism. Parliamentary representation is often pictured as an instrument of society against the state, with the purpose of keeping the bureaucratic state under control after its great expansion under monarchical absolutism. Whatever the merits of this view, our data show that parliaments and elections could become a crucial channel through which the state itself (and the leading strata of its personnel) could be represented. The data also suggest that the basic distinction between state and society may be too simplistic. As a result of the great process of state-building, which had taken place during the pre-parliamentary era, the state via its officers had become a leading component of society. Society had become 'state-shaped' and representation plausibly reflected this situation.

The countries of the group which display the lowest levels of legislators with a public sector background are France, Italy, Spain, and the United Kingdom. The differences between the four cases in terms of levels of bureaucratic development and of the length of a unitary state tradition seem at first to defy a common explanation. But in all cases, a closer look reveals the existence of obstacles to a larger representation of the state bureaucracy. In the United Kingdom, it is the relative weakness of the central state apparatus compared to most of the continental countries, which was expressed rather than caused by strict incompatibility rules that prevented civil servants from standing in national elections. In the French and Spanish cases, the low levels of public sector representation find a plausible explanation in the regime discontinuities (and the problems of regime legitimization) that have characterized both countries: bureaucrats were possibly less ready than in other countries to risk their careers in such a dangerous political arena. In Italy, the recent tradition of a unified state is not in itself a sufficient factor to limit the parliamentary representation of public servants, since Imperial Germany, also a latecomer, shows much higher levels. But differences between the two histories might help explain this. While the German unification in 1871 was a merger of integral states, this was not the case in Italy where only the state of Piedmont had accepted unification. The other Italian states (and their bureaucracies) had rejected it together with the parliamentarization of politics. The propensity of these bureaucracies to become part of the first parliamentary establishment was therefore reduced.

The last indicator to be introduced is the share of lawyers. From Max Weber onward, many studies have underlined the characteristic features of this profession that make it easily adaptable to political life (Weber 1947; orig. 1919). The predisposition of lawyers to deal with other people, and to work as advocates of their interests, combined with the flexibility of their work, put them in a particularly favourable position in the political market, especially when electoral politics still had a strong local dimension and representation concerned individuals or small groups, rather than the masses. We could, therefore, expect a stronger presence of lawyers where electoral politics had such characteristics and where the availability of other strong contenders for this role was limited. The importance of lawyers is well documented in many of our countries. In Italy, France, and the Netherlands, they were one of the largest categories of parliamentarians, while in Hungary and the United Kingdom their share was significant. In contrast, they were much less important in Imperial Germany, Norway, and in Finland. Here, an extended suffrage, coupled with the strength of other contenders for legislative recruitment (such as bureaucrats, nobles, and landowners) may be a possible explanation, since it pre-empted opportunities for lawyers. It could be asked why France had such a large proportion of lawyers when, from the point of view of the extension of suffrage, it fits better with the latter group of countries. The answer might be that, in spite of bureaucratic centralism, political life in France remained strongly localized (probably linked to the weaker role of parties) and thus provided leeway for the representation by lawyers.

This synoptic analysis of the initial stage of parliamentary representation has revealed some significant differences. It has also shown that differences are not linked in a simple way to external factors, such as the level of economic development or the chronological timing of suffrage extensions. Rather, they suggest a mix of factors pertaining to the supply of potential representatives, to selection mechanisms (where variations in the social structure, as well as patterns of political organization, appear relevant), and possibly also to the demand by the electorate for different models of representation.

Trying to put the various findings together, we can delineate a variety of profiles. In Germany and in Hungary, the data indicate that a blend between state, nobility, and landed property dominated the first legislatures. Parliament was a pretty clear reflection of an established order where feudal and statist traditions mixed together well. Public sector and nobility also played a crucial role in the Netherlands, but here they were part of a much more clearly urban coalition. As expected, the share of the traditional strata of society was significant in the United Kingdom but contrary to the previous cases, the state apparatus (with the exception only of the military sector) did not contribute significantly to shaping the representation of the nation. Given the greater weakness of the bureaucratic state compared to the other countries on the continent, it was rather the 'market' with its emerging sector of capitalist enterprise that supplied the new recruits to the House of Commons. In Italy, Spain, the Netherlands, France, and the United Kingdom, a class of political intermediaries—the lawyers—had a particularly strong role. In the Nordic countries, more than in any other European nation, one can find from quite early on an important state sector coexisting with a socially more 'democratic' component rooted in an agricultural base.

4.2. Transformations of the Original Parliamentary Establishment between the 1880s and 1920s

Moving to the final two decades of the nineteenth century, and to the first of the twentieth, we see a thorough transformation of the original picture with structures of opportunity for legislative recruitment changing profoundly. In countries with limited suffrage, the franchise was extended, and in all the countries the mobilization of the lower classes was promoted by the creation of new parties linked to them. These changes posed a significant challenge to the first parliamentary establishment. However, before looking at this from a qualitative perspective, the circulation of the parliamentary personnel, that is, the mechanism by which the exit of old parliamentarians and the entrance of a new type may change the makeup of legislatures, has to be assessed.

Our data indicate that the renewal of parliamentary elites follows a path generally characterized by a predominance of continuity over change: the percentage of newcomers is in most elections below the 40% level (Fig. 13.16). On average, among the countries examined, the Netherlands (until World War I) show the lowest levels of turnover (partly explained by the higher frequency of elections), while France, Germany, and Norway tended to have higher rates of circulation. The few cases of exceptionally high turnover can be located in the first elections of a new regime (as in the case of Imperial Germany and of the French Third Republic) when the new parliamentary elite was not yet stabilized. In any case, the influx of new members soon declined and overall there was no great variance in the levels of turnover. The stabilization of representative elites is confirmed by the steady growth of tenure (at the turn of the century, the mean number of elections in which MPs had successfully stood for parliament oscillates between 2.5% and 3.5%), with the result that the share of experienced parliamentarians became quite substantial (Fig. 13.15). In many countries, however, this period of stability—the *belle époque* of Parliaments—gave way to turbulence around World War I. In some cases, the accelerated change is to be explained simply by the delay of elections due to the country's participation in the war (e.g. the United Kingdom), in others by regime discontinuity associated with military defeat (e.g. Germany and Hungary), by franchise transformations (e.g. Italy), by party system restructuring (e.g. Germany, Italy), or by combinations of these factors. In all countries under observation, the crisis-ridden interwar period was ushered in by a substantial circulation of the political personnel.

The next question to be addressed is to what extent turnover is associated with change in the social makeup of legislatures. However, the relationship between these two aspects is not easily determined. If low levels of turnover necessarily mean an incremental change in the profile of parliamentarians, the opposite does not need to be true. A high turnover must not necessarily open the doors to a new brand of parliamentarians, it may simply reproduce a legislature with the same characteristics, except, of course, for tenure.

If we go back to the main indicators used to define the profile of parliamentary representation (education, nobility, economic sector, professional background), our data reveal that important changes had taken place after the turn of the last century. But the picture we get is one of gradual change until World War I, whereby the old establishment did not disappear abruptly and new breeds of politicians emerged slowly. The decline of nobility as a means of access to a parliamentary career is one of the clearest trends of this period in all those countries where it had formerly played an important role (Fig. 13.5). After many centuries, one of the traditionally most important (and peculiar) actors of European political life leaves the scene. The most dramatic change took place in Germany where, between 1880 and 1920, the percentage of representatives from the nobility fell from approximately 35% to less than 5%. The German paradox—the country with one of the most democratic suffrages but also the most aristocratic Parliament—started to disappear with the political mobilization after the 1880s and was finally wiped away by the regime discontinuity after World War I. In comparison, in countries such as the United Kingdom, the Netherlands, and Italy, transformation was much more gradual.

Whereas nobility was the epitome of the *ancien régime*, a primary sector background was also strongly correlated with the predominance of the traditional components of society in the representative processes (Fig. 13.7). There were, however, some important exceptions, such as the Netherlands, where the nobility had a distinctively urban background, and the Nordic countries, where the primary sector had a much more 'democratic' character (i.e. it comprised smallholders rather than large landowners). Our data reflect these different stories. The countries where representatives with a primary sector background were predominantly upper-class landowners are characterized by a clear downward trend of this category. The decline is particularly dramatic in Parliaments where this component had initially been very strong, for example, the United Kingdom and Portugal, followed with little delay by Germany. The trend is more gradual in France and Italy where this process started on intermediate levels.

The trend in the Nordic countries was completely different. Denmark, Norway, and later Finland, show that the primary sector, far from declining, managed to maintain a strong role in parliamentary representation, even expanding its influence with the process of democratization. In Denmark and Norway, the very high proportions of parliamentarians with a primary sector background that we had found at the beginning show a steady increase during the decades either side of the turn of the century. The decline begins much later than in the other countries, but even so, the primary sector maintained its importance well into the 1960s. Finland, in spite of its late arrival on the scene, follows the same pattern. This peculiar development is linked to the rather different relevance of the primary sector in the Nordic countries, and to the peculiar developments of their party systems where a specific party was strongly identified with the democratic mobilization of the farmers and of the periphery. These conditions enabled agriculture to preserve a significant influence well into the age of full democratization.

The third major component (albeit with significant cross-country variations) of the original mid-nineteenth-century pattern of legislative recruitment was experience in the public sector (Fig. 13.10). In most of the countries, this gave a rather *étatiste* tinge to parliamentary representation (with the Netherlands, Germany, and Norway at the top, Britain and France at the bottom of the continuum). As with the nobility, a clear common downward trend emerges, so that by the time of World War I the share of this component had been drastically reduced. Quite a clear relationship can be found between the original importance of this element and the pace of the downward trend, with the rate of decline being particularly evident in countries where the importance of this type of background was greater initially. In Germany, Norway, and the Netherlands, the 'retreat of the state' from parliamentary representation is striking: between the 1870s and the 1920s, the percentages are more or less halved. In Italy, one of the countries with a less *étatiste* Parliament, the decline is not so dramatic, yet clearly noticeable. Only in France, probably because the original level was so low comparatively, are variations not particularly significant. Political mobilization, if not able to dispel the strong bureaucratic tradition that had impregnated politics from the outset of the modern state completely, was at least able to counterbalance it somewhat, and to open access to the heart of sovereignty to new forces in society. In any case, as we shall see later, this was not the end of the story, although it was, for good or for worse, a major transformation of politics.

The predominance of the upper strata of society in the first stages of parliamentary life was attested to, not only by the frequency of incumbents from the nobility, but also by high levels of education. Indeed, one of the main indications of the democratization of representative elites in the decades following this period is the significant decline in the number of parliamentarians with a university degree. In some countries, the transformation is particularly striking (Figs. 13.1 and 13.2). For example, in Germany and the Netherlands, where university-educated parliamentarians were once in a large majority, by the 1920s they had been reduced to a minority. Their decline is understandably less marked in the three Nordic countries where they had been far fewer from the outset. The most significant exceptions to this trend are, however, Italy and Spain, where the already strong share of this group remained fairly constant. This even increased slightly in the first decades of the twentieth century, with the result that these two Southern European parliaments had a distinctively more 'elitist' character than the representative assemblies of the other countries.

With regard to the role of lawyers in parliament during this period, three groups of countries can be distinguished (Fig. 13.9): those where the share was limited (e.g. the Nordic countries and Germany), those in the middle (e.g. France, Netherlands, and the United Kingdom) and those where it was very high (e.g. Italy and Spain). While in the first two groups the proportion of lawyers remained generally stable during this period, or even declined gradually (as in the Netherlands), the Italian case differs significantly because of the clear and constant growth of this category until World War I. Here we find a key to the Italian exception with regard to university education: since the legal profession requires an academic training, its expansion also increased the share of MPs with a university degree. Italy (and to some extent France) can be interpreted as cases of a relatively strong 'proto-professionalization' of politics: lawyers acted as representatives for social groups and interests that in other countries intervened more directly or via parties in the representative process. This 'semi-professional elite' survives where party organizations are weak, while the 'functionary' (rooted in party and trade union organizations) takes over where organizations control the arena of mass politics (Fig. 13.12).

In sum, the forty years between the end of the nineteenth century and the beginning of the twentieth were years of gradual but momentous change for European parliamentary representation. With the help of a selection of indicators, we have documented the significant transformations of the original picture of the representative elites which, with some national variations, can be typified by the decline of the traditional components of the social and political establishment, that is, of privileged social status (particularly aristocratic background), land-ownership, state officialdom, and university education. Political elites underwent a process which had two faces: the face of 'democratization' and the face of *de-étatization*. During this period, the process was particularly clear in some countries (such as Germany, Norway, and the Netherlands), while it was more ambiguous in others. The Italian case is an interesting example of the latter: the decline of some of the typical components of the traditional establishment (nobles, landowners, state officials) did not mean a democratization of parliamentarians but the growth of a special group of 'semi-professional' representatives, the lawyers.

4.3. Representative Elites in the Age of Mass Democracy from the 1920s to the 1960s

As our data clearly indicate, the 1920s are the turning-point between two cycles of transformation. So far, our attention has been focused on aspects in decline, which can be described as the passing of the traditional establishment; we should now pay more attention to the political personnel who replaced those of the old establishment, and look into the developmental cycle of these new elites.

The interwar years (at least in those areas where competitive democracies survived) and the first years after World War II, are the period of the most 'democratic' and at the same time least *étatiste* recruitment pattern in Europe. It is the time when new strata of a politicized society gained access to parliamentary representation. In terms of social stratification, recruitment became significantly more 'representative' of the whole societal spectrum, so that even if a faithful mirroring of society was far from being attained, the pool of potential contenders for elective office was significantly broadened. Not only did the large and varied world of the middle classes provide the new recruits for parliament, but increasingly the working classes themselves. Thus, the percentages of parliamentarians with a blue-collar-worker background rose in all countries, peaking generally between the 1920s and 1940s (Fig. 13.13). However, because national occupational classifications are often different, and sometimes ideologically biased, cross-national comparisons can be difficult. Consequently, it was not always easy to establish whether we were dealing only with parliamentarians coming directly from the factory or whether their numbers had been inflated by those who were no longer active blue-collar workers but were now party or trade union officials. However, if we collapse both occupational categories, the trend is homogeneous and the democratization of recruitment becomes obvious, particularly if we read these data in combination with the proportion of MPs with only a basic education (Fig. 13.1).

This qualitative change in recruitment became possible because new political and social organizations offered potential representatives a functional substitute for the prestige, skills, and relationships previously derived from social status, property, or high state office. The new mass parties and politically engaged trade unions provided the organizational milieux where the 'functionary' could emerge as a pivotal political figure. Consequentially, the number of parliamentarians gaining their living from a party or trade union became particularly significant where democratization was channelled through organizations. Germany, in the years of the Weimar Republic, sets the upper limits of this development, but Denmark, Finland, and the Netherlands follow, albeit somewhat later, and on a significantly lower level. In Italy, the two elections after World War I show the beginnings of the same trend which, due to the Fascist take-over, only gained momentum after the democratic restoration of 1946 when there was a rapid upsurge in the proportion of functionaries. In most of the countries, the first decades after World War II see a general continuation of the same trend. For Denmark, Finland, Italy, the Netherlands, and Norway, the early 1970s are the peak of a mediation of parliamentary representation by organizations.

The importance of party organization is also shown by the proportion of parliamentarians who held leading positions in party organizations. The data available for the period after World War II show, albeit with significant inter-country differences, high rates of members of parliament who before their first election to parliament had held a position of leadership in party organizations at local or national level (Fig. 13.4). In many countries (Finland, Italy, Netherlands, Norway), a growth in this indicator of 'partyness' (Katz 1986) of parliamentary recruitment can be seen up to the early 1970s. Thereafter, it levels off or even declines. Germany lags behind these countries until the end of the 1960s but then shows a significant increase.

Although most trends that had begun at the end of the nineteenth century continued into the post-World War II era, two important indicators—university education and public sector background—show a sharp U-turn after 1945 (Figs. 13.2 and 13.10). With regard to university education, the clear downward trend that had characterized all the countries (exceptions being Italy and Spain) throughout the first half of the twentieth century, was completely reversed after World War II. An upward trend characterized Finland, France, Germany, the Netherlands, the United Kingdom, and, albeit at a lower level, Denmark and Norway. Only Italy, because of its earlier saturation, was not affected by the growth of university education among parliamentarians. Behind this general phenomenon, two concurring factors were working. The first was the opening of access to universities which made education at tertiary level less socially exclusive than previously, and significantly enlarged the supply of university-educated personnel available for a political career, especially after the 1960s. The second had to do more with the mechanisms of representation. In the first part of the century, the (social) 'democratization' of the parliamentarians had been pushed on the 'demand' side by the newly enfranchised and mobilized lower classes demanding representatives more closely related to their social situation, and symbolically representing their political grievances. At the same time on the 'supply' side, the development of the organized mass parties had enabled socially disadvantaged challengers to pursue a political and electoral career successfully. Eventually, however, this kind of 'symbolic representation' lost some of its original appeal to working-class voters who had become more interested in the effectiveness of their parliamentarians than in their symbolic value. At the same time, the class parties, once they had been fully incorporated in the governing system, became more ready to sacrifice the class purity of parliamentary representation to the need to recruit a more professionally qualified personnel; a trend which was also encouraged by their increased bureaucratization. In addition, the growing embourgeoisement of left-wing parties after World War II is confirmed by the declining proportions of working-class parliamentarians in their ranks (Fig. 13.13).

With regard to public sector representation, after the long and continuous decline in most of our countries, the postwar data consistently indicate a 'return of the state'. Formerly, the 'opening' of the political system to the representation of previously excluded sectors of society had meant a drastic reduction in opportunities for state officials. The political mobilization of the lower classes challenged the traditional officialdom of the state, perceived as being too closely coupled with the upper strata of society and hostile to popular demands. However, once the state had been 'conquered' by the new political forces and had extended its welfare function, the compatibility, or even affinity, between legislative recruitment and public sector experience was progressively restored. This had to do with the fact that the whole state administration and its personnel had been deeply changed as a consequence of the democratization of politics, and that the greatly expanded bureaucracy of the advanced welfare states also produced a strong demand for representation of the state's own interests. In order to capture the whole cycle of relations between state administration and representation with a simple formula, one could say that European parliaments had moved from a (partial) 'guardianship' of the authoritarian state over electoral representation through the predominance of politicized society to a new and more balanced combination of the two.

5. ONGOING DEVELOPMENTS

The homogenization of the European continent (except for some peripheral areas) under the 'democratic model' may lead one to think that an 'end of history' has been achieved. This is not totally without foundation: the history of the difficult process through which the democratic model has affirmed its primacy over authoritarian regimes (both traditional and post-traditional) does seem to be complete (although we should not assume the final victory of this model in every European country). This does not mean, however, that other 'histories' are also complete. As can be learned from older democracies, such as that of North America, a history of the transformations of democracy is well under way. That is, within the broad framework of democracy, important changes continue to take place through which the meaning of democracy itself may be subtly changed. In this perspective, the convergence towards the model of the party-centred professional politician that we have found in our analysis of the elected national politicians may also not necessarily mean the end of history.

Our data, in fact, provide some evidence that changes are still happening. The most striking change still under way concerns the gender composition of European legislatures (Fig. 13.6). The picture is clear. The dramatic underrepresentation of women among MPs that had characterized all the countries of our sample for decades (with the exception of Finland which already had a significantly higher level in the 1950s) begins to crumble in the 1970s, followed by a process of rapid change. Paradoxically, it is precisely the beginning of this change that produces an increase in diversity among European countries in that the take-off points and the pace of change are different. The Nordic countries, followed closely by the Netherlands, clearly lead the process. The take-off starts in the 1970s, and by the 1980s the differences between these countries and the others are huge (about 30% between the two extreme cases, i.e. Norway and the United Kingdom). However, with change accelerating in the 1990s, and including Western and Southern Europe, the gap overall begins to close.

How should this be interpreted in terms of representation models, and how can it be explained? With regard to the first question: does the increase of female MPs mean a trend in the direction of 'representation by identity', that is, women asking to be represented by women, or does it herald the end of gender-based discrimination in the field of legislative recruitment, and with it the disappearance of gender among the relevant factors in the 'recruitment function'? Or, is it a supply-side phenomenon, that is, the result of a greater availability of female candidates, thus enabling voters to spread their preferences more evenly on the basis of other criteria (be they collective political platforms or personal skills)? Probably both elements concur in this important transformation. We know that in all Western countries the demand for a gendered representation became a focal point from the 1970s onward, although it is difficult to evaluate to what extent this request by vocal minorities has been shared by the mass of female voters, or to what degree it has transformed electoral behaviour. It is easier to assume that these ideas have had effects upon the supply side of female representation. On the level of selectorates, the demand by feminist groups for a more gendered representation has often produced formal or informal rules, or at least new patterns of behaviour, which have purposefully increased the supply of female candidates. But independent of such feminist requests, other societal changes (such as changes in the labour market, particularly the increase of female employment in the public sector) have also contributed to extend the pool of women available for elective political offices. This larger supply might also have produced an increase of elected female MPs because of voters voting in a gender-neutral way, that is, voting for the candidates available, among whom there are now more women.

Other dimensions of ongoing change are less substantial and less homogeneous. In some countries, a decline in leading party officials can be observed in recent elections (Fig. 13.4). At the end of the 1970s, the number of MPs with a political background in party offices declined in Finland, Norway, Italy, and—to a lesser degree—in the Netherlands. A similar trend can be seen in the time series for professional pressure groups and party officials (Fig. 13.12). In Finland, Italy, and Norway, there is also a decrease in the number of MPs with a background in local elective offices and in the public sector (Figs. 13.3 and 13.10). In these data, we can perhaps read the first effects on the recruitment of parliamentarians of the new political trends detected in party organization by studies such as those of Katz and Mair (1995) concerning the 'cartel party', and perhaps also of the beginning of a retrenchment of the 'big state'. The signs, however, are still not very clear and not yet common to all the countries of our sample. Germany, for example, does not seem to follow these trends. At the end of the twentieth century, we may have some indications that the profile of legislative recruitment is bound to change from the predominant model of the past decades, but we do not yet have a clear picture of the new model that will take its place.

6. THE TRANSFORMATION OF LEGISLATIVE RECRUITMENT: A CASE IN POINT FOR POLITICAL MODERNIZATION?

The data presented here have put some of the crucial assumptions of modernization theory, and in particular the concept of political development, to the test. If we ask whether the passing of traditional society in Europe was accompanied by a converging transformation of legislative recruitment, the answer will have to take the persistent autonomy and distinctiveness of the political sphere into consideration. Indeed, Gaetano Mosca's (1939; orig. 1922) statement that 'the main differences between political organisms can be seen in the way in which the ruling classes are recruited and how they act' has only recently lost some of its validity.

At first sight, many of the time series presented in this volume fit well into the conceptual frameworks of modernization theory for, while the shares of the primary sector and the nobility in parliamentary recruitment have decreased to residual values since 1848, the representation of women has increased after the introduction of female suffrage and eligibility. Thus, the results expected from the extension of suffrage, the rationalization of authority, and the routing of rural elites can be seen to have occurred. However, closer examination reveals some striking deviations from the expected course of the time series which particularly violate the criteria of progressiveness, synchronicity, and convergence over extended periods. For example, in the case of primary sector representation, there was a rise in the late nineteenth or early twentieth centuries in countries like Germany, Denmark, Norway, and Finland, while during the late 1860s, the United Kingdom, which was the first industrial nation, displays the highest share of landed interests of all parliaments under investigation. Obviously, there was no direct connection between the shifting social significance of certain economic sectors and their parliamentary representation. It was rather the endangered than the endangering classes who initially asserted themselves in the process of parliamentary recruitment.

A similar picture emerges when we look at the representation of MPs with an aristocratic background. Although there was a marked decline of representatives with family affiliations to the nobility in all countries with a significant native aristocracy before World War I, there was an astonishing ability of noble incumbents to cope with political competition and with the extension of suffrage. Whereas, in most European countries, World War I was a watershed after which parliamentary representation by nobles sank below the 5% threshold, in Britain, deference for the old upper class remained significant, and was confirmed via the ballot box until the late 1950s. Female representation also seems to follow this pattern of retarded adaptation, this time disfavouring a latecomer category in the political arena. For about sixty years after the introduction of female suffrage and eligibility, female parliamentary representation hovered around its low starting-point, only exceeding the 10% threshold in the case of Finland, which had pioneered female suffrage in 1907.

These results show a persistent resistance of traditional patterns of parliamentary representation, even under the conditions of an extension of suffrage and fundamental social change. From this perspective, long-term change of parliamentary representation could be interpreted as a process of *retarded* political development, whereby parliamentary recruitment works as a kind of 'lock', delaying political change and separating it from the dynamics of change in other sectors of society. Therefore, the idea of progressive development, fundamental to modernization theory, could be maintained, although the theorems of synchronization and convergence would have to be dropped. However, a totally different picture emerges if we include indicators for the differentiation of structures in our review: here we have synchronization and convergence but progress is missing.

A case in point is the time series for public service employees, which displays a U-shaped cycle. According to the 'differentiation of structures' theorem, in the process of political development an increasing dissociation between different sectors of the power structure should have occurred, thus reflecting the 'division of powers' on the level of political roles and parliamentary recruitment. And indeed, until the 1930s, trends in most countries conformed to this assumption, converging at a relatively low level in a narrow corridor. High-ranking officials, members of the judiciary, and university teachers who had played an important role in the processes of state and nation-building during the nineteenth century became rather marginal categories in the era of mass democracy and party rule. In many cases, these 'dignitaries' were replaced by 'functionaries', that is, representatives who were directly drawn from party or trade union organizations. However, after World War II this trend was reversed and public servants once more became the most important occupational category from which European MPs were recruited. Although this development was complemented by a change in the composition of public sector employees represented in parliaments, namely, by an upsurge of schoolteachers who had become particularly numerous in socialist and social democratic parliamentary parties (Fig. 13.11), some fundamental similarities grounded in the nineteenth century should not be overlooked: namely, a distance towards the productive sector of the economy, a protected status with regard to the risks of labour markets, a higher availability for public offices than in other occupational categories, and an especially intimate relationship with the state as employer, patron, and source of authority. It is plausible, therefore, to assume that there is a connection between the marked state orientation of continental European economic and social policies and the recruitment of the respective legislatures.

The earlier success of the functionary and the return of the public sector employee as main actors on the parliamentary stage signalled the demise of the free political entrepreneur, personified in the lawyer, who lost ground in most European parliaments. Even in their former strongholds in the Italian and French chambers, the share of lawyers decreased to 10%, or even lower. What we see here is a result of changing role requirements for representatives, which restrain their function as independent intermediaries and tie them closely to party organizations. With regard to the assumptions of modernization theory, this result and its interpretation are ambivalent: while the free political entrepreneur appears hopelessly anachronistic in a situation where party organizations have taken over control, they incarnate the separation of powers and offer an 'independent position of trust' (Weber 1947; orig. 1919). Finally, it is interesting to see that the growing control of party organizations over parliamentary recruitment was not complemented by a declining involvement of MPs in local offices—with the exception of the Weimar Republic when there was a virtual uprooting of German political elites from local politics. Eventually, however, after World War II, Germany rejoined the other European democracies in this respect and now conforms to the pattern we have seen on several occasions: convergence without progress.

In an overview of the long-term trends of European parliamentary representation, those deviating from that which could be expected following the assumptions of modernization theory can be easily seen. In some areas, recruitment patterns resisted the pressure of general social change for decades, in other areas they followed a cyclical course or diverged, while there was no diffusion of modernity. Britain and France, in particular, the two 'model polities' for parliamentary democracy in Europe, maintained distinctly traditional features in their parliamentary recruitment patterns for extended periods. On the other hand, the Weimar Republic displayed the most 'modern' parliamentary representation of the time, being dominated by political professionals and closely tied to powerful party organizations. However, if this was modernity, it was by no means a contribution to the stability of German democracy because it ushered in its breakdown in 1933. Seen in comparison, legislative recruitment is a rather conservative element of the power structure and one might speculate whether this structural conservatism is directly (and positively!) linked to the performance of parliamentary democracies.

Although it is not appropriate to describe the long-term change of European legislative recruitment patterns as one coherent, homogeneous, synchronic, and progressive process of 'modernization', we have seen, however, developmental patterns which were convergent and which followed distinctive paths. These developmental paths were directed both by democratization, that is, the extension of the social niches from whence the electors and the elected were drawn, and by professionalization, that is, the establishment of a fairly autonomous field of political action with specific (although mostly informal) rules for access and reward. As mentioned earlier, both trends are contradictory since democratization is socially inclusive, while professionalization is exclusive, in that it creates a division between spheres of insiders and outsiders. Thus, long-term trends of European parliamentary recruitment did not result in a harmonious community between electors and elected, but in the inherently conflictual (although in most cases peaceful) coexistence between, in Max Weber's terms, professional politicians, who are living from and for politics, and amateur politicians, that is, all who are only incidentally involved in politics (1947, orig. 1919). Much of today's criticism of politicians against their alleged distance towards the electorate and ruthless pursuing of self-interest, is based on the contradictory logic of the processes of professionalization and democratization.

If we combine both dimensions of change and just distinguish between high and low levels of democratization and professionalization, a taxonomy with four cells results, into which the social figures dominating legislative recruitment in different historical periods can be allocated (Fig. 13.17). Thus we can associate low democratization and low professionalization with a high share of dignitaries and notables such as those who populated parliaments in many European countries throughout most of the nineteenth century. They owed their legislative recruitment to restrictive electoral laws or, where suffrage was already more extended, to a social control of the electoral process by traditional elites and the deference paid to them by large parts of the electorate. Their professionalization was low, not only with regard to direct payments received for their electoral offices and the time

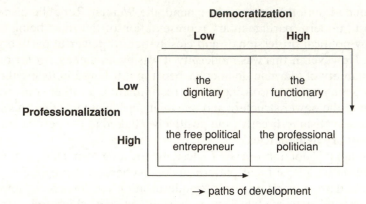

Fig. 13.17. A typology of legislators

budget devoted to them, but also with regard to their independence from the social and institutional settings from which they were recruited. They were very much representatives of the classes, or rather estates, to which they belonged, be they the landed aristocracy, the civil service, or the entrepreneurial bourgeoisie.

The political figure contrasting with the dignitary in this taxonomy is the fully professionalized politician in modern mass democracy who owes his or her office to a mandate gained in universal elections, whereby recruitment is, in most cases, mediated and sponsored by parties. MPs are now fully professionalized, not only with regard to an income directly related to their electoral office and a full commitment to their political career, but also with regard to the separation from their social background and the loyalties devoted to it. They become politicians *purs et durs*, for whom the rules of the political field determine their actions and expectations. In such a setting, social background loses its value as an element of the social capital to be invested in the competition for offices, since neither selectorates nor electorates expect that social background has any significant impact on the parliamentary behaviour of candidates after their election (Putnam 1976: 42). For fully professionalized politicians, the relevance of their social and particular occupational background lies mainly in its impact on the availability for and its compatibility (in terms of skills) with electoral offices.

The two remaining cells of the taxonomy represent transitory stages, when either full professionalization or full democratization is not yet achieved. The related political figures are the functionary and the free political entrepreneur. The free political entrepreneur—usually incarnated by the lawyer—flourishes particularly well where the political game on the parliamentary stage has gained a considerable degree of autonomy and involves the full-time budget of those acting on it. On the other hand, the power base of this type of politician rests mainly on his or her ability to mobilize the support of informal caucuses and networks of those who control the selection process of candidates and are able to trade votes for political influence. Therefore, a fully developed mass democracy in a highly polarized ideological setting is not a friendly environment for free political entrepreneurs. Thus, it is not surprising to find them being particularly strong in those polities where electoral laws are restricted and/or parties are relatively weak, and where parliaments have a strong position in the constitutional setting.

The reverse is true for functionaries. They are companions of mass democracy and particularly frequent in settings where parties and other intermediary organizations are closely linked to certain segments of the electorate. Here, paid positions in mass organizations or party apparatuses are relevant starting-points for careers through elective offices and into legislative mandates. Particularly before allowances were granted, or as long as they were insufficient to support political careers, organizational support compensated for private means. In so far as functionaries were actually paid by their employers for holding elective offices, they were professional politicians. However, financial support, sponsorship, and the safety of entrenchment in a powerful organization comes at the price of independence. Functionaries are kept on a short lead by their supporting agencies and have to follow the rules of their gratifying or sanctioning overseers, thus failing to fulfil the criterion of autonomy as a necessary condition for becoming fully fledged professional politicians. Since economic interest parties—like old-style working-class parties and agrarian parties—tended to tie their MPs to one social class and related political issues, they provided particularly fruitful ground for the rise of the functionary as a central political figure.

The two transitory cells were the moulds in which the modern European representative took shape, but it was primarily institutional factors, like the paths towards the extension of suffrage, the timing of the introduction of allowances, the constitutional position of parliaments in the policy-making process, and the strength and shape of the party system that decided into which of the two transitory cells individual countries were allocated or which countries became borderline cases. Eventually, however, European developmental paths converged into the figure of the fully professionalized politician in the context of an 'inclusive' mass democracy. The fact that this is a contradictory configuration, laden with conflictual expectations by the different political actors involved, assures us that we have not reached, and probably never will, a perfect solution to the challenge of combining the practices of representation with the promises of democracy.

References

Blondel, J., and Thiébault, J.-L. (1991). *The Profession of Government Minister in Western Europe*. London: Macmillan.

Eulau, H., and Sprague, J. (1961). *Lawyers in Politics: A Study in Professional Convergence*. Indianapolis: Bobbs-Merril.

Huntington, S. P. (1968). *Political Order in Changing Societies*. New Haven: Yale University Press.

—— (1971). 'The Change to Change: Modernisation, Development and Political Change'. *International Social Science Journal*, 145: 379–404.

Katz, R. S. (1986). 'Party Government: A Rationalistic Conception', in F. G. Castles and R. Wildenmann (eds.), *Visions and Realities of Party Government*. Berlin: de Gruyter.

—— and Mair, P. (1995). 'Changing Models of Party Organisation and Party Democracy: The Emergence of the Cartel Party'. *Party Politics*, 1: 5–28.

Linz, J. J. (1995). 'Some Thoughts on the Victory and Future of Democracy', in A. Hadenius (ed.), *Democracy's Victory and Crisis: Nobel Symposium No. 93*. Cambridge: Cambridge University Press, 404–26.

Mosca, G. (1939; orig. Ital. 1922). *The Ruling Class*. New York: McGraw-Hill.

Norris, P. (ed.) (1997). *Passages to Power: Legislative Recruitment in Advanced Democracies*. Cambridge: Cambridge University Press.

Pedersen, M. (1972). 'Lawyers in Politics: The Danish Folketing and the United States Legislature', in S. C. Patterson and J. C. Wahlke (eds.), *Comparative Legislative Behaviour: Frontiers of Research*. New York: Wiley, 25–63.

Pitkin, H. F. (1967). *The Concept of Representation*. Berkeley: University of California Press.

Putnam, R. D. (1976). *The Comparative Study of Political Elites*. Englewood Cliffs, NJ: Prentice-Hall.

Riddell, Peter (1995). 'The Impact of the Rise of the Career Politician'. *The Journal of Legislative Studies*, 2: 186–91.

Sartori, G. (1987). *Theory of Democracy Revisited*. Chatham: Chatham House Publishers.

Weber, M. (1947; orig. 1919). 'Politics as a Vocation', in H. H. Gerth and C. Wright Mills (eds.), *From Max Weber: Essays in Sociology*. London: Routledge & Kegan Paul Ltd.

INDEX